JOHN G. TURNBULL, Ph.D., Massachusetts Institute of Technology, is Professor of Economics and Industrial Relations and Associate Dean of the College of Liberal Arts, University of Minnesota. Dr. Turnbull is widely recognized for his work in the field of social security and labor relations. He has recently written a monograph on economic insecurity and has been a regular contributor to such journals as the *Harvard Business Review, Personnel, Labor Law Journal,* and *Industrial and Labor Relations Review.*

C. ARTHUR WILLIAMS, JR., Ph.D., Columbia University, is Professor of Economics and Insurance in the School of Business Administration, University of Minnesota. He is a past president of the American Risk and Insurance Association and a co-author of a text on risk management and insurance. He has contributed articles to the *Journal of Risk and Insurance,* the *Journal of Finance,* the *Journal of the American Statistical Association,* and other periodicals.

EARL F. CHEIT, Ph.D., University of Minnesota, is Executive Vice-Chancellor and Professor of Business Administration at the University of California, Berkeley. He is also a member of the Institute of Industrial Relations at that institution and has taught at St. Louis University. Recognized as an authority on social insurance, Dr. Cheit is the author of several volumes including *Medical Care Under Workmen's Compensation,* written for the United States Department of Labor, Bureau of Labor Standards.

ECONOMIC AND SOCIAL SECURITY

JOHN G. TURNBULL
UNIVERSITY OF MINNESOTA

C. ARTHUR WILLIAMS, JR.
UNIVERSITY OF MINNESOTA

EARL F. CHEIT
UNIVERSITY OF CALIFORNIA, BERKELEY

THIRD EDITION

THE RONALD PRESS COMPANY • NEW YORK

Library of Congress Catalog Card Number: 67–11890

PRINTED IN THE UNITED STATES OF AMERICA

Preface

This is a volume on the nature of economic insecurity, the factors that give rise to it, the ways in which society has sought to adjust to insecurity, and the consequences of problems and programs. In our approach to this subject matter we focus on principles. We obviously cannot bypass facts —and the pages herein are full of them—but these facts are only a means to the end of understanding man's quest for security.

We should like to repeat here a number of ideas which we expressed in the first and second editions. First, we treat not only the customary fields of social insurance and assistance, but also private insurance and substandard conditions. We conceive of the problem of economic security as relating essentially to the operation of the labor market, and on that basis these inclusions are logical. We have found this method particularly useful in our own courses in the several institutions in which we teach.

Second, our approach makes it necessary that we deal with a broader framework of subject matter than if we analyzed only social—or private—assistance and insurance. We have not, however, tried to be less exacting in our treatment of these areas than are several excellent volumes in this field.

Third, we have limited our discussion of economic insecurity essentially to the operation of the labor market, as this operation relates to job-oriented insecurity. Substandard conditions in housing could be included in a work on economic insecurity and, in fact, have been by some analysts. But we view this type of problem as somewhat outside the scope of our treatment. We have had to limit our boundaries in order to secure a manageable volume, and our decisions are reflected in the following pages.

Fourth, our approach is essentially economic in nature. We cannot claim competence as legal practitioners, political scientists, or social workers. Hence we do not treat in detail these phases of the subject matter involved. We hope, however, that this volume reflects training and interest beyond the narrow confines of economics as such.

Fifth, we make no claim to have pioneered in our analytical techniques, in our evaluations, and in our proposals for improvements in the American economic security system, although we have tried to introduce some differing ideas on the nature of economic security.

But, sixth, we do feel that we have applied a newer approach in the treatment of the subject matter. Within each of the sub-areas in the field of economic security we have attempted to synthesize and integrate public and private approaches to the problem and to show how society in the larger sense has sought to adjust itself to the issues involved.

One additional comment needs to be made in this Preface, a comment which in a sense could not have been made in earlier editions. The field of economic security is not only becoming more complex, it is ever widening. Increasingly one finds broader concerns exhibited, broader subject matter included. Thus the general problem of poverty, which we did not treat in the first two editions, is included in these pages. The "war on poverty" has become much more a part of conventional economic security policy and programming in the past five years.

Again, in this Third Edition we have tried to retain that which others have indicated they found useful, to respond to comments and suggestions, and to eliminate that which no longer appears to serve its purpose. While the format remains essentially unchanged from earlier editions, we have done a good deal more than merely update, though we hope we have accomplished that also. In particular, we have restructured the presentation in many ways, and have sought to incorporate newer analytical methods where useful.

We are indebted to many individuals in this revision; to the reviewers and users of this text who contributed many constructive criticisms; to Robert J. Myers for carefully reviewing several chapters, and to Joseph Borus, Lenore A. Epstein, Robert C. Goodwin, A. Edward Hunter, Louis Levine, Harry Malisoff, Ida C. Merriam, William Papier, Paul Smith, Ray Solem, and Donald T. Strand for technical information or comment; to our students at the Universities of California and Minnesota for ideas and suggestions; to the American College of Life Underwriters for their help in surveying teachers in the Chartered Life Underwriter study program, in connection with the Second Edition, and to the teachers who responded; to Stephen Engleman and Margaret Frantz for their help in researching and writing Mr. Cheit's chapters; to Nancy Lestina, Ilona Hanka, and Mary M. Pepple for editorial assistance; and to our families, now no larger but older than in 1956 and 1961, for patiently sitting out this revision.

As always, we remain responsible for those views with which the reader may not agree and for those errors of fact we may not have caught.

JOHN G. TURNBULL
C. ARTHUR WILLIAMS, JR.
EARL F. CHEIT

Minneapolis, Minnesota
Berkeley, California
January, 1967

Contents

ECONOMIC AND SOCIAL SECURITY

1

Economic Security in Our Society

> "Having combed the Literature from 2000 B.C. to 1966
> A.D., we have concluded that insecurity and security—
> economic or otherwise—are most vexing issues."
>
> —The Authors, 1966 A.D.

INTRODUCTION

In the first two editions of this volume—written ten and five years ago respectively—we sought to describe and analyze two basic issues:

— The nature, causes, and consequences of economic insecurity in our society,

— The ways in which society has attempted to meet such insecurity through an increasingly integrated approach that combines public and private programs.

With the passage of time, two characteristics relating to the basic issues noted above are becoming increasingly clear:

— The forces giving rise to economic insecurity have been subjected to re-examination and it is now frequently suggested that two underlying types of problems can be recognized: (1) those involving "temporary" or "transitory" income curtailment such as might arise out of an industrial accident or short-term unemployment; and (2) those that result from more fundamental forces and that tend to be of longer duration—and here "poverty" provides a frequently cited example.

— The pluralistic approach—of public and private techniques—which we sought to characterize in earlier editions has, in fact, been borne out,

3

and we now have a highly complex and multi-faceted system of economic security programming. But, more than that: while temporary income curtailment problems have continued to receive their share of attention, increasing emphasis has been placed upon long-term and more basic income issues, and here the Economic Opportunity Act of 1964 affords an example of such attention.

With these introductory comments in mind, let us note the nature and scope of the subject matter treated in these pages. We focus upon "security"—the quality of being protected against or safe from dangers and threats of diverse kinds. Security has many faces. Some are collective in nature, as, for example, in the case of national security—the safety of a country from forces without. Some are individual, and here again diverse types are to be found. There is, for example, physical security—protection against bodily harm. Or, emotional security, which is equated with psychological well-being.

We focus in this volume upon still another form, that of economic security. This kind of security may be defined as protection against the loss of income, such as might arise out of job separation, or against extra expenses such as might result from extended illness. We limit our treatment for two reasons. First, there is not space enough in a volume of this size to treat the many dimensions of security. (It is difficult enough to treat economic security adequately.) But, second, even if there were, we do not possess the necessary competence. We have been trained as economists, and hence are not capable of analyzing such issues as mental health or international relations. Even in the economic security area we shall have to limit our discussion to keep the treatment within manageable bounds; we shall not analyze, for example, the insecurities involved in business risk-taking (such as introducing a new product line) or personal risk-taking (such as building an investment portfolio). We focus instead upon *personal income and expense* insecurity: income insecurity as it is influenced by personal circumstances (such as employee illness) and by labor market processes; expense insecurity as it is affected by accidental injury or sickness to the breadwinner or members of his family.

PLAN OF THE BOOK

Following this introductory section, each of the major categories of economic insecurity is discussed systematically. The approach includes (1) a discussion of the nature of the problem; (2) the actions society has taken in trying to solve the problem, including both public and private methods; and (3) an analysis of the consequences of the actions taken.

Throughout the volume, emphasis is placed upon the broader features of problems and programs and upon basic principles rather than detailed facts and statistics. This volume is designed to provide a basis for understanding the nature and causes of economic insecurity in our society and the social adjustments to it. It is not a handbook designed to answer such technical questions as to whether an individual can collect unemployment compensation in a given state under a given set of complex job separation circumstances. Such queries can best be answered by the administrative agencies set up for such purposes.

Nor is this volume a statistical compendium of facts and figures on economic security; this information can be obtained readily from published reports. Such materials tend to be short-lived, and therefore of limited usefulness in a book of this type. This should not be taken to imply that we will have no concern with facts and figures. Obviously, this could not be the case. But our emphasis will be upon understanding, rather than upon memorization, upon the more basic economic and social forces involved, rather than upon administrative complexities, legal niceties, or statistical detail.

NATURE AND CAUSES OF ECONOMIC INSECURITY

As noted in the Introduction, recent analysis of economic insecurity has tended to distinguish between two fundamental categories of causal forces. But whatever the category, a common thread is to be found. This is the factor of insufficiency of income, whether for the normal necessities of life or for the added expenses that arise from cases such as extended illness. Insufficiency may be viewed as total or relative: total in the sense of complete curtailment of income; relative in the case where some income is received but not enough to meet minimal budgets.

1. In one category of causal forces, two characteristics are relevant. First, the insecurity tends to be of "long duration." Although this term is not precisely quantifiable, it is regarded as something longer than the period of incapacitation due to a routine industrial accident or longer than that arising out of unemployment resulting from a typical layoff. At the other extreme, the duration may be for a generation or more, as the welfare roles would indicate for some families or individuals. Second, the individual involved is considered as "contributing" in some way to the insecurity, contributing in the sense that emotional, educational, or other difficulties are among the causal factors at work. "Poverty stricken" is a term frequently applied to one of the subgroups experiencing this form of insecurity.

2. In the second category, the same two characteristics are applicable, but in a different way. First, the insecurity tends to be of short (or

shorter) duration; a few weeks or months instead of, say, a generation. Second, the insecurity is regarded as arising from forces outside of the individual; that is, he does not "contribute" to it.

Now it is apparent that this twofold classification is both elusive and overlapping. It is elusive because it is difficult if not impossible to define "personal responsibility." When *does* an individual "contribute" to his own economic insecurity? If he deliberately maims himself at his work place? If he refuses to seek employment? Certainly these would be regarded as the extreme types of cases. But one gets into serious difficulties when one tries to pin down further responsibility in such instances. Moreover, the classes overlap, since what starts out as short-term insecurity may well develop into long-term; and the individual (say one who is unemployed) may suffer emotional damage to the point where he no longer has any initiative to seek employment. Yet, these difficulties notwithstanding, this twofold classification does provide a useful approach if for no other reason than that the evolving forms of economic security programming recognize it.

Let us look more closely at the causal forces at work in these two categories, recognizing that a precise dividing line cannot be drawn between them.

Prolonged Economic Insecurity

Income Insufficiency Characteristics. Income loss may be "total," in which case substitute income must be provided; or, it may be partial and the individual (and his family) may be regarded as living in poverty. While it is difficult to set a point at which poverty exists, a commonly used figure is a $3,000 annual budget for a family of four.[1] By this standard, in the decade of the 1960's, one-fifth of American families (and nearly one-fifth of the total population) were poor.

Personal Factors. The importance of education as a factor in poverty is illustrated time and again in current data. Families whose head had more than twelve years of education were only one-fifth as numerous as those where the head had eight years or less. Insofar as lack of education arises from economic factors, it would fall in the external factor category discussed below; insofar as it is not, it is relevant here. Physical and mental disabilities play a part, as does lack of motivation. These forces are most difficult to quantify, however, and it is equally difficult

[1] See the discussion in *Economic Report of the President, 1964* (Washington, D. C.: U. S. Government Printing Office, 1964), chap. 2, "The Problem of Poverty in America."

to prescribe for them; what can be done about poor motivation? We shall return later to these issues.

Factors External to the Individual. Numerous forces give rise to this type of economic insecurity. Economic causes are important; the level of business activity is not high enough so that all who want jobs can find them; low productivity is reflected in low rates of pay; localities exhaust their natural resources; discrimination in employment opportunities affects certain groups; an individual cannot afford the education that his abilities would permit. "Substandard conditions" are a particular class of economic factors associated with insufficient income, particularly when low wages (rather than long hours or subminimal working conditions) are involved. At issue is not the inability of an individual to secure a job, but rather his inability to get an employment contract that meets the minimum standard under which society will permit its members to be employed. Other diverse factors also play their parts: technology changes, and retraining programs do not exist to qualify individuals for new jobs; mobility is made difficult because of commitment to a given area. Economic opportunity and operational efficiency play twin and important roles.

Transitory Economic Insecurity

Income Insufficiency Characteristics. In partial contrast to the prolonged case, described above, income curtailment tends to be total: An individual is laid off and his wages or salary cease; the same is true for temporary "total" accidental injury and sickness. There are minor exceptions: An unemployed individual may find some work; a partially disabled employee may be able to do certain tasks.

The adjective "transitory" needs particular qualification in this context. First, what began as transitory may turn out to be prolonged. Thus, an individual who is laid off and told to return in four weeks may find the weeks stretching to months and the months to years. Or, an injured employee, instead of suffering a temporary, partial disability, may be the victim of permanent and total incapacitation. The outstanding illustration is, of course, retirement. An individual stops work at sixty-five and lives for fifteen more years. How can this possibly be classed as transitory? The answers to these vexing issues fall into two categories. First, long-term unemployment and permanent disability are the exception rather than the rule. Hence, the basic generalization holds. Second, while the retirement period—for ten or fifteen years—hardly tends to be temporary, the opportunity does exist to plan for it. Hence, it can be anticipated.

Personal Factors. It is with respect to this set of characteristics that a major difference is held to exist between prolonged and transitory insecurity. In the former case the individual is viewed as "responsible"— even if only in part—for his problems. In the latter case, a frequently used expression is that the individual's insecurity arises through no fault of his own.

As was noted earlier, this issue of "personal responsibility" for economic insecurity is vexing, and, some would suggest, without foundation. We admit that an ultimate definition of responsibility leads one down treacherous paths. We would, however, suggest that there is a usefulness to the distinction and that this usefulness is borne out by current economic security programming.

— In the case of transitory economic insecurity, program emphasis is placed upon the "system"; upon such factors as increasing the flow of information about job availabilities.

— To the contrary, where prolonged insecurity is involved, much greater emphasis is placed upon the "individual" and his rehabilitation or retraining.

Factors External to the Individual. It is here that one finds the customary analysis of the forces that affect an individual's economic well-being. The following causes are invariably treated in any discussion of the subject.

Job Separation Arising from Old Age. We do not discuss at this point whether an older worker should or should not retire or, if he should, at what age. It is sufficient to say that a retirement custom has developed in this country, that "compulsory retirement" (and hence job separation) is the rule, and that the age of such retirement is most commonly sixty-five. Unless, however, the retiring employee has accumulated a fund upon which to live, this very fact of job separation creates for him an economic insecurity.

It is interesting to note that programs designed to overcome this type of insecurity may not seek to solve the problem by keeping the individual at work (nor incidentally by having him live with children or relatives). Rather, such programs seek to permit the individual to accumulate a fund so that when job separation does occur at retirement, economic insecurities are not created.

Job Separation Arising from Accidental Injury or Sickness, with Death as the Extreme Case. In these cases it is also apparent that the very fact of job separation creates an income (salary or wage) loss. But such illness may include additional economic hazards. These are the expenses arising out of medical care, or burial expenses in the case of death; and possible future losses in earning power if the accidental injury involves loss of a bodily member such as a hand or leg, or death in the extreme case. If permanent and total disability results from the accidental injury or sickness, the degree of economic insecurity created becomes particularly critical. But even temporary and partial disability may be serious. Until recently, public programs designed to meet these types of insecurities protected the employee only, and then only against job-connected accidental injuries and later certain job-connected sickness. Increasingly, however, there is a tendency to protect the employee and his family also against these hazards, regardless of the source.

Job Separation Arising from "Economic" Causes. Old age, accidental injury, and sickness all contain an element of "economic" causality in that the individual's productivity diminishes, becoming zero in the case of total incapacitation. But there are cases where individual productivity does not change at all and yet job loss occurs for economic reasons beyond the individual's control. This is the familiar case of economic "unemployment"—where business conditions require employers to curtail their work forces, for whatever reason.

The above three cases typify the major forces giving rise to economic insecurity. In general, our analysis will stop at these "causality" levels. If one goes much beyond these stages, one finds himself in technical areas beyond the boundaries of the field of economic security as it is viewed here. For example, the prevention of industrial accidents, as a phase of programs designed to reduce one type of economic insecurity, involves individual physiological and psychological factors requiring the attention of specialists. Or, the further analysis of unemployment leads one into the field of fiscal and monetary theory, and again the role of the expert becomes evident.

Conventional treatment of the topics of income and expense security and insecurity tends to stop with the types of subject matter discussed above. When this is the case, the term "social security" frequently has been used to denote public approaches to the problems, although in this text we discuss private approaches also. And, if the emphasis has been upon public insurance programs designed to combat the insecurities involved, "social insurance and related programs" customarily has been the applicable term. In the larger sense, of course, "social security" can be applied to the vast range of security problems faced by any society: disease, war, pestilence, upheaval. The dimensions of these problems are obviously beyond the scope of our treatment. (These matters of terminology will be more fully noted in a later section in this chapter.)

Two Specific Causal Factors

While conventional treatment of economic insecurity has tended to stop with the topics noted above, two additional factors have received increased attention in recent years as contributing to the problems under consideration. These include substandard conditions and price level changes. Their impacts may be prolonged or transitory depending upon their characteristics. Thus, a moderate price increase in one year followed by a long period of stability is one thing; a steady rise over a generation is another. Hence, we treat these two—substandard conditions and price level changes—separately at this point.

Substandard Conditions. "Substandard conditions" is a term applied to wages, hours, and other phases of employment. "Substandard" is viewed as below some socially acceptable minimum. At issue is not the inability of an individual to secure a job, but rather his inability to get an employment contract that meets the minimum standards under which society will permit its members to be employed.[2]

Price Level Changes. Since the publication of the first edition of this book, greater attention has been directed to the possibility that increasing prices—"inflation"—may create economic insecurities. The reasoning runs as follows. Programs designed to combat insecurity frequently make use of a "fixed" fund of savings or a "fixed" set of income payments. Thus after retirement, an individual receives a fixed income from an annuity. If the price level increases, there is an erosion of purchasing power; if prices increase enough, the insecurity may become critical. This problem has become more acute in the last twenty years and has led to programs designed to create "flexible" income payments: the variable annuity, automatic adjustments in unemployment compensation. This problem may be more of a "complicating factor" than a basic issue; we shall nevertheless comment upon it where relevant.

SOCIAL ADJUSTMENT TO ECONOMIC INSECURITY

General Approaches Employed

If society does not sit back and passively accept the consequences of economic insecurity, a number of alternative courses are open. These courses may be followed individually or collectively. Historically, society

2 Professor Stefan A. Riesenfeld was a pioneer in this approach. See Stefan A. Riesenfeld and Richard C. Maxwell, *Modern Social Legislation* (Brooklyn: The Foundation Press, 1950). But see also, for an earlier view, Barbara N. Armstrong, *Insuring the Essentials* (New York: The Macmillan Co., 1932).

has attacked the insecurity problem in a number of ways. In spelling these out at this point we are basically interested in providing a kit of tools—a framework of ideas—which the student can then use continuously throughout the text. We do not include examples except where they are an aid to understanding. Nor do we apply these approaches here to the American economic security system; that will come later in this chapter.

There are various ways of classifying social adjustment; we shall utilize several of these so as to set out as clearly as possible the diverse ways in which society has tackled the problem of economic insecurity.

Basic Elements in Approaches to Economic Security

Three key elements are involved in any discussion of economic insecurity.

The Economic System. It is this system which—in its public and private sectors—provides employment and hence the means of achieving economic security. And it is the efforts to make the system operate more effectively that aid in such achievement. Thus, policies designed to maintain a high level of economic activity, to facilitate job creation and stabilization in the private sector, to increase desirable labor mobility, and to provide educational opportunities are all indicative of efforts designed to improve the economy's operating performance and hence to lessen the threats of economic insecurity.

The Individual. It is the individual—and his dependents—who constitutes the human family upon which the impacts of insecurity fall. Economic security programming not only seeks to improve the operating efficiency of the system; it also focuses upon this individual in that system. Education, motivation, training, and retraining—all constitute examples of the ways in which society seeks to make the individual less "insecurity prone" as he lives and works within the economic system. Current emphasis upon the high-school dropout and his problems provides a particularly relevant case in point. Summing this up in a different way, it is not enough for the economy to be able to operate at a high level of activity; there must also exist individuals with educational attainments sufficient to meet the job requirements that exist and also sufficiently motivated to make the best use of their opportunities.

Income Maintenance Programs. In cases where the economic system fails to provide the necessary opportunities or where the individual falls victim to a peril (such as an industrial accident or death), some type of substitute income must be provided. The nature of the insecurities—in terms of their causes—and the programs designed to protect against them form the content of this volume.

We thus have an economic system with humans working and living within it. Improving the functioning of the system and motivating and educating the people in it constitute important ways in which society seeks to lessen the threat of economic insecurity. But when the system fails to provide opportunities (or when forces giving rise to insecurity still persist) or when the individual still has difficulties, income maintenance programs of diverse types have evolved.

Operational Approaches Employed in Economic Security

The classification above outlined the nature of the key elements in the economic security sphere. Indirect reference was made to some of the ways in which policies and programs were applied to lessen insecurity or to compensate for it when it does occur. But it is possible to spell out more precisely the operating approaches used. It will be useful to do this here; then in the remaining discussion it will not be necessary each time to repeat these basic points.

Prevention (or Reduction in Incidence) of the Event Giving Rise to the Economic Insecurity. This approach may focus upon the previously noted economic system or upon the individual. Thus, policies designed to maintain high levels of economic activity illustrate emphasis upon the system; programs seeking to increase a person's motivation relate to the individual. Prevention may be "true" prevention, which seeks to eliminate or reduce the chance of loss; the use of safety guards on plant equipment is an example. Or the approach may seek to minimize the severity of loss; prompt medical attention in the case of accidents is illustrative. But whatever the specific focus or method, the purpose is to reduce the possibility of undesirable insecurities or to minimize their severity.

Alleviation of the Undesirable Economic Consequences of the Event Giving Rise to the Economic Insecurity. In the "nature of things," prevention can never be 100 per cent successful. An industrial accident does take place; a wage loss is incurred; medical expenses are created. One social approach to such problems is to compensate the individual for the medical expenses and for a portion of the wage loss. This is "curative" rather than "preventive" medicine; that is, in and of itself, such a method of assisting the individual seeks to alleviate consequences rather than prevent occurrences. Note also that this approach is essentially economic in nature; there is no payment for physical pain, psychological suffering, and so on. The alleviative approach is essentially the substitute income maintenance approach. (Students have sometimes noted semantic difficulties here. If one takes out life insurance against the undesirable economic consequences of premature death, does not one seek to "prevent" these consequences? The answer is yes. But, in order to provide clarity in the use of terms, prevention is applied to the causal force itself, e.g., unemployment; alleviation to the consequences, e.g., unemployment insurance. We shall use this distinction throughout the volume.)

Government Regulation. In one respect, regulation is found in any program of prevention or alleviation where the government is concerned. (And "regulation" also exists in the private sector, as in the case of a collective agreement that specifies compulsory retirement at age sixty-five.) But regulation may be pinpointed in particular cases of governmental activity, primarily those of substandard conditions. Regulation may be preventive or punitive in nature. Thus, in certain jurisdictions, children below a certain age may be prohibited from seeking gainful employment. Or, women may be prohibited from working in certain types of establishments between the hours of midnight and 7:00 A.M. Or, women and children may not be allowed to work over a certain number of hours in given types of operations. In other cases the regulation may impose penalties. Thus, a forty-hour ceiling may be placed upon the work week. If this were an absolute prohibition, forty hours would be the outside limit. But the regulation instead may be punitive: an employer may work his employees over forty hours per week, but only upon paying them a penalty rate, such as time-and-one-half for the excess hours.

Methods of Combating Economic Insecurity: Private Approaches

Prevention, alleviation, and regulation (working in both the preventive and alleviative cases) constitute the principal approaches to the problems of economic security. In turn, there are a number of ways in which they can be applied; these can be divided into two basic categories, private and public. Let us consider these categories in turn without seeking to analyze or evaluate them at this point.

Private Preventive Approaches. Here the individual, the employer, the union, or others seek to reduce the possibility of the insecurity, whether it arises from premature death, old age, economic unemployment, or illness. Examples are numerous and readily found: employment stabilization plans and safety programs are but two of many illustrations.

Private Alleviative Approaches, Without the Use of Insurance. In this case the individual or group seeks to combat the risks of insecurity, where it does arise, through a variety of non-insurance means.

One alternative involves the individual only. Through his own resources the individual may seek to protect himself from the undesirable economic consequences of specific insecurities. This alternative is frequently called "assumption" or "retention" and may be informal or formal in its application. A systematic savings program would illustrate the formal variety; a "catch-as-catch-can" pay-as-you-go program would illustrate the informal.

A second alternative involves the individual and his family and/or friends. Should the insecurity occur and place the individual in impoverished circumstances, his family, friends, or a private agency may take care of him temporarily or permanently. This alternative (and the insurance method noted below) involves a "transfer" of the risk to friends, relatives, private charities, or insurance carriers. It might be noted that if the individual does nothing to prepare for possible contingencies, he is really transferring the problem to society.

Private Approaches Utilizing a System of Insurance. This method is an extension of that discussed above. Instead, however, of "saving" in the individual sense, the person pools his risks with others and employs a practice commonly called insurance.[3] An individual uses this method when he buys an annuity for old age from a commercial insurance company. The same is true when life or health insurance is purchased.

Formal groups as well as individuals as such may utilize this method. Thus, fraternal associations, labor organizations, and others, either by themselves or through collective negotiations, use insurance programs. And again, although the insurance approach is basically alleviative, prevention may accompany it, as in the linkage between health and safety programming and workmen's compensation.

Private insurance—individual and group—has come to play a very important part in present-day attacks upon economic insecurity in the United States. Whereas the non-insurance method was important in an earlier day, it has become less so today in the cases of premature death, old age, accidental injury, and sickness.

Mixed Private Approaches. Realistically this mixed system typifies present practice in the United States. For some individuals and/or groups and for some risks, insurance systems are used; for other individuals or risks, they are not. Detailed discussion of these programs will constitute a major portion of this book.

[3] See p. 21 for a more formal definition of insurance.

Methods of Combating Economic Insecurity: Public Approaches

In addition to private approaches, there are different ways in which public bodies may seek to attack the problems of economic insecurity. Here also one finds alternative methods, and in real life political bodies tend to use various combinations.

Government Preventive Programming. Just as private individuals and groups seek to prevent or minimize the losses associated with economic insecurity, so do public bodies. Government actions are perhaps most effective in the area of economic unemployment. Through the use of monetary and fiscal policies the government may exert a strong influence on the well-being of the economy. The Employment Act of 1946 provides an example of one way in which a government formally seeks to undertake a preventive economic security program. Public bodies also frequently cooperate with private individuals and groups in other preventive programs in the areas of premature death, old age, and illness. Since considerable "discretionary action" is usually involved in such programs, they are not customarily viewed as "regulation." This latter method we consider next.

Government Regulation. Here regulation exemplifies a specific type of prevention. Laws seek to rule out the force giving rise to the insecurity. Thus, in substandard conditions, the government spells out a framework of rules, seeking to eliminate certain "causes" of insecurity. The Fair Labor Standards Act of 1938 (the Wage and Hour Law) provides the best illustration of this type of governmental regulation. Here the federal government has set down a framework of regulations including a floor on wages and a ceiling on hours. A federal agency administers the Act in its various phases. But beyond this the government is not in "business," and the only obligation business enterprises have is to comply with the statute.

Government Regulation, with a "Service" Function Undertaken by Private Agencies. In this case, there is also a government control. But compliance in this case involves the provision of continuing "service," either by the covered business enterprise or, through it, by other private agencies. This method is primarily alleviative although some preventive phases are intertwined.

The treatment of industrial accidents illustrates this case. A state enacts a law placing certain responsibilities upon the employer as to indemnification of wage losses suffered and medical costs incurred by an employee injured on the employer's premises. The law may permit the employer himself, under certain circumstances, directly to assume the financial responsibilities, that is, to become "self-insured." Most employers will, however, comply with the law by taking out an insurance policy with a commercial company writing this type of coverage. Thus, while the state legislates the framework of regulation, it is the private agency—the employer himself or an insurance company—that undertakes the activity required for compliance.

Government Regulation, with the "Service" Function Also Provided by the Government. In addition to writing a framework of economic security regulation, governments may also undertake the operations required by the regulation. This may be done in two ways: by providing services directly, or by making income payments to individuals and permitting them to purchase the service. These methods are primarily alleviative; they seek to provide assistance as the insecurity arises.

1. Direct provision of economic security service is found in a variety of situations. A given county in a state sets up a poorhouse, a mental hospital, or an old people's home. In such cases the service—food, lodging, clothing, medical care—is provided directly on a service basis to the needy person, and there is customarily no intermediate transfer of money.

2. Income payment systems have become increasingly important since the middle of the 1930's. Such systems may be of two basic types. In one case the government makes the income payments to the individual in need, who then, within certain limitations, is free to spend the income to meet his needs. Here the government acts as a sort of middleman: it raises monies from various sources, and then passes them on to individuals for use in combating the insecurities they face. The "dole," "poor relief," and "old-age assistance" are examples of this approach.

In the other case the government also uses the income approach, but it engages in continuing business activity. This method exists, first, on the federal level in the Old-Age, Survivors, and Disability Insurance (OASDI) program, wherein the government is in the insurance business, particularly the life and death branches. On the combined federal-state level, the Unemployment Compensation (UC) program provides an illustration: here the several states, operating within a federal framework, are in the unemployment insurance business. Finally, in some states, the state is in the liability insurance business, underwriting workmen's compensation risks.

Indirect Public and Private Approaches
to Economic Insecurity

In addition to the types of programs noted above, there are other and somewhat more indirect approaches to economic insecurity. These include both public and private methods, in which preventive aspects are perhaps more strongly stressed. Two illustrations can be given. Public actions that strengthen, say, the banking and financial intermediary system indirectly contribute to economic stability and hence lessen the possibilities of insecurity. Many such examples are to be found.

In the private sector of the economy, measures that business enterprises take to increase their stability contribute to a lessening of economic insecurity. This is true whether merely an informal improvement in procedures is introduced or whether formal actions are applied.

In the United States today we utilize all the foregoing direct and indirect public and private systems. The proportions vary, depending upon the specific causal factor in economic insecurity for which the program is set up. The body of this book will concern itself with discussing and analyzing the variety of programs existing in the framework sketched above.[4]

ECONOMIC SECURITY APPROACHES:
SOME IMPORTANT DISTINCTIONS

In spelling out the above approaches we used a number of specific terms such as "assistance," "insurance," and "service and income programs." These terms possess additional distinctive characteristics. Again it will be well to clarify these characteristics at an early stage so that we can use the terms with understanding in future sections of this book. Let us therefore examine in greater detail these several important distinctions in society's approaches to economic insecurity.

Service Versus Income Payments

As noted earlier, under a service program, the recipient receives payments in kind instead of in cash, while under an income program the recipient receives cash which he may use to purchase the services he needs and desires. Both service and income programs exist in the United States today although, as will be seen, the latter tends to predominate.

[4] Although the subject matter is beyond the scope of this book, it is clear that collective bargaining and its related public policy are designed to make employees more secure through their own efforts.

The recipient of service benefits must accept the program benefits, but the recipient of income benefits can purchase those services which he deems most important. The recipient loses freedom of economic choice when a loss of income is replaced with specific services. For example, there is a loss of freedom if an individual is provided with free room and board instead of, say, a cash payment of $100 a month when he reaches age sixty-five. The loss of freedom is less, however, when the program provides specific services instead of reimbursing the individual for expenses incurred in purchasing the specific types of services. In fact, the loss of freedom may be very slight if the services under the service program may be obtained from all or most of the available providers of that service. For example, a medical expense program may provide service benefits or cash reimbursements for expenses incurred. In either case, the program is limited to medical services. The loss of freedom under the service program depends upon the ability of the insured to choose his own doctors, hospitals, nurses, and other suppliers of medical service. If the service program makes available all or most of the medical facilities of the nation on equal terms, the relative loss of freedom of choice is slight.

A variety of other considerations, some administrative, some economic, are relevant to the issue of service versus income payments. Among them are the following:

1. Service benefits make it possible for the sponsoring body to exercise more control over the quality and cost of the services.
2. An insured person may use cash payments for purposes which are not socially or economically desirable; hence service programs provide more rigorous controls, not only in quality and cost, but also in use.
3. Service benefits may, however, be more costly to administer, for there may be many more administrative and other details to be considered.
4. Public service benefits may make it necessary for the government to enter an area which, in the past, has been reserved for private enterprise.
5. Service benefits may not be affected directly or immediately by price changes; income benefits are. For example, a promise to provide hospital care in a semi-private room for thirty days is not reduced by an increase in the costs of providing this service. A $10 per day allowance may be sufficient to pay all the cost when the promise is made but only part of the cost later when the insured is hospitalized.
6. Service benefits replacing lost income are less "popular" than income benefits because of the loss of freedom of economic choice, although recently enacted medical expense programs for the aged

are service-oriented. Therefore, some who are eligible do not apply for the benefits. This tends to reduce the cost of the program. Freedom of choice is frequently a critical factor.

Nevertheless, because of the importance attached to the freedom of economic choice by our population, most of the alleviative payments under the American economic security system are payments in cash.[5] Certain service programs do, however, loom large currently on the American economic security scene. The distribution of surplus food to needy families provides an example of a public system utilizing the service approach. In recent years, for example, this U. S. Department of Agriculture program was distributing food to over six million persons. A currently important private illustration is provided by certain non-profit medical expense associations in which alleviation is in the form of direct provision of the service rather than a cash payment. And, the new medical expense programs for the aged, under the Social Security Act, afford an important example.

Public Assistance Versus Social Insurance [6]

Public assistance programs tend to be "charity" programs. Public assistance benefits customarily are paid only to those individuals who can demonstrate need, and the amount of the benefit is based upon the extent of the demonstrated need. Final decisions on both eligibility and benefit amounts are made on a discretionary basis by the officials administering the public assistance programs.

Social insurance and related programs provide benefits as a matter of right instead of on the basis of demonstrated need. (It is of course true, if an assistance program exists, and need is demonstrated, that a "right" to such assistance may be presumed. But this is a "right" of a different order.) Social insurance benefits are paid regardless of need to all persons who satisfy certain eligibility requirements. The benefit amounts are also determined on some basis other than actual need, although under many social insurance programs one factor affecting general benefit schedules is the presumed average need of the beneficiaries. The actual need may be more or less than the social insurance benefits. The officials administering the social insurance programs exercise little or no discretion in the determination of eligibility or benefit amounts in the general case.

[5] Eveline M. Burns, *Social Security and Public Policy* (New York: McGraw-Hill Book Co., 1956), pp. 5–9. This excellent book discusses in detail the major questions arising in connection with public social security programs.

[6] For an extensive discussion, see Eveline M. Burns, *The American Social Security System* (Boston: Houghton Mifflin Co., 1951), pp. 28–39. As noted in Mrs. Burns' volume, some programs are "hybrids," such as "income conditioned" systems.

Other differences between public assistance and social insurance programs may be summarized as follows:

1. The only direct participants under a public assistance program are the recipients. The direct participants under a social insurance plan are the insureds, only a small fraction of whom are beneficiaries at any given time. Thus, many more persons are directly concerned with social insurance programs.
2. Many persons who otherwise would be eligible for public assistance benefits do not apply because of the test of need. Participation in most social insurance programs is compulsory (with possibly a few exceptions), but the participants need not claim their benefits. Of course, very few persons who are eligible for social insurance benefits refuse to make a claim, for there is no stigma attached to the receipt of the benefits.
3. Because of the character of public assistance programs, they are usually financed out of general revenues which usually are derived from a more progressive tax system than earmarked revenues. Social insurance programs, on the other hand, are generally financed out of earmarked taxes, and there is usually some relationship between an individual's benefit and the contributions made by the individual or on his behalf. It is held generally desirable to maintain some relationship between contributions and benefits because of the presumably favorable effect on economic incentives.
4. Federal, state, and local funds are used to finance public assistance programs, but the programs are administered only by state or local government units. The amount of discretion involved in the programs is the principal reason advanced for the lack of federal administration. Federal and state funds plus private "contributions" are used to finance social insurance programs. Because the amount of discretion involved is slight and because uniformity among the states is highly desirable, many of the programs are administered solely or in part by the federal government.
5. Public assistance benefits are difficult to forecast because of the discretionary means test for both eligibility and benefit amounts. Therefore, most American families do not consider public assistance benefits in their economic security plans (except as emergency measures) because they do not expect or want to be needy. Social insurance benefits, on the other hand, can be reasonably forecast and participants are eligible for the benefits as a matter of right. Therefore, social insurance benefits are and should be included in the economic security plans of the American family.

Social insurance programs are much more "popular" than public assistance programs because definite benefits payable as a matter of right are preferred to indefinite benefits payable on the basis of need. Therefore, as interest in more adequate public economic security schemes has increased, social insurance programs have gradually replaced public assistance programs as the basic approach to these financial problems. Public assistance programs today protect only those persons who are both needy and ineligible for adequate social insurance benefits. Such programs are relatively least important in economic insecurities involving premature death and old age, for which social insurance programs are highly developed, and most important in cases such as poor health where economic security programs are less adequate.

Social Insurance Versus Private Insurance

Insurance may be defined as a social device by means of which the risks or uncertainties of many persons are combined through actual or promised contributions to a fund out of which claimants receive benefits as a matter of right.[7] Because the proportion of losses becomes more predictable as the number of persons or objects independently exposed to the loss increases, the risk or uncertainty of the insurer is slight if the insured group is large. Thus insurance is beneficial because it (1) reduces risk and its undesirable consequences and (2) substitutes many small losses in the form of premiums for a few large losses, thus reducing the *real* economic burden on society. The economic burden is less because, according to the law of diminishing utility, the loss in utility is much less if $100 is taken from each of 1000 families than if $10,000 is taken from each of ten families.[8]

Ideally, an insurable risk should possess the following characteristics: [9] First, the number of insureds should be large and they should be independently exposed to the potential loss. Otherwise the risk is not reduced sufficiently to permit safe operation. Second, the losses covered should be definite in time, place, and amount to facilitate loss adjustments. Third, the chance of loss should be measurable. Otherwise the cost of the program is indefinite. Fourth, the loss should be accidental from the viewpoint of the insured. It is unwise to insure against losses which the insured can bring about or against losses which are bound to happen.

---

[7] We define private insurance so as to include all types of definite benefit plans, because all such benefit plans of which we are aware can and usually do involve some pooling of the risks of many persons. Furthermore, under our definition, a "self-insured" employee-benefit plan is not insurance from the viewpoint of the employer but is insurance from the viewpoint of the employee.

[8] See Paul A. Samuelson, *Economics* (6th ed.; New York: McGraw-Hill Book Co., 1964), pp. 418–19; Allan H. Willett, *The Economic Theory of Risk and Insurance* (New York: Columbia University Press, 1901. Reprinted, Philadelphia: University of Pennsylvania Press, 1951); and Irving Pfeffer, *Insurance and Economic Theory* (Homewood, Ill.: Richard D. Irwin, Inc., 1956).

[9] For a discussion of the extent to which risks covered by common forms of insurance possess these characteristics, see C. A. Williams, Jr., and R. M. Heins, *Risk Management and Insurance* (New York: McGraw-Hill Book Co., 1964), pp. 53–55.

(Death, for example, is "bound to happen"; but the date of death is uncertain.)

Private insurance plans generally possess the following characteristics, although there are some important exceptions primarily associated with group insurance.

1. The protection is voluntary. Insureds must be "sold" on the need for protection. As a result, some persons buy either no protection or inadequate protection. On the other hand, they do retain their freedom of economic choice.

2. The insurance contract is a legal instrument which, except in unusual cases, cannot be changed without the consent of the insured, and which can be enforced in the courts.

3. The cost of each individual's protection is determined on an actuarial basis. His benefit amounts and his loss and expense-producing potentialities are considered in determining the price, for the price of the protection should equal the expected cost. It is true that most insureds are not rated individually, for there is a desire to base rates on past experience and the experience of a single insured is not usually credible. (This is obvious in the case of death.) Moreover, rating each person individually is a complicated procedure. Therefore, usually all insureds with *approximately* the same loss and expense characteristics are grouped together in a class and charged the same rate. For example, life insurance premiums vary with the amount and type of life insurance purchased, but for a given benefit the rates depend upon only one factor—age. There are undoubtedly differences among standard lives in the same age groups, but these differences are assumed to be slight.[10] Insofar as practical considerations will permit, price equals expected cost.

   Private insurers may become bankrupt if their premiums plus assessments, if any, are consistently not sufficient to pay their actual expenses and losses, which may differ considerably from their expected losses and expenses. Private insurer experience in this respect has, however, been excellent.

4. The protection is provided by many insurers of various types who compete with one another for insureds. There are stock insurers, mutual insurers, self-insurers, medical service associations, and many others. Competition forces these insurers to reassess their contracts and prices periodically.

Social insurance, as defined in the first two editions of this text, included a variety of insurance arrangements. Under this earlier definition, social insurance included all insurance arrangements in which the govern-

---

[10] Substandard lives may pay a higher premium, but there are relatively few substandard lives.

ment acted as the insurer, subsidized the operation, or required the insureds to purchase the protection. At one extreme this definition included the type of private insurance required by law, such as workmen's compensation insurance, and public insurance, such as government life insurance for World War II veterans, which operate on essentially the same basis as private insurance. At the other extreme it included programs which differ from private insurance in many respects and which some persons believe should not be considered insurance. However, these programs do satisfy the definition of insurance used in this text.

The most important social insurance program—Old-Age, Survivors, and Disability Insurance—is the best example of this latter "extreme." This program carries out a social and economic public policy decision: it provides a floor of protection for all participants against financial losses caused by premature death, disability, or old age.[11] It differs from the most common forms of private insurance in four important respects:

1. Participation is compulsory (with a few exceptions) for all eligible persons. Otherwise some individuals would elect not to be covered and the policy objective of a floor of protection for all members of a defined group would be thwarted.
2. The benefits are prescribed by law. There are no contracts, and it is possible (but highly improbable) that Congress will rescind the benefits in the future. Periodic changes in the benefit structure are very likely through changes in the law.
3. The system redistributes income in addition to providing protection through a pooling arrangement. The lower-income groups, the insureds with many dependents, and the participants who were elderly when the system was inaugurated receive more benefits for their contributions than most other participants. If this were not true, it would be impossible to achieve the public policy objective of a floor of protection for all participants, since some insureds would be unable to afford adequate protection. Old-age benefits during the early years of the system would also be limited. The benefits are not equitable in the private insurance sense, but they are not meant to be. Other standards of performance have been deemed more important. In short, the system stresses "social adequacy" rather than "individual equity."[12] The contribution

[11] For a concise description of the principles underlying this program, see J. Douglas Brown, "Concepts in Old Age and Survivors Insurance," *Proceedings* of the First Annual Meeting of the Industrial Relations Research Association, 1948, pp. 100–06.

[12] For the original statement of this feature of OASDI in these terms by an actuary for the Metropolitan Life Insurance Company, see R. A. Hohaus, "Equity, Adequacy, and Related Factors," in W. Haber and W. Cohen, *Social Security: Programs, Problems, and Policies* (Homewood, Ill.: Richard D. Irwin, Inc., 1960), pp. 61–63. This article appeared originally in the June, 1938, issue of *The Record*, a publication of the Institute of Actuaries.

rates are scheduled, but Congress may and has revised the schedule periodically. Consequently, bankruptcy is impossible as long as the government has an effective taxing power, although it is conceivable that the taxes may become unbearable. An individual's contribution may vary yearly even though the tax rate remains fixed, for the base (annual income) upon which the tax is levied may fluctuate from year to year. These fluctuations may have little or no effect on the benefits.

4. The government system is a monopolistic system. However, public pressure forces a continual reassessment of benefits and contribution rates.

In 1964 the Committee on Social Insurance Terminology,[13] one of the operating committees of the Commission on Insurance Terminology of the American Risk and Insurance Association, recommended a more restrictive definition of social insurance, which will be used in this text. "Social insurance and related programs" will be used to mean what social insurance meant in previous editions. Unfortunately, no one has yet coined a satisfactory term for these related programs.

According to the definition adopted by the Committee, if an insurance program is to be labelled "social insurance," it must possess the following characteristics:

1. Persons eligible for coverage must be covered except in unusual cases.
2. Eligibility for benefits is derived, in fact or in effect, from contributions having been made to the program by or in respect to (a) the claimant or (b) the person as to whom the claimant is a dependent; there cannot be any requirement that the individual demonstrate inadequate financial resources, although a dependency status may have to be established.
3. The method for determining the benefits is specifically prescribed by law.
4. The benefits for any individual can be directly related to contributions made by or in respect to him but this should not usually be the case; instead, most "social insurance" programs would be expected to redistribute income in such a way as to favor certain groups such as those with low former wages or a large number of dependents. In other words, the usual program stresses social adequacy.

13 This committee included private insurance representatives, a risk manager for a large business, social insurance personnel, a union spokesman, and several academicians. For explanatory comments on the definition, see *Bulletin of the Commission on Insurance Terminology*, I, No. 2 (May, 1965), 2–4. For a discussion of the alternative definitions considered, see C. A. Williams, Jr., " 'Social Insurance'—Proper Terminology?" *Journal of Insurance*, XXX, No. 1 (March, 1963), 112–28.

5. There is a definite plan for financing the benefits that is designed (even though the design may be unsuccessful in view of the many long-range imponderables) to be adequate in terms of long-range considerations. The adequacy of the financing arrangements may involve reliance on some financial support from taxes or from contributions made with respect to *new* entrants.
6. The cost of the program is borne primarily by contributions which are usually made by covered persons, their employers, or both. Although some contributions may be made from general governmental funds, these contributions should not be the major source of financial support.
7. The plan is administered or at least supervised by the federal, state, or local government. Direct supervision, however, may be limited to the settlement of contested cases or checking compliance with insurance requirements, with most of the daily operations being conducted by private insurance.
8. The plan was not established by the government solely for its present or former employees. Social insurance programs must cover some persons other than government employees.

Under this definition the following programs (to be described later in this text) *are* social insurance programs because they meet all the prescribed conditions:

Old-Age, Survivors, and Disability Insurance

Unemployment Compensation or Insurance

Workmen's Compensation

Compulsory Temporary Disability Insurance

Railroad Retirement System

Railroad Unemployment and Temporary Disability Insurance

The following programs are *not* social insurance programs because they fail to meet at least one of the prescribed tests:

Civil Service Retirement System, because this plan was established by the government solely for its employees.

National Service Life Insurance, because it is not compulsory and because it was established by the government solely for its present or former employees.

Public assistance, because the individual must demonstrate that he has inadequate financial resources, the method of determining the benefits is not prescribed by statute, and the cost is not borne primarily by employers and their employees.

Veterans' benefits, because the plan is wholly financed out of general revenues, because it was established by the government solely for its former employees, and because some of the benefits require the individual to demonstrate that his income falls below a specified level.

On the other hand, all of those programs except public assistance and the veterans' benefits involving an income test are "related programs."

The issues created by the establishment in 1965 of Hospital Insurance and Supplementary Medical Insurance are considered in Chapter 11.

In one respect, the above definition has not been adopted in this text. The definition does not limit social insurance programs to the risks associated with death, accidental injury, sickness, family breakdowns, unemployment, and the like; but the text does. The only major subject that is not discussed because of this omission is automobile compensation, which would, at least in some modified form, apply the principles of workmen's compensation to automobile accidents. At the present time there are no automobile compensation plans in the United States, but the concept is attracting increasing attention.[14]

Notice that social insurance programs still include different types of insurance arrangements but these differences are much less marked than under the earlier definition. Variety is still possible with respect to (1) the relative roles of social adequacy and private equity, but the program that stresses private equity is an unusual one; (2) contributions from general governmental funds may or may not be involved, but in any event their role should be minor; and (3) the government may either function as a monopoly insurer or exercise various degrees of supervision over private insurers. Consequently other social insurance programs such as workmen's compensation are not as different from private insurance as is OASDI, an "extreme" case, but OASDI is a less extreme case than was true under the earlier definition. We shall not consider here these other programs but as each is discussed in detail in later chapters, the student should compare and contrast that program with private insurance in order to increase his appreciation and understanding of the important differences between private and social insurance. Since the purposes of the two devices differ, we should not be surprised to find differences in their nature and application.

One final note should be made here concerning the differences between private insurance and social insurance. Because the benefits and the contribution rates may be made non-contractual and flexible, and

---

[14] For those interested in exploring the social problem of automobile accident costs and the ways in which they are or could be handled, the following two books are highly recommended: A. F. Conard, J. N. Morgan, R. W. Pratt, Jr., C. E. Volz, and R. L. Bombaugh, *Automobile Accident Costs and Payments* (Ann Arbor: The University of Michigan Press, 1964); R. E. Keeton and J. O'Connell, *Basic Protection for the Automobile Accident Victim* (Boston: Little, Brown, & Co., 1966).

because the government has the taxing power, some risks which are non-insurable by sound private insurance standards are insurable under social insurance programs. For example, Old-Age, Survivors, and Disability Insurance, as it presently exists, could not be underwritten by a private insurer because there are too many unpredictable variables in the program. Another case in point is unemployment insurance, which is not underwritten by private commercial insurers because they consider the chance of loss to be unpredictable and the exposure units to be interdependent. However, some employers have developed self-insured unemployment "insurance" plans, to be discussed subsequently.

THE AMERICAN ECONOMIC SECURITY SYSTEM

Let us now use the above framework in presenting a bird's-eye view of the American economic security system. Classifying the various programs included in this system is a difficult task, if for no other reason than that the system is very complex.[15] In the presentation of this system we shall use the following classification:

1. The two major headings will be prevention and alleviation with regulation introduced as the occasion demands.
2. *Within* each of these major headings the classification will be by type of insecurity: death, old age, unemployment, and so on. This is the way the American system is customarily described and hence our approach is realistic.
3. In turn, for each type of insecurity, note will be made of specific public and private plans and the variations within them.

(Earlier in the chapter we emphasized *approaches;* we were interested in providing a basic tool kit. Here we emphasize specific *programs* and show how the various approaches are applied. In so doing we seek to present a recognizable picture of the American economic security system.)

Preventive Programs

Most people do not think of preventive programs when economic security measures are being discussed, but the preventive approaches decrease the cost of non-preventive programs and produce greater social and economic benefits when they are successful. Preventive efforts include programs aimed at one or both of the following objectives: (1) re-

[15] For a useful classification of the public social security programs, see *Systems of Social Security: United States* (Geneva: International Labour Office, 1953). See also, Edwin E. Witte, *Five Lectures on Social Security* (Rio Piedras, Puerto Rico: University of Puerto Rico, 1951).

duction or elimination of the chance of loss ("true" prevention); (2) minimization of the severity of the losses.[16] The preventive efforts may be general programs aimed at problems affecting all or most of our population or they may be selective programs designed to aid one person, firm, area, or other subdivision of the population. Preventive programs operate so as (1) to provide a safer environment in which to live and work and (2) to educate and protect the individual within that environment.

Death, Old Age, and Illness.[17] Since the preventive programs dealing with the problems of death, old age, accidental injuries, and sickness overlap to a large extent, they will be treated in this discussion as one unit. All levels of government participate in the extensive public preventive programs. It is impossible to enumerate all of these activities, but an example of each approach will indicate their nature. General programs illustrating the true prevention and minimization objectives are quarantine programs and inspections under pure food and drug acts. Illustrative selective programs are physical examinations of school children and rehabilitation programs for veterans. Private efforts may be divided into the same categories. Illustrative general programs are medical research into the causes of certain diseases and first-aid classes. Illustrative selective programs are physical examinations for employees and the assignment of a lighter work load to an employee following a heart attack. It is interesting to note that while all the above measures have an important job-oriented relationship, it is indirect in many cases. Of course, any method an individual uses to protect his health and safety is preventive in this respect. But, in general, in this text, we shall be concerned with the more direct job-related relationships.

Unemployment. Public preventive measures against unemployment may be categorized in the same way. Most of the programs are sponsored by the federal government. True prevention includes monetary and fiscal policies aimed at maintaining full employment. The same policies when aimed at re-achieving full employment following a decline in economic activity illustrate the minimizing approach. Other examples are public works programs and "automatic stabilizers," such as the income tax whose burden decreases in periods of unemployment, thus tending to increase purchasing power. Public employment services for veterans illustrate a selective preventive approach, while the allocation of government contracts to critical unemployment areas is a selective

---

[16] A. H. Mowbray and R. H. Blanchard, *Insurance* (4th ed.; New York: McGraw-Hill Book Co., 1955), pp. 30–36.

[17] We use "illness" here and later in the text as a generalized term which includes accidental injuries and sickness.

minimizing approach. Private industry also has introduced stabilization programs which attempt to reduce unemployment through various techniques. Anything an employee does to improve his job marketability is relevant also.

Substandard Conditions. Government intervention in substandard conditions is fundamentally preventive in nature. There are no alleviative aspects to these programs. Before we investigate the scope of this intervention, we should note two facts. First, any improvement in substandard conditions indirectly improves the condition of the population with respect to the economic insecurities associated with death, old age, illness, and unemployment. Second, any public actions designed to increase the average real wage of employees indirectly attack substandard conditions.

Government intervention in substandard conditions essentially consists of a set of rules with which employers are expected to comply. The federal Fair Labor Standards Act contains the most important set of rules, for it establishes a minimum wage and a maximum work week at standard rates for most employment in interstate commerce. The Act also regulates the use of child labor. The Davis-Bacon Act and the Walsh-Healey Act provide for the payment of prevailing minimum wage rates by private firms serving the government. The Walsh-Healey Act, which applies to suppliers, also establishes a maximum work week at standard rates, prohibits child labor, and specifies certain health and safety standards.

All states have child labor laws and laws which regulate in some way the maximum work week for women. A few have laws which regulate the maximum work week for men. Nine have minimum wage laws applying to all workers, while twenty-two have similar laws applying to women and children only. Other working conditions such as minimum work space are also prescribed under some state laws.

Private attempts to improve the working conditions of the wage earner include the voluntary action of employers, the efforts of labor unions, collective actions through collective bargaining, and measures of one type or another inspired by the public conscience.

Alleviative Programs

Preventive programs are only a partial solution to the problem of economic security. There may be limitations as to what can be accomplished; for example, premature death can probably never be eliminated. In other cases, the results do not justify the commitment of more economic resources to the preventive program.

Alleviative programs not only supplement but are the alternative solution when preventive efforts fail. They reimburse the insured for the financial loss that he or his family suffers when he becomes ill, dies prematurely, terminates his earning career because of old age, or is unemployed. In this section we shall list the alleviative programs dealing with each of these problems and classify them as social insurance programs, public assistance programs, or private approaches. Whether the programs provide service or cash benefits will be indicated in the text.

Death and Old Age. 1. *Social insurance and related programs.* The most important program providing death and retirement benefits is the Federal Old-Age, Survivors, and Disability Insurance System established under the Social Security Act of 1935. The social insurance program pays benefits in cash, and its coverage is becoming almost universal.

Other programs, all of which are underwritten by the federal government and all of which pay income benefits, are the Railroad Retirement System, the Civil Service Retirement System, government life insurance for servicemen and veterans, veterans' benefits (though certain of these may be income-conditioned benefits), and retirement programs of the armed services. State and local governments also have retirement systems for certain of their employees. That these programs are designed for special groups is evident from their titles.

Death due to occupational causes is covered under both federal and state workmen's compensation laws. The state acts are the most important. These acts require employers to pay cash benefits to the beneficiaries of deceased employees whose deaths were job-connected. Employers may self-insure this obligation with the state's permission, but usually the employer is insured by a private insurer or a state insurer. Six states have monopolistic state funds, while twelve have funds which compete with commercial insurers.

2. *Public assistance.* The public program dealing specifically with old age is Old-Age Assistance. The federal government makes grants-in-aid to approved state programs which are in turn administered by state and local governmental authorities. A similar program—Aid to Families with Dependent Children—provides benefits for children who are deprived of parental support because of death, incapacity, or absence of a parent or, at least temporarily, the unemployment of a parent. Both programs pay income benefits.

3. *Private approaches.* The most important private measure is private insurance, which consists primarily of individual insurance contracts issued by commercial insurers and group insurance plans underwritten by commercial insurers or self-insured by employers and/or unions. Reliance on relatives and charity, while still extensive, is less important than in the past.

Unemployment. 1. *Social insurance and related programs.* Each of the fifty states has an unemployment insurance system covering most of the employees in the state. The federal government participates indirectly, for it levies a tax on employers to pay the administrative costs of the state funds. The tax is reduced if the employer contributes to a state unemployment insurance scheme. Thus the states have a strong incentive for maintaining an unemployment compensation fund. Moreover, all taxes paid to the states are deposited in a federal unemployment insurance fund from which the states withdraw needed benefit amounts. The state plans provide cash payments to the *temporarily* unemployed.

The only other active unemployment insurance system is the federally written Railroad Unemployment Insurance System which provides similar benefits for a special class of workers.

2. *General assistance.* General assistance provides a type of "residual" protection, available under a variety of circumstances, but importantly useful in situations involving economic unemployment. Temporarily, at least, Aid to Families with Dependent Children also provides some unemployment assistance.

3. *Private approaches.* No commercial insurer underwrites unemployment insurance, but we do have private unemployment "insurance" and, more commonly, supplementary unemployment insurance self-insured by an employer or union. The benefits are cash payments. Work and wage guarantees, including supplementary unemployment insurance, are of interest currently.

Reliance on relatives and charity is necessary in some cases; here benefits may be in cash or in kind.

Accidental Injury and Sickness. 1. *Social insurance and related programs.* The Federal Old-Age, Survivors, and Disability Insurance System provides two types of benefits in case of disability caused by accidental injury or sickness. The first benefit is a monthly income for certain totally and permanently disabled persons. The second benefit enables a totally and permanently disabled person to retain the death and retirement benefits to which he was entitled at the date the disability began. A Hospital Insurance program and Supplemental Medical Insurance provide medical care for the aged.

The other programs provide benefits for only (1) job-connected injury or disease or (2) special groups.

The federal and state workmen's compensation laws protect most employees against loss of income and medical expenses caused by job-connected injuries and disease. Income benefits are paid in cash; medical bills are paid by the insurer. These laws have already been discussed as an alleviative approach to the financial problems caused by death.

Federal programs dealing with special groups include (1) the Railroad Retirement System, which pays a lifetime income in case of total and permanent disability, (2) the Railroad Temporary Disability Insurance System, which pays income benefits to participants who are totally disabled for a short period, (3) the Public Health Service, which, in addition to its other functions, provides free medical services in its hospitals for qualified seamen, (4) a federal law which requires that shipowners continue the wages and provide full medical care for a seaman during a voyage and, in the event of continued illness, for a reasonable time thereafter, (5) the disability pensions and medical care services provided by the Veterans Administration, and (6) the continued salary and medical benefits for members of the armed services.

Four states—Rhode Island, California, New Jersey, and New York—have enacted temporary non-occupational disability insurance legislation, which affects most of the industrial workers in those states. The purpose is to provide income to workers who are disabled for short periods because of non-occupational injuries and sickness. The California act also provides cash allowances toward hospital bills. The insurance is provided by a monopolistic state fund in Rhode Island; the other three states have competitive state funds.

2. *Public assistance.* Special public assistance programs providing income benefits in case of disability include Aid to Families with Dependent Children (already mentioned in connection with death), Aid to the Blind, and Aid to the Totally and Permanently Disabled. Under all four special public assistance programs—these three and Old-Age Assistance—medical care allowances are included in the assistance payments made to recipients. Direct payments are also made to suppliers of medical service under these plans and this practice has been encouraged over cash allowances in recent years. Medical assistance for the aged makes direct payments in behalf of *medically* needy aged and under certain conditions a state can establish a program which will make vendor payments in behalf of the medically needy aged, blind, or disabled or dependent children.

3. *Private approaches.* Private approaches are especially important in this area because the public programs are so limited. The insurance approach is, by far, the most important. Many types of insurers are active, the two leading types being the commercial insurers and the Blue Cross and Blue Shield associations. Commercial insurers under individual or group contracts promise income benefits in case of long-term or short-term disability and pay cash allowances toward medical expenses. They also protect an individual against the loss of his life, retirement, or health insurance through his inability to pay premiums while totally and permanently disabled. Blue Cross and Blue Shield associations provide medical expense protection, usually on a service basis. Other plans, called independent plans, include a variety of approaches to the medical expense problem.

As in the case of other risks, it may be necessary to rely on assistance from relatives or gifts from non-relatives. The benefits may be in cash or in kind.

General. 1. *Public assistance.* Needy persons who do not qualify for benefits under any of the social insurance and related programs or special public assistance programs may receive aid from the general assistance programs financed and administered by the states, local governments, or both. Payments are made in cash or in services to persons who can demonstrate need, regardless of the cause, if they satisfy the eligibility requirements. These are residual programs whose importance depends upon the coverage and benefit levels of other programs as well as upon general economic conditions.

2. *Private approaches.* Assistance from relatives and gifts from friends, charities, and help from employers, unions, and others are the basic private approaches available. The benefits may be in cash or in kind.

RECENT GROWTH

The American insurance system, as a component of the American economic security system, has expanded tremendously in the past twenty-five years. Table 1.1 shows how the financial protection of a "typical" United States employee's family against death, old age, unemployment, and illness improved from 1929 to 1966. The table "does not present an average and is not symbolic of all workers, but it shows the situation of some millions of workers." [18] The most striking feature of the table is the increase in the number of kinds of public and private protection against economic insecurity.

Most of the public programs were initiated under the Social Security Act, which was not passed until 1935. Workmen's compensation was the only important public program in existence prior to that time. Other countries had adopted extensive public social insurance programs at a much earlier date. Germany had a fairly complete national insurance system in operation by the close of the nineteenth century. Great Britain introduced a series of public programs during the first two decades of the present century. Other foreign countries were also active about the same time. Why did the United States lag behind?

This lag has been explained by the superior economic status and individualistic nature of our population, our federal form of government, and

---

[18] Chester C. Nash, "The Contribution of Life Insurance to Social Security in the United States," *International Labour Review*, LXXII, No. 1 (July 1, 1955), 39. The comparison presented in the text is based on a table in this article. We have used the Nash table and brought it up to date.

TABLE 1.1

Financial Protection of a "Typical" United States Worker's Family
Against Death, Old Age, Unemployment, and Accidental Injury
and Sickness, 1929, 1954, and 1966

Type of Protection	1929	1954	1966
Death:			
Old-Age, Survivors, and Disability Insurance	None	Up to $200 monthly while children are dependent	Up to $368 monthly while children are dependent
Private life insurance [a]	$3,000	$8,000	$18,000
Old age:			
Old-Age, Survivors, and Disability Insurance	None	Up to $162.80 monthly for worker and spouse	Up to $252 monthly for worker and spouse
Private annuities and pensions [b]	None	$100 monthly	$160 monthly
Unemployment:			
State unemployment compensation [c]	None	$35 weekly	$50 weekly
Illness:			
Occupational:			
Workmen's compensation	Yes	Yes	Yes
Non-occupational:			
Old-Age, Survivors, and Disability Insurance	None	None	Up to $368 monthly while children are dependent for disabilities lasting more than one year
Hospital insurance	None	None	Hospital services during old age
Supplemental medical insurance	None	None	Medical services other than hospital services during old age
Private temporary disability insurance income [c]	None	$35 weekly for short-term disability	$50 weekly for short-term disability
Private medical expense insurance	None	Most medical expenses associated with short-term illnesses	Most medical expenses associated with short-term illnesses and a considerable portion of the larger bills

[a] Average life insurance per insured family.

[b] Crude estimates based on median incomes of employed males and three-to-one weighting of benefits under pattern plans and conventional plans reported in 1955 and 1965 editions of *Study of Industrial Retirement Plans* by the Bankers Trust Company of New York City.

[c] Common maximum weekly benefits.

the retention by the states of powers not expressly delegated to the federal government, social and economic variations among the states, and competition among the states for business interests.[19] The Great Depression and changes in our social mores lessened the retarding effect of these factors and an extensive social insurance program was born. However, the program characteristics reflect the continuing importance of these factors.

Private insurance, on the other hand, was important thirty-five years ago, but it was much less developed and much less popular than it is today. In fact, private insurance in the United States dates back to the colonial period, but the industry was a very small one until the middle of the nineteenth century when it began a period of steady growth. The Depression marked the beginning of a period of extremely rapid growth. The factors favoring the tremendous increase in the benefits and the proportion of the insured population are the Depression experiences, the excellent record of the private commercial insurers during this period, increased public interest in economic security, the introduction of public programs, the increasing importance of industry programs for employees, the government insurance program for servicemen and veterans, the changes in income distribution, an improved insurance industry sales force, the introduction of new coverages, and a higher average level of education among our population.

Forecasting is a hazardous occupation, but we can be almost certain that the protection afforded the typical employee will continue to improve. The existing types of benefits should more adequately cover his losses, and new benefits such as private long-term disability income insurance will probably be included in the list by 1975.

BASIC PROBLEMS IN ECONOMIC SECURITY PROGRAMS

This bird's-eye view omits, of necessity, detailed information about each part of the American economic security system; this information will be presented in later chapters of this book. We shall want to be systematic, however, in our presentation of the details. Let us note, therefore, the basic problems that must be considered in thinking about and spelling out any economic security program.

At this point we do not, however, discuss the more basic issues that need to be considered in order to evaluate a given program and decide if it should or should not be introduced or should or should not be eliminated. For the moment we accept the system as it is. This is not an unrealistic point of view, since it is hard to conceive, for example, of the

---

[19] Mowbray and Blanchard, *op. cit.,* pp. 492–94.

Old-Age, Survivors, and Disability Insurance System being wiped off the books. This neither suggests that such programs cannot be amended or improved, nor does it mean that they cannot be criticized. But for purposes of exposition in this text, it is perhaps better to present first the system as it exists and then later evaluate it on the basis of specific criteria set up for the purpose.

The operational questions involved in any given economic security program are as follows.[20]

Who Shall Be Covered by the Program? In the case of public programs, administrative, constitutional, economic, political, and other pressures are intertwined, along with "need," in determining coverage. The Old-Age, Survivors, and Disability Insurance program will serve as an example. In the early years following the passage of this act, certain classes of employees such as agricultural laborers and domestic servants were excluded, partly because of administrative difficulties involved in handling their records. As record-keeping experience was gained by the OASDI administration, this became less of a problem, and such employees have since been brought under the act. Or, there is little doubt that economic considerations were important in originally excluding farm groups, for example, from coverage. Again, the political representation of medical practitioners was probably instrumental in enabling them to remain out of the OASDI program until the amendments of 1965.

In the case of unemployment insurance, differences in coverage have been in part based upon the number of employees the employer had and, additionally, in some states, upon the size of the community in which the company was located. Thus, in a case in point, eligible employers of *one* or more employees in towns of 10,000 and over would come under the act, but in towns of less than 10,000 only employers of *eight* or more (after December 31, 1955, four or more) employees would be covered. The logic of the community size factor was based in part, at least, upon the belief that in small towns employment was "inherently" more stable, and also that where unemployment did occur, the individual frequently had other resources, such as a quarter-acre of land to help tide him over. Thus, it was argued that the same degree of need did not exist.

Similar considerations enter into private programs, such as employer-sponsored or collectively bargained pension programs or "guaranteed wage" programs. A wage guarantee may be extended only to employees with two years' service with the company, this restriction arising in part out of the belief that the company does not have such an obligation to employees who do not intend to remain with it, that is, to "floaters." Or,

[20] For a useful reference, see Burns, *Social Security and Public Policy, op. cit.*

if such a plan is collectively bargained, it may extend only to "seniority" workers. In part, this may be based upon cost factors, in part upon ethical considerations noted above. Other reasons may also be involved, varying to some extent with the specific program concerned.

In general, there is a tendency for the coverage of economic security programs to become more extensive. This is true for public as well as private programs. The increase in OASDI coverage illustrates this for public programs, and the extension of company and union health and welfare programs to the family of the employee provides an example for private programs. There are some exceptions; unemployment insurance is a case where coverage has been extended relatively little. And there are some cases where the program contracts because of the well-being of the economy or because of the substitution of other programs. Thus, the county poor farm is gradually becoming a thing of the past as newer programs of economic security take its place.

What Are Qualifications for Collection of Benefits? Where economic security programs involve the payment of benefits, as to an injured, retired, or unemployed individual, it is customary to require that the "covered" individual also meet certain other requirements. These are usually of three types.

First are requirements relating to coverage itself. Thus the individual frequently must have been in the program for a certain minimum period of time and in some cases also must have had certain minimum wages or earnings. The specific requirements vary with program types, and again are a result of a combination of administrative, economic, political, and other considerations. The reasoning behind such requirements is that benefits should only be payable to one who has a "genuine" attachment to the labor force or to a given company and there should be some sort of "ethical" minimum to this attachment. Thus, for example, it is not held to be economically or ethically desirable to pay unemployment benefits to a housewife who works as a retail clerk during the Christmas season but who retires from the labor force after the season is over. (This is not universally true: a covered employee is protected by workmen's compensation the moment he begins on the job. The reader should ask himself why the difference.)

A second requirement relates to the specific factor "causing" the economic insecurity. Thus, where discharge is for cause, or where an individual quits for certain reasons, unemployment insurance may be denied or there may be a longer waiting period required. Parallel illustrations can be given for accidental injury and for old-age security programs. Private economic security systems probably are currently less restrictive in these respects than are public. Subsequent to job separation, other qualifications are also found. In unemployment compensation, for example, a person must be able to work and willing to work before he can become an eligible claimant; the previously mentioned housewife who worked at Christmas would not be eligible for benefits (assuming that she had sufficient coverage) if she dropped out of the labor force on January 1 and did not make herself available for employment.

Third, some public programs involve continuing requirements, once benefits have started. Thus, under unemployment compensation, a beneficiary may lose part or all of his benefits if he earns above a certain maximum amount in part-time, casual, or other employment while he is technically unemployed. The same is true of a beneficiary under OASDI, who, if he is in a certain age group and earns more than a certain sum, has his benefits reduced.

The net effect of all these restrictions is to set up a series of rules under which benefits can or cannot be claimed. Ethical and economic reasons underlie such requirements, with political pressures evident in a variety of instances. Public assistance programs illustrate, in a different way, all of the above characteristics.

What Benefits Should Be Paid the Recipients of Economic Security Programs in Varying Situations? Here public and private programs differ markedly. In the private insurance program there is usually a close correspondence with actuarial principles. A person collects what is related actuarially to the specific cost outlays made under the program; under a given annuity plan a higher in-payment will result in an actuarially related higher benefit. Hence the major determinant is impersonal and mathematical. In the non-insurance type of private economic security program, such as the dismissal wage or the wage guarantee, actuarial relations do not hold, and the benefit levels are usually a matter of individual or pooled judgment, as well as of collective bargaining.

In the public insurance programs, such as OASDI or UC, actuarial relations are less important. This is true not only for the relation between over-all total benefits and over-all total costs of the program, but also for individual benefits and costs. These social insurance systems emphasize the social aspect more than they do the actuarial. (Indeed, some critics have held that social "assurance" or other variants would be more logical terms.) Thus, under OASDI, per given dollar of in-payment, a low-wage worker receives a proportionately greater benefit than does the high-wage earner. This is true because the benefit computation formula is structured so as to pay a higher percentage benefit for the lower wage increments. Under public assistance programs "need" is critical in determining benefits. The influence of political pressures is apparent with respect to the above.

What Are the Costs? A complicated set of factors lies behind cost considerations, of which the following are among the more basic.

Costs are, of course, closely related on one side to need and on the other to the ability and willingness of the individual, company, or governmental unit to bear the cost. Thus, a given county's ability to take care of its aged poor or needy (assuming no grants are available from other political units) depends not only upon the degree of need, but upon how much revenue can be directed to this purpose.

If there is leeway in how much can be expended, the actual expenditures will be determined by a number of factors. First are the benefit levels desired. For example, there is a considerable difference in the benefits collectible under the Railroad Retirement Act as compared with OASDI. But there is also a considerable difference in the level of inpayments. Political pressures may influence benefit levels; thus under UC, experience rating has probably contributed to keeping benefits down in order to keep costs down. Second, for private plans, where the actuarial relationship is much tighter, it is more obvious that the benefit structure desired will have a direct bearing upon costs. Here, also, political pressures are evident, though they are the pressures of management, unionism, and collective bargaining, rather than of government. If a wage increase is forthcoming, the union membership may prefer it in "here-and-now pay raises" rather than as part of an increase in security benefits.

Who Shall Pay the Costs? Here again diverse pressures are evident. In public programs, political and constitutional considerations are relevant. Thus, in the OASDI program, both employer and employee contribute. In the UC program, only the employer contributes. Why this difference? One reason is that it was felt the UC program would have a greater chance of meeting the test of constitutionality if the given approach were used. Another was that old age is inevitable and hence both parties should "help" whereas unemployment might not fall upon everyone. In private programs, both ethics and economics are involved. Some persons hold that the employee as well as the employer should contribute to security programs as a matter of "right." Against this is set the fact that, dollar for dollar, contributions made only by the employer are the more economical, since they are tax deductible, while the employee's are not. Also, it has been held that it is much more economical to administer a program where only the employer contributes. Compromise, not necessarily in the worst sense of the term, usually produces the final result.

What Method of Financing Should Be Used? Should the program be put completely upon a pay-as-you-go basis or should the system be set up so as to provide also for an accumulation of funds for past service (as in the case of retirement) as well as for possible future increases in costs?

In general, the type of insecurity involved, and hence the program utilized, has an important bearing upon the answer to this last question. For example, most health insurance programs tend, by their inherent nature, to be operated upon a pay-as-you-go basis; there is little logic in any other approach. Public unemployment insurance programs stand in an intermediate position; in part the employer (given varying state laws) pays in yearly on a pay-as-you-go basis. But, if he builds up the account for his own enterprise, and his firm has little unemployment, his rates in subsequent years may be lowered. At the other extreme are situations, primarily involving retirement, where a choice can be made between pay-as-you-go and other systems. Thus, a university may provide for its retired employees by meeting retirement payments through a year-by-year budgetary allowance. This was, in fact, the way many such institutions operated until 1930–1935. But this approach entails heavy financial burdens if the retirement rolls grow and if no reserve has been built up. Hence, in most private retirement programs the pay-as-you-go approach has been abandoned in favor of other more financially sound means. In the OASDI program the approach has veered from one extreme to the other, with political and other pressures as important as economic ones. In passing, it ought to be noted that the same type of financial logic need not necessarily hold for both public and private programs. Thus, "pay-as-you-go" may have different implications for private in contrast to public programs.

A final comment on financing relates to public programs only. Some critics have taken the point of view that it would be cheaper to finance, say, an economic security program such as OASDI by direct government payments raised from general revenue sources without any intermediate in-payment plan.[21] At present such proposals do not seem likely to be adopted generally in the social insurance field though they are important in grants-in-aid approaches, as, for example, in the categorical public-assistance programs, and are now found to some extent in programs such as Hospital Insurance and Supplemental Medical Insurance for the Aged.

How Shall the Program Be Administered? In the case of public programs, administrative procedure is basically a matter of law. The administrative agency is conventionally set up by statute, as is the broad framework within which it operates. Within this framework the agency

[21] See, for example, Lewis Meriam, *Relief and Social Security* (Washington, D. C.: The Brookings Institution, 1946), pp. 84–88.

exercises, of necessity, some degree of discretion in its day-by-day operations. Thus, within limits, the agency makes rulings on eligibility,
disqualifications, and the thousand-and-one phases of administration that
are encountered daily. Commonly, there are provided procedures for
appeal, so that a person or group aggrieved by the ruling of an administrator has the opportunity to petition for review. The exact nature of
the administrative organization and process is in part a result of conscious
planning, in part a result of the vagaries of lawmaking, and in part a
result of the specific administrators named or elected and their policies.

In the case of private programs, the administrative organization and
procedure are largely a matter of what the party or parties wish, with
some external regulation imposed. Thus a given pension plan may be
self-administered or it may be turned over to a third party, such as an
insurance company. The Labor Management Relations Act of 1947, as
amended in 1959, contains restrictions for those plans arrived at through
collective bargaining. These restrictions relate mainly to the fact that
"joint" administration must be exercised and that out-payments must meet
certain stipulations; they cannot, for example, be used for other than
benefit payments. Additional controls were imposed as of January 1,
1959.

In addition to the broad phases of administration, there are many
matters of detail involved in economic security programs. In one respect
these may be viewed as program features which, nevertheless, have administrative implications. Thus, in a private pension program, a pertinent question is: What pension rights does an individual employee carry
with him when he leaves a given employer? This is the problem of
"vesting," and it is but one of many detailed features of economic security
programs.

The above comments indicate the basic questions involved in any
economic security program. These ideas have been deliberately developed on a general level so they can be used in subsequent discussions
without repeating them each time. Then, we can subsequently proceed
directly to the specific subject matter in each type of economic security
program.

One further note. Government intervention in substandard conditions also requires answers to the questions listed above, although the
importance of the different questions varies. Thus, "coverage," "benefits,"
and "administration" would be very important matters in the above sense;
"costs" would be pertinent also, but in a different way because of the
very nature of the programs. Thus, an employer "improves" his working
conditions; this is a "once-and-for-all" process. Or, overtime is eliminated, or, children under a given age are prohibited from working.

THE WAR ON POVERTY

In recent years considerably increased emphasis has been placed upon poverty, its causes and its cures. Although we shall not devote a separate chapter to this issue, it will be worthwhile to outline here some of the major characteristics of problems and programs.[22]

Poverty—as a form of economic insecurity—has many roots. These include low rates of pay resulting from low productivity which in turn can reflect lack of education and training, physical or mental disability, poor motivation, discrimination, low bargaining power, exclusion from minimum wage coverage, inadequate knowledge of opportunities, and immobility.[23]

Poverty has long been recognized and studied, and many proposals have been advanced for its elimination or mitigation.[24] But it has been only recently that a determined and integrated national attack has been made upon the problem, culminating in the Economic Opportunity Act of 1964 (signed into law August 20, 1964). The main thrust of this Act is directed at the roots of poverty, particularly at helping the children of the poor, and augments other government programs for education, training, and health and welfare services which are directed less specifically at poverty.

It will be useful to look at provisions of the Act since it deals specifically with the problems of protracted economic insecurity and focuses upon both the economic system and the individual in a more comprehensive fashion than much economic security legislation.

The Act consists of six titles.

Title I sets up job corps (residential camps) where jobless youths learn work habits and job skills; creates neighborhood youth corps permitting employment on a variety of jobs and helping the individual to stay in school or increase his employability; and provides for a work study program in which low-income college students can secure part-time jobs to help them through school.

Title II authorizes formation of local councils to combat poverty and creates "Project Head Start," set up by these councils to provide guidance clinics through which poor youngsters may catch up to a kindergarten or first-grade level.

22 Two useful sources with respect to poverty are *The Economic Report of the President*, January, 1964, and January, 1965 (Washington, D. C.: U. S. Government Printing Office), chaps. 2 and 4, respectively.

23 See *ibid.* (1964 *Report*), p. 66.

24 See the discussion in John G. Turnbull, *The Changing Faces of Economic Insecurity* (Minneapolis: University of Minnesota Press, 1966), "Conclusions."

Title III provides for the making of low-interest loans to poverty-stricken farm families and locally devised programs to aid migrant workers.

Title IV affords a basis for making low-interest small business loans.

Title V involves special efforts to help the unemployed heads of households in welfare families to become self-sufficient through vocational or educational training.

Title VI sets up the administrative machinery for the Act and establishes a Domestic Peace Corps.[25]

The Act has been in effect too short a time to make any conclusive judgments about its effectiveness. Programs have got under way, but, as is typical in new legislation, many problems have been encountered in getting them under way, ranging from general uncertainty at one extreme to specifics at the other, such as the matter of discipline in job corps. We would venture the prediction, however, that the Act will be effective, though it would be rash to suggest quantitatively what the impact will be on the reduction in poverty. But it is an Act which, unlike much earlier programming, seeks to get at the individual and his role in economic insecurity. And the approach is through the preventive route.

Other programs such as area redevelopment, manpower retraining, and education, all of which seek also to get at many of the problems delineated here, will be treated in later sections of this book, particularly in the chapters dealing with unemployment.[26]

THREE CONCLUDING TOPICS

Yardsticks for Evaluating Economic Security Programs

In this book we shall want to do more than describe and analyze. We shall wish to make some evaluation of economic security programs. If one is to assess, standards of evaluation are necessary. We shall apply three major types of yardsticks.

1. Did the economic security program accomplish its purpose? Or, was it self-defeating? For example, in a narrower sense, was a minimum wage law self-defeating in that it reduced the total wage bill? In a

[25] For a detailed account of the Act, the problems it seeks to attack, and some consequences of the implementation of the Act see Sam Newlund, Richard P. Kleeman, and Frank Premack, "The War on Poverty," a series of ten articles running in the *Minneapolis Tribune,* commencing August 30, 1965. For a critical view see Nathan Glazer, "The Grand Design of the Poverty Program," *New York Times Magazine,* February 27, 1966, pp. 21, 64, 69–73.

[26] For an analysis of the problems of poverty and education—and prescriptions therefor—see Committee for Economic Development, *Raising Low Incomes Through Improved Education* (New York: Committee for Economic Development, 1965).

broader sense, do economic security programs "reduce" incentives to the point where the economy is worse off than if the program had not been introduced?

2. Is the specific economic security program soundly structured and administered? Subsidiary standards are involved here: What is meant by soundly structured? By soundly administered? The second question is easier to answer than the first; we would suggest that sound administration involves, first, execution of the program in terms of its intent and, second, that such execution be honest. Recent experiences with some private health and welfare programs provide examples of poor administration. Structural soundness implies not only an economical plan, but one whose features make sense organizationally.

3. Does the program produce undesirable economic consequences? Does it artificially distort resource allocation? Pricing? What is its impact upon the functioning of the economy? For example, do different state unemployment insurance laws artificially influence the location of industry? Does experience rating in unemployment compensation add to cyclical movement rather than act as a counter-cyclical force? Do private pension programs unduly restrict labor mobility?

The criteria problem not only involves the choice of yardsticks, but also requires the collection of information so as to apply the yardsticks. Information is becoming increasingly available in many areas of economic security, and this is perhaps a less difficult problem than the specification of standards. We shall use the above-noted three criteria throughout the book as we discuss economic security programs.

Three Value Judgments

Value judgments are important in a field such as economic security. To make our position clear on several important points—which will come up from time to time—let us briefly indicate our beliefs.

1. Some causes of insecurity, such as industrial deaths, have decreased over time; others, such as non-occupational highway accidents, have increased. On balance it is not easy to say which trend is uppermost. But insecurity is *not* a problem which has been solved at present. Hence continuing attention is necessary.

2. What happens to incentive as security increases? To progress? These are not easy questions to answer. And, empirical evidence is mostly lacking.[27] One ingenious set of empirical tests has, however, been

---

[27] Though literary allusions are not. If one broadens his notion of security, one is deluged by mankind's conclusions. To cite but one example, listen to Macbeth:

> As you all know, security
> Is mortals' chiefest enemy.

made by W. Cris Lewis. He made two comparisons: (1) United States labor force participation and unemployment rates, and the growth of economic security programs and (2) the relative level of social security expenditures in seven countries and their respective labor force participation and unemployment rates. His thesis was that increasing economic security programs should be accompanied by increasing unemployment and decreasing labor force participation rates. Over time (in the United States), and at a given time (among seven countries), he did *not* find this to be the case. He concluded, therefore, that insofar as unemployment and labor force participation rates serve as a measure of incentive, the case is not proved that economic security programming weakens such incentive.[28]

We would tentatively conclude (a) that the present economic security system in the United States has not damaged our well-being; but that (b) abuses and dangers exist and should be guarded against. We would, for example, doubt the wisdom of 100 per cent wage restoration under, say, an unemployment insurance program.

3. The government has a legitimate role to play in economic security programming. In some cases, as in the regulatory field, it may be the only body capable of doing the job. We further hold that it plays a useful role in providing a "floor of protection."

But, beyond regulation, government action and activity may be necessary, this based upon the principle of "subsidiarity." [29] This principle suggests that "higher" levels should not undertake to meet responsibilities if "lower" levels can. Thus, private action is to be preferred over public, state over federal. But, where lower levels cannot meet the responsibility, the higher must. Thus, in the case of unemployment, the preventive approach (maintaining high levels of economic activity) has become a basic responsibility of the public (federal level) sector. The alleviative approach is, however, largely at state, local, and private levels. It has become increasingly accepted that government plays a useful role in providing a "floor of protection." Our judgment is, however, that given these constraints, the area in which private enterprise can operate should be maximized.

A Note on Terminology

We have noted in this chapter many terms used in the field of economic security. Here we should like to present a more detailed picture

[28] W. Cris Lewis, "An Empirical Analysis of Security and Incentive" (unpublished paper prepared for one of the author's economic security classes, 1965).

[29] We are indebted to A. Edward Hunter of the Minnesota Department of Employment Security for provocative discussions on this topic. The principle has had a long standing among political scientists and public administration specialists.

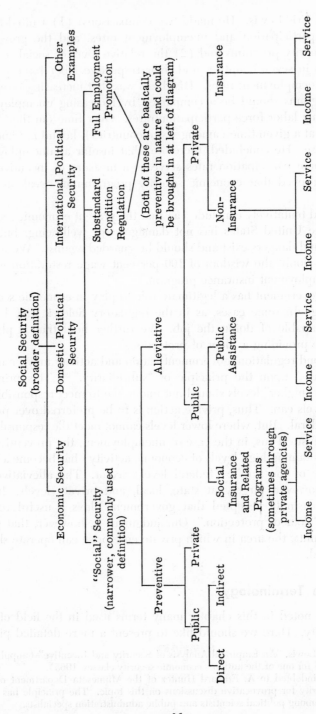

Figure 1-1. Principal Economic Security Terms and Their Relationships.

and, in so doing, provide an over-all view of the pattern of terminology. Then, in future sections of this book, the meaning of and relationship among terms should be clear.

Our presentation is in diagrammatic form, with appended explanation where needed. (See page 46.) It should be noted that preventive, alleviative, and regulatory methods are intertwined in a complicated fashion.

A FINAL COMMENT

The American approach to economic security seems unnecessarily complicated when judged on a strictly logical basis. We may wonder how such a complex system came into being. The major reason is that the system was developed piecemeal in response to what seemed to be the most important need at the time. This statement applies to both public and private programs.

Political factors as well as social and economic needs were important in public programs, while a private insurance program had to promise safe operation before it could be initiated. Thus our system is a compromise between the desire to provide the optimum economic security at the minimum cost, make the system self-supporting, maintain individual responsibility, respect states' rights, and please the voting public. Few, if any, persons are completely satisfied with the present system, but the critics, with feelings ranging from mild to intense, are not united in their objections. Some argue for a completely logical system, however that may be defined. Others believe that some, but not all, of the other considerations should be ignored, while still others believe that it is possible to establish a superior compromise system. Each of these three groups may be divided into many subgroups on other bases, such as the method of implementing their proposals.

We shall not attempt to evaluate the system at this point because we need to know more about the provisions and operations of these programs. We will, however, present a series of evaluations in the final chapter of this text.

We shall now explore in some detail the nature of the financial problems caused by death, old age, unemployment, accidental injury and sickness, and substandard conditions and the public and private programs providing some degree of economic security against these risks.

SUMMARY

This introductory section has been designed to trace the principal features of the subject of economic insecurity. Such insecurity arises out of the loss of income and/or the creation of additional expenses for the individual. In turn, the most important cause giving rise to the loss of income is the loss of gainful employment: the insecurity is job-oriented. Additional expenses may be incurred through accidents or sickness; here there may or may not be an accompanying job loss. Society may try to adjust to these forms of economic insecurity in a variety of ways: allevi- ation of the undesirable consequences, reduction or prevention of the incidence, and government regulation. Both public and private methods to combat insecurity may be utilized, and in the United States a com- bined system, in fact, exists.

The conventional treatment of the problem of economic security tends to limit itself to the topics of public and private assistance and insurance as they seek to combat insecurity of the types noted above. But, sub- standard conditions in wages, hours, and other conditions of employment are also important causal factors in economic insecurity.

The American economic security system includes preventive and al- leviative programs, public and private. The preventive programs in- clude general and selective efforts to reduce or eliminate the chance of loss due to death, superannuation, illness, and unemployment, or to mini- mize the extent of such losses, as well as government regulations such as the Fair Labor Standards Act which establish sets of operating rules affecting such working conditions as the wage rate and maximum work week.

The alleviative programs include social insurance and related pro- grams, public assistance, and private approaches of which the most im- portant is private insurance. Social insurance differs from public assist- ance primarily in that the benefits are established by formula and are available as a matter of right, while public assistance payments are determined on a discretionary basis and are payable only to the needy. It is difficult to compare social insurance with private insurance because each type includes many different types of programs, but the most im- portant social insurance program, Old-Age, Survivors, and Disability In- surance, can be contrasted with the most important private insurance protection, individual insurance contracts issued by commercial insurers. OASDI is compulsory, the benefits are prescribed by law and subject to change, the system redistributes income in addition to pooling the risks, and the government is a monopoly insurer. Individual life insurance written by commercial insurers is voluntary, the benefits are prescribed in a contract, the price is determined by the cost of the benefits insofar as practical considerations will permit, and there is intense competition.

Some programs provide service benefits, but most pay cash benefits. The loss of freedom of economic choice under a service program is great- est when lost income is replaced by limited specific services.

Social insurance programs providing death and retirement benefits include OASDI and programs for special groups. Workmen's compensation laws provide protection against death due to occupational causes. Public assistance programs attacking these perils specifically are Old-Age Assistance and Aid to Families with Dependent Children. Private protection consists primarily of individual or group insurance.

Social insurance programs providing unemployment insurance benefits include the state unemployment insurance funds and the special federal program for railroad workers. Private protection is afforded through self-insured industry plans.

Social insurance attacking accidental injury and sickness consists of the OASDI provisions providing an income for certain totally and permanently disabled persons and preventing a loss of retirement and death benefits due to total and permanent disability, Hospital Insurance and Supplemental Medical Insurance for the Aged, workmen's compensation insurance, and programs for special groups. Public assistance programs include cash payments under Aid to the Blind and Aid to the Totally and Permanently Disabled programs and medical expense allowances or payments under all federally supported state programs. Private protection includes individual and group insurance underwritten primarily by commercial insurers and non-profit medical expense associations.

Residual protection for the needy is provided through state and local general public assistance programs. Private residual protection includes reliance on relatives and charity.

SUGGESTIONS FOR ADDITIONAL READING

BOULDING, KENNETH E. *Principles of Economic Policy.* Englewood Cliffs, N. J.: Prentice-Hall, Inc., 1958.
See Chapter 10, "Income Maintenance Policy," for a series of penetrating and humane comments on insecurity.

BURNS, EVELINE M. *Social Security and Public Policy.* New York: McGraw-Hill Book Co., 1956.
A highly respected student of social security presents a brief and stimulating discussion of the historical development of social security measures and the important decisions to be made before establishing a program.

CARLSON, VALDEMAR. *Economic Security in the United States.* New York: McGraw-Hill Book Co., 1962.
An historical and analytical treatment of economic security in this country. It is useful not only for its treatment of the development of problems and programs, but also for the ways in which economic security approaches are analyzed in terms of the market mechanism.

CHAMBERS, CLARKE A. *Seedtime of Reform: American Social Service and Social Action, 1918–1933.* Minneapolis: University of Minnesota Press, 1963.
A detailed history of the social welfare movement in the United States from

World War I to the era of Franklin Delano Roosevelt. Written by an historian, the volume covers topics such as unemployment, but also treats many broader issues and developments.

Monthly Labor Review, LXXXVI, No. 6, June, 1963.

The entire issue is devoted to the topic "Worker Security in a Changing Economy." Topics include the nature of workers' goals, the responses of society—including public and private sectors—to these goals, and indexes of workers' wealth and welfare. There is a useful chronology of worker security, 1961–63.

MYERS, ROBERT J. *Social Insurance and Allied Government Programs.* Homewood, Ill.: Richard D. Irwin, Inc., 1965.

An analysis of public programs in the areas of old age, premature death, health, unemployment, and work-connected injury and disease. The discussion is particularly valuable with respect to financing issues.

SHOSTAK, ARTHUR B., and GOMBERG, WILLIAM (eds.). *New Perspectives on Poverty.* Englewood Cliffs, N. J.: Prentice-Hall, Inc., 1965.

A series of readings on poverty in America, including (1) a general view, (2) reforms for specific problems, (3) the war on poverty, (4) models for action.

TURNBULL, JOHN G. *The Changing Faces of Economic Insecurity.* Minneapolis: University of Minnesota Press, 1966.

A qualitative and quantitative comparison of economic insecurity 1910–60 and of social adjustments thereto. The volume analyzes trends of the past half-century.

2

Problems of Death and Old Age

INTRODUCTION

Each person faces the possibility that premature death will cut short his earning period or that he will live to such an advanced age that his earning power will have stopped and he will have consumed all of his accumulated assets. Both situations pose serious financial problems that most persons are anxious to solve in advance through private or public means. We start our discussion in this text with the topics of death and old age, since these are the most "final" forms of job severance. Unemployment, injuries, and sickness are usually of limited duration.

In this chapter we shall explore the nature and importance of the financial problems associated with premature death and old age. We shall also consider the probability that a person will die prematurely and the probability that a person will survive to retirement age and beyond, and how these probabilities are related to economic insecurity.

The general preventive and alleviative approaches to these problems will then be discussed so as to emphasize the important roles played by social insurance, public assistance, and private insurance. Each of these approaches is discussed in detail in the next three chapters.

Finally, note will be made of the current economic resources of survivors and the aged, from all private and public sources, in order to indicate the need for improvements in the present approaches to the problems of death and old age.

THE ECONOMIC PROBLEMS OF PREMATURE DEATH

Nature and Importance

Premature death causes two types of financial loss to dependents. First, the deceased's earning power stops. Second, extra expenses are incurred in the form of burial expenses, probate costs, estate and inheritance taxes, forced liquidation losses, and others.

The earning power loss is the more important for most families, but few persons appreciate its possible magnitude. An example will illustrate this point. Assume that an individual, aged thirty-five, is earning $6,000 a year after income taxes. In order to simplify the explanation, further assume that his salary is not expected to change until age sixty-five, at which time he expects to retire. Under these assumptions, his future income will total $30 \times \$6,000 = \$180,000$. If he should die at age thirty-five, this income will never be earned. However, it is not fair to state that his dependents will suffer a loss of $180,000 because, first, he would have consumed some of this income if he had lived and, second, this income would have been spread over a thirty-year period.

If it is assumed that $1,500 would have been required each year to maintain the deceased and prepare for his retirement, the annual income loss to the dependents is $4,500, making a total income loss of $135,000. The fact that this income would have been spread over a thirty-year period means that some allowance must be made for the interest earnings on a lump sum available at the present time. In more technical terms it is necessary to discount the future incomes in order to determine their present values. If it is assumed that this lump sum can earn 3 per cent interest after taxes compounded annually and that the incomes would have been available at the end of the year in which they were earned, the lump sum (or the present value of the future incomes) is computed as follows:

$$\$4500 \, (1 + .03)^{-1} = 4500 \, (.9709)$$
$$4500 \, (1 + .03)^{-2} = 4500 \, (.9426)$$
$$4500 \, (1 + .03)^{-3} = 4500 \, (.9151)$$

$$\cdot \quad \cdot \quad \cdot \qquad \qquad \cdot \quad \cdot \quad \cdot$$

$$4500 \, (1 + .03)^{-28} = 4500 \, (.4371)$$
$$4500 \, (1 + .03)^{-29} = 4500 \, (.4243)$$
$$\underline{4500 \, (1 + .03)^{-30} = 4500 \, (.4120)}$$

$$\$88,200, \text{ approximately}$$

In other words, if $88,200 is invested at 3 per cent interest compounded annually, periodic withdrawals of $4,500 at the end of each year for thirty years would exhaust the fund. Therefore, $88,200 is a good *estimate* of the earning power loss to the dependents in this case. Even if it were in error by as much as $20,000 or $30,000, it is still a useful figure because it reveals the magnitude of the loss.

The earning power loss varies directly with the level of future earnings, inversely with age. When the individual whose situation was discussed in the last paragraph reaches age fifty, the possible earning power loss will have dropped to approximately $53,700. At retirement age, it will be zero. Because annual income typically increases in the early years of employment, the drop in earning power loss is usually not as rapid as in the case discussed.[1] However, it is still generally true that, other things being equal, the family suffers the greatest earning power loss when the breadwinner dies at an early age.

The earning power loss also varies inversely with the assumed interest rate. For example, in the case cited the loss would be about $101,000 under a 2 per cent interest assumption and $77,800 under a 4 per cent assumption.

Probability of Premature Death

Because of medical advances and improved social and economic conditions, premature death is much less likely to occur today than it was in the earlier part of the twentieth century. However, a large number of people still die early in life and the probability that this will happen is greater than most people choose to believe. Table 2.1 shows the mortality rates at various ages over the first decades of this century. Notice that most of the improvement has occurred at the younger ages. This improvement is expected to continue, but at a less rapid pace, in the future.

Table 2.2 presents the most recent data in a different setting. It indicates the probability that a person aged twenty, thirty, forty, fifty, and sixty will die before reaching age sixty-five, which is a typical retirement age. On the average, on the basis of 1959–61 mortality rates, about one out of four persons, aged twenty, will have his earning period shortened by a premature death.

---

[1] If the difference between the starting and final incomes is great, it is possible that decreasing interest discounts on the future larger salaries may result in an increasing earning power loss during the first few years. For a more detailed and sophisticated discussion of the human life concept, and tables expressing the human life value as a multiple of present gross earnings for selected occupations and ages, see Alfred E. Hofflander, Jr., "Human Life Value Concepts," unpublished doctoral dissertation, University of Pennsylvania, 1964. For example, the multiple for an engineer, aged twenty-five, is thirty-six.

TABLE 2.1

Deaths Per 1,000 Total Population Living at Specified Ages
at Ten-Year Intervals, 1910–60 *

Age	1909–11	1919–21 †	1929–31 †	1939–41	1949–51	1959–61
0	114.62	80.25	62.32	47.10	29.76	25.93
10	2.27	2.11	1.47	.90	.53	.37
20	4.68	4.27	3.18	2.17	1.35	1.15
30	6.51	5.73	4.13	3.07	1.79	1.43
40	9.39	7.50	6.79	5.24	3.68	3.00
50	14.37	11.74	12.78	10.76	8.76	7.74
60	28.58	24.62	26.44	22.51	19.77	17.61
70	59.52	54.63	57.96	48.73	42.49	38.66
80	130.28	119.73	129.97	114.91	98.41	92.08
90	249.62	238.19	245.50	230.81	212.49	227.09
100	401.91	442.44	470.37	360.05	389.04	392.42

* Death registrations were not available for all states until 1933.
† Data for 1919–21 and 1929–31 apply to white males only.

Sources: U. S. Department of Commerce, Bureau of the Census, *United States Life Tables: 1910, 1930, 1940, and 1950* (Washington, D. C.: U. S. Government Printing Office, 1916, 1936, 1946, and 1954). Data for 1959–61 are from U. S. Department of Health, Education, and Welfare, Public Health Service, *United States Life Tables: 1959–61* (Washington, D. C.: U. S. Government Printing Office, 1964).

TABLE 2.2

Probability of Dying Prior to Age 65, 1959–61

Present Age	Probability
20	.26
30	.25
40	.24
50	.20
60	.10

Source: *United States Life Tables: 1959–61.*

THE ECONOMIC PROBLEMS OF OLD AGE

Nature and Importance

Old age also presents serious economic security problems. Earnings may stop or be considerably reduced, but expenses continue. The economic security problem involved is how to meet expenses not covered by current earnings. Again it is fair to say that the average person does not appreciate the magnitude of this problem. For example, assume that a retired person, aged sixty-five, has expenses totaling $3,000 a year. If these expenses are to be paid at the end of each year solely out of interest payments on accumulated investments, the principal would have to be $100,000 if the interest return after taxes is 3 per cent, $75,000 if that return is 4 per cent.

If it is assumed that expenses are to be paid out of periodic with-drawals of the principal plus interest on the unpaid balance, one would have to know how many years the person will live in order to determine the amount he must have accumulated by the date of retirement. If he will live ten more years, the required principal is about $25,600 at 3 per cent interest, $24,300 at 4 per cent. If he will live twenty more years, the required principal is $44,600 at 3 per cent interest, $40,800 at 4 per cent. If he will live to age one hundred, the amount required is $64,500 at 3 per cent interest, $56,000 at 4 per cent. The amount varies directly with the living expenses and the number of years, inversely with the interest rate.

Even a short period of retirement, therefore, requires the accumula-tion of a large sum of money. One never knows, however, whether he will live to retirement age and, if so, how long he will live after retiring. Consequently the problem is compounded because the amount which an individual would have to accumulate if he handled this problem on his own is unknown.

Probability of Survival to Retirement Age and Beyond

A person either dies or lives. Consequently the chance that a person will live to reach a certain age is equal to unity minus the probability that he will die before reaching that age. Therefore, Table 2.3, which shows the probability that a person aged twenty, thirty, forty, fifty, or sixty will reach age sixty-five, is based upon the data presented in Table 2.2.

Table 2.3 also indicates the average life expectancy for each age or the average number of years that persons in that age group will live

TABLE 2.3

Probability of Survival to Age 65 and Average Life Expectancy
at Specified Ages, 1959–61

Present Age	Probability	Average Life Expectancy	Average Life Expectancy Beyond Age 65
20	.74	52.58	7.58
30	.75	43.18	8.18
40	.76	33.92	8.92
50	.80	25.29	10.29
60	.90	17.71	12.71

Source: *United States Life Tables: 1959–61.*

beyond their present age. For ages twenty and forty, the median number of remaining life years is slightly higher than the average; for age sixty, the median is less. The third column in the table shows the number of years by which the average life expectancy will carry the person beyond sixty-five. Notice that these figures increase as the person grows older because he has moved closer to age sixty-five and his chances of surviving to that age have improved.

As mortality rates decrease over a period of time, the probability of surviving to retirement age and beyond increases. Table 2.4 shows how average life expectancies at birth and at ages twenty, forty, sixty, and eighty have increased over time. Improvements at the older ages have been slight, but those at the younger ages have been great. However, the improvement at the younger ages from 1949–51 to 1959–61 was less impressive than during earlier intervals.

TABLE 2.4

Average Life Expectancies at Specified Ages
at Ten-Year Intervals, 1910–60 *

Age	1909–11	1919–21 †	1929–31 †	1939–41	1949–51	1959–61
0	51.49	56.34	59.12	63.62	68.07	69.89
20	43.53	45.60	46.02	48.54	51.20	52.58
40	28.20	29.86	29.22	31.03	32.81	33.92
60	14.42	15.25	14.72	15.91	17.04	17.71
80	5.25	5.47	5.26	5.73	6.34	6.39

* Death registrations were not available for all states until 1933.
† Data for 1919–21 and 1929–31 apply to white males only.

Sources: *United States Life Tables: 1910, 1930, 1940, 1950, and 1959–61.*

Factors Other Than Age Causing Variation in Mortality Rates

Mortality rates also vary according to factors other than age. The most important variables are sex, race, marital status, occupation, and residence. The effects of sex and race are illustrated in Table 2.5. The average effect of all six variables upon mortality rates can be summarized as follows: [2]

1. Females experience lower mortality rates than males at all ages and their advantage is increasing.

[2] For a much more detailed discussion, see Mortimer Spiegelman, *Significant Mortality and Morbidity Trends in the United States Since 1900* (rev. ed.; Philadelphia: American College of Life Underwriters, 1964).

2. At all except possibly the most advanced ages, the non-white population has higher mortality rates than the white population.
3. The mortality rates for married persons at all age levels are less than those for single persons. Widowed persons, on the other hand, have higher mortality rates than single persons, except at the more advanced ages. Divorced persons experience the highest mortality rates at all ages.
4. Except for agricultural laborers, mortality rates for semi-skilled workers and laborers exceed those for professional workers and technical, administrative, and managerial workers. These differences are apparently declining in importance.
5. Urban areas have a higher level of mortality than rural areas but the margin between the two groups is also decreasing.

TABLE 2.5

Average Life Expectancy Classified by Age, Sex, and Race, 1959–61

Age	White		Non-Whites		All Races	
	Male	*Female*	*Male*	*Female*	*Male*	*Female*
0	67.55	74.19	61.48	66.47	66.80	73.24
20	50.25	56.29	45.78	50.07	49.77	55.60
40	31.73	37.13	28.72	32.16	31.42	36.61
60	16.01	19.69	15.29	17.83	15.94	19.52
80	5.89	6.67	6.87	7.66	5.95	6.72

Source: *United States Life Tables: 1959–61.*

Causes of Death

The five leading causes of death in 1964 and the proportion of the 939.7 deaths per 100,000 population for which they were responsible were as follows: [3]

Cardiovascular diseases	54 per cent
Malignant neoplasms	16 per cent
Accidents	6 per cent
Certain diseases of early infancy	3 per cent
Influenza and pneumonia	3 per cent

In 1900, the five leading causes, in order of importance, were pneumonia and influenza, tuberculosis, diarrhea and enteritis, cardiovascular diseases, and accidents.

[3] U. S. Department of Health, Education, and Welfare, *Health, Education, and Welfare Indicators,* December, 1965 (Washington, D. C.: U. S. Government Printing Office, 1965), p. 54.

Age Composition of the Total Population

As Table 2.6 indicates, the proportion of the population that is aged sixty-five and over has more than doubled since the turn of the century. The increase in the *number* of aged persons has been even more dramatic. Increased life expectancy, low birth rates during the 1930's, and reduced immigration rates have combined to produce this result, which has caused society to pay increasing attention to the social and economic problems of the aged.

Table 2.6 also shows that the proportion of the population that is aged sixty-five and over is not expected to change much in the remainder of this century and may actually decrease. The estimated proportions of aged persons in this table are smaller than in previous population estimates, but the proportions are still high. Furthermore, the proportion of aged persons should begin to increase rapidly again after 2010.[4]

TABLE 2.6

Age Composition of the United States Total Population
at Twenty-Year Intervals, 1900–2000

	Per Cent of Population in Each Age Group		
Year	*Under 20*	*20–64*	*65 and Over*
1900	44	52	4
1920	40	54	5
1940	34	59	7
1960	38	53	9
1980	36–41	54–50	10–9
2000	34–42	56–50	10–8

The first figure for each age group in the projections for 1980 and 2000 is the "low" population estimate which is based on the fertility of women during the Great Depression. The second figure is the "high" population estimate based on prevailing fertility levels since World War II. Under the low estimate the population will be 291 million in the year 2000. The high estimate is 362 million.

Source: Jacob S. Siegel, Meyer Zitter, and Donald S. Akers, *Current Population Reports, Population Estimates,* Series P-25, No. 286, July, 1964.

GENERAL APPROACHES TO THE ECONOMIC PROBLEMS OF PREMATURE DEATH

Society has attacked the problems of premature death in many ways. Both private and public bodies have applied both preventive and alleviative methods to these problems.

[4] For a valuable analysis of population trends, see Robert J. Myers, "The Population Explosion and the United States," *Journal of the American Society of Chartered Life Underwriters,* XX, No. 1 (Winter, 1966), 85–93.

Preventive Methods

Preventive methods have reduced mortality rates, as evidenced by the data presented in Tables 2.1 and 2.4. Advancements in medical knowledge and the more extensive application of that knowledge have been the most important factors, but higher average standards of living have also contributed to the increasing life span.

Private Preventive Measures. Private preventive measures assume many forms and involve many different groups. The following five measures illustrate their nature and importance. The first is health education which may consist of personal conversations between a physician and his patient or may instead be a program affecting many persons. Health education may be sought and paid for by an individual or it may be sponsored by an employer, a union, a non-profit foundation, a commercial insurer, or some other private institution. The major objective of health education is to teach persons how to conserve their health, how to recognize danger signals, and why they should seek early treatment. Medical care itself is a second preventive technique whose importance is obvious. A third example is a safety program aimed at preventing or reducing the effects of accidents on the job, on the highway, in the home, or elsewhere. At least some parts of most safety programs can be viewed as a kind of health education but the program usually includes some measures such as the removal of unsafe machinery that fall outside the scope of education as such. Employers, unions, non-profit foundations such as the National Safety Council, and commercial insurers are especially active in this area. A fourth example is individual health examinations which, it is hoped, will reveal at an early date conditions that, if not treated in time, might result in death. This examination might be a condition or privilege of employment, part of an application for an insurance contract, a service sponsored by a non-profit foundation, or part of an individual's program of preventive medicine. The fifth and final example is medical research which seeks to push back the frontiers of medical knowledge. Conducted by individuals, universities, hospitals, drug firms, and other groups, this research is sponsored by the four groups named as well as by non-profit foundations, commercial insurers, and others.

Public Preventive Measures. Our society first recognized the need for public methods on an effective scale about a century ago.[5] Government action was requested because (1) only the government had the authority to *require* the public to supply information, meet certain standards, or

---

[5] The enactment of the New York Metropolitan Health Bill of 1866 is considered to be a turning point in the history of public health in the United States. See George Rosen, *A History of Public Health* (New York: M.D. Publications, Inc., 1958), p. 247.

stop practices considered to be undesirable and (2) certain services such as sewage disposal were obviously more economically and efficiently provided by the government. At first state and local governments were almost entirely responsible for public health activities. A National Board of Health functioned from 1879–83 [6] but it was not until the second decade of the present century when the Public Health Service, the Children's Bureau, and some other federal agencies were established that the national government became an important factor. At present the national health authority is responsible for international and interstate quarantines, assembles and disseminates vital statistics, conducts research itself and encourages research by others, inspects and establishes standards for food and drugs, and stimulates through several grants-in-aid programs varied activities of state and local governments. Specialized services which cannot be obtained at the local level are also provided by the federal government.[7] The activities of the federal government were considerably increased by the Social Security Act of 1935 which provided for the allocation of considerably more funds among the states to establish and maintain adequate public health services and to promote the health of mothers and children.

Examples of activities of state and local governments are quarantine regulations, water sanitation and sewage disposal, immunization requirements and services for school children, inspection of food handlers, fluoridation of community water supplies, industrial and highway safety campaigns, school lunch and milk programs, physical examinations for school children, provision of hospital and medical facilities, health education, and medical research.

Many public methods are only indirectly job-oriented, and in keeping with the focus of this book, we shall not analyze them in detail. As noted in the Preface, substandard housing is an example of such an indirectly related item.

Preventive methods can never be completely successful, however, and there is tremendous variation in the extent to which they are used by each person. Furthermore, our society is continually creating new possible causes of premature death, such as the automobile and the airplane. For these reasons, alleviative measures are also necessary.

Private Alleviative Methods

Private methods of alleviating the financial loss caused by premature death have changed materially since the beginning of the Industrial

---

[6] *Ibid.*, p. 249.

[7] *Ibid.*, p. 470. The federal government also provides medical services for certain groups such as the Coast Guard, American Indians, and Alaskan Eskimos.

Revolution. As long as families were largely self-sufficient—a common occurrence in a predominantly agricultural economy—the dependents of a deceased person were welcome in some relative's home because they were able to make valuable contributions to the household's consumption needs. Today these dependents can usually make a positive contribution only if they have some source of money income, such as wages or savings.

Furthermore, even if the dependents have sufficient money income, it has become less "convenient" for relatives to care for them because of smaller living quarters, longer and more expensive dependency periods for children, varied interests, a desire for a higher standard of living, and increased mobility. Moreover, the size of the average family has decreased and hence there are fewer relatives to turn to for support. Finally these relatives may reside in widely scattered geographical locations and may not have maintained close family ties.[8]

Dependents still move in with relatives (for example, a widowed daughter and her children still may live with her parents), but in general, social and economic forces have reduced the frequency and effectiveness of this approach to the problem.

Private charities help in alleviation, but this aid is necessarily very limited. United Fund agencies exemplify this approach. Churches, labor unions, fraternal societies, and charitable institutions of various types have also been active in providing assistance. However, if private aid of this sort is the only support available, a drastic reduction in the family's standard of living is almost certain to result. Furthermore, most families do not consider charity to be an acceptable solution to their financial problems.

The meager support provided by relatives and private charities is indicated in a 1957 survey conducted by the Social Security Administration.[9] The survey dealt with the income of "young" (persons under sixty-five were considered to be young) survivors who had filed for OASDI benefits. Attention here will be focused upon the income of young widows with children under eighteen in their care.

According to the survey, only 7 per cent of the widow-children groups received $25 or more in cash contributions from relatives outside the home. About one-quarter of the widow-children groups lived with relatives but less than 3 per cent received housing without direct expense to them, less than 15 per cent received medical care at someone else's expense, less than 10 per cent received free food, and less than 3 per cent re-

---

[8] About one out of every five families moves during a year. "Facts About Families," *Social Security Bulletin*, XXII, No. 5 (May, 1959), 10.

[9] Mollie Orshansky, "Income of Young Survivors," *Social Security Bulletin*, XXII, No. 9 (September, 1959), 10–15, 24. This article is the source of almost all the data in this section.

ceived free clothing. Even these figures overstate the assistance from relatives and private agencies because they include support in kind from such non-relatives as doctors and neighbors and from public agencies. On the other hand, it is true that the existence of public alleviative measures and the taxes supporting these measures reduces both the necessity and the resources available for private support of this type.

The survivors may, of course, be able to support themselves through earnings or accumulated assets. For example, a young widow without any children may be able to work, but her income may be less than the support previously provided by her husband. A young mother may also be able to work but her home life is likely to suffer as a result of her absence. In many cases it is impossible for the mother to work.

The Social Security Administration survey cited above illustrates the limited role of earnings in meeting the problems created by premature death. In late 1957 only about half the young widowed mothers were employed and the proportion was less when there were several children. At the close of 1960 this situation was unchanged.[10] About 9 per cent more were not then working but had worked at other times during 1957. Many working mothers apparently worked part-time or in low-paying jobs because one-fourth earned less than $600 a year and only one-fifth earned $3,000 or more.

Accumulated capital in the form of real estate, savings accounts, securities, and the like may be an important source of income for middle-aged survivors but, as explained on page 71, there are many reasons why it may be difficult to accumulate substantial assets even by the age of retirement. Younger persons are, of course, much less likely to have substantial accumulated capital.

Private life insurance is an excellent way to accumulate capital in case of premature death. This device is particularly useful for young survivors because through a life insurance contract an insured can leave his dependents a large sum of money even if he should die at an early age.

Private life insurance, however, is by no means a complete solution to the problem. Some applicants do not qualify for insurance issued on an individual basis [11] because of poor health or other reasons, while other persons consider the cost too high for them. Many individuals with dependents mistakenly feel that they need little or no insurance.

Group insurance, which is usually associated with the individual's place of employment and which originated in this century, has been a very important development because every member of an eligible group

[10] Mollie Orshansky, "Money Income Sources of Young Survivors, December, 1960," *Social Security Bulletin*, XXIV, No. 10 (October, 1961), 16.

[11] The differences between individual insurance and group insurance are explained more fully in Chapter 5.

is eligible for insurance and because the wholesale merchandising of the coverage cuts the cost. However, many persons are not members of an eligible group and the amount of protection available under a group plan is usually limited.

Private life insurance has expanded tremendously since World War II. The amount of life insurance owned by all families at the end of 1965 was $900 billion.[12] This is an impressive total but the average amount of insurance per family was only $14,700 or 1.93 times the average annual disposable income. About 86 per cent of the heads of families including both the husband and the wife had some life insurance coverage, but the range in protection was great.

The 1957 Social Security Administration survey revealed that widowed mothers received little support from assets accumulated through life insurance or in any other way. Only half of the widowed mothers had *any* liquid assets. Sixty-two per cent had no income from assets, liquid or non-liquid, and only one-fourth received net rents, dividends, or interest exceeding $25 during the year. On the brighter side, about one-half owned their own homes and about half of these homes were free of mortgage debt.

Still another private approach to the financial problems created by premature death is to cut expenses by becoming more self-sufficient. More than very limited use of this approach, however, is not easy or in some cases even possible. In the 1957 survey, for example, less than 10 per cent of the widow-children groups raised any of their own food.

Public Alleviative Methods

Because the financial loss caused by premature death is so great, and because most families for various reasons have not voluntarily protected themselves adequately against this loss, the government has often been forced to aid the deceased's dependents. Poorhouses and orphanages represent the major approach used prior to the twentieth century. Limited state cash assistance programs made their appearance at the beginning of this century, but these programs varied greatly among states and, in general, were very inadequate.

The Social Security Act of 1935 was responsible for the first large-scale use of public alleviative methods. This Act provided, among other things, for federal grants-in-aid to state public assistance programs dealing with the problems caused by premature death. In 1939 the social insurance provisions of the Act were amended to include what Congress considered to be basic minimum death benefits. Because the provisions of the Social

[12] *Life Insurance Fact Book, 1966* (New York: Institute of Life Insurance, 1966), pp. 21–22.

Security Act are discussed in detail in Chapters 3 and 4, the Act will not be described here, but it should be mentioned that the benefits under these programs are sizable and affect most of the population.

According to the Social Security Administration survey noted above, about half the widows with children in their care were receiving OASDI benefits and another 11 per cent would have received benefits except for the fact that their earnings exceeded the work-test limit described in Chapter 4. About 10 per cent of the group received federally aided public assistance.[13] In December, 1960, 54 per cent were receiving OASDI benefits and 13 per cent public assistance.[14]

Death benefits are also available under the federal government's Railroad Retirement System, Civil Service Retirement System, veterans' programs, and armed services' programs, a selective discussion of which is found in Chapter 13. The special occupational death benefits payable under workmen's compensation statutes are discussed in Chapter 10.

Layers of Protection

The average American family then has two layers of protection against the financial loss caused by premature death. Social insurance provides the basic layer, while private insurance supplements this coverage. In many cases this private insurance consists only of individual insurance, but for a large and increasing number of families, group insurance is the second layer and individual insurance the third.

Money Income of Survivors

The adequacy of the present alleviative programs, both public and private, depends upon the standard of living that is adopted as a yardstick but the following finding of the 1957 Social Security Administration survey on the money income of survivors would seem to indicate that our protection is still not adequate, given most any standard. Of the young widows with children who were entitled to OASDI benefits, 7 per cent had less than $1,200 in money income including earnings. Almost 40 per cent had money incomes of less than $2,400 and only 11 per cent had money incomes of $5,000 or more.[15] On the other hand, it should be

---

[13] Orshansky, "Income of Young Survivors," *op. cit.,* 11.

[14] Orshansky, "Money Income Sources of Young Survivors . . . ," *op. cit.,* 16.

[15] No specific yardstick has been suggested for survivor groups, but in 1960 the Department of Labor developed a "modest but adequate" budget for an urban worker, aged thirty-eight, his wife, a son, aged thirteen, and a daughter, aged eight, who live in a rented dwelling. The amounts for Chicago, Minneapolis, and Philadelphia were $6,567, $6,181, and $5,898 respectively. If the worker dies, the modest but adequate budget would of course be much lower for several reasons but it would exceed $2,400.

recognized that this situation will improve with time even if no substantial changes are made in our system, solely because relatively more survivors will in the future receive benefits under the public and private insurance portions of our system and the average dollar benefit will be larger. Whether the average *real* benefit will be larger will depend upon the relative change in prices.

GENERAL APPROACHES TO THE ECONOMIC PROBLEMS OF OLD AGE

Methods of attacking the economic problems of old age are largely alleviative, but the preventive programs discussed in connection with premature death do diminish the old-age problems if a larger proportion of the persons attaining advanced ages are capable of earning a limited income and if a place can be found to employ their talents. Otherwise, increasing average life expectancies intensify the problems of old age.

Preventive Methods

Preventive efforts, then, take the form of continued employment, but the prospects for this approach are not bright. As Table 2.7 indicates, the proportion of the labor force that is aged sixty-five or over has not increased despite the fact that the aged now constitute a much larger percentage of the total population than they did in 1900. This proportion has remained fairly stable because the percentage of aged males who belong to the labor force has decreased steadily. The proportion of aged females belonging to the labor force was slightly higher in 1965 than in 1900 but less than in 1960.

One reason why more aged do not belong to the labor force may be that the demand for their services is not adequate to absorb all the qualified aged persons. Other possible explanations are that (1) the aged prefer not to work, (2) many of the aged are in poor health or do not possess the talents that are in demand, or (3) institutional pressures cause forced retirement.

Work Experience and the 1963 Survey of the Aged. A 1963 Survey of the Aged by the Social Security Administration has shed further light on the work experience of the aged in 1962.[16] About 38 per cent of the aged

"The City Worker's Budget," *Monthly Labor Review,* LXXXIII, No. 8 (August, 1960), 785–808. See pp. 73–75 of this text for a discussion of the application of this standard to retired couples.

[16] Erdman Palmore, "Work Experience and Earnings of the Aged in 1962: Findings of the 1963 Survey of the Aged," *Social Security Bulletin,* XXVII, No. 6 (June, 1964), 3–14, 44.

males and 14 per cent of the aged females had some work experience during 1962, but only 15 per cent of the males and 4 per cent of the females had full-time, year-round jobs. As might be expected, age is an important factor affecting employment rates. For example, among males aged sixty-two through sixty-four, 80 per cent had some work experience in 1962, with 47 per cent having full-time, year-round jobs. Only 47 per cent of the males aged sixty-five through seventy-two had some work experience, and only 18 per cent had regular full-time jobs. For males aged seventy-three and over, the two corresponding percentages were 23 per cent and 6 per cent.

TABLE 2.7
Aged Persons in the Labor Force, 1900–65 *

Year	Proportion of Labor Force 65 Years and Over		Proportion of Persons 65 Years and Over in the Labor Force	
	Men	Women	Men	Women
1900	4.5	2.6	68.4	8.5
1910	4.2	2.5	63.7	8.6
1920	4.4	2.4	60.2	7.9
1930	5.1	2.6	58.3	7.9
1940	4.6	2.2	41.5	5.8
1950	5.4	3.1	41.0	7.3
1960	4.6	3.8	33.1	10.8
1965	4.1	3.7	27.9	10.0

* 1900–30 data are for the gainfully occupied. 1940–65 data relate to the labor force.

Sources: Data for 1900–40 based on Tables 1 and 4 in S. J. Mushkin and Alan Berman, "Factors Influencing Trends in Employment of the Aged," *Social Security Bulletin*, X, No. 8 (August, 1947), 18–23. Data for 1950 from U. S. Department of Commerce, Bureau of the Census, *Seventeenth Census of the United States, 1950*, II, Part I, 97, 247. Data for 1960 based on *Employment and Earnings*, VII, No. 7 (January, 1961), xii. Data for 1965 from *Employment and Earnings*, XII, No. 7 (January, 1966), 74.

Compulsory retirement ages and maximum hiring ages do keep many able aged out of the labor force. The arguments against hiring workers at advanced ages or retaining them beyond age sixty-five can be summarized as follows: The elderly employees are often in poor health, they are relatively inflexible at a time when our economy demands flexibility, they raise insurance and pension costs, they resent being supervised by younger people, and they block the promotion lanes for other younger persons. Furthermore, because of minimum wage laws and collective bargaining, the production of the aged is often exceeded by the wages they must be paid. A discretionary policy would permit a firm to select the more able among the aged but many businessmen believe that a discretionary retirement policy is unworkable, breeds discontent, and hinders programs preparing older workers for retirement.

The 1963 Survey of the Aged confirms the results of earlier studies [17] which suggested that while liberalizing retirement and hiring policies may help to increase the proportion of the aged in the labor force, other causes are more important.[18] According to this survey, among the wage and salary workers who had retired since 1957, 63 per cent retired by their own decision. Thirty-five per cent retired because of poor health, 19 per cent because they preferred leisure, and 9 per cent for other reasons. Of the 37 per cent who were retired by their employers, 19 per cent were retired because of a compulsory retirement age, 6 per cent because of poor health, 8 per cent because they were laid off or their job was discontinued, and 4 per cent for other reasons. The major reason for retirement, therefore, is poor health, which accounted for 41 per cent of the retirements. Among self-employed persons who retired since 1957, 53 per cent did so because of poor health.

On the other hand, poor health was a less important reason for retirement in the 1963 survey than in a 1951 survey. The most striking change from the earlier survey was the increase in the proportion who retired because they preferred leisure. The proportion who were retired because they reached a compulsory retirement age also increased significantly, but this increase was more than matched by a decrease in the proportion who were laid off or had their job discontinued.

Among those not at work during the survey week, 69 per cent did not consider themselves well enough to work. Among those well enough to work, over half were not interested in work. These findings, when compared with earlier studies, also support the hypothesis that the health of the aged is improving and that more of the aged prefer leisure time.

The 1963 survey also revealed that men in the higher-paid occupations are less likely to retire. Although they have the financial means to retire, their work is more interesting, more rewarding, and less physically demanding. They are also in better health; their compulsory retirement age, if any, is likely to be higher; and their services are more likely to be needed.

The availability of retirement benefits is apparently a major factor affecting a decision to retire because nearly all of the aged workers who planned to stop work or to work less in 1963 were already eligible or would shortly become eligible for such benefits. About one-third of the

[17] See the discussion on pp. 54–56 in the Second Edition of this text, on Peter O. Steiner and Robert Dorfman, *The Economic Status of the Aged* (Berkeley and Los Angeles: University of California Press, 1957).

[18] Erdman Palmore, "Retirement Patterns Among Aged Men: Findings of the 1963 Survey of the Aged," *Social Security Bulletin*, XXVII, No. 8 (August, 1964), 3–10.

aged who were not currently OASDI beneficiaries said that they planned to retire for this reason.

The proportion of men aged sixty to sixty-four in the labor force has also declined. Automation, other technological and structural changes, the ineffectiveness of programs designed to prevent age discrimination in employment, union bargaining for increased severance payments, more liberal unemployment benefits, and OASDI changes providing for retirement at age sixty-two at reduced benefits have been cited by one highly respected observer as explanations for this decline.[19]

According to the 1963 Survey of the Aged, about 28 per cent of the men aged sixty-two through sixty-four were receiving OASDI retirement benefits. Most of these early retirants had a low income. Poor health was the reason for retirement for over half of these men; another 18 per cent had been laid off or had their job discontinued.

Arguments for Increasing Employment Opportunities. The survey concludes that if "the present trends toward less work and less earnings among the aged were to continue, by the end of this century there would be virtually no earnings or work experience of the aged left to analyze." [20] Some close observers claim, however, that these trends can and should be reversed. They argue that many of the aged who do not consider themselves well enough to work might change their attitude if they had something challenging to which they could look forward.[21] Furthermore, many of the aged might have retained their health if they had continued their normal work.[22]

These authorities remind us that employers are placing increasing emphasis on training and decreasing emphasis on physical strength, which should improve employment opportunities for the aged. They point to the fact that the educational levels of the aged and the non-aged will be more alike in the future. In addition, aged workers in their opinion are more responsible, loyal, and stable. They believe, therefore, that modern

[19] See Margaret S. Gordon, *National Retirement Policies and the Displaced Older Worker,* Reprint No. 250 (Berkeley: Institute of Industrial Relations, University of California, 1965), pp. 591–92. Mrs. Gordon expresses concern that many workers will be forced through unemployment to accept reduced OASDI benefits, which may cause them to have inadequate incomes after they reach age sixty-five. She argues for joint consideration of extended unemployment compensation, disability benefits, and early retirement provisions.

[20] Palmore, "Work Experience and Earnings of the Aged in 1962 . . . ," *op. cit.,* 14.

[21] Floyd Bond, discussion of Robert Dorfman, "The Labor Force Status of Persons Aged Sixty-Five and Over," and Peter O. Steiner, "The Size, Nature, and Adequacy of the Resources of the Aged," *American Economic Review,* XLIV, No. 2 (May, 1954), 634–60, 673.

[22] Elizabeth Wallace, discussion of Dorfman article, *ibid.,* 675.

industry should take another look at compulsory retirement ages and maximum hiring ages because many able persons have been forced to retire too early in life, thus wasting human resources and destroying for the individual the non-economic attractions of work.[23]

In short, they argue that a retirement philosophy that was appropriate when the aged formed a relatively small segment of the population or when jobs were very scarce because of a great economic depression is not appropriate now and will not be appropriate in the future. This viewpoint is attracting more interest each year and merits serious consideration. On the other hand, there is no doubt that the aged will be more employable to the extent that they are able to retain their health and modernize their skills, regardless of retirement and hiring policies.

Older Americans Act of 1965. The Older Americans Act of 1965, which created a new Administration of Aging within the Department of Health, Education, and Welfare, has established as one of its many objectives programs to help older persons obtain employment. The general purpose of the Act, however, is much broader—to help older people enjoy "wholesome and meaningful" living, which includes non-economic values (such as independence, honor, and dignity) as well as economic values (such as income, housing, and employment). To accomplish its objectives the new Administration of Aging will develop plans for and conduct research and demonstration projects, provide technical assistance to state and local programs, gather statistics on the aged, make research grants, and engage in other related activities.

Private Methods of Alleviation

The importance of private and public alleviative measures increases as the percentage of the aged who are employed decreases. Attention will be centered first upon private methods.[24]

Despite the small proportion of the aged with earnings, most of the private money income of the aged comes from this source, thus emphasizing the limited contributions of private alleviative methods. According to Table 2.8, private money income of the aged in 1962 accounted for only about 51 per cent of their aggregate income, and earnings accounted

[23] For example, work may be attractive because it enhances a person's self-respect and provides associations with others, opportunities for service to mankind, and a check on anxieties. See Otto Pollak, *The Social Aspects of Retirement,* Pension Research Council Monograph Series (Homewood, Ill.: Richard D. Irwin, Inc., 1956).

[24] This section is based almost entirely upon seven articles on the 1963 Survey of the Aged appearing in the March, June, July, August, November, and December, 1964, and May, 1965, issues of the *Social Security Bulletin.*

for about 60 per cent of this private component. No data are available concerning the median income of the aged from private sources, but their median income from both public and private sources in 1962 was only $2,875 for married couples and $1,130 for non-married persons.

It is particularly interesting that group pensions and individual annuities provided only 6 per cent of the aggregate money income from private sources and that so few of the aged were receiving any income from these sources. By 1975 the proportion receiving pension benefits may increase to 25–30 per cent but, as indicated earlier, the proportion with earnings is expected to decline.

The asset position of the aged must also be considered in determining their economic status. According to the 1963 Survey of the Aged the median value of the asset holdings of aged couples was $11,180 including their equity in a home. More than one-third of the couples had assets of $15,000 or more but another one-sixth had assets of less than $1,000. Two-thirds of the couples owned non-farm homes, the median equity of these owners being $10,100. The median value of financial assets was $1,340. About 15 per cent of the married couples reported financial assets (bank accounts, securities, and other readily convertible holdings) of $15,000 or more but nearly 40 per cent had less than $500 in these assets. Investment in real estate (other than a non-farm home), farms, or non-farm businesses accounted for the remaining one-quarter of the assets of these couples. The cash value of life insurance, equity in annuities or retirement plans, and the value of automobiles and personal effects were not included in the survey, but these values were probably small.[25] As one might expect, the couples with the higher money incomes also tended to have the larger assets, particularly financial assets. To illustrate, about 60 per cent of the OASDI beneficiary couples in the lowest income third had less than $500 in financial assets, but only about 10 per cent of the couples in the top income third had so few financial assets. One encouraging note is that about 75 per cent of the aged couples had no debts. Furthermore, personal debts (not including mortgage or home-improvement loans) were small in relation to assets at each income level, the median debt being $385 for those with debts.

In general, non-married beneficiaries had fewer assets. The median value of total asset holdings was $2,900 for non-married men and $3,285 for non-married women. About one-sixth of these persons had assets of $15,000 or more, but about 40 per cent had less than $1,000 in assets. About one-third owned non-farm homes, the median equity being $7,270 for men and $9,070 for women. The median value of financial assets was $2,740 for the men and $2,200 for the women. Less than 10 per cent of

[25] The median face value of life insurance for couples with insurance was $2,580, but 32 per cent had no insurance.

the non-married had financial assets of $15,000 or more but nearly half reported less than $500 in assets of this type. Fortunately about 90 per cent of these non-married persons had no debts, the median debt being $410 for men with debts and $290 for women in the same situation.

These data suggest that, although the situation is improving, largely because of the growth and liberalization of private pension plans, present private sources of support are inadequate for most families. Of course it must be recognized again that these private sources might have been greater if it had not been for the existence of public sources which meet part of the need and perhaps siphon off some funds which would otherwise become private sources of support.

TABLE 2.8

Private Sources of Money Income for the Aged, 1962

| Source | Per Cent of Aged Receiving Money from Source | | Shares of Aggregate Money Income from Private Sources |
	Married Couples	Non-married Persons	
Earnings	55%	24%	32%
Cash contributions from friends or from relatives not living in the same household	3	5	1
Interest, dividends, and rents	63	48	15
Individual annuities	4	3	} 3
Group pension plans	16	5	

Source: Adapted from Lenore A. Epstein, "Income of the Aged in 1962: First Findings of the 1963 Survey of the Aged," *Social Security Bulletin,* XXVII, No. 3 (March, 1964), 3–8.

Reasons usually given to explain the inadequate private sources of support (other than current earnings) for the aged include the relatively low income status of a large part of the population, an upward trend in prices, high income taxes, the importance to Americans of "keeping up with the Joneses," the bank and business failures of the 1930's, personal misfortunes, the weakening of family ties, and a human tendency to postpone preparation for retirement. Most of these forces are beyond the control of the individual, but the last is definitely not.

Public Methods of Alleviation

Before the twentieth century, government assistance to the aged consisted almost entirely of poorhouses. A few states made cash grants to the needy aged during the first thirty years of this century, but, until the federal government through the Social Security Act made grants-in-aid to the states, the vast majority of the states made no cash grants and those that did paid very small amounts to very few people. At present, all fifty states have public assistance programs for the aged. About 11 per cent of the aged received over $2 billion in benefits during 1965.

Social insurance plans for the aged originally took the form of retirement plans for persons rendering service to the government. State and local government employees, federal government civil service employees, and members of the armed services have been covered for the greater part of this century. Railroad workers became the first non-governmental employees to be covered under a social insurance plan when the Railroad Retirement System began to operate in 1937 as a substitute for private employer plans. The most important social insurance program—Old-Age, Survivors, and Disability Insurance—began to operate in the same year and has expanded in coverage and benefits since that time. About 80 per cent of the aged received over $13 billion in benefits under OASDI in 1965.

Layers of Protection

The average American family has three or four layers of protection against the financial dilemma posed by old age: social insurance, savings and investments, and individual annuities and life insurance contracts; or, social insurance, group pensions, savings and investments, and individual annuities and life insurance contracts. The social insurance provides a floor of protection; the private investments and insurance make it possible for a person with initiative, foresight, and some luck to convert this minimum level of income into a more comfortable one. The provisions of social insurance and private insurance plans are discussed along with public assistance plans in the next three chapters.

Money Income of the Aged

One measure of the adequacy of the combined public and private layers of protection against old age is the present money incomes of the aged, including their earnings. Table 2.9 indicates that in 1962 about 5 per cent of the married couples, 32 per cent of the non-married men, and 49 per cent of the non-married women had money incomes from all public and private sources of less than $1,000. Only 47 per cent of the married couples, 16 per cent of the non-married men, and 7 per cent of the non-married women had total money income in excess of $3,000. On the other hand, the picture is much brighter than in 1951 when, for example, 38 per cent of the married couples had incomes of less than

$1,000 and only 22 per cent had incomes of more than $3,000. The increase in the median incomes shown in Table 2.9 is another way of indicating this encouraging trend. However, because consumer prices increased about 16 per cent over this period, the gain is not this great in real terms. Even this adjustment may underestimate the effect of price changes because certain items which have increased most in price (such as medical expenses) are relatively more important for the aged than for the worker's family whose cost of living changes are measured by the Bureau of Labor Statistics consumer price index. Furthermore, the position of the aged has remained about the same relative to that of the remainder of the population. While the median incomes of families with an aged head were increasing from $1,956 in 1951 to $3,204 in 1962, an increase of 63 per cent, the median income of all families increased from $3,709 to $5,956 over the same period, an increase of 61 per cent.

TABLE 2.9

Percentage Distribution of the Aged by Total Money Income Class, by Marital Status, and by Sex, 1951, 1959, and 1962

Money Income Class	Married Couples			Non-married Men			Non-married Women		
	1962	1959	1951	1962	1959	1951	1962	1959	1951
Less than $1,000	5	13	38	32	44	70	49	66	87
$1,000–$1,999	24	25	26	37	29	16	34	20	8
$2,000–$2,999	25	19	14	16	11	6	10	6	2
$3,000–$3,999	16		9	6			3		
$4,000–$4,999	11	43	6	3	16	8	1	8	3
$5,000–$9,999	15		7	6			3		
$10,000 or over	5			1			*		
Median income	$2,875	$2,600	$1,390	$1,365	$1,160	$660	$1,015	$670	$270

* Less than 0.5 per cent.

Sources: 1962 data from Lenore A. Epstein, "Income of the Aged in 1962: First Findings of the 1963 Survey of the Aged," *Social Security Bulletin*, XXVII, No. 3 (March, 1964), 8. 1959 and 1951 data from Lenore A. Epstein, "Living Arrangements and Income of the Aged," *Social Security Bulletin*, XXVI, No. 9 (September, 1963), 7.

Comparison with Modest But Adequate Living Standard. One way to measure the adequacy of the money incomes of the aged is to compare them with the cost of a "modest but adequate" level of living developed by the Bureau of Labor Statistics.[26] An aged couple living alone would require $2,500 a year in money income to maintain this standard of living.

[26] Epstein, "Income of the Aged in 1962 . . . ," *op. cit.*, 8 (see source citation at Table 2.8).

Non-married persons living alone would need $1,800.[27] The Bureau
originally developed cost figures for retired couples renting their home
in the fall of 1959 in twenty large cities (for example, $3,366 in Chicago,
$3,111 in Los Angeles, and $3,044 in New York). The new figures are
adaptations of these earlier estimates to allow for reduced costs for
homeownership, lower costs in the smaller communities, and differences
in costs for those living alone instead of with relatives. The following
quotation provides a more concrete explanation of the standard of living:

> The standard for the retired couple's budget has been translated into specific
> quantities to permit pricing. Although no couple would buy in exactly the
> manner of the budget, these quantities make it possible to visualize the level
> provided. The budget provides, for example, not quite an egg a day per person
> for the table and for use in cooking and about a half-pound of meat, poultry,
> or fish—barely enough for two small servings per day. For the entire year, it
> provides for a total of 15 restaurant meals. Since the couple was assumed to
> be in good health for their age, there was no provision for a special diet and
> practically none for household help or the expensive types of medical care that
> are all too often associated with the terminal illness that strikes 1 in 10 couples
> every year.
> Five-sixths of the couples were assumed to have a telephone for which they
> paid the minimum rate. The budget assumes the couple has an average inven-
> tory of clothing and house furnishings. Following are examples of certain types
> of clothing that could be purchased to maintain their inventory: The man can
> replace his topcoat only every ninth year, and his wife can buy three dresses
> each year, including housedresses. Ownership of an automobile was assumed
> for about one-fifth of the couples—with the percentage varying somewhat with
> the size of the city—and replacement was allowed every 7 or 8 years. For those
> without automobiles, four bus or trolley fares a week were included. Husband
> and wife could thus ride together to church, or to visit friends, or to shop, or
> to go to the movies in the 1 week in 4 that they had the cash to pay the
> admission fee.[28]

About 42 per cent of the aged couples, at least 60 per cent of the non-
married men, and at least 75 per cent of the non-married women do not
have cash incomes high enough to maintain this standard of living if they
live alone. However, many of the aged—particularly widows and other
non-married women—live with relatives, and these aged account for a

[27] Professor Juanita Kreps has argued that these two amounts should be increased
to $2,800 and $2,000, respectively, because there should be some increase in the allowance for automobile ownership and for medical costs. For her interesting analysis of
the economic status of the aged, see Juanita M. Kreps, "The Aged Poor," *Poverty:
The Sick, Disabled and Aged,* Second Report of the Task Force on Economic Growth
and Opportunity (Washington, D. C.: Chamber of Commerce of the United States,
1965), pp. 239–63. An alternative standard based on an economy food plan developed by the Department of Agriculture would require incomes of about $1,800 for
aged couples and $1,300 for non-married persons. See *ibid.,* pp. 249–50, and Mollie
Orshansky, "Counting the Poor: Another Look at the Poverty Profile," *Social Security
Bulletin,* XXVIII, No. 1 (January, 1965), 3–29.
[28] Epstein, "Income of the Aged in 1962 . . . ," *op. cit.,* 14.

disproportionate share of the low-income aged. For example, in 1959 the median income in metropolitan areas of 250,000 or more was $890 for non-married women who were living alone or with non-relatives but only $410 for those who lived with relatives except as the head of the family.[29]

Potential Income of the Aged. The Social Security Administration has also constructed a distribution of "potential" income which combines information on the money income and the asset holdings of the aged. The procedure has been explained as follows:

Assets were assumed to be capable of earning a 4 per cent annual rate of return. The principal and the appropriate interest amounts were divided over the expected remaining years of the unit's life in equal annual sums so that the assets would be exhausted at the end of that period. The annual amount computed in this way was added to the current money income less income actually received from assets.[30]

The median potential income for aged couples is $3,130 excluding equity in a home and $3,795 if this equity is included. For non-married men these two figures are $1,560 and $1,845, respectively, and for non-married women $1,130 and $1,395. Inequalities in the distribution of income were accentuated by this measure because those with high money incomes tend to control the most assets. Furthermore, 36 per cent of the aged couples, at least 50 per cent of the non-married men, and at least 70 per cent of the non-married women still lack sufficient income to maintain a "modest but adequate" standard of living.

The Aged Poor. Of the 34 million Americans who lived in 1964 "on an income that must be rated insufficient for daily needs by even a most conservative standard," [31] more than five million were at least sixty-five years old. An additional one-third would be considered poor if it were not for the fact that they shared the homes of relatives who had more money than they did. About half of these aged poor live alone. Of the three million aged women living alone, two million were considered poor. In short, the aged constitute a more than proportionate share of the poor.

Sources of Money Income. The sources from which the aged drew their money income in 1962 are indicated in Table 2.10. As noted earlier,

[29] Epstein, "Living Arrangements and Income of the Aged," *op. cit.,* 5.

[30] Janet Murray, "Potential Income from Assets: Findings of the 1963 Survey of the Aged," *Social Security Bulletin,* XXVII, No. 12 (December, 1964), 3–4.

[31] Mollie Orshansky, "Who's Who Among the Poor: A Demographic View of Poverty," *Social Security Bulletin,* XXVIII, No. 7 (July, 1965), 3. For the method used to derive the poverty line which recognizes differences in the poverty level for different family types, see Mollie Orshansky, "Counting the Poor: Another Look at the Poverty Profile," *op. cit.;* also see footnote 27.

if present trends continue, earnings will become a less important source of income in the future. Private pension plans will become a more important source, but most of the aged will not receive benefits from this source for at least the next two decades. By 1975, the proportion receiving benefits from OASDI is expected to reach 90 per cent, and the average OASDI benefit is also likely to increase. The persons who become aged in the next decade should have their benefits based on higher wage levels than their predecessors, but the difference between the median earnings ($2,900 for couples) of present OASDI beneficiaries, aged sixty-five to seventy-two, and the median earnings ($2,430 for couples) of present older beneficiaries suggests that the position of the future aged may be only moderately improved by funds from this source.[32] OASDI beneficiaries entitled to small benefits will probably continue to depend almost solely on these benefits.

TABLE 2.10

Sources of Money Income for the Aged, by Marital Status
and by Sex, 1962

Source	Per Cent Having Income from Specified Source			Per Cent of Aggregate Income from Specified Source
	Married Persons	Non-married Men	Non-married Women	
Earnings	55	28	23	32
Retirement benefits	84	72	64	39
OASDI	79	68	60	30
Other public programs	12	8	7	6
Private group pensions	16	10	3	3
Veterans' benefits	14	11	6	4
Interest, dividends, and rents	63	45	50	15
Private individual annuities	4	1	3	–
Unemployment insurance	3	1	1	4
Contributions by relatives or friends not in households	3	1	6	–
Public assistance	8	18	17	5

Source: Lenore A. Epstein, "Income of the Aged in 1962 . . . ," *Social Security Bulletin*, XXIV, No. 1 (March, 1964), 4, 6.

Conclusion. On the basis of these data, we conclude that the economic status of many aged persons is disturbingly low. The situation is improving for most persons in this age group, but no dramatic improvement in the proportion with substandard incomes should be expected in the next decade or two under present arrangements.

[32] Epstein, "Income of the Aged in 1962 . . . ," *op. cit.*, 22–23.

Public Versus Private Action

The need for some level of public action is obvious. However, since increased public benefits may occur at the expense of increased or present private benefits, it is not clear at present whether the two types of action have been combined in the optimum proportions. An answer to this question would, of course, contain important policy implications for the future. However, in order to discuss the question, it is necessary to understand the major characteristics of the present public assistance, social insurance, and private insurance plans. We shall consider the public plans in Chapters 3 and 4 and the private plans in Chapter 5.

SUMMARY

Premature death causes a loss of earning power and unexpected expenses such as funeral expenses and estate taxes. For most families, the most important loss is the loss of the present value of future incomes. About one out of four persons, aged twenty, will die prior to age sixty-five.

When a person reaches an advanced age, his earnings may stop or be reduced but his expenses continue, even if at a lower level. He must save during his earning career to prepare for retirement, but he does not know how much to save because the date of death is unknown. On the average, about three out of four persons, aged twenty, will reach age sixty-five. Decreasing mortality rates, low birth rates during the Depression, and reduced immigration have increased greatly the proportion of our population faced with the problems of old age.

Preventive methods such as medical research and safety programs have reduced the probability of premature death, but alleviative methods are still essential. Prior to the Industrial Revolution, the dependents of deceased persons moved in with relatives, but social and economic forces have reduced the importance of this solution. Insurance is the most acceptable and effective private alleviative approach, but relatively few persons are adequately protected through this medium for various reasons.

The Social Security Act initiated the first extensive public programs dealing with premature death. State public assistance programs became eligible for federal grants-in-aid in 1935 and the social insurance system was amended in 1939 to include death benefits.

The current incomes of many young widows with children in their care are still too low, however. About 40 per cent of the young widowed mothers had money incomes in 1957 of less than $2,400.

The most important preventive approach to the problems of old age is continued employment of the aged. About one-third of the *total* money income of the aged comes from this source. However, in 1962, less than 40 per cent of the aged males and 15 per cent of the aged females had some work experience during a year, and this labor force participation by the aged is declining. Compulsory retirement ages are only one reason for this decline. Poor health and, increasingly, a preference for leisure are other important reasons. Interest, dividends, and rents provide about half as much income as earnings for the aged. Private pension plans, though growing in importance, account for less than 3 per cent of the total money income of the aged.

Not only is the total private money income of the aged low, but the distribution of this income is very uneven. The inadequacy of these private sources other than earnings has been attributed to many factors including the low income status of part of the population, high taxes, and personal failures to prepare for retirement.

The Social Security Act also initiated the public programs dealing with old age. State public assistance programs were made eligible for federal grants-in-aid and a social insurance pension system was established.

Despite the public and private layers of protection and the continued employment of some aged persons, the current economic resources of the aged are inadequate. In 1962, for example, aged couples had a median money income of $2,875. About 42 per cent of these couples had less than the $2,500 income required to provide a "modest but adequate" standard of living.

SUGGESTIONS FOR ADDITIONAL READING

CORSON, JOHN J., and JOHN W. McCONNELL. *Economic Needs of Older People.* New York: The Twentieth Century Fund, 1956.
The economic problems of the aged are discussed in some detail in this extensive study, particularly in Chapters 1 through 5.
DUBLIN, LOUIS I., and ALFRED J. LOTKA. *The Money Value of a Man,* rev. ed. New York: The Ronald Press Company, 1946.
A detailed discussion of a method for measuring the value of a human life in terms of earning power.
EPSTEIN, ABRAHAM. *Insecurity, A Challenge to America,* 2d rev. ed. New York: Random House, Inc., 1938. Chapters 6–11.
A strong advocate discusses the need for social insurance programs providing protection against premature death and old age.
EPSTEIN, LENORE A. "Income of the Aged in 1962: First Findings of the 1963 Survey of the Aged," *Social Security Bulletin,* XXVII, No. 3 (March, 1964), 3–24.

This article and the later reports in the *Social Security Bulletin* on the 1963 Survey of the Aged were the source for most of the data in this chapter on the economic status of the aged.

GORDON, MARGARET S. "Aging and Income Security," *Aging and Society: A Handbook of Social Gerontology,* Clark Tibbitts (ed). Chicago: University of Chicago Press, 1960. Pp. 208–60.
A carefully prepared statement of the economic problems of the aging and the public and private programs dealing with these problems.
HUEBNER, SOLOMON S. *The Economics of Life Insurance,* rev. ed. New York: Appleton-Century-Crofts, 1944.
A pioneering discussion of human life values and their relationship to property values.
ORSHANSKY, MOLLIE. "Income of Young Survivors," *Social Security Bulletin,* XXII, No. 9 (September, 1959), 10–15.
This article provided most of the data in this chapter on the economic status of young survivors.
SHANAS, ETHEL. *Financial Resources of the Aging.* Research Series 10. New York: Health Information Foundation, 1959.
A different approach to measuring the financial resources of the aging which it is instructive to compare with the Social Security Administration approach.
STEINER, PETER O., and ROBERT DORFMAN. *The Economic Status of the Aged.* Berkeley and Los Angeles: University of California Press, 1957.
A comprehensive study of the economic status of the aged in the early 1950's which contains some interesting observations on the employability of the aged.
U. S. DEPARTMENT OF HEALTH, EDUCATION, AND WELFARE, PUBLIC HEALTH SERVICE. *United States Life Tables: 1959–61.* Washington, D. C.: U. S. Government Printing Office, 1964.
Detailed mortality tables applicable to the total population.

3

The Social Security Act: Public Assistance

INTRODUCTION

The need for some public protection against the financial problems of death and old age has been discussed in Chapter 2. In this chapter we shall consider the Social Security Act and its relationship to these problems.

First we shall describe the conditions that led to the passage of the Social Security Act. Then we shall analyze the public assistance programs established under the Act which deal with death and old age. The nature of the federal support, the characteristics of the state programs, and important trends are issues that will bear analysis.

HISTORICAL DEVELOPMENT

Prior to the passage of the Social Security Act in 1935, only limited public financial assistance was available for the aged and for the dependents of deceased workers. Because practices in this country during that period were based largely upon the poor laws in England, our discussion will begin with a brief review of some historical developments in the mother country.[1]

---

[1] See "Poor Law," *Encyclopaedia Britannica,* XVIII, 1964, 215–24. Also see Stefan A. Riesenfeld and Richard C. Maxwell, *Modern Social Legislation* (Brooklyn: The Foundation Press, Inc., 1950), pp. 685–92, 763–65.

The English Poor Laws

Prior to the sixteenth century, the feudal system provided security (although at a low level) for a good share of the English population, and the Church assumed primary responsibility for helping others in need. With the passing of the feudal system and, to a lesser extent, the dissolution of monasteries, poverty became a more acute problem and the dissatisfactions it created worried governmental authorities. On the assumption that any able-bodied person could find employment if he tried, the state concentrated its attention in 1531 on a law designed to stamp out vagrancy. Under this law only the aged and the impotent were permitted to beg, and they had to restrict their activities to their own neighborhood. Relief of the poor was left to the conscience of local authorities. However, a 1536 statute, which some historians consider to be the first English poor law, made local authorities responsible for the collection of voluntary contributions to be used to employ able-bodied "paupers" and to provide direct relief for others. Poor children were to be apprenticed and all begging was prohibited. Relatives were expected to assume primary responsibility for the poor of all types. Only the larger cities developed workable programs under this law; some of these cities imposed a compulsory poor rate instead of depending upon voluntary contributions. In 1572 a compulsory poor rate was imposed on a national scale.

A major bench mark in the development of the English poor law was the passage in 1601 of what is popularly known as the Elizabethan Poor Law or the "Old Poor Law." Under this law parishes were made the unit of administration. With funds obtained from a compulsory poor rate, the aged poor were to be granted relief, poor children were to be apprenticed, and the able-bodied poor were to be assigned jobs. As in earlier times, relatives were held primarily responsible for supporting the poor in each of these groups. Increasingly, the system of local administration caused difficulties because the poor tended to seek out those parishes with the most satisfactory relief arrangements. As a result, the parishes began to restrict benefits to established residents. A 1662 Law of Settlement and Removal legalized and strengthened this practice by permitting the overseers of a parish to petition the local justices to move back to his place of settlement any new resident who did not rent a fairly substantial dwelling or who could not guarantee that he would not become a public burden in the future. Under the Elizabethan Poor Law the aged and the sick apparently received better treatment than other poor persons. Children were often apprenticed under unsatisfactory arrangements merely to reduce the cost of supporting them on relief and only feeble attempts were made to employ the able-bodied poor.

In 1723 a general act permitted parishes to refuse relief to those who would not enter workhouses. These workhouses "everywhere rapidly degenerated into mixed receptacles of misery where every class of pauper, vicious or unfortunate, young or old, sick, well or lunatic, was dumped." [2] Increasing humanitarian concern about these workhouses resulted in a 1782 act that permitted parishes to combine resources to build institutions for all paupers except the able-bodied, who were to receive relief or to work outside the institution.

Toward the end of the eighteenth century, a series of events causing price increases made the wages of many workers inadequate. Although one solution would have been to raise wages, such action would not have been consistent with the prevailing mercantilist obsession with maintaining a favorable balance of trade. This solution was also opposed by the ruling landowning aristocracy who wanted a good supply of cheap agricultural labor.[3] The problem seemed to be temporary. Consequently, at a meeting at Speen in 1795, the Speenhamland system was adopted, under which wages were to be supplemented by relief payments if they did not provide a minimum standard of living.

With the advent of the Industrial Revolution and the increasing popularity of the laissez-faire philosophy espoused by Adam Smith, David Ricardo, and others, the Speenhamland system was increasingly criticized as an unjustified interference of the state with individual freedom and responsibility, an undesirable influence on the moral character of the population, a subsidy for the landowning class, and a deterrent to labor mobility. The system was also imposing an almost impossible financial burden on many parishes. Consequently, a royal commission was appointed in 1832 to study the system, and its recommendations were largely responsible for the "New Poor Law" of 1834.

The 1834 law was based upon the harsh philosophy that all the poor were poor because of their own failings. Able-bodied workers and their dependents were to be granted relief only in workhouses in which they could be closely supervised and in which conditions would be such that the worker would clearly prefer regular employment. Other poor persons such as the aged, the sick, and the young were subjected to the same rigid discipline. Recipients lost their right to vote and were required to wear special uniforms to indicate their second-class status.

By the middle of the nineteenth century, public sentiment began to change and the system began to be liberalized on a piecemeal basis. Outdoor relief became more common, separate institutions were created

2 "Poor Law," op. cit., p. 218.
3 The Law of Settlement had been supported by this English ruling class for the same reason. For an excellent analysis of the effect of prevailing economic thought upon the English poor laws, see Valdemar Carlson, Economic Security in the United States (New York: McGraw-Hill Book Co., 1962), chaps. 3 and 4.

for women, children, and the aged, and more visitors were permitted to inspect the almshouses. In 1905 a Royal Commission on the Poor Laws was appointed. Although its highly critical report in 1909 did not result in any immediate amendments to the Poor Law, it did result in a more liberal administration of that law. An Old Age Pensions Act in 1908 provided pensions for needy aged on a more humane basis, and a National Insurance Act in 1911 provided sickness and unemployment insurance benefits for some workers on a contributory basis. Because subsequent developments in England are less relevant to the United States' experience, they will not be discussed here, but it should be noted that in 1948 a new National Assistance Act was enacted which was designed to supplement a comprehensive national insurance law passed in 1944.

Early Poor Laws in the United States

Except for the fact that their poor laws were based even more heavily on a deterrent philosophy, the experience of the American states and local communities with poor laws parallels very closely that of England.[4] Initially, the local governments assumed responsibility and arranged on a limited basis for outdoor relief, for indentures, and for boarding out needy persons. The first poor law, which, like its English precedents, provided for local responsibility and settlement requirements, was passed by the Massachusetts Bay Colony in 1639. The first poorhouse was established in Massachusetts in 1660, but it was not until the next century that the poorhouse became the most popular approach to helping needy persons. Apparently the Speenhamland system had little effect upon American legislation, and the poor were almost continuously regarded as inferior persons. After 1870, however, there was increasing discontent with mixed poorhouses and their administration, and legislation was enacted to provide special treatment for such indigent groups as the insane, the blind, the deaf, and the dumb.

Shortly after the turn of the century, Massachusetts became the first state to establish a commission to study the problems of the aged. Other states followed suit. These commissions reflected a shift in prevailing attitudes with respect to public assistance for the needy aged and needy dependent survivors in that these groups were increasingly assumed to be more the victims of circumstances than, say, low-paid workers and the unemployed. In 1909, there was a White House Conference on the Care of Dependent Children, and in 1911 Missouri and Illinois passed laws establishing "pension" systems for needy widowed mothers. In 1914 Arizona passed a "pension" law, which also covered the aged, but it was shortly declared unconstitutional. Although Alaska passed a similar law

4 Carlson, *ibid.*, p. 38.

in 1915, it was so limited in effect that the Montana law, passed in 1923, is generally considered to be the first old-age "pension" law.

The 1921 recession awakened more interest on the part of the states in the needy aged and widowed mothers. Energetic social reformers wrote and talked at length about the problem. One of the most notable of these reformers was Abraham Epstein who served as Research Director of the Pennsylvania Commission on Old-Age Pensions created in 1917, worked for the Fraternal Order of Eagles during 1922–23 in their drive for pensions throughout the country, and in 1927 established the American Association for Old-Age Security, later renamed the American Association for Social Security. This association was probably the most effective promoter of social security legislation from its establishment until Mr. Epstein's death in 1942.[5] Although its primary concern initially was old-age pensions, it later concentrated its attention on social insurance.

In spite of this increased activity, only seven states had passed old-age assistance laws prior to the Great Depression, and two of these laws had been declared unconstitutional. More than half of the states had passed mothers' pension laws which provided cash payments for needy widowed mothers, but the benefits were small. The federal government itself had taken no action, although bills had been introduced in the Congress at various times, beginning as early as 1909.

The Depression increased and dramatized the problem. Annual unemployment rates rose to about 25 per cent, soup kitchens and bread lines became commonplace, and many conservative, thrifty, industrious workers exhausted their savings and lost their homes through mortgage foreclosures. Man, it became clear to more and more people, does not always control his own destiny. Consequently, the legislative pace was quickened and over half the states had an old-age assistance law by the middle 1930's. However, these laws covered only a very small segment of the aged population because of severe age, citizenship, residence, income, and property requirements. In addition, during the depth of the Depression, only about one out of every ten eligibles was actually receiving a pension, primarily because of financial problems experienced by state and local governmental units. All but two states had mothers' aid laws, but these programs were also badly in need of financial assistance. Relief for other categories of the poor was left to local communities and voluntary charities, but by 1932 seven states, led by New York State in 1931,

[5] For a more detailed account of Mr. Epstein's work, see E. Wight Bakke, "Life of Abraham Epstein: An American Epic," *Social Security*, XVI, No. 7 (September–October, 1942), 3–6. Another social insurance pioneer whose name deserves mention in a text on this subject was Dr. I. M. Rubinow, considered by many to be the father of modern social security because of his 1913 volume on *Social Insurance*. For an account of Dr. Rubinow's life, see "Dr. I. M. Rubinow Passes On," *Social Security*, X, No. 7 (September–October, 1963), 3–4.

had assumed some responsibility for the unemployed.[6] Wisconsin established an unemployment insurance system in 1932, and similar programs were being considered in other states.

The Townsend Plan

During 1933 another movement which was to influence social security legislation first became prominent. Dr. Francis E. Townsend, a former physician who had been driven by the Depression from South Dakota to California, advocated a plan that was designed to improve the purchasing power of the aged and to eliminate the Depression by restoring purchasing power. Dr. Townsend advocated a monthly pension of $200 for all citizens sixty years of age or over who promised: (1) not to engage in any employment and (2) to spend the $200 within thirty days. The pensions were to be financed by a 2 per cent business transactions tax. Economists criticized the inadequacy of the transactions tax and its incidence, the cost of administering the plan, and its inflationary aspects,[7] but in spite of these deficiencies, the plan appealed to many aged persons and future events underscored their political power. During the remainder of the 1930's, Townsend Clubs appeared throughout the nation; although the Townsendites were unable to gain acceptance of their plan, they were influential in bringing about some legislation.

The Social Security Act of 1935

Pressure for some federal action increased as the Depression situation worsened. By 1931 President Hoover was convinced that the federal government should intervene in some direct fashion. Later that year at his suggestion Congress established the Reconstruction Finance Corporation, which made loans to businesses and banks in danger of failing. Under the Emergency Relief and Construction Act of 1932, this agency also made loans to states to be used in connection with public works projects and, later, for relief payments. This legislation encouraged many additional states to establish state emergency relief administrations. Franklin Delano Roosevelt advocated more extensive federal action during the 1932 presidential campaign and his election was considered to be a mandate for more federal legislation. In 1933 the Federal Emergency Relief Administration (FERA) was established to make grants to states for direct relief and for work relief. Some of these grants required match-

[6] Charles I. Schottland, *The Social Security Program in the United States* (New York: Appleton-Century-Crofts, 1963), p. 31. Chapter 4 of this book contains a concise but comprehensive discussion of the effects of the Great Depression and the events leading to the Social Security Act of 1935.

[7] John J. Corson and John W. McConnell, *Economic Needs of Older People* (New York: The Twentieth Century Fund, 1956), pp. 118–19.

ing expenditures from state funds; others did not. Some closely related programs established under the "New Deal" included (1) the Civilian Conservation Corps (1933), which employed young men on conservation projects; (2) the Public Works Administration (1933), a Hoover-conceived project, which made loans and grants to states for large public building projects; (3) the Civil Works Administration (1933), which made funds available to those local governments that could arrange work relief projects on short notice; (4) the Federal Surplus Relief Corporation (1933), which distributed surplus foods to the needy; and (5) the Works Progress Administration (1935), which replaced the PWA and the CWA. The WPA, which did not limit itself to construction projects, continued to operate until World War II eliminated the need for its existence.

In June, 1934, President Roosevelt appointed a Committee on Economic Security to study the general problem of economic security. This action was prompted by the obvious need, the growing interest in and acceptance of social legislation, and the fear that some unwise proposal might be adopted without careful study. The Committee was composed of several cabinet members and the head of the Federal Emergency Relief Administration. Professor Edwin Witte of the University of Wisconsin was appointed Executive Director.[8] General advisory committees, a technical board of specialists from within and outside the government, and a special committee of four private actuaries aided the Committee in its work. After extensive deliberations concerning the perils to be included, the approaches to be used, the employments to be covered, the benefits to be provided, and the method of financing, the Committee reported its findings in January, 1935. In response to this report [9] Congress passed, just seven months later, the Social Security Act—the most extensive piece of social legislation in our history.

The original Act provided for the following:

1. Grants to the states for assistance to the needy aged, blind, and dependent children.[10]
2. Grants to the states for the administration of state unemployment compensation systems.

---

[8] For the Executive Director's own account of this period, see Edwin E. Witte, *The Development of the Social Security Act* (Madison: University of Wisconsin Press, 1962).

[9] Although Congress accepted in principle most of the Committee's recommendations, it did not accept all of them. For example, a proposal to set up a government insurer to sell annuities in competition with private insurers was rejected. See Schottland, *op. cit.*, p. 37.

[10] Professor Carlson argues that categorical programs were established only for the aged, the blind, and dependent children because Congress was made more aware of the needs of these groups and because its preference for outdoor relief caused it to concentrate on those groups for whom institutional care seemed to be the least adequate. See Carlson, *op. cit.*, p. 90.

3. Increased grants to the states for public health services and re-habilitation facilities and increased appropriations for the Public Health Service and the Federal Vocational Rehabilitation Service.
4. Grants to the states for maternal and child health services, services for crippled children, and child welfare services, and an increased appropriation for the Children's Bureau.
5. Federal old-age insurance benefits.
6. Taxes on employers and employees to support the old-age insur-ance benefits.
7. Taxes on employers designed to encourage the establishment of state unemployment compensation systems.

Important amendments to the Act were passed in 1939, 1946, every two years beginning in 1950, and in 1961, 1962, and 1965. The most sig-nificant changes are the following:

1. Grants are now also extended to the states for assistance to the needy permanently and totally disabled and for medical expense programs for medically needy persons among the aged, the blind, the permanently and totally disabled, and dependent children.
2. The Public Health Service and the Federal Vocational Rehabilita-tion Service provisions have been expanded and transferred to the Public Health Service Act and the Vocational Rehabilitation Act, respectively.
3. The federal old-age insurance benefits have become old-age, sur-vivorship, and disability insurance benefits.
4. A hospital insurance system and a supplementary medical expense insurance program have been established for the aged.
5. The tax provisions have been transferred to the Internal Revenue Code. The part of the code dealing with OASDI and hospital in-surance contributions is called the Federal Insurance Contributions Act. These tax provisions were originally assigned to separate titles in the Social Security Act and deliberately not related to the other titles in order to prevent any attack upon their constitution-ality from destroying the other provisions. Their constitutionality, however, was upheld by the United States Supreme Court in 1937.[11] The change to the Revenue Code was made in 1939 at the same time that Congress appropriated all tax collections from this source to the OASDI system.

The grants under the public assistance programs were designed to solve an immediate problem by strengthening and extending state special public assistance programs. The OASDI system and the medical expense insurance programs represent a long-range approach to the problems of death, old age, and poor health. The other grants deal with preventive

[11] *Carmichael v. Southern Coal and Coke Co.*, 301 U.S. 495, *Steward Machine Co. v. Davis*, 301 U.S. 548, and *Commissioner v. Davis*, 301 U.S. 619.

approaches, which have already been discussed, or unemployment compensation, which will be discussed later.

SPECIAL PUBLIC ASSISTANCE PROGRAMS

Under the Social Security Act, the federal government makes grants-in-aid to states having public assistance programs for the needy (including the medically needy) aged, blind, permanently and totally disabled, and dependent children. Unlike the social insurance programs to be discussed later, the public assistance programs (1) distribute funds only in the case of need and (2) rely usually upon general revenues for their support. The social insurance programs do not eliminate the need for public assistance because many persons are not covered under these programs, while others, who are covered, are not eligible for adequate benefits and require supplementary assistance.

Since old age and death are the insecurities under consideration in this chapter, the discussion will be limited to the programs providing aid for the needy aged and needy dependent children. The other special public assistance programs are discussed in Chapter 11.

Federal Grants for Old-Age Assistance Programs

All fifty states (plus the District of Columbia, Guam, Puerto Rico, and the Virgin Islands) now have old-age assistance programs that are eligible for federal aid. The purpose of federal grants-in-aid is to provide financial support for state programs that meet certain minimum standards; however, the detailed provisions and administration of the programs are left to the state and local governmental units.

At the present time, the federal government pays, in addition to one-half the administrative expenses and 75 per cent of the cost of providing certain "social services" described below, the following portion of the average *monthly* pension [12] provided under an approved state program:

$\frac{31}{37}$ of the first $37, plus

50–65 per cent of the next $38.

The second fraction is 50 per cent for states with above-average per capita income and ranges from 50–65 per cent for the other states. [13] For this

[12] The pension may include payments to vendors for medical services. For a discussion of the effect of the 1960 and later amendments on these payments, see pp. 360–63 in Chapter 11.

[13] The proportion, which is bounded by 50 per cent and 65 per cent, is determined as follows:

$$\text{Proportion} = 1.00 - .50 \frac{(\text{State per capita income})^2}{(\text{National per capita income})^2}$$

reason and because the federal government's share of the benefits is greatest when the average pension payment is low, the formula favors the poorer states and those wealthier states that make a large number of low average grants.[14] This same matching formula is used to determine federal participation in the cost of state programs providing aid to the blind and to the permanently and totally disabled.

The basic minimum requirements for federal approval are as follows; [15] the logic underlying each requirement is appended in parentheses.

1. The program must cover all counties in the state, but it may be administered by local governmental units. (Otherwise certain counties could be discriminated against.)
2. A single state agency must either administer the program itself or supervise the local governmental units administering the program. (This promotes uniformity of treatment among localities.)
3. The state must participate financially in the program. (The state government should aid the local government units in the same way that the federal government is aiding the state.)
4. Personnel in the administrative unit must be selected and retained through the merit system. (This provision is designed to improve the caliber of employed personnel.)
5. The Secretary of Health, Education, and Welfare is entitled to any information he may require concerning the operation of the program. (This information is used primarily to determine whether the minimum federal requirements are being met, and for informational and research purposes.)
6. Information divulged by applicants and recipients must be regarded as confidential, but state legislation may permit interested persons to look at the rolls under certain conditions so long as it prohibits the use of such information for political or commercial purposes. (The privacy of the individual is to be preserved, but some persons believe that open rolls cut costs by discouraging fraudulent applications.)
7. The age requirement must be sixty-five years or less. (Sixty-five is the retirement age under the OASDI program. The federal government, however, participates only in the benefits to persons aged sixty-five or more.)
8. The residence requirement must not exceed five out of the preceding nine years and one year immediately preceding the date

[14] The 1965 amendments provided that a state would not receive the additional federal funds provided under those amendments except to the extent that they resulted in increased benefits to individual recipients. The funds could not be used merely to cut state costs.

[15] U. S. Department of Health, Education, and Welfare, Welfare Administration, "Characteristics of State Public Assistance Plans under the Social Security Act," *Public Assistance Report No. 50, 1964 Edition* (Washington, D. C.: U. S. Government Printing Office, 1964).

of application. (The durational residence requirement should be as short as possible.)

9. The citizenship requirement must not exclude any citizen of the United States.

10. Benefits must be granted only in case of need. An applicant's income and assets must be considered in determining his needs. In determining need, however, a state may disregard the first $20 of earned income and half of the next $60 of a recipient's earnings. It *may* also choose to exempt *any* income up to $5 per month. On the other hand, a state may include provisions for recovery of assistance paid from the recipients during their lifetime or from their estate. (This requirement follows from the nature of the grants. The exemptions represent an increasing tendency to encourage some earnings and savings on the part of recipients.)

11. A dissatisfied applicant must have the right to a fair hearing before the supervising state agency. (This right is regarded as essential in a democracy.)

12. A state authority must establish and maintain standards for public and private institutions housing recipients of the benefits. The federal government, however, does not participate in benefits to those persons who are inmates in a non-medical *public* institution.[16] (If it were not for these standards, some institutions might profit at the expense of the public assistance program. The original Act, which sought to eliminate poorhouses and payments in kind, provided for federal assistance only with respect to cash grants. Later it was recognized that for some recipients such as the infirm aged, public institutional care has many advantages. Private institutional care was possible even under the original Act.)

The state administration costs must be necessary and proper. A 1956 amendment made it clear that the cost of providing social services designed to help applicants or recipients (past, present, *and potential*) to attain or retain some ability for self-care or self-support is a proper cost of administration. An example of such services is arranging for specialized help that will enable an aged person to remain in his own home instead of entering a nursing home. A 1962 amendment increased federal participation in the cost of providing certain of these services (including the cost of training skilled personnel) to 75 per cent. The Secretary of Health, Education, and Welfare was made responsible for defining the services eligible for this higher federal participation.

[16] Until the 1965 amendments, the federal government did not participate in benefits to patients in a tuberculosis or medical institution. Under those amendments, a state became eligible for additional federal funds for payments to these persons but only to the extent that it increased its expenditures for mental health purposes under public health and public welfare programs.

A 1965 amendment permits the state to make protective payments to some third party interested in the aged recipient if that recipient is unable to manage his money properly because of some physical or mental incapacity.

Another change introduced by the extensive Public Welfare Amendments of 1962 permits the states to combine (1) their programs of assistance for the aged, the blind, and the disabled or (2) these three programs and medical assistance for the aged. One advantage of such a combination is that the separate and additional federal financing for vendor payments for medical care for OAA recipients described in Chapter 11 would be extended to the blind and the disabled. (A 1965 amendment that, like this 1962 amendment, is also described in more detail in Chapter 11, permits the states to establish a single medical assistance program for direct payments to vendors of medical care and services under all of the categorical public assistance titles.) A second possible advantage is that because the average benefit used to determine federal participation is the average under the combined program, an average benefit under one of three separate programs in excess of $75 may be offset by an average benefit in another program below $75 to produce an average of $75 or less.

Experimentation in public assistance programs was encouraged by a 1962 provision that waived the standard requirements for those states that want to conduct approved experimental, pilot, or demonstration projects designed to promote program objectives. Federal funds were also made available to meet all of the costs of these projects.

The Bureau of Family Services, a unit of the Welfare Administration of the Department of Health, Education, and Welfare, is charged with the administration of all the public assistance grants-in-aid programs included under the Social Security Act. In addition to approving state programs and making the federal grants, the Bureau works with the states to improve their programs and their staffs, collects and interprets nationwide data on public assistance, and suggests changes in federal legislation and policy that it considers necessary and desirable.

State Old-Age Assistance Programs

The fifty state programs meet these federal standards; but given these minimal standards, there are considerable differences in the details of state programs, especially as regards the concept of need and the amount of the benefits. These differences reflect variations among the states with respect to economic conditions including financial need and fiscal resources, the length of operation of the plan, and the philosophy of the citizenry as determined by a host of factors. The most important features of the current state programs as of early 1964 are summarized in the following paragraphs.[17] By that time fifteen jurisdictions (fourteen states plus Puerto Rico) had already combined OAA with their programs for the blind and for the permanently and totally disabled.

All state programs except one require that the recipient be at least sixty-five years of age. The Colorado program lowers the age requirement to sixty for persons who have resided in that state for the thirty-five years immediately preceding their application for benefits. In about four-fifths of the states, there is no citizenship requirement and in most of the other states long-term residence in the United States is accepted as a substitute for citizenship. In about two-thirds of the states, the residence requirement is less than the federal requirement for approval. Some states have reciprocal agreements with other states which reduce the durational residence requirements for some applicants. Although there is considerable variation in details among the states, particularly with respect to private institutions, the restrictions on institutional care tend to parallel those in the matching federal provisions.

An applicant is generally considered to be "needy" if he has insufficient income or other resources to provide reasonable subsistence compatible with decency and health. A few states consider a person to be needy if his income or other resources are less than a specified dollar amount. As of April, 1964, only twenty-two states disregarded some earnings in determining need but this possibility was not permitted until the 1962 amendments. Almost all states set definite limits on the amount of property which an applicant may own in order to be considered needy. These property limits tend to reduce the amount of discretion involved in individual cases. They vary by amount, the method of valuation, and the type of property included. Usually real estate used as a home can be retained but there may be a dollar value placed on this property. Other real estate must be sold. The person may have a limited amount of cash, life insurance, and other personal property including a low-valued automobile for essential transportation. An applicant who disposes of property in order to qualify for assistance is ineligible under almost all state laws.

Slightly less than one-third of the states require children to support their needy parents and withhold public assistance or reduce it in amount even if the support is not forthcoming. About two-fifths of the states require support from the children but give the parent assistance even if the children refuse to help their parents. The remaining one-third of the states have no support requirement by law or policy.[18]

17 "Characteristics of State Public Assistance Plans under the Social Security Act," *op. cit.*

18 Alvin L. Schorr, *Filial Responsibility in the Modern American Family* (Washington, D. C.: U. S. Government Printing Office, 1960), pp. 23–24.

The amount of assistance required is determined by subtracting the applicant's resources from his personal requirements as determined by the administering agency. The requirements of the claimant are computed in accordance with a state standard which specifies the quantity and cost of stated essentials. State standards vary markedly with respect to the content of these standards and the frequency with which they are revised. Local variations are permitted with respect to such objective factors as local prices. Special needs of individual families may also be recognized. The applicant's resources may include money income, non-cash income, and assets. As stated earlier, some earnings may be disregarded in determining these resources.

A few states have established statutory minimums for assistance plus other income. The system used by these states is sometimes referred to as a "flat-grant minus" or an "income conditioned" system but the minimums in these state laws may be and often are exceeded.

About three-fifths of the states have a specified maximum benefit. About half of the limits are statutory, while the others are administrative. A few states, by policy, pay only a reduced proportion of the determined need.

About three-fifths of the states reserve the right to recover at least part of the assistance granted from the recipient or his estate. Usually this claim is not enforceable against any house or homestead if there is a surviving spouse or minor children.

In almost three-fifths of the states, the program is administered by a state agency. In the other states it is administered by the local governments under the supervision of the state government. About forty states provide social services that qualify them for 75 per cent federal matching of expenditures. The other states provide social services but not those defined by the Secretary of Health, Education, and Welfare for increased federal participation.

Trends in Old-Age Assistance

The old-age assistance programs have been liberalized in various ways over the years. Property limits have been raised; certain earnings have been disregarded; the circle of relatives considered legally responsible for the support of aged persons has been narrowed and, in some cases, eliminated; statewide standard budgets have been developed to reduce administrative difficulties, encourage uniformity of treatment, and safeguard the privacy of the individual; pensions are now paid to persons in approved public medical institutions; monthly benefits have been considerably increased; and greater emphasis has been placed on the provision of social services in addition to financial assistance.

The formulas that have been used since 1935 to determine the contribution of the federal government are given in Table 3.1. Three important changes have occurred. First, the contribution has been considerably increased through increases in the maximum monthly benefits included in the average and the fraction of the average benefit paid. Second, instead of contributing the same percentage of all average benefits, the federal government now pays a larger share of the low average grants than of the high average grants. Third, the federal government currently varies its grants according to the per capita income of the states.

TABLE 3.1

Formulae for Determining Federal Contributions to State Old-Age Assistance Programs, 1935–65

Year	Maximum Monthly Benefits Included in Average	Fraction of Average Benefit Paid by Federal Government
1935	$30	½
1939	40	½
1946	45	⅔ of first $15, ½ of balance
1948	50	¾ of first $20, ½ of balance
1952	55	⅘ of first $25, ½ of balance
1956	60	⅘ of first $30, ½ of balence
1958	No limit	⅘ of first $30, 50–65% of next $35 depending upon state per capita income
1961	No limit	⅘ of first $31, 50–65% of next $35 depending upon state per capita income
1962	No limit	$29/35$ of first $35, 50–65% of next $35 depending upon state per capita income
1965	No limit	$31/37$ of first $37, 50–65% of next $38 depending upon state per capita income

Because it is more convenient to discuss the operations of old-age assistance plans at the same time that we discuss the operations of the plans providing aid to families with dependent children, we shall consider next the nature of the latter group of plans. An evaluation of both groups of plans will follow the discussion of their operations.

Federal Grants for Programs Providing Aid to Families with Dependent Children

All states in the Union (plus the District of Columbia, Guam, Puerto Rico, and the Virgin Islands) have federally approved plans providing aid to families with dependent children. In 1962 the name of these programs was officially changed to "Grants to States for Aid and Services to Needy Families with Dependent Children." Although this title clearly identifies the new emphasis on rehabilitation and other services, the more popular label, AFDC, will be used in this text. These benefits are payable in cases where the father has died, become mentally or physically disabled, or is continually absent from the home because he has divorced his wife or deserted his family. The children need not be legitimate to receive these benefits. A 1961 amendment to the Social Security Act permitted states to extend their programs until June 30, 1962, to provide aid to children deprived of parental support or care because of a parent's unemployment. This extension, which in 1962 was continued for another five years, is discussed in more detail in Chapter 7. A few states also make payments for other reasons, but the federal government does not contribute to these special benefits.

As in the case of old-age assistance, the federal government pays one-half the general administrative expenses and 75 per cent of the cost of providing certain social services defined by the Secretary of Health, Education, and Welfare and designed to help applicants and recipients (including past and potential applicants and recipients) to attain or retain some ability for self-support or to help them maintain and strengthen their family life. It also pays the following portion of the *average* monthly benefit per recipient (not family):

5/6 of the first $18, plus
50–65 per cent of the next $14, depending upon the state per capita income as under the OAA formula

Eligible recipients include the dependent children, the mother, the father (but only if he is disabled or unemployed), and, if the children are in the care of someone other than the parents, one adult caretaker.

The requirements for federal approval are essentially the same as those established for old-age assistance plans, but the residence requirement is considerably more liberal from the viewpoint of the recipient. No state may impose a residence requirement which denies aid to any child residing in the state (1) who has resided in the state for one year immediately preceding the application or (2) who was born within one year immediately preceding the application if his parent or other relative with whom he is living has resided in the state for one year immediately preceding the birth. No age requirement is necessary for approval, but the federal government will contribute only to those cases involving dependents under eighteen unless the child is attending high school or college on a regular basis or is taking vocational training, in which case the federal government will participate in payments until the child is aged twenty-one. The federal government will not match payments to children living in public or private institutions. Until 1961 there was also no matching of payments to children living in foster homes but the federal government now participates in these payments when the children are removed from their homes by court order and placed in foster-family homes or in a non-profit child-care institution and when certain other conditions are met. The 1961 amendments also provided that federal funds would not be withheld for any period before September 1, 1962, because a state statute denied aid to a child because of "unsuitable" conditions (such as the presence of illegitimate children) in the home in which the child is living. The 1962 amendments permit such denials so long as the child receives in some other way adequate care and assistance.

A late 1961 administrative change required states to notify law enforcement officials immediately when a father abandons or deserts his family in order that they might help to locate him. The Public Welfare Amendments of 1962 also established some additional requirements for approval of state AFDC programs. In keeping with the new emphasis on rehabilitation, the state plan must now include some program for providing welfare and related services for each child recipient, according to his need. This program must be coordinated with the child welfare services program developed under the maternal and child welfare title of the Social Security Act. States must now also consider all expenses associated with employment in determining need; formerly such consideration was optional.

Another important change in 1962 authorized federal financial participation in payments for work performed by an adult relative with whom a dependent child is living. Payment for this work must be not less than the prevailing community rate for such work and the work itself must meet certain standards. For example, it must be safe and useful, and must not result in the displacement of regular workers. The state must recognize the additional expenses attributable to work in determining need and must not deny aid when refusal to work is for a good cause. A person assigned to a work project must be given the opportunity to seek other employment and to obtain appropriate training or retraining for this purpose. The state must cooperate with the state employment service and with state adult education agencies to return these recipients to the regular labor force as soon as possible.

Another incentive for employment provided under the 1962 amendments allows all or any portion of a family's earned income to be set aside for the future identifiable needs (such as education) of a dependent child. A 1965 amendment provided further incentive by permitting states in determining need to disregard up to $50 of earnings per child per month but not more than $150 per family. Up to $5 per recipient per month of *any* income may also be exempted.

If a state questions whether the AFDC payments are being used for the child's benefit, it can, as a result of the 1962 amendments, provide counselling and guidance in the management of these payments and other funds. Protective payments may be made to another person interested in or concerned with the child if the relative is unable to manage the payment. If serious mismanagement is likely to continue despite special efforts to improve the relative's ability to manage funds, the state is permitted to seek the appointment of a guardian or legal representative.

State Programs Providing Aid to Families with Dependent Children

The details of the state programs in early 1964 may be summarized briefly as follows: [19] Under almost three-fifths of the plans, the dependent child must be under eighteen years of age. Under most of the other programs, a dependent child must be under sixteen or under eighteen if regularly attending school. The minimum-age requirement is sixteen but some require that children of school age must be attending school if possible; the maximum age is twenty-one. Only one plan has a citizenship requirement. Four-fifths of the plans have the residence requirement established for federal approval; the others have none except that the family must be resident at the time of application. About one-fourth of the plans provide payments on behalf of unborn children.

In almost all states, the child recipient must be living with a close relative. About half of the states approve a foster home or a private child-care institution. In over two-fifths of the states the family home must be "suitable." The child is generally assumed to be needy if he or the persons with whom he is living has insufficient income or other resources to provide the child with a reasonable subsistence compatible with decency and health. Only one state automatically considers a need to exist if the income or other resources are less than a specified amount. Almost one-third of the states provide for the conservation of certain earnings of the child for future identifiable needs such as education. Almost all the programs set limits on the property owned by the child and his family. As in the case of old-age assistance, these property limits vary by amount, the method of valuation, and the type of property involved.

[19] "Characteristics of State Public Assistance Plans under the Social Security Act," *op. cit.*

The amount of the benefit is determined in the same way as the old-age assistance benefit. About three-fifths of the states have established a maximum benefit. Most of these are administrative; the others are statutory. Some states pay, by policy, only a fraction of the determined need.

Most states do not reserve the right to recover payments made to an infant. This policy differs from the one adopted in the case of old-age assistance. The aid does not represent a loan against future earning power.

If a state agency administers directly the old-age assistance program, it also administers directly the aid to families with dependent children. A similar correspondence exists with respect to state agencies that supervise local administrating agencies.

All programs provide services as well as financial aid. Only one program does not provide the defined services that would qualify it for increased federal matching of expenses associated with these services.

Trends in Aid to Families with Dependent Children

The aid-to-families-with-dependent-children programs have been continually liberalized since the 1930's in the same ways as the old-age assistance programs. The changes in the federal contribution formula over the years are given in Table 3.2.

TABLE 3.2

Formulae for Determining Federal Contributions to State
Aid-to-Families-with-Dependent-Children Programs: 1935–65

	Maximum Monthly Benefits Included in Average		Fraction of Average Benefit per Recipient Paid by
Year	First Child	Each Additional Child	Federal Government
1935	$18	$12	$\frac{1}{3}$
1939	18	12	$\frac{1}{2}$
1946	24	15	$\frac{2}{3}$ of first $9, $\frac{1}{2}$ of balance
1948	27	18	$\frac{3}{4}$ of first $12, $\frac{1}{2}$ of balance
1950	27 plus 27 per adult	18	$\frac{3}{4}$ of first $12, $\frac{1}{2}$ of balance
1952	30 plus 30 per adult	21	$\frac{4}{5}$ of first $15, $\frac{1}{2}$ of balance
1956	32 plus 32 per adult	23	$\frac{14}{17}$ of first $17, $\frac{1}{2}$ of balance
1958	No limit	No limit	$\frac{14}{17}$ of first $17, 50–65% of next $13 depending upon state per capita income
1965	No limit	No limit	$\frac{5}{6}$ of first $18, 50–65% of next $14 depending upon state per capita income

Until 1939 the federal government paid less than half the average benefits under the state programs. Until 1946 the federal contribution was a fixed percentage of all average benefits, but since that date the federal contribution has been relatively greatest for low average benefits. Until 1950 the federal government contributed nothing toward payments on behalf of the adults with whom the children live. The per capita income of the state was recognized explicitly for the first time in 1958. The total federal contribution has increased significantly over the years. The Public Welfare Amendments of 1962, through their emphasis upon rehabilitation and other social services, incentives to work, and protective payments gave the program a new direction and purpose.

Operations

A study of the more important operations of these two special public assistance programs enables one to understand more clearly their nature and scope.

The changes over time in the number of recipients, total payments, and average monthly payments under the public assistance programs are given in Table 3.3. The number of old-age recipients increased up to 1950 except during the war years, but it has decreased since 1950 when OASDI was extended to cover many new groups of employees. The number of recipients under the aid-to-families-with-dependent-children programs has increased very rapidly except for temporary reductions during World War II and 1952–53. The average monthly payments for both old-age assistance and aid to families with dependent children have more than quadrupled. The future should be marked by a further decline in old-age assistance recipients as more people become eligible for OASDI, but the number of persons receiving support under the aid-to-families-with-dependent-children programs will probably increase because OASDI provides assistance only in case of death or disability. Only 7 per cent of the AFDC child recipients are survivors. On the other hand, about 8 per cent receive benefits because of the unemployment of the father and if the temporary provision providing benefits for this group is permitted to expire, the number of AFDC recipients may temporarily decrease. The new emphasis on social services should also tend to reduce the number of recipients. The average monthly payments will probably continue to increase as long as the trend of the price level is upward.

Part of the change in the number of recipients is due to the changing age composition of the population and the size of the population. Table 3.4 indicates that the number of old-age assistance recipients relative to

TABLE 3.3

Public Assistance: Recipients, Total Payments, and Average Monthly Payments, by Program, 1936–65

| Year | Recipients (in thousands) * | | | | Total Payments † (in millions) | | Average Monthly Payment * | | |
| | Old-Age Assistance | Aid to Families with Dependent Children | | | Old-Age Assistance | Aid to Families with Dependent Children | Old-Age Assistance | Aid to Families with Dependent Children | |
		Families	Total Recipients	Children				Per Family	Per Recipient
1936	1,106	162	——	404	$ 155	$ 50	$18.79	$ 29.82	——
1938	1,776	280	——	648	393	97	19.56	31.96	——
1940	2,066	370	——	891	475	133	20.26	32.38	——
1942	2,227	348	——	849	595	158	23.37	36.25	——
1944	2,066	254	——	639	693	135	28.43	45.58	——
1946	2,196	346	——	885	822	209	35.31	62.23	——
1948	2,498	475	——	1,214	1,133	364	42.02	71.88	——
1950	2,789	652	2,234	1,662	1,470	554	43.95	72.42	21.13
1952	2,646	570	1,992	1,495	1,533	554	50.90	83.83	23.98
1954	2,565	604	2,174	1,640	1,593	594	51.90	86.24	23.96
1956	2,514	616	2,271	1,732	1,677	663	57.99	95.05	25.79
1958	2,455	756	2,851	2,185	1,830	895	64.08	106.59	28.29
1960	2,332	806	3,080	2,377	1,928	1,062	68.45	114.86	30.07
1962	2,226	943	3,828	2,873	1,962	1,395	75.46	125.95	31.02
1964	2,159	1,030	4,292	3,221	2,045	1,649	78.89	140.96	33.82
1965	2,127	1,069	4,457	3,358	2,054	1,825	79.87	148.09	35.55

* Data shown are for December of each year.
† Includes vendor payments for medical care from 1950 on.

Sources: *Social Security Bulletin, Annual Statistical Supplement,* 1963, pp. 114–15, and *Social Security Bulletins.*

TABLE 3.4

Proportion of Population Receiving Assistance, by Program, 1938–65

December of Year	Number of Old-Age-Assistance Recipients Relative to 1,000 Population Sixty-five and Over	Number of Child Recipients Relative to 1,000 Population Under Eighteen
1938	208	16
1940	228	22
1942	232	22
1944	203	15
1946	202	21
1948	216	27
1950	224	34
1952	200	30
1954	181	29
1956	167	29
1958	154	34
1960	141	35
1962	126	41
1964	119	45
1965 *	117	46

* June of 1965.

Sources: U. S. Department of Health, Education, and Welfare, *Health, Education, and Welfare Trends,* 1960 and 1964 Editions (Washington, D. C.: U. S. Government Printing Office, 1960 and 1964), and U. S. Department of Health, Education, and Welfare, *Health, Education, and Welfare Indicators* (Washington, D. C.: U. S. Government Printing Office, monthly).

the number of persons sixty-five or over has declined markedly, while the number of child recipients relative to the total population under eighteen has increased, but not as rapidly as the absolute number has increased.

The variations among states are very wide. In June, 1965, the number of old-age assistance recipients per 1,000 aged population ranged from twenty-two in New Jersey to 497 in Louisiana. The number of dependent children receiving aid per 1,000 population under eighteen ranged from fifteen in New Hampshire to 120 in West Virginia. The average old-age assistance benefit, including vendor payments for medical care, varied between $28.74 in Mississippi to $120.33 in North Dakota. Mississippi also paid the lowest average AFDC benefit per recipient, $9.16, while New Jersey paid the highest, $50.35. The variations in the assistance expenditures per inhabitant are also of interest. During fiscal year 1961–62, OAA expenditures per inhabitant averaged $10.08, but ranged from $1.47 in Delaware to $35.33 in Oklahoma. AFDC expenditures per inhabitant averaged $7.11 but ranged from $1.79 in Texas to $21.04 in West Virginia. These variations are caused by differences in the economic status of the state populations, the percentage of the populations covered under OASDI, and the provisions of state plans and their interpretation, particularly with respect to the amount of assistance.

Federal contributions have become more important over the years, as would be expected from the formula changes discussed earlier. In 1936, the federal government paid 42.8 per cent of the expenditures for assistance and administration under the old-age assistance programs. The state paid 45.0 per cent and the local units paid 12.2 per cent. In 1964, the three corresponding figures were 64.9 per cent, 30.8 per cent, and 4.3 per cent.[20]

Federally approved aid-to-families-with-dependent-children programs were not enacted as rapidly as old-age assistance programs, and federal aid to these programs was more limited in the beginning. Therefore, the increasing importance of the federal contribution to these programs is even more marked. In 1936 the federal government paid 12.9 per cent of the expenditures, while the state paid 26.1 per cent and the local units 61.0 per cent. In 1964 the three corresponding figures were 56.3 per cent, 32.2 per cent, and 11.5 per cent.

The importance of federal aid varies among states depending upon the economic status of the state and the willingness of the state to appropriate funds for public assistance purposes. In 1964 the percentage of expenditures for old-age assistance payments supplied by the federal government ranged from 81.6 per cent in Mississippi to 48.1 per cent in California. The federal share of AFDC payments varied between 82.4 per cent in Florida and 41.7 per cent in Massachusetts.

Evaluation [21]

The original purpose of the special programs providing aid to the aged and to families with dependent children was to provide minimum subsistence to the needy persons in these two groups. Since 1962, in the words of the late President Kennedy, there has been "a new approach—stressing services in addition to support, rehabilitation instead of relief, and training for useful work instead of prolonged dependency." The objective now "is to prevent or reduce dependency and to encourage self-care and self-support—to maintain family life where it is adequate and to

[20] U. S. Department of Health, Education, and Welfare, Welfare Department, Bureau of Family Services, Division of Program Statistics and Analysis release dated June 17, 1965, *Source of Funds Expended for Public Assistance Payments, Calendar Year Ended December 31, 1964.*

[21] For a list of recommended changes in the entire public assistance program, see "Public Assistance: Report of the Advisory Council," *Social Security Bulletin,* XXIII, No. 2 (February, 1960), 10–22, 36.

restore it where it is deficient."[22] This enlarged objective adds greatly to the value of these programs. It may also answer some of the major criticisms that have been levied against OAA and, more particularly, AFDC. During the slight recession of the early 1960's when unemployment rates increased, some intense opposition to these public assistance programs developed on the ground that they encouraged indolence, illegitimate children, and poor financial management. The most extreme example of this opposition involved the Newburgh, New York, City Council, which unsuccessfully sought to grant relief only under very restrictive regulations.[23] For example, service benefits (food, clothing, rent, etc.) were to be provided instead of cash if this could be done without "basic harm" to the intent of the law. All able-bodied adult male recipients were to be assigned to the Chief of Building Maintenance of the city for work assignments on a forty-hour-week basis and relief was to be denied to any recipient who refused private employment *of any kind.* The "rehabilitation" approach introduced by the Public Welfare Amendments of 1962 is a more humane and, it is believed, a more effective way to attack the same inadequacies of public assistance that bothered the Newburgh Council and other critics. It is more in keeping with the prevailing social conscience. Whether the particular measures introduced in 1962 are the best way to accomplish rehabilitation is more debatable, but they are sufficiently promising to merit a reasonable testing period.

The possibility of combining OAA with programs for the blind and the permanently and totally disabled is also an encouraging step that should lead to a better coordinated program, more equitable treatment of the various groups, and an administratively more economical operation. Some observers favor, for basically the same reasons, one public assistance program covering all the needy, including those not covered under any of the four categorial federal–state plans.

Public assistance programs are superior to the older almshouse approach in that recipients are given a cash allowance, which they may spend according to their individual needs and desires. On the other hand, some of the institutional restrictions that were originally inserted into the Act for the purpose of achieving this result were too severe and have gradually been relaxed.

Basing eligibility and the amount of the benefit upon demonstrated need has the advantage of tailor-making the assistance to the need, but it

[22] Quoted in Wilbur J. Cohen and Robert M. Ball, "Public Welfare Amendments of 1962 and Proposals for Health Insurance for the Aged," *Social Security Bulletin,* XXV, No. 10 (October, 1962), 10.

[23] For the Council's thirteen-point proposal and the negative reaction of the Supreme Court of New York, see *State Board of Social Welfare v. Newburgh,* 28 Misc. 2d 539, 220 NYS 2d 54 (1961).

also involves an invasion of privacy of the individual and may damage his self-respect. Emphasis upon demonstrated need may also destroy the prospective recipient's incentive to save. The needs test, however, is by definition an essential part of assistance programs designed to supplement a wage-related contributory social insurance program. To remove the test would raise the cost and alter the entire complexion of our public social security system.

Steps have been taken instead to reduce the disadvantages of the needs test without destroying the basic character of the assistance programs. The balance achieved is necessarily a compromise between competing goals. To cite two examples: First, cost standards have been developed to reduce the subjectivity and the questioning involved in determining whether an applicant is eligible and the amount of assistance to which he is entitled. Further work along these lines should and can be expected. Second, because a claimant is permitted to hold some assets and still be declared needy, he has some incentive to save.

The problem of relatives' responsibility, especially in old-age assistance, is a delicate one.[24] The major argument in favor of holding relatives responsible, in addition to a possible reduction in cost, is that society will benefit from a strengthening of mutual family economic responsibility. On the other hand, placing the burden on the children may actually cause friction between the children and the needy parents and may reduce to dangerous levels the standard of living of the children's families. In addition some needy parents do not apply for OAA benefits because they do not wish to place a burden upon their children or incur their displeasure. Finally, administering this requirement is fraught with difficulties. Sample problems are the unwilling, but able relative; the amount of support to be requested from a relative whose own financial position is only slightly above the subsistence level; and the out-of-state relative. In those states where filial support is not required, the policy of considering voluntary contributions by the children as part of the parents' resources does not provide any incentive for the child to provide this support.

Perhaps the major objection to these programs is the great heterogeneity among the states. This is the price that must be paid to preserve states' rights, but steps could be taken within the existing framework to make the programs less diverse. For example, more reciprocal arrangements should be made that prevent the loss of benefits when a person moves from one state to another. A more drastic solution would be more restrictive requirements for federal approval of the state plans.

[24] For a more complete discussion, see Eveline M. Burns, *Social Security and Public Policy* (New York: McGraw-Hill Book Co., 1956), pp. 80–86, and Schorr, *op. cit.*

TABLE 3.5

Need Under State Cost Standards Met by Payments Under Old-Age Assistance and Aid to Families with Dependent Children, by Region, End of 1958

			Region		
Item	United States	Northeast	North Central	South	West
	Old-Age Assistance				
Average recipient's monthly requirements [a]	$89.49	$111.80	$91.71	$73.87	$110.93
Average recipient's income	20.83	22.79	22.32	17.24	26.56
Need	68.66	89.01	69.39	56.63	84.37
Average assistance payment	64.96	88.52	66.94	50.18	83.86
Per cent of need met	94.6%	99.4%	96.5%	88.6%	99.4%
	Aid to Families with Dependent Children				
Average recipient's monthly requirements [b]	39.44	42.25	43.59	32.96	46.34
Average recipient's income	6.74	6.51	7.58	6.50	6.45
Need	32.70	35.74	36.01	26.46	39.89
Average assistance payment [c]	28.01	35.50	31.14	18.03	39.01
Per cent of need met	85.7%	99.3%	86.5%	68.2%	97.8%

[a] Includes requirements for (1) basic needs and (2) special needs and medical care covered completely by either vendor payments or money payments to recipients.

[b] Same basis as OAA requirements except that expenses covered by vendor payments are excluded.

[c] Excludes vendor payments.

Source: Ellen J. Perkins, "Unmet Need in Public Assistance," *Social Security Bulletin*, XXIII, No. 4 (April, 1960), 6.

While average benefits have increased significantly over the years, much of this increase has been offset by increases in the cost of living. For example, in current dollars the average OAA benefit moved from $20.26 in 1940 to $78.90 in 1964, but in 1964 dollars the benefit changed only from $44.90 to $78.90. The average AFDC benefit increased from $9.85 to $33.85 over the same period, but in 1964 dollars the change was only from $21.85 to $33.85.

One measure which has been used by the Social Security Administration to test the adequacy of the OAA and AFDC benefits is the relationship between the payments under these programs and the need as represented by the requirements determined through the use of the state-cost standards mentioned earlier.[25] Table 3.5 shows the percentage of need met on this basis under both programs in the United States as a whole

[25] Ellen J. Perkins. "Unmet Need in Public Assistance," *Social Security Bulletin*, XXIII, No. 4 (April, 1960), 3–11.

For similar data for the July–September, 1960, period, see the 1962 Social Security Administration Public Assistance Report No. 48. As this section of the text was being

and in each of the four regions in late 1958. Although this study is not current, its major findings are still relevant because the changes in OAA and AFDC benefit levels have not been that dramatic. The differences among the regions with respect to the standard cost requirements and the percentage of need that was met by assistance payments are particularly noteworthy. Even more striking are the differences between the standards and the adequacy of the assistance under the two programs. In part this reflects the greater need of the aged for medical care (which it was not possible to separate in the table from the requirements or the assistance payments), but more important is the fact that over 60 per cent of the case load under AFDC results from divorce, separation, desertion, or unmarried parenthood, and the public is much less sympathetic to these causes of dependency.[26] It has been argued that AFDC contributes to these causes but it has been counter-argued that the children should not be penalized for the failures of their parents and that the real causes cannot be attacked by withholding adequate financial assistance. One suggestion is that in order to avoid putting a premium on broken homes the program be extended to include any financially needy children living with any relatives. The temporary extension in 1961 to include children deprived of parental support because of unemployment and the new emphasis on social services are steps in this direction.

These data were also analyzed by states instead of regions. Thirteen out of forty-nine states (including the District of Columbia) [27] whose programs were studied met all of the OAA need, twenty-six states met 90 per cent or more but not 100 per cent of the requirements, and ten states met less than 90 per cent. Under AFDC, the states numbered twelve, twenty-one, and sixteen respectively.

A second measure of adequacy attempts to eliminate the effect of variations in state standards. In this instance, the average recipient's basic requirements were assumed to be twice the amount for food included in the low-cost plan of the Department of Agriculture unless the state standard was higher, in which case it was used. The resulting requirements were considered to underestimate the true basic needs of the recipients. On the basis of the average cost in each region,[28] the percentage of OAA

---

written in early 1966, the Welfare Administration of the Department of Health, Education, and Welfare was preparing a more recent report.

[26] Lenore A. Epstein and Alfred M. Skolnik, "Social Security Protection After Thirty Years," *Social Security Bulletin*, XXVIII, No. 8 (August, 1965), 17.

[27] Data were not available for Alaska and Hawaii.

According to Public Assistance Report No. 48, *op. cit.*, average income available per old-age assistance recipient was less than the average subsistence standards set by thirty-four states in July–September, 1960.

[28] Estimates were also prepared using the average cost in the United States and an adaptation of the standard plan for the South but the results were about the same. Perkins, *op. cit.*, p. 7.

basic need which was satisfied was 94.4 per cent for the United States, 99.3 per cent for the Northeast, 96.1 per cent for the North Central, 88.4 per cent for the South, and 99.4 per cent for the West. The respective percentages for AFDC were 57.1, 71.4, 60.5, 38.2, and 78.6. In addition to emphasizing the inadequacy of the benefits, this analysis also highlights the inadequacy of many state standards and again suggests the need for more research in this area on both the state and federal levels. No attempt was made to determine whether the resources of the needy were overvalued.

The Social Security Administration has summarized the situation aptly as follows: "Comparisons with the past give cause for pride. Comparison of today's assistance payments with need . . . indicates cause for concern about the effects of inadequate assistance payments on needy persons, particularly children in many states." [29]

The recommendation of a 1965 task force of the Chamber of Commerce of the United States is also noteworthy in this connection. This task force recommended that public assistance programs provide "minimum-decency" living standards based upon carefully developed market baskets of goods and services. They urged businessmen to take more interest in state public assistance programs because they believe that inadequate state programs will encourage further dependence upon the federal government.[30]

The variation among state laws and their interpretation is caused primarily by differences in income in the various states and their willingness to tax this source. It is generally agreed that less heterogeneity in assistance standards and benefits is desirable but the poorer states are doubly disadvantaged—a larger proportion of their aged and dependent children are needy and the taxable per capita income is low. A rich state could pay the same absolute benefit with relatively little strain on its citizens. Consequently there is a movement toward "equalization" of the tax burden among the states and the formula changes, especially those beginning in 1958, have all been in that direction.[31] Such a trend is necessary if less heterogeneity is our goal.

On the other hand, it must be recognized that it is not feasible or desirable to achieve this goal completely and continuously. If the standards in those states with low standards were to be raised substantially, a larger proportion of the population would become eligible under the program and the average benefit to existing recipients would be increased.

[29] *Ibid.*, p. 4.

[30] *Poverty: The Sick, Disabled, and Aged,* Second Report by the Task Force on Economic Growth and Opportunity (Washington, D. C.: Chamber of Commerce of the United States, 1965), p. 73.

[31] Partly for political reasons, however, increased federal monies for the poorer states have also been accompanied by increased federal monies for the other states. See Burns, *op. cit.,* pp. 242–43.

This double-barrelled effect would increase greatly the public funds required to support the program. In addition the fact that even greater proportions of the population would be placed on the relief rolls would have serious adverse social and economic implications for the entire state as well as the recipients.[32] Consequently, although more uniformity among the states may be desirable, it is impractical and unwise to assume that this can be accomplished solely through revising the public assistance programs. The real solution is to strengthen the general economy of the poorer states in order to reduce the proportions of their population receiving assistance, but acceptable programs aimed at achieving this solution are not easily formulated and must necessarily aim at long-range results. The Economic Opportunity Act, described in Chapter 11, and other parts of the War on Poverty are important in this respect.

From the evidence available, it appears that the administration of the special public assistance programs has been honest, but many claimants have complained about inequitable treatment and, as noted earlier, some critics have complained about lax administration because benefits have been paid to some undeserving persons. Such complaints are bound to arise when administrative discretion is involved, but fortunately, the amount of discretion is being reduced. The federal requirement that employees be hired and discharged on a merit basis has raised the general level of competence, but high caseloads, relatively low salaries, and a nationwide shortage of social workers continue to affect the quality of the services provided.[33] Some improvement should result from provisions in the 1962 amendments that increased to 75 per cent federal matching of the cost of training staff to provide the new social services. These amendments also authorized the Secretary of Health, Education, and Welfare to provide fellowships and traineeships at institutions of higher learning for present and potential personnel and to contract for special short courses of study for training purposes. Unfortunately Congress has not yet appropriated any funds to implement this authorization.

SUMMARY

The Social Security Act, which, among other contributions to economic security, created the first extensive public programs dealing with the economic problems of death and old age, was an outgrowth of the Depression.

[32] Perkins, *op. cit.*, p. 18.

[33] For a recent discussion of the role of the caseworkers and the skills required, see Helen B. Foster, *Services in Public Assistance, The Role of the Caseworker,* Public Assistance Report No. 30 (Washington, D. C.: U. S. Government Printing Office, 1965).

In addition to establishing a social insurance program, to be discussed in the next chapter, the Act provided for federal grants-in-aid to states having public assistance programs for the needy aged and for needy families with dependent children who are deprived of parental support through death, continued absence from the home, or physical or mental incapacity of a parent. A 1961 amendment added unemployment to the list of covered perils, but this extension is supposed to be temporary. To be eligible for federal support, the programs must meet certain minimum standards, but the state and local governments are responsible for the detailed provisions and the administration of the programs.

The state plans vary greatly. Important characteristics of the state programs are the age, citizenship, and residence requirements they impose, the responsibility of relatives, the definition of need, and the method in which the amount of assistance is determined.

The plans are becoming more liberal and the application of the needs test and the determination of the assistance amount are becoming more objective through the use of statewide cost standards. However, the unmet need under assistance programs is still substantial, especially in the poorer states and under the aid-to-families-with-dependent-children programs.

The trend in the formulae for determining the federal grants favors the poorer states. The principle of a grant based on a state's per capita income was adopted for the first time in 1958.

The recipients under the old-age assistance programs are decreasing but the recipients under the aid-to-families-with-dependent-children programs are increasing. The important Public Welfare Amendments of 1962 increased federal participation in the cost of providing social services and introduced several other measures designed to change the emphasis under these programs from relief to rehabilitation.

SUGGESTIONS FOR ADDITIONAL READING

BURNS, EVELINE M. *The American Social Security System.* Boston: Houghton Mifflin Co., 1951. Chapters 11 and 12.
    Although dated, this treatment remains one of the most complete descriptions of the public assistance programs.
———. *Social Security and Public Policy.* New York: McGraw-Hill Book Co., 1956. Pp. 19–26, 58–59, 64–65, 80–89, 171, 212–48, 251–66.
    In the pages cited, the author discusses important public assistance issues.
CARLSON, VALDEMAR. *Economic Security in the United States.* New York: McGraw-Hill Book Co., 1962.
    Chapters 3 and 7 present an interesting economic analysis of public assistance approaches before and after the Social Security Act of 1935.

Characteristics of State Public Assistance Plans under the Social Security Act, 1964 Edition, Public Assistance Report No. 50. Washington, D. C.: U. S. Government Printing Office, 1964.
A detailed description of the state public assistance programs.

CORSON, JOHN J., and JOHN W. McCONNELL. *Economic Needs of Older People.* New York: The Twentieth Century Fund, 1956. Chapters 6 and 7.
A discussion of the political implications of the aged and an analysis and evaluation of old-age assistance programs.

EPSTEIN, ABRAHAM. *Insecurity: A Challenge to America.* New York: Random House, Inc., 1938.
An interesting discussion of the problems of economic security and their possible solution by one of the most active workers for "pension" laws and social insurance.

GAGLIARDO, DOMENICO. *American Social Insurance,* rev. ed. New York: Harper & Row, 1955.
A description of the historical development of old-age assistance, the current old-age assistance programs and their operations, and some trends in these programs.

HABER, WILLIAM, and WILBUR J. COHEN (eds.). *Social Security: Programs, Problems, and Policies.* Homewood, Ill.: Richard D. Irwin, Inc., 1960.
Most of the readings in this volume deal with social insurance but many pages describe and evaluate public assistance.

MYERS, ROBERT J. *Social Insurance and Allied Government Programs.* Homewood, Ill.: Richard D. Irwin, Inc., 1965.
Chapter 2 on public assistance programs contains a detailed discussion of the application of the federal matching formulae.

Public Assistance: A Report of the Findings and Recommendations of the Advisory Council on Public Assistance. Washington, D. C.: U. S. Government Printing Office, 1960.
The recommendations and findings of a council established under the 1958 amendments to the Social Security Act to review the public assistance programs. A report of the council appointed in 1964 will be published shortly.

Report to the President of the Committee on Economic Security. Washington, D. C.: U. S. Government Printing Office, 1935.
The committee report which led to the passage of the original Social Security Act.

SCHOTTLAND, CHARLES I. *The Social Security Program in the United States.* New York: Appleton-Century-Crofts, 1963.
Chapter 4 on the Great Depression and the battle for the Social Security Act, and Chapter 7 on the special public assistance programs are excellent supplementary reading for this chapter.

WITTE, EDWIN E. *The Development of the Social Security Act.* Madison: University of Wisconsin Press, 1962.
A monograph by the chairman of the Committee on Economic Security on the history of that committee and of the Social Security Act of 1935.

4

Old-Age, Survivors, and Disability Insurance

INTRODUCTION

The major social insurance program created under the Social Security Act is known as Old-Age, Survivors, and Disability Insurance, or OASDI in abbreviated form. This system provides certain protection against the problems created by death, old age, and disability. Hospital Insurance and Supplementary Medical Insurance, which began to operate in 1966, are in many respects separate programs, but the Social Security Administration has broadened the designation, OASDI, to Old-Age, Survivors, Disability, and Health Insurance, or OASDHI in abbreviated form. Although this practice has much to recommend it and will probably become universal, this text will treat HI and SMI as "separate programs." To be consistent it could be argued that there are four programs—OASI, DI (Disability Insurance), HI, and SMI because there are four separate trust funds. However, some disability benefits are paid out of the OASI trust fund and, as will become apparent in Chapter 11, there seems to be more reason to regard the two medical expense programs as separate from OASDI. Nevertheless, the text does defer the discussion of the disability benefits under OASDI until Chapter 11. Only the provisions dealing with retirement and survivorship benefits are discussed below. These provisions are subject to change each time the Congress meets, but a study of the current provisions and the changes that have occurred will help one to understand and appreciate the nature and magnitude of this operation.

In order to emphasize the major features of the system and the important issues involved, no attempt has been made to cover all of the situations that can arise under the program. On the other hand, the treatment is detailed enough to provide a good working knowledge of the system.[1]

The plan of the chapter is to present first a factual analysis of the program and its operations that will provide background for understanding the important issues to be discussed in the concluding sections.

COVERAGE

Classes of Coverage

With one exception, to receive OASDI benefits, a person must be either "fully insured," "currently insured," or both. Fully insured persons are eligible for most of the survivorship and retirement benefits provided by the system; currently insured persons are eligible only for some survivorship benefits.

Persons who become age seventy-two before 1968 are eligible for payments of $35 a month even though they have never worked in covered employment if they are not receiving public assistance. Married couples, both of whom are seventy-two years of age or over, receive $52.50 a month. However, persons receiving a pension from a state or local government, a veteran's pension or any other pension from the federal government (including OASDI and Railroad Retirement) are not eligible for these benefits, except that if such pension is smaller, the difference is payable.

Quarters of Coverage and Covered Employment

In order to understand how one may become fully or currently insured it is necessary to define "a quarter of coverage." A quarter of coverage for a wage earner is a calendar quarter during which he received $50 or more in "covered" employment.

Most employments are covered employments on a compulsory or elective basis. The easiest way to define covered employment is to consider the employments that are excluded from coverage or included only under special conditions. The excluded occupations are:

1. Family employment except when the service is performed in a trade or business by a parent or a child twenty-one years of age or over.

---

[1] The reader who is interested in a detailed explanation of the laws and regulations affecting OASDI is referred to U. S. Department of Health, Education, and Welfare, *Social Security Handbook on Old-Age, Survivors, and Disability Insurance* (Washington, D. C.: U. S. Government Printing Office, latest edition).

2. Local newsboys under eighteen years of age.
3. Student nurses.
4. Student workers in institutions of learning.
5. Students performing domestic services for college clubs, fraternities and sororities.
6. Long-service (over ten years) railroad workers.
7. Policemen and firemen covered under an existing retirement system (except in some states where the situation is similar to that explained below for state and local government employees).
8. Federal government civilian employees covered by a retirement system established by a law of the United States.
9. Some special types of federal and state civilian employees.[2]

The occupations included under special conditions are the following:

1. Self-employment is covered employment if the net earnings are $400 or more.
2. Agricultural labor is considered covered employment if the laborer earns $150 or more from any one employer in a calendar year or if he works for one employer on twenty or more days for cash pay figured on a time basis rather than a piece-rate basis.
3. Non-farm domestic workers and casual laborers must earn $50 or more from one employer in a calendar quarter for that quarter to be a quarter of coverage.
4. Clergymen and members of religious orders (except those who have taken a vow of poverty) may elect individually to be considered in covered self-employment. This decision must be made on or before the due date of the individual's tax return for his second taxable year after 1954 in which he has net earnings of $400 or more, any part of which was derived from his duties in the ministry.
5. Members of recognized religious sects such as the Amish who, in adhering to the teaching of their sect, are conscientiously opposed to receiving any private or public insurance benefits in case of death, old age, or poor health may elect not to be covered as to their self-employment income.
6. In order for employees of non-profit organizations to be covered, the employer must consent. All new employees are automatically covered but current employees have a choice. Coverage may be made retroactive for up to five years. Any employee who elects not to be covered cannot change his mind unless he acts within twenty-four months after the end of the first month of the calendar quarter in which the coverage for the group becomes effective.
7. State and local government employees not already under a retirement system may be covered if the state agrees. The employees under a retirement system may be covered if the state consents

[2] For example, the President of the United States.

and at least half the employees under each separate system agree. In several states a retirement system can be divided into two parts (those who want coverage and those who do not) to obtain coverage for the members who want it. All new members of the total system are automatically covered. Coverage may be made retroactive for up to five years.

The exclusions have been justified on the following grounds. Railroad workers are covered under a separate public retirement system as are the federal employees excluded under the Act. As indicated in Chapter 13, however, the Railroad Retirement System is closely coordinated with OASDI. Because non-profit organizations have a tax-exempt status, they cannot be taxed without their consent. States also cannot be taxed without their consent. Some state and local government employees fear that they will lose their benefits under their present public retirement systems if they are covered under OASDI. The exclusion of certain religious sects such as the Amish is considered necessary to assure these people religious liberty. In order to be exempt, however, the sect must have been in existence since 1950 and its members must have a reputation for making reasonable provision for dependent members. Most of the other occupations are excluded for administrative reasons. Either the administrative problems seem insoluble at the present time or the efforts necessary to solve the problems are not justified by the benefits to be gained.

For earnings prior to 1951, the wage earner receives credit for four quarters of coverage for each year in which his income in covered employment was $3,000 or more. For earnings during 1951–54, during 1955–58, during 1959–65, and after 1965 the same rule applies, but the annual income figures are $3,600, $4,200, $4,800, and $6,600, respectively.

Self-employed persons, a group who first became eligible for coverage in 1951, receive credit for four quarters of coverage for each year in which their annual self-employment income is $400 or more.[3]

Determination of Insured Status

To determine whether an individual is *fully insured* at retirement age or death, the first step is to count the number of years elapsing between December 31, 1950 (or the end of the year in which he became twenty-

[3] Self-employed farmers have an optional way of figuring self-employment earnings. If a farmer's gross farm income is $2,400 or less, he may report his actual net farm earnings or two-thirds of the gross income. If his gross farm income is more than $2,400, and his actual net farm earnings are less than $1,600, he may report his actual net earnings or $1,600. Otherwise, he must report his actual net farm earnings.

Farm laborers also receive special treatment. A farm laborer is credited with one quarter of coverage for each $100 of annual wages, the maximum annual credit being four quarters of coverage.

one, if later) and the beginning of the year in which he became (or would become if the individual is a male retiring early) sixty-five years of age (sixty-two for women) or died. If the quarters of coverage credited to this person since January 1, 1937, are equal to at least this number, he is fully insured. However, he must have at least six quarters of coverage [4] and he is not required to have more than forty quarters of coverage. Furthermore, years included wholly or partly in a "period of disability" are not counted as elapsed years.[5]

Illustrations

The following illustrations should clarify the above definition.

1. Assume that a male will be sixty-five in March, 1969. If he earned $5,000 a year in covered employment during 1958–64 inclusive, he has been credited with twenty-eight quarters of coverage. He is fully insured because the number of quarters of coverage exceeds the number of years (eighteen) that have elapsed between December 31, 1950, and January 1, 1969. Note that if he were retiring at age sixty-two in 1969 the requirement would be twenty-one quarters of coverage. For a female retiring at age sixty-two in 1969, the requirement would be only eighteen quarters of coverage.

2. Another worker will reach age sixty-five in July, 1972. If he has earned at least $50 per quarter in covered employment during 1960–69, inclusive, he has forty quarters of coverage. It is not necessary to apply the elapsed-years rule in this case to determine whether he is fully insured because he has satisfied the maximum requirement. In fact, he needs only twenty-one quarters under the elapsed-years rule.

3. A student will be twenty-one years of age in December, 1969. He expects to work in covered employment for five years beginning January

[4] Persons who reached retirement age (sixty-five for men and sixty-two for women) in 1956 qualify for benefits of $35 a month beginning at age seventy-two if they have five quarters of coverage. Those who reached retirement age in 1955 qualify for these benefits if they have at least four quarters of coverage; those who reached retirement age in 1954 or earlier need have only three quarters of coverage. Wives of retired persons qualifying under this provision receive $17.50 a month at age seventy-two if they were aged sixty-nine or over in 1965. A widow of a worker in this category is eligible at age seventy-two for $35 a month if she was aged sixty-nine or over in 1965.

The purpose of this "transitional insured status" is to make it easier for many of the aged with limited periods of covered employment to qualify for benefits by relaxing the minimum requirement of six quarters. In order to have six quarters, these workers would have to have more than one quarter of coverage for each of the years elapsing after 1950 and before the year in which they reached retirement age.

Persons aged seventy-two before 1968 are better off under this transitional insured status than under the special provision noted on p. 112 because there is no assistance exclusion and no "other public pension" offset.

[5] For more details on the effect of a disability upon this determination, see Chapter 11.

1, 1970, after which time he expects to go into some non-covered employment. He will not be fully insured when he reaches age sixty-five, for he will have only twenty quarters of coverage. This case is not typical. Most students will qualify by working ten years in covered employment. Some will be well on their way to a permanent fully insured status by the time they graduate (because of part-time work in college).

It is possible to achieve *currently insured* status at an early date, for the only requirement is that the person have six quarters of coverage out of the last thirteen quarters including the quarter in which he dies or becomes entitled to old-age or disability benefits. However, the quarter in which he becomes disabled is not counted in the thirteen-quarter period unless it is a quarter of coverage. Under this rule a young man could enter covered employment in June, 1968, at a salary of $200 a month and be currently insured in July, 1969. It is, of course, possible to be currently insured without being fully insured and vice versa.

BENEFITS

The benefits under the system may be divided into retirement, survivorship, and disability benefits. Only the first two types of benefits will be described here. *Unless otherwise specified*, a person must be fully insured to qualify for retirement benefits, but the survivorship benefits are provided for fully insured individuals in all instances (unless otherwise specified) and for currently insured persons for certain types of such benefits.

Retirement Benefits

1. *The primary insurance amount.* When an insured worker reaches age sixty-five, he is entitled to a monthly income for life (called the "old-age insurance benefit") equal to the primary insurance amount. All other benefits are expressed as a per cent of this amount.

A worker may elect to receive his (or her) monthly retirement income as soon as he reaches age sixty-two, but his monthly income is reduced by 5/9 of 1 per cent for each month prior to his sixty-fifth birthday that the benefits begin. For example, if his benefits begin on his sixty-third birthday, the amount of his monthly payments will be 86⅔ per cent of what he would receive if he were sixty-five. If there are any months before he reaches age sixty-five for which his benefit is *withheld* because he works, his benefit is automatically recomputed when he reaches age sixty-five to take account of these months. In addition, because of the less liberal base period used to determine a male's primary insurance amount (described in the next section), if a male works *at all* after his entitlement to reduced benefits, his benefit is automatically recomputed when he reaches age sixty-five (or dies) to take into account these additional earnings (or to shorten the period used in the computation in case of death).

Describing the computation of the primary insurance amount under all possible situations would be a complex procedure because of the many amendments to the original Act, but for most persons it is a fairly simple process. The first step is to compute the individual's *average monthly earnings* subject to OASDI taxes. Except in those unusual cases where using 1936 as the "starting" year instead of 1950 would produce a higher benefit, the average is computed for the n years in which the worker's credited earnings were the highest, n being equal to the number of years elapsing after 1955 (or the year in which the person was twenty-six years of age, if later) and before the year in which he attains age sixty-five if a male, attains age sixty-two if a female, or dies if this occurs earlier. Years included wholly or partly in a "period of disability" are not counted unless this would be to the person's advantage. The base *must* include at least two years. Using 1955 instead of 1950 as the starting point for computing n in effect permits the worker to omit his five years of lowest credited earnings after 1950 or, if later, after the year in which the person was twenty-one years of age. To illustrate the application of this rule, if a male attains age sixty-five in 1971, his average monthly earnings will be computed on the basis of his *credited* earnings in the fifteen years after 1950 in which those credited earnings were the highest. The average monthly earnings will be equal to the credited earnings over these fifteen years divided by the number of months (180) in these fifteen years. For example, if he was credited with $4,000 in six of these years, $3,000 in four other years, and nothing in the remaining five years, his average monthly earnings would be $200. If this male were retiring in 1971 at age sixty-two, the average monthly earnings would be based instead upon the eighteen years after 1950 in which his credited earnings were the highest.

These n years of highest earnings may include years before the person was twenty-two years of age, the year in which the person reaches age sixty-five, if a male (age sixty-two, if a female), or later years. This rule will be important for persons who work beyond the minimum retirement age in the near future because it will permit many of them to raise their average monthly earnings closer to the present maximum of $550. Prior to 1951, the maximum average monthly earnings were $250 because the annual earnings were taxed only up to $3,000. The annual credited earnings were increased in 1951 to $3,600, in 1955 to $4,200, in 1959 to $4,800, and in 1966 to $6,600. The five years that are to be dropped from the earnings record in all instances enable persons who have earned the maximum amount subject to tax since 1950 to drop out the years 1951–55. Some of the years 1956–65 can be replaced by the year in which the person reaches sixty-five (sixty-two if a female), or any later years if the person continues to work after age sixty-five (or sixty-two if a female). Thus, if a male worker who reaches age sixty-five in 1968 after earning $10,000 a year since 1950 continues to earn this amount in 1968, 1969, and 1970, he will raise his average monthly earnings from $412 to $462.

The next step is to apply the primary insurance amount formula to the average monthly earnings. The following formula is applied to the average monthly earnings derived as stated above:

62.97 per cent of the first $110 of average monthly earnings plus
22.90 per cent of the next $290 of average monthly earnings plus
21.40 per cent of the next $150.

Because this formula is so complex,[6] and because the amounts it develops must be increased slightly in some cases for average earnings under $85, a benefit table has been prepared that is reproduced as Table 4.1. To illustrate the use of this table, note that if the average monthly earnings are $400, the primary insurance amount is $135.90. The primary insurance amounts for average earnings of $250 and $550 are $101.70 and $168, respectively. There is a minimum primary insurance amount of $44 except for workers who retire early, in which case the minimum amount is scaled down in the usual fashion. The maximum primary insurance amount is $168. The meaning of the first two columns in this table will be explained shortly.

If the person has elected to retire at sixty-two years of age, the corresponding old-age insurance benefits are

.80 ($135.90) = $108.80
.80 ($101.70) = $ 81.40
.80 ($168.00) = $134.40

This formula represents a compromise between the desire to provide a floor of protection that might be the same (except for price level differences) for all families and the desire to preserve some relationship between taxable average monthly earnings and benefits. The primary insurance amount increases as the average monthly earnings increase but the ratio of the primary insurance amount to the average monthly earn-

[6] This complex formula is basically the 1954 Act formula adjusted for (1) increases in the maximum average monthly earnings, (2) an increase of 7 per cent in the cost of living from 1954 to 1958, and (3) except for monthly earnings in excess of $400, an increase of 7 per cent in the cost of living from 1958 to 1965. The 1954 Act formula applicable to average monthly earnings of $110 or more was 55 per cent of the first $110 and 20 per cent of the next $240, $.55(1.07)^2 = .6297$, $.20(1.07)^2 = .2290$, and $.20 (1.07) = .2140$.

ings decreases as the earnings increase. Figure 4.1 presents this relationship in graphic form. For some evaluations of this benefit formula, see
pages 151–54.

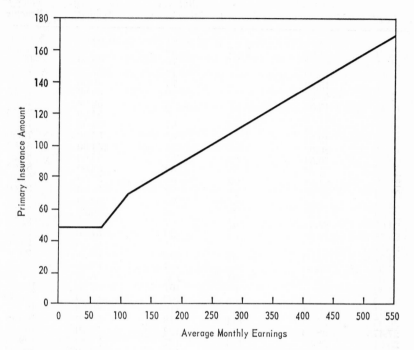

Figure 4.1. Primary insurance amount as a function of average monthly
earnings.

If the individual had at least one quarter of coverage before 1950, a
primary insurance *benefit* is computed using a 1950 amendment formula
and an average wage computed on earnings after 1936, and the benefit
is converted to a primary insurance *amount* with the aid of a conversion
table.[7] If this result is larger than that from the normal method, it is used.
The formula is as follows:

> 40 per cent of the first $50 of average monthly wage plus
> 10 per cent of the next $200 of average monthly wage plus
> 1 per cent of the sum of the two preceding items times the number of
> years prior to 1951 in which the employee earned $200 or more in
> covered employment

The conversion table is included in Table 4.1. To illustrate its use, assume that a worker was in covered employment from January, 1939, until

---

[7] If the individual attained age twenty-two after 1950, the procedure can be used
only if he did not have six quarters of coverage after 1950.

TABLE 4.1

Primary Insurance Amounts and Maximum Family Benefits

Primary Insurance Benefit		Average Monthly Earnings		Primary Insurance Amount	Maximum Family Benefits
At Least	But Not More Than	At Least	But Not More Than		
	$13.48		$ 67	$ 44.00	$ 66.00
$13.49	14.00	$ 68	69	45.00	67.50
14.01	14.48	70	70	46.00	69.00
14.49	15.00	71	72	47.00	70.50
15.01	15.60	73	74	48.00	72.00
15.61	16.20	75	76	49.00	73.50
16.21	16.84	77	78	50.00	75.00
16.85	17.60	79	80	51.00	76.50
17.61	18.40	81	81	52.00	78.00
18.41	19.24	82	83	53.00	79.50
19.25	20.00	84	85	54.00	81.00
20.01	20.64	86	87	55.00	82.50
20.65	21.28	88	89	56.00	84.00
21.29	21.88	90	90	57.00	85.50
21.89	22.28	91	92	58.00	87.00
22.29	22.68	93	94	59.00	88.50
22.69	23.08	95	96	60.00	90.00
23.09	23.44	97	97	61.00	91.50
23.45	23.76	98	99	62.10	93.20
23.77	24.20	100	101	63.20	94.80
24.21	24.60	102	102	64.20	96.30
24.61	25.00	103	104	65.30	98.00
25.01	25.48	105	106	66.40	99.60
25.49	25.92	107	107	67.50	101.30
25.93	26.40	108	109	68.50	102.80
26.41	26.94	110	113	69.60	104.40
26.95	27.46	114	118	70.70	106.10
27.47	28.00	119	122	71.70	107.60
28.01	28.68	123	127	72.80	109.20
28.69	29.25	128	132	73.90	110.90
29.26	29.68	133	136	74.90	112.40
29.60	30.36	137	141	76.00	114.00
30.37	30.92	142	146	77.10	116.80
30.93	31.36	147	150	78.20	120.00
31.37	32.00	151	155	79.20	124.00
32.01	32.60	156	160	80.30	128.00
32.61	33.20	161	164	81.40	131.20
33.21	33.88	165	169	82.40	135.20
33.89	34.50	170	174	83.50	139.20
34.51	35.00	175	178	84.60	142.40
35.01	35.80	179	183	85.60	146.40
35.81	36.40	184	188	86.70	150.40
36.41	37.08	189	193	87.80	154.40
37.09	37.60	194	197	88.90	157.60
37.61	38.20	198	202	89.90	161.60
38.21	39.12	203	207	91.00	165.60
39.13	39.68	208	211	92.10	168.80
39.69	40.33	212	216	93.10	172.80
40.34	41.12	217	221	94.20	176.80
41.13	41.76	222	225	95.30	180.00
41.77	42.44	226	230	96.30	184.00
42.45	43.20	231	235	97.40	188.00
43.21	43.76	236	239	98.50	191.20
43.77	44.44	240	244	99.60	195.20
44.45	44.88	245	249	100.60	199.20
44.89	45.60	250	253	101.70	202.40
		254	258	102.80	206.40
		259	263	103.80	210.40
		264	267	104.90	213.60

TABLE 4.1 (Continued)

Primary Insurance Benefit		Average Monthly Earnings		Primary Insurance Amount	Maximum Family Benefits
At Least	But Not More Than	At Least	But Not More Than		
		$268	$272	$106.00	$217.60
		273	277	107.00	221.60
		278	281	108.10	224.80
		282	286	109.20	228.80
		287	291	110.30	232.80
		292	295	111.30	236.00
		296	300	112.40	240.00
		301	305	113.50	244.00
		306	309	114.50	247.20
		310	314	115.60	251.20
		315	319	116.70	255.20
		320	323	117.70	258.40
		324	328	118.80	262.40
		329	333	119.90	266.40
		334	337	121.00	269.60
		338	342	122.00	273.60
		343	347	123.10	277.60
		348	351	124.20	280.80
		352	356	125.20	284.80
		357	361	126.30	288.80
		362	365	127.40	292.00
		366	370	128.40	296.00
		371	375	129.50	298.00
		376	379	130.60	299.60
		380	384	131.70	301.60
		385	389	132.70	303.60
		390	393	133.80	305.20
		394	398	134.90	307.20
		399	403	135.90	309.20
		404	407	137.00	310.80
		408	412	138.00	312.80
		413	417	139.00	314.80
		418	421	140.00	316.40
		422	426	141.00	318.40
		427	431	142.00	320.40
		432	436	143.00	322.40
		437	440	144.00	324.00
		441	445	145.00	326.00
		446	450	146.00	328.00
		451	454	147.00	329.60
		455	459	148.00	331.60
		460	464	149.00	333.60
		465	468	150.00	335.20
		469	473	151.00	337.20
		474	478	152.00	339.20
		479	482	153.00	340.80
		483	487	154.00	342.80
		488	492	155.00	344.80
		493	496	156.00	346.40
		497	501	157.00	348.40
		502	506	158.00	350.40
		507	510	159.00	352.00
		511	515	160.00	354.00
		516	520	161.00	356.00
		521	524	162.00	357.60
		525	529	163.00	359.60
		530	534	164.00	361.60
		535	538	165.00	363.20
		539	543	166.00	365.20
		544	548	167.00	367.20
		549	550	168.00	368.00

December, 1948. He reaches sixty-five years of age in February, 1968. If his determined average monthly wage is $100, his primary insurance *benefit* is:

$$.40 \ (\$50) + .10 \ (\$50) + .01 \ (10) \quad \text{(Sum of two preceding terms)}$$
$$\text{or } \$20 \qquad + \$5 \qquad + .10 \ (\$25) = \$27.50.$$

The primary insurance *amount,* according to the conversion table, is $71.70.

The number of years of service is included in the older *benefit* formula, but not in the normal formula, because it was felt that this feature of the older formula placed too much emphasis on the relationship between total taxable earnings and benefits. It penalized especially the dependents of wage earners who died at an early age. However, periods not spent in covered employment do tend to reduce the average monthly earnings and consequently the primary insurance amount.

Persons who were in the armed forces between September 15, 1940, and January 1, 1957, receive a wage credit of $160 for each month of service during this period if they were honorably discharged. (Effective January 1, 1957, members of the armed services became eligible for full social security coverage on the same basis as those in other covered employments.) These wage credits may (1) enable a veteran to achieve fully or currently insured status at an earlier age and (2) increase the average monthly wage. These military wage credits are not counted if monthly benefits based at least in part on this military service period are paid under the Army, Navy, Civil Service, or other federal retirement systems except that for persons in service after 1956, 1951–56 wage credits are counted.

2. *Dependents' benefits.* The benefits for dependents of the retired worker are the following:

(a) Life income to wife of retired worker. The wife of a person receiving a primary insurance amount (or a lesser amount because of early retirement) for life will receive 50 per cent of that amount if she is sixty-five years of age at time of first eligibility and has been married to the retired worker at least one year. If the husband is receiving a reduced amount because he elected to retire earlier than age sixty-five, the wife's benefit is based on the amount her husband would have received if he had been age sixty-five when he retired. This same rule applies to all of the other dependents' benefits.

If she wishes she may take reduced benefits beginning as soon as she reaches age sixty-two. The reduction in benefits is $^{25}\!/_{36}$ of 1 per cent times the number of months prior to age sixty-five that the benefits begin.

Thus if she elects to receive benefits beginning on her sixty-third birthday, she will receive 83⅓ per cent of the amount she would receive if she waited until she was sixty-five.

A divorced wife is eligible for benefits if she had been married to the worker for at least twenty years and if her divorced husband was making or was obligated to make a substantial contribution to her support when he became entitled to benefits. She loses her benefit rights if she remarries, but she regains those rights if her subsequent marriage ends.

(b) Income to age eighteen or, if the child is attending an accredited school as a full-time student, to age twenty-two for unmarried children of a retired worker. (For the effect of disability upon the continuance of this benefit and the mother's benefit described below, see Chapter 11.) Each child of a person receiving a primary insurance amount will receive 50 per cent of that amount until he reaches eighteen (twenty-two, if a full-time student) or marries. At the time the benefit is applied for, the father must be supporting the child or have some legal obligation to do so. The child may be a stepchild, a legally adopted child, or even an illegitimate child. It is not necessary that the child have the status of a child under the varying provisions of state inheritance laws.

(c) Income to a mother until her youngest child eligible for a child's benefit is eighteen years of age. The wife of a person receiving a primary insurance amount will receive 50 per cent of that amount as long as she has under her care an eligible child of the worker under eighteen years of age. Divorced wives are eligible for these benefits under the conditions discussed above.

(d) Life income to husband of retired worker. The husband of a woman receiving a primary insurance amount will receive 50 per cent of that amount if he is sixty-five years of age and can prove that he depended upon his wife for at least one-half of his support at the time she filed for benefits. This benefit is available only if the wife is both *fully and currently insured.* If he wishes, the dependent husband can also start to receive reduced benefits as early as age sixty-two.

The maximum family benefit for a retired worker and his dependents is 80 per cent of the first $370 of average monthly earnings plus 40 per cent of the next $180 (applied to the top figure in each monthly earnings bracket in Table 4.1). However, the application of this rule is not permitted to reduce the family benefit below one and one-half times the primary insurance amount. Hence, the maximum "maximum family benefit," the one corresponding to average monthly earnings of $550, is .80 ($370) + .40 ($180) or $368. The maximum family benefit for average monthly earnings of $400 is $309.20. These maximum monthly benefits are, in essence, scaled downward if the worker retires early.

Illustrations

The following cases show the application of these rules. All examples have been rounded to the nearest dollar to simplify the illustrations.

1. A worker, aged sixty-five, who retires has an average monthly wage of $200. His primary insurance amount is $90. If his wife is also sixty-five years of age, the family benefit will be (1.00 + .50) $90, or $135. The maximum benefit rule does not affect this benefit.

If his wife is sixty-two and elects to receive a reduced benefit, the family benefit will be [1.00 + (.75) .50] $90 = $124.

If the worker has a wife, aged forty-five, with a child, aged ten, in her care, the computed family benefit will be (1.00 + .50 + .50) $90, or $180. The maximum family benefit rule applies here, and the family will receive $162 a month for eight years until the child reaches age eighteen. If the child is then a full-time student, the family will receive (1.00 + .50) $90 or $135 until the child reaches age twenty-two. Unless the wife elects to receive a reduced wife's benefit between age sixty-two and age sixty-five, the worker will receive $90 a month for the next eight years until his wife is sixty-five years of age. The benefit will then be increased to $135.

2. A worker, aged sixty-five, who retires has an average monthly wage of $300. His primary insurance amount is $112. If he has a wife, aged fifty-five, and two children, aged seventeen and fifteen, the computed initial family benefit is (1.00 + .50 + .50 + .50) $112, or $280. However, the maximum benefit is (.80) $300 or $240. Therefore, the family will receive $240 a month until the first child is eighteen years of age. Unless the wife elects to receive a reduced wife's benefit between ages sixty-two and sixty-five, if neither child is a full-time student after age eighteen, the benefit will be $225 for two more years, $112 for the next seven years, and $169 after the wife is sixty-five years of age. If both children are full-time students to age twenty-two, the benefit will continue at $240 for two more years and then become $225 for the next two years as both children are at school, $169 for the two years while only the younger child is a student, $112 for the next three years, and $169 after the wife is sixty-five years of age.

3. A worker, aged sixty-five, who retires has an average monthly wage of $100. His primary insurance amount is $63. If his wife is the same age, the computed family benefit is (1.00 + .50) $63, or $95. If the maximum benefit were computed on the 80 per cent basis, it would be less than this, but this rule is not applied because it would reduce the benefit to less than one and one-half times the primary insurance amount.

Survivorship Benefits

The survivorship benefits provided under OASDI are the following:

1. Life income to widow. The widow of a *fully insured* person will receive 82.5 per cent of the deceased's primary insurance amount if she is sixty-two years of age and has not remarried. If she has remarried, she will still receive this benefit if that subsequent marriage has ended. If she remarries after attaining age sixty, she remains eligible for a benefit equal to 50 per cent of the deceased's primary amount.

A widow may elect to take reduced benefits as early as age sixty. The percentage reduction in benefits is 5/9 of 1 per cent for each month prior to her sixty-second birthday that the benefits begin.

A divorced wife of a deceased worker is eligible for a widow's benefit under the same conditions as the divorced wife of a retired worker.

2. Income to age eighteen for children of a fully or currently insured deceased worker or to age twenty-two if the child is a full-time student at an accredited school. Until he reaches age eighteen (twenty-two if a full-time student) or marries, each child of a deceased worker will receive 75 per cent of the deceased's primary insurance amount. (For the effect of disability upon the continuance of the benefit and the mother's benefit described below, see Chapter 11.) The child may have been a stepchild, an adopted child, or an illegitimate child but he must have been dependent upon the deceased at the date of death. It is not necessary for the child to have the status of a child under provisions of state inheritance laws, which vary greatly from state to state.

3. Income to the widow of a fully or currently insured worker until her youngest eligible child reaches eighteen years of age. A widow will receive 75 per cent of her husband's primary insurance amount as long as she has an eligible child of the deceased under eighteen years of age in her care and has not remarried (unless she qualifies under 1). If she remarries, her benefits stop but her children's benefits continue even if they are adopted by their stepfather. Her benefit right is restored if the subsequent marriage ends. If she was divorced from the deceased at the time of his death, she must have depended upon him for at least one-half of her support at the time of his death.

4. Life income to widower. The widower of a *fully and currently* insured woman will receive 82.5 per cent of the deceased's primary insurance amount if he is sixty-two years of age, has not remarried, and depended upon his wife for at least one-half of his support when she died. Widowers who remarry after age sixty-two remain eligible to receive a

benefit equal to 50 per cent of the deceased spouse's primary insurance amount.

5. Life income to parents. Each parent of a *fully insured* deceased will receive 75 per cent of the primary insurance amount if he is sixty-two years of age, depended upon the deceased for at least one-half of his support, and has not remarried since the death of the deceased. The benefit is 82.5 per cent if only one parent is receiving this benefit.

6. Lump-sum death benefit. A lump-sum death benefit equal to three times the primary insurance amount, but in no case more than $255, is paid to the widow or widower, if eligible. Otherwise the person(s) paying the burial expenses can be reimbursed (but no more than such expenses).

The minimum benefit for a single survivor is $44. If a mother's benefit is payable, the minimum family benefit is $66. The maximum family benefit payable to survivors is determined the same way as the maximum family retirement benefit.

Illustrations

A few examples, all of which have been rounded to the nearest dollar, will illustrate the application of these benefits.

1. A currently insured worker dies leaving a wife, aged thirty-five, and one child, aged eight. If his average monthly wage was $250, his primary insurance amount is $102. The lump-sum benefit is $255, and the wife and child will receive $(.75 + .75) \$102 = \$153$ for ten years. If the child is then a full-time student, he will continue to receive his benefit of $.75 (\$102) = \$76$ for four more years. If the worker had been fully insured, the widow would also begin to receive $(.825) \$102 = \$84$ after she reaches age sixty-two. If she wished, she could start receiving a reduced amount of $73 at age sixty.

2. A fully insured person dies leaving a wife, aged fifty-two. If his average monthly wage was $450, his primary insurance amount is $146. The wife will receive a lump-sum benefit of $255, but she will not receive any monthly income for ten years, at which time she will begin to receive $(.825) \$146 = \$121$. She could, however, elect to receive a reduced monthly benefit of $104 beginning at age sixty. If her husband had been only currently insured or if she had remarried before age sixty, she would not receive the income benefit.

3. A fully insured worker dies leaving a wife, aged thirty-five, and two children, aged eight and thirteen. If his average monthly wage was $500, his primary insurance amount is $157. The lump-sum benefit of

$255 will be paid to the wife, and the family will receive at first a monthly benefit of $348. The computed initial benefit is $(.75 + .75 + .75)$ $157 = $353, but the maximum family benefit rule applies. If both children go to college until they are aged twenty-two, the family will receive this $348 for nine years until the oldest child is twenty-two years of age. The benefit will then drop to $(.75 + .75)$ $157 = $236 for one year and, because the youngest child will then be aged eighteen, to $(.75)$ $157 = $118 for the next four years. The income then stops until the widow becomes eligible for $(.825)$ $157 = $130 a month when she reaches sixty-two years of age. If she elects a reduced benefit beginning at age sixty, the monthly benefit will be $112.

LOSS OF BENEFITS

Benefits are *terminated* for several reasons, most of which have been implied in the preceding discussion. A mother loses her benefit if for any reason she no longer has under her care a child under eighteen entitled to benefits. A child loses his benefit if he reaches eighteen (twenty-two if he is a full-time student), marries, or is adopted by anyone other than his stepparent, grandparent, aunt, uncle, brother, or sister. A widow (unless she marries after age sixty), a widower (unless he remarries after age 62), a surviving mother, or a surviving parent loses her benefit if she or he remarries. However, remarriage to another survivor beneficiary does not result in termination. A wife's benefit continues only so long as she remains married to the insured, unless at the time of her divorce she had been married to him for at least twenty years. Death, of course, terminates the benefit of any deceased person as of the preceding month.

There is one very important reason why the monthly payments may be *reduced*. If a retired worker under seventy-two years of age earns more than $1,500 in any calendar year in covered or uncovered employment, the total family benefits are reduced by an amount equal to (1) one-half of the first $1,200 that he earns in excess of $1,500 plus (2) all of what he earns in excess of $2,700. For example, $100 is withheld if he earns $1,700, $400 if he earns $2,300, and $900 if he earns $3,000. As a result, if taxes and any extra expenses associated with working are ignored, the beneficiary always gains by working. The rule also states that benefits shall not be reduced for any month during which a person earns $125 or less in wages and does not render substantial services in self-employment, even if his annual earnings are in excess of $1,500. The major purpose of this provision is to make it possible to pay benefits beginning with the first month of retirement to a person who retires in the middle or toward the close of the year. A consequence of the rule is that a person may have very high earnings in one month and receive full benefits for the other eleven months.

The rule with respect to the earnings of dependent beneficiaries is the same except that only the dependent's benefit is affected. For example, if a widow, aged 35, with two children under eighteen, should earn more than $5,000, only her benefit would be affected.

The purpose of the earnings test is to pay benefits only to those workers and their families whose earnings have been stopped or reduced substantially by reason of retirement or death. What is perhaps more important, the test cuts the cost of the program.

Other less common reasons for suspending payment are employment outside the United States in non-covered employment on seven or more calendar days; deportation because of illegal entry or conviction of crime; and conviction of treason, sedition, sabotage, or espionage.

Benefits are not duplicated, the largest being paid. For example, the wife of a retired worker may be eligible for a lifetime income based on her own earnings record in addition to a wife's benefit based on her husband's record. She will receive, in effect, only the higher of these two benefits.

FINANCING

Taxes

The special benefits payable to persons aged seventy-two and over even if they have never worked in covered employment are paid out of general revenues. Otherwise, OASDI benefits are financed by a tax on the worker and his employer. The employee has been asked to contribute because (1) the problems created by death and old age are not entirely due to employment, (2) employer contributions alone would not provide adequate benefits, (3) most employees apparently want to contribute to the cost, (4) a direct contribution reminds employees that increased benefits means increased costs, and (5) an employee contribution strengthens the employees' claim for a voice in the program. Although the law and Congressional intent are silent on this point, the tax schedule and the benefit formula are designed to give each beneficiary at least as much protection as his *own* contributions would provide on a private insurance basis. The employer's contribution is justified by the fact that the employer has a moral obligation and a business interest with respect to the welfare of his own employees and a social obligation with respect to the entire system. The cost of adequate protection against the problems of death and old age is considered a proper charge against business operations and, presumably, part of this charge can be shifted to consumers.[8]

In 1967–68, the employer and the employee each pay 3.90 per cent on the first $6,600 of the employee's wage. A self-employed person pays 5.9 per cent on his net earnings. The 5.9 per cent figure represents a compromise between 3.90 per cent and 2(3.90) = 7.80 per cent. These tax rates include a .35 per cent tax on employees and on employers and a .525 per cent tax on the self-employed, which go to the disability insurance trust fund discussed in Chapter 11. These rates do not include contributions for Hospital Insurance.

Wages include all payments in cash or in kind, with certain exceptions such as the employer's OASDI and unemployment compensation contributions or payments in kind to domestic and farm workers. Tips are not included as wages unless they exceed $20 in a month in which case they are reported by the employer but only the employee contribution is paid. Net self-employment earnings do not include interest, dividends, and rent unless the self-employed person receives them in the course of his business as a real estate or securities dealer.

After 1968, the tax rates including the disability tax noted above are scheduled to increase as follows:

Tax Rate

Year	Employer	Employee	Self-employed
1969–72	4.40	4.40	6.6
1973 on	4.85	4.85	7.0

The purpose of the gradually increasing tax rates is to avoid the adverse effects, political and economic, of the sudden imposition of a large tax increase. This approach is feasible because the benefit payments are lower at present than they are expected to be in the future. The funding implications of this approach will be discussed later.

All persons in covered employment pay the tax even if they derive no benefit from the payment. For example, a fully insured person, who could retire with a maximum benefit, must pay a tax if he works in covered employment after age sixty-five.

Each employer withholds the social security tax from the pay of covered employees and sends twice this amount to the District Director of Internal Revenue with a detailed report on the employees covered. Self-employed persons pay their tax in connection with their income tax return.

[8] Ida C. Merriam, "Social Security Financing," *Bureau Report No. 17* (Washington, D. C.: Federal Security Agency, Social Security Administration, 1952), pp. 12–13.

The Trust Fund

The funds collected less the disability taxes are appropriated to the Old-Age and Survivors Insurance Trust Fund. The disability tax receipts are placed in a separate fund. (This separation explains why the abbreviation OASI will sometimes be used in this text instead of OASDI in the sections on financing.) The Secretary of the Treasury is the Managing Trustee of the fund with broad powers over it. The other members of the Board of Trustees are the Secretary of Labor and the Secretary of Health, Education, and Welfare. That part of the fund that is not needed to pay the benefits and administrative costs is invested in interest-bearing United States government obligations or securities guaranteed as to principal and interest by the United States.

The fund does not represent a legal policy reserve of the type required to be established by private life insurers. A private life insurer must carry as a liability item on its balance sheet the difference between the present value of future benefits promised under its contracts in force and the present value of future premium payments for these contracts. The private insurer could (and may be forced to) stop selling contracts at any time, and, if its interest and mortality assumptions are correct, future premiums plus an amount equal to this liability item accumulated at interest would be sufficient to pay all future claims. The OASI Trust Fund is not this large, but the current amount in the fund plus future tax contributions and interest on the assets of the fund is expected to be sufficient to pay all future benefits and administrative expenses as they come due over the next seventy-five years. This feature of the OASI Trust Fund is explored in more detail on pages 146–47.

Until 1960 the Board of Trustees was required to report annually on the operation and status of the fund during the next ensuing five years. The Board was to report immediately to the Congress whenever it believed (1) that during the ensuing five years, the amount in the fund would exceed three times the highest annual expenditures during that period or (2) that the fund was unduly small. Congress was not required to act on this report. The 1959 Advisory Council on Social Security Financing recommended repeal of this provision because of the implied limitations on the size of the fund. While not a full reserve fund, the trust fund is more than a contingency fund and through interest earnings will reduce to a limited extent the burden of future payroll taxes.

ADMINISTRATION

Old-Age, Survivors, and Disability Insurance is administered by the Social Security Administration which is in turn a part of the Department of Health, Education, and Welfare. The Social Security Administration has regional and district offices located throughout the country.[9]

Each worker covered under OASDI has a social security number which is used to keep a record of his earnings. The benefits are computed on the basis of this earnings record. This record is kept by the Social Security Administration at its central office in Baltimore, Maryland, and insureds are encouraged to check on their accounts every three years, since certain corrections must be made within approximately four years after the wages are paid.

Benefits must be applied for at a social security office. If the insured believes that there has been an error in his earnings record or in computing his benefit, he may ask the Social Security Administration to reconsider his case. Either after this reconsideration or without it, he may request a hearing before a referee. The referee's decision may be appealed to the Bureau of Hearings and Appeals of the Social Security Administration. Further appeal may be made to the federal courts, if necessary.

OPERATIONAL TRENDS [10]

Since its original passage in 1935, the Social Security Act has been considerably liberalized by enlarging the scope of covered employment, reducing the requirements for insured status, adding new benefits, increasing their amount, and, during its early history, postponing scheduled tax increases. A consideration of the major amendments may indicate further the types of changes to be expected in the future.

Covered Employment

Under the original Act, only six out of ten gainfully employed persons were in covered employment. Excluded were agricultural laborers, do-

[9] The offices are invaluable as information centers. If the student has any technical questions on OASDI or other programs administered by this agency, he will be able to get answers to them from such an office. The Social Security Administration publishes a series of useful informational booklets, copies of which can be secured from these offices.

[10] Two excellent references on these trends are the following: Robert J. Myers, "Old-Age, Survivors, Disability, and Health Insurance Provisions: Legislative History, 1935–65," Social Security Administration, July, 1965, and "OASDI Program: History of the Benefit Formula," *Social Security Bulletin*, XXIII, No. 9 (September, 1960), 3–9.

mestic employees, employees of federal, state, and local governments, casual laborers, employees of non-profit charitable, religious, scientific, literary, or educational institutions, and self-employed persons. The arguments advanced in favor of these exclusions were similar to those cited on page 114, but administrative difficulties seemed much more important in 1935 than now. For example, in 1935 the inclusion of any agricultural laborers, domestic workers, or self-employed seemed administratively impossible. The 1950, 1954, and 1956 amendments reduced the exclusions considerably. The 1965 amendments added self-employed doctors of medicine and interns, an important group who had been excluded previously because the American Medical Association had maintained that the earnings test would deprive most doctors from receiving retirement benefits until age seventy-two. The exemption of certain religious sects was also a 1965 change. At present more than nine out of ten gainfully employed persons are in employments that make them eligible for coverage. This fraction may eventually become unity.

Insured Status

Under the original Act, a worker aged sixty-five was entitled to retirement benefits if he (1) had worked in covered employment on at least one day in each of five years between December 31, 1936, and his sixty-fifth birthday and (2) had earned at least $2,000 in covered employment. No survivorship benefits were available. This eligibility requirement was restrictive, and no benefits would be payable until 1942 (even though it could be met early in 1941).

In 1939, the eligibility requirements were liberalized because it was believed that the existing provisions were too strict in connection with the retirement benefits and were not entirely suitable for the newly added survivor benefits. The terms "fully insured" and "currently insured" were introduced and defined in the same way as at present, except that the starting point was January 1, 1937, instead of January 1, 1951,[11] and the quarters of coverage required for fully insured status were at least one-half of the elapsed quarters instead of one-fourth.

The number of covered employments was greatly increased by the 1950 amendments and the starting date for measuring fully insured status was moved up to January 1, 1951, in order to make it easier for new entrants to qualify at an early date. When the list of covered employments was further extended in 1954 and 1956, the starting date was not changed because so few years had elapsed since 1950 and the new entrants were not nearly as numerous. However, special rules were adopted

[11] Until 1946 the requirement for currently insured status was six out of the last twelve quarters, not including the quarter in which the insured died or retired. The present provision is more liberal.

which enabled many new entrants to qualify with fewer quarters of coverage than the standard rule would require. The 1960 amendments substituted one-third for one-half as the required proportion of quarters of coverage to achieve fully insured status. The fraction was further reduced to the present one-fourth in 1961. The 1965 amendments introduced the "transitional insured status" for persons who reached retirement age in or before 1956. The transitional benefits payable to persons seventy-two years of age and over before 1968 even if they had never worked in covered employment were added in 1966.

Benefits

Until 1939 the only benefit was a monthly income for a retired worker based on the total wages on which an OASDI tax should have been paid. The formula was as follows:

> ½ per cent of the first $3,000, plus
> $\frac{1}{12}$ per cent of the next $42,000, plus
> $\frac{1}{24}$ per cent of the excess.

The formula recognized both the level and duration of earnings.

The maximum benefit was $85; the minimum was $10. No benefit was payable for any month in which the worker was engaged in "regular" employment. If a worker died before he had received at least 3.5 per cent of his total taxed wages, the difference was returned to his estate. If he failed to qualify for monthly benefits at sixty-five, 3.5 per cent of his total taxed wages was returned to him in a lump sum. This return was considered to be a return of the worker's contributions plus interest.

The 1939 amendments made extensive changes in the benefits. The first important change was in the formula. Average monthly earnings were to be computed in essentially the same way as at present, except that the starting date was always January 1, 1937. Because only the first $3,000 of income was taxed, the maximum average monthly wage was $250. The primary insurance benefit, as it was called at that time, was computed according to the formula discussed on page 119 except that there was no limitation on the credit for years of coverage.

The effective maximum primary benefit was $40 plus ($.40 times years of coverage); the minimum was $10. The maximum family benefit was $85. No benefit was payable for any month in which the claimant earned at least $15 in covered employment.

These changes accomplished the following objectives. First, the benefit depended upon the average taxable earnings over the base period, instead of upon the total taxable earnings. This procedure increased the benefits available to those persons who were approaching retirement age at the time the formula was introduced. It also favored those who spread their total earnings over more years in the base period, the argument being that the person who pays taxes over a longer period of time should receive more benefits. Second, the formula favored low-income groups relatively more than did the old formula. The benefit was recognized more as a floor of protection than as a savings program. The reduction of the maximum benefit, and the introduction of dependents' allowances (as discussed in the next paragraph) were steps in the same direction. Finally, the introduction of a $15 earnings limit eliminated the discretionary determination of what was regular employment.

The second important 1939 change was the addition of new retirement benefits—the wife's and children's benefits, and survivorship benefits—the widow's, mother's, children's, and parent's benefits; and the lump-sum benefit. The maximum family benefit was twice the monthly primary benefit, 80 per cent of the average monthly wage, or $85, whichever was the smallest.

No more extensive changes were made until 1950 when the increment for years of coverage after 1950 was omitted from the primary insurance *benefit* formula. For the first time a primary insurance *amount* formula, which applied to averages computed on the basis of earnings in 1951 and later, was introduced (50 per cent of the first $100 of average monthly earnings and 15 per cent of the next $200). In addition, the primary insurance *benefits* computed on the basis of the revised *benefit* formula and earnings since 1936 were to be converted to larger primary insurance *amounts* by means of a conversion table. These liberalizations reflected increases in the cost of living and in wage levels. The children's benefit, the parent's benefit, the maximum taxable earnings, the maximum and minimum individual and family benefits, and the limitation on earnings of beneficiaries were all liberalized. The survivorship benefits for aged widowers and divorced wives with eligible children and the retirement benefits for aged husbands and wives with eligible children were also added in this year.

The cost of living continued to increase and minor amendments in 1952 increased all of the following: the benefits for the first $100 of average earnings, the earnings limitation on beneficiaries, and the maximum and minimum individual and family benefits.

In 1954 some extensive changes were made. The formula was further liberalized, the maximum and minimum individual and family benefits were increased, and the earnings limitation was changed to $1,200 in a year with one month's benefit being withheld for each $80 or fraction thereof in excess of $1,200. Finally, in computing his average monthly wage, the insured was permitted to "drop out" some years of low earnings. Since the cost of living had increased only slightly, these changes increased the adequacy of the benefits.

The 1956 amendments lowered from sixty-five to sixty-two the age at which female workers, wives, widows, and female dependent parents could draw benefits and liberalized the drop-out provisions slightly to their present form. The 1958 amendments substituted the present tabular presentation for the benefit formula, increased the general benefit level around 7 per cent because of the cost of living increase since 1954, and raised the maximum and minimum individual and family benefits.

In 1960 the child's survivorship benefit was increased to 75 per cent per child and the present earnings test was adopted except that the lower limit was $1,200 instead of the present $1,500 and the upper limit was $1,500 instead of the present $2,700.

In 1961, men were also permitted to retire as early as age sixty-two; aged widows', widowers' and some parents' benefits were increased to 82.5 per cent; minimum benefits were raised; and the upper limit under the earnings test was changed to $1,700.

The 1965 amendments made extensive changes. Benefits for average monthly earnings under $400 were increased by about 7 per cent to reflect increases in the cost of living since 1958.[12] The maximum average monthly earnings amount was increased to $550. The minimum benefit was also increased. Benefits for dependent children were continued to age twenty-two if they were full-time students attending an accredited school. The definition of "child" was broadened and the conditions under which a divorced wife can receive benefits were liberalized. Widows were permitted to elect reduced benefits as early as age sixty and to receive reduced benefits if they remarried after they reached age sixty. Maximum family benefits were increased and the earnings test was considerably liberalized with the lower limit being increased to $1,500 and the upper limit to $2,700.

If, as many economists believe will be the case, prices and earnings continue to rise, we may expect further increases in the earnings subject to tax and in the benefits provided. The lower income groups will probably benefit most from the changes, but this depends to some extent upon political fortunes.

The Tax Structure

In 1937 the employer and employee were each asked to pay a tax of 1 per cent on the first $3,000 of the worker's earnings. It was stipulated that this tax would increase by ½ per cent every three years until 1949 when it would have reached 3 per cent. As stated earlier, the purpose of the graduated increase was to lessen the impact of the tax.

[12] See footnote 6.

Because a tax increase is unpopular and because many persons questioned the necessity for an increase for reasons to be discussed shortly, the original rates were not increased as scheduled. However, it was not until 1947 that this original tax schedule was abandoned in favor of one which called for a tax of 1 per cent in 1948–49, 1½ per cent in 1950–51, and 2 per cent thereafter.

The tax was increased in 1950 according to this revised schedule, but the important 1950 amendments in coverage and benefits also produced a new tax schedule. The tax was to remain at 1½ per cent until 1954 when it would be increased to 2 per cent. In 1960 the tax would jump to 2½ per cent, in 1965 to 3 per cent, and in 1970 to 3¼ per cent, the maximum figure. Self-employed persons were to pay one and one-half times the employee tax. The maximum taxable earnings were increased to $3,600.

In 1954 the tax was increased as scheduled, but a revised tax schedule was adopted which required employees and employers to pay a maximum tax rate of 4 per cent from 1975 on. Maximum taxable earnings were again increased to $4,200. In 1956 each of the tax rates in the 1954 schedule was increased to cover the cost of the disability benefits added in that year.

A new tax schedule was introduced in 1958 that imposed a rate of 2½ per cent on employers and on employees on the first $4,800 of covered annual earnings. Under this schedule the tax rate for 1960–62 was 3 per cent, for 1963–65 3½ per cent, for 1966–68 4 per cent, and from 1969 on 4½ per cent. This change was necessitated because of liberalized benefits and because benefit expenditures were exceeding previous estimates. In 1957 the total assets in the trust fund had declined for the first time since it had been established. In 1961 the employer-employee tax rates in the 1958 schedule were all increased by ⅛% (self-employed rates went up about .2 per cent) and the year in which the maximum rate was to be effective was advanced from 1969 to 1968. The present tax schedule was adopted in 1965 with a 3.85 per cent rate applicable to employee earnings in 1966.

Tax increases have been postponed in the past, but it is probable that there will be fewer postponements in the future as benefits are increased and the cost of the program both mounts and becomes more apparent. A higher tax schedule is expected to accompany any further extension of benefits.

The Trust Fund

Until 1940 the excess of the income over expenditures was kept in an Old-Age Reserve Account which was administered by the Secretary of the Treasury. The balance was invested in special 3 per cent government bonds. On January 1, 1940, the funds were transferred to the Old-Age and Survivors Insurance Trust Fund, which was to be administered by a Board of Trustees. The funds were to be invested in public issues bought on the open market or in special bonds bearing the average rate of interest on the public debt. A separate fund was created in 1956 for the disability tax receipts. The 1956 amendments also changed the interest rate on the special bonds to the average coupon rate of interest on all marketable obligations of the United States not due or callable until at least five years after the original date of issue. The 1960 amendments changed the rate on the special bonds to the average market yield on all bonds that will mature four or more years after the date of the special issue and changed to a statutory obligation the practice of the Managing Trustee to purchase marketable obligations only if such purchase is in the public interest.

The intent behind the original tax schedule was to accumulate a sizable trust fund as soon as possible in order that the interest on the trust fund might be used to pay a substantial proportion of the costs. For example, by 1980 the interest on the fund was expected to equal about 40 per cent of the disbursements. From the beginning, however, the fund was assumed to be less than that required of a private insurer because it was assumed that the system would operate indefinitely into the future. Strong opposition to the philosophy supporting a sizable trust fund had existed prior to its adoption but this opposition later became more outspoken and effective. Among the arguments were the following:

1. Because the old-age insurance system covered such a sizable segment of the voting population, because it could be expected to operate indefinitely, and because the federal government possessed the taxing power, there was no need to accumulate a sizable trust fund.[13]

2. The benefits provided under the 1935 amendments were inadequate. In order to provide the more reasonable benefits that were considered essential and to operate under the original reserve philosophy, high payroll tax rates would be required. These rates would not only be deflationary; they would also be an impossible burden.

3. A large trust fund might serve as an excuse for an unjustifiable liberalization of benefits.

4. The fund that was contemplated at this time (late 1930's) would rival the then-existing national debt in magnitude. The federal government might be provided with funds which it did not need and as a result might be encouraged to make unwise expenditures. Diversion of some of these funds into private investments would not be in keeping with our national philosophy.

[13] See p. 130.

Those favoring a large trust fund argued as follows:

1. A sizable trust fund was necessary to protect the rights of future recipients. Congress, they thought (perhaps naively), would respect the purpose of the trust fund and the present generation would be less dependent upon a future generation and its elected representatives.
2. A trust fund of the 1935 variety would reduce the financial burden passed on to future generations.
3. If a small trust fund were accumulated, the short-run costs would be deceptively low and might serve as an excuse for unjustifiable liberalizations.
4. Long-range social insurance policy should not be sacrificed in favor of short-run political and economic considerations.[14]

At the same time that the tax schedule was being debated, a much more liberal benefit schedule was being studied, and it was recommended that the government contribute to the cost. It was argued that the government should bear at least part of the cost for those who would contribute for only a few years before retiring, since it was thought to be unfair to tax the younger employees to pay for these benefits. It was also argued that the inclusion of these retirants would reduce the social assistance programs supported out of general revenues, thus lessening the financial burden of the federal government. The opposing argument was that introducing a government contribution might lead to an even greater participation in the future and threaten the contributory principle underlying the insurance system.

The intent of the changes actually made in 1939 in the financial provisions of the law is not clear. The tax increase scheduled for 1940 was postponed but no increase was recommended in later years to make up for this reduction. As a result the trust fund's progress was slowed down considerably, particularly since the benefits were liberalized substantially by the same amendments. On the other hand, the federal government did not pledge itself to participate in the program. It was at this time that the Board of Trustees was asked to report immediately when the fund was unduly low or exceeded the maximum established by the "rule of three." This appeared to set a maximum limit on the fund, but the maximum was exceeded almost immediately and Congress did nothing except to continue postponing tax increases until 1947 when a stop-gap

---

[14] James S. Parker, "Financial Policy in Old Age and Survivors Insurance, 1935–50," *Social Security Bulletin*, XIV, No. 6 (June, 1951), 3–10. This list of arguments and much of the discussion herein on the trust fund are based upon this article.

measure was enacted. The tax freezes were strongly opposed by the Commissioner of the Social Security Administration who argued that the immediate economic problems of the 1930's no longer existed.

The result of the freezes was that a larger share of the financial burden was passed on to future OASDI taxpayers. It also became apparent that the tax schedule was not sufficient to make the system self-supporting and the Revenue Act of 1943 authorized Congress to make direct appropriations when necessary to finance the benefits provided.

In 1950 Congress reversed itself and declared that the system was to be self-supporting. It adopted a new higher tax schedule, and the tax increase scheduled for 1954 became a reality. The benefit increases in 1954 and later years were accompanied by an even higher tax structure. The 1956 disability income benefits are paid out of a separate fund. As a result the trust fund today is not as great as intended in 1935, but it is more than a contingency fund and, according to Congress, should be sufficient with future taxes to pay all benefits and expenses for the next seventy-five years.

OPERATIONAL DATA

Old-Age and Survivors Insurance is, by far, the most important insurance operation in the country. In December, 1965, total covered employment was estimated at 66.2 million, including 2.8 million in the armed forces. About 79 million persons worked in covered employment sometime during 1965. About 95 million people had already achieved fully insured or currently insured status by the end of 1965, and millions of non-workers were entitled to benefits as dependents of covered workers.

The increases in the number of insured living workers, the number of workers with taxable earnings, the number of new entrants, the amount of taxable earnings, the average taxable earnings per employee, and the number of employers reporting taxable wages are indicated in Table 4.2. All of the "sudden changes" appearing in the table can be attributed to amendments to the Social Security Act and to the impacts of World War II. The effect of the 1950 amendments, which greatly extended the scope of covered employment, is the most noticeable. The number of living workers insured at the end of 1961 increased markedly over those insured at the end of 1959 because of the 1960 and 1961 liberalizations in the requirements for fully insured status. Steady increases in wage levels have also been partly responsible for an increase in the average taxable earnings per worker.

Among the 95.2 million insured living workers at the beginning of 1966, 56.7 million were permanently fully insured, 34.8 million were fully

TABLE 4.2

Old-Age, Survivors, and Disability Insurance: Insured Living Workers, New Entrants, Workers with Taxable Earnings, Taxable Earnings, and Employers Reporting Taxable Earnings, 1937–64

Year	Living Workers at Beginning of Following Year (in thousands) Insured	Uninsured	New Entrants (in thousands)	Workers with Taxable Earnings During Year (in thousands)	Taxable Earnings Total (in millions)	Average per Worker	Employers Reporting Taxable Wages (in thousands)
1937	——	——	32,904	32,904	$ 29,615	$ 900	2,421
1939	22,900	17,800	4,450	33,751	29,745	881	2,366
1941	27,500	23,500	6,436	40,976	41,848	1,021	2,646
1943	34,900	30,500	7,337	47,656	62,423	1,310	2,394
1945	40,300	32,100	3,477	46,392	62,945	1,357	2,614
1947	43,400	33,700	2,685	48,908	78,372	1,602	3,246
1949	45,700	34,900	1,958	46,796	81,808	1,748	3,316
1951	62,800	25,000	5,999	58,120	120,968	2,081	4,440
1953	71,000	21,800	3,094	60,839	136,003	2,235	4,350
1955	71,400	26,800	4,756	65,203	157,772	2,420	5,050
1957	77,000	26,100	3,350	70,500	181,421	2,573	5,100
1959 *	79,700	27,300	3,120	71,695	202,346	2,822	5,200
1961	89,100	21,800	2,920	72,819	209,886	2,882	5,320
1963 *	92,100	22,800	3,500	75,760	225,660	2,979	5,450
1964 *	n.a.	n.a.	n.a.	77,700	236,600	3,045	5,510

* Preliminary estimates.
n.a. = not available. About 95 million workers were insured at the end of 1965.

Sources: *Social Security Bulletin, Annual Statistical Supplement,* 1963, p. 25, and *Social Security Bulletin* (June, 1966), p. 44.

insured but that status was not permanent, and 3.7 million were currently insured only.

The number of persons receiving monthly benefits at the end of each five-year interval between 1940 and 1965 and the total monthly benefits that they were receiving are shown in Table 4.3. The data are also classified by type of benefit. The increase in the number of beneficiaries and in monthly benefits for each type of benefit and for all benefits combined is the most important fact revealed by the table. The retirement beneficiaries and benefits have become a more important part of the total beneficiaries and benefits as the number of persons becoming eligible for these benefits has increased. The mother's benefit and the child's benefit, which are generally survivorship benefits, have become less important, partly because of lower mortality rates at the younger ages and partly because death benefit rolls reach maturity more quickly than the number and amount of old-age benefits.

TABLE 4.3

Old-Age, Survivors, and Disability Insurance: Number of Beneficiaries Receiving Benefits at End of Year and Monthly Benefits Received, by Type of Benefits, 1940–65 *

(NUMBERS AND AMOUNTS IN THOUSANDS)

Year	Total		Old-Age		Wife's or Husband's		Child's †		Widow's or Widower's		Mother's †		Parent's	
	Number	Amount	Number	Amount	Number	Amount	Number	Amount	Number	Amount	Number	Amount	Number	Amount
1940	222	$ 4,070	112	$ 2,539	30	$ 361	55	$ 668	4	$ 90	20	$ 402	1	$ 11
1945	1,288	23,801	518	12,538	159	2,040	390	4,858	94	1,893	121	2,391	6	81
1950	3,477	126,856	1,771	77,678	508	11,995	700	19,366	314	11,481	169	5,801	15	535
1955	7,961	411,613	4,474	276,942	1,192	39,416	1,276	46,444	701	34,152	292	13,403	25	1,256
1960	14,157	888,320	8,061	596,849	2,269	87,867	1,845	88,578	1,544	89,054	401	23,795	36	2,178
1965	19,128	1,395,817	11,101	931,532	2,614	114,035	2,535	141,802	2,371	174,883	472	30,882	35	2,683

* Disability benefits are not included in this table.

† The child's benefit column includes payments to children of deceased or retired workers. The mother's benefit column includes only survivorship benefits; benefits paid to the mothers of retired workers' children are listed under the wife's benefit column.

Source: *Social Security Bulletin*, April, 1966.

Table 4.4 shows how improved benefits and rising wages have increased the average monthly benefit of each type.

TABLE 4.4

Average OASDI Monthly Benefit Being Received at End of Year, by Type of Benefit, 1940–65

Year	Old-Age	Wife's or Husband's	Child's	Widow's or Widower's	Mother's	Parent's
1940	$22.60	$12.13	$12.22	$20.28	$19.61	$13.09
1945	24.19	12.82	12.46	20.19	19.83	13.06
1950	43.86	23.60	27.68	36.54	34.24	36.69
1955	61.90	33.07	36.40	48.69	45.91	49.93
1960	74.04	38.72	48.04	57.68	59.29	60.31
1965	83.92	43.63	22.23	73.75	65.45	76.03

Source: Based on Table 4.3.

Although the number and the amount of OASDI benefits have continually increased, certain individuals have had their benefits withheld or terminated. About 695,000 benefits were being withheld on June 30, 1965. The reason for withholding over 90 per cent of these benefits was the employment or self-employment of the beneficiary or an old-age beneficiary on whose earnings the benefit was based.[15] Over 1,670,000 benefits were terminated in 1963. As would be expected, death was the most important cause of termination, except in the case of the children's and mother's benefits, where attainment of age eighteen by the child was the most important reason. Another important reason for the loss of the mother's benefit was her remarriage.[16]

The growth of the OASI Trust Fund since 1937 is shown in Table 4.5. Taxes, transfers from the Railroad Retirement account,[17] appropriations by Congress from general funds to cover the additional payments arising from the extension of survivors' insurance protection to certain veterans of World War II under the 1946 amendments, and interest on investments exceeded the benefits and administrative expenses every year until 1957 when the trust fund assets declined for the first time. The tax schedule increases enacted in 1958 and 1961 reversed this trend in 1963 as compared with 1962. At the close of 1965, the fund consisted of $1.6 billion in cash, $3.5 billion in public issues of government bonds, and $13.1 billion in special issues.

[15] *Social Security Bulletin*, XXVIII, No. 11 (November, 1965), 37.

[16] *Social Security Bulletin, Annual Statistical Supplement*, 1963, p. 74.

[17] The purpose of these transfers is to put both funds in the position they would now be in if railroad employment after 1936 had been under OASDI.

TABLE 4.5

Receipts, Expenditures, and Assets of OASI Trust Fund,
1937–65

(In Millions)

Year	Receipts		Expenditures		Total Assets
	Net Tax Contributions *	Interest †	Benefit Payments ‡	Administrative Expenses	
1937	$ 765	$ 2	$ 1	**	$ 766
1939	580	27	14	**	1,724
1941	789	56	88	$ 26	2,762
1943	1,239	88	166	29	4,820
1945	1,285	134	274	30	7,121
1947	1,558	164	466	46	9,360
1949	1,670	146	667	54	11,816
1951	3,367	417	1,885	81	15,540
1953	3,945	414	3,006	88	18,707
1955	5,713	461	4,968	119	21,663
1957	6,825	558	7,347	162	22,393
1959	8,052	532	10,124	184	20,141
1961	11,285	548	12,194	239	19,725
1963	14,541	521	14,639	281	18,480
1965	16,017	593	17,173	328	18,235

* Includes Congressional appropriations in 1946–51 to meet cost of benefits for certain World War II veterans.

† Includes interest on amounts held in the Railroad Retirement account to the credit of the OASI trust fund during 1954–57.

‡ Includes transfers to the Railroad Retirement account in 1958 and each succeeding year. The transfer in 1965 was $436 million.

** Administrative expenses before 1940 were, in effect, deducted from contributions before the latter were credited to the fund.

Sources: *Social Security Bulletin, Annual Statistical Supplement,* 1963, p. 29; *Social Security Bulletin,* XXIX, No. 4 (April, 1966), p. 51.

Actuaries of the Social Security Administration periodically prepare actuarial cost estimates that include an analysis of the probable future progress of the fund. The estimate prepared in 1965 on the assumption that the 1965 benefit schedule and tax schedule would remain in effect will serve as an illustration of the actuarial principles involved.[18]

[18] This section is based on Robert J. Myers and Francisco Bayo, "Hospital Insurance, Supplementary Medical Insurance, and Old-Age, Survivors, and Disability Insurance: Financing Basis Under the 1965 Amendments," *Social Security Bulletin,* XXVIII, No. 10 (October, 1965), 17–28. For a thorough discussion of the actuarial methods and principles involved, see Robert J. Myers, *Social Insurance and Allied Government Programs* (Homewood, Ill.: Richard D. Irwin, Inc., 1965), pp. 107–39.

The estimated progress of the OASI trust fund under the 1965 Act is shown in Table 4.6. Note that there are three estimates: a low-cost estimate, a high-cost estimate, and an intermediate-cost estimate. The intermediate-cost estimate includes a short-range estimate for 1965–72 and a long-range estimate for 1975–2025. All three long-range estimates were based upon the assumption that we would have close to full employment with average earnings at about the level prevailing in 1963. The low-cost and high-cost estimates indicate the plausible variation in future costs depending upon what happens with respect to many other factors such as mortality rates, birth rates, migration rates, retirement rates, disability rates, the ratio of insured persons to the total population, marital and parental status, remarriage rates, the proportion of potential beneficiaries at work, the proportion of beneficiaries with duplicate benefits, average benefits, administrative expenses, and interest rates. Until 1964 the actuaries made assumptions concerning what would happen to these factors into the indefinite future, but the 1963–64 Advisory Council on Social Security Financing suggested that the period for long-range cost estimates be changed from perpetuity to seventy-five years. This suggestion has been followed in the 1965 estimates. The plausible range represented by the two extreme estimates is not intended to be the maximum possible range. The intermediate long-range estimate is the average of the high- and low-cost estimates. It is not necessarily the most probable estimate, but it is a convenient estimate to use for comparative purposes.

The intermediate short-range estimate is also a relatively new feature suggested by the 1963–64 Advisory Council on Social Security Financing. Only an intermediate short-range estimate is prepared because more confidence can be placed in a single set of assumptions in the short run. Another difference between the short-range and long-range estimates is that under the short-range estimate the level of average earnings is assumed to rise gradually in accordance with recent trends. This assumption increases contribution income over what would be received if average earnings remained the same. Benefit outgo is also increased by this assumption, but much less so for three reasons: (1) Benefits, being based on average monthly earnings in the past instead of final earnings, would not respond as quickly to increases in earnings, (2) benefits are not adjusted for changes in the earnings level after retirement, and (3) the benefit formula is weighted in favor of lower average monthly earnings (see Figure 4.1). The result is that the trust fund at the end of 1972 under the short-range estimate is higher than would be developed under the long-range estimates. The long-range estimates, therefore, are conservative in the sense that if average earnings rise and the benefits in the

TABLE 4.6

Estimated Progress of OASI Trust Fund Under 1965 Act,
Low-Cost, High-Cost, and Intermediate-Cost Estimates

(IN MILLIONS)

	Receipts		Expenditures		
Calendar Year	Net Tax Contributions *	Interest †	Benefit Payments ‡	Administrative Expenses	Assets at End of Year
	Low-Cost Estimate				
1975	$29,426	$1,633	$24,664	$361	$ 50,193
1980	32,080	2,767	28,101	398	81,283
1990	38,017	5,316	34,882	469	151,886
2000	45,377	9,525	38,365	515	270,603
	High-Cost Estimate				
1975	$28,209	$ 906	$25,659	$418	$ 30,989
1980	30,129	1,212	29,816	464	40,370
1990	33,235	537	38,383	550	18,064
2000	37,362	**	43,487	603	**
	Intermediate-Cost Estimate				
1965	$16,014	$ 570	$17,422	$351	$ 17,936
1966	18,848	546	18,965	377	17,988
1967	20,687	580	20,036	363	18,856
1968	21,568	634	20,808	369	19,881
1969	24,958	733	21,700	377	23,495
1970	26,328	900	22,579	385	27,759
1971	27,163	1,082	23,456	393	32,155
1972	28,041	1,271	24,362	401	36,704
1975	28,818	1,212	25,161	390	40,044
1980	31,105	1,895	28,958	431	59,891
1990	35,623	2,689	36,629	510	82,433
2000	41,370	3,287	40,926	559	101,233
2025	51,345	4,476	62,118	769	132,792

* Includes payments to the fund under the Railroad Retirement financial interchange. No such payments are predicted under any estimate until around 1990.

† At rates of 3¾ per cent under the low-cost estimate, 3¼ per cent under the high-cost estimate, and 3½ per cent under the intermediate-cost estimate.

‡ Includes payments from the fund under the Railroad Retirement financial interchange.

** Fund exhausted in 1993.

Source: Robert J. Myers and Francisco Bayo, "Hospital Insurance, Supplementary Medical Insurance, and Old-Age, Survivors, and Disability Insurance: Financing Basis Under the 1965 Amendments," *Social Security Bulletin*, XXVIII, No. 10 (October, 1965), 22–23.

law are unchanged, the trust fund will be larger than estimated, other things being equal.[19]

Under the low-cost long-range estimate, the trust fund would continually increase, but under the high-cost estimate the fund would be exhausted in 1993. Under the intermediate-cost estimate, the trust fund was expected to reach a maximum of about $160 billion about 2015 and then decrease. If the trust fund should be exhausted at some future date and if benefits exceed contributions (as was assumed to be the case eventually under the high-cost assumptions), Congress would have to raise the OASDI payroll tax rates or appropriate general revenue funds to help pay the benefits, but Congress has stated its intention not to do the latter.[20] On the other hand, if the low-cost assumptions are correct, Congress would undoubtedly delay the application of scheduled increases in payroll taxes, increase the benefits, or even reduce the tax rates.

Under the low-cost estimate, the benefit payments were expected to increase to 9.95 per cent of taxable payroll by 2040. Under the high-cost estimate the figure was 15.01 per cent and under the intermediate-cost estimate 11.95 per cent. These rates are interesting because in 2040 employees and employers would have to pay combined rates equal to these amounts if the OASI portion of the system were operated entirely on a pay-as-you-go basis. The corresponding 1975 rates would be 7.47 per cent, 8.10 per cent, and 7.78 per cent.

Another informative measure is the level-contribution rate that would have to be paid annually if the system were to operate for seventy-five more years and remain self-supporting with a contingency fund at the end of that period equal to one year's disbursements. Table 4.7 shows the estimated level-contribution rates under the low-, high-, and intermediate-cost assumptions.

The level contribution expressed as a percentage of taxable payroll is equal to the present value of future benefit payments and administrative expenses expressed as a percentage of the present value of future taxable payrolls *less* interest on the existing trust fund expressed as a percentage of the present value of future taxable payrolls.

Under the low-cost estimate, the equivalent value of the present contribution rate exceeded the required rate, but the opposite was true

---

[19] However, if benefits are increased to keep pace with average earnings, the trust fund will be smaller relative to taxable payroll than currently estimated because interest on the existing trust fund will become a smaller percentage of taxable payroll.

[20] In 1969 Congress will appropriate monies from general revenues to reimburse the fund for the special payments beginning in 1966 to some persons aged seventy-two and over without any insured status. Until that time the trust fund will carry the cost, which will cause it to grow less rapidly in the next few years than predicted under the short-range estimate.

under the high- and intermediate-cost estimates. According to the intermediate-cost estimate, the required combined rate was 8.84 per cent,[21] while the combined level-contribution rate under the current schedule was 8.74 per cent. If the assumptions turn out to be correct, this annual shortage of .10 per cent of payroll would cause the fund to decline after about 2015.

TABLE 4.7

Estimated Level-Cost Rates of the OASI System, 1965 Estimate

	Present Value as a Percentage of Future Taxable Payrolls		
Present Value of	Low-Cost Estimate	High-Cost Estimate	Intermediate-Cost Estimate
Benefit payments	7.82	10.25	8.87
Administrative costs	.11	.15	.13
Interest on Existing Trust Fund	−.17	−.15	−.16
Net level-contribution rate	7.76	10.25	8.84
Scheduled contributions	8.74	8.74	8.74
Actuarial balance	.98	−1.51	−.10

Sources: Same as Table 4.6, and letter from Robert J. Myers to authors dated May 15, 1966.

Some indication of the many variables that must be considered in preparing these estimates has already been presented on page 144. Consequently the estimates are crude and new estimates must be made periodically. The operating question is whether the estimated required rate is reasonably close to the actual rate. Traditionally Congress considered the permissible variation to be .25 per cent of payroll for OASI and .30 per cent for OASDI when the costs were measured in perpetuity. Now that the estimates are prepared on a seventy-five-year basis, the permissible variation for the combined OASDI program has been reduced to .10 per cent of payroll. Because the actuarial balance for the disability insurance system is +.03, the actuarial balance for the combined system is −.07, which is within the permissible tolerance.

It should be re-emphasized that even if the assumptions were correct, the adoption of an 8.84 per cent level-contribution rate from now on would not make it possible to terminate OASDI at some time in the

[21] Of the 8.83 per cent present value of benefit payments (8.87 per cent including the financial interchange with the Railroad Retirement system), primary benefits for retired workers account for 6.27 per cent, widows' benefits for 1.11 per cent, children's benefits for .67 per cent, wives' benefits .51 per cent, and all other benefits .27 per cent.

future, continue payments to current benefit recipients, and make actuarially fair payments to other contributors. The assumption of an indefinite operation is crucial.

It should also be emphasized that if OASDI had been terminated at the end of 1964, the trust fund of $19 billion would not have been sufficient to pay the approximately $123 billion present value of OASI benefits to current recipients. However, since few persons expect the system to stop operating, this may be an academic issue.

EFFECT OF OASI ON PUBLIC ASSISTANCE PROGRAMS

The Social Security Act provided for a social insurance program at the federal level and for grants-in-aid for public assistance programs at the state level. It was believed that the importance of the public assistance programs would decline as the number of persons attaining insured status under OASDI increased. Actually the number of persons receiving old-age assistance and aid to families with dependent children is larger now than in the early 1930's. It is true, however, that the number of old-age recipients has decreased substantially since 1950.

The increase in the number of persons receiving old-age assistance until 1950 was due primarily to the rapidly increasing aged population, the many excluded employments under OASI during the first fifteen years of its operations, the tighter requirements for insured status, the expanding adequacy of OAA, and the inadequacy of the OASI benefits received by some of the beneficiaries covered under that system. The increasing number of persons receiving aid to families with dependent children has been accompanied by a change in the principal cause of dependency from death of the father to absence of the father, usually because of marital difficulties, a contingency that is not covered under the insurance system.

In spite of their continued importance, these two public assistance programs have been affected considerably by OASI. They would have been far more important if there had been no OASI. While the proportion of OAA recipients to the aged population has been declining from 22 per cent in June, 1940, to 12 per cent in June, 1965, the proportion of OASI aged recipients to the aged has increased from 1 per cent to 75 per cent. Nearly 85 per cent are either drawing OASI benefits or would get them if they retired. More than 90 per cent of those currently reaching age sixty-five are eligible for OASI benefits.[22] Current receipt of both OAA and OASI benefits has also increased. In 1950 the proportion of the aged receiving both benefits was about 2 per cent; by 1965 the proportion was about 5 per cent. The proportion of OAA recipients receiv-

[22] Ida C. Merriam, "Overlap of Benefits Under OASDI and Other Programs," *Social Security Bulletin,* XXVIII, No. 4 (April, 1965), p. 22.

ing OASI benefits increased more than fourfold over this period, but the proportion of OASI beneficiaries receiving OAA benefits was reduced substantially.

The *number* of children receiving assistance under the AFDC program *because of the death of the father* has actually declined while the number of survivor children receiving OASDI benefits has increased markedly as shown in Table 4.3. In 1965 about 5 per cent of the population under age eighteen were receiving AFDC benefits.

EVALUATION

Although Old-Age, Survivors, and Disability Insurance is designed primarily to achieve a social objective—a floor of protection for all participants on a quasi-contractual basis—it possesses some modified private insurance characteristics. Except for some special benefits to certain persons aged seventy-two or over, benefits under the system are related to some extent to earnings and contributions instead of being related entirely to presumed need. On the other hand, the benefits are a larger proportion of low average earnings and are directly related to the number of dependents, while the tax is a specified percentage of the earnings up to $6,600.

The objective of a protective floor makes it impossible to relate the benefits exactly to the taxes paid because the lower income groups and those with many dependents cannot afford to pay the entire cost of their own benefits. On the other hand, it has been considered desirable to maintain some relationship between benefits and earnings on which contributions are paid because this relationship emphasizes the distinction between OASDI benefits and charity, appeals to most Americans, serves as a check on unjustifiable liberalizations, is assumed to encourage enterprise and initiative, and produces a benefit that varies with the recipient's standard of living.

The merger of these two concepts, however, has produced many misunderstandings concerning the nature of the system and has increased administrative costs. In addition, there is much disagreement concerning whether the two concepts have been combined in the correct proportions and in some instances whether they should have been combined at all. This is a danger associated with all compromise solutions. In reading the discussion that follows on specific issues, it is important to keep in mind this compromise nature of the system and the basic disagreements over the blend of individual equity and social adequacy. The position one takes on this fundamental point can determine his views on specific issues. The authors believe that the values of the compromise exceed its costs, but that we should all be aware of its true nature.

Coverage

The closer the system approaches universal coverage, the fewer the problems created by "in-and-out employment" and, more significantly, the less important becomes the role of public assistance programs. Consequently, as long as the system has existed, there has been substantial support for expanding the types of employment covered and for liberalizing the conditions under which a covered person can attain insured status. Because the system now covers almost all types of employment, the pressure for increasing the kinds of workers covered under the system has lessened substantially. However, because federal government employees covered under the Civil Service Retirement System constitute one of the most important groups still outside the system and because, it is argued, there is no reason for this special treatment of federal employees, there is a movement to coordinate the Federal Civil Service Retirement system with OASDI in a manner somewhat analogous to the Railroad Retirement system.

A more extreme suggestion, which was restated in 1965 by a task force of the Chamber of Commerce of the United States,[23] is that some OASDI benefits should be granted immediately to all aged persons. In a surprise amendment to a 1966 bill increasing taxes because of the Viet Nam conflict, Congress moved in this direction when it made certain persons aged seventy-two or over eligible for some minimum benefits even though they have never worked in covered employment. The Chamber and other supporters of "blanketing-in" all aged persons argue that this would provide a better current indication of the final costs of the system, eliminate or at least lower the cost of the old-age-assistance programs, and remove an important inequity under the system—the loss that some uncovered persons suffered simply because they did not meet stipulated requirements. At present about 7 per cent of the aged have no protection under any public retirement system.

On the other hand, however, extensive blanketing-in would have serious ramifications. It would be inconsistent with the contribution-benefit relationship principle and would raise some difficult questions. For example, what benefit should these people receive? Should it be the same in all areas? Should it equal the current average public assistance benefit? If so, should this benefit become the minimum OASDI benefit for all recipients? In its 1966 action Congress adopted a uniform benefit substantially less than the average public assistance benefit or the

---

[23] *Poverty: The Sick, Disabled, and Aged,* Second Report by the Task Force on Economic Growth and Opportunity (Washington, D. C.: Chamber of Commerce of the United States, 1965), pp. 71–73.

minimum OASDI benefit, but many members of Congress favored a payment equal to the OASDI minimum. Unless general revenues are used to support these payments, as is currently the case, shifting some of the cost from public assistance to OASDI would change the primary financial support from progressive income taxes to payroll contributions, which many consider to be regressive. With regard to the inequities involved, it must be remembered that some of these persons chose not to be covered. Furthermore, although current OASDI participants have experienced windfall benefits, they were required to have made some contributions to the system. If windfall benefits had not been paid, the total benefits paid in the early years would have been small and misleading. Nevertheless, there is considerable support for blanketing-in more persons as evidenced by the fact that the Senate version of the 1966 program would have paid larger benefits to all persons aged seventy or over. Cost considerations were largely responsible for the less liberal proposal developed by a conference committee.

Benefits

The proper benefit formula and level of benefits are constant sources of contention. The objective is a floor of protection with some relationship to average earnings and contributions. Unfortunately, the floor of protection is a subjective concept. Relatively few observers favor such a high level of benefits that most families would have little need for private supplementation, but this still leaves room for wide differences of opinion. Is the floor a subsistence level, a "modest but adequate" level, or some other standard of living? Should all insured families receive benefits determined in accordance with one selected standard or should the definition of a floor vary depending upon the average monthly earnings? Should any one receive benefits below the floor? More efforts should be directed toward a more precise statement of the objective of the system in order to resolve these arguments. In its January 1, 1965, report, the Advisory Council on Social Security did state that "one goal must be that . . . a low-paid worker will get benefits high enough so that he will not have to turn to public assistance to meet regular living expenses." The Council established this objective, however, only for "regular full-time workers at low earnings levels." [24]

The variety of suggestions concerning the proper benefit level reflects different opinions concerning the proper floor of protection and the proper combination of socially adequate benefits and wage-related ben-

[24] "Report of the Advisory Council on Social Security: The Status of the Social Security Program and Recommendations for its Improvement," *Social Security Bulletin*, XXVIII, No. 3 (March, 1965), 28.

efits. Some would raise benefits for persons in all income groups (although not necessarily by the same per cent or amount) [25] whereas others would maintain or, if possible, cut benefits at all levels. Still others would agree to further increases in benefits for lower-income groups but not for middle- and upper-income families. The most radical suggestion along these lines is to substitute a flat benefit for the present wage-related benefit. This latter suggestion denies the importance of the benefit-contribution relationship and the geographic and other differences in the level of a "floor of protection."

The effect of variations in prices and earnings upon benefit adequacy has been handled through periodic increases in the maximum annual earnings to be included in calculating the average monthly wage, the introduction of dropout provisions, and liberalizations in the benefit formula applicable to current and prospective benefits. Since the Social Security Act was passed in 1935, there has been a marked upward trend in prices and earnings. Consequently the changes just noted have been necessary (1) to prevent the system from providing the same benefits (the maximum benefit) for a large proportion of the recipients and (2) to maintain the adequacy of the benefits.[26] However, these changes have not been automatic and the impact of the change in the maximum earn-

[25] For example, the 1965 amendments raised primary insurance amounts for average monthly earnings under $400 by 7 per cent. See footnote 6. The Advisory Council on Social Security, however, recommended that the level be increased about 15 per cent, about half of which would be necessary to restore purchasing power lost by price increases since 1958. The other half would have improved the real value of the benefit. The cost of living increase was to be applicable at all benefit levels, but the real value increase would be accomplished by raising the amount to which the higher percentage in the formula applies from $110 to $155. The Council reasoned that because of increases in average earnings, the definition of a low-paid worker should be revised upward. Persons with earnings below $110 would not benefit from this change, but most of these people were assumed not to have worked regularly under the program and, if a couple, to be already eligible for benefits almost as large as their average monthly earnings. See Report of the Advisory Council on Social Security, *ibid.*, 27–28.

The Task Force on Economic Growth and Opportunity of the Chamber of Commerce of the United States has recommended that the minimum benefits represent an adequate floor of protection against the loss of job-related income and reflect changes in living standards, the cost of living, and the economy. The present $44 is, in their opinion, much too low. See *Poverty: The Sick, Disabled, and Aged, op. cit.*, pp. 69–71.

[26] For an interesting analysis of the effect of changes in the benefit formula, see "OASDI Program: History of the Benefit Formula," *op. cit.*, 7–9. The article indicates some improvement in the adequacy of the benefit level since 1950. For example, the monthly retirement benefit based upon the 1950 formula and the median earnings in that year was 28 per cent of those earnings. The monthly benefit based upon the 1958 formula and the median earnings in 1958 was 32 per cent. On the other hand, long-term contributors without dependents would have been better off under the 1935 formula if earnings had remained static since that time.

ings is never felt immediately because the benefits are based upon career earnings instead of final earnings. The changes also contradict to some extent the contributory nature of the system. In order to make the benefits more responsive to variations in price levels and earnings, it has been suggested that benefit levels and the maximum earnings taxed should fluctuate automatically with selected economic indicators such as the Consumers' Price Index or the median average earnings in covered employment.

That Congress probably intends to adjust the benefit level to changes in the Consumers' Price Index is best evidenced by the fact that this was the reasoning behind the benefit level increases under the 1958 and 1965 amendments. Few people disagreed with these changes and the reasoning involved. The philosophy underlying the maximum earnings figure, however, is less clear and much more debated. Under the original $3,000 base, 92 per cent of the covered payroll was taxed and 98 per cent of the workers had all their earnings covered. A base of $14,500 would have been required in 1965 to restore this relationship. Some members of the last Advisory Council on Social Security recommended a move toward this goal, but the Council advocated as a more practical alternative the 1950 situation. In 1950 the new base of $3,600 would have covered 86 per cent of covered payrolls and the entire earnings of 81 per cent of all workers. A base of $7,200 in 1968 would, it was estimated, achieve the desired result.[27] On the other hand, others have challenged the current $6,600 maximum because it exceeds the current average wage of full-time workers, which is another standard that might be used.[28]

Proposals for *automatic* changes in the benefit level, the maximum earnings base, or any other part of the system have not received widespread support because of (1) technical difficulties; [29] (2) differences of opinion concerning (a) the philosophies that determine the nature of these automatic changes and (b) whether these underlying philosophies should themselves change over time; (3) a belief that changing any features of the system automatically may make it more difficult to generate support for changes in other parts of the system; (4) a political preference for assigning credit to each Congress for liberalizations made

[27] "Report of the Advisory Council on Social Security," *op. cit.*, 12–13.

[28] Ray M. Peterson, *An Appraisal of the Social Security Amendments of 1965*, an address to the Conference of Actuaries in Public Practice, New Orleans, Louisiana, October 4, 1965.

[29] For a discussion of how the technical problems involved in changing the earnings base might be handled, see Robert J. Myers, "A Method of Automatically Adjusting the Maximum Earnings Base under OASDI," *The Journal of Risk and Insurance*, XXXI, No. 3 (September, 1964), 329–40. For discussions of this paper and the general subject of automatic changes, see the Communications section of *The Journal of Risk and Insurance*, XXXII, No. 3 (September, 1965), 465–73.

in the system; and (5) a fear that automatic benefit changes, in addition to weakening the contribution principle, would intensify swings in the business cycle.

Many people are surprised to find that a widowed mother receives benefits only until her youngest child entitled to benefits is eighteen and that a widow's benefit does not begin until age sixty. Some suggest the elimination of this gap but to do so would increase the cost of the system substantially. It would also mean that widows could claim benefits at a much earlier age than female workers, a situation that some would consider unfair. The 1965 amendments did liberalize the program slightly in this direction by the continuation of the child's benefit to age twenty-two for students and the reduction in the starting age for the widow's benefit from age sixty-two to age sixty.

Other controversial proposals would provide benefits for dependent sisters or for children who are supported by a worker who is not their parent, raise the widow's benefit to 100 per cent of the primary insurance amount, increase the number of dropout years in the benefit formula, reduce the ending point of the period for figuring a man's average monthly earnings from age sixty-five to age sixty-two, permit a wife to collect a benefit based on her own earnings record in addition to a dependent's benefit, and continue the mother's benefit if a child aged eighteen or over receives a benefit because he is attending school.

Loss of Benefits

The earnings test is another highly debatable issue. Those who favor granting retirement benefits to all eligible persons past the retirement age, regardless of their earnings, maintain that these persons have a pro-prietary interest in the benefit that is being denied and that the test reduces national output and OASDI contributions by forcing benefit recipients out of the labor force. The latter argument becomes more persuasive as the proportion of the aged in the population increases. The contrary view is that the benefit is designed to be paid only to those persons who have retired from full-time employment; none of the present retirement beneficiaries can claim that they have paid for all the benefits to which they would be entitled except for the earnings test; and removing the test would increase the cost substantially (about 10 per cent) in order to meet a relatively unimportant need. In addition, according to this view, the earnings test causes only a relatively small loss of national output because the current sliding-scale approach permits a reasonable amount of partial employment and because persons who are otherwise inclined to continue full-time employment are not likely to retire simply to receive retirement benefits that are much less than their current full-time earnings. Less extreme proposals would reduce the age at which the test does not apply or eliminate the test for a child's benefit or a mother's benefit.

Retirement Age

The retirement age itself has been the subject of some discussion. Some would permit early retirement without reducing the benefit, others would raise the retirement age, and still others would increase the benefit paid to those persons who retire after age sixty-five. Although some have argued that the gradually improving health status and educational level of the aged favor increasing the retirement age, automation and resulting unemployment among many older workers have created more effective pressures for reducing the minimum retirement age. Some authorities believe that permitting reduced retirement benefits at age sixty-two is a questionable way to handle the problem of workers forced out of the labor force by poor health or deteriorating employment opportunities because the benefits to which these people are entitled are likely to be inadequate. They urge further consideration of more liberal disability pension and extended unemployment benefits for this group.[30] The cost of paying unreduced benefits at age sixty-two or earlier would increase the cost of the system substantially. The proposal to increase the benefits for those who retire after age sixty-five has been supported or rejected with arguments similar to those advanced in connection with the earnings test.

Financing

Since OASDI benefits the entire population directly or indirectly and the vast majority are affected directly, it has been argued that the government should pay the entire cost of the program out of general tax revenues. As a result, high-income groups would bear a larger share of the cost of the program than they do at present and employers would have less reason to resort to labor-saving devices. However, the direct benefits of the program are so much more important than the indirect benefits that, it is argued, it would not be equitable to tax those persons who are not participants. Furthermore, an earmarked payroll is superior to a general revenue tax in that it emphasizes the cost of the benefits and supports the contributory principle. Chapter 14 further analyzes these matters, along with other economic issues.

[30] Margaret S. Gordon, *National Retirement Policies and the Displaced Older Worker,* Reprint No. 250 (Berkeley: Institute of Industrial Relations, University of California, 1965), p. 599.

A much stronger argument can be made for using a government contribution to pay the interest on the unfunded accrued liability, thus reducing the payroll tax to that which would be necessary if the system were to begin operations now and only new entrants into the labor force participated. The cost of benefits for new entrants would still be emphasized and the contributory principle would remain intact. Key questions that remain to be answered, however, are (1) whether it is more equitable to distribute the excess costs among the participants and their employers (who may be able to shift the tax to consumers and workers) through payroll taxes or among the total population through progressive federal income taxes and (2) what effect a change in the taxing method would have upon incentives, national output, and demands for more liberal OASDI benefits. Support for some contribution from general revenues has increased in recent years and may become a major issue in the next decade. General revenues have already been used in the new health insurance programs for persons aged sixty-five or over and to pay the cost of the special benefits to persons aged seventy-two and over who have not worked enough in covered employment to have earned any insured status.

The arguments advanced for and against a trust fund have not changed much since the late 1930's, but there seems to be more general agreement that because of the peculiar nature of a broad-coverage public fund, some departure from full reserve principles is desirable. Those who approve the present reserve system or would prefer to build an even larger trust fund argue that the maintenance of some trust funds reduces the tax burden of future generations, encourages more honest accounting concerning the cost of proposed benefit increases, increases the moral obligation of future Congresses to continue the benefits equal to at least the current level, and more adequately preserves the contribution principle in the system.

Those persons favoring a more complete pay-as-you-go system oppose a trust fund because they believe that the fund may be used as an argument in favor of further liberalizations in the law or because they consider the fund to be an unnecessary complication. They also fear that the taxes necessary to accumulate more than a contingency fund constitute a "fiscal drag" upon the economy. They counter the argument that a trust fund reduces the burden on future generations in three ways. First, they claim that the trust fund makes it possible for the government to borrow instead of taxing the present generation more heavily in other ways. Second, many of the public expenditures financed by the present generation (for example, those for national defense and education) will benefit future generations. Third, reducing the tax burden of future generations is not the only objective of a trust fund. If the payroll tax is lower in 2010 than it would have been without a trust fund, but there are no more goods and services than there would have been under a pay-as-you-go plan, the sole effect of the trust fund will be to improve slightly the position of the taxpayer relative to that of OASDI beneficiaries. A trust fund makes a real contribution to the economic welfare of future taxpayers only if it transfers funds from current consumption to investment, thus increasing production in the future. How effective the trust fund has been in this respect is a matter of conjecture.

The Advisory Council on Social Security reported in 1965 that the "social security program as a whole is soundly financed, its funds are properly invested, and on the basis of actuarial estimates that the Council has reviewed and found sound and appropriate, provision has been made to meet all of the costs of the program both in the short-run and over the long-range future." [31] They did suggest, however, that the trust funds be held to reasonable contingency levels, the interest on which would supply 4 to 5 per cent of benefit costs instead of the 10 to 15 per cent under the schedule in effect until 1966. Larger trust fund accumulations, they feared, would be too deflationary and, because the system is expected to operate indefinitely, were unnecessary. This is the philosophy that currently prevails.

Some authorities have questioned whether the outlook is this optimistic.[32] They maintain that the real test of social security financing is still to come when the tax burden increases and the windfall benefits disappear. These observers are especially disturbed by the fact that the value of the contributions by the average new entrant and his employer exceeds by far the value of his own benefits. As a result many younger workers can already obtain superior protection from *private* insurers for the taxes paid by them and by their employers. With the passage of time more people will find themselves in this situation. As more younger workers become aware of this fact and as the tax rate mounts, these people may rebel and may through their votes (1) act to suspend or reduce benefits under the system, (2) press for still higher benefits with no increase in taxes, thus compounding the problem, or (3) ask for support from general revenues. The situation will become even more acute

[31] "Report of the Advisory Council on Social Security," *op. cit.*, 29.
[32] Two interesting dissents are the following:
Ray M. Peterson, "Misconceptions and Missing Perceptions of our Social Security System (Actuarial Anesthesia)," *Transactions of the Society of Actuaries*, XI (November, 1959), 812–51 and the discussions and the author's reply, 852–919. Also see Peterson, *An Appraisal of the Social Security Amendments of 1965, op. cit.*
Frank G. Dickinson, "The Social Security Principle," *The Journal of Insurance*, XXVII, No. 4 (December, 1960). Dr. Dickinson proposes a tax rate that increases as the person ages. See also the discussion of this article by W. R. Williamson, R. M. Peterson, R. J. Myers, and F. G. Dickinson in *The Journal of Insurance*, XXVIII, No. 2 (June, 1961), 111–27.

when the "aging of the electorate" (i.e., the increase in the proportion of adults aged fifty or over that has occurred since 1900) is replaced by a "younging of the electorate" by the end of this century.[33]

In reply it has been argued that the fear concerning the future unwillingness of new entrants to pay taxes is unfounded for at least two reasons. First, OASDI participants are not generally aware of the benefit-cost factors involved, and, second, even if they were, the problem will not become acute until the cost to a very large number of persons exceeds that of equivalent private insurance.[34] Furthermore, insofar as their own contributions are concerned, most covered persons will pay less than the actuarial value of their benefits. The employer contributions are not and should not be allocated to individual employees since the social insurance system is designed to provide social adequacy rather than strict individual equity. Many private plans do not allocate the employer contributions to individual employees. Private plans also commonly recognize prior service in their benefit structure and there is often an unfunded accrued liability. Finally, the social adequacy feature of social insurance, which is one reason why some workers benefit less from OASDI than from private protection that could be purchased with their own and their employers' contributions, reduces public assistance costs and income taxes.

Only time will tell whether these fears are well-grounded. The observations do remind us, however, that there probably is some limit beyond which we cannot push the disparity between the value of the benefits and the tax rate without endangering the system or requiring support from general revenues. Many observers believe that for this reason new proposals for increased OASDI benefits are likely to authorize the use of general revenue funds.[35]

[33] Frank G. Dickinson, "The Century Cycle," *The Spectator*, CLXXIII, No. 10 (October, 1964), 47–48, 88–89. Dr. Dickinson argues that there are now two older voters for every three younger voters but that by 2000 this ratio will be cut in half. According to the population estimates presented in Table 2.6, the ratio will drop to one-half by 2000 and then begin to increase again. See Robert J. Myers, "The Population Explosion and the United States," *Journal of the American Society of Chartered Life Underwriters*, XX, No. 1 (Winter, 1966), 90–93.

[34] A third argument heard less often is that no private insurance contract provides equivalent protection. For example, OASDI benefits vary with the number of dependents. Furthermore, OASDI benefits are almost certain to be adjusted as prices and earnings rise.

[35] In anticipation of such a proposal, Roy M. Peterson, a private life insurance company actuary and a highly respected critic of many facets of OASDI, has advanced an interesting proposal in an unpublished memorandum dated June 16, 1966. In this memorandum Mr. Peterson suggests that OASDI tax rates be increased to finance any proposed benefit increases, that OASDI taxes be deductible from personal taxable income, and that OASDI benefits be included in taxable income. The contribution of general revenues would be the difference between the cost of deductible employee contributions and the revenue from taxing benefits.

The maximum earnings base also has tax implications because taxes can be increased by raising either the tax rates or the maximum earnings base. The impact of the increase is different, however, because lower-paid workers and employers in industries with lower-paid workers are much less affected by an increase in the earnings base. Another consideration is that as the taxable wage base rises, the amount of additional revenue produced by further increases becomes less and less. For example, removing the ceiling completely would produce additional revenue equal to less than 1 per cent of taxable payroll. Some additional views on the optimum size of this base have already been presented in the benefit evaluation section above.

In its 1965 report the Advisory Council on Social Security recommended that the ultimate rate for self-employed persons be no more than 1 per cent of earnings greater than the rate paid by employees. The Council "does not believe that self-employed workers should as a rule be charged rates for their own coverage beyond the rates needed to pay for the protection they are provided by the program in order to help meet the cost of the protection provided to others." [36] The employee rate plus 1 per cent would approximate the cost of the protection for a person covered by the system over a whole working lifetime at the maximum covered amount. Congress has not accepted this philosophy because of the loss of revenue and because many members believe that the present rate already represents a concession to self-employed persons who, as employers, should also contribute the cost of protection of others.

Administration

The administration of the system is highly mechanized and efficiently conducted. Administrative expenses in 1965 were about 2¼ per cent of the benefits paid. This excellent record may be due in part to the non-discretionary aspects of the program, but the federal civil service program is also contributory.

Economic implications of the program will be analyzed in greater detail in Chapter 14. The discussion now turns to private approaches to the economic problems of old age and premature death as they provide supplements to the floor of protection afforded by the social security system.

SUMMARY

Old-Age, Survivors, and Disability Insurance is a social insurance program established under the Social Security Act of 1935. Unlike the pub-

[36] "Report of the Advisory Council on Social Security," *op. cit.,* 13.

lic assistance programs, OASDI is entirely federally supported and, except with respect to disability benefits, federally administered.

Except for some special benefits payable to persons aged seventy-two and over even though they did not work in covered employment, in order to receive OASDI retirement or survivorship benefits, which are the only ones discussed in this chapter, a person must be either "fully insured," "currently insured," or both. Fully insured persons are eligible for most of the survivorship and retirement benefits while currently insured persons are eligible only for some of the survivorship benefits.

The basic benefit is a retirement benefit for an insured person at age sixty-five with reduced benefits available as early as age sixty-two. The benefit formula is a compromise between the desire to provide a floor of protection for all families and the desire to preserve some relationship between taxable earnings and benefits.

The benefits for the dependents of a retired worker are a life income to the wife after age sixty-two, income to a mother until her youngest child is age eighteen, income until age eighteen for children unless they are attending school in which case the benefit is continued until age twenty-two, and a life income to the dependent husband of a retired female worker after age sixty-two.

The death benefits are a life income for a widow after age sixty or a dependent widower after age sixty-two, income to a mother until her youngest child reaches age eighteen, income for children until age eighteen or, if the child is attending school, until age twenty-two, a life income to dependent parents after age sixty-two, and a lump-sum death benefit.

The most important reason for a reduction in benefits is annual earnings by a beneficiary in excess of $1,500.

Except for the special minimum benefits for persons aged seventy-two or over, OASDI benefits are financed entirely by a payroll tax paid by the worker and his employer. The 1967–68 tax rate on each is 3.90 per cent on the first $6,600 of the employee's earnings. Self-employed persons pay 5.9 per cent. Tax rates are scheduled to increase until 1973 but this schedule can be changed by Congress, as in the past.

The most important liberalizations of OASDI since its introduction in 1935 have been the addition of the survivorship benefits, benefits for dependents of retired workers, disability benefits (see Chapter 11), the health insurance benefits for persons aged sixty-five or over, the extension of coverage to more employments, the reduction of the eligibility requirements, and increases in all benefit amounts.

Arguments over the purpose and desirability of the trust fund have been frequent, extensive, and continuing.

OASDI has not replaced the special public assistance programs, but it has reduced their relative importance.

SUGGESTIONS FOR ADDITIONAL READING

CORSON, JOHN J., and JOHN W. MCCONNELL. *Economic Needs of Older People.* New York: The Twentieth Century Fund, 1956.
Chapters 6 through 8 present an analysis of both old-age assistance and social insurance for the aged. Chapters 9 through 11 present useful data on private pension plans.

HABER, WILLIAM, and WILBUR J. COHEN (eds.). *Social Security: Programs, Problems, and Policies.* Homewood, Ill.: Richard D. Irwin, Inc., 1960.
This book of selected readings contains several excellent articles dealing with the topics covered in this chapter.

MERRIAM, IDA C. *Social Security Financing.* (Bureau Report No. 17.) Washington, D. C.: Federal Security Agency, Social Security Administration, 1952.
The various ways in which social security programs can be financed are discussed in this report.

MYERS, ROBERT J. *Social Insurance and Allied Government Programs.* Homewood, Ill.: Richard D. Irwin, Inc., 1965.
Chapters 3 through 10 provide an authoritative discussion of OASDI by the Chief Actuary of the Social Security Administration. Chapter 8 presents the methodology for OASDI actuarial cost estimates.

Report to the President of the Committee on Economic Security. Washington, D. C.: U. S. Government Printing Office, 1935.
The committee report which led to the passage of the original Social Security Act.

TASK FORCE ON ECONOMIC GROWTH AND OPPORTUNITY. *Poverty: The Sick, Disabled, and Aged.* Washington, D. C.: Chamber of Commerce of the United States, 1965.
A recent report by a Chamber of Commerce Task Force that includes several suggestions for improving OASDI, including blanketing-in all aged persons.

U. S. DEPARTMENT OF HEALTH, EDUCATION, AND WELFARE. *Annual Report.* Washington, D. C.: U. S. Government Printing Office, latest edition.
The annual reports of the Department comment on the current operations of the special state public assistance programs and OASDI.

U. S. HOUSE OF REPRESENTATIVES. Executive Hearings Before the Committee on Ways and Means, 89th Congress, 1st Session. *H. R. 1 and Other Proposals for Medical Care for the Aged.* Washington, D. C.: U. S. Government Printing Office, 1965.

U. S. SENATE. Hearings Before the Committee on Finance, 89th Congress, 1st Session. *Social Security.* Washington, D. C.: U. S. Government Printing Office, 1965.
Hearings on the latest amendments to the Social Security Act. Earlier hearings before these two committees on the Social Security Act are also valuable references.

5
Private Approaches:
Death and Old Age

INTRODUCTION

OASDI provides a floor of protection against financial problems caused by premature death and old age. The coverage is extended on a compulsory basis and the benefits are paid for through taxes. OASDI does not, and should not, provide complete protection against these problems, for it is generally agreed that the complete elimination of individual responsibility would affect adversely the moral and mental fiber of our population. Therefore, the individual who wants more than a floor of protection must supplement OASDI with private alleviative methods.

Private methods of alleviating the financial losses caused by premature death and old age were discussed in Chapter 2. Private insurance, which is easily the most important of these methods, is the subject of this chapter.

We shall first consider individual life insurance and annuity contracts issued by commercial insurers. The nature and uses of the basic types of contracts and some important special contracts will be discussed. The possible stumbling block of uninsurability will also be considered.

The second part of the chapter deals with group life insurance and group pension plans. Group life insurance is primarily underwritten by commercial insurers, but group pension plans are commonly underwritten by both commercial insurers and employers or unions. We shall trace very briefly the historical development of group insurance and pensions and note their distinctive features and contributions to economic security.

INDIVIDUAL INSURANCE

Most of the private insurance in force today is purchased by persons acting as individuals. The responsibility for purchasing the insurance and paying the premiums is almost always the insured's. Ideally the protection is tailor-made to meet the insured's needs and desires.

Types of Life Insurance Contracts

Individual insurance contracts may protect the insured or his dependents against financial losses caused by premature death, old age, or both.

Term insurance is the simplest form of life insurance. If the insured dies during the term of the policy, the face amount of the policy is paid to his beneficiary. If he does not die, the insurer pays nothing. The period of a term insurance policy may be any number of years such as one year, five years, ten years, twenty years, or the years to age sixty-five.

Because there is no savings element in the term policy, the premium is relatively low. For this reason, term insurance is an excellent temporary form of protection against premature death. For example, term insurance may be purchased so as to complete the payments on a mortgage were the insured to die before the mortgage has been paid off. A person who will be currently insured under OASDI in a few months may purchase term insurance to protect his family in the interim. A young man with excellent prospects but little current income may purchase term insurance to protect his family in the early years of marriage.

One of the major disadvantages of term insurance is that the protection terminates at the end of the period. This would not be important in the first and second examples cited above, but it would be extremely important in the third example because the need for protection continues and the insured may become uninsurable before the end of the term. However, term insurance policies are available that are renewable at least once without evidence of insurability. Each time the policy is renewed, the premium is increased because the probability of death increases. The premiums charged by one non-participating life insurer [1]

---

[1] About 56 per cent of the life insurance in force is written by mutual insurers, while about one-sixth of the insurance issued by stock insurers is written on a participating basis. This means that under about 64 per cent of the life insurance in force, dividends to policyholders must be subtracted from the premiums paid in order to determine the actual cost of continuing the insurance in force.

Participating insurers typically charge a higher initial premium than non-participating insurers, but the dividends will determine whether the actual cost of continuing the contract will be more, the same, or less.

Non-participating premiums as of 1965 are quoted in this text because they are actual cost figures. A fair illustration of the cost of continuing participating contracts would require dividend estimates as well as a table of the initial premiums.

TABLE 5.1

Annual Premium Rates Charged by One Non-participating Life Insurer
for $10,000 Five-Year Renewable Term Insurance *

Age	Premium per $1,000	Age	Premium per $1,000
20	$5.08	45	$10.88
25	5.13	50	15.74
30	5.48	55	22.05
35	6.58		
40	8.28		

* Minimum policy amount issued is $5,000. Premium rates decrease as the policy amount increases. For example, the premium rate at age 35 is $7.38 per $1,000 insurance for a $5,000 policy and $6.18 if the policy amount is $20,000.

for its five-year renewable term insurance contracts are presented in Table 5.1. At the advanced ages, the premiums are so high that the policy will probably be dropped or at least reduced. However, if the term insurance is also convertible, it may be converted within a specified period to a non-term contract as of the original date of issue or at the attained age.

The basic non-term contracts are *the straight life contract, the limited payment life contract, and the endowment contract.* Under the first two contracts, called whole-life contracts, the insurer promises to pay the face amount when the insured dies. The two contracts differ from one another in that under the straight life contract the insured pays premiums until death, but under the limited payment life contract the insured pays premiums until death or until the expiration of a stated period, if earlier. Examples of limited payment contracts are twenty-payment, thirty-payment, and paid-up at sixty-five contracts. Under an endowment contract the insurer promises to pay the face amount immediately if the insured dies within the endowment period *or* at the end of the period if the insured is still living. Examples of endowment contracts are twenty-year endowments, thirty-year endowments, and endowments at age sixty. Premiums charged for four principal non-term contracts by the same non-participating insurer whose term insurance rates have been quoted in Table 5.1 are presented in Table 5.2.

If a male insured continues the protection from age twenty-five to age sixty, he will pay out $3,707 to protect his family under a $10,000 five-year renewable term insurance policy issued by this insurer. The premiums on a straight life policy would total $4,746. However, this comparison is unfair, for possible interest earnings are ignored. If the premiums could have been invested at 3 per cent interest after taxes, compounded annually, the true cost of continuing the term protection is $5,666, while the straight life policy would cost him $8,445.

TABLE 5.2

Annual Premium Rates Charged Males by One Non-participating Life Insurer for $10,000 Straight Life, Limited Payment, and Endowment Contracts *

| | Type of Contract | | | |
Age	Straight Life	Twenty-Payment	Paid-up at Sixty-five	Twenty-Year Endowment
20	$11.76	$20.57	$13.51	$43.83
25	13.56	22.94	15.78	43.98
30	15.86	25.73	18.80	44.28
35	18.82	29.03	22.97	44.89
40	22.76	32.95	28.78	46.00
50	33.82	43.32	51.87	50.77
60	52.92	59.50	——	62.09

* Rates decrease as the amount of insurance increases. For example, at age 35 a $5,000 straight life policy would cost $19.62 per $1,000 insurance. The rate for a $20,000 policy would be $18.42. Females pay lower rates. For example, the rates for $5,000, $10,000, and $20,000 straight life insurance policies issued to a female, aged 35, are $17.76, $16.96, and $16.56, respectively.

On the other hand, there is one very important difference between non-term insurance contracts and term insurance contracts. Under non-term contracts, the insurer accumulates at a guaranteed interest rate the differences between the level-premium and the insured's share each year of the expected death benefits and administrative expenses. This accumulation process accomplishes two objectives. First, the cost of paying death benefits does not increase as rapidly as the mortality rate because the increasing accumulations are part of the face amount paid the beneficiary and the "net amount at risk" (the face amount less the accumulation) decreases. In fact, except during the first year or two, when the administrative expenses are high, the level premium less the insured's share of the expenses plus the interest credited for the year is always more than enough to pay the insured's share of the expected benefits for that year. Consequently the accumulations continue to grow.

Second, the insured may claim these accumulations (called non-forfeiture values) at any time. For example, he may elect to retire at age sixty-five and use the accumulations to help finance his retirement. There are usually three non-forfeiture options. The insured may elect to take the accumulations in cash, use them as a single premium to purchase paid-up insurance, or use them as a single premium to purchase extended term insurance. The paid-up insurance is a policy of the same type as the original contract in a reduced amount. The extended term insurance provides the original amount of protection for a limited number of years.[2] For example, under the $10,000 straight life policy for which the premium has been quoted, the insured may at age sixty stop paying premiums and obtain $4,900 in cash, have $7,750 of insurance protection continued for life, or have $10,000 of insurance protection continued for about sixteen years.

The amount of the cash value at the end of each policy year depends upon the type of contract, the age at issue, and the actuarial assumptions made by the insurer. Under all non-term contracts, the cash value continues to grow throughout the life of the contract, but the pattern of growth differs by policy type. Under a straight life contract, the cash value grows steadily until it equals the face value at age 100. The cash value must equal the face value at this age, for insurance actuaries have assumed in their premium calculations that no one will live beyond age 100.

Under a limited payment life contract, the cash value grows more rapidly during the premium-paying period because the premiums are higher. The cash value continues to grow at a less rapid pace after the premium-paying period because the interest on the cash value is more than is required to pay the insured's share of the benefits which the insurer expects to have to pay to the beneficiaries of the deceaseds. At age 100 the cash value equals the face value for the reason already cited.

Under an endowment contract, the cash value grows very rapidly and equals the face amount at the end of the endowment period. In a sense, the straight life and limited payment life contracts are endowments at age 100.

Thus, in addition to providing protection against financial losses caused by premature death, all non-term insurance contracts help the insured to acquire a retirement fund through a systematic savings plan.

Methods of Paying Proceeds

The death proceeds under life insurance contracts are payable in a lump sum or according to some settlement option selected by the insured or his beneficiary. An increasing number of insurers also permit the insured to select some settlement option if he wishes to surrender the policy for cash before his death.

The four most common settlement options are the following:

---

2 If the original contract is an endowment contract, the extended term insurance does not run beyond the maturity date of the original endowment contract. If the cash value is more than the premium required for term insurance to the maturity date, the excess is used to purchase a promise that some reduced amount will be paid to those who live to the maturity date.

1. Interest option. The proceeds are left with the insurer for some specified period and interest payments are made to the beneficiary. The beneficiary may or may not have the right to withdraw part or all of the principal.
2. Fixed amount option. The beneficiary receives a specified monthly income for as many months as the proceeds and the interest on the unpaid balance will afford.
3. Fixed period option. The beneficiary receives for a specified period a monthly income of whatever amount the proceeds and the interest on the unpaid balance will afford.
4. Annuity option. An annuity payable under this option may take one of several forms. It may be a straight life annuity under which the insurer promises to pay the beneficiary a monthly income for life. Usually, however, it is either an instalment refund annuity, a cash refund annuity, or an annuity with a period certain.

   Under an instalment refund annuity, the payments are continued during the lifetime of the beneficiary, but if the annuitant should die before the annuity payments have equalled the proceeds, the payments are continued to another beneficiary until this equality is achieved. A cash refund annuity differs from the instalment refund annuity only in that upon death of the beneficiary the difference, if any, between the proceeds and the sum of the monthly payments is paid in cash to another beneficiary. Under an annuity with a period certain, the insurer promises to pay a monthly income for life, but the income is guaranteed for at least a specified period.

For proceeds of a given amount, the monthly income differs depending upon the option selected because of the differences in the guaranteed amounts and the loss of interest for varying periods. The annuities with some guaranteed amounts are a wise choice when dependents survive the beneficiary, but the price is a reduced monthly income for the beneficiary.

A table of settlement options appearing in one insurance contract is reproduced as Table 5.3. The values presented in the table are the minimum amounts this insurer promises to pay; actual payments may exceed these amounts depending upon the insurer's investment experience. These options are useful because they enable the insured to have the proceeds paid in the manner he deems best. He may or may not give the beneficiary the right to change the program he sets up. If the insured does not elect any options, the beneficiary may usually elect them. The options provide a safe investment, with at least a guaranteed rate of interest and no management problems. The present tax code also favors their use. Only the interest portion of the income is taxable and, except under the interest option, spouses have a $1,000 federal income tax exemption applicable to this interest.

TABLE 5.3

Settlement Option Values Used by One Insurer

Fixed Instalment Options		Monthly Life Income per $1,000 Proceeds				
Number of Years	Monthly Income per $1,000 Proceeds	Age		Five Years Certain	Ten Years Certain	Fifteen Years Certain
		Male	Female			
5	$17.70	35	40	$3.34	$3.33	$3.32
10	9.39	40	45	3.60	3.59	3.56
15	6.64	45	50	3.95	3.92	3.87
20	5.27	50	55	4.38	4.32	4.22
25	4.46	55	60	4.92	4.81	4.64
30	3.93	60	65	5.62	5.42	5.10

If the settlement option privilege also applies to cash values, the insured may usually elect a joint and survivorship annuity. This annuity provides a specified income per month during the lifetime of two beneficiaries plus a reduced income during the lifetime of the survivor. For example, a husband and wife may receive $100 a month, with $66.67 a month being paid to the surviving spouse.

When the settlement options may be applied to both death proceeds and living benefits such as cash values and matured endowments, nonterm insurance contracts provide comprehensive protection against the financial problems associated with both premature death and old age. For example, an insured may purchase a straight life contract to protect his family and at retirement age have the cash value converted into a lifetime income. When the options may not be applied to living benefits, the only contribution to old-age protection is the accumulation of a retirement fund.

Settlement Options and Planning an Insurance Program

One of the important uses of a table of settlement options is the determination of the amount of insurance that is needed to carry out the desires of the insured. A highly simplified example follows. Assume that a young man, aged thirty-five, has a wife, aged thirty-five, and a son, aged three. If this young man were to die today, how much insurance would be required to provide the following benefits for his family? Assume that his needs are as follows:

$2,000 for taxes and funeral expenses;
$200 a month for the widow and child until the child reaches age eighteen; and
$100 a month for life for the widow after the child reaches age eighteen.

In order to simplify the problem, assume that the young man is not entitled to OASDI benefits [3] and that all of the family needs are to be met through the purchase of new private insurance. In actual practice, the benefits provided under social insurance programs, existing private insurance, and other resources such as savings accounts are deducted from the family needs in order to determine the need for new private insurance.

One way of paying out life insurance proceeds that would provide the desired benefits is the following:

$2,000 in a lump sum;
$100 a month according to the settlement option that provides a lifetime income for the widow beginning at age fifty; and
$200 a month during the fifteen years following death composed of two parts: (1) interest payments on the amount held at interest until age fifty to provide the lifetime income beginning at that age and (2) the remainder according to a fixed instalment option.

If the settlement option values in Table 5.3 are applicable [4] and the monthly amount payable under the interest option is $2 per $1,000 of insurance, the following amounts of insurance will be needed in addition to the $2,000 lump sum:

$$\frac{\$100}{\$3.87}\text{ [5]} \times \$1,000 = \$26,000, \text{ approximately; and}$$

since $26,000 at interest provides $52 a month during the fifteen years following death, a remainder of

$$\frac{\$148}{\$6.64} \times \$1,000 = \$22,000, \text{ approximately.}$$

The total insurance required is close to $50,000.

In actual practice the problem is far more complicated and the solution much more thorough. It is necessary to recognize changes over time, retirement needs, tax factors, existing social insurance, private insurance and non-insurance assets, and many other factors. Several solutions are possible and the particular circumstances and desires of the insured

[3] This is an important assumption in this instance because the mother and son could receive as much as $255 in a lump sum, $252 a month until the son reaches eighteen years of age, $126 a month while the son is in school and is aged eighteen, nineteen, twenty, and twenty-one, and $139 a month after the widow reaches age sixty-two.
[4] The reader is reminded that these values are *minimum* amounts.
[5] Because the difference between the five- and fifteen-year certain amounts is so small at this age, the fifteen-year certain amount was selected. The insurance required under the five-year certain assumption would have been $25,000. Theoretically a straight life annuity would be sufficient but this form is not generally provided by this insurer and in any event the difference would be small.

determine which is best. Considerable skill is required in order to construct a satisfactory program. The example, however, illustrates valid insurance planning principles.

Annuity Contracts

Life insurers issue annuities as separate contracts in addition to those issued as supplementary contracts under the settlement option provisions. These separate contracts may be classified into two major groups—immediate annuities and deferred annuities. The emphasis in these contracts is upon financial preparation for old age.

Under an immediate annuity, the annuitant pays the insurer a lump sum and receives a monthly income for life under one of the annuity forms discussed in connection with settlement options. The savings may be accumulated through some method other than insurance.

The more common type of annuity is the deferred annuity under which a person normally pays premiums from the issue date to the retirement date, at which time the insurer begins to pay him a monthly income according to the terms of one of the various annuity forms. Under a pure deferred annuity, no benefit is paid if the insured dies prior to reaching retirement age, but few contracts of this type are issued. Usually the premiums, or, if higher, the cash value is refunded in case of death.

An important recent development is the variable annuity contract. A variable annuity differs from a conventional annuity in that (1) the premiums are usually invested entirely in equities and (2) at the retirement date the insured is promised a fixed number of units each month for the remainder of his life instead of a fixed number of dollars. The value of each unit fluctuates with the performance of the invested assets. Because equities tend to rise and fall in value as consumers' prices rise and fall, the variable income tends to provide constant real purchasing power. However, because equities tend to fluctuate more in value than consumers' prices, it is recommended and sometimes required that an equal amount be invested in a conventional annuity. In 1952 New York granted permission to a special insurer, which restricts its policies to staff members of colleges, private schools, foundations, and research organizations, to issue the first variable annuity.[6] This special permission was required because of (1) statutory restrictions on the proportion of a life insurer's assets that could be invested in equities and (2) doubt concerning whether authority to underwrite annuities included variable annuities. Until 1963, the only other insurers to issue variable annuities were a few

[6] For a discussion of the variable annuity concept, see William C. Greenough, "Pensions—Meeting Price Level Changes," *Pensions: Problems and Trends* (Homewood, Ill.: Richard D. Irwin, Inc., 1955), pp. 138–60.

companies organized specifically to issue this product. None of the leading life insurers issued a variable annuity until that year because of (1) strong differences of opinion within and outside the insurance business concerning the desirability of this product, (2) state legal barriers, and (3) some requirements imposed by the Securities and Exchange Commission. In that year, the SEC granted a "no-action" letter to one major insurer in connection with a variable annuity contract written on a group basis. Insurers can now write group variable annuities in many states; only a few have done so, but their number is expected to increase. Because of continuing legal obstacles, the future of individual variable annuities is less certain but more insurers will probably also enter this field.

Special Life Insurance and Annuity Contracts

Numerous modifications and combinations of term insurance contracts, basic non-term insurance contracts, and annuities are sold by insurers. The reader is referred to any standard text on life insurance for a detailed discussion of these contracts and life insurance in general.[7] However, a few special contracts are so important in the search for economic security that they merit a brief description here.

1. Under a *modified life contract*, the protection is for life, but the premium is less in the first three or five years and higher thereafter.
2. A *family income contract* is a whole life contract plus decreasing term insurance. If the insured dies within some specified family income period, such as ten or twenty years, the insurer will pay a monthly income of usually $10 or $20 per $1,000 of whole life protection until the expiration of what remains of that family income period. The face value of the whole life policy is payable at the end of the period. If the insured lives to the end of the family income period, the decreasing term insurance expires and the policy continues as a whole life policy. The family income policy is especially designed for a young man with a family whose need for protection is greatest when his children are young.
3. A *family policy* covers all members of a family under one contract. The most common combination is $5,000 of whole life or endow-

[7] For example, see J. B. Maclean, *Life Insurance* (9th ed.; New York: McGraw-Hill Book Co., 1962); R. I. Mehr and R. W. Osler, *Modern Life Insurance* (3rd ed.; New York: The Macmillan Co., 1961); S. S. Huebner and K. Black, *Life Insurance* (6th ed.; New York: Appleton-Century-Crofts, 1964); D. McGill, *Life Insurance* (Homewood, Ill.: Richard D. Irwin, Inc., 1959); and D. Gregg (ed.), *Life and Health Insurance Handbook* (2nd ed.; Homewood, Ill.: Richard D. Irwin, Inc., 1964). For a detailed discussion in a general insurance text see R. Riegel and J. Miller, *Insurance Principles and Practices* (5th ed.; Englewood Cliffs, N. J.: Prentice-Hall, Inc., 1966).

ment insurance on the husband, $1,000 or $1,250 term insurance to age sixty-five on the wife, and $1,000 term insurance to age twenty-one on the children, including children born after the contract becomes effective.

4. A *retirement income annuity* is a deferred annuity plus decreasing term insurance. For each $10 of monthly income provided at retirement age by the annuity, there is a promise that $1,000 will be paid to the beneficiary if this amount exceeds the cash value.

5. *Preferred risk policies* or *specials* are usually straight life contracts or contracts paid up at some very advanced age which are sold at reduced rates because applicants must meet superior underwriting standards or, what is more likely, because they are sold only above certain minimum amounts with subsequent expense savings. Specials have decreased in importance since the introduction of quantity discounts such as those indicated in Tables 5.1 and 5.2. Until 1956 it was illegal to apply quantity discounts to all policies because insurers were not permitted to discriminate among insureds according to policy size. Since the policy type sold as a special was not available on a regular basis, the use of specials was considered to be discrimination by policy type and not by size.

6. A *guaranteed insurability rider* attached to a life insurance policy gives the insured the right to purchase additional insurance at specified ages at standard rates. In other words, the insured is protected against loss of his insurability.

Branches of Individual Insurance

The most important branch of individual insurance sold by commercial insurers is the ordinary insurance branch. These policies are written in amounts of $1,000 or more; premiums are designed to be paid annually but may be paid semi-annually, quarterly, or monthly; and all premiums other than the first are paid directly to the branch or home office of the insurer.

Another branch of commercial life insurance, which is declining rapidly in relative importance, is industrial insurance. "Industrial" policies have provisions which differ slightly from those in ordinary policies and are usually written in amounts of $1,000 or less. In most cases, premiums are collected weekly or monthly at the home of the insured. The premiums are higher than the premiums for equivalent ordinary insurance, primarily because of the collection service. This insurance is designed to appeal to low-income groups.

Contracts similar to those sold by commercial insurers are issued by fraternal societies in all states and by mutual savings banks in Connecticut, Massachusetts, and New York.

Insurance in Force, 1910–65

The spectacular growth in the total amount of private individual life insurance and the increasingly important role played by commercial ordinary insurance are illustrated by the data in Table 5.4.

TABLE 5.4

Individual Life Insurance in Force in the United States, 1910–65

(In Millions)

Year	Commercial Insurance *		Fraternals	Mutual Savings Banks †
	Ordinary	Industrial		
1910	$ 11,783	$ 3,125	$ 8,596	$ 1
1915	16,650	4,279	9,444	4
1920	32,018	6,948	10,500	15
1925	52,892	12,318	10,289	38
1930	78,576	17,963	9,539	77
1935	70,684	17,471	6,719	110
1940	79,346	20,866	6,676	203
1945	101,550	27,675	7,422	331
1950	149,071	33,415	8,811	580
1955	216,600	39,682	10,507	860
1960	340,268	39,563	14,235	1,243
1965	497,630	39,818	16,316	2,110

* Individual credit life insurance issued through a lending agency to cover payment of a debt in case of death is not included in these data. In 1965 individual credit life insurance in force was $7,690 million. In 1950 the corresponding figure was only $720 million.

† Insurance in force for mutual savings banks includes some group insurance in recent years.

Sources: Institute of Life Insurance, *Life Insurance Fact Book, 1966*, pp. 19, 103; U. S. Department of Labor, Bureau of Labor Statistics, "Operation of Savings Bank Life Insurance in Massachusetts and New York," *Revision of Bulletin 615*, 1941; Alfred M. Best Co., *Best's Life Insurance Reports* (New York: 1941 and 1946).

Almost all individual annuity contracts are sold by commercial insurers. The amount of annual income to be provided at maturity date under individual commercial annuity contracts increased from $375 million in 1935 to about $622 million in 1954. Individual annuities then declined in importance until 1961 when the annual income to be provided at maturity was reduced to $564 million. This decline, compared with the rapid growth of life insurance in force, was due in part to the tremendous increase in group annuities to be discussed later and in part to the threat of inflation. This decline was also one of the reasons for the interest in the variable annuity discussed earlier. Since 1961 individual annuities have regained some of their popularity as insurers have increased the rate of return earned on their invested funds. At year-end 1965, the annual income at maturity under individual annuities in force was $669 million.[8]

Types of Contracts in Force

In Table 5.5 the ordinary life insurance contracts in force at the end of 1950, 1957, and 1962 are analyzed according to contract type. Basic non-term insurance contracts accounted for about 60 per cent of the insurance in force. Clearly, most of the insurance in force is designed to protect the insureds against financial losses caused by both premature death and old age. However, contracts providing protection only against premature death, particularly decreasing term insurance and family income policies, are becoming increasingly important.

TABLE 5.5

Ordinary Life Insurance Contracts in Force in the United States, by Type of Contract, 1950, 1957, and 1962

Type of Contract	Per Cent of Total		
	1950	1957	1962
Straight life	37.2	36.7	37.7
Limited payment life	25.3	20.4	16.9
Endowment	15.0	9.7	7.1
Retirement income annuity	5.8	4.1	2.4
Term			
Regular	⎰4.6	4.9	5.1
Decreasing	⎱	2.8	4.1
Extended term	1.2	1.5	1.7
Family policies			
Non-term	—	1.9	5.0
Term	—	1.5	3.7
Other combination policies			
Non-term	⎰11.1	7.0	6.8
Term	⎱	9.5	9.5
Total	100.0	100.0	100.0

Source: Institute of Life Insurance, *Life Insurance Fact Book, 1966*, p. 25.

Uninsurability

An individual must be insurable from the viewpoint of the insurer before he can obtain a policy. The sources of information consulted by

[8] Institute of Life Insurance, *Life Insurance Fact Book, 1966*, p. 33.

an insurance underwriter are the prospective insured's application, the agent's statement, an inspection bureau's report, and, in about two out of three cases the results of a medical examination by a doctor. If there is no medical examination, a detailed non-medical form must be completed. Personal history, family history, physical condition, and personal habits are considered in making the underwriting decision.

No one knows how many persons fail to apply for insurance because they or their agents know that they are uninsurable, but data are available that indicate how many applicants are refused insurance because of the underwriting requirements. Only 3 per cent of the applications received in 1962 for ordinary life insurance were declined by the insurers.[9] Six per cent were rated substandard, chiefly because of physical impairments or hazardous occupations, and as a result usually paid higher premiums than the standard lives. Over the years, underwriting restrictions have been liberalized.

Hence, individual insurance is a readily available form of protection against the economic insecurities of premature death and is an important part of the American economic security system.

GROUP LIFE INSURANCE AND PENSIONS

Development

Group life insurance and pensions provided at the place of employment have played an increasingly important role in the average American's search for economic security. The characteristics of group life insurance and pensions are discussed in detail later in this chapter, but first we shall look at some of the historical background.[10]

At the turn of the century, the social and economic status of the average worker was far from Utopian, as will be noted in Chapter 15. Most workers were expected to solve the problems caused by death, disability, and old age on their own, but few were financially able to do so. Some workers, however, belonged to mutual benefit associations which provided small benefits in case of death or disability. These associations included the employees of a given firm or the members of a trade union. Participation was almost always voluntary, and many workers did not join even though they were eligible. Employees usually managed the plans, with the employer contributing directly to the cost in about one-third of the plans. The employer contributed indirectly to the cost of

---

[9] *Ibid.*, p. 91.

[10] See Louise Wolters Ilse, *Group Insurance and Employee Retirement Plans* (Englewood Cliffs, N. J.: Prentice-Hall, Inc., 1953) and *Private and Public Pension Plans in the United States* (New York: Institute of Life Insurance, 1963).

other plans by performing some of the administrative duties or permitting employees to handle them on company time.[11]

Very few employees, other than railroad workers, received company pensions when they retired. Most of the pension plans that did exist were informal plans, with the amount and duration of each pension being determined by the employer at the date of retirement. Pensions were paid out of current income and varied with that income. There were a few formal pension plans that contained a formula for determining the benefit, but there was no guarantee that the given pension might not be discontinued. Since these pension funds also operated on a pay-as-you-go basis or, at best, with a partial reserve, the discontinuance or reduction of these benefits was a distinct possibility, and often happened.

Because each of the mutual benefit associations and pension funds covered a small number of persons, the benefit payments tended to vary greatly from year to year. This was especially noticeable in the case of death and disability, and many of the mutual benefit associations either failed or faced financial difficulties because of adverse loss experience in a single year.

In 1910 Montgomery Ward and Company decided to increase the death and disability benefits provided by its mutual benefit association. The company was concerned about possible unstable loss experience and thought that this risk could be eliminated by insuring the benefits with a commercial insurer. The negotiations with insurers were lengthy because the idea was novel, but an insurance contract was finally issued in 1912.[12] All employees at Chicago and Kansas City who had worked for the company for at least six months were covered, regardless of their individual insurability status. The company paid the entire premium. Because of the savings involved in wholesaling the benefits, the cost of the group protection was less than that of equivalent individual insurance contracts.

During this period, employers were becoming increasingly interested in providing death and disability protection for their employees, and the new group life insurance and group health insurance contracts appealed to them. Several reasons have been advanced to explain this employer interest in welfare benefits. Some argue that employers became more humanitarian and wanted to improve the lot of the workers for unselfish reasons. Others believe that selfish motives predominated. According to the latter, employers began to realize that a worker is more productive if he does not have to worry about possible or actual financial losses caused by death and poor health; he develops loyalty to the firm; and he is less likely to leave the firm or to strike against the employer. Still

[11] Ilse, *Group Insurance and Employee Retirement Plans, op. cit.,* p. 24.
[12] See *ibid.,* chap. ii, for a more detailed discussion.

others believe that employers were aware of the developing trends and attempted to wrest the initiative from labor leaders. Certainly, not all employers had the same motives, and many were probably motivated by all three factors. Part of the movement also can be credited to the salesmanship of the insurance industry.

Labor unions initially opposed the new group insurance idea as an example of paternalism that would destroy the union movement. Fraternals and a large segment of the commercial insurance industry also questioned the soundness of the idea, because there was no individual underwriting. They also argued that the contracts were discriminatory, threatened the continued existence of individual insurance, and emphasized term insurance, which they considered to be unsatisfactory except in special instances. The press and the general public, however, were generally sympathetic to the plan.

In order to assure sound underwriting and placate opposition in the insurance industry, many states passed legislation which limited the conditions under which group insurance could be written, and listed certain provisions the sense of which had to be included in every group insurance contract. Unions generally remained opposed to employer-sponsored benefits, but in the twenties many unions began to insure their own members under group insurance plans, in some cases forming their own insurance companies to underwrite the plans.

In 1926 the Amalgamated Association of Street and Electric Railway Employees became the first union to introduce life and disability insurance into a collective bargaining agreement.[13] Although in later years collective bargaining agreements were to become a most important force in the growth of group insurance, until the forties most unions preferred to press directly for higher wages, shorter hours, and improved working conditions, and not for these "fringes."

The pension movement also grew, but much less rapidly. Over 200 new plans, all of which were self-insured, were established between 1910 and 1920. Pension costs, of course, were much higher than the cost of other fringe benefits. The growth in pension plans that did occur was due to the increased employer interest already discussed. However, in connection with pensions, two additional reasons for this employer interest should be added to the list. First, pension plans made it possible to retire older persons in a more graceful fashion when their usefulness declined. Second, the promotion lanes were continually being opened up for younger employees and their incentives increased as a result.

Shortly after 1920, some employers, impressed by the success of the group life insurers, agreed to insure their pension plans on a group basis with commercial insurers. The major advantage to be gained through

13 *Ibid.*, p. 339.

such an approach was the contractual guarantee of the insurer.[14] In the late twenties insured pension plans became popular, and during the thirties and early forties most of the new pension plans were insured plans.

During World War II, there was a tremendous increase in the importance of group life insurance, group health insurance, and pension plans. Wage increases were limited under the wartime government stabilization program, but welfare benefits customarily were not. Therefore, many employers, on their own or, more commonly, through collective bargaining, substituted insurance benefits for wage increases. The high excess profits tax structure reduced the actual cost to employers. Employees also benefited taxwise because the employer's contributions to a plan qualified with the Internal Revenue Service were not considered taxable income to the employees.[15]

This growth continued after the war as many of the larger unions pressed for and obtained welfare benefits clauses in their collective bargaining agreements. Pensions were highlighted in these union demands. Some unions argued that the depreciation and obsolescence of manpower are proper charges on industry. (This argument, incidentally, has been attacked on the grounds that a man ages even if he does not work.) A more common and more powerful argument advanced by the unions held that pensions are deferred wages. Current wages are reduced in order to provide pension benefits. However, unions were willing to accept plans under which the employees lost their deferred wages if they terminated their employment prior to retirement age. This concession was probably a wise tactic at the time because it reduced the cost of pensions to employers. Coverage under self-insured plans also began to grow more rapidly than the coverage under insured plans because of the greater flexibility they permit with respect to benefit formulas, budgeting arrangements, and types of investments.

An important benchmark in the pension movement was the establishment of the United Mine Workers Retirement Plan which became effective in 1947. The plan provided initially, in addition to certain death and accidental injury and sickness benefits, $100 a month to workers aged sixty who have completed twenty years of service. The fund is administered by three trustees representing the union, the public, and the coal operators and is financed entirely by the operators through the payment of a "royalty" rate per ton of coal mined. Because the payments into the fund have been less than expected, the benefits have had to be reduced.

[14] The relative merits of insured and self-insured pension plans are discussed on pp. 193–94.
[15] This point is important enough to merit a more extended discussion later. See pp. 180–81.

In the development of pension programs, several important Supreme Court decisions were rendered two years later. In 1946 the Inland Steel Company of Chicago had refused to bargain with the United Steel Workers' Union on the issue of a compulsory retirement age in an existing retirement plan. The National Labor Relations Board ruled in 1948 that pensions were a form of wages and that the provisions of a pension plan were conditions of employment. Therefore, the company was required to bargain with the union on company pension plans. The NLRB issued a similar ruling concerning group life insurance benefits in the same year. Both rulings were sustained by the Supreme Court in 1949, and union interest in welfare benefits soared now that the legal status of collective bargaining on these benefits had been clarified. The United Steel Workers and the United Automobile Workers negotiated important retirement plans in the same year. Union and employer interest in group insurance and pensions has continued to the present time.

CLASSIFICATIONS OF GROUP INSURANCE AND PENSIONS

Before turning to a detailed discussion of group life insurance and pension plans, we should note that group insurance plans (not limited to group life insurance and commonly referred to as welfare plans) and pension plans can be classified in several ways. First, the plans may differ according to the type of group insured. The group may be the employees of a single employer, the employees of two or more employers in an industry, an area, or an industry within an area (called a multi-employer group),[16] the members of a professional association, the debtors of a common creditor, or some other group. From this point on we will concern ourselves exclusively with plans providing protection for employees. In fact, in the more detailed analyses which follow this section on the classifications of group plans, we shall restrict our attention primarily to plans covering the employees of a single employer because this simplifies the discussion and more than 80 per cent of the employees covered under group insurance and pension plans belong to single-employer groups.[17]

[16] Multi-employer groups usually include the members of a labor union or certain labor unions. Sometimes they include employees of employers belonging to an employers' association.

[17] A survey of group life insurance in force by type of group covered at the end of 1963, exclusive of dependent coverage, credit life insurance, and the federal employees' group plan, showed that groups related to the members' employment or occupation accounted for about 90 per cent of the insurance in force. Single-employer groups covered through master contracts issued to their employers, alone accounted for about 86 per cent of the amount of insurance in force. See *Life Insurance Fact Book, 1966* (New York: Institute of Life Insurance, 1966), p. 28.

According to the U. S. Department of Labor, there were in 1963 about 1,000 negotiated multi-employer plans covering about 4 million workers. Other multi-

Second, employee-benefit plans can be classified according to whether they were established unilaterally by the employer(s) or in accordance with some collective bargaining agreement. Over half of the plans fall in the latter category and this proportion is increasing.

Third, employee-benefit plans may be administered by the employer(s), by an employee organization(s), or jointly by an employer-employee board of trustees. In 1965, among plans covering more than twenty-five persons, 91.2 per cent of the welfare plans were administered by employers, 2.1 per cent by employee organizations, and 3.4 per cent by joint employer-employee boards of trustees. The other 3.3 per cent were not classified or were administered in some other way. For pension plans, the respective percentages were 76.9 per cent, 19.6 per cent, 0.9 per cent, and 2.6 per cent.[18]

Fourth, the plans may be financed by employers, employees, or both. Both contributed to the cost of about half the welfare plans in 1965. Employers paid the entire cost in about 36.0 per cent of the plans, employees in about 9.6 per cent, and unions (out of general funds) in about 1.0 per cent. The remaining 3.4 per cent were not classified or were supported in some other way. For pension plans, the five percentages were 23.5 per cent, 72.9 per cent, 0.8 per cent, 9.2 per cent, and 2.6 per cent, respectively.[19]

The trend is toward non-contributory (employer-pay-all) plans. The major advantages of a non-contributory plan are as follows:

1. The member does not have to pay an income tax on the premiums paid in his behalf if the group insurance expenditures by the firm are "reasonable." In the case of pensions, he can defer and in some cases escape the tax if the pension plan is qualified with the Internal Revenue Service. In order to be qualified, a pension plan must, among other things, be for the exclusive benefit of the employees and must not discriminate in favor of certain classes of highly paid employees.
2. All eligible members of the group are insured.
3. The administrative costs are less because there is less record-keeping.

---

employer plans usually cover public employees and employees of religious, charitable, and educational institutions. About 24 million workers, excluding annuitants, were covered under pension plans at that time. See *Public Policy and Private Pension Programs—A Report to the President on Private Employee Benefit Plans*, by President's Committee on Corporate Pension Funds and Other Private Retirement and Welfare Programs (Washington, D. C.: U. S. Government Printing Office, 1965), p. 7.

[18] U. S. Department of Labor, Labor-Management Services Administration, *Characteristics of 163,500 Plans Filed as of July 1, 1965* (Washington, D. C.: U. S. Government Printing Office, 1966), p. 11.

[19] *Ibid.*, p. 14.

The principal advantages of a contributory plan are the following:

1. The plan can provide larger benefits if both the employer and the employees contribute.
2. The member may take a greater interest in the plan and may as a result derive more satisfaction from the protection.
3. The plan is less likely to be discontinued.

Tax considerations and the inclusion of insurance benefits in collective bargaining agreements are the primary factors favoring the current trend toward non-contributory plans.

Fifth, the plans may be classified according to whether they are self-insured by the administrator or insured with an outside agency. Because about 91 per cent of the welfare plans covering more than twenty-five persons in 1960 were insured,[20] a study of death-benefit plans is almost entirely a study of group life insurance underwritten by commercial insurers and our analysis will be limited to this subject. On the other hand, about three-fourths of the pension participants are covered under self-insured plans [21] and our analysis must, therefore, include both self-insured plans and those insured by commercial insurers. We now turn to these more detailed analyses.

Group Life Insurance

Individual underwriting and the cost of individual insurance contracts plus the difficulties involved in selling life insurance to individuals tend to restrict the extension of ordinary and industrial insurance. Group life insurance, which is designed to attack these problems, is insurance of a group of persons bound together by some common interest. The contract is issued to the head of the group such as the employer, the labor union, or the trustees of a welfare fund. The participating members receive individual certificates.

Group underwriting is substituted for individual underwriting. If the group is acceptable to the insurer, all members of the group are acceptable even if they would be unable to pass the individual underwriting standards. The cost is relatively low because of the reduction in administrative expenses due to the wholesaling principle and the fact that the head of the group usually performs some of the administrative duties. Moreover, the head of the group usually pays part or all of the cost.

[20] U. S. Department of Labor, Office of Welfare and Pension Plans, *Welfare and Pension Plans Statistics 1960* (Washington, D. C.: U. S. Government Printing Office, 1963), p. 3. For a discussion of self-insured plans, see Robert D. Eilers and Robert M. Crowe (eds.), *Group Insurance Handbook* (Homewood, Ill.: Richard D. Irwin, Inc., 1965), chaps. 40 and 41.
[21] See Table 5.7.

Gregg illustrates how greatly group life insurance has extended life insurance coverage as follows: "At the end of 1960, about 41 million workers in the United States were covered by group life insurance. Probably about 25 per cent of this group, over 10 million persons, had no individual policies of life insurance. In addition it is estimated that about 70 per cent of the persons covered by group life insurance had less than $1,000 of life insurance under individual policies." [22]

If an insurer limits group life insurance protection to those groups that have an expected mortality rate approximating that underlying the premium charged, group insurance is feasible. As a rule, the expected mortality rates are assumed to differ among groups only because of differences in the age composition of the groups.

In order to avoid adverse selection against the insurer and in order to maintain a low stable premium, insurers first sought groups possessing the following characteristics: [23]

1. Insurance should be an incidental purpose of the group.
2. Membership in the group should require a certain minimum degree of physical activity and health.
3. New entrants should be required to show a minimum grade of health.
4. There should be a continuous withdrawal of aged and impaired lives and a steady inflow of young and healthy lives.

The most insurable type of group, according to these criteria, is a group of employees under a common employer. Insurers have become much more liberal in recent years with respect to the types of groups they will underwrite.

Of course, not all groups of an acceptable type are eligible for insurance. The group must be of a certain minimum size. The minimum size for a group of employees of a single employer is usually twenty-five but many insurers write group life insurance on as few as ten lives and the trend is toward smaller group minimums. The major purpose of this requirement is to reduce the overhead expense per insured. Moreover, underwriters feel that the proportion of impaired lives in an eligible group decreases as the size of the group increases.

If the members of the group do not pay any of the cost, all members of an eligible class must be covered. If the members pay part of the

---

[22] Reprinted by permission from Davis W. Gregg, *Group Life Insurance* (3rd ed.; Homewood, Ill.: Richard D. Irwin, Inc., 1962), p. 21.

[23] Davis W. Gregg, *An Analysis of Group Life Insurance* (Philadelphia: University of Pennsylvania Press, 1950), pp. 27–30.

cost, all members of a specified class must be eligible to participate, and in the case of individual employer groups, at least 75 per cent, say, of those eligible must participate. If it were not for this requirement, the proportion of impaired lives among the employees might be abnormally high; some insurers have relaxed this requirement.

In addition to meeting these general requirements, each group must satisfy the insurer's underwriter that there are no special reasons why it should not qualify for group insurance.

The group insurance contract itself contains some additional underwriting safeguards. First, eligibility requirements are stated. What constitutes membership in the group is clearly defined; a probationary period of membership may be required in order to avoid the high cost of insuring "floaters"; and there may be a requirement that the member be actively at work or able to present some other evidence of reasonably good health. If the insurance is voluntary, eligible members usually must apply for the insurance within thirty days after the date of their eligibility if they wish to obtain the insurance without evidence of insurability.

Second, the amount of insurance is determined automatically by the member's earnings, position, years of membership, debt, or some other criterion. It may be a flat amount for all group members. The earnings basis has proved the most satisfactory for the employee group, and the amount of group life insurance is often some multiple of the annual earnings. If the amount of insurance were not determined automatically, the persons in poor health would tend to purchase the largest amounts of insurance.

Third, there is a minimum and maximum amount of insurance per person. A minimum of $500 of insurance is usually established in order to avoid unduly high expenses of administration. The maximum amount is a function of the total insurance in force and because of legal restrictions in many states, usually does not exceed $40,000. However, amounts in excess of $100,000 have been written. Setting a minimum and maximum amount in this way produces a safer distribution of insurance amounts from an underwriting point of view. Otherwise the insurer might have most of his eggs in a few baskets.

Group Renewable Term Insurance. Over 90 per cent of the group life insurance in force is one-year renewable term insurance. From the member's point of view, the insurer will pay the face amount to his beneficiary if he dies while insured as a member of the group, but there is no cash value if he leaves the group. The proceeds are payable in a lump sum or according to one of the optional modes of settlement, but the annuity and the interest options are generally not available.

The major disadvantage of individual one-year renewable term insurance is that each year the premium rate increases and at the advanced ages the premium becomes prohibitive for most people. Fortunately, however, the total premium rate for a group does not change unless the age and benefit composition of the group changes.[24] If the group is carefully selected, these changes should be slight. If the head of the group pays the entire cost, it is possible for him to provide this low-cost protection at an almost constant rate. If the plan is contributory, each member's share of the cost is usually kept constant during his period of participation and seldom exceeds 60¢ per month per $1,000 of insurance. In this case the head of the group pays the almost constant additional cost per $1,000 of protection. Under a contributory plan, the cost for the very young may exceed the premium for individual term insurance, but after a few years the cost will be much less. If the plan is voluntary, some of the younger members may wait until the group protection is cheaper than the individual contract, but they may become uninsurable in the meantime and be unable to participate.

A simplified example of the procedure commonly used to compute the total annual premium rate for a group term life insurance contract will illustrate these principles. Assume that the group consists of 200 members grouped as follows:

Age	Benefit	Number
20	$1,000	50
30	1,000	45
40	2,000	40
50	2,000	35
60	2,000	30

The total initial premium is obtained by (1) multiplying the "gross" premium rate (i.e., the net premium rate [25] increased by one-third of itself to provide for those expenses that vary with the premium) for each age by the amount of insurance in force at that age, (2) summing the resulting products, (3) adding $2.40 for each $1,000 of insurance under $40,000 to cover those expenses that are a function of the amount of insurance in force, and (4) if the premium calculated up to this point is $2,400 or more, reducing this premium by an advance expense adjustment factor in recognition of the fact that expenses do not increase proportionally with the size of the premium. This adjustment factor ranges from 1 per cent if the premium is at least $2,400 but under $3,000, up to 20 per cent if

---

[24] The total premium, but not necessarily the premium rate, would change if the size of the group increased or decreased.

[25] The net premium rate includes no allowance for expenses. It depends upon only the expected mortality rates and the assumed investment return.

the premium is $720,000 or more. Therefore, the total premium rate for this group is computed as follows:

Age	Total Amount of Insurance	"Gross" Premium Rate	Premium
20	$ 50,000	$ 2.75	$ 137.50
30	45,000	3.15	141.75
40	80,000	5.28	422.40
50	70,000	12.51	875.70
60	60,000	29.72	1,783.20
	$305,000		$3,360.55

Total premium = $3,360.55 + $2.40(40) − .02($3,456.55) = $3,387.42
Total premium rate = $3,387.42 ÷ $305 = $11.11

If no new members join the group and coverage is continued on all the old members, the total premium will increase over time, but if the older members are dropped from the group after a certain age and younger members take their place, the total cost will be fairly constant over time. Note that it is the age composition of the group that must remain fairly constant, not the average age. It costs more to insure two people, aged thirty and fifty, than two people, both aged forty, but the average age of the two groups is the same.

The actual cost of the group protection will probably be less than the computed premium, for participating insurers return dividends to policy-holders and non-participating insurers make retroactive adjustments of the premium. The size of the dividends and the retroactive adjustments depend partly upon the total group experience of the insurer and partly upon the experience of the particular group. Insurers pay more atten-tion to the experience of the particular group when that group includes many persons.

An insured who terminates his connection with the group (other than a debtor group) has the right to purchase an individual life insurance contract up to the amount of the group coverage without evidence of in-surability. Application for this coverage must be made within thirty-one days and the premium is that in effect for his attained age at the date of termination. Term insurance coverage is sometimes granted for one year, but usually the converted contract must be some form of non-term in-surance. If the insurer or the employer terminates the group insurance, members who have been insured for five years (sometimes three) may convert their insurance under the same conditions, but the converted amount may not exceed $2,000. This conversion privilege is extremely important if a terminating member becomes uninsurable while a member of the insured group, but there is no premium advantage for *standard* lives.

Other Forms of Group Life Insurance. A major problem with group term insurance is that the conversion privilege is of little value to members retiring at an advanced age because the premiums on the individual contracts are very high. For this reason, insurers now underwrite two additional forms of group insurance: group paid-up insurance and level-premium group permanent insurance. In the description of these forms we shall assume a group of employees under a common employer.

A group paid-up plan combines term insurance with paid-up insurance. The total amount of insurance for each employee is determined in the same way as under a group term insurance plan, but the composition of the total differs. Usually small units of paid-up insurance are purchased annually during the insured's participation under the plan, while term insurance is written for the difference. If the total amount of protection is constant, paid-up insurance represents an increasing portion of the total, while the term insurance decreases. Two common plans are (1) the annual purchase of a specified number of units of paid-up insurance and (2) the annual purchase of a decreasing number of units of paid-up insurance with the employee's constant contributions. Under the second plan, the amount of paid-up insurance will depend upon the number of years of participation *and* the age at which the employee entered the group. If none of the paid-up insurance was purchased by employer contributions, the employee is entitled to the paid-up protection when he leaves the group. Paid-up insurance, like individual insurance, may be surrendered for its cash value if the insured wishes. In addition, the usual conversion rights apply to the term insurance portion of his protection. However, if the employer has contributed to the cost of the paid-up insurance, he may establish certain conditions that must be satisfied before the employee may claim that portion of the paid-up insurance purchased with his contributions. These conditions are called vesting conditions and plans may provide for no vesting at any time, full vesting immediately upon becoming a group member, or full or partial vesting after a specified age, years of membership, or both. (The problem of vesting is discussed more fully on pages 191–92 and in Chapter 14.)

Group permanent or level-premium life insurance plans emphasize the retirement aspects of insurance more than group paid-up plans. In fact they are more often used as pension plans instead of life insurance plans because of the sizable cash values available at retirement age and some tax factors. Straight life, limited payment life, endowment, or retirement income contracts are issued to individuals on a group basis. They contain paid-up insurance and cash value options, and settlement options, except for the interest option. If an employee terminates his connection with the group, his claim to the non-forfeiture value will depend upon the vesting conditions mentioned in the preceding paragraph. If he wishes, he may convert in the usual way the difference between the total group coverage and the amount of the paid-up insurance.

The most common solution to the problem of retired employees, however, is to continue their insurance in a reduced amount under the regular group term contract.

Trends. Important trends in group insurance include the extension of group insurance to new types of groups and smaller groups; an increase in the maximum amount of group insurance written on a single life and in the average size of a group certificate; more frequent use of settlement options in paying out policy proceeds; liberalization in the conversion privilege by permitting the insured to convert his group protection to term insurance for at least one year; and an increase in the use of group permanent insurance or reduced group term insurance to solve the problem of the retiring member.

Group Life Insurance in Force, 1912–65. Group life insurance is the fastest growing branch of insurance. The tremendous increase in the amount of group insurance in force since its introduction in 1912 is shown in Table 5.6. Less than half of the nation's civilian wage and salary workers were covered by group insurance at the close of 1954; the proportion is now over 63 per cent. Until 1947 the amount of industrial insurance in force exceeded the amount of group insurance in force, but there is now almost $7,700 of group life insurance in force for each $1,000 of industrial insurance. Over the same period, the ratio of the amount of group insurance in force to the amount of ordinary insurance in force has increased from about 26 per cent to 62 per cent.

TABLE 5.6

Group Life Insurance in Force in the United States, 1912–65

(In Millions)

Year	Amount *	Year	Amount *
1912	$ 13	1940	$ 14,938
1915	100	1945	22,172
1920	1,570	1950	47,793
1925	4,247	1955	101,300
1930	9,801	1960	175,434
1935	10,208	1965	306,113

* These data do not include the amount of group credit life insurance in force. See the footnote to Table 5.4. In 1965 this insurance totaled $49,303 million; in 1950, $3,169 million.

Source: Institute of Life Insurance, *Life Insurance Fact Book, 1966,* p. 27.

Group Pension Plans

The amount of group life insurance in force is less than the individual life insurance in force, but group pension plans provide much more protection against old age than individual annuity contracts. These pension plans may be formal or informal; they may be financed on a pay-as-you-go or on some funding basis. Since almost all the important pension plans are formal funded plans, the discussion will be limited to this type.

We shall further limit our detailed discussion to those plans which cover the employees of a single employer, but in recent years, as a result of collective bargaining, pooled welfare funds covering the employees of more than one employer have become more common, especially among craft unions which include members working for a large number of small employers. Examples are the plans of the United Brotherhood of Carpenters and Joiners of America, the International Brotherhood of Electrical Workers, and the United Mine Workers of America. These multiemployer plans are usually financed entirely by employer contributions based on some measure such as the number of hours worked or tons of coal mined and are jointly administered by employers and unions. One noteworthy characteristic of these plans is that an employee's pension status is not lessened by movements from one employer to another included under the same plan. These plans are still relatively few in number but they cover many employees and have come to play an important role in our search for economic security.[26]

Retirement Benefits. Benefits under these formal funded plans are determined in one of two ways.

Under a *defined contribution plan,* the benefit is the amount that can be provided on the basis of specified annual contributions to the plan. Negotiated plans that state the employer's obligation in terms of stated amounts per hour of work or dollars of payroll fall in this category. Among single-employer plans of this type it is customary to express the contributions as a percentage of the employee's earnings. This plan is seldom used except by public bodies and non-profit organizations, because the benefits cannot easily be explained and they decrease rapidly as the age of the entrant increases. Furthermore, the benefit depends more upon the earnings in the early years than those in the later years because the early contributions are credited with compound interest over a longer

[26] For a more complete discussion of these multi-employer plans, see Joseph J. Melone, *Collectively-Bargained Multi-Employer Pension Plans* (Homewood, Ill.: Richard D. Irwin, Inc., 1963) and Meyer Melnikoff, "Multi-employer Pension Plans," Chapter 43 in Davis W. Gregg (ed.), *Life and Health Insurance Handbook,* 2nd ed. (Homewood, Ill.: Richard D. Irwin, Inc., 1964), pp. 564–76.

period of time. The advantage to the employer is that the cost is known and it varies with his payroll.

Under a *defined benefit plan*, the benefit is a flat amount for all retirants or a specified function of earnings, service, or both. The contribution is the amount necessary to provide the benefit. Examples of defined benefit formulas include the following: $100 per month for all eligible retirants; 50 per cent of final earnings; 50 per cent of average earnings over the past five years; $3 per month for each year of service; [27] 2 per cent of final earnings for each year of service; 2 per cent of average earnings during the past ten years for each year of service; and 2 per cent of average earnings for each year of service. The last example, which develops a benefit that depends upon both the level of compensation and the length of service, illustrates the type of plan that is the most common, but there is a definite trend toward the use of average earnings during the past five or ten years instead of the career average. Retirants, past and future, tend to judge plans on the relationship between their pension and their final earnings, not their average earnings; and over most earning careers, the final earnings are much greater than the average earnings. During periods of inflation they are markedly so.

Whenever length of service is a factor in determining the amount of the benefit, as it is in the case of most plans, a distinction is made between service rendered prior to and after the installation of the pension plan. Most plans count at least part of the past service in addition to the future service. Otherwise, employees approaching retirement age at the time the plan was introduced would receive a very small benefit. If the benefit depends upon career earnings, it is customary to assume for administrative reasons that the annual earnings prior to the installation of the plan were equal to the present earnings. Because this assumption almost always results in an overestimate of past earnings, a smaller percentage is applied to past earnings than to future earnings to determine the benefit.

Because most employees will receive OASDI retirement benefits, which the employer has paid for in part, the benefits under most private pension plans are affected in some way by OASDI.[28] It is customary to (1) deduct the social security benefits actually received from the private pension benefit, (2) exclude earnings under the maximum OASDI earnings base from the private pension plan, or (3) apply a smaller rate of

[27] This benefit formula is associated with "pattern" plans negotiated by certain unions such as the United Automobile Workers with individual employers or groups of employers. These plans are usually non-contributory. In its *1965 Study of Industrial Retirement Plans,* the Bankers Trust Company of New York found that about one-fourth of the plans in the study were pattern plans. All but a few of these pattern plans were self-insured plans.

[28] The integration with OASDI must not discriminate in favor of the more highly paid employees or the Internal Revenue Service will not qualify the plan.

benefit to those earnings.[29] When the last two methods are used, and they are by far the most common methods, the usual objective is to produce a maximum total benefit (OASDI plus private pension benefit) expressed as a per cent of earnings which decreases as the earnings increase to the maximum OASDI earnings base and remains the same for all higher incomes.

Retirement income is always paid during the lifetime of the pensioner, but there may be additional payments if the pensioner dies. The annuity form may be a straight life annuity, a cash refund annuity, an instalment refund annuity, a joint and last survivor annuity, or an annuity with a period certain. These annuity forms have been described on page 167. The cash refund and instalment refund annuity forms are usually modified to the extent that the refund is limited to the employee's contributions to the plan.

Benefits under a pension plan are specified in terms of one annuity form, usually the straight life annuity or a cash refund annuity, but the employee almost always has the right to receive an actuarially equivalent income under another form. If the employee wishes to elect a form with larger death benefits, he must usually elect this form a stated number of years prior to retirement because of the possibility of adverse selection.

About two-thirds of the university pension plans (underwritten by the special life insurer noted on page 170) and an increasing number of industrial pension plans provide a variable annuity or adjust the monthly benefit to changes in the Consumers' Price Index.[30] As noted on pages 170–71, since 1963 private insurers have been able to write group variable annuities for pension plans in an increasing number of states. Several insurers have already issued group variable annuity contracts or plan to do so shortly.

Qualification for Retirement Benefits. In order to qualify for retirement benefits, an employee must first have been eligible to participate under the plan. Participation may be limited to those employees who satisfy one or more of the following types of criteria: minimum age, maximum age, minimum length of service, minimum earnings, type of remuneration (hourly wage or salary), and type of work. For example, one plan may cover all employees over thirty years of age with at least five years of service. Another may cover all salaried employees earning over $6,600 a year. The minimum age and service requirements cut the cost of ad-

[29] For a discussion of the relative merits of each method of integration, see Dan M. McGill, *Fundamentals of Private Pensions*, 2nd ed. (Homewood, Ill.: Richard D. Irwin, Inc., 1964), pp. 74–81.

[30] For more details on the university plans, see William C. Greenough and Francis P. King, *Retirement and Insurance Plans in American Colleges* (New York: Columbia University Press, 1959).

ministration by excluding temporary employees; the maximum age limitation excludes those employees for whom it would be very expensive to provide pensions. The minimum earnings requirement is designed to integrate the plan with OASDI. The other requirements may be used to cut the cost or may arise out of the special circumstances surrounding negotiated plans.

In order to receive the full retirement benefits, employees must almost always have attained a normal retirement age, usually sixty-five. Sometimes there is also a minimum service requirement. If an employee wishes to continue working beyond the normal retirement age, he may be able to do so under some circumstances, although institutional rules may make it increasingly difficult. However, there are seldom any further contributions to the plan in his behalf. The benefits may start at the normal retirement age even if he continues working, but usually the income is postponed until the actual retirement date. The deferred benefit may be the same as that which he would have received at the normal retirement age or it may be the actuarial equivalent; that is, it may be adjusted upward to reflect additional interest earnings and the advanced age.

Early Retirement, Termination, and Death Benefits. Some plans do not permit an employee to retire prior to the normal retirement date; others make an exception only in the case of total and permanent disability. However, most plans permit early retirement if the retirant meets a minimum age or minimum age and service requirement. The employer's consent may or may not be required. For example, the plan may permit an employee to retire with the employer's consent if he has attained the age of fifty-five. Another may require that a person reach fifty-five years of age and complete ten years of service before he can retire. If early retirement is permitted, the benefit is usually the actuarial equivalent of the normal retirement age benefit. This actuarial equivalent is much less than the benefit at the normal retirement age because fewer contributions are made to the plan, the period of compound interest earnings is much less, the cost of providing an income beginning at an earlier age is much higher, and many of the early retirants are persons in poor health who would not have attained the normal retirement age. Some pattern plans providing benefits of a stated number of dollars per month for each year of service simply discount the amount by, say, 0.5 per cent for each month by which the employee retires prior to his normal retirement age.

If an employee withdraws from employment prior to the normal or early retirement age, he is entitled to his own contributions to the plan, with or without interest. The vesting provisions of the plan determine his right to the benefits provided by the employer's contributions. There may be full, partial, or no vesting; the vesting may be immediate or, as is usually the case, there may be certain service or age and service requirements; and the vested amount may be returned in cash or as a paid-up annuity. For example, one plan may provide for immediate full vesting, but the employee must take his own and the employer's contributions in the form of a paid-up annuity. Another may entitle the employee to 25 per cent of the employer's contributions in cash after five years of service, 50 per cent after ten years, 75 per cent after fifteen years, and 100 per cent after twenty years. A third may provide full vesting of the employer's contributions in cash or as a paid-up annuity for all eligible employees with ten years of service. According to the U. S. Department of Labor, in 1963 about two-thirds of the pension plans covering twenty-five workers or more provided some vesting rights.[31] These plans covered three-fifths of the workers included under the plans surveyed.

Death benefits prior to retirement are usually limited to a return of the employee's contributions with or without interest, but death benefits equal to one year's income or $1,000 per $10 of retirement income are sometimes included. Some pension plans provide a "widow's pension" under which the widow receives a lifetime income. This income is usually related to the deceased's accrued retirement benefit at the time he died.

In 1965, about 71 per cent of the pension plans covering at least twenty-five persons provided disability retirement benefits; over 80 per cent included some death benefits.[32]

Funding Methods. The subject of funding methods, i.e., the ways in which the pension costs are budgeted over time, is too complex a subject to be covered in detail in this text.[33] It is important to note, however, that most employers set aside funds before the date on which they are needed to pay benefits. This funding increases the likelihood that the benefits will be paid, apportions the cost of the pension plan more equitably over time, and, because of interest earnings, reduces the total dollar outlay by the employer. Possible disadvantages are that the employer may be able to earn a better return by investing the funds in his own business, the accommodation of a sizable fund may encourage undue benefit liberalizations, and a funded plan is more complicated and expensive to administer.

The reader should realize, however, that few plans are fully funded; i.e., the fund is seldom sufficient to pay all benefits earned up to the present by active and retired members if the plan were to be terminated. On the other hand, most private pension plans do have enough assets to continue benefits to those persons who have already retired and pay some benefits to active workers.

[31] *Public Policy and Private Pension Programs, op. cit.,* p. 33.
[32] *Characteristics of 163,500 Plans, op. cit.,* p. 12.
[33] See McGill, *op. cit.,* pp. 247–52.

Funding Agencies and Instruments. As stated earlier, the pension plan may be self-insured by the employer or insured with an insurer. Under a self-insured trusteed plan, a consulting actuary advises the employer who transfers funds periodically to a trustee such as a bank. The trustee invests the money and commonly sends out the pension checks at the direction of the employer. The plan is highly flexible with respect to the benefit formula that can be used, the budgeting arrangements that can be selected by the employer, and the investments that can be made. Common stocks usually constitute a sizable proportion of the investments, and since World War II these securities have been rewarding investments. The primary disadvantage of a self-insured operation is that no third party such as an insurer has absorbed any of the risks. There is no guarantee that the contributions by the employer will be sufficient to pay the benefits.

Under an insured plan, the contributions are paid to an insurer who administers them in one of the following ways. Small firms usually use an *individual policy arrangement* under which the employer transfers funds to a trustee who purchases an individual level-premium retirement annuity or retirement income annuity contract for each eligible employee. However, the insured plans covering the most persons are *group annuity plans* under which the employer purchases each year from an insurer a number of paid-up deferred group annuities. Usually the benefit is expressed as a percentage of earnings for each year of service, and the annuity purchased in any year is sufficient to provide this benefit at the retirement date. Under either of these plans, the insurer guarantees performance under the contract purchased. The plans, however, are relatively inflexible and the yield on the invested funds, although it has improved markedly during the past five years, has been lower than that on the self-insured funds because life insurers are generally required by law to place most of the funds they receive in connection with these contracts in fixed obligations.

Insurers also operate three more flexible plans—*deposit administration plans, immediate participation guarantee contracts,* and *separate account contracts.* Under a deposit administration plan, annuity contracts are not purchased until an employee retires. Annual employer contributions to the insurer are accumulated at a guaranteed minimum rate of interest and may be used to purchase an annuity at a price fixed at the time the contribution is made. Employee contributions, if any, are accumulated at interest in individual accounts or used for immediate purchases of deferred annuities. The employer contributions are made on the basis of an actuarial estimate by the insurer's actuaries or a consulting actuary, but there is no guarantee that they will be sufficient to provide the benefits specified under the plan. The insurer guarantees the benefits for retiring employees only. The deposit administration plan is becoming more popular because of the flexibility in financing that it affords the employer and because it may be used to fund the more popular final-pay type of benefit. The principal differences between this plan and the self-insured plan are that the deposits must be invested in legal investments for insurers and the benefits for retired persons are guaranteed by a third party.

Immediate participation guarantee contracts are even more flexible in that the insurer administers the retirement fund as if it were a self-insured trusteed fund, but the insurer reserves the right to convert the plan into a deferred group annuity plan if the fund drops to the level where it is just sufficient to provide the benefits for retired workers. In this way, the retired workers receive a guarantee that their income will not be disturbed.

A separate account contract is basically a deposit administration or immediate participation contract with one additional feature.[34] Part or all of the employer's deposit fund is allocated to one or more separate accounts, which are held separately from all other assets of the insurer. The funds in a separate account may be invested solely in common stocks or some other type of investment or in some combination of investments. Although an individual separate account may be established for a large employer, most separate accounts pool the funds of many policyholders. This approach to pension funding was impossible until 1960 when Connecticut became the first state to pass the necessary enabling legislation. Only a few states still prohibit insurers from issuing separate account contracts. Fixed dollar annuities for retirants are still required under most state laws, but in an increasing number of states, the separate account contract may be used to provide a variable annuity. (See pages 170–71 and page 190.)

Trends. The important trends in group pensions include an increase in the number of persons covered, a reduction in age and service eligibility requirements, increased benefits, new benefit formulas including cost of living adjustments and variable annuities, a movement from inflexible insured plans to more flexible insured plans and self-insured trusteed plans, more liberal vesting provisions, and the growth of industry-wide negotiated plans. Collective bargaining has played a significant role in these developments.

Pension Plans, 1930–65. Table 5.7 shows the rapid growth of pension plans since 1930 and the more rapid relative growth of self-insured pen-

[34] For a discussion of this new approach to pension funding, see John C. Bowling, "Separate Accounts—The Quiet Revolution in Pension Funding," *The Journal of the American College of Chartered Life Underwriters*, XIX, No. 3 (Summer, 1965), 217–19.

sion plans following the end of World War II. The 28 million employees covered under pension plans at the close of 1965 constituted almost half of the wage and salary workers in private industry. In 1954 this proportion was only 31 per cent.

TABLE 5.7

Pension Plan Coverage in the United States, 1930–64

Year	Employees Covered * (in thousands)	
	Insured	Self-insured
1930	100	2,700
1935	300	2,500
1940	700	3,400
1945	1,500	5,000
1950	2,600	7,200
1955	3,800	11,600
1960	4,900	16,300
1961	5,100	17,100
1962	5,200	17,900
1963	5,400	18,400
1964	6,000	18,600

* Includes some pay-as-you-go plans. Excludes pensioners.

Sources: *Private and Public Pension Plans in the United States* (New York: Institute of Life Insurance, 1963), pp. 3, 11–14, and 16; Alfred M. Skolnik, "Ten Years of Employee-Benefit Plans," *Social Security Bulletin*, XXIX, No. 4 (April, 1966), 11.

The number of insured plans of each type and the number of persons covered under each type are presented in Table 5.8. The deposit administration plans, which include immediate participation guarantee and separate account plans, are the fastest growing types of insured plans

TABLE 5.8

Number of Insured Pension Plans and Number of Persons Covered, by Type of Plan, 1965

Type of Plan	Number of Plans	Number of Persons Covered *
Group annuities	7,980	2,275,000
Deposit administration	7,700	3,410,000
Individual policy pension trusts	43,580	795,000
Other	7,000	560,000
Total	66,260	7,040,000

* Includes about 790,000 pensioners.

Source: Institute of Life Insurance, *Life Insurance Fact Book, 1966,* p. 36.

with respect to both the number of plans and the number of persons covered. Table 5.8 does not indicate the increasing importance of separate account plans among deposit administration plans, but they expanded rapidly during 1965. Many observers expect separate account plans to enable insurers to increase their share of the pension business.

OPERATIONS

The life insurance industry is the largest private agency dealing with the financial problems of premature death and old age. Its operations are indicative of private activities in this area.

TABLE 5.9

Income of United States Life Insurers, 1920–65

(IN MILLIONS)

Year	Premium Income *	Investment and Other Income †	Total
1920	$ 1,381	$ 383	$ 1,764
1925	2,378	640	3,018
1930	3,517	1,077	4,594
1935	3,673	1,399	5,072
1940	3,887	1,771	5,658
1945	5,159	2,515	7,674
1950	8,189	3,148	11,337
1955	12,546	3,998	16,544
1960	17,365	5,642	23,007
1965	24,604	8,563	33,167

* Health insurance premiums included in 1950, 1955, 1960, and 1965 figures. Health insurance premiums in 1965 were about $6.3 billion.
† Other income includes proceeds left with the insurers under settlement options.

Source: Institute of Life Insurance, *Life Insurance Fact Book, 1966,* p. 50.

Over 60 per cent of the total population and over 80 per cent of adult males own some form of life insurance, and the percentages are increasing each year.[35] The total amount of life insurance in force at the close of 1965 was about $901 billion which is 2.4 times the amount in force ten years ago. About 7.5 million persons owned annuities providing about $3.7 billion in annual income at maturity. Ten years ago the annual income figure was about one-half its present value.

The significant growth in the income of the life insurance industry is shown in Table 5.9. Note that the annual income is now over $33 billion.

[35] For a more detailed recent analysis of the age, sex, income, residence, and other characteristics of the persons with life insurance contracts, see the latest *Life Insurance Fact Book, op. cit.*

Benefits have also increased, but not as rapidly. Table 5.10 shows that annuity payments have shown the greatest increase since 1940, but death benefits are the most important type of benefit. Note, however, that the total living benefits listed approach the death benefits. The living benefits listed do not include settlement option payments on contracts maturing in past years.

TABLE 5.10

Benefit Payments in the United States, 1940–65

(IN MILLIONS)

Year	Death Benefits	Matured Endowments	Annuity Payments	Surrender Values
1940	$ 995	$269	$177	$ 652
1945	1,280	407	216	211
1950	1,590	495	319	592
1955	2,241	614	462	896
1960	3,346	673	722	1,633
1965	4,831	931	1,039	1,932

Source: Institute of Life Insurance, *Life Insurance Fact Book, 1966*, p. 37.

Because income exceeds expenses and benefits, the assets of life insurers have grown rapidly and were about $158.9 billion at the close of 1965. Table 5.11 records the growth of these assets and of the policy reserves, which are the most important liability items. Almost all the assets are invested in interest-bearing debt securities and mortgages.

TABLE 5.11

Assets and Policy Reserves of the United States Life Insurers, 1920–65

(IN BILLIONS)

Year	Assets	Reserves *
1920	$ 7	$ 6
1925	12	10
1930	19	16
1935	23	20
1940	31	27
1945	45	39
1950	64	55
1955	90	75
1960	120	98
1965	159	128

* Health insurance reserves included in 1950, 1955, 1960, and 1965 figures. Health insurance reserves in 1965 were $1,432 million.

Source: Institute of Life Insurance, *Life Insurance Fact Book, 1966*, pp. 59, 64.

To complete this picture of the operations of private insurers, self-insured pension plans will be compared with the pension plans underwritten by private insurers. The number of persons covered under insured and self-insured plans has already been discussed. With respect to contributions, in 1950 employers and employees paid about $1 billion to insured pension plans and about $1.2 billion to self-insured plans. In 1964 the corresponding contributions were $1.8 billion and $5.0 billion. Benefit payments in 1950 were $80 million under insured plans and $290 million under self-insured plans. In 1964 the benefits were $640 million and $2,120 million respectively. Finally, at the end of 1950 the assets of insured funds totaled $5.6 billion, while self-insured funds had $6.5 billion worth of assets. At the close of 1964, the corresponding assets were $25.2 billion and $51.9 billion.

EVALUATION

Private life insurers have made sizable contributions to the economic security of our population.[36] Most American families look to private life insurance and annuities as their major supplement to the floor of protection provided by OASDI.

The commercial insurer is, by far, the most important underwriter of private insurance. In this evaluation of private insurance, therefore, we shall discuss primarily the types of protection afforded, the underwriting practices, and the premium structures of commercial insurers, but some attention will also be paid to self-insured pension plans.

Types of Protection Afforded

Commercial insurers issue a wide variety of life insurance and annuity contracts. Numerous combinations of pure protection against premature death and a systematic savings plan are obtainable from most of the leading insurers.

Very few persons question the advantages of life insurance as pure financial protection against premature death, but the following advantages of life insurance and annuity contracts as a systematic savings plan are less widely understood and appreciated. (1) Insureds are much less inclined to skip premium payments than savings bank deposits or security purchases. (2) The insurer guarantees a minimum interest rate on the savings fund. (3) Actual interest returns are usually higher than the guaranteed minimum and compare favorably with returns on fixed-dollar investments of similar quality. (4) The insured does not have to worry

---

[36] See p. 34.

about managing the fund. (5) The present tax code favors saving through insurance. (6) The chance that the insurer will not be able to pay the savings fund on demand is almost nil. For these six reasons, life insurance and annuity contracts are an excellent way for most families to accumulate at least the minimum savings fund required for old age. In addition, annuity contracts and annuity settlement options on cash values or death proceeds make it possible to avoid exhausting the savings fund before the date of death.

The contracts contain many liberal provisions. For example, if the insured dies two or more years after the life insurance contract is issued, the insurer cannot refuse to pay the death claim because of misrepresentations by the insured at the time he applied for the contract even if fraud is involved. The contracts are also flexible, as evidenced by the nonforfeiture options and the settlement options.

The promises of the life insurers are secure. State regulatory bodies restrict the investments of commercial insurers to high-grade securities and require them to establish a policy reserve item on the liability side of their balance sheets. This policy reserve is equal to the difference between the present value of estimated future benefits and the present value of expected future premium payments under contracts already in force. The policy reserve differs from the OASDI Trust Fund in that an indefinite operation is not and cannot be assumed. If a commercial insurer sold no new contracts, the premium payments under the contracts in force plus assets corresponding to the policy reserve amounts should be sufficient to discharge the obligations of the insurer.

However, it cannot be argued that all persons have received the optimum protection for their premium dollars. One of the most common failings is an overemphasis on contracts with savings fund aspects at a time when protection against premature death is the most important need. For example, many young workers with dependents have twenty-payment life contracts, but renewable and convertible term insurance would seem more appropriate in most instances. On the other hand, the authors do not agree with the fairly common suggestion that most persons would be better off (some might be) if they limited their life insurance programs solely to pure term insurance contracts.

This less-than-optimum protection in individual cases may be ascribed to many factors, the most important of which are (1) a lack of knowledge and appreciation of basic insurance principles by insureds and (2) the poor advice provided by what is fortunately a small proportion of insurance agents or other advisers. Both situations are being rectified. Insureds have more opportunity than ever before to learn the basic principles of life insurance. Journals and magazines print more feature articles on insurance; competent authors have written helpful books on the subject; [37] and college insurance courses for the non-specialist are becoming more common. As for the agents, the caliber of the average insurance agent has improved greatly during the past two or three decades. Agents are required to know more about insurance contracts, law, rates, and reserves than in the past. Life insurance programming—a survey of the private insurance needs followed by the selection of the best insurance contracts and settlement options to meet those needs—has become a fairly common procedure. Some excellent training and educational programs have been established, one of which leads to the professional designation of Chartered Life Underwriter (C.L.U.).

In the opinion of the authors, the insurance industry in the past has tended to de-emphasize term insurance to such an extent that it was not used in cases where it was the most appropriate form of protection. In recent years, however, many types of term insurance have become more readily available, and the insurance industry has enthusiastically supported the sale of the attractive family income contracts. Table 5.5 documents the effect of these changes. Some insurers and agents, however, still fail to appreciate the value of term insurance in many situations.

The inadequacy of fixed-dollar obligations, such as life insurance and annuity contracts, during a long period of steady upward price movements is obvious. This inadequacy is primarily responsible for the interest in the variable annuity that is currently being offered by several insurers on a group basis and by some insurers on an individual basis. Several other insurers have formed or associated themselves with mutual funds and sell a life insurance–mutual fund package. One insurer has developed a life insurance policy under which the face value will, except under unusual conditions, rise and fall with the Consumers' Price Index, but is never less than the original amount. More thought is being devoted to handling the technical problems associated with developing a life insurance contract of this sort.

Underwriting Practices

Relatively few persons are unable to purchase private individual life insurance because they are uninsurable. Another relatively small group can purchase only substandard insurance, which is either more expensive or more restricted than the contracts issued to standard lives. A very small number of persons will always be uninsurable, and contracts may on rare occasions have war and aviation exclusions, but individual underwriting procedures have been continually liberalized.

[37] See the life insurance texts cited in footnote 7. For a different viewpoint, see consumer education books such as the one by Jerome B. Cohen and Arthur W. Hanson, *Personal Finance*, 3rd ed. (Homewood, Ill.: Richard D. Irwin, Inc., 1964), chaps. 7 and 8.

Group insurance provides relatively inexpensive protection for all participants and is especially valuable to persons who are uninsurable by individual insurance standards. The continuation of group insurance on retired workers is an encouraging development. On the other hand, the protection is not tailor-made for the individual. At present, group life insurance plans cover about 63 per cent of the wage and salary workers in private industry, and benefits are gradually being extended and improved. The over-all development of group insurance appears satisfactory, but a few insurers have underwritten groups and benefit amounts that appear unsound, or threaten the continued existence of individual insurance and tailor-made protection. On the other hand, the legislation of some states appears unnecessarily restrictive.

Premium Structures

Private insurance premiums should not, on the average, exceed the expected losses and expected reasonable expenses plus a reasonable margin for contingencies and profit. In addition they should distribute the cost equitably among insureds. Life insurance premiums are satisfactory on both counts. The manner in which premiums vary among insureds has been discussed at various points in this chapter. A few additional facts concerning the general level of rates should be noted here.

The initial cost of a life insurance or annuity contract is determined by the insurer's expected mortality rates, interest rates earned on invested assets, and expenses. If the actual experience is more favorable than the expected experience, the policyholders usually gain because, as indicated previously, most life insurance is issued on a participating basis. Moreover, competition forces the non-participating insurers to make their estimates as realistic as possible.

Mortality rates have been decreasing, thus decreasing actual life insurance costs and increasing annuity costs. Interest rates declined from about 5 per cent in 1930 to 2.88 per cent in 1947, but since that date they have increased to about 3.5 per cent in 1955, 4.1 per cent in 1960, and 4.6 per cent in 1965. Most life insurance investments are limited by choice and by statute to debt obligations whose yield has been greatly affected by the monetary and fiscal policies of the federal government. Expenses average about 17 per cent of total income. Increasing mechanization, group coverages, and high-minimum policies tend to reduce the expenses, but increasing wages, rents, taxes, and other costs operate in the opposite direction. The expense ratio varies greatly among contracts and branches of insurance. All these factors vary among insurers. Many insureds underestimate the resulting variation in premium rates among insurance companies.

Pension Plans

Private pension plans, both insured and self-insured, are of such great importance that they have been the subject of a recent report by a special committee appointed by the President.[38] The committee justified this public interest in private pension plans by noting that these plans (1) provide economic security for millions of workers, (2) affect significantly the national savings stream and financial markets, (3) influence incentives, mobility of labor, and employment opportunities, and (4) have received indirect federal subsidies through federal tax concessions. As a result of its deliberations, the committee concluded that private pension plans have served an important social purpose and that they should continue to be a major element in the economic security program of the average worker. Consequently, public policy should continue to encourage the sound growth of private pension plans through tax incentives, labor relations statutes, standards for fiducial obligations of trustees, and legislation requiring public disclosure of various aspects of retirement and welfare plans.

On the negative side, the committee did raise some questions about possible adverse effects on the mobility of labor, the extent to which pension promises will actually be fulfilled, and possible inequities in the tax law as it applies to pensions. Among their recommendations were the following:

1. Employers should be encouraged to adopt plans that do not develop significantly higher costs for older workers.
2. In order to receive favorable tax treatment, pension plans should be required to include some reasonable graded vesting provisions.
3. The funding requirements for favorable tax treatment should be tightened considerably. Defined benefit plans, for example, should be fully funded no more than thirty years after their installation.[39]
4. Some mechanism should be developed for permitting the accumulation and transfer of pension credits when a worker changes jobs.
5. Plans should not qualify for favored tax treatment if they cover only salaried or clerical workers or if the waiting period for coverage exceeds three years.

[38] *Public Policy and Private Pension Programs, op. cit.*

[39] As pension plans become more flexible with respect to (1) benefit formulae which may involve variables such as final pay that are difficult to estimate in advance, (2) funding methods, and (3) investment media, the security of the pension promise is weakened even though these developments may be desirable on other grounds. The report of the President's Committee reflects increasing concern over this feature of pension plans. For a comprehensive statement of the problem, see Dan M. McGill, *Fulfilling Pension Expectations* (Homewood, Ill.: Richard D. Irwin, Inc., 1962).

6. Pension plans should not be permitted to invest more than 10 per cent of their assets in the stock or obligations of the employer, and disclosure requirements on investments should be increased.

Some labor and management representatives have objected to these recommendations, particularly the second and the third. They believe that the imposition of vesting and funding requirements may unduly hamper the development of new plans and may cause some old plans to be abandoned. Furthermore, by dictating the vesting and funding patterns, these requirements would take away from pension planners some desirable management discretion concerning the allocation of resources among the various aspects of a pension plan such as benefit levels, eligibility requirements, vesting, and funding. Some of these observers deny that full funding is required to assure the actuarial solvency of *all* defined contribution pension plans. Some argue that the best assurance that the pension promises will be fulfilled is that the employer continue a successful business operation.

In a much discussed private study,[40] Professor Merton Bernstein has expressed concern over the hazards to pension eligibility created by employee turnover, plan terminations, mergers, sales, and plant shut-downs. When these hazards are coupled with the fact that less than half of the labor force is now covered under pension plans, he concludes that a relatively small proportion of the labor force will actually qualify for benefits and that the average benefit will be much less than is suggested by the typical plan illustration for long-term employees. Furthermore, even the benefit for these employees is inadequate. Consequently, he argues for the extension of pension coverage, more liberal vesting provisions, more adequate benefit levels, and a clearing house for handling pension benefits earned in several different employments. He also suggests taxation reforms including a tightening of the funding requirements. Because Professor Bernstein's conclusions so closely parallel those of the President's Committee, which indeed were influenced by the Bernstein study, the objections that have been raised with respect to the vesting and funding suggestions made by the President's Committee also apply to the Bernstein study.

As Professor Bernstein acknowledges in his preface,[41] despite these suggestions for improvements, private pension plans are generally acknowledged to have made significant strides, especially in the past two decades. Furthermore, most persons actively involved in pension plan formulation and administration are well aware of the shortcomings in

[40] Merton C. Bernstein, *The Future of Private Pensions* (New York: The Free Press of Glencoe, 1964).

[41] *Ibid.*, p. v.

their plans. Many argue, however, that some of the solutions suggested by Professor Bernstein and the President's Committee would create more problems than they would solve.[42]

Abuses in Administration of Welfare and Pension Plans: A Special Note

The Taft-Hartley Act of 1947 required that welfare and pension plans established after 1945 by a labor representative with employer contributions be administered by a board of trustees representing management, labor, and the public. The purpose of this provision was to insure honest administration, but some cases of dishonest and irresponsible administration have occurred. For example, the trustees have in certain cases acted in collusion with insurance agents to embezzle premiums. Fortunately, however, such cases are definitely in the minority. This is especially true of pension plans which are subject to some controls by the Internal Revenue Service.

In 1958, however, because of growing concern for sound administration, Congress passed the Federal Welfare and Pension Plan Disclosure Act, which requires the administrators of all plans covering more than twenty-five persons to file plan descriptions and annual reports with the Secretary of Labor. The Secretary, however, has no enforcement powers. A 1962 amendment increased the amount of information required. Similar reports are also required in five states.[43]

The 1959 Labor-Management Reporting and Disclosure Act provides that certain designated personnel of union-created or administered (including jointly administered) funds be bonded.

Private insurers are in addition rather closely regulated by the states.

A Comment on Some Economic Issues

The existence of private insurance has important economic consequences. The over-all effect of private insurance is that of increasing the fund of savings available for investments in the economy. Annuity pre-

[42] For a recent comprehensive statement of the arguments against compulsory vesting requirements, see Joseph J. Melone, "Implications of Vested Benefits in Private Pension Plans," *The Journal of Risk and Insurance*, XXXII, No. 4 (December, 1965), 559–69. Dr. Melone argues that such legislation would impose an additional burden only on those employers who provide pensions for their employees, would favor covered employees over those with no pension plan, and might be followed by legislation requiring all employers to establish private plans. He urges further analysis of the basic objectives of the private pension movement. His arguments, he notes, are based on the assumption that private pensions are a clear-cut voluntary addition to OASDI, but he recognizes that other positions are both possible and tenable.

[43] Connecticut, Massachusetts, New York, Washington, and Wisconsin.

miums and the portions of life insurance premiums that are used to build up cash values represent a type of forced savings, which insurers must invest, thus increasing the production in the future when the insureds plan to retire. Private pension plans apparently not only result in forced savings but encourage savings in other ways.[44] The term portions of the premiums probably also lead to an increase in available short-term investment funds, for the insurer can invest these amounts for the period elapsing between the payment of the premiums and the payment of the expenses and benefits. If investment opportunities are not available, private insurance may simply reduce current spending and hence national income.[45]

One important consequence of private programs is their effect upon labor mobility, as affected particularly by group insurance. The effect of group life insurance is slight because the employee's only loss in moving from one employer to another may be a period of no coverage during the waiting period. As already noted, group pensions are a more important factor, especially when the vesting provisions are a function of the length of service. Older workers are more likely to be affected by this consideration than younger workers. It should also be remembered that seniority carries with it other advantages, which the worker must also consider.[46] Group insurance exerts its greatest influence when the proposed movement is from a firm with group insurance to one with no group insurance. Chapter 14 further analyzes these and other issues.

A Concluding Comment

As long as we wish to preserve the freedom and responsibility of the individual, private insurance will continue to play an important role in our quest for economic security. Social insurance will provide the floor of protection; private insurance makes it possible to carpet this floor. It is hoped and expected that the thickness of the carpet will increase in the future.

---

[44] For a discussion of some reasons why private pension plans probably increase aggregate consumer savings substantially, see Walter Williams, "Implications of Retirement Security Systems for Consumer Behavior," *The Journal of Risk and Insurance,* XXXII, No. 3 (September, 1965), 349–66.

[45] See Chapter 14 for further discussion of finance and investment issues.

[46] Daniel H. Brill, "Economic Impact of Private Pension Plans," *Pensions: Problems and Trends* (Homewood, Ill.: Richard D. Irwin, Inc., 1955), pp. 86–87.

See also Robert M. Ball, "The Economics of Pensions" in W. Haber and W. J. Cohen (eds.), *Social Security: Programs, Problems, and Policies* (Homewood, Ill.: Richard D. Irwin, Inc., 1960), pp. 477–93, and Robert Tilove, "Social and Economic Implications of Private Pensions," *Industrial and Labor Relations Review,* XIV, No. 1 (October, 1960), 24–34.

SUMMARY

Private life insurance and annuities include (1) individual life insurance and annuities, (2) group life insurance, and (3) group pension plans.

The basic types of individual life insurance contracts are term insurance contracts and non-term contracts including the straight life contract, the limited payment contract, and the endowment contract. Term insurance provides temporary protection against death losses only. Non-term contracts combine protection against death losses with a systematic savings plan.

The death proceeds are payable in a lump sum or according to some settlement option selected by the insured or his beneficiary.

The savings fund under non-term contracts may be used to continue some life insurance protection if the insured wishes to stop paying premiums. If the insured prefers, he may receive the savings fund in a lump sum or according to some settlement option.

Annuity contracts are primarily designed to protect the insured against the problems of old age. The basic annuities may be classified as immediate or deferred annuities and as straight life, instalment refund, or cash refund annuities. Annuities may also be classified according to whether they provide fixed or variable benefits.

Applicants for individual insurance must be insurable, but less than 3 per cent of the applications for ordinary insurance are declined.

Group life insurance was first written by a commercial insurer in 1912 for Montgomery Ward employees. Commercial insurers entered the group pension field in the twenties. Self-insured group pension plans were also important by that time. Almost all the early group plans were employer-initiated, but group insurance benefits are now an important issue for collective bargaining.

Each member of an eligible group is eligible for group life insurance even if he is not individually insurable. Another advantage to the insured is that the cost is lower than the cost of equivalent individual insurance.

Most group life insurance is yearly renewable term insurance. An insured who leaves the group may without proving insurability replace the group protection with an individual life insurance contract.

Group pension benefits are computed according to a defined benefit or a defined contribution formula. The benefits are specified in terms of one annuity form, but usually other forms may be elected.

Benefits available to employees terminating their employment at an early date depend upon the vesting provisions. Death benefits are usually limited to a return of the employee's contributions.

The pension plan may be a self-insured plan or an insured plan. The insured plans include a pension trust, a group annuity plan, a deposit administration plan, an immediate participation guarantee plan, and a separate account plan. Most pension plans are insured, but the self-insured plans cover more employees.

Most new group insurance plans are non-contributory, primarily because of the tax advantages and collective bargaining.

SUGGESTIONS FOR ADDITIONAL READING

BERNSTEIN, MERTON C. *The Future of Private Pensions.* New York: The Free Press of Glencoe, 1964.
A thought-provoking evaluation of the effectiveness of private pension plans.

DEARING, CHARLES L. *Industrial Pensions.* Washington: The Brookings Institution, 1954. Chapters 3 through 5.
A clear exposition of the nature and increasing importance of collective bargaining on industrial pensions and a concise description of the differences between single-firm and multi-firm plans.

GREGG, DAVIS W. *An Analysis of Group Life Insurance.* Homewood, Ill.: Richard D. Irwin, Inc., 1962.
The theory and the practice of group life insurance are examined in this authoritative volume.

GREGG, DAVIS W. (Ed.). *Life and Health Insurance Handbook,* 2nd ed. Homewood, Ill.: Richard D. Irwin, Inc., 1964.
A handbook of current practices and procedures in the life and health insurance fields.

EILERS, ROBERT D., and ROBERT M. CROWE (Eds.). *Group Insurance Handbook.* Homewood, Ill.: Richard D. Irwin, Inc., 1964.
A recently published handbook on group life and health insurance.

HAMILTON, JAMES A., and DORRANCE C. BRONSON. *Pensions.* New York: McGraw-Hill Book Co., 1958.
A comprehensive treatment of pension plans.

ILSE, LOUISE WOLTERS. *Group Insurance and Employee Retirement Plans.* Englewood Cliffs, N. J.: Prentice-Hall, Inc., 1953. Chapters 1 through 6; 12 and 13.
This text emphasizes the historical development of the group insurance movement.

MELONE, JOSEPH J. *Collectively-Bargained Multi-Employer Pension Plans.* Homewood, Ill.: Richard D. Irwin, Inc., 1963.
The most complete treatment of multi-employer pension plans available.

McGILL, DAN MAYS. *Fundamentals of Private Pensions,* 2nd ed. Homewood, Ill.: Richard D. Irwin, Inc., 1964.
An excellent description and analysis of the fundamentals of group pension plans.

McGILL, DAN MAYS. *Fulfilling Pension Expectations.* Homewood, Ill.: Richard D. Irwin, Inc., 1962.
  The master report on an investigation by several task forces into the reliability of private pension promises.

Public Policy and Private Pension Programs. A Report to the President on Private Employee Retirement Plans, by the President's Committee on Corporate Pension Funds and Other Private Retirement and Welfare Funds. Washington, D. C.: U. S. Government Printing Office, January, 1965.
  A report by a special committee appointed by President Kennedy to study pension and welfare plans.

1965 Study of Industrial Retirement Plans. New York: Bankers Trust Company, 1965.
  A study of recent trends in retirement plans and a tabulation of the provisions of over 200 retirement plans.

6

Problems of
Unemployment

INTRODUCTION

Interest in unemployment—problems and programs—has increased significantly since 1960, for a number of reasons. For one thing, the Kennedy and Johnson Administrations have been committed to lines of action seeking to lower the unemployment rate, which was hovering between the 5 and 7 per cent level. Also, there developed an extensive analytical debate over the relative roles of "aggregate demand" versus "structural" factors as causes of unemployment. This combination of analysis and policy made debate and discussion more intense than it had been for some years.

We are concerned in this section with "economic" unemployment—that arising from a reduction, relative or absolute, in the demand for labor. In the previous chapter we analyzed unemployment associated with old age; in the next we treat that related to illness. If unemployment, as a source of income curtailment, is viewed as arising from all three sources noted above, there is little doubt that it is the prime factor giving rise to economic insecurity. But, even if one looks only at the "economic" variant, one cannot help being struck by its significance. The generation—including the authors'—which felt the post-1929 impacts of economic unemployment was particularly aware of its devastating effects. But even today, unemployment affects millions.

This chapter deals with three major topics: (1) the concepts of employment and unemployment, (2) their measurement, and (3) the ways in which society has sought to prevent or lessen unemployment.

THE PROBLEM OF UNEMPLOYMENT

General Nature

The economist has traditionally concerned himself with involuntary unemployment—the case where, at a given wage level and with a given set of working conditions, there are more job seekers than jobs available. We shall enlarge upon the details of this shortly. "Involuntary" is, however, an elusive term. What of the person who has been unemployed for so long a period that he has lost the motivation to continue to look for work? What of the rarer case, the person who would prefer welfare to work? When does involuntary become voluntary? Since these cases involve problems outside the range of competence of the economist he has tended to leave them to social workers and other specialists. Instead, he has concerned himself with the creation and maintenance of employment opportunities and with the allocation of labor to them.

Involuntary unemployment may be defined, as noted above, as the difference between the quantity of labor services offered at a given level of wages with a given set of working conditions, and the quantity of labor services taken at such levels. If job seekers outnumber job offers, involuntary unemployment exists. Translated into individual terms, this means simply that a given person may not be able to find employment or may lose what he has.

But factors other than wage level relationships are causally important in unemployment. Because of particular forces in a given economic situation, it may be possible that even an adjusted wage level would not reduce unemployment. Thus, in a declining industry, say railroad passenger transportation, a reduction in wages may not be a feasible means to increase, let alone maintain, employment. Or, in certain seasonal operations such as processing foodstuffs, if the raw materials are non-existent at the moment, wage rate changes may be able to accomplish little in providing work opportunities. Thus it is necessary to distinguish between *aggregate* involuntary unemployment arising out of deficiencies in labor demand related to wage levels, and *selective* involuntary unemployment arising out of deficiencies in labor demand caused, even if only temporarily, by structural economic factors such as production conditions, changes in technology, and changes in consumer preferences.

The labor market does not, however, operate as impersonally as this type of discussion might indicate. "People" seek jobs; "people" offer jobs. All sorts of human decisions are involved in the process, some of them non-rational. Hence, some individuals might find it difficult to secure employment irrespective of the state of economic activity.[1] If employer hiring selectivity increases as conditions worsen, the problem is compounded for some individuals. Thus, this "personal" factor is important.

Therefore, several factors are at work in creating unemployment: first, the impersonal operation of the labor market, reflecting aggregate demands for and supplies of labor at various wage levels (and with possibilities of involuntary unemployment at different wage levels); second, the more selective though still impersonal structural problems of indus-tries or companies, reflecting demands for labor not necessarily wage related; and third, the personalized hiring *and* job-getting process, that is, the personal operation of the labor market as seen by the individual. Notwithstanding this classification, unemployment cannot yet be handled on the basis of statistical probability as was done for life expectancy in Chapter 2. The implications of this for policy are clear.

Unemployment is not an easy term to define precisely or to quantify, either conceptually or empirically, let alone in terms of the above three-fold classification.[2] We have focused above on involuntary unemployment, on the basis that voluntary unemployment, by its very definition, has no relevance for the problem of economic insecurity. But, as we noted, "voluntary" is an elusive term: an individual may be "voluntarily" idle in the sense that his search for work has been discouraging and he has temporarily removed himself from the labor force or in the sense that he is only interested if a certain type of job comes along. How much of this "involuntary voluntarism" exists is not definitely known; probably it is not large except for older age groups, where it may be significant. But there is little doubt that conceptually it creates a problem in the measurement of unemployment.

"Partial" employment poses another issue. In the midpoint of the decade (1960–1970 inclusive), data for July, 1965, showed that out of 61,823,000 persons at work, 12,350,000 or 20 per cent worked less than thirty-five hours. Table 6.1 points this up. Not all of this partial employment has an equivalent unemployment counterpart. For example, certain classes of employees, such as housewives, may prefer to work (and may be able to work) only a restricted number of hours per week. To the extent that this is true, productive capacity is expanded by any participation on their part in the labor force and theirs is not involuntary unemployment. But there is no doubt that among these 12,350,000

[1] See Joseph W. Garbarino, *The Unemployed Worker During A Period of Full Employment,* Reprint No. 50 (Berkeley: University of California, Institute of Industrial Relations, 1954).

[2] The reader interested in a detailed discussion is referred to *The Measurement and Behavior of Unemployment,* A Report of the National Bureau of Economic Research (Princeton: Princeton University Press, 1957).

women there are many who are only "partially" employed and who would prefer a longer work week. (In mid-1966, the entire structure had moved upward, there were fewer partially employed, and average hours worked had increased. This was the consequence of the tightened labor market that developed in 1966.)

TABLE 6.1

Hours Worked, Survey Week, July, 1965

Total at work	66,823,000
1–4 hours	831,000
5–14 hours	2,947,000
15–34 hours	8,570,000
35–40 hours	31,177,000
41 hours and over	23,296,000
Average hours, total at work	41.3

Source: U. S. Department of Labor, Bureau of Labor Statistics, *Employment and Earnings* (August, 1965), p. 8.

"Disguised" unemployment is a further problem that is both conceptually and realistically important, though quantifying it is an extremely difficult task. This type of unemployment occurs when persons are not placed in jobs where their capacities are utilized to the fullest. Such unemployment implies that a norm or standard of employment is not being met. Examples of such under-utilization are common: excess numbers of persons in given industries such as agriculture, or in given regions such as the South, who would make a greater contribution to national productivity if labor mobility operated so as to place them elsewhere. Or in a given company, industry, or area a similar case exists when an individual is not producing to capacity because the placement process has not located him where his abilities would be best utilized.[3]

The Focus of This Chapter. In this chapter we shall be concerned essentially with involuntary and total unemployment. Partial and disguised unemployment will receive some attention, the former in the general discussion on unemployment, the latter in a more special way. However, any detailed analysis of and prescription for disguised unemployment not only raises broad issues of economic policy, but also leads us to a consideration of education, counseling, placement, and other topics far beyond the scope of this book. Partial unemployment, while

[3] For a useful discussion of both the above topics see the paper, "The Meaning and Measurement of Partial and Disguised Unemployment," by L. J. Ducoff and M. J. Hagood in the previously cited National Bureau of Economic Research volume, *The Measurement and Behavior of Unemployment*. See also Fernando Sierra Berdecia and A. J. Jaffe, "The Concept and Measurement of Underemployment," *Monthly Labor Review*, LXXVIII, No. 3 (March, 1955), 283–87.

involving some specialized characteristics, is of such a nature as to permit treatment under the analysis of general unemployment.

The Measurement of Unemployment: Aggregate Data

Not until 1940 was information available on a comprehensive and continuous basis on the extent of unemployment. Census data were available in earlier years in the form of gross figures on those totally unemployed during the census survey week. But these data are not entirely comparable from one census to another, and of course they did not constitute continuous annual series. Private estimates were prepared at least as far back as 1897, but they also are subject to limitations of various sorts.

Unemployment Data, 1929 to Date. Beginning with the application of the "labor force" concept in 1940, data have been available continuously since that year, and have been carried back to 1929. The data are published in *Employment and Earnings,* issued by the Department of Labor. While the specialist might wish to question the concepts utilized in this labor force framework, the statistical techniques employed (though basic changes and improvements were made in 1954 and 1957), and the possible sampling errors in the estimates, the data are nevertheless reliable indicators of *changes* in the volume of employment and unemployment. And they are far better than anything we have had in the past. (The "labor force" measurements were developed in the Bureau of the Census, U. S. Department of Commerce. For many years they were issued by that Bureau in the form of a release titled *Monthly Report on the Labor Force,* or *MRLF.* Beginning in 1959 the Bureau of Labor Statistics in the U. S. Department of Labor took over the analysis function, with, however, the Census Bureau still collecting and tabulating the data. The *MRLF* is now part of a more comprehensive monthly BLS publication titled *Employment and Earnings.*)

The relevant definitions in this labor force conceptual framework are as follows: [4]

1. *Employed.* Employed persons comprise those who, during the survey week, were either (a) "at work"—those who did any work for pay or profit, or worked without pay for 15 hours or more on a family farm or business; or (b) "with a job but not at work"— those who did not work and were not looking for work but had a

---

[4] See the monthly publication *Employment and Earnings.* For a discussion of conceptual and statistical problems, see President's Committee to Appraise Employment and Unemployment Statistics, *Measuring Employment and Unemployment* (Washington, D. C.: U. S. Government Printing Office, 1962).

job or business from which they were temporarily absent because of vacation, illness, industrial dispute, bad weather, or because they were taking time off for various reasons.

2. *Unemployed.* Unemployed persons include those who during the survey week (a) did not work at all and were looking for work; or (b) did not work at all and were (1) waiting to be called back from layoff; (2) not in school and were waiting to report for a job scheduled to begin in the next 30 days; (3) would have been looking for work except temporarily ill or believed no work was available in their line.

3. *Labor force.* The civilian labor force comprises the total of all civilians classified as employed or unemployed in accordance with the criteria described above. The total labor force also includes members of the armed forces stationed either in the United States or abroad.

Using these definitions, data on employment and unemployment are available from 1929 on. Table 6.2 summarizes this information.

Unemployment Data, 1900–29. Additional data, going back to 1897 in one case, have been developed by Paul Douglas, John P. Herring, the National Industrial Conference Board, and others.[5] The data, however, tend to be set in a framework different from that of "labor force." The most comprehensive statistics have been prepared by Stanley Lebergott.[6] His figures show unemployment fluctuating between a low of 0.8 per cent in 1906, and a high of 11.9 per cent in 1921, with the median between 4.4 and 4.8 per cent.

Other Sources of Unemployment Data. In conjunction with the operation of the Unemployment Insurance program, the Bureau of Employment Security prepares weekly figures on initial unemployment claims as well as on insured unemployment. For July, 1965, insured unemployment under state programs was 1,164,800, this comparing with a labor force unemployment total figure of 3,415,000.[7] Of necessity, insured unemployment figures are lower; for, quite apart from technical statistical differences, not all the unemployed are covered under the unemployment

[5] See Paul H. Douglas, *Real Wages in the United States, 1890–1926* (Boston: Houghton Mifflin Co., 1930), Table 172, p. 460; John P. Herring, *Labor Force, Employment and Unemployment* (Seattle: University of Washington Press, 1951), p. 47; National Industrial Conference Board, *Economic Almanac* (New York: 1945–46), pp. 38–39.

[6] See his "Annual Estimates of Unemployment in the United States, 1900–1950" in the previously cited National Bureau of Economic Research volume, *The Measurement and Behavior of Unemployment*, particularly Table 1 on pp. 215–16, and his volume, *Manpower in Economic Growth: The American Record Since 1800* (New York: McGraw-Hill Book Co., 1964).

[7] For these kinds of data see current issues of *Unemployment Insurance Statistics.* Total insured unemployment (including other programs) was 1,256,000 in July, 1965.

TABLE 6.2

Employment–Unemployment, 1929–65

Annual Average	Total Including Armed Forces	In Labor Force			
		Civilian Labor Force			
		Civilian	Employed	Unemployed	
				Number	Per Cent
1929	49,440	49,180	47,630	1,550	3.2
1930	50,080	49,820	45,480	4,340	8.7
1931	50,680	50,420	42,400	8,020	15.9
1932	51,250	51,000	38,940	12,060	23.6
1933	51,840	51,590	38,760	12,830	24.9
1934	52,490	52,230	40,890	11,340	21.7
1935	53,140	52,870	42,260	10,610	20.1
1936	53,740	53,440	44,410	9,030	16.9
1937	54,320	54,000	46,300	7,700	14.3
1938	54,950	54,610	44,220	10,390	19.0
1939	55,600	55,230	45,750	9,480	17.2
1940	56,030	55,640	47,520	8,120	14.6
1941	57,380	55,910	50,350	5,560	9.9
1942	60,230	56,410	53,750	2,660	4.7
1943	64,410	55,540	54,470	1,070	1.9
1944	65,890	54,630	53,960	670	1.2
1945	65,140	53,860	52,820	1,040	1.9
1946	60,820	57,520	55,250	2,270	3.9
1947	61,608	60,168	58,027	2,142	3.6
1948	62,748	61,442	59,378	2,064	3.4
1949	63,571	62,105	58,423	3,682	5.9
1950	64,599	63,099	59,748	3,351	5.3
1951	65,832	62,884	60,784	2,099	3.3
1952	66,426	62,966	61,035	1,932	3.1
1953 *	66,965	63,815	61,945	1,870	2.9
1954	67,819	64,468	60,890	3,578	5.6
1955	68,896	65,847	62,944	2,904	4.4
1956	70,387	67,530	64,708	2,822	4.2
1957	70,744	67,946	65,011	2,936	4.3
1958	71,284	68,647	63,966	4,681	6.8
1959	71,946	69,394	65,581	3,813	5.5
1960	73,126	70,612	66,681	3,931	5.6
1961	74,175	71,603	66,796	4,806	6.7
1962	74,681	71,854	67,846	4,007	5.6
1963	75,712	72,975	68,809	4,166	5.7
1964	76,971	74,233	70,357	3,876	5.2
1965	78,357	75,635	72,179	3,456	4.6

* Beginning in 1953 a new sample was used, and in 1957 definitional changes were made, both of which affect comparability. Data include Alaska and Hawaii beginning in 1960.

Source: U. S. Department of Labor, Bureau of Labor Statistics, *Employment and Earnings* (August, 1961), p. 1, and subsequent issues. For the effects of changes in estimating procedures upon the historical comparability of the data, see *Employment and Earnings* (May, 1962), p. xiv.

insurance system. The data are useful, however, for comparative purposes.

State agencies frequently provide monthly, annual, or other time-period estimates, useful on the local or regional level.[8]

The Measurement of Unemployment: Specialized Data

Unemployment has dimensions other than weekly, monthly, or annual aggregates for the economy.[9] Data—detailed in some cases, fragmentary in others—are available for various of these other dimensions and are discussed below. To a considerable extent these data can be fitted into the previously noted "selective" and "personal" categories of unemployment. A knowledge of these dimensions is important because attempts to deal with unemployment must recognize them. The problem is more complex than merely finding a given number of additional jobs for the economy as a whole.

General Employment and Earnings. The Bureau of Labor Statistics, in its monthly publication *Employment and Earnings*, provides data on employment, employment trends, and labor turnover—this in addition to the *Monthly Report on the Labor Force*, included in the same publication. These data are technically not of the same dimension as those in the labor force noted above, but they are useful complements. The lack of comparability arises from the fact that the labor force approach uses household reporting (receives its information from households) while the other BLS series use establishment reporting (information obtained from business firms). The approaches are likewise conceptually different: the BLS measures the number of jobs; the MRLF, the numbers of individuals with jobs.

Unemployment by Regions. Unemployment tends to vary by geographic regions. Such unemployment may result from various causes: resource depletion, changes in demand for the products turned out by industries in the region, natural catastrophes such as floods. Regional unemployment may persist for long periods as in textiles in New England or coal mining in West Virginia, or it may be more short-lived as in automobiles in Detroit or steel in Pittsburgh. There were indications, however, arising out of the 1957–58 and 1960–61 recessions that the depressed

---

[8] Such data can customarily be obtained, without cost, from the appropriate unemployment insurance administrative agency in the state.

[9] See the papers by P. M. Hauser, and D. L. Kaplan and L. Levine in the previously cited National Bureau of Economic Research volume, *The Measurement and Behavior of Unemployment*.

area problem was becoming more critical.[10] The Bureau of Employment Security presently classifies major labor markets ("regions") into six groups ranging from labor shortage areas (with less than a 1.5 per cent ratio of unemployment to total labor force) to labor surplus areas (with an unemployment ratio of 12 per cent or more). At mid-1965, there were no labor shortage areas, but 46 were classified as "low unemployment" (1.5 to 2.9 per cent) areas and only two—both in Puerto Rico—were in the labor surplus category. This was a distinct improvement over 1961, and as the economy moved into 1966, the improvement trend continued. (The improvement continued also in "smaller" labor markets for which data are maintained.[11])

Unemployment by Occupation and Industry. Unemployment also varies by occupation and industry. Thus, in 1965, the occupational breakdown shown in Table 6.3 can be found.

TABLE 6.3

Unemployed Persons, by Occupation of Last Job, July, 1965

Occupation	Unemployment Rate	Per Cent Distribution
TOTAL	4.6	100.0
White-collar workers	2.0	18.1
Professional and technical	1.3	3.2
Managers, officials, and proprietors	.9	1.9
Clerical workers	2.7	8.7
Sales workers	3.1	4.3
Blue-collar workers	4.8	38.7
Craftsmen and foremen	3.0	8.1
Operatives	5.5	21.8
Non-farm laborers	6.5	8.7
Service workers	5.2	14.9
Private household workers	5.0	3.3
Other service workers	5.3	11.6
Farm workers	1.9	2.8
Farmers and farm managers	.1	.1
Farm laborers and foremen	3.3	2.7
No previous work experience	—	25.4

Source: U. S. Department of Labor, Bureau of Labor Statistics, *Employment and Earnings* (August, 1965), p. 4.

[10] See the Hearings of the Senate Special Committee on Unemployment Problems, Eugene J. McCarthy, Chairman (Washington, D. C.: U. S. Government Printing Office, 1959–60). See also the variously published accounts of the Depressed Area legislation introduced during the Kennedy Administration, and subsequent Congressional Hearings on automation and unemployment.

[11] See *Area Trends in Employment and Unemployment* (July, 1965), pp. 1–11.

These differences can be explained by demand and supply and the forces behind them: changing consumer preferences, changing technology, the nature of the occupation and the skills it requires, its seasonality, and the "fixed" versus "variable" cost nature of differing vocations.

Other variations are also found. Thus, industrial employment may decrease at a given time, but non-industrial may increase. Or, one may find construction with a high percentage of unemployment, self-employed with a low, with others in between. In part, the self-employment figures may be misleading, since many of the self-employed may continue in marginal businesses rather than look for employment elsewhere.[12]

Unemployment by Age and Sex. Hauser and Pearl found, except for the war years, no "striking differences over the past decade [1940–50] between the unemployment rates of men and women."[13] In absolute numbers there have been changes, however, with unemployed men outnumbering unemployed women three to one in 1940, but only two and one-half to one or so at the end of the decade. By age there appears to be a higher rate for the teen-age group, tapering off to ages forty-five to fifty-four and then tending to rise again. This is the familiar "U-shaped" curve. The reasons for this are almost self-evident in terms of employer and union policies, and of American cultural factors.

Unemployment by Duration of Unemployment. Table 6.4 summarizes this information. While short-term unemployment has its various consequences, it is the individual who exhausts his right to unemployment compensation who, with his family, faces the critical problem. In periods of high-level employment the number of such cases may not be large, but there may be industry or regional cases which do pose serious problems.[14] Duration of unemployment appears to be higher for men than for women, for older as compared to younger persons, and to be on the increase since World War II.[15]

Other Dimensions. The unemployment rate in the United States is consistently higher for non-white than for white workers, and this is true

[12] For an interesting discussion of these cases, see T. C. Fichlander, cited in W. S. Woytinsky and Associates, *Employment and Wages in the United States* (New York: The Twentieth Century Fund, 1953).

[13] See Philip M. Hauser and Robert B. Pearl, "Who Are the Unemployed?" *Journal of the American Statistical Association*, XLV, No. 252 (December, 1950), 486–89, and the article by Philip M. Hauser, "Differential Unemployment in the United States," in the previously cited National Bureau of Economic Research volume, *The Measurement and Behavior of Unemployment*.

[14] See the monthly publication, *Unemployment Insurance Statistics*.

[15] For a detailed discussion see U. S. Department of Labor, Bureau of Employment Security, *Persistent Unemployment—Problems and Programs*, Mimeographed Release, October, 1959.

even during periods of "full" employment.[16] There is an inverse correlation between income group and unemployment. Here again the reasons are largely those of occupational association, lower income tending to be associated with occupations having independently a higher unemployment rate. Seasonal rates vary as do those for "secondary" employees.[17] Still other dimensions could be noted, but the above examples illustrate the availability of aggregate selective, and personal unemployment data.

TABLE 6.4

Unemployed Persons, by Duration of Unemployment, July, 1965

Duration of Unemployment	Thousands of Persons	Per Cent Distribution	Category	Thousands of Persons	Per Cent Distribution
TOTAL	3,602	100.0	TOTAL	3,602	100.0
Less than 5 weeks	1,888	52.4	Persons on temporary		
5 to 14 weeks	1,127	31.3	layoff	130	3.6
5 and 6 weeks	453	12.6			
7 to 10 weeks	495	13.7	Persons scheduled		
11 to 14 weeks	180	5.0	to begin new jobs		
15 weeks and over	587	16.3	within 30 days	136	3.8
15 to 26 weeks	250	6.9			
27 weeks and over	337	9.4	All other unemployed	3,336	92.6
Average (mean) duration	10.5	——			

Source: U. S. Department of Labor, Bureau of Labor Statistics, *Employment and Earnings* (August, 1965), p. 5.

Full Employment and the Historical Pattern of Unemployment

If one accepts the maintenance of a high level of employment as a desirable goal of society, then it may be instructive to measure past performance of the economy with this yardstick. A "high level of employment" may, of course, be interpreted in different ways. In turn, the performance record will vary depending upon the standard selected.

At one extreme is the criterion of "full employment." Defined in its more rigorous sense the concept has been interpreted as

Full employment . . . means having always more vacant jobs than unemployed men . . . it means that the normal lag between losing one job and finding another will be very short.[18]

[16] See Garbarino, *op. cit.*, pp. 16–23.

[17] See the article by Richard C. Wilcock in the previously cited National Bureau of Economic Research study, *The Measurement and Behavior of Unemployment*.

[18] See William H. Beveridge, *Full Employment in a Free Society* (New York: W. W. Norton & Co., 1945), p. 18.

A somewhat less rigorous definition, though not necessarily incompatible with Beveridge's, is found in a United Nations Report:

. . . We define full employment as a situation in which unemployment does not exceed the minimum allowances that must be made for the effects of seasonal and frictional forces.[19]

A yardstick that appears still less exacting is given in the 1953 *Economic Report of the President,* where it is noted:

And it is assumed for purposes of this study that unemployment, which during the past 2 years has been below the 2-million mark, could rise to as much as 2½ million by 1955 without presenting a general unemployment problem. Such an unemployment figure in a considerably larger labor force would not depart so markedly from the Nation's legislated objective of "maximum employment" as to call for new counteracting public measures. . . .[20]

Two and one-half million out of a labor force of 68.6 million (the 1955 projection) would amount to a percentage of 3.6. Various other views of "high-level" employment are to be found, ranging up to unemployment levels of 5 per cent or so.[21] (In some cases a range of percentages is used, with variations allowed for seasonal and frictional factors.) While 5 per cent was a "popular" figure in the 1950's, 4 per cent is more frequently heard these days, and has been accepted as an intermediate target by the Kennedy–Johnson Administrations.

If one takes the least rigorous concept of "full employment" (or "high-level employment")—say 4 per cent unemployment—then using the Lebergott data, in forty-two of the last sixty-five years, unemployment has been higher. Moreover, nine of the years in which unemployment was lower were war years. The record is somewhat better since 1940; unemployment was over 4 per cent in only fifteen of the twenty-five years 1941–65.

[19] See *National and International Measures for Full Employment* (Lake Success: United Nations, 1949), p. 13.

[20] *The Economic Report of the President,* January, 1953 (Washington, D. C.: U. S. Government Printing Office), p. 83.

[21] See Lloyd Reynolds, *Labor Economics and Labor Relations* (3rd ed.; Englewood Cliffs, N. J.: Prentice-Hall, Inc., 1959), p. 367, where he notes: ". . . something like 5 per cent unemployment may be close to the point of price balance in our economy." In his 4th edition, Reynolds notes there is no single figure for full employment, and a trade-off of reducing unemployment versus increasing prices is involved. A 4 per cent level is the judgment of the Committee for Economic Development. Others would think 5 per cent too high. See John Dunlop, "Public Policy and Employment," in *Studies in Unemployment,* prepared for the Senate Special Committee on Unemployment, Eugene J. McCarthy, Chairman (Washington, D. C.: U. S. Government Printing Office, 1960). For a comprehensive discussion see the article by Albert Rees in the previously cited *The Measurement and Behavior of Unemployment.* See also *The American Economy in 1961,* Statement of the Council of Economic Advisers, Walter W. Heller, Chairman, March 6, 1961, in which 4 per cent is viewed as an intermediate target.

And, with both major political parties committed to some type of "full employment" policy, it is not likely that we shall see in our lifetime a duplication of the experiences of the 1930's. But the reduction of unemployment is not a cost-free process, particularly if accompanied by rising prices. To a considerable extent, as we move along in the 1960's, the preoccupation of economists is not with *deflation* and unemployment, but with trying to approach high-level employment, while keeping a rein on inflation.[22]

The Impacts of Unemployment

Thus far we have talked about the dimensions of unemployment without specifying in any detail why it is an undesirable phenomenon. In one respect the answer may appear obvious; in others it may be well to be more specific.

Impacts upon the Economy. Unemployment has negative impacts upon the level of economic activity in the national economy, the region, or the locality. (We make no distinction here as to "cause" and "result.") The experience of the United States in the 1930's, of various textile mill areas in the North for a longer period, or of the western "ghost town" illustrates this point. The impact upon industries and firms, and upon other businesses in various areas, is also clear, as is the influence upon future supplies of skilled labor.

While aggregate unemployment has been less in the last two decades than in earlier periods, selective unemployment persists and in some regions has become chronic. It has been said that unemployment frequently serves a useful "corrective" economic function. This has a grain of truth to it, but the process is still inherently "cruel" and in many cases of selective unemployment it does *not* provide the adjustment necessary.

Impacts upon the Individual and His Family. The direct income loss impacts are obvious. But there are indirect and non-economic consequences. While it is hard to quantify these impacts, or even estimate their seriousness in some cases, there seems to be little doubt that they are undesirable in nature. There appears to be some loss of skill in protracted unemployment, a worsening of the mental outlook, some increase

[22] Indeed, some labor economists view unemployment as a phenomenon which has a psychotic hold on the American consciousness and they suggest that overexpansion rather than deflation has been the tendency in the past fifty years. See, for example, Orme W. Phelps, *Introduction to Labor Economics* (New York: McGraw-Hill Book Co., 1950), pp. 155–59. For a summary of many of the issues see *Wages, Prices, Profits and Productivity* (New York: Columbia University, The American Assembly, 1959) and William G. Bowen, *The Wage-Price Issue* (Princeton: Princeton University Press, 1960).

in delinquency, physical debilitation, very frequently of children in the family, and some deterioration of the family unit.[23]

Impacts upon Social Institutions. Unemployment reaches beyond the individual, the family, and beyond economic forces to society as a whole. It affects social institutions of many types, changing the direction toward which political parties move, instituting new beliefs and new groups—Technocracy and the Technocrats, the Townsend plan and the Townsendites—and making for a realignment of the structure of society.[24]

Whether these social changes can be held to be essentially undesirable (as were the impacts upon the individual and his family) is a matter of opinion. Certainly, however, unemployment has been an important instrumentality in making for change. Unemployment has been, to be sure, only a symptom of deeper-lying causes, yet there is little doubt that it was one of the symbols seized upon in the pressures of social change.

THE TYPES OF UNEMPLOYMENT

There are many ways of classifying the "types" of unemployment or, what is similarly construed, the "causes" of unemployment. This "causal factor" problem is of current importance—and has been since 1961—not only because of its analytical aspects, but, more critically, since policy alternatives depend upon the relative significance of varying causes.

The classification used here is the same as found earlier in this chapter and includes the following three basic categories: [25]

1. "Aggregate" unemployment, reflecting "secular" or "cyclical" causal factors, including the idea of "permanent underemployment"
2. "Selective" or "structural" unemployment, reflecting seasonal, technological, casual, and other causal factors; this category tended to receive particular emphasis in the 1960–61 recession

[23] Several useful, though older, sources which discuss this problem are Philip Klein, *The Burden of Unemployment* (New York: The Russell Sage Foundation, 1923); Stuart A. Rice, "The Effect of Unemployment upon the Worker and His Family," in *Business Cycles and Unemployment* (New York: McGraw-Hill Book Co., 1923); and *Men without Work, A Report Made to the Pilgrim Trust* (Cambridge: Cambridge University Press, 1938). Areas of interest change, and we have relatively little research of this type today as compared with a quarter-century ago. Perhaps the last big wave of data concerns the physical and mental condition of members of the armed forces in World War II and the relation of such condition to economic experiences in the post-1929 period. There appears, however, to have been some increase in interest following recent recessions.

[24] For an interesting analysis, see Robert S. and Helen M. Lynd, *Middletown in Transition* (New York: Harcourt, Brace & World, Inc., 1937); and Frederick Lewis Allen's two books, *Only Yesterday* and *Since Yesterday* (New York: Harper & Row, 1931 and 1939 respectively).

[25] For a broader set of concepts, see *National and International Measures For Full Employment, op. cit.,* pp. 11 ff.

3. "Personal" unemployment, largely involving human beings in the labor market: the ways people get jobs and the ways in which employers operate in the labor market.

We shall take up each of these in turn.

Aggregate Unemployment

This type of unemployment is at first instance a reflection of the *aggregate* demand for labor. Given this statement, different analysts in the labor field approach the problem somewhat differently, although two main lines of thought can be found.

1. The first type of aggregate unemployment arises out of the idea that the customary state of the economy, particularly an industrialized economy, is characterized by an insufficiency and instability of effective demand. The key to understanding this effective demand problem lies in recognizing the fact that, under a private enterprise system, the decisions to save and to invest are to a considerable extent independent of each other. This approach reflects the course of developments culminating in Lord Keynes' *General Theory* in 1936. If permanent underemployment is not only a theoretical possibility but a real-life tendency, then appropriate counter-measures must be found, whether privately or publicly originated. Both major American political parties, whether they would grant the existence of such a type of underemployment (at least on a permanent basis), are seemingly committed to monetary and fiscal policies which would prevent its occurrence.

2. A second type of aggregate or "mass" unemployment is that caused by cyclical forces.[26] The drop in production—and employment—may be triggered by a drop in spending occurring anywhere in the economy, but is most likely to develop in capital expenditures, government outlays, or consumer purchases of durables, with probably the first and second items the more important.[27] It is cyclical unemployment which has been the most serious and the most prolonged type in the United States. Reference to Table 6.2 reveals the pattern of this type of unemployment.

[26] See, for example, Reynolds, *op. cit.*, pp. 362 ff. It is interesting to note that, except for an indirect citation on p. 441, Reynolds does not mention Keynes—nor does he discuss permanent underemployment. Nor in the 4th edition is Keynes to be found. Fashions change in this field as well as in others.

[27] Here is an example of where our analysis stops at the proximate stage; to get at the reasons for the change in expenditures would lead us into topics outside the province of this discussion. Obviously, however, any monetary and fiscal policy which tackles the unemployment problem cannot stop at the proximate level, but must go deeper.

Selective or Structural Unemployment

In contrast to "mass" unemployment, with its impact upon the economy as a whole, there are numerous other types of unemployment affecting only particular individuals or groups in the economy. Such unemployment is sometimes called "normal," since some authorities hold it to be expected in a dynamically functioning economy. Given causal factors lie behind each of these types. These causal factors are all demand-deficiency oriented, but the deficiency is specialized rather than generalized as is the case in mass unemployment, and it arises out of structural features of the economy. Inasmuch as solutions to each type involve an understanding of causes, it is desirable to spell them out.

1. Seasonal unemployment is the single most important type of non-mass unemployment. Woytinsky notes that in the pre-World War II period, seasonal changes tended to make October (the high month) employment some 4.1 to 4.3 million higher than in the low month of January, although the latter month was not the seasonal trough for all industries.[28] Seasonality is essentially a function of two factors: first, weather conditions, influencing agriculture and outdoor construction, and second, "custom," affecting demand and production in industries such as automobiles, apparel, and retail trade. These two major factors exhibit some interdependence. Since there is likewise an interdependence among business enterprises in the economy, the economic impacts of seasonality may extend outward like the ripples made when a stone is cast into a mill-pond.

2. Casual unemployment can be viewed as a foreshortened form of the seasonal type. In this case the work is also intermittent in nature, but on a daily or weekly basis rather than by seasons. Longshoring provides a case in point. In such industries and occupations the problem may be heightened further by the attachment of an excessive labor force.

3. Technological unemployment results from the "displacement of men by machines." We do not argue here whether in the aggregate or in the long run such unemployment actually exists. In the short run and for certain individuals and groups, there is little doubt of the reality of job separations from this cause.[29] "Automation" affords a current illus-

[28] See Woytinsky, *op. cit.*, pp. 336–41, and U. S. Department of Commerce, Bureau of the Census, Current Population Reports, Series P-50, No. 82, "Seasonal Variations in the Labor Force, Employment, and Unemployment" (April, 1958). There has been considerable controversy recently over seasonal adjustments in unemployment figures.

[29] For two analyses, see the Work Projects Administration project reports, *Survey of Economic Theory on Technological Change and Employment*, and *Unemployment and Technological Change* (Philadelphia: 1940).

tration of this phenomenon.[30] Congressional hearings in the 1960's on automation attest to the contemporary importance of—and fears about—the process.

4. Secular declines in demand for specific types of goods and services—and hence declines in the derived demand for labor—are causes of unemployment. Again, while the long-run effects of such changes may be debatable, there is little doubt about the short-run displacement. Illustrations in this field are numerous: diesel for steam power, the synthetic revolution in fabrics, the change in styles of women's headgear, the decline in the use of men's hats. The first two of the above illustrations indicate demand changes linked with broad-scale changes in technology; the latter two are indicative of changes in fashion.

5. Conversion-reconversion unemployment, noted in particular from 1940 on as the United States converted twice to war and back to peace again. While this form of displacement may be short-lived, and may not even result in a change of employers by the individuals involved, it may be sufficiently serious locally to warrant calling it an emergency. This type of unemployment is accentuated by the ebb and flow of government contract allocation in the defense field and by changes in the location of military installations.

6. In all the above cases, regional unemployment may be a resultant. Thus, technological change may leave a community with heavy unemployment. Or, changes in demand for goods and services may do the same. But stranded areas may result from other causes: depletion of local natural resources, the migration of industry, or natural disasters. This "depressed area" problem has been receiving increased attention, with Congressional investigations, enacted legislation, and Presidential vetoes. At the time of revising these materials in mid-1966 the newspapers and economic journals were still full of accounts of depressed area matters.[31]

7. Finally, in the area of specific unemployment, there may be a miscellany of causes: industrial disputes, the failure of a specific business enterprise, temporary natural disasters (spring floods provide a recurring illustration), and other factors.

[30] See Clyde E. Dankert, "Automation and Unemployment," in *Studies in Unemployment,* prepared for the U. S. Senate Special Committee on Unemployment Problems, Eugene J. McCarthy, Chairman (Washington, D. C.: U. S. Government Printing Office, 1960). The reports of this Committee are an invaluable source of information on unemployment, as are subsequent Congressional Hearings on automation and unemployment.

[31] See the articles by John R. Fernstrom and William H. Miernyk in *Studies in Unemployment, ibid.* Also see W. H. Miernyk, *Depressed Industrial Areas—A National Problem* (Washington, D. C.: National Planning Association, 1957), and *Distressed Areas in a Growing Economy* (New York: Committee for Economic Development, June, 1961).

The above seven types are different from mass unemployment essentially in terms of the causes and of the numbers of people involved. On this basis the remedy to be applied may likewise be expected to be different. It is for this reason the story is spelled out in some detail.

Personal Unemployment

The above two major categories may be viewed as impersonal in form, in that the specter of unemployment beckons impartially. (We exempt here cases of "favoritism" in layoffs and discharges; the developing application of seniority and the use of grievance procedures have tended to lessen this.) But some individuals may find it difficult to obtain their first job; others, once displaced, may find re-employment difficult; and in the extreme case, the "unemployable" may result. In other instances, where workers are displaced for whatever cause, they may find other employment, but it may take an uneconomical amount of time. This problem is related to two factors: (1) the job-getting process: the way applicants look for jobs and the way in which employers look for employees (or, more broadly speaking, the process through which the labor market matches man and job), and (2) institutional restraints upon employment possibilities of various classes of people.[32]

The unemployment solution in such cases is quite different from that of aggregate or selective unemployment. In these latter two cases the approach is essentially through the "creation" of more jobs or through their regularization. In personal unemployment the approach is through the improvement of the job marketing process, and through the "improvement" of the individual by training and retraining. "Frictional" unemployment of some magnitude is to be expected in any changing economy. But the duration of such unemployment can no doubt be lessened through the wide dissemination of information about job openings and through other techniques designed to bring applicant and job together. Moreover, a more efficient labor marketing process would make for a better matching of applicant and job and thus tend to decrease disguised unemployment. Finally, a re-evaluation of employment standards may make possible a reduction in the hard core of the unemployables.

---

[32] For a basic reading list, the student should consult L. G. Reynolds and Joseph Shister, *Job Horizons* (New York: Harper & Row, 1949); L. G. Reynolds, *The Structure of Labor Markets* (New York: Harper & Row, 1951); E. W. Noland and E. W. Bakke, *Workers Wanted* (New York: Harper & Row, 1949); Herbert J. Parnes, "Research on Labor Mobility," *Bulletin 65* (New York: Social Science Research Council, 1954); *Labor Mobility and Economic Opportunity* (Cambridge: The Technology Press, 1954); and William Haber *et al.* (eds.), *Manpower in the United States* (New York: Harper & Row, 1954).

The Debate of the 1960's

The discussion generated by the Council of Economic Advisers under Chairman Walter W. Heller began in early 1961 with the first report issued by the new Council.[33] The question was not whether there existed both aggregate and structural causal forces; the reality of both was readily recognized. The question was rather: Was the increase in unemployment since the mid-1950's primarily a result of aggregate demand deficiency or of structural factors? The answer given in this first report, subsequently reaffirmed in later reports, and since generally accepted, was that aggregate demand deficiency was the root problem.[34]

Hence, policy prescription, while not neglecting structural problems, was directed primarily toward lifting the level of aggregate demand. The income tax cut of 1964 and the excise tax reduction of 1965 illustrate this type of approach. But structural factors also received attention, as witnessed by the passage of the following acts: the Area Redevelopment Act (1961); the Manpower Development and Training Act (1962 and 1963); the Economic Opportunity Act (1964); and the Civil Rights Act (1964).[35]

APPROACHES TO THE PROBLEM OF UNEMPLOYMENT

In this chapter we shall concern ourselves essentially with public preventive measures, reserving for the next chapter a discussion of the chief public alleviative measure (unemployment insurance) and for the following chapter a discussion of private approaches to unemployment.

Aggregate Unemployment: General Issues

Any analysis of the prevention (or reduction) of aggregate or mass unemployment requires a prior consideration of five issues.

[33] "The American Economy in 1961: Problems and Policies" (mimeographed), Statement of the Council of Economic Advisers Before the Joint Economic Committee, March 6, 1961.

[34] Put in simple terms, the method used to analyze the question was as follows. The unemployed were classified into various categories: by age, sex, occupation, geographic area, and so on. These groups were then "counted," for a base year such as 1957, and then for later years. If it were shown that the increase in unemployment was concentrated in one or more of these categories, the existence of structural causes might be presumed. But such was not the case; the increase was spread generally across the board.

[35] For a useful discussion on structural vs. non-structural unemployment (and a view that the hard core of unemployment is a core of ice, not iron) see Paul A. Samuelson, Economics (6th ed.; New York: McGraw-Hill Book Co., 1964), pp. 783–84.

1. What is the line at which mass unemployment is construed as beginning? The answer is of paramount importance because public measures of one type or another may not be set into motion until this point is reached or approached. While there is no unanimous answer to the question, there is some agreement about a 3 to 5 per cent zone, with allowable variations for frictional and seasonal impacts. Interestingly enough, these figures result from two different types of beliefs. The first is that if unemployment becomes higher than, for example, 4 per cent, a danger point has been reached, and mass unemployment, with detrimental effects upon the economy, is the next step. The second is that if *less* than 4 per cent unemployment is reached, inflationary pressures may throw the economy out of balance in the other direction. Trying to walk the 4 per cent tightrope is an obvious impossibility; even trying to walk the 3 to 5 per cent plank is not easy. In the thirties the United States economy was well over the figure, with deflationary consequences; in the forties the picture was the opposite. The best one can probably hope for is that excess pressures do not develop in either direction.[36]

2. As a corollary of the above, if underemployment is viewed as undesirable, so likewise is overemployment, with its possible inflationary pressures. Whereas the specter of the thirties was unemployment and deflation, the problem of the two decades since then has trended (except for four short periods) in the opposite direction. And it may well be that the outlook for the near future is in a direction opposite from that of deflation. Hence public policy should be expected to deal with over- as well as with mass underemployment.[37]

3. In this type of analysis it is not necessary to enter the equilibrium-at-less-than-full-employment controversy, nor to try to distinguish between those measures designed to counter cyclical mass unemployment and those to counter long-run equilibrium employment, if such is a possibility. There are two reasons for this. First, the anti-unemployment policies that have been suggested are in certain measure the same whether the phenomenon is cyclical or long-run. Second, at the present time, one has no way of knowing empirically whether any "downturn" is merely a cyclical indication or whether it has other implications.

4. In general, mass unemployment requires an attack on other than the industrial relations front. That is, actions by employees, unions and/or

[36] These lines were written in 1955–56. In revising them a decade later, one is struck by the persistence of this problem.

[37] As Paul Samuelson has noted: "Can business, labor, and agriculture learn to act in such a way as to avoid inflation whenever private or public spending brings us anywhere near to full employment?" See Samuelson, *Economics* (4th ed.; New York: McGraw-Hill Book Co., 1958), p. 360. In subsequent editions this sentence is missing, but the thought remains. Moreover, we may encounter still another problem: a rising price level accompanied by unemployment at uncomfortably high levels.

employers are not, in themselves, likely to be enough to solve aggregate unemployment problems. Moreover, solutions which seek to reduce the labor supply to a given demand level clearly are not as desirable as those of raising demand. Given these conditions, mass unemployment requires action on broader monetary and fiscal fronts. These problems are discussed in greater detail in Chapter 8, where it will be seen that the stabilizing activities of employers and unions, while of considerable value, are not in themselves sufficient to counteract mass unemployment movements.

5. If a broad attack is required, then governmental action is necessary. To some people and groups this intrusion by government may be undesirable. Such opposition is less than it used to be, however, and there seems to be an increasing acceptance of the role of government in maintaining the well-being of the economy.[38]

Aggregate Unemployment: Preventive Measures

Two basic preventive approaches exist in the United States today. The first involves the use of "automatic" devices, wherein unemployment (and a lowering of economic activity) call forth their own compensatory devices. The second includes using discretionary and consciously planned actions.[39]

The first category of devices includes what have come to be called "built-in stabilizers." There are a number of such stabilizers presently existent in the economy, some linked directly to employment, others not. Among the principal stabilizers are the following.

Unemployment Insurance and Other Welfare Payments. An increase in unemployment does not curtail purchasing power by an equivalent amount, because unemployment insurance shores up in part the purchasing power of the covered unemployed. This program is planned to be counter-cyclical in nature, collecting more in taxes than is paid out in benefits in prosperous times, and vice versa. (The program may not turn out to be entirely counter-cyclical, insofar as "experience rating" modifies this characteristic.) Other transfer payments, such as public assistance, play an important role.[40]

[38] See both majority and minority views in Report of the Senate Special Committee on Unemployment Problems, Eugene J. McCarthy, Chairman (Washington, D. C.: U. S. Government Printing Office, 1960).

[39] For a useful discussion, see the articles in *Policies To Combat Depression*, A Report of the National Bureau of Economic Research (Princeton: Princeton University Press, 1956).

[40] For an excellent discussion of built-in economic security stabilizers see Ida C. Merriam, "Social Security Programs and Economic Stability," *Policies To Combat Depression, ibid.*

The Graduated Income Tax. This tax is of such a nature that a given increase in income occasions a greater than proportional increase in the tax, and vice versa. Thus, as economic activity lessens and incomes decrease, the income tax decreases more than proportionately. With given consumption patterns, this stabilizer also is counter-cyclical.

Other Measures. There are other types of built-in stabilizers. These include farm-aid programs, in which compensatory payments tend to move in directions opposite from that of the cycle, and corporate and family savings which tend to exhibit the same tendency.

While these built-in stabilizers are of some counter-cyclical importance, they are not at present viewed as being sufficient to create a "balance" in the economy. Therefore, other measures have been suggested and utilized in the past, of which public works and monetary and fiscal policy are the most important.

Public Works. As counter-cyclical devices, public works have been exhaustively analyzed, discussed, and utilized, particularly in the thirties.[41] It will be useful, however, to comment briefly on such measures.

The rationale of the public works approach is simple. Since various public projects—roads, airports, dams, office buildings, schools—must be undertaken from time to time, why not undertake such projects (or the majority of them) when the economy is operating below capacity? Two purposes would be served by such an approach: first, "excessive" construction, adding fuel to the flames, would be avoided in prosperous times and, second, the economy would be shored up by the introduction of such construction in depressed times.

Various problems are raised by such an approach. One is planning. For a sound system to be used, there should be advance planning, so that construction undertaken returns the greatest possible yield per dollar of investment. On this basis we would hold that projects of this type are preferable to those which merely seek to get money into circulation. This in turn implies that the program should not seek to maximize direct employment at the expense of efficiency, and conversely that public works employees should be regarded as bona fide workers, not as relief clients, and should be paid going wages.

Another problem is timing, which raises a number of difficult issues. The public cannot postpone indefinitely all projects. This means that construction may have to be undertaken in prosperous times, defeating

[41] For useful summaries, see Arthur D. Gayer, *Public Works in Prosperity and Depression* (New York: National Bureau of Economic Research, 1935); and J. M. Clark, *Economics of Planning Public Works* (Washington, D. C.: U. S. Government Printing Office, 1935). The Public Works Acceleration Act of 1962 provides a current example of the use of this technique.

in part the counter-cyclical process. The school-building program since World War II illustrates this point. (There is little doubt, of course, that this building program has helped in part to create prosperity.) Again, while it is not likely that the public will "run out" of projects, some problems of this type might develop locally. Here again advance planning is useful. Still another difficulty is deciding when to turn on public works and when to turn them off. Turning them on may be easier than turning them off; thus, if a "danger point" of X per cent unemployed is reached, the program may be set in motion. But since projects require a definite construction period, it may not be so easy to curtail the program when unemployment falls below the danger point by a given amount.

Also, such projects may be of limited usefulness at the local level if they are financed and administered essentially at that level. A recent study concludes that even if state and local public works programs had been stabilized to the greatest degree practicable in the period 1920–39 they would have changed gross national product in the average year by only a fraction of 1 per cent.[42] The study further raises serious doubts as to the potency of timed public works for alleviating the consequences of cyclical contractions. But, it is also noted that if federal money were made available on a sufficient scale, 25 per cent of the unemployment slack could be taken up by public works. Hence, there is a useful role to be played by such programs, though they may not be the primary measures they were once thought to be. Therefore other approaches must also be used.

Monetary and Fiscal Policy. The broadest public approach to the employment problem is through monetary and fiscal policy. Through changes in the structure of tax rates, through changes in the level of government expenditure, through debt increases or retirement, and via other means (including public works as noted above), public bodies may seek to maintain a high-level employment economy. These control techniques appear to be powerful, and there is evidence they work. The test of such techniques is that they should accomplish the purposes for which they are introduced; they should neither be self-defeating nor have injurious side effects. Thus, public programs should not reduce the willingness of businessmen to make private capital expenditures nor should they unstabilize private investment. (As a passing comment, there is no evidence that public programs in the United States have had these negative results; as an illustration one can look at private business expenditure

[42] See W. E. Upjohn Institute for Community Research, *Public Works and Employment From the Local Government Point of View* (Chicago: Public Administration Service, 1955). A critical reader of the first edition of our text wondered why local dollars are of any less value than federal. They are not; it is just that there are so many more of the latter.

figures during political administrations allegedly "unfriendly" to private enterprise.)

In general, it appears that monetary and fiscal techniques can play an important role in maintaining the well-being of the economy.[43] This is true not only in the "direct" sense, but also insofar as they may be used indirectly to encourage the stability of private investment in a private enterprise economy. The indirect control approach may be the only feasible one for such an economy. Indirect monetary control methods tend to be more effective in placing upper limits to investment than in preventing downward movement. But special tax incentives may be instrumental in regularizing investment. And, where fluctuations in private investment still persist, countervailing public investment—a direct method—may be used. Obviously, such programs require careful planning and timing by the appropriate authorities.

Selective or Structural Unemployment

Selective unemployment is normal in a dynamic economy. To reduce this type of unemployment to zero would be equivalent to making the economy more rigid. But there is little doubt that a reduction is possible in given cases, that critical instances of such unemployment might be treated on some sort of emergency basis, and that the readjustments called for in this type of unemployment should be made as expeditiously as the situation allows.

There are a number of methods by which such selective unemployment can be attacked. First, employers and unions can seek to regularize employment, as, for example, in the case of seasonal variations; to assist in readjustment where job severance is involved, through the use of dismissal wages; to plan rationally the introduction of new equipment; to develop employment and wage guarantees. All these private methods are discussed in Chapter 8. Likewise, the government can seek to improve the operation of the labor market in providing information about jobs and job openings, and in trying to bring demands for and supplies of labor together. This method—the public employment service—is developed in the next section in this chapter.

There are other ways, however, in which selective unemployment can be tackled, particularly by government agencies. Among such methods are the following.

Allocation of Government Defense or Other Contracts. Thus, if labor market area A is classed as a labor supply area and if it has certain types

[43] This has been increasingly borne out by the measures adopted 1961–65. See Chapter 14 for further discussion.

of productive facilities, the government may specifically allocate contracts to it, and indeed has used this approach in various periods. The usefulness of this method in reducing pockets of unemployment is obvious. The dangers are that it may become a political pressure problem with all the attendant dangers. This is pointedly illustrated in a converse problem: the closing of (or attempts to close) army and navy installations of various types.

Non-Emergency "Financial" Relief Afforded to Industries or Regions. The following mechanisms come to mind: stockpiling programs; accelerated depreciation allowances as for defense industries; changes in credit terms as for housing, automobiles, and home appliance producers; direct subsidies for various industries, such as shipbuilding; tariff changes, as for the watchmaking and bicycle industries; and so on. These selective measures may be disadvantageous to the consumer at large (as in the tariff illustration) and they may be unwise economically, but they may be of direct help in the local employment situation.

Direct Emergency Assistance. In the case of natural or other disasters —droughts, floods, hurricanes, tornadoes—government agencies may seek to assist in the restoration of business activity (and employment) by direct loans, emergency grants, and other measures.

Relief and Reclamation of Depressed Areas. Both public and private bodies have developed various types of depressed area proposals.[44] But haste is made slowly here. At the time of writing the first edition of this text, the Congress was considering various plans. A depressed area bill was enacted in 1960 but vetoed by President Eisenhower as being "too broad." In 1961, such legislation was enacted by the Kennedy Administration; it provided for a broad attack upon the problem through techniques designed to operate on both supply and demand factors.[45]

The advantages of all the above procedures are obvious. The dangers are twofold. First, government assistance may be based primarily upon partisan political considerations. And, second, the assistance may perpetuate an already uneconomical situation. Thus, governmental measures to maintain farm employment opportunities would be open to serious debate, since one of the logical solutions of this problem appears to be increasing mobility *from* the farm. (Here is an exception to the rule of increasing demand rather than reducing supply; in this case a reduction in supply is called for.) Yet if these measures are sensibly used, there

[44] See the various *Economic Reports of the President;* many of those issued to date are valuable sources of information.

[45] See Sar A. Levitan, *Federal Aid to Depressed Areas: An Evaluation of the Area Redevelopment Administration* (Baltimore: Johns Hopkins Press, 1964).

is little doubt that they can assist in minimizing the readjustment problems associated with selective unemployment.

Personal Unemployment

The two categories of unemployment noted above tend to be impersonal in nature. But the labor market functions in a personal way: individuals try to get their first jobs, individuals become unemployed, given employers offer jobs, and so on. And in order for individuals to know of jobs and facts about them, and for employers to know of job applicants, it is necessary that the labor market maximizes its flow of information. In so providing a two-way flow of information, the labor market will not only make it easier to secure the first job, but also facilitate the employment readjustments necessitated by mass or selective unemployment. This labor market procedure may be developed in two ways: first, by "structuring" an unstructured market, and second, by increasing the flow of information in a structured market.

An unstructured labor market may be viewed as one in which the only "link" is cash.[46] Structuring introduces other considerations into the market: occupational groupings, attachments of employers for given types of employees and vice versa, developing a flow of information about the job market, using rational techniques in job marketing. While certain of these structural characteristics impose restraints upon the market, others help to improve its operation. Interestingly enough, the entry of a union may assist in structuring a labor market, through the introduction of job classes, wage "rationalization," information on job availability, and other procedures.

The employment exchange or service is the major mechanism by means of which the structured market increases the flow of information. In the United States two principal types of agencies, the private and the public employment services, are found. While many private employment agencies had poor reputations in the past, public regulation has been imposed, and many of them perform a useful function today in bringing together job offerer and job seeker in clerical, secretarial, professional, and other fields. Many employers and unions have maintained employment services in one form or another: the hiring hall, preferential hiring, and maintenance of job opportunity lists illustrate these approaches. While these methods may be discriminatory in some instances—as in the case of the preferential treatment given union members—it is probable

[46] For a more sophisticated treatment, see Clark Kerr, "The Balkanization of Labor Markets," *Labor Mobility and Economic Opportunity* (Cambridge: The Technology Press, 1954), particularly p. 95.

that the net result has been to increase the structured operation of the labor market.

Although the public employment service approach has a history dating back at least to the early 1900's, it was not until 1933, with the passage of the Wagner-Peyser Act, that the system was fully formalized. This Act set up a federal-state system of public employment offices, the purposes of which were to structure the labor markets and to bring together those seeking and those offering jobs.[47] The system was federalized in 1942 as part of the war manpower program and was returned to the states shortly after the war.

The employment service performs a number of functions, including the following: (1) seeking to match workers and jobs through the local employment service office, (2) acting as a service arm of the unemployment insurance system in that those who have applied for unemployment insurance are required to register at such an office, and (3) performing broader service functions such as providing counseling and testing services and making labor market surveys.

The employment service is a meeting place for buyers and sellers. An unemployed individual may register for work. An employer may list job openings, specifying in some detail relevant job information. When a job request is received, the employment service provides a referral service by sending applicants to the job. There is no pressure upon the individual to accept the job (except the implicit incentive that exists in the case of an applicant drawing unemployment insurance).

The role of the employment service has become increasingly important in the United States.[48] Not only has the abstract objective of increasing the efficiency of labor markets been influenced, but the concrete goal of job placements has annually increased. The employment service operates under a number of difficulties: the problem of securing all the relevant information about jobs and applicants, pressures from both job seekers and job offerers who each want "something better," the use of the service in many cases by "marginal" employers and employees, and the stigma of a political operation. While the quality and quantity of results vary from one state to another, it may be said in general that the service has been increasingly accepted by employers and applicants, that it has become increasingly effective in placement operations, particularly in the blue-collar job category, and that it has had a positive effect in

[47] For a general summary see William Haber, "The U. S. Employment Service in a Changing Economy," in the previously cited Studies in Unemployment.

[48] Useful sources of information are Employment Security Review and Area Trends in Employment and Unemployment, both publications of the U. S. Department of Labor, Bureau of Employment Security.

increasing the economic operation of the labor market. It still has a way to go, however, before its operation can be called "ideal." [49]

The Manpower Services Act of 1966 is a step in the direction of improving the service. Among other things, it provides for a network of multi-job market clearance centers, better trained counselors, and labor market forecasting. The service would also aid job hunters at all occupational levels.

The labor market should also channel information about job requirements and opportunities to institutions preparing the youth of the country for vocational pursuits. In turn, these institutions should provide means for evaluating the varying job aptitudes of these youths. Increasingly, vocational testing and counseling are being given in high schools, colleges and universities, and elsewhere. Likewise, the Manpower Development and Training Act and the Economic Opportunity Act should prove useful in increasing the employability of many individuals. Such an approach not only increases the efficient functioning of the labor market, but equally importantly, it helps minimize the amount of disguised unemployment.

PROBLEMS AHEAD

What are the major employment problems ahead in the next half-decade? The following appear as basic issues.[50]

Job Creation. Approximately 1.5 million new jobs a year will need to be created through the early 1970's to absorb the growing labor force and to reduce or hold unemployment to the 4 per cent level. This level of job creation is more than double that which took place a decade ago, but approximates that of the mid-1960's.

Manpower Resource Development. It will not prove sufficient to create jobs; it will also be necessary to have those who would fill the jobs possessed of the requisite skills. The jobs cannot be downgraded to the capabilities; the inverse must be the case. Hence, what is called for is increased emphasis upon education and training—and re-education and retraining.

[49] See, for example, J. J. Corson's statement: "After twenty years' development, the public employment service is far from an effective national placement institution to provide the service needed by society and the individual." ("The Placement Function in an Industrial Society," in National Manpower Council, *Improving the Work Skills of the Nation*. New York: Columbia University Press, 1955, p. 178.)

[50] *The Economic Report of the President* for recent years (which includes *The Annual Report of the Council of Economic Advisers*) and *The Manpower Report of the President* also for recent years are sources for the discussion developed here.

Improving the Functioning of the Labor Market. Employers must have a means of making known their manpower needs; workers must have knowledge of alternative employment opportunities. Effective labor market operation would also call for additional characteristics such as elimination of discrimination, providing for necessary labor mobility, and special services for those who are disadvantaged in the job-getting process —the inexperienced, older workers, the handicapped.

Improving Income Maintenance Programs. For those individuals adversely affected by unemployment, adequate income maintenance programs must be developed. "Adequacy" would call for an improvement in the present system, particularly as respects coverage and benefit levels. These issues are treated in the next chapter.

AN EVALUATION

Tremendous strides have been made in the United States in the last twenty-five years in the identification and measurement of employment and unemployment. While a critic might not necessarily agree that the labor force concept, and the currently used definitions of employment and unemployment, are the most sophisticated possible, it is true that this approach is a great improvement over a quarter-century ago. And it is likely that continuing improvements will be made, increasing the accuracy of the measurements.

The approach to the unemployment problem requires as well an approach to the overemployment problem, or at least to the problem of a level of employment that invokes inflationary pressures. The American economy became so deflationary-conscious during the thirties and forties that it may well be that the opposite possibility is the greater future threat. There may be more truth than sophistry to the "Uneasy Triangle" argument that a society can have *no more* than any *two* of the following three objectives: free collective bargaining, full employment, and stable prices.[51] In the last decade we have chosen the first two, and the burden has fallen upon those whose incomes did not rise as fast as the average increase in prices. If the past presages the future, then over- as well as underemployment may be a critical problem, to say nothing of the possibility of unemployment with rising prices.

[51] See "The Uneasy Triangle" in *The Economist,* issues of August 9, 16, 23, 1952, pp. 322–23, 376–78, and 434–35, respectively. This trilogy was propounded earlier in this country by C. O. Hardy. For skepticism about its validity, see the paper by Milton Friedman in *The Impact of the Union,* edited by D. McC. Wright (New York: Harcourt, Brace & World, Inc., 1951), particularly pp. 226 ff. For a current analysis of the issues involved see Bowen, *op. cit.,* pp. 34–60.

All the techniques we have examined here—monetary and fiscal policies, public works, selective emergency measures, employment exchanges —seem capable of performing useful roles in the prevention or reduction of unemployment. In general, where various of these policies have been applied, the performance record has been good, including even the emergency "alphabet" agencies of the New Deal. But there seems to be little doubt that some measures may produce undesirable economic consequences. Thus, measures to prevent mass unemployment may lead to overemployment. Or, emergency measures designed to reduce unemployment in critical areas may do so, but may also perpetuate uneconomic situations instead of, say, encouraging the labor mobility necessary to rectify the situation.

In conclusion, the unemployment-overemployment problem is one of delicate balance. There is no necessary guarantee that the marketing mechanism will automatically achieve and maintain this balance for society. And if the government, broadly defined, seeks to assist in maintaining equilibrium, it has powerful tools at its command, but it also has several pressing problems. First, it may have to make a choice with respect to the alternatives that are open to society: free collective bargaining, full employment, and stable prices. Second, it must administer its policies so as to achieve the alternative it selects. This requires establishing criteria of various "levels" of employment, securing a continuous flow of information thereon, choosing the correct policy, and timing the actions carefully.[52] The best we can probably hope for is achievement within a limited range. But there is little doubt that we can avoid the debacle of the thirties. And, with wisdom and a little courage, we should be able to avoid the opposite extreme. This is not wishful thinking, though we must admit we are not quite as optimistic about the outcome as we were five years ago.

SUMMARY

"Economic unemployment" has been one of the most important causal factors giving rise to economic insecurity in the United States in this century. While unemployment is neither easy to define precisely nor to measure exactly, it is possible to visualize three major types: aggregate, selective, and personal. Such a breakdown is useful, since programs to combat this type of insecurity have approached the problem on these three fronts. While unemployment data are not collected on the basis of the above threefold classification, the data we do have provide an increasingly reliable picture of employment and unemployment, particularly on

[52] See in this connection Charles D. Stewart, "Uses of Unemployment Statistics in Economic Policy," *Monthly Labor Review*, LXXVIII, No. 3 (March, 1955), 279–82.

a relative basis. Additionally, selective unemployment data of various types are becoming increasingly available: unemployment by regions, by occupation and industry, by age and sex, by duration of unemployment, and in other dimensions.

Aggregate unemployment requires for its minimization the maintenance of a high level of economic opportunity. While industry and labor can undertake useful positive action, governmental monetary and fiscal policies are likely to be the more important, particularly in critical periods. Selective unemployment may also require government assistance for its solution, although one should note that such solutions may tend to perpetuate an uneconomic situation, particularly where political pressures are strong. Personal unemployment can be attacked on a broad front through a series of measures which seek to improve the operation of the labor market by making more efficient the ways in which jobs are offered and sought.

There is little doubt that we have at our command today powerful tools which, on the one hand, should make unlikely a repetition of the period 1930–40, and, on the other, should make for a more effective labor market operation. But vigilance needs to be exercised so that in our desire to avoid the insecurity of unemployment we do not fall heir to other dangers.

SUGGESTIONS FOR ADDITIONAL READING

BOWEN, WILLIAM G., and FREDERICK H. HARBISON (Eds.). *Unemployment in a Prosperous Economy.* Princeton: The Industrial Relations Section and The Woodrow Wilson School of Public and International Affairs, 1965.
   A series of essays on the dimensions of unemployment, the aggregate-demand approach, and selective manpower policies.
COMMITTEE FOR ECONOMIC DEVELOPMENT. *Raising Low Incomes Through Improved Education.* New York: Committee for Economic Development, 1965.
   A policy statement, including an analysis of education as a road to more productivity and employment.
GALENSON, WALTER. *A Primer in Employment and Wages.* New York: Random House, Inc., 1966.
   A well-integrated and clearly presented discussion of the labor market, the determination of wages and employment, and unemployment and poverty.
NATIONAL BUREAU OF ECONOMIC RESEARCH. *The Measurement and Behavior of Unemployment.* Princeton: Princeton University Press, 1957.
   A useful series of essays relating to many of the problems discussed in this chapter.
OKUN, ARTHUR M. (Ed.). *The Battle Against Unemployment.* New York: W. W. Norton & Co., Inc., 1965.
   A series of readings on the nature and consequences of unemployment, problems of employment and price stability, and the uses of fiscal and monetary policy.

Ross, Arthur M. (Ed.). *Employment Policy and the Labor Market.* Berkeley: University of California Press, 1965.

A series of papers presented at a 1964 conference. The topics deal with the causes and measures of unemployment and the approaches to it.

———. *Unemployment and the American Economy.* New York: John Wiley & Sons, Inc., 1964.

A general analysis of the problems of and policies for unemployment. The papers in this volume provide a comprehensive view of the issues involved.

Wolfbein, Seymour L. *Employment, Unemployment, and Public Policy.* New York: Random House, Inc., 1965.

A comprehensive analysis on (1) identifying the unemployment problem, (2) economic growth and public policy as they relate to unemployment, and (3) manpower policies. The latter section provides a particularly useful summary of current approaches.

A decade ago one would have been hard pressed to find in summary form information on unemployment: nature, concepts, causes, "cures." If, however, the reader peruses the above mentioned eight volumes he will obtain an excellent overview of the entire topic.

7

Unemployment Insurance

INTRODUCTION

The major public program in the United States for the alleviation of the undesirable consequences of unemployment is the unemployment insurance (or compensation) system which was developed in the Social Security Act of 1935. In addition to this basic system, there are a number of special programs to be found, as, for example, for railroad employees, which are discussed in Chapter 13.

The terms unemployment "compensation" and "insurance" as used above are commonly employed interchangeably. In the early days of the program "compensation" was used. After 1937, when the Social Security Act was declared constitutional, there was a tendency to use the term "insurance." [1] Technically, "compensation" might be a better term in light of the actuarial nature of the problem. Or, social "assurance" would be appropriate. But since "compensation" and "insurance" are both found in ordinary usage, we shall follow this custom here.

As was noted in Chapter 6, there are various ways in which society can approach the unemployment problem: prevention, or reduction, on a public or private basis; alleviation on the same grounds or some combination of these two. The public preventive approach has been discussed in the last chapter; private systems will be covered in Chapter 8. This chapter, then, will focus upon the remaining major area—public alleviative programs of which unemployment compensation is the outstanding example.

One additional comment may be made at the outset. It was indicated in Chapter 6 that extensive analysis of, and prescriptions for, the unem-

[1] See Ruth Reticker, "Twenty Years of Unemployment Insurance," *Social Security Bulletin,* XVIII, No. 12 (December, 1955), 3–10, and *Unemployment Insurance Review* for August, 1965, which provides a thirty-year summary.

ployment problem have occurred in the past five years. To the contrary, "innovation" in unemployment insurance has been at a minimum for a variety of reasons to be noted later. This has led to a heightened interest in "federal standards" upon which we shall also comment later in this chapter.

DEVELOPMENT OF THE PRESENT SYSTEM

If one accepts the premise that the unemployed are a fixed cost to society, though they may be a variable cost to the employer, then the question that must be answered is how society will provide for this overhead item. Various alternatives are to be found. At one extreme is the case where society lets the unemployed take care of themselves through private means: personal resources, relatives, friends, private charities. At the other extreme would be some complete public "cradle to the grave" system. The trend in the United States has changed from the almost completely private approach to one with a significant degree of public intervention. The chronological sequence of these alleviative program developments is interesting to note.

Individual Initiative

There has always been a belief in the United States that, wherever possible, individuals themselves should make provision for economic emergencies such as might arise from unemployment. Although this doctrine has been tempered considerably through the years, for a long period it was the basis for social action. Applying this doctrine meant in turn that while society would not stand by and permit an individual to starve, it would provide assistance only in the critical case and not as the general rule. Private charities for many years carried the bulk of alleviative programs.

The "Relief" Doctrine

Where public assistance was provided, it was commonly done under the "poor relief" or "work relief" doctrine.[2] Such relief might be "indoor," as in an almshouse, "outdoor," as through the receipt of cash, or "work relief," wherein the community sought some service in return for assistance. Such relief was customarily administered on the local or state level,

[2] For a useful summary see Florence Peterson in D. D. Lescohier and E. Brandeis, *History of Labor in the United States, 1896–1932* (New York: The Macmillan Co., 1935), III, chaps. xi and xii—Unemployment Relief.

was enmeshed in legal intricacies that frequently denied help to an individual, and tended to "disfranchise" the needy in a variety of ways, as, for example, in defining them as paupers.

Development of Federal Relief

After a series of depressions in this country, beginning with the period of 1893–94, there was an increasing tendency to formalize public assistance and to apply it in a somewhat more systematic social manner. (Prior to 1893–94 there seems to have been little organized public response to the economic consequences of depression conditions.) And after 1929 there was increasing participation by the federal government in unemployment relief, culminating in the comprehensive programs developed in the New Deal era.

"Unemployment Insurance" Plans

In addition to private and public *relief* approaches, a number of employers and/or unions sought to develop "unemployment insurance" plans of various types. These plans, to be discussed more fully in the next chapter, were insufficient to meet the general problem, though they were of some help in scattered instances. There was no attempt in this country to follow such European plans as those of Berne, Switzerland, or Ghent, Belgium, which, in the period 1893–1901 and later, provided for subsidization of private programs by municipal, provincial, and national governments.

Unemployment Compensation Laws

Hence, the non-relief developments in the United States took the turn of governmental programming of unemployment insurance systems. Early attempts were made on a state basis, in Massachusetts in 1916, in Wisconsin, with the Huber bill in 1921; and, on a federal basis, with resolutions or bills introduced in the Congress in 1916, 1928, 1931, and 1934. Nothing developed from these sources, however, in no small measure because of the opposition of labor organizations. Such opposition arose because of a fear of government as such and a further fear that a system of this type could be turned against employees on strike. By 1932 the forces of economic necessity diminished labor opposition, and in that year Wisconsin passed the first unemployment compensation law in the United States. The law was a deferred statute, however, not to go into effect for two years. Four other states passed unemployment insurance laws prior to the Social Security Act of 1935, but only the New York law became effective.[3]

Social Security Act of 1935

The insurance approach was crystallized in the Social Security Act of 1935, in which one of the several major components related to unemployment compensation. As noted in Chapter 3, in 1934 a national Committee on Economic Security had been created; out of its deliberations had come a series of recommendations, including a national system for old-age insurance, and a federal-state system in the unemployment field. Preference for a federal-state tax-offset plan rather than for a national system or a tax-rebate plan was based in part upon the belief that such an approach would be the most likely to survive the test of constitutionality; in part upon the fact that the committee included among its influential members persons who were responsible for the Wisconsin plan; in part upon disputes between adherents of different types of funds, which disputes could be resolved by letting each state go ahead; and in part upon a belief that a faster job could be done if each state were encouraged to act on its own. The 1935 Act, with subsequent modifications, is that which has come down to the present day and which we shall examine after commenting upon the compensation principle and its application in this field.

THE COMPENSATION PRINCIPLE

If the labor market operated so that the principle of equal net advantage were fully applicable, then one would expect that wage rates for individual occupations would reflect their relative advantages and disadvantages, so that the final wage rate would equalize the advantages and disadvantages among all occupations.[4] And it would therefore follow that, other things being equal, occupations where the incidence of unemployment was high would pay correspondingly higher wage rates than similar occupations where the incidence was low. Demand and supply factors operating in such a labor market would work so as to bring about these optimal conditions.

Do wage rates, in fact, reflect such differences in the risks of unemployment? To some extent, yes. Various building trade rates for a long

---

[3] See Harry Malisoff, "The Emergence of Unemployment Compensation," *Political Science Quarterly*, LIV, Nos. 2, 3, 4 (June, September, December, 1939), 237–58, 391–420, and 577–99, respectively.

[4] See the parallel reasoning applied in Chapter 9 on workmen's compensation, in which field this type of argumentation has been used more extensively.

period tended to take account of the pressures of seasonal unemployment. But these cases are few; we have little correspondence, for example, of rates with the risks of cyclical, secular, or technological unemployment.

If this is the case, what alternatives are open to society if it wishes to take positive action? One approach would be for wages to be set legislatively or administratively so as to reflect differing unemployment risks. The serious ethical implications and enormous administrative difficulties in such an approach are readily apparent.

An alternative approach is to use the compensation principle, in which the cost of production includes a charge (tax) for the specific unemployment risk. If this cost is shared by the public (through higher prices), the employer (through reduced profits), and the employee (through lower wages), the burden is distributed. The utility of the compensation payment at the time of unemployment is greater than that of incremental increases in the wage rate which would occur under wage adjustment. Thus this method is more economically rational than that of administrative wage setting, to say nothing of being more feasible operationally.[5] Even if it is assumed that the employee bears the *full* burden of the cost, this method has merit. First, while it may be *forced insurance,* thus limiting freedom of choice, it is there, and the employee can draw upon it in time of need. (There is no assurance, for example, that "compensatory" wage rates would be used by the individual to provide for unemployment needs.) Second, the cost of the risk is spread beyond the particular risk, thus forcing a social sharing of the burden. (It should be noted, however, that experience rating—to be discussed in Chapter 14 —may narrow this risk spreading to a point where "self-insurance" is evident.) Hence there is both administrative feasibility and economic logic to the "compensation" or "insurance" principle.

This compensation approach is, in fact, the system embodied in the Social Security Act of 1935, to which the discussion now turns.

UNEMPLOYMENT PROVISIONS OF THE 1935 SOCIAL SECURITY ACT

It should be noted initially that the federal Act had two distinguishing characteristics. First, it was an enabling Act designed to encourage the states to pass their own laws. And second, it provided a set of minimum standards for state laws, permitting the states to enact more liberal, but not more restrictive, laws. The basic elements in this federal statute are as follows.

[5] See Chapter 9 for a more detailed analysis of the applicability of this approach in workmen's compensation.

Coverage

Coverage is a matter of numbers as well as of employment types. Taking numbers first, covered employers were those who employed eight or more different individuals on any twenty or more days in the calendar year, each day being in a different week. This is a "minimum-minimum"; thus, an employer who meets the above requirement is covered for the year, and pays taxes on his employees for the full year, even though he has, say, only seven or fewer employees for the balance of the year. In 1954, in one of the few amendments to the Act, the Congress lowered the limit from eight to four employees, effective January 1, 1956, and blanketed-in civilian employees of the federal government as of January 1, 1955.

Employment types excluded are agriculture, domestic service, casual labor, certain public service, and non-profit charitable, educational, literary, religious, and scientific pursuits. These criteria are applied to the employee in terms of the types of work he does, and not to the employee as employee. The 50 per cent rule is applied to determine coverage: if over 50 per cent of the work an employee does is within the meaning of the Act, he is covered for all his employment; if less than 50 per cent, he is excluded. This makes for administrative simplicity and does not work an injustice. While OASDI has greatly broadened its coverage, the same has not been true in unemployment compensation, for reasons to be noted later. The Act originally covered employees in interstate transportation, but separate legislation is now provided for them.

Why these exclusions? The reasons are found in a complex of administrative, economic, and political circumstances. Thus, there was some belief that smaller employers could handle implicitly their unemployment problems; moreover, the administrative difficulties were felt to be of such a nature that it would not be feasible to include the employer of fewer than eight. Twenty weeks was used as a cut-off, since it would eliminate most seasonal employment related to agriculture. Certain employment classes—such as casual labor or domestic service—were excluded, partly because of administrative difficulties in blanketing-in such groups, and additionally in the former case because of the belief that one should have some permanence of attachment to the labor force before one could rightly make a claim upon the system. Agricultural labor was excluded, in part for administrative and political reasons, and also because of the belief that the depressed farm economy could not bear the costs.

Qualifications for Benefits

The Act leaves to the states the right to determine specific qualifications for benefits, such as allowable reasons for job separations, interpretations of the terms "able to work" and "available for work," and "allowable earnings" while unemployed. The federal Act does specify, however, a number of situations in which a state may not deny compensation to an otherwise eligible applicant. These include the stipulations that the applicant shall not be ineligible if he refuses to accept new work under any of the following conditions: (1) if the job opening is available because of a strike, lockout, or other labor dispute, (2) if the wages, hours, or working conditions are substantially less favorable than those prevailing for similar work in the locality, and (3) if as a condition of employment the individual must join a company union, or resign from, or refrain from joining a bona fide labor organization. The logic of these specifications is clear; they are designed to prevent an undercutting of desirable labor standards, and to preserve the neutrality of the state *vis-à-vis* employers and labor organizations, and in labor disputes.

Benefit Levels

Benefit levels as such are not specified in the federal Act. There are, however, several indirect stipulations. First, such benefits as are paid must be paid through public employment offices or such other agencies as may be approved. Second, all money withdrawn from the unemployment fund of a state shall be used solely in the payment of unemployment compensation, with certain administrative and disability exceptions. The reasons for such requirements are clear.

Costs and Financing

It is here that the major feature of the federal Act is found. A federal tax of 3 per cent was levied upon the wages and salaries paid by covered employers, as previously defined. Up to 1939 the tax was levied on total wages; in that year an amendment set a limit of $3,000. The limitation was imposed because of the disparate relation between in-payments and possible benefits for higher income groups.[6]

---

[6] It is interesting to note that, while the OASDI tax base has gone to $6,600, the unemployment insurance base has held at the above-mentioned $3,000. The student should ask himself why this is so. He might also ask whether an increase in the tax base is more likely now than in 1955 when the first edition of this text was written.

The 3 per cent rate was selected for two basic reasons. First, it represented an "actuarial" figure that would have provided benefits at levels envisaged in a number of proposed bills for the period 1920–32. Second, it was a compromise between "disaster relief" and "high benefit" plan proponents.

The important "enabling innovation" in the federal Act was as follows. The specified 3 per cent tax was to be paid to the federal government. If, however, the state in question had an approved unemployment insurance law with its own tax structure, 90 per cent of the federal tax could be deducted, or "offset." (Numerically, if an employer's federal tax was, for example, $3,000, then $2,700 of it might be offset for the state.) The remaining 10 per cent (or $300) was to be paid to the federal government for administrative costs. (Beginning in 1961 the 3 per cent was increased to various different levels, in part to take care of increased operational costs, in part for the purpose of repayment of monies advanced by the federal government to finance temporary extensions of unemployment insurance benefits. The underlying logic, however, remains the same. Thus, in 1961 the tax rate became 3.1 per cent. The offset was still $2,700, but in this case $400 was retained by the federal government. In some states, however, depending upon the method adopted for paying back the advances under the temporary unemployment extensions of 1958 and 1961, the offset might be reduced. Thus, in Minnesota, the maximum credit of 2.70 per cent was reduced to 2.55 for 1963 and 2.40 for 1964.) A state law would, of course, keep the "monies at home" for use within the state, instead of having them go to the federal government for commingled use in various states. There was thus considerable incentive for a state to pass its own law; and this, in fact, was what happened in all the states.

Technically, *all* the monies collected by a state are sent to the Secretary of the Treasury and put into an Unemployment Trust Fund, thus centralizing and safeguarding the reserve. The "title" to a state's monies is, however, retained by it, and a separate book account maintained for it. The funds, other than those needed for current state withdrawals, are invested in United States bonds, either regular or special issues. Interest earned on these bonds is periodically added to the reserve. A state may draw on its account, but only to the limit of its balance, and only for the purpose of paying unemployment benefits. (A 1946 amendment permitted the states utilizing employee contributions to withdraw such contributions to pay disability benefits.) The federal Act does not require employee contributions, but does not prohibit them. Although ten states have at various times levied an employee tax, only three do so today.[7]

---

[7] Under OASDI, both employee and employer contribute. The student should ask himself why this is not also the case for unemployment compensation.

In order to assist in providing an economic incentive for the reduction of unemployment, an "additional credit" provision was incorporated in the Act. A state may write into its own program a provision whereby an employer with a favorable employment experience (low unemployment) pays a lower tax. But the federal offset applies only to such taxes as the employer pays to the state. Hence, unless a special provision were made, the employer with a reduced state tax would technically pay the balance to the federal government. Special provision, in fact, has been made in the law via the "additional credit" proviso. Hence, the employer with a reduced state tax is permitted to deduct not only what he *does* pay to the state, but what he *would have paid* had he paid the maximum tax, subject to the federal offset. In order to prevent abuse of this tax reduction procedure, the experience rating provisions (that is, the provisions which permit low unemployment employers to pay lower rates) of state acts must meet minimum federal standards. The federal standards require in general that an employer have a certain minimum time experience (formerly three years; as of January 1, 1955, one year) or have a certain maximum balance in his reserve account before he can become eligible for a reduced tax.

Administration

The federal law is administered by the Secretary of Labor through the Bureau of Employment Security. The states retain considerable autonomy; their major responsibility is to comply with federal specifications, but, given that, they exercise the day-to-day administration of the state laws. The federal administrative specifications are five in number. The state must: (1) administer its law in such a way as will, within reason, permit full payment of unemployment compensation when due, (2) cooperate with state agencies administering public works or employment, (3) provide for a review system for denied claims, (4) make the necessary reports to the federal administration, and (5) after 1939, apply the merit system to its administrative staff. Hence, there is considerable variation in the details of state administration. Administrative costs are borne by the federal government through its retention of 0.4 of the tax, and by subsequent reimbursement to the states.

STATE UNEMPLOYMENT INSURANCE ACTS

In attempting to portray the present state unemployment insurance system in the United States, one faces a dilemma. On the one hand, a detailed presentation does not serve the purpose of this text, whose aim is analysis and evaluation. Moreover, a detailed presentation would become out of date as quickly as it was printed, so rapid are developments in this field.[8] Yet it is obvious that one cannot analyze and understand if one does not have some fund or stock of information with which to work. Hence, we shall adopt the compromise of sketching in the main informational threads without attempting in any way to suggest that this provides a definitive treatment of the full range of available data.[9]

Coverage

As was previously noted, the federal law sets a floor below which the states cannot go in restrictiveness. The states can, however, adopt more liberal provisions, and this is the trend that has developed. The following data illustrate the picture as of January 1, 1966.

First, as to the size of the firm, twenty-six jurisdictions went beyond the federal Act and covered employees in firms with work forces ranging from one to four employees. Moreover, twenty-nine states require the specified number of employees to be employed for a period shorter than the federal Act's twenty weeks. Additionally, all states which limit coverage by firm size provide that employing units with fewer than the required number of employees may elect to have them covered under the state law. The contractual relationship of employer and employee and the location of employment have come to be defined in ways such as to broaden coverage.

Second, as noted previously, the federal Act excludes various categories of employees on the basis of the type of employment. Except for the District of Columbia, Hawaii, and Puerto Rico, which do not exclude agricultural labor, the other states tend to follow the federal law. Only New York and Hawaii cover domestic servants in private homes; only

---

[8] This is even more the case in unemployment compensation, workmen's compensation, and public assistance than in old-age insurance, for in the latter instance there is only a single federal law; in the former the complex diversity of state laws is apparent.

[9] The authors have found two techniques useful in approaching this problem. The first technique is to include, as part of the textual materials for the course, copies of the following: the latest issue of the U. S. Department of Labor's *Comparison of State Unemployment Insurance Laws;* current issues of Health, Education, and Welfare *Indicators* (monthly), and *Trends* (annual); *Social Security Bulletin, Employment Service Review, Unemployment Insurance Review,* and *Unemployment Insurance Statistics.* It is obvious that a text cannot help being dated almost immediately as to the factual data; even the government reports are always somewhat behind the times. Yet the publications listed above do provide a set of comprehensive source materials. (The larger institution also is likely to have in its library a labor reporting service of some type through which one can keep completely up to date if this is felt desirable.) The second technique is to take the unemployment insurance law of the state in which the college or university is located, use it as a prototype, and subject it to detailed inquiry, spending a week or more upon presentation and analysis. Copies of the state law usually can be secured without difficulty. The specific sources used in the following section are: U. S. Department of Labor, Bureau of Employment Security, *Comparison of State Unemployment Insurance Laws as of January 1, 1966,* with supplements.

California covers self-employment; only Alaska, Colorado, the District of Columbia, and Hawaii cover employees in non-profit organizations. Thus the tendency here is to hew close to federal specifications.

Given these coverage qualifications, the average number of employees blanketed under the state acts was 52 million as of January, 1966, with over 1½ million eligible employing units. This compares with approximately 20 million employees covered in 1938. The rate of growth of covered employees has been larger than the rate of growth of the labor force. Coverage varies rather widely in different industries: manufacturing and wholesale and retail trade account for the bulk of total coverage, while mining and finance run low.

But more employees than the "average" tend to have some wage credits at one time or another during the year. The numbers with some wage credits approximate one-half to one-third again as many as the average number of employees covered, tending toward the latter figure of late. Of these, somewhat over 80 per cent have enough wage credits (to be defined shortly) to qualify for at least minimum benefits. Protection is thus broader than "average" coverage figures would indicate.

Qualifications for Benefits

It is here that many of the complexities of state laws are to be found. But these are complexities of detail; the underlying approach is similar. Let us look systematically at both similarities and differences.

Eligibility Conditions. These represent the "affirmative statement of the risks selected for coverage under the program"; they are the "conditions *precedent*" to the risk which the program insures against.[10]

Eligibility conditions are three in number: (1) extension of unemployment beyond the waiting period (2) by a claimant who has established himself as part of the labor force by having earned qualifying wages in covered employment and (3) who has a continuing attachment to the labor force (being able to work and available for work) indicated by registration for work at an employment office.

The "waiting period" is discussed below under benefit levels. Let us merely note here that it is most commonly one week and that an individual must be unemployed beyond it before he is "eligible."

"Attachment to the labor force" is the second eligibility condition. The purpose of this condition is to admit to participation in the benefits of the system only such employees as have a bona fide attachment. Such attachment is measured by requiring that the individual earn a specified amount of wages or work for a certain period of time within his base

---

[10] We have extensively used here L. G. Williams, "Eligibility for Benefits," and P. H. Sanders, "Disqualification for Unemployment Insurance," both in *Vanderbilt Law Review*, VIII, No. 2 (February, 1955), 286–306 and 307–37, respectively.

period, or both. (The "base period" or "base year" is a period of time, commonly one year, which precedes the period in which benefits start, usually with a lag of one quarter.) There is an increasing use of "earnings within the high quarter" as a criterion of eligibility. Thus, instead of so many dollars within the base year, the requirement is so many dollars within the high quarter in that base year.

Earnings requirements may be stated in a number of ways. The simplest is the stipulation of a flat amount. As of January, 1966, only four jurisdictions used this method; $800 was the high earnings figure, $700 the low. The remainder use one of two other principal alternatives, with certain variations. A minority of the remainder utilize an earnings-time requirement, such as 20 weeks of employment at an average of $20 or more, or $750 and wages in two quarters. The majority use the "benefit multiple" approach: a multiple of either the weekly benefit or the high-quarter wages. The most common benefit multiple is 30. Thus if the weekly benefit were $20, the individual would need $600 in his base period. The high-quarter approach utilizes an eligibility requirement such as one and one-half times such wages.

Some estimates suggest that the above requirements reduce the number of otherwise eligible claimants by 20 per cent plus or minus. The trend appears to be toward tightening rather than relaxing this eligibility requirement. [The student might ask himself two questions here: (1) should only employees "genuinely attached" to the labor force be eligible for benefits and (2) if so, how "genuinely attached" should be measured.]

But the labor force attachment must not only have been in the past; it must exist at present and into such future period for which the individual wishes to be eligible. Such continuing attachment is measured by the individual's being able to work and available for work. Here the states set their own eligibility requirements, since there are no federal specifications except the labor standard provisions. "Able to work" implies physical and mental ability. The unemployment insurance system as presently structured is an economically oriented system; it is not set up for the purpose of providing accident or sickness benefits (which may be covered in part by workmen's compensation or by private accident and health plans). One evidence of ability to work is the filing of a claim and registration for work at a public employment office, which is required under all state laws, ordinarily on a weekly basis.

Availability for work is a more complex issue.[11] The customary interpretations of availability include the following: (a) indication of availability as evidenced by registration at the appropriate public employment

[11] For a useful analysis and discussion, see Ralph Altman, *Availability for Work: A Study in Unemployment Compensation* (Cambridge: Harvard University Press, 1950).

office, (b) actively seeking work or making a reasonable effort to obtain work, and (c) willingness to accept suitable work (to be defined shortly).

Disqualifying Provisions. These represent negative conditions or the "conditions *subsequent*" to the risk. "Precedent" and "subsequent" should be viewed here in terms of the *processing* of an individual's claim: eligibility conditions are first checked after which it is ascertained whether the individual is otherwise "disqualified." In terms of what the individual "does," the disqualifying action may actually be the first event in time; for example he may be discharged for cause, which "disqualifies" him.

A major cause of disqualification arises out of the method of job separation; certain types of separations disqualify an individual (either temporarily or permanently) from receiving benefits. The purpose of such qualifications is to restrict benefits to those who become unemployed through no fault of their own; that is, it is generally held that an employee who "voluntarily" leaves his job should take the consequences.

The series of disqualifying reasons includes: voluntary separation from work, discharge for misconduct, refusal of suitable work, and unemployment due to a labor dispute. In some cases and in some states the disqualification results in a denial of benefits for a temporary period. In other cases the disqualification may be "permanent" (for the duration of unemployment). In some cases the disqualification is mandatory, in others it may be optional and at the discretion of the administrative agency.

In general, the above listed reasons for disqualification admit of exceptions, depending upon the circumstances involved. Thus, as of January 1, 1966, all states disqualified an individual for voluntarily leaving his employment without "good cause." But if the quit was for "good cause," benefits were not denied. (What constitutes "good cause" becomes, of course, a complicated matter and one with which administrative agencies have to concern themselves regularly.) The penalty for discharge for misconduct may result in disqualification for the duration of unemployment, or it may be scaled down according to the type of misconduct. Thus, "aggravated misconduct" disqualifies for a longer period than "lesser misconduct."

Refusal to accept suitable work also disqualifies an individual. In addition to the federal specifications on suitable work, other criteria have been developed to evaluate the suitability of an offer of work. These include: (1) the degree of risk to a claimant's health, safety, and morals; (2) the claimant's physical fitness, prior training, experience, and earnings; (3) the length of his unemployment and local job market prospects, and (4) the distance of the job from his home. It should be noted that the suitable work criteria are imposed not only as an initial test, but throughout the period of unemployment, whereas the job separation cause is a "once and forever" action. Labor dispute disqualifications, in general, last as long as the labor dispute, though there is a pattern of exceptions and qualifications for lockouts, location of the dispute, and indirect actions. Finally, certain special groups of individuals are disqualified: students not available for work while attending school and women who quit their jobs to assume marital obligations or to bear children.

Even though an individual meets all the above requirements, there are still certain factors that may prevent him from starting to collect benefits or from continuing to receive benefits once he has started. Fraudulent misrepresentation not only disqualifies an individual, but all state laws contain some provision for recovery of benefits paid. Other income received may disqualify an individual, usually through a reduction in benefits. Thus workmen's compensation, old-age benefits, private pensions, wages in lieu of notice, or dismissal payments may restrict unemployment benefits. Partial employment does not disqualify an individual, but it may reduce his benefits. Thus in 1966, all states allowed an individual to earn some sum each week without reducing his benefits; the size of the sum varied from $2 to one-half the weekly benefit amount, with $6 a median figure.

All the above restrictions are designed to carry out the intent of the unemployment insurance system, given its basic premises. One may quarrel with these basic premises, but if one accepts them, the subsequent regulatory framework logically flows out of the system. It is apparent, of course, that one may differ with specific regulations or their application.

Benefit Levels

If an individual meets all the above qualifications, what benefits can he collect? The following seeks to provide an answer to this question.

First, it should be noted that the federal Act sets no standards for unemployment insurance benefits. This, unlike coverage and financing, has led to the development of different and complex formulae for determining employee benefit rights. The following are the principal factors involved in benefit calculation.

Benefit Year. The period in which an employee may receive his benefits is called a "benefit year." This is usually a one-year period; in most jurisdictions it is an "individual benefit year" related to the date of his unemployment. In other states the potential benefit year begins for all claimants on a date specified in the law, usually April 1, or the first week in July.

Waiting Period. All but three states require a waiting period before benefits are payable. This is an "uncompensable period" in which the employee must have been otherwise eligible for benefits. One week (with modifications) is the most common initial period. In seven jurisdictions, the waiting period does become compensable if certain stipulations are met, such as the payment of benefits for a given number of weeks. The purposes of such a period are two in number. First, it excludes from coverage those unemployed who secure re-employment within this period; that is, it permits unemployment compensation to be applied to those who more fully need it. The belief here is that an individual should be expected to, and be able to, finance a week of unemployment. Second, like a "deductible insurance," it reduces the cost or, conversely, for a given premium it permits a higher benefit.

The Weekly Benefit Amount. Numerous formulae are used to compute the weekly benefit amount, but they all depend upon certain basic factors. First, benefits vary with the employee's past wages (customarily during the base period or some portion thereof) within minimum and maximum limits. Second, the formulae are generally weighted so that the lower paid employee receives a proportionately larger benefit than does the higher paid. The minimum effective weekly benefit in 1966 was $3; the maximum, without dependents' allowances, was $65. With dependents' allowances, the maximum was $75.

Three principal methods are used in benefit calculation. The majority of states use a "high-quarter" formula which bases benefits upon wages in that quarter of the base period in which such wages were the highest. Benefits are computed by applying a fraction, such as $\frac{1}{26}$, to the high-quarter wages. (For workers with thirteen weeks of employment in the high quarter this fraction provides benefit restoration of 50 per cent, subject to minimum and maximum benefit limitations.) Since workers may have some unemployment even in the high quarter, some twenty-six states use fractions larger than $\frac{1}{26}$ ($\frac{1}{20}$ currently being the maximum). Half of these states use a weighted schedule which gives a greater proportion of high-quarter wages to lower paid workers.

Eight states use an "annual-wage" formula. A benefit "schedule" or "table" is set up which directly relates benefits to base-period wages. As an example from one state, base-period wages of $520 would afford weekly benefits of $12; wages of $3,000 would yield $38. Such schedules tend to be weighted so as to provide a proportionately higher benefit restoration for the low wage earner.

Nine states use an "average-weekly-wage" formula in which benefits are calculated as a percentage of average weekly wages in the base period. For example, benefits may be two-thirds of the first $45 and two-fifths above $45, up to a statutory maximum.

In all cases there are statutory benefit minimums and maximums. The minimums are all specified in dollar terms; in 1966 $3 was the lowest. The maximums may be specified in dollar terms (the most common practice) or "flexibly," as up to 50, 52½, or 55 per cent of the average weekly wage in the state. The 1966 maximum was $65 (without dependents).

Dependents' Allowances. Eight states provide dependents' allowances. A rather rigorous set of restrictions defines dependency. The allowance formulae vary from a fixed sum per dependent ($1 to $9) with a maximum allowed amount (such as $25), to systems whereby the supplementary payment depends upon the "primary" weekly benefit. Several states use a "variable maximum" system in which the benefit limits depend upon high-quarter or average wages as well as the number of dependents.

Duration of Benefits. In 1966 thirty-nine weeks was the maximum effective period during which a claimant could collect benefits. Twenty-six weeks was the median figure. The exact maximum for a given individual depended upon the specific formula used, the formula in the majority of the states being related to the weekly benefit amount. Thus, in one state using the annual-wage formula, minimum base-period earnings afforded a total benefit of $216 at $12 a week for 18 weeks; maximum base-period earnings afforded $988 at $38 a week for 26 weeks. In 1966, eight states had "triggered" benefit extensions. When unemployment in the state reaches a certain level (such as 6 or 7 per cent), benefits could be extended for, e.g., another thirteen weeks. In these states 39 weeks then becomes the maximum.

The net effect of the weekly benefit calculation is to weight benefits in favor of the lower bracket wage earner. This is true even though benefit duration is shorter for the lower wage earner. A question here: Does this "discriminate" against the high wage earner? The low? At present, although benefit weeks have lengthened, average benefits do not come up to the 50 to 65 per cent of wages envisaged in the 1935 Act.[12] As we shall see in the next chapter, this has been one of the bases upon which labor organizations have built their supplementary unemployment benefit approach.

Temporary Unemployment Compensation (TUC and TEUC). A new benefit approach was introduced during the recession of 1957–58. This was temporary unemployment compensation, the "TUC" program, created by an Act of June 4, 1958. The Act provided that in states which chose to participate in the program additional benefits could be paid to jobless

---

[12] Analysts differ on the 50 and 65 per cent figures. This is the effective range, however, within which most opinions fell.

workers who exhausted their regular benefits after June 30, 1957 (or some later date selected by the participating state). In effect the program provided for a 50 per cent increase in benefit duration. The Act was effective June 19, 1958, was to terminate March 31, 1959, but was extended to June 30, 1959.

Thirty-four states elected to participate in the program, and five others undertook programs on their own. The program was to be financed by state repayments, either directly or, commencing in 1963, by a reduction in the federal offset. Alternative repayment measures have since been enacted.

Under the federal and state extension programs over 2 million individuals received $601 million in benefits. (Yet 1.2 million exhausted their temporary benefits also.) The average weekly benefit was $30.44, and the average duration was 9.8 weeks. As noted earlier, eight states have continued the extension practice, paying extended benefits when unemployment in the state exceeds a given percentage.

A second federal TUC program (titled TEUC) was undertaken in March, 1961. The Act was signed on March 23, 1961, and was to apply to those who had exhausted their benefits between July 1, 1960, and March 31, 1962. Benefits were to be extended for 50 per cent of the original allowance, but for not more than thirteen weeks (with an outside allowable limit of thirty-nine weeks). Benefit advances were to be made by the federal government. It was anticipated in April, 1961, that 700,000 exhaustees would benefit immediately from the program. By the end of the program, in 1962, nearly 2.8 million unemployed had received benefits to an aggregate figure of $771 million. The average claimant received a weekly payment of $31 for nine weeks. Approximately three out of every five claimants used up all of their extended benefit entitlement.

Financing was to be accomplished by a 0.4 per cent tax on employers in the years 1962 and 1963. This would make the total tax 3.5 per cent, of which 0.8 would go to the federal government. The tax was later altered to make the total rate 3.5 per cent for 1962 and 3.35 for 1963 with the state offset remaining the same. The program was to be effective only in those states which agreed to participate, *but* all employers were to be taxed irrespective of whether the state participated or not. Hence, as might be expected, all states participated.

A special kind of temporary program, enacted in Public Law 87-31, which amended Title IV of the Social Security Act, was signed by President Kennedy on May 8, 1961. This law made available, for a fourteen-month period (since extended) beginning May 1, 1961, federal grants to states wishing to extend their programs of aid to dependent children to those children (and the relatives caring for them) who have been deprived of parental support or care because of a parent's unemployment.

The extension of a state's program of aid to dependent children to include the children of unemployed parents was optional with the state, and the definition of unemployment as a condition of eligibility is left to the state. Technically, of course, this is a grant-in-aid program, and it has been previously mentioned in Chapter 3. But it illustrates in an interesting way the interrelationships between various kinds of insecurities and the programs that have been developed to meet them.

Costs—Financing

The federal Act specified a 3 per cent tax on employers against which could be offset up to 90 per cent of any state contributions. (As of January 1, 1961, the rate became 3.1 per cent, with the federal government retaining the extra increment. In 1962 and 1963 the rates went to 3.5 and 3.35 per cent, respectively. The purpose of these latter increases was to recapture advances made under the temporary extension Act of 1961.) Additionally, the employer could be credited with any reductions under an approved experience rating plan. No tax on employees was provided for in the Act. We shall cover the principal cost-finance topics under a number of subheads.

Employee Contributions. Although ten states at one time or another utilized employee contributions, only Alaska, Alabama, and New Jersey did so in 1966. (California, Rhode Island, and New Jersey utilize employee contributions for a related system of disability insurance.) The tax in Alabama and New Jersey is on the first $3,000 of wages, and in Alaska on the first $7,200. The rates vary: in Alabama, from 0.25 per cent to 0.5 per cent as the employer's rate varies under experience rating; in New Jersey the rate is 0.25 per cent; in Alaska, 0.6 per cent.

Experience Rating. Unemployment insurance is essentially an alleviative system. But it also contains a "preventive" component whereby an employer who reduces his unemployment (or who is so placed that his employment is "normally" stabilized) can have his tax reduced. The procedure used is called experience rating. In Chapter 14 we shall discuss more fully the economic ramifications of this procedure; here we will present some of the details of application.

Experience rating formulae of the different states vary greatly, but they all contain a number of common elements. First, all formulae measure the employer's experience with unemployment: how much unemployment he has had in his establishment in some specified period. This factor is customarily measured in terms of benefit payments to employees severed from jobs in his company. Second, this measure is compared with a measure of "exposure," usually the payroll for the period in question. In a sample formula, the benefits paid are put in the numerator and the "exposure" (payroll) in the denominator. A fraction results from the division; this is the "experience ratio." What tax the employer then pays may depend not only upon this ratio (a higher ratio would require a higher tax) but also upon the size of the state unemployment reserve fund (a smaller size fund moves the tax structure up and vice versa) and upon the employer's individual reserve (unless a specified reserve is reached and maintained, a tax reduction is not allowed).[13] All states now have in effect some experience rating system. The reason is clear; no state feels it can put its industry at a competitive disadvantage by not having such a plan. While social insurance costs are but one of many factors involved in plant location (attraction of new industry or retention of present), they are one over which state legislatures can exercise directly some degree of control.

The result of experience rating has been to change the effective tax "paid" by the state from 2.7 per cent to a lower figure. Calculations for the decade 1950–60 indicate that the average contribution (tax) rate for fifty states was 1.4 per cent. (The annual average cost rate for the decade was 1.6 per cent; as will be seen it was possible to have a cost rate higher than a tax rate through the means of drawing down the unemployment trust fund.) The decade tax rate for Colorado averaged 0.6 per cent; for Alaska and Rhode Island it was 2.7 per cent.[14] In the next half-decade the effective tax paid increased markedly as unemployment insurance trust funds were drawn down (to pay benefits) and then had to be rebuilt. Yet, the effective state rate still averaged less than 2.7 per cent; in 1964, for example, it was 2.2 per cent. Another result of experience rating probably has been to keep the benefit structure lower than it would otherwise have been. This has happened for two reasons. First, given a lower tax rate, employer pressures have tended to resist any increase in benefits which would require an increase in tax rates. Second, state legislatures have been reluctant to raise rates unless such a raise were general among the states; to do so unilaterally would be to add a factor of competitive disadvantage. This should not be taken to imply that there have been no benefit increases. Benefits (levels and duration of) have climbed since the passage of the federal Act. But they have not kept pace with wage changes, and it is probable that experience rating has had a braking effect upon benefit liberalization.

[13] The student should secure a copy of the plan used in his state and work out arithmetic examples using different figures. The best over-all exposition of different plans is still to be found in D. Gagliardo, *American Social Insurance* (rev. ed.; New York: Harper & Row, 1955), pp. 261–71.

[14] U. S. Department of Labor, Bureau of Employment Security, *State Unemployment Insurance Statutory Provisions and Experience, 1960* (BES No. U–192), 1960.

Other Cost-Financing Details. State laws contain various other financing features designed to make the system operate more efficiently. Let us examine the more important of these.

1. In 1966, eighteen states had tax bases higher than the $3,000 specified under federal law; eleven of the eighteen were at $3,600; one (Alaska) at $7,200. Thirty-one states provided for rates above 2.7 per cent (3.0 per cent in four; 7.0 per cent in one—North Dakota). Given the unemployment compensation "solvency problems" of the past decade it is no accident that there has been an upward drift in the rate structure. (In 1960 only seventeen states had rates above the 2.7 level.)

2. Twenty-five states permit "voluntary contributions" by means of which an employer can "buy back." That is, by making a voluntary contribution he can improve his experience ratio. The contribution systems are so structured as to save the employer more than the amount of his voluntary contribution.

3. "Non-charging" of benefit clauses exists in all state laws. Such non-charges are of several types. First, the employer may not be charged for benefits based upon employment of short duration or for appealed cases which are reversed, or, in nine states, for dependents' allowances. Second, in discharge or voluntary quit cases, where benefits ultimately may be paid, the employer may not be charged. The intent here is to relieve the employer of charges for unemployment due to circumstances beyond his control. (It should be noted, however, that the "system" must in some way recover the monies paid in benefits for such cases.)

4. All state laws specify the conditions under which the experience record of a predecessor employer may be transferred to an employer who acquires the business. In a minority of states, "total" transfer is required; in the others partial as well as total is allowed.

5. What employer is to be charged for the benefits paid an unemployed claimant? If the claimant had only one base-period employer the answer is easy. But what if there was more than one such employer? The majority of states charge benefits against all base-period employers in proportion to wages earned, this on the basis that unemployment results from general conditions. Fourteen states charge base-period employers in inverse chronological order, while ten charge one employer, commonly the most recent.

Administration

Since there are no specific requirements in the federal Act as to the form of the state administration or its place in the state government, a number of differing agency types have developed. The most common type in 1966 was the independent board or commission found in fourteen states. A second common type found in eighteen states was an independent department of the state department. Finally, seventeen states have the administrative agency located in the state department of labor, with one in the state's workmen's compensation agency. To some extent the form of the administrative agency is an accident of political pressure, of existing state government units, and of historical growth. But, irrespective of the form, the purpose is clear: to administer the state act in conformity with its intent as well as content.

The administrative procedure set up for the processing of claims is similar in all states. The unemployed individual files a claim for benefits following specified steps and using specified forms. This is usually done at his local public employment office, although in unpopulated areas another public official may substitute for an employment office. The claim is then centrally reviewed (in some states locally) and benefit amount and duration determined. Benefit claimants customarily receive their checks by mail, but must report regularly (usually weekly) at the local public employment office. All states provide an appeals procedure for the individual whose claim is denied. The appeals agency is an impartial tribunal, variously composed in different states. In all but four states in 1966 an additional second appeals stage was provided. Appeal agency decisions can be reviewed by the courts, but only as to matters of law and not of fact. All but three states provide for an advisory council—usually with equal employer and union representation—whose purpose is to help in policy formulation and administrative problem solving.

The administration of the state acts is financed by the federal government, through grants from the general federal treasury. After January 1, 1961, the 0.4 per cent federal tax was reserved for employment security purposes. (This is apart from the extra taxes imposed to repay the costs of the TEUC program.) The annual excess (if any) of such taxes over the cost of administration is to be placed in a federal Unemployment Account (an emergency reserve) until a total of $550 million is reached. Subsequent excess collections are to be allocated to the various state accounts in the proportion their covered payrolls bear to the aggregate, this after a second administrative expense account of $250 million has been built up.

Administrative provision is also made for the handling of interstate claims. At present the principal procedure is for the "liable" state to make the original determination of eligibility and benefits, and the "agent" state to receive and initially transmit the claim and subsequently pay the benefits (reimbursed by the "liable" state) and make subsequent determinations. The advantage of this procedure in permitting desirable labor mobility is obvious.

OPERATIONAL DATA AND TRENDS IN
UNEMPLOYMENT INSURANCE

The above material was designed to present an over-all view of the nature of state unemployment insurance programs. Without burdening the reader with excessive details, it may prove desirable to highlight a few operational statistics and indicate trends in the program.

Coverage and Claims

Table 7.1 presents data on coverage and claims for selected years of operation under the state unemployment insurance system.

TABLE 7.1

Coverage, Claims, and Payments Under Unemployment Insurance—
State Programs

		Payrolls Covered		Initial Claims (weekly average) (in thousands)	First Payments (in thousands)	Exhaustions (in thousands)
Year	Coverage (in thousands)	Amount (in millions)	Per Cent of Civilian Wages- Salaries			
1940	23,096	$ 32,352	65.7	214	5,220	2,590
1950	32,887	102,835	72.7	236	5,212	1,853
1951	34,858	118,243	72.9	208	4,127	811
1952	35,557	127,320	72.9	215	4,383	931
1953	36,667	138,657	73.8	218	4,228	764
1954	35,372	136,594	73.3	303	6,590	1,769
1955	36,590	158,439	78.8	226	4,508	1,294
1956	39,200	175,342	80.4	226	4,730	1,020
1957	39,900	184,837	80.7	268	5,647	1,191
1958	38,400	183,936	80.0	370	7,941	2,599
1959	39,900	199,912	80.5	281	5,867	1,703
1960	40,500	209,707	80.2	331	6,753	1,603
1961	40,400	214,140	79.7	350	7,066	2,371
1962	41,600	228,554	79.8	302	6,074	1,638
1963	42,400	240,055	79.7	297	6,041	1,569
1964	43,600	257,361	80.5	268	5,498	1,371
1965	n.a.	n.a.	n.a.	232	4,817	1,086

n.a. = not available.

Sources: *Unemployment Insurance Statistics; Social Security Bulletins.*

While coverage has increased 75 per cent since the beginning of operations and has resulted in the inclusion of a greater proportion of the civilian labor force (57 per cent in 1965 in contrast to 43 per cent in 1940), this has been accomplished by the growth of employment in already covered industries rather than by blanketing-in new occupations. (If railroad, federal worker, and armed forces programs are included, the proportion covered rises to over 65 per cent.)

The number of initial claims follows closely the level of economic activity. In the full-employment economy of 1943–44 there were few claims. Conversely, in each of the four post-war recessions (1949–50, 1954–55, 1957–58, 1960–61) claims increased.

Various analysts have suggested that disqualifications and appeals have increased more than proportionately because of an increasing tightening of state administrative standards and the application of more rigorous standards.

Beneficiaries and Benefits

Table 7.2 presents data on beneficiaries and benefits. From this table one can derive several bits and pieces of information: (1) the trend in beneficiaries given post-war prosperity and recession and (2) the countercyclical stabilizing nature of benefit payments.

TABLE 7.2

Beneficiaries and Benefits Under Unemployment Insurance—
State Programs

Year	Number of Beneficiaries (average weekly number)	Amounts of Benefits (in thousands)	Average Actual Duration of Benefits (weeks)	Average Weekly Payment for Total Unemployment (dollars)
1940	982,392	$ 518,700	9.8	10.56
1950	1,305,000	1,408,079	13.0	20.76
1951	796,900	842,645	10.1	21.09
1952	873,600	1,001,776	10.4	22.79
1953	812,100	1,003,919	10.1	23.58
1954	1,614,900	2,134,532	12.8	24.93
1955	1,099,500	1,437,940	12.5	25.08
1956	1,037,000	1,441,643	11.4	27.06
1957	1,250,200	1,819,532	11.6	28.21
1958	2,255,000	4,061,981	14.8	30.58
1959	1,675,000	2,635,304	13.1	30.41
1960	1,709,000	2,867,051	12.7	32.87
1961	2,290,311	4,156,316	14.7	33.80
1962	1,783,118	3,012,610	13.1	34.56
1963	1,805,816	2,926,409	13.3	35.27
1964	1,312,538	2,670,743	13.0	35.96
1965	1,128,186	2,176,239	12.2	37.17

Sources: *Unemployment Insurance Statistics; Social Security Bulletins.*

The Unemployment Trust Fund

Table 7.3 presents a picture of the unemployment trust fund from its inception through 1965. As can be seen, the fund has a cycle all its own, which in its larger dimensions is unrelated to the four post-war periods of prosperity and recession. Up to 1953 unemployment was underestimated in terms of the tax structure applied; from 1953 to 1962 the reverse was true; since 1961 the fund has been again increasing.

TABLE 7.3

The Unemployment Trust Fund—
State Programs

Year	Collections (in millions)	Benefits (in millions)	Interest (in millions)	Balance (in millions)	Ratio of Benefits to Collections and Interest (per cent)
1936	$ 65	(less than $500,000)	$ 1	$ 65	—
1937	567	$ 2	8	638	(less than 1)
1938	829	404	9	1,072	48
1939	830	429	27	1,500	51
1940	861	517	60	1,805	56
1941	1,008	342	58	2,516	32
1942	1,139	344	74	3,379	28
1943	1,328	78	89	4,711	06
1944	1,317	63	55	6,016	05
1945	1,161	461	129	6,833	36
1946	916	1,104	144	6,775	104
1947	1,097	787	147	7,217	63
1948	989	852	246	7,572	69
1949	998	1,762	176	6,954	150
1950	1,191	1,342	163	6,948	99
1951	1,495	845	175	7,757	51
1952	1,372	996	194	8,310	64
1953	1,350	970	217	8,892	62
1954	1,136	2,027	199	8,219	152
1955	1,208	1,350	185	8,264	97
1956	1,463	1,381	200	8,574	83
1957	1,544	1,744	220	8,662	99
1958	1,471	3,513	199	6,953	210
1959	1,956	2,279	178	6,892	107
1960	2,289	2,727	195	6,643	110
1961	2,450	3,423	176	5,802	130
1962	2,952	2,675	173	6,273	86
1963	3,019	2,775	195	6,648	86
1964	3,048	2,522	225	7,296	77
1965	2,954	2,165	266	8,336	67

Sources: *Social Security Bulletin, Annual Statistical Supplement, 1955*, p. 12; *Unemployment Insurance Reviews; Social Security Bulletins.*

But, what size should the fund be? The answer one gets depends upon how one views the fund: as a "contingency" fund, as an "earnings" fund, or as some other kind of reserve. A currently accepted view is that the fund should be between one and one-half and two times the largest amount of benefits paid in any previous twelve-month period. Given this view, the "fund" in 1965 was within this range and hence "safe."

One might get the impression from above that the fund is a federal fund. This, of course, is not the case. The totals presented in Table 7.3 merely represent the summation of individual state funds (technically "reserve accounts"). From this fact flows a problem hidden by the fund aggregation shown above. This problem arises because not all states have the same unemployment experience.[15] Some are hit much harder than others in periods of economic recession: Massachusetts and Rhode Island in 1949–50; Michigan and Pennsylvania in 1957–58.

Hence, at different times, individual state funds have approached dangerously low levels. The affected state has several alternatives open to it. While it is difficult to cut benefits, increases can be forestalled. Since there is customarily a relationship between individual state fund size and tax rates under experience rating, a lowering of the fund may call for increased tax rates. This is a second alternative and one most commonly followed. Thus in the four post-war recessions one finds states such as Massachusetts, Michigan, Pennsylvania, and Rhode Island at effective rates of 2.7 per cent or higher, while the average for the country stood at 1.6 per cent or thereabouts.

A third alternative is to secure an interest-free loan from the federal Unemployment Account.[16] A state is eligible for such a loan whenever its reserves available for benefits at the end of a calendar quarter are less than the amounts of benefits paid out in the twelve months ending with that calendar quarter. States make use of the loan fund: in 1958, for example, Michigan borrowed $113 million; in 1959 Pennsylvania bor-

[15] Many states have recently conducted studies to analyze in detail their employment-unemployment experience, the operation of their state funds, and thence to make projections as to future patterns. This provides a base for policy action. The interested student can check to see if such a report has been made in his state. Several examples of such studies include E. L. Bowers, P. C. Craig, and W. Papier, *Financing Unemployment Compensation: Ohio's Experience* (1956); G. Seltzer (Director), *Economic Guidelines for Unemployment Insurance, Minnesota, 1958–1967* (1958); W. H. Andrews, Jr. and T. Miller, *Employment Security Financing in Indiana* (1956). Federal studies are also to be found.

[16] This was originally set up in 1944 as a federal Emergency Reserve, designed to handle what was expected to be the vast immediate post-war unemployment problem. It was abolished in 1952 and re-established in 1954. Given the increase in the federal tax from 0.3 to 0.4 per cent (as of January 1, 1961) additional changes were made in the structure and operation of the fund. For a useful discussion, see Robert J. Myers, *Social Insurance and Allied Government Programs* (Homewood, Ill.: Richard D. Irwin, Inc., 1965), pp. 178–82.

rowed $96.44 million. At the end of 1959 the federal loan fund was nearly exhausted. The increase in the federal tax rate from 0.3 to 0.4 per cent as of January 1, 1961 has built up the fund, since certain portions of these monies were allocated to it.

AN EVALUATION OF THE UNEMPLOYMENT INSURANCE SYSTEM

What can be said by way of evaluating the unemployment insurance system? In Chapter 1, three general criteria were laid down. They included the questions: (1) Did the program accomplish the purpose(s) for which it was designed? (2) Was the program rationally structured and soundly administered? (3) Did the program produce undesirable economic consequences? We shall generally reserve for Chapter 14 the discussion of the third criterion, and shall concentrate here upon the first two.

Purposes and Accomplishments of Unemployment Insurance

In a general sense the purpose of the unemployment insurance program was to alleviate the undesirable economic consequences arising out of short-term unemployment which regularly employed individuals would experience even though the aggregate demand for labor was not insufficient. This general purpose was carried into effect by the law in two specific ways: first, by providing a high benefit level, designed to approximate 50 to 65 per cent of the unemployed individual's previous income; and second, by extending the benefit level over a relatively short period of time (sixteen weeks was the maximum in the first state laws passed since 1935).

Appraising performance in terms of the general purpose, one might conclude that unemployment insurance has accomplished the objective for which it was designed. The specifics, however, have not been met in the form in which they were set up. In place of 50 per cent of previous wages, the average has dropped to 30 to 40 per cent (though some individual states have maintained a higher ratio). However, the benefit period was lengthened to a median figure of twenty-six weeks in 1966. Thus the trend has been to provide a lower relative benefit for a longer period of time.

With a given in-payment structure, one or the other of benefit levels or benefit duration must be the limiting or balancing factor; both cannot be indefinitely extended. Hence, it is not fully justifiable to criticize the failure of benefits to keep pace with wage and price-level increases, for the duration of benefits has increased at the same time. Thus, if one took the net amount receivable (by multiplying benefit by duration) by an unemployed person, this would not exhibit quite the same lag characteristics as would benefit levels alone. One has to make a choice between what one wants (or what combination one wants) in benefit levels and benefit duration.

If one took the sentiments of employers and unions and arrayed them against each other, one would find generally opposing views, though with different emphases. Labor views would be critical of general accomplishment; not only has the system not "improved," but it has not kept pace. Labor would also be critical of some specialized aspects: administration, experience rating, and disqualifications. Management, while not generally unsympathetic toward the system, would criticize administration (on opposite grounds from labor) and financial procedures.

Before trying to present our evaluation of general accomplishments, let us suggest a number of improvements.

Unemployment Insurance: Suggestions for Improvement

In the following section we list a number of ways in which we believe the unemployment insurance system could be strengthened and improved. These proposals arise out of the authors' service with state unemployment insurance advisory councils and the proposals of analysts and critics of the existing system.

Improvements in the present framework might be made through (1) "federal standards," i.e., changing the specifics of the federal enabling act or (2) alterations in the state laws. Federal standards are proposed for two reasons. First, it is held that economic logic sustains this position; the pattern of unemployment is not so varied among the states as to justify separate treatment. Second, operating efficiency could well be improved by one uniform system. But irrespective of the stand one takes on federal standards, one can spell out suggested changes. We shall do so in a systematic fashion.[17]

Coverage. If the employing unit size were lowered from four to one and if the employees of non-profit institutions were included some 4 million additional persons would be brought under the Act, increasing coverage by about 7 per cent. At the moment it is more difficult to visualize covering the self-employed and domestic and agricultural workers, though proposals are found here.

[17] For a discussion of "federal standards" see Merrill G. Murray, *Proposed Federal Unemployment Insurance Amendments* (Kalamazoo, Mich.: The W. E. Upjohn Institute for Employment Research, 1966).

Benefits. Benefits could well be "flexibly" set, say at 50 per cent of regular earnings, with the maximum set at say 66⅔ per cent of average wages in covered employment. One shortcoming of the present system is that benefits may not be flexible (in which case legislative action is required to improve them). More important, however, is the fact that at present benefit maximums thwart flexibility, and with a majority of beneficiaries at the maximum, one really approaches a flat benefit system.

Benefit Duration. Uniform duration is recommended. At present the low wage earner usually has the shorter duration, but he is the very person who, through lack of seniority or skill, tends to be unemployed the longest. But what period of uniform duration? There are no standards available by means of which an easy answer can be obtained. Studies of benefit duration lead one to suggest that thirty weeks has merit as a reasonable "approximation." We would also encourage study of the feasibility of varying benefit duration (and perhaps amount) with the level of economic activity.

Financing. An ideal financing system would not only embody basic insurance principles but also would be counter-cyclical in nature. Such a system appears to be far in the future. For the interim we would recommend further study of the feasibility of a "level-rate" approach.[18]

Other Phases. Numerous suggestions have been made over the years as to qualifications for benefits, disqualification, and administration. We would make only one general point here: that the benefit structure should be liberalized, but liberal benefit payments require and presuppose careful setting and administration of standards.

We would conclude that the present system has not failed of its basic purpose, but that it has not accomplished what it might have, and that it could be made a much more effective system at a relatively small marginal cost.[19]

Federal Standards: Proposed Legislation

Federal standards *have* received increasing attention in the Congress. At the time of this writing none has been enacted, but there was introduced in 1965 a far-reaching series of proposals (H.R. 8282 and S. 1991).

[18] See the comments by Richard A. Lester, "Financing of Unemployment Compensation," *Industrial and Labor Relations Review,* XIV, No. 1 (October, 1960), 52–67.

[19] One can find a vast body of literature appraising unemployment insurance, literature ranging from careful government analyses to popular magazine exposures of maladministration. Our conclusions would lead us to believe that the system is not "perfect" but that its merits far outweigh its shortcomings.

In brief compass, the proposals included:

1. A federal program of extended benefits to begin July 1, 1966.
2. Weekly benefits (under state laws) to be set at at least half of average weekly wages, up to a maximum, set high enough so that most workers can have their benefits set by their own wages rather than by the statutory maximum. (The ultimate maximum, to be set by 1971, would be 66⅔ per cent of statewide average wages.)
3. A tax base increased by steps to $6,600 in 1971, with additional provisions of federal grants to states meeting benefit standards.
4. Extension of coverage to some 5 million additional employees.
5. Additional standards with respect to disqualification provisions, interstate claims, and other administrative aspects.

There is every likelihood that these proposals will continue to receive increasing attention as time passes, though one can only conjecture (1) whether they will, in fact, be enacted into law and (2) if so, when.

SUMMARY

In the United States the major public program for the alleviation of the economic consequences of unemployment is the unemployment compensation (or insurance) system. This is a combined federal-state program, with the federal government setting down a framework of minimal specifications within which the several states are free to write their own acts, which all have done.

An unemployment insurance program requires answers to a number of basic questions: who is to be covered, what shall be the eligibility requirements for benefit collection, how much benefits shall be and for how long they shall be paid, who shall pay the costs and how much they shall be, and how the program is to be administered. While the federal government imposes certain minimal requirements upon the states in the answering of these questions, the states are given considerable latitude in the programs they enact. Hence, one finds an extremely complicated as well as diverse set of laws in this country. The state programs have been amended continually, but because of interstate competitive relations, such changes have tended to be less marked than for wholly federal laws such as the OASDI program.

In concluding this chapter it may be noted first, that the unemployment insurance system *has* been an effective instrument in alleviating the undesirable economic consequences of short-term unemployment. But, second, it may be suggested that the program falls short of the goals it could achieve, and hence there is need for a continuing examination so as to create a more fully effective unemployment insurance system in the United States.

SUGGESTIONS FOR ADDITIONAL READING

BECKER, JOSEPH M., S. J. *Shared Government in Employment Security.* New York: Columbia University Press, 1959.
An analysis of the role of advisory councils in policy formulation and administration in economic security programs.

————. "Twenty-Five Years of Unemployment Insurance," *Political Science Quarterly,* LXXV, No. 4 (December, 1960), 481–99.
An interesting and "unorthodox" examination of unemployment insurance.

Industrial and Labor Relations Review, XIV, No. 1 (October, 1960).
This issue is devoted to the social security system in the United States and has pertinent articles on unemployment insurance.

LESTER, RICHARD A. *The Economics of Unemployment Compensation.* Princeton University, Industrial Relations Section, 1962.
An analysis of the economic impacts of the UC program, particularly useful in the area of benefits and income maintenance.

MALISOFF, HARRY. *Cost Estimation Methods in Unemployment Insurance, 1909–1957.* New York: New York State Department of Labor, 1958.
A useful historical and analytical examination of the actuarial aspects of unemployment insurance.

————. *Simplifying Unemployment Insurance Objectives.* Pasadena: California Institute of Technology, Benefits and Insurance Research Center, Industrial Relations Section, 1960.
An incentive appraisal of unemployment insurance, its objectives, and the practicalities and realities of simplification.

McKEAN, EUGENE C. *The Taxable Wage Base in Unemployment Insurance Financing.* Kalamazoo, Mich.: The W. E. Upjohn Institute for Employment Research, 1965.
An analysis of the arguments for and against a higher wage base in financing unemployment insurance, and the implications for effective tax rates.

SELTZER, GEORGE (Director). *Economic Guidelines for Unemployment Insurance, Minnesota, 1958–1967.* St. Paul: Minnesota Department of Employment Security (Frank T. Starkey, Commissioner), 1958.
A re-examination of the Minnesota economy and its implications for the unemployment insurance program. The student will want to look at similar reports for other states.

"Twenty Years of Unemployment Insurance in the U.S.A., 1935–1955," and "Unemployment Insurance in the U.S.A., 1956–1960," *Employment Security Review,* August, 1955 and August, 1960 respectively, and *Unemployment Insurance Review,* August, 1965 (issue devoted to the 30th anniversary of unemployment insurance).
Useful historical summaries.

8

Private Approaches:
Unemployment

INTRODUCTION

This chapter is more appropriately titled private "approaches" than "supplements," since the approaches taken by employers and unions against unemployment are not only preventive as well as alleviative, but also broader than supplements to the public system of compensation as discussed in Chapter 7. The major approaches include private unemployment insurance programs; dismissal compensation or the severance wage as it is sometimes called; employment stabilization; and work and wage guarantees, including the conventional guaranteed annual wage (GAW) and the newer supplementary unemployment payment (SUP) or supplementary unemployment benefit (SUB). We shall discuss each of these methods in turn and attempt to relate them to the over-all American economic security system.

GENERAL COMMENTS

The methods used in private approaches to unemployment are clear: the employer, either by himself or through collective bargaining, seeks to reduce unemployment in his establishment and, for such cases as do arise, may additionally seek to supplement public alleviative measures. Why should the employer do this? There are several very good reasons, based on humanitarian as well as economic grounds. On the preventive side, stabilizing employment affords operational advantages to the employer: manpower savings through reduction in the costs of labor turnover and machine savings in the more intensive utilization of equipment. Stabilization also permits a reduction in unemployment insurance taxes through the experience rating system, and, if accompanied by an approved guarantee, provides exemption from the overtime provisions of the Fair Labor Standards Act. On a humanitarian basis, stabilization reduces the incidence of unemployment and, hence, employee fears about the threat of economic insecurity.[1] On the alleviative side—that of the private unemployment supplement—one finds the same reasons as are found for pensions and accident and illness insurance: namely, to supplement what is considered an otherwise inadequate level of benefits.

How far should an employer go in seeking to stabilize employment? The answer here is the same as for any dollar and cents business decision: to the point where the additional cost of stabilizing is equal to (or at least does not exceed) the additional benefit, this assuming that the employer has some degree of control in the situation (which realistically is the usual case). There is a point below which stabilization is socially undesirable (in that labor mobility is unduly restricted) and also beyond which the costs of further reduction exceed the gains.

Private supplements to unemployment compensation are a new development. The first collective agreement embodying this approach was signed in 1955. Under present practice, protection via the private supplement is provided by the employer on the basis of a contribution of so many cents per hour into a fund which then can be used to pay the supplements. Customarily, the cents-per-hour fund payment is part of the total wage package or settlement. Hence, employer decision-making on this problem involves determining jointly with the union (or unilaterally in the non-unionized case) what portion of the over-all wage bargain will be allotted to the supplement. We shall discuss these matters more fully later in this chapter, after discussing other types of programs.

PRIVATE UNEMPLOYMENT INSURANCE SYSTEMS

Private unemployment insurance systems (other than the newer unemployment compensation supplements) are primarily of historical interest, but they are worth a brief comment, since they highlight employer and union attempts to deal with this form of insecurity.[2]

Private unemployment insurance programs can be classified into three groups, depending upon the originating parties involved: those developed by unions, those developed by employers, and those collectively bargained. (So far as the authors know, a fourth alternative, unemployment insurance written on an actuarial basis by a commercial insurance com-

---

[1] For a fuller discussion, see J. L. Snider, *The Guarantee of Work and Wages* (Boston: Harvard University, Graduate School of Business Administration, 1947), pp. 109–10; and H. Feldman, *Stabilizing Jobs and Wages* (New York: Harper & Row, 1940), pp. 10–11.

[2] For a useful reference, see B. M. Stewart, *Unemployment Benefits in the United States* (New York: Industrial Relations Counselors, 1930).

pany, never came into being, although some carriers were working upon such policies in the 1920's.)

Trade-union plans, dating back to at least 1831, never developed more fully than to provide protection for between approximately 35,000–60,000 or so union members under some thirteen international and twenty additional local union programs in the 1920's. Yet some protection was afforded in specific cases (though the benefits were very low), and the experimentation was useful. Company plans, of which some thirteen were paying benefits in the early 1930's, varied from the employment guarantee approach to the out-and-out unemployment benefit, as found in the Dennison Manufacturing Company. In this company plan, benefits were liberal; up to the middle of 1930, employees with dependents received 80 per cent of their weekly earnings, with a waiting period of but one day. Collectively bargained plans covered more employees— some 63,500 in 1928—than either union or company plans. Again, the approach varied from guarantees to benefits. The most outstanding benefit plans were found in the clothing industry, with some attempt being made to approach actuarial soundness through the use of risk pooling and the setting up of reserve funds.

The passage of the Social Security Act in 1935 led to predictions that private plans would either terminate or function under public regulation. As a matter of course, the former generally happened. All these private plans are interesting for two reasons: (1) they illustrate company and union concern with a burdensome type of economic insecurity and (2) they also illustrate the incredible difficulties involved in trying to combat this form of insecurity on a piecemeal basis, where actuarial data do not exist and where many forces are beyond the control of the employer and the union. (It might not have been too difficult to undertake a modest program on a "limited liability" basis, as was the case in the clothing industry. But a piecemeal approach such as this was not likely to lead to comprehensive and systematic coverage for the economy as a whole.)

Dismissal Compensation or Severance Pay

Private unemployment insurance, insofar as the benefit payments technique was used, made no *formal* distinction as to whether a man was laid off and was expected to return, whether he was laid off and his return was uncertain, or whether he was permanently severed, say, for economic reasons. The evidence, however, leads one to presume that the benefit approach was tied principally to job separation due to layoffs, where the man was expected to return, rather than to cases where he was permanently separated. For this latter case, a different technique developed —that of dismissal compensation or severance wages.

Dismissal compensation may be defined as "the payment of a specific sum, in addition to any back wages or salary, made by an employer to an employee for *permanently terminating* the employment relationship for reasons beyond the control of the employee" [3] (italics supplied). In general, dismissal compensation is paid for a severing of the employment relationship, rather than for a period of unemployment; thus, payments are not contingent upon the former employee's remaining unemployed. Such compensation is not customarily paid if discharge is for cause, including fault, incapacity, or incompetence.[4]

While exact figures are not available on the extent of dismissal compensation plans in industry, estimates would indicate a coverage of over five million employees in 1965. Over 25 per cent of union agreements appear to contain a separation allowance provision, covering at least 35 per cent of employees under union agreements.[5]

Why should an employer be interested in providing this form of protection against economic insecurity? One can visualize employer interest in protective plans where the employee is expected to remain with the company—pension, and accidental injury and sickness plans, for example. But in the other case the employment relationship is permanently severed. Two reasons appear for employer interest in situations where his employee leaves "permanently." One is the increasing belief that the cost of doing business—the cost of production—should include a charge for those employees "scrapped" because of the changes wrought by a dynamic economy. The other is that labor organizations have evinced increasing interest in this type of protection; and, since collective bargaining is a two-way process, union interest is likely to evoke employer response.

Details of Dismissal Compensation Plans

The following summarizes the basic operational details of severance pay plans.

Coverage. While earlier plans tended to be restrictive in coverage—including, for example, only white-collar employees of the company, or,

---

[3] E. D. Hawkins, *Dismissal Compensation* (Princeton: Princeton University Press, 1940), pp. 5–6. This is a very useful source book on dismissal compensation, along with the National Industrial Conference Board analysis, "Severance Pay Plans," *Studies in Personnel Policy No. 141* (New York: 1954). See also footnote 5 below.

[4] Some recent cases indicate that severance pay is now being given for "temporary layoffs," though not for discharge for cause.

[5] "Severance Pay Plans," *AFL-CIO Collective Bargaining Report,* IV, No. 10 (October, 1959), 57–62; Leon E. Lunden and Ernestine M. Moore, "Severance Pay and Layoff Benefit Plans," *Monthly Labor Review,* LXXXVIII, No. 1 (January, 1965), 27–34.

if blue-collar, only a select group—the present tendency is to widen the umbrella of protection to, say, all employees who have passed their probationary period.

Qualification for Benefits. The fact that coverage has tended to increase recently does not mean that a "covered" employee thereby is automatically eligible to receive benefits. Two additional qualifications are found. The first is that the employee must be a certain age (a much less common requirement today) or have had some degree of attachment to the company, ranging all the way from three months to ten years, with one year the most common. (There is an increasing tendency to get away also from the "attachment" qualification by requiring that the individual be merely a "regular" employee of the company—"regular" being defined as having passed the probationary period.) The second qualification relates to the manner of job separation. Usually the job separation must be for reasons beyond the control of the employee; hence, voluntary quits and discharges for cause commonly disqualify the individual. Some companies have escape clauses in which dismissal pay is not required where acts of God, national emergencies, or other forces are the "cause" of the separation. Conversely, some companies make such payments for separations due to total incapacity, military service, retirement, or death.

Benefit Levels. The following variables are most commonly taken into account in calculating dismissal pay: (1) the wage or salary at the time of separation (or for some average period prior to that), (2) length of service, and (3) age and need. The latter—age and need—are less commonly applied today than previously and are tending to disappear. The common forms of benefit calculation provide either a "uniform payment" system, such as that all severed employees shall receive two weeks' pay or a "service rule" where pay is graded on the basis of length of service. Thus, an individual might get one week's pay for each year of service. Or, there might be a system of classes set up, such as one week's pay for one to two years of service, two weeks' pay for two to three years of service, three weeks' pay for three to ten years of service, and so on. More complex formulae are sometimes found, taking into account age, need, or possible moving expenses. (To give a concrete example of one program, in 1966 a General Motors employee with 30 years' service would receive 2,080 hours pay.)

Here again in these benefit structures is an illustration of the "cultural" belief that loyalty to the company (evinced by a long employment attachment) should be rewarded. The rewards do not, however, go up proportionately in most plans: a twenty-year man does not get twenty times as much as a one-year man.

Benefit payments are commonly made on a lump-sum basis, although some periodic and combination payment plans exist. Not all states permit unemployment insurance payments to be made if the individual receives severance wages, the belief being that this constitutes "double payment." As a result of recent decisions made in conjunction with supplementary unemployment benefit payments, this "double payment" objection is likely to decrease in the future.

Costs, Financing, and Administration. In the majority of present cases, the employer finances the plan, frequently on a pay-as-you-go basis, though as noted below there is a trend toward funding such plans. If the dismissal pay plan is negotiated, then both its content and administration may be subject to joint determination. Commonly, however, the employer is given administrative initiative in operating the plan, with the union having the right to protest management actions where it feels it has been aggrieved.

Trends. In addition to increasing coverage a number of other trends are evident. First, instead of financing on an out-of-pocket basis the tendency is to make regular payments into a severance pay fund. This, of course, increases the safety of the plan. Second, such plans are being supplemented by other aids for employees who are separated, such as continuing their health and welfare plan coverage for the year or until they find another job. Third, liberal severance pay is being used to encourage older workers to retire in cases where a work-force contraction is called for. This prevents the younger employee from being severed.

Evaluation

Since dismissal compensation has many characteristics in common with wage guarantee plans, particularly the new supplementary unemployment benefit plans, we will defer evaluation until later in this chapter.

EMPLOYMENT STABILIZATION

Employment stabilization may be defined as the process whereby an employer seeks to regularize his business operations so as to provide as nearly continuous employment as possible for his work force. At one extreme, such stabilization may be very informal; at the other, it may become formalized and may be accompanied by explicit work and/or wage guarantees to the employees. We shall discuss these guarantees in the next section of this chapter, concentrating at this point upon stabilization itself and upon the procedures used.

The common sense of employment stabilization has already been commented upon: it affords both monetary and non-monetary advantages to the employer, and in so doing also benefits the employee and the community. Employment stabilization is not a cost-free process, however; employing economic logic only, the sensible approach would be to push stabilization to the point where the additional benefits were equal to (or were not exceeded by) the additional costs of the program. Non-monetary factors—such as the social standing of the plant in the community —frequently may influence economic standards, and hence the employer may make stabilization decisions which take these other factors into account.

Formal data on the extent of employment stabilization as such do not exist. Certainly, its use must be very widespread, however, for the very logic of business operations would seem to call for it. If one took a range of possibilities and labeled one extreme "no stabilization" (a fiction as far as actual operations are concerned) and the other "perfect stabilization" (also a fiction), there is little doubt that most companies have purposefully moved, or tried to move, *further* away from the "no stabilization" extreme. It is probably true also that most companies have a long way to go before getting close to the other extreme (the reaching of which, incidentally, would be both impossible and undesirable, economically and socially).

Granting the logic of stabilization, can business enterprises achieve it in some degree? That is, can they move toward employment stabilization? The answer seems to be Yes; while certain unstabilizing forces are outside the control of any company, and while certain other forces affect different companies differently, there are various stabilization procedures that *all* companies can utilize, and there are certain others that *specifically situated* companies can employ. Hence, it *is* possible to move toward the "perfect stabilization" end of the spectrum, even if different companies move at different rates and come to rest at different points. And, while "perfect stabilization" would make for undesirable rigidities (if, indeed, along with "no-stabilization," it made any sense), there is little doubt of the logic of movement toward stabilization.

Approaches to Employment Stabilization

Employment stabilization is a two-step process: (1) uncovering unstabilizing forces and measuring their significance where possible and (2) introducing appropriate measures to counteract them.

Unstabilizing forces are of two general types: those "internal" to and those "external" to the company, though in some cases this distinction is blurred. Internal forces are those arising out of inefficient internal business procedures: erratic selling, poor materials scheduling which idles part of the work force part of the time, and poor over-all production planning. Internal pressures are less serious insofar as their impacts may be short-lived. Likewise, their remedy is essentially found in educating management to use "better business methods." External pressures can be classified on the basis of the unemployment categories developed in Chapter 6. Thus, these unstabilizing forces may be secular, cyclical, seasonal, and technological.

Given the unstabilizing force (or forces), the approach is to overcome it (or them) to whatever degree possible through the use of counteracting measures. As noted previously, there is little doubt that employers have some degree of freedom in the application of these counteracting measures. Thus, while there are some unstabilizing forces about which he can do little, the employer normally has some "elbow room." But he must *want* to act, and he must have or acquire the knowledge with which to act. If these conditions are met, three basic categories of counteracting measures are found: those associated with markets and products, with production methods and general operations, and with personnel practices. We shall discuss each of these in greater detail.[6]

Markets and Products. By stabilizing the markets for its products, the company can stabilize production, and thus employment. The market-product approach can take various turns. Thus, a cyclically affected company may seek to add product lines whose sales tend to be more fully maintained in a depression. A seasonably affected company does the same: the classic illustration is the handling of both ice and fuel oil. A company engages in research so as to have new products continually emerging, thus preventing the possibility of secular decay.

The approach need not necessarily be in terms of adding or changing products as such. It may rather involve timing the introduction of given (as well as new) products. Thus, a company changes the time of new model introduction so that the slack season comes in the summer months, when the entire plant can shut down for vacation. Or, new product (or new model) introduction can be coordinated in various ways so as to minimize unstabilizing impacts.

Market techniques of various types, for given product lines, can be applied as regularizing devices. Thus at one extreme, the company may seek, through advertising or other means, to lessen a seasonally unstable

---

[6] There are many source materials on stabilization techniques. See, for example, American Legion, Employment Stabilization Service, *To Make Jobs More Steady and to Make More Steady Jobs* (St. Paul: Webb Publishing Co., 1942); Ernest Dale, "Annual Wages and Employment Stabilization Techniques," *Research Report 8* (New York: American Management Association, 1945); Industrial Relations Counselors, *Steadier Jobs* (New York: 1954).

consumer demand. In its relations with wholesalers, jobbers, and others, the company may seek to regularize their purchases by offering off-season discounts, by guaranteeing delivery at specified prices and times, and by providing warehousing services.

Production Methods. The integration of sales forecasting with production planning provides a concrete basis for stabilization. Such integration involves a forecast of sales, setting up of production levels, and control of stock levels. Production for "stock" is a frequently used procedure. Shifting to maintenance work in slack seasons also has been widely used, although this may be difficult if the company is unionized and craft lines are involved.

Personnel Methods. Centralizing personnel functions and records is a useful device in that it permits the company to operate with an eye on its over-all operations; thus, one department is not hiring from the outside at the same time that another is laying off. Training for versatility, using interdepartmental transfers, and scheduling vacations during slack periods are other personnel procedures that have been used successfully in the past.

In all the above cases, the business logic is simple: it may be good business (depending upon cost-benefit relationships) to apply operating procedures that seek to stabilize sales, production, and employment ("stabilize" here as elsewhere making allowances for growth potentials). It is probably the case that most employers could do something more than they are doing in the way of stabilizing. And while the greatest successes of stabilization are in overcoming seasonal fluctuations, other causal forces can be attacked successfully to some degree.

In the management of manpower, advance planning is an absolute necessity; this is true whether "stabilization" as such is involved, or whether such problems as job changes are at issue. Advance notice to employees is also a must, and in a variety of situations negotiation with the union representing the employees may be necessary.[7]

WORK AND WAGE GUARANTEES

An employer who regularizes his business operations may wish to go further and offer the fruits of stabilization to his employees in the form of various types of work or wage guarantees. Such guarantees not only serve useful industrial relations functions, but also may exempt the employer from the overtime provisions of the Fair Labor Standards Act, and reduce his state unemployment tax. For conventional guarantee plans,

[7] See Rudolph Oswald, "Easing Job Changes by Advance Notice," *The American Federationist*, LXXII, No. 12 (December, 1965), pp. 13–17.

to be defined shortly, stabilization is a necessary prerequisite condition. This is true because the very nature of such guarantee "demands" a prior stabilization condition if the employer is not going to be forced to default when the chips are down. Stabilization is not as vital an issue in the new supplemental unemployment benefit programs, since such plans commonly call for the employer to build up a reserve benefit fund and also limit his obligations to the assets in the fund, plus any agreed-upon and continuing cents-per-hour out-of-pocket payments.

Nature of Conventional Guarantee Plans

Conventional guarantee plans "guarantee" to the eligible employee a given amount of work per year with no specification as to income, a given income per year (in the strictest sense the "Guaranteed Annual Wage") or provide a similar arrangement for some shorter period. The term "guarantee" was put in quotation marks in the above sentence because the conventional plans customarily contain escape clauses of one type or another. *The important point to note in conventional guarantee plans is that the emphasis is upon fulfilling the guarantee through keeping the employee at work;* or, phrased another way, *the focus is upon the employee who is kept on the job.* Technically, such conventional plans need not inevitably work out in this manner; but historically, it is the way that a majority of them have evolved. *In contrast, and as will be noted in greater detail later in this chapter, the newer supplemental benefit plans focus upon the employer who is displaced from his job.*[8] The immediate connection in conventional guarantees is through the whole complex array of techniques designed to stabilize employment; in the new plans the direct relation is through an addition to labor cost of so many cents per hour.

Extent and History of Conventional Guarantee Plans

The most recent detailed analysis of conventional guarantee plans was made by the Bureau of Labor Statistics in 1945. The results of this survey were incorporated in the Latimer Report, published in 1947. While there

---

[8] The literature on guarantee plans is voluminous. For useful source materials on these plans, see J. W. Garbarino, *Guaranteed Wages* (Berkeley: University of California, Institute of Industrial Relations, 1954); Jack Chernick and G. C. Hellickson, *Guaranteed Annual Wage Plans* (Minneapolis: University of Minnesota Press, 1945); A. D. H. Kaplan, *The Guarantee of Annual Wages* (Washington, D. C.: The Brookings Institution, 1947); and M. W. Latimer, *Guaranteed Wages*, O. W. M. R. Report (Washington, D. C.: U. S. Government Printing Office, 1947). The first item is an accurate and popular style pamphlet; the last, the "Bible" on the subject. The second and third items present factual details on many types of plans. Little new material has appeared since 1955.

have been some changes since this date in conventional guarantee plans (primarily in the form of additions), the 1945 data present an accurate picture of the nature and development of such plans. The Bureau of Labor Statistics canvassed some 90,000 employers in March, 1945, as to the use of guarantee plans. The criterion of acceptability for such plans was that they guarantee in advance a period of employment equal to at least three months a year, or an equivalent amount of wages.

The results of the survey were as follows. A total of 347 plans were tabulated. Of these, 196 plans were still in operation, and 151 had been discontinued, the latter including 96 cases which operated under the Wisconsin unemployment compensation law in 1934–35. As of January, 1946, the 196 plans covered approximately 61,000 employees. A 1964–65 Bureau of Labor Statistics examination of collective agreements (covering 1,000 workers or more) indicated that approximately 513,000 workers were covered by agreements containing weekly work or income guarantee clauses though not all the 513,000 were eligible. Annual guarantee clauses were in agreements covering 12,450 workers, though again not all were eligible for the guarantees.[9]

The first of such plans (or among the first) was started in 1894 as a result of negotiations between the National Association of Machine Printers and Color Mixers and the National Wall Paper Company. The guarantee was for eleven months, and in 1896 was extended to twelve months. The greatest period of growth was in the 1930's and 1940's, with some 102 plans started in 1934, 96 of which were passed under the tax exemption provisions of the Wisconsin unemployment insurance law. As of January, 1946, the median number of years current plans had been in existence was eight. The majority of plans (111 plans) were in companies with less than 100 employees, and in turn the majority of plans (100 plans) were in wholesale or retail trade, or food and kindred manufactured products. These two sets of statistics point up the types of economic factors conducive to stabilization. The student should ask himself: Would plans of this type be easily introduced in "prince and pauper" industries? In the large corporation? Why, or why not?

Of the 347 listed plans, 151 had been discontinued, and among these were the 96 abortive Wisconsin cases. But why the mortality among the other 55 plans? Opinions differ. The Latimer Report indicates that discontinuance was largely the result of special individual circumstances, in a number of cases related to the general state of business conditions at the time, but more specifically the result of problems facing the individual employer. Other analysts are less charitable in their comments. Thus

[9] "Supplemental Unemployment Benefit Plans and Wage-Employment Guarantees," *Bulletin No. 1425–3*, U. S. Department of Labor, Bureau of Labor Statistics, June, 1965.

W. A. Berridge and C. Wolfe critically suggest that inherent instability may also have been important.[10]

Examples of Present Conventional Plans

The "Big Three" among conventional plans, and the best known, are the Procter & Gamble Company, George A. Hormel & Company, and Nunn-Bush Shoe Company plans. The first two are work or income guarantee plans; the latter, a flexible wage plan. Other newer conventional plans are similar in nature and scope to the earlier plans. We shall examine here briefly the details of a number of such plans, focusing upon an annual, not weekly, guarantees.

Coverage. In collectively bargained plans, employees most commonly had to qualify as "permanent" employees, that is, pass the probationary period before they were eligible, although in the Hormel Plan, workers were covered as soon as hired.[11] In some employer-initiated plans a worker must have as much as a year's attachment before being eligible. But, not all plans extended guarantees to all workers even though they were "permanent" (however defined). Thus, the Michigan Sugar Co.–American Federation of Grain Millers plan covered only 108 workers in 1965, though 1,200 were under the collective agreement. The Nunn-Bush Shoe Co. plan applied only to 705 "Class A Workers"; the St. Louis Area Companies–Teamsters plan extended to the first 267 employees on the master seniority list. Hence, there is some tendency to restrict work or wage guarantees to certain classes of employees in the same way that restrictions are imposed in unemployment insurance or dismissal compensation.

Two reasons appear for such restrictions. The first is the conventional belief that the employee should have some "permanence" about his attachment to the company before it is obligated to him; this is essentially the type of ethical belief we have noted in conjunction with other programs. The second reason is cost and safety: limiting the guarantee to some portion of the work force makes it less likely that default will be necessary if heavy economic weather is encountered. Thus, conventional guarantees tend to have some limitations in coverage, and while this coverage is tending to expand rather than contract, there is less than complete protection for all employees in the companies in question.

[10] See W. A. Berridge and C. Wolfe, *Guaranteed Employment and Wage Plans* (New York: American Enterprise Association, Inc., 1948), particularly pp. 21–27.

[11] See footnote 9 above and "Experience under Three Guarantee Wage Plans," *Monthly Labor Review,* LXXVII, No. 7 (July, 1954), 769–70.

Qualifications for Benefits. In general, in work and wage guarantee plans, "coverage" and "eligibility" are more nearly synonymous than is true in other security programs; the "covered" employee is "eligible." There are, however, additional qualifications found in some plans. Voluntary quits, discharge for cause, absence beyond regularly provided sick leave or vacation, failure to report for work or to accept suitable work are among the more important disqualifying factors. Except for these restrictions, the eligible employee is blanketed under the guarantee.

Benefits. Benefits under guarantee plans are, of course, the guarantees themselves: so many hours of employment in the given period, so much income, or some other arrangement. Thus, the Procter & Gamble plan guarantees 48 weeks of work per year to eligible employees. The Hormel plan guarantees 52 paychecks per year. The Nunn-Bush flexible wage plan does not guarantee any definite amount of hourly pay. The Company allocates to a fund X per cent of the value added by manufacture. From this "wage fund" a specified number of eligible employees are guaranteed wages during a 52-week period. The amount paid out in wages is directly dependent upon company revenues.

Costs and Financing. Conventional plans appear to have been explicitly financed, where necessary, on a pay-as-you-go basis by charges against payroll. There appears to have been little tendency to "fund" against future contingencies. The fundamental approach to guarantees has, however, been of a different nature: an approach that would minimize the necessity for any explicit outlays to meet the guarantees. This approach involves the precedent step of "stabilization" and hence of meeting the obligation simply through the process of doing business in such a way that the people to whom the guarantee is extended are kept at work. While this method may have been less applicable to those companies which abandoned their plans than for those who retained them, it probably characterizes the majority.

Administration. Since the majority of guarantee plans have been employer initiated, it would be expected that the employer would exercise administrative control over them. This has tended to be true also in several of the earlier plans where the company—or some part of it—was unionized. In several of the newer plans in unionized companies, the certified labor organization has tended to play a more important role in administration.

Administration has presented two major issues: first, those matters concerned with stabilization as such, and, second, the problems that arise if the guarantee is not "automatically" met by stabilization. In this latter case, conscious "remedial" steps must then be taken so as not to default on the guarantee.

Evaluation of the conventional stabilization approach may be deferred until after we present, in the next section, some highlights on the "new look" in guarantee plans.

THE NEW APPROACH TO GUARANTEE PLANS

The new types of guarantee plans, oriented toward supplementing unemployment insurance payments for employees separated from their jobs, had their genesis in the years of World War II. During this period and earlier, a number of CIO unions, particularly the United Steelworkers of America, had interested themselves in wage and employment guarantees as part of their long-range wage policy. In 1943, the steelworkers included, as part of the negotiating pattern with the "Big Steel" companies, a demand for a guarantee for forty hours' straight-time pay for each week of a proposed two-year contract. The disputed case was brought before the National War Labor Board, which, while rejecting the demand, urged that an official study be made of the problem. This led to the Office of War Mobilization and Reconversion inquiry, headed by Murray W. Latimer and subsequently to the publication of the so-called "Latimer Report." [12]

The Latimer Report noted that conventional guarantees would be difficult to achieve in a cyclical industry such as steel, but suggested that an "unemployment compensation supplement" would be feasible.[13] Action was not seriously pressed during subsequent full-employment years by the unions, which concentrated instead upon securing health, welfare, and pension plans. Both the steelworkers and the United Automobile Workers (CIO) did, however, continue to work upon the details involved in such plans, and to make them part of token demands upon the employers. In 1951–52 the issue was argued again by the steelworkers, this time before the Wage Stabilization Board as that agency was constituted during the Korean conflict. Again the union request was denied. Still later, after further action, the issue was joined in the 1955 negotiations between the UAW and Ford and General Motors, with an historic contract, embodying a modified new-type guarantee, being signed with Ford on June 6, and with General Motors shortly thereafter.[14] We shall ex-

---

[12] See the reference in footnote 8.

[13] See the Latimer Report, *op. cit.*, pp. 97–124, for details.

[14] A good résumé up through 1953 is to be found in Industrial Relations Counselors, "The Guaranteed Wage: An Active Issue," pp. 2–5. An excellent analysis and summary is found in Jack Chernick, "A Guide to the Guaranteed Wage," *Bulletin No. 4* (New Brunswick: Rutgers University, Institute of Management and Labor Relations, 1955).

amine these plans in greater detail after a brief look at their composition before modification.

Early Versions of New-Look Plans

The new-look plans were best typified in their "tentative versions" by those of the autoworkers and the steelworkers.[15] While the plans differ in details, particularly as to financing, they had certain common elements which we shall discuss.

"One-Week" Guarantee to "All Employees." The *one-week* guarantee to *all employees* characterized the UAW plan. This short-term guarantee would require the employer to pay the employee for a full week unless the latter were properly notified previously that his services would not be needed for the ensuing week. This is actually equivalent to "40-hour call-in pay," and was designed to put pressure upon the employer to regularize his week's work schedule. This part of the plan did not appear in the final contractual version. [In the 1961 settlement with General Motors, the short work week benefit was recognized. The settlement provided that (1) where management schedules less than 40 hours work, employees will receive 65 per cent of their regular pay for each hour under 40 and (2) where the short work week is unscheduled, half-pay will be received for each hour under 40.]

"One-Year" Guarantee to "Eligible Employees." A *one-year* guarantee to *eligible employees* characterized both plans. In the case of the steelworkers' plan, eligible employees would be those with three years of service; in the autoworkers', all those employees with seniority status. In the steelworkers' version, the amount of the guarantee would be 30 times the employee's basic hourly wage rate, running for 52 weeks from the date of unemployment, with all benefits paid by the state unemployment insurance system deducted from company payments. The plan envisaged a guarantee of about 75 per cent of straight-time wages. The UAW plan provided for a 52-week guarantee. Payments would supplement unemployment compensation and would be such as to permit employees to "maintain the same standard of living as when fully employed." This could be viewed as 100 per cent of take-home pay. Both plans contained elaborate "incentive" guarantees to prevent their abuse: guarantees that would preclude the separated employee from merely sitting back and drawing benefits if work were available.

[15] For full details see USW–CIO, *A Guaranteed Wage Plan for the Workers in the Steel Industry* (Union exhibit before the Wage Stabilization Board, Case No. D–18–C), and UAW–CIO, *Preparing a Guaranteed Employment Plan* and *Questions and Answers about the UAW–CIO Guaranteed Employment Plan* (Detroit: UAW–CIO Education Department Publications 321 and 330, respectively).

Financing and Administration. In the steelworkers' plan, a trust fund would be set up, with the employer paying, for example, 10 cents per hour per man into the fund. Employer liability would be limited to this obligation. As hours worked decreased (as in a cyclical downturn), the in-payment obligation would be reduced. The UAW plan involved a combination of trust fund, pay-as-you-go, and re-insurance. The added pay-as-you-go obligation presumably would offer an extra incentive to the employer to stabilize; if he did not stabilize, he would have the equivalent of a partial payroll to meet without having employees performing productive operations. Thus, pay-as-you-go would make this week's lay-offs raise this week's costs immediately. Both plans envisaged an employer-union administrative agency of some type not only for purposes of over-all supervision, but more importantly to adjudicate cases of individual eligibility (initial and continuing) as they arose. This unit would be over and above any applicable state unemployment insurance administrative agency.

The "one-year" guarantee plan discussed above brings out sharply the differences between conventional and new-type guarantees. While an implicit "stabilization" approach is found in both UAW and USW plans, and is formalized to some extent in the UAW pay-as-you-go proposal, the major emphasis is upon the displaced worker and upon supplementing his unemployment compensation.

How intensely the unions were wedded to these particular plans is not readily apparent. At one extreme, they could be viewed as bargaining points, to be modified in the face of the realities of collective negotiation. At the other, one could look at them as plans in which the unions had a strong belief. The 1955 negotiations, which resulted in the introduction of these new-style guarantees, did modify rather markedly the proposals outlined above. But we do not know if the unions will be content with the modified versions of 1955, or if they will eventually seek to obtain the original versions. There is some evidence that the unions will push ahead toward trying to secure something like the original versions; indeed, subsequent settlements confirm this.

Current Versions of New-Look Plans

It is now over a decade since the new-style guarantees were instituted. What are their present characteristics? Let us examine certain of these features.[16]

---

[16] These details were obtained from a miscellany of current sources and from Dorothy R. Kittner, "Supplemental Unemployment Benefit Plans in Major Agreements," *Monthly Labor Review*, LXXXVIII, No. 1 (January, 1965), 19–26.

Coverage. Approximately two million employees are covered by such plans. Concentration is found in the following industries: automobiles, apparel (women's), glass, maritime, certain retail situations, rubber, and steel. Usually one year of service is required to qualify for benefits; in steel, two years is the minimum.

Qualifications for Benefits. All plans pay a weekly unemployment benefit to wholly unemployed workers. Some nine-tenths of the plans provide special or short-week benefits for partially employed workers. About half the plans pay separation and moving allowances. Temporarily disabled workers are eligible for benefits under a minority of plans. A small number of plans—chiefly in the glass industry—give the employee a vested right to the company's contributions; these are tantamount to "savings account" plans. All plans provide for specific ways in which the employee is to build up "wage credits" through length of service. The majority of plans stipulate that the employee shall receive "credit units" at the rate of one-half unit for each week in which pay was received.

Benefits. Regular unemployment benefits are computed in the following way. Workers must qualify for state unemployment insurance benefits. The SUB plans then pay the difference between the UI benefits and some "maximum." The most common maximum was 60 per cent of before-tax earnings. Thus, if an individual had a before-tax weekly wage of $100 and he received $45.00 from unemployment insurance, SUB would provide the other $15.00. A majority of plans pay dependents allowances, such as $1.50 per week per dependent. Dollar maximums are found in all SUB plans. The majority of plans limit SUB payments to $40.00. That is, irrespective of the weekly wage, the SUB payment itself may not exceed $40.00 ($55.00 in the most liberal plans). Most plans permit benefits to be paid as long as 52 weeks.

Special weekly benefits are payable under most plans. For example, in the steel industry, a partially employed and eligible worker is paid the difference between his lost wages in excess of eight hours and his full-time pay in excess of eight hours less his unemployment insurance benefits. Nine out of ten plans pay benefits to employees not working a full work week.

Costs and Financing. All plans are financed solely by the company; the majority require contributions to be paid into a separately maintained trust fund. Two to ten cents per hour is the range within which company payments fall (with five cents the most common). Company contributions vary with the size of the fund. Variations are found in cases such as the individual account plans in the glass industry, where the maximum accumulation per account is $600. After this figure has been reached, company contributions continue, and the excess is used to increase employee vacation benefits.

Experience Under the Plans

The recession of 1957–58 provided the first real test for the SUB plans. There is no comprehensive summary available for this period, but some bits and pieces of information can be put together.[17] At the time of this writing no reports were available on 1961 experiences.

Qualitatively, the AFL–CIO suggests (1) the plans worked fairly smoothly, with few grievances or hitches considering the large number of layoffs and the newness of the plans, (2) reaction to the operation of the plans has been favorable, particularly as respects the shoring-up of purchasing power.

Quantitatively it has been estimated that during the worst six months of 1958 SUB payments were averaging $10–12 million per month. [Unemployment compensation payments (state programs) during this period averaged $350 million per month.] The total number of employees who received SUB payments during 1958 has been put at over 300,000. In particular local situations SUB proved to be especially useful, though in some areas, such as Detroit, the program could not begin to cope with the problem.

The drain on some company funds was such as to require cutting back benefits. This experience was in contrast to sentiments expressed a year earlier during the relatively prosperous part of 1957 when it was contended that the funds were of sufficient size to permit benefit increases.

In 1960, approximately $100 million was paid out in SUB benefits, compared to $3.02 billion for all types of public unemployment insurance programs. Unemployment rates for those eligible for SUB appear to have been about half of those for the labor force at large. In subsequent years in the decade, the SUB payout drifted upward, but remained at about the same proportion—slightly over 3 per cent—to total unemployment insurance benefits. The plans encountered fewer financing problems than was the case in the 1958 period.

---

[17] See particularly "Supplemental Unemployment Benefits," *AFL–CIO Collective Bargaining Report*, III, No. 12 (December, 1958), 73–78. We have also used a miscellany of business publications and labor reporting services. For a more detailed discussion see Richard A. Lester, "The Economic Significance of Unemployment Compensation," *The Review of Economics and Statistics*, XLII, No. 4 (November, 1960), particularly pp. 369–72. The AFL–CIO report also contains a useful description of the National Maritime Union Plan.

PROBLEMS AND PROGRAMS OF THE DECADE

One of the most important problems currently facing business enterprises, employees, and labor organizations is how, on the one hand, to provide for flexibility in the introduction of technological change, yet on the other, not to require that the worker bear the brunt of such change in the form of displacement and unemployment.

A major breakthrough has been made in the form of specific programs introduced in recent years. We shall examine several of these.

Possibly the most publicized of such programs is that negotiated in 1960 by the International Longshoremen's and Warehousemen's Union and the Pacific Maritime Association. The terms of the agreement provide essentially: [18]

1. Employers are given, in effect, a free hand in the introduction of new machinery and work methods.
2. Employees are provided with various forms of economic security should such changes result in displacement.

The advantages to employers are impressive: unloading 10,000 tons of raw sugar in sacks required 6,000 manhours; if handled in bulk, only 1,000 manhours. Warehouse operations required 80 men if the sugar was handled in sacks; 8 men if handled in bulk.

Employee protection against the consequences of such change is financed by employer payments into a trust fund and takes various forms. These include, among others:

1. West Coast longshoremen fully registered are guaranteed 35 hours' work opportunity per week or the equivalent in pay.
2. There can be no layoffs of fully registered longshoremen; either the guarantee of earnings or early retirement goes into effect.
3. If it is necessary to reduce the size of the work force, early retirement takes place and the retirement benefit is $320.00 a month. Hence, separation is "off-the-top," not the bottom as is normally the case.

As the parties have noted, the plan is not without its problems. Yet, withal, it is a major step, it is imaginative, and it appears to have worked to date.

A second plan is that concluded by the Kaiser Steel Corporation and the United Steelworkers of America, which became effective March 1,

[18] See Otto Hagel and Louis Goldblatt, *Men and Machines* (San Francisco: International Longshoremen's and Warehousemen's Union and Pacific Maritime Association, 1963).

1963.[19] The program contains a number of features outside immediate interest here, such as sharing the gains of productivity increases.

But, a basic component of the plan is to be found in its employment guarantees. Again, the company is given a high degree of flexibility in its introduction of technological change; employees are provided with protection against separation.

The basic features of this part of the plan include the following. A basic standard was first developed—the number of employees required to produce a ton of steel in 1961. (In fact, standards were set for various levels of production, since the number of employees varies.) This number of employees provides a figure called the company's "maximum employment obligation."

If, in succeeding months, the same amount of steel is produced but fewer employees are needed to produce it, the average number displaced are regarded as "technologically displaced." The individual actually "displaced" has several options. He may bump another employee with less seniority. He may accept a place in the employment reserve, in which "other" work is found: substituting for absentees, doing maintenance, making products the company now buys, and so on. Or, he may prefer to be laid off, in which case he would collect unemployment compensation as well as supplemental unemployment benefits. It should be noted that those who are bumped—and hence severable—have the same privileges; the process continues to the individual with the lowest seniority. But, if the layoff is for "lack of work"—an entirely different causal factor—the above options (UC-SUB excepted) do not apply.

Irrespective of the work he does, each employee receives at least his regular rate of pay for the job formerly held, for a maximum of 52 weeks. The maximum employment obligation can be modified by the Company, thus providing it with an additional element of flexibility. If 1,000 employees were required to produce a given tonnage, and the number decreases to 900, the new figure could become the standard provided no one were on layoff and hence not either in the employment reserve or receiving UC or SUB. The plan is still to be tested in the crucible of experience, but it is in being and operable.

A third plan was not negotiated by the parties but arose from a federally enacted compulsory arbitration statute affecting the railroads. After protracted but fruitless collective bargaining and a series of governmental inquiries, Congress passed P.L. 88–108 (approved August 28, 1963) creating an arbitration board to decide upon the use of firemen (helpers) in specified railroad operations.

The nub of the dispute revolved about the question: Were firemen (helpers) "necessary" in the manning of crews for given operations? The

[19] See National Industrial Conference Board, *The Kaiser-Steel Union Sharing Plan,* Studies in Personnel Policy, No. 187 (New York, 1963).

majority of the board—with the union representatives dissenting—concluded the firemen were not. But, the "unnecessary personnel" were not thrown on the industrial scrap heap. Instead, various forms of economic cushioning were provided. Those who had less than two years' service on the effective date of the award could be separated with a lump-sum separation award as provided by a carrier-union agreement. Those hired prior to two years but whose monthly earnings had not exceeded $200 during the last 24 months could be separated, but with a termination allowance equal to 100 per cent of their earnings during this 24-month period. Those hired prior to two years but who had not performed service could be separated with no allowance. All others with less than 10 years of service retained their job rights; those with 10 or more years of service retained their rights to protect engine service assignments as provided by existing rules. The net effect of the award was, therefore, to permit the carriers to eliminate certain groups of employees; but the award also provided temporary income maintenance—in the form of severance pay—for those separated.

The above three plans typify—though in different ways and via different procedures—current interest in two problems: (1) maximizing employer flexibility in the introduction of new technology and thereby increasing efficiency, and (2) providing economic safeguards for those displaced. We believe such experimentation is valuable.

PRIVATE UNEMPLOYMENT APPROACHES: SOME EVALUATORY COMMENTS

Private approaches to unemployment are of various types. In turn, each of these types is many-dimensioned and capable of being discussed on various levels and in innumerable detail. We shall select a number of major headings upon which to concentrate our discussion.[20] Let us

[20] While much of the literature available on this subject sheds more heat than light, it is nonetheless instructive. Most of the source material focuses upon employment stabilization and wage guarantees, both old and new styles. The following are suggested to the student as comprising a reasonably balanced list. For stabilization programs, see the volumes by J. L. Snider and H. Feldman, cited in footnote 1. For a discussion of conventional guarantee plans see A. D. H. Kaplan, cited in footnote 8. For union positions on the new plans see particularly the two UAW publications cited in footnote 15. For employer positions on the new plans, see Chamber of Commerce of the United States, *The Economics of the Guaranteed Wage,* and *Jobs? or Jobless Pay?*, Washington, D. C., 1954, 1955, respectively, and National Association of Manufacturers, *Guaranteed Annual Wage and Its Implications to a Free Economy* (New York: 1954). For the views of outside analysts, see especially S. H. Slichter, "Labor's New Victory," *The Atlantic Monthly* (September, 1955), 63–66, and "One View of the Effects of the Ford-GM Contracts," *Monthly Labor Review,* LXXVIII, No. 10 (October, 1955), 1115–18. As a final suggestion, see H. J. Ruttenberg, "Pay By The Year," *Harper's,* CCXI, No. 6 (December, 1955) 24, 29–33.

first look at the arguments as they appeared during the height of the heat of discussion in 1955–56. After that we may re-examine the problem from a more dispassionate point of view, a decade later.

Some General Conclusions of the Critics: Conventional Plans

The following typify some of the more general conclusions that various analysts have reached concerning conventional private unemployment approaches.

First, employer stabilization programs are both desirable and useful, though some critics doubt how effective such programs can really become and other critics feel that such approaches should be purely voluntary—that if labor organizations can use these approaches as collective bargaining pressure levers, much of the "desirability" is lost. Sentiment exists that such programs may accomplish their purposes in a limited way. Further, given the types of programs thus far developed, undesirable results are not likely except for some possible "rigidities" imposed upon the company using them.

Second, probably because of its limited use thus far, dismissal compensation has not been publicized and discussed to the degree that other programs have. There is, however, some feeling that the cost of production ought to include a readjustment allowance for the worker who is permanently separated from his job for technological or other reasons. On this basis, there is likewise some sentiment that dismissal compensation would be a feasible mechanism for providing such a readjustment allowance. There are, however, numerous specific problems associated with this approach that are also common to guarantees. We shall examine these shortly.

And third, conventional guarantee plans have also tended to receive general approval, provided they were "voluntarily" introduced. (There has been considerable doubt expressed, however, as to how extensive such plans could ever become in the economy and there has been interindustry criticism.) This matter of "voluntarism" is interesting. As long as the employer was free to experiment with such plans on his own, employer associations and others had not been particularly critical, although, conversely, unions had not been very enthusiastic or optimistic. When various unions began to suggest bargaining collectively over these plans, employer groups marshaled weighty evidence to show why, from their point of view, the approach was not feasible, at least not for the economy at large. Many of the arguments developed have also been applied to the new types of plans.

The Unemployment Supplement Plans

If employers and unions were not particularly vocal about the conventional plans noted above, the dam broke when the new plans crystallized; torrents of argumentation and discussion appeared on both sides as well as from "neutrals." [21]

We shall select for discussion a number of "problem areas" associated with new-type guarantee plans.

"Duplicate" Unemployment Systems. One of the major criticisms leveled against the new plans was that they duplicated programs existent in an already complex security system, proliferating administrative agencies in a wasteful way, and uneconomically utilizing resources. There is little doubt that these charges contained a grain of truth. But this is one of the prices paid for free collective bargaining. Moreover, it takes two to make a bargain, and a number of employers agreed to such union demands in 1955. One alternative approach would be to deny to employers and unions the right to bargain over certain matters. A moment's reflection indicates, however, the incredible difficulties involved in trying to stake out allowable areas of collective bargaining, though this ought not to stop us from trying to make decisions about the "good" and the "bad."

It has been said sometimes that if unemployment compensation benefit levels had kept pace with changes in the price level, these new plans would not have developed. If benefits had averaged around 50 to 65 per cent—which appears to have been the original intention of the unemployment insurance system—instead of slipping well below that, it is claimed that the existing system would have been acceptable. Further, it is held that if the states had been willing to adjust their plans even as late as 1955, the new plans would not have appeared on the bargaining agenda.

One cannot prove what would or would not have happened had circumstances been different. But we feel that by 1955 the die had been cast, the unions' stake in these plans was high, and, irrespective of what changes took place in unemployment insurance, it was likely that the unions would press their claims. And, writing in 1966, no matter what the states do in the near future to increase benefit levels, union interest in

[21] See the references cited in footnote 20. See also the papers and comments by Arthur Larson, S. E. Harris, Nat Weinberg, E. P. Schmidt, and S. Brandwein in "The Impact of Employment Security Problems," *Proceedings* of the Seventh Annual Meeting of the Industrial Relations Research Association, 1954; and W. Papier, "Guaranteed Annual Wage Proposals: Their Implications for Unemployment Compensation," *Industrial and Labor Relations Review*, VIII, No. 2 (January, 1955), 265–74. For an over-all analysis of many broader issues, see S. E. Harris, *The Economics of Social Security* (New York: McGraw-Hill Book Co., 1941).

the new plans is not likely to abate. Hence, it is unrealistic to say that these plans are uneconomical duplication and thereby to wish them away. If they are uneconomical, this is the price of employer and legislative shortsightedness in refusing to adjust benefits to price-level changes. It is also the price of free collective bargaining and the right of unions to act as "idea men." These are not fatalistic views, but they are, perhaps, realistic.

"Unethical" Systems. It is also charged that the new plans are unethical: Why should an employee who, as an accident of fate, works for an employer with a supplement plan be entitled to collect more for being unemployed than another employee not so fortunately placed? Again, there is more than a grain of merit in this contention. But life is full of such differentials: Is it not equally unethical for an employee to have a higher wage merely because he is lucky enough to work for a prosperous company? By parity of reasoning, one could extend the argument to many other facets of the job and the wage. If the unemployment supplement is financed by an employer payment of X cents per hour into a fund, isn't this merely a foregone direct wage increase? Would the same objection be raised if the X cents were paid directly to the employee as wages? If these new plans are unethical on this basis, then any differential advantage that was obtained by individual A over individual B might be so construed. Improving the unemployment insurance system so as to provide parity of treatment for the unemployed would be a much more equitable approach. But, if employers and unions are free to bargain, these differentials are likely to result, at least in the short run. And, since unionism is presumed to "pay off," this is one of the gains it may try to secure for those who are its members.

The Incentive Effect. Critics claimed that the new plans would destroy incentive: Why should a man seek work if he can collect a 100 per cent benefit when idle? At the moment the question is partially academic, since the plans negotiated in 1955 and revised since settled approximately at a 75 per cent compromise level rather than the 100 per cent original proposals. But there is some evidence that the unions intend to push eventually for the 100 per cent figure. As was noted in Chapter 1, there is a scarcity of proof as to the "disincentive" level for an individual, let alone for a group. It is our belief, however, that a 100 per cent benefit level would have extremely undesirable disincentive consequences (quite apart from the cost considerations involved); this would be true even if an elaborate system were set up to protect the 100 per cent plan from abuse. Here is an instance in which the contemplated plan has not yet been adopted. And it might be desirable to take a long, hard look before figuratively or actually accepting a feature of the plan about which there

is such an absence of favorable evidence. But in contrast to these conjectures, the evidence available from the application of SUB in the
1957–58 and 1960–61 recessions does not indicate any "incentive" problem.

Economic Issues. Numerous economic issues have arisen in conjunction
with the new supplement plan. We shall look at two in particular.[22]

One criticism is that such plans put another block in the pathway of
labor mobility. Insofar as the plans are on a company-by-company basis,
with no interchange, this charge is true. The impediment is less serious
than in the case of, say, pensions where an employee must attach himself
in most cases to a given employer for a much longer period of time in
order to be eligible. But there may be short-term immobility, immobility
which would not be created if the unemployment insurance system were
expanded. Mobility is, however, a vexing problem. One of the purposes
of an employment program in any company is to reduce labor turnover to
whatever minimum is economically feasible. To do this, the employer
utilizes a variety of personnel practices of which the unemployment supplement may be one. Yet, the very accomplishment of reducing turnover
may reduce desirable mobility. We need to know more about desirable
mobility levels before we can say much about the effect of the new-type
plans. In general, however, it is safe to conclude that such plans do reduce mobility. Whether they reduce it to an undesirable level is a matter
of conjecture.

A second economic issue involves the impacts of the plan upon the
ability of businesses to survive. It is claimed that such plans are likely
to cause serious financial difficulties for business enterprises and, if imposed upon the small enterprise, to drive it out of business. If the supplemental plan is financed by a fixed cents-per-hour contribution to a
fund, if there is no additional out-of-pocket cost, and if the liability of
the firm is limited to the fund, then it is hard to see why such a plan
should cause a company any more difficulties than would any other wage
charge. Moreover, if fund in-payments vary directly with work-force
size, then burden decreases as layoffs (and presumably an unfavorable
economic climate) increase. The fear for the small employer rests upon
the assumption that his employment instability is greater. This is not
necessarily true, and hence the small company may be in no more of a
disadvantageous position than the large one. The plan may have serious
consequences, however, for the unstable firm, possibly adding to its problems if the union is able to bargain through a supplement. (We have
seen little evidence—writing in 1966—of dislocation caused by these
plans.)

[22] See Chapter 14 for additional discussion. See also Campbell McConnell, "Pros
and Cons of the Guaranteed Annual Wage," *Labor Law Journal,* VII, No. 7 (July,
1956), 414–24.

Operational Issues. Another set of criticisms relates to the operating practices of companies and unions. For example, it is held that a company which formerly subcontracted certain operations will now no longer do so, since by doing them at home employment can be maintained at a time when layoffs might otherwise have occurred. Thus, it is claimed that this new system will operate so as to shift the layoff burden to a whole host of suppliers. There is little doubt that this is a possibility. But with the guarantees extending generally at present only to the one-year or more service employee, the need for such changes in company operations is likely to be small.

A more pressing operational problem exists for the union, particularly the union with an increasing proportion of high seniority workers. Suppose the supplemental benefits are paid substantially to the short service worker, with seniority protecting the long service worker. Yet, payments made into the fund are on the basis of total payroll. Why should not the long service employee prefer the X cents per hour added directly to his wage, since there is little likelihood of his ever getting it through an unemployment supplement? (This type of pressure, incidentally, was sufficient to prevent the introduction of the plan in several companies in 1955 and probably has been a retarding factor since then.) The glass plan, in which an individual has a fully vested personal security account, is not as subject to this pressure. If employees view the other plans as quasi-insurance types—as, say, fire insurance—where one collects only if the undesirable event happens, then it is not likely that serious pressures will build up. But if the plans are viewed as individual forced savings-deferred payment plans, then difficulties are likely to arise. One suspects that employees accept the latter more than they do the former view. Therefore, it is likely that some difficulties will be encountered in this direction, though by 1966 they were not particularly evident.

Political Issues. It has been suggested that the piecemeal introduction of guarantee plans will lead to political problems within and among states.[23] Thus, it is held that employers who have such plans will push for increases in unemployment compensation benefits in their states, reducing demands on their own funds and in effect transferring part of the burden elsewhere. This may lead to conflicts of various types among employers on the state level. The same problem may be repeated between states. An additional result may be the transference of deliberations over unemployment insurance from the legislature to the bargaining table. There is little doubt that all these problems are real and that they

[23] For an excellent analysis of this, see W. Papier, *op. cit.*, pp. 265–74. It is doubtful (writing in late 1966) if much pressure of this kind has built up. One of the authors sat in the Unemployment Insurance Advisory Council in his state and saw little evidence that this was occurring even though SUB played some role in the state.

may be heightened by the further partial introduction of supplement plans. It is hard to envisage a way out of these conflicts except to note in an almost trivial fashion that differences of various types have existed and persisted in these areas for long periods.

A Brief Reappraisal

Let us briefly reappraise private unemployment approaches from the vantage point of five years' additional time.

Stabilization programs as such have received relatively little direct attention in this period; the same holds true for conventional employment guarantees. The emphasis has been on other problems such as the depressed area, not amenable to treatment by such programs. (One indication of the lack of attention has been the lack of literature; relatively little has appeared on these topics in recent years.)

Dismissal compensation or severance pay has become much more important during this time. Coverage increased markedly: the very rough estimates we have indicate over seven million employees had this type of protection in 1965 compared with one million in 1955. These plans are likely to increase in importance.

SUB plans went through their first baptism of fire in 1957–58 and 1960–61, with the results relatively favorable given incomplete returns on operations. Few if any of the dire economic, ethical, operational, and political consequences predicted in 1955 have materialized.

The economics of severance pay and supplemental unemployment benefit plans are relatively simple if, as is increasingly true, the program is funded. Employer payments into such a fund represent a part of the wage package which is simply taken in a form different from that of a direct wage increase. There may be a "time-lock" built into such a program; that is, a direct wage increase is obtained here and now whereas, say, severance pay requires a specified length of service with the company. And, while all may share in a direct increase this is not necessarily true in the other programs. In effect, the total work force of an employer is insuring itself against certain contingencies and not all will "collect." Hence all these programs can be viewed as "wages" simply taken in a different form.

A Concluding Comment

In evaluating private approaches to unemployment the following conclusions appear.

First, such approaches permit useful experimentation. There are some dangers, but the benefits are likely to outweigh the dangers—benefits that would include among others augmenting our built-in stabilizers, stimulating technical progress, and increasing industrial expansion.

Second, we have seen the limited coverage of severance wage plans and conventional guarantee programs. And supplemental plans at best are likely to reach only a small fraction of the employees now covered under unemployment insurance.[24] Where the supplements may be needed most is where they are least likely to develop. There are significant gaps in the protection afforded by private plans. Hence, as was concluded in the last chapter, *there is a real need to press for a more adequate system of unemployment compensation.* This is a goal toward which real effort should be extended. This we stated in 1955; we repeated it in 1961, and we emphasize it again in 1966.

SUMMARY

Private approaches to the economic insecurity created by unemployment have had a long history in the United States, antedating unemployment compensation by a half-century.

Approaches of employers and unions to the unemployment problem have taken various forms. Private insurance systems of various types were experimented with on a limited basis. Although such systems were restricted in their usefulness, and although they were superseded after 1935, they afford an interesting example of one approach to an economic and social problem. A current variant of such an approach is found in the increasingly important system of the dismissal wage, which seeks to compensate an individual severed from a job through no fault of his own.

The most important current private approach is that of employment stabilization, wherein the employer seeks to regularize his operation so as to maximize the work opportunities of his employees. Employment stabilization may be accompanied by a formal work or wage guarantee. In conventional guarantee plans the emphasis is upon keeping the employee at work. Newer guarantee plan types focus upon the employee who is displaced and seek to provide a supplement to his unemployment benefits.

Notwithstanding the realized or potential usefulness of such private plans, the federal and state unemployment insurance approach does have a fundamentally important place in our society, and efforts should be extended to make it as effective as possible.

[24] See S. H. Slichter, *op. cit.*, p. 66. The late Professor Slichter, as of the end of 1955, did not believe such plans would become widespread, and indicated that at best the fraction would be 25 per cent. This was optimistic; we have seen figures of two million employees covered for both 1956 and 1966.

SUGGESTIONS FOR ADDITIONAL READING

CHERNICK, JACK. *A Guide to the Guaranteed Wage.* Bulletin No. 4. New Brunswick: Rutgers University, Institute of Management and Labor Relations, 1955.
An account of old and new-style guarantees. Particularly helpful at the level of the individual firm.

HAWKINS, EVERETT D. *Dismissal Compensation.* Princeton: Princeton University Press, 1940.
One of the best available descriptions and analyses of "voluntary and compulsory plans used in the United States and abroad." The book is particularly useful in its treatment of historical analysis and administrative operations.

LATIMER, MURRAY W. (Research Director). *Guaranteed Wages* (Report to the President by the Advisory Board). Washington, D. C.: U. S. Government Printing Office, 1947.
The standard authority on the subject and well worth careful study. See especially the appendixes, particularly Appendix F on the economics of wage guarantees.

NUNN, HENRY L. *Partners in Production.* Englewood Cliffs, N. J.: Prentice-Hall, Inc., 1961.
A discussion of the Nunn-Bush Shoe Company's "52 Paychecks-a-Year Plan": its details, inception, evolution, philosophy.

SLICHTER, SUMNER H., JAMES J. HEALY, and E. ROBERT LIVERNASH. *The Impact of Collective Bargaining Upon Management.* Washington, D. C.: The Brookings Institution, 1960.
A detailed analysis of the ways in which collective bargaining has influenced management functions and practices. Chapter 16 on Income Security and Severance Pay Plans is particularly relevant.

YODER, DALE, H. G. HENEMAN, JR., JOHN G. TURNBULL, and C. HAROLD STONE. *Handbook of Personnel Management and Labor Relations.* New York: McGraw-Hill Book Co., 1958.
A discussion of the principal policy issues and problem areas an employer faces in his relations with employees and labor organizations. The chapters on financial services and employment stabilization provide a useful checklist.

9

Problems of Occupational Disability

INTRODUCTION

When a worker is forced to leave his job because of injury or sickness, he may incur a greater risk to his economic security than if he left because of changing economic circumstances. Serious disability may cause prolonged unemployment, and may have severe personal and economic consequences in addition to the cost of the unemployment.

Job-connected disability, however, presents a less important aggregate problem in economic security than does unemployment, because fewer people are affected, either directly or indirectly, by industrial disability; and because economic losses due to long-term unemployment are far greater than those caused by disabilities.

Occupational disability became a serious threat to economic security when, in the late nineteenth century, our nation's work place shifted from agrarian to industrial grounds. It was the first hazard to economic security to inspire social insurance legislation in the United States over a half-century ago. Injuries and sickness from non-work causes began to come under private and public insurance systems much later. In this chapter we will discuss the problem of occupational disability, its origins, and the development of workmen's compensation legislation which seeks to deal with it. The following chapter discusses these laws in greater and evaluative detail. Chapters 11 and 12 will consider non-occupational disability.

THE PROBLEM OF OCCUPATIONAL DISABILITY

Scope of the Problem

According to the U. S. Bureau of Labor Statistics, an occupationally disabled worker is one who, because of a job-connected accident or sickness, is unable to perform his usual work one or more days after his injury.[1] Disabilities fully repaired by healing are classified as "temporary." Those involving more serious injuries and permanent impairment or loss of a member or of its function are termed "permanent disabilities." Both temporary and permanent disabilities may be totally or partially disabling depending upon the degree of physical impairment caused by the injury.

Hence, industrial disability figures may include, on the one hand, a worker who is forced to miss a day's work because of a sprained ankle and, on the other, a worker who has permanently lost his sight. Included, too, are occupational diseases, which tend to be understated by reported occupational injury data since many evolve over long periods of time. The list of illnesses that come as a natural consequence of employment is nearly inexhaustible: "The fisherman's rheumatism, the waiter's fallen arches, the surgeon's hypertension, the miner's silicosis, the boilermaker's deafness, the bus driver's peptic ulcer, and the housemaid's bursitic knee are all, like a thousand other complaints, more or less directly attributable to the environmental conditions under which their victims work." [2] But, in cases of occupational disease, the causal relationship between disabling disease and the occupation in which the individual is engaged is often more obscure than in the case of a traumatic injury.

Job-connected injuries, sickness, and deaths are a frequent occurrence in an industrial economy. The occupationally disabled far outnumber war casualties, and they are more numerous than motor vehicle accident victims. In fact, job-connected disabilities account for nearly one-fifth of all accidental injuries each year.

Judging by the experience shown in Table 9.1, we can expect nearly two million disabling work injuries annually (including disease). About 14,000 of these workers will die as a result of their injuries, and another 85,000 will be permanently maimed or crippled. These figures do not

[1] The complete definition of disabling work injury, as approved by the American Standards Association, may be found in "Techniques of Preparing Major BLS Statistical Series," *Bulletin 1168* (Washington, D. C.: U. S. Department of Labor, Bureau of Labor Statistics, 1954), p. 34. Students interested in the concepts, background, and scope of the Bureau's work-injury studies are advised to consult Chapter 5 of this bulletin: "Work-Injuries and Accident-Cause Statistics."

[2] Berton Roueché, *The Incurable Wound and Further Narratives of Medical Detection* (Boston: Little, Brown & Co., 1957), p. 72.

include an estimated six to seven million minor injuries which, because they do not cause lost work days, are not "work injuries" by the accepted definition.

TABLE 9.1

Estimated Number of Disabling Work Injuries, All Industries

Year	All Disabling Injuries	Deaths	Permanent Disabilities	Temporary Total Disabilities
1942	2,267,700	18,100	102,000	2,147,000
1947	2,059,000	17,000	91,800	1,950,200
1957	1,890,000	14,200	80,800	1,795,000
1958	1,820,000	13,300	76,700	1,730,000
1959	1,960,000	13,800	83,200	1,863,000
1960	1,950,000	13,800	82,200	1,854,000
1961	1,930,000	13,500	80,500	1,836,000
1962	1,990,000	13,700	83,300	1,893,000
1963	2,020,000	14,200	84,800	1,921,000
1964	2,050,000	14,200	85,800	1,950,000

Sources: U. S. Department of Labor, Bureau of Labor Statistics, "Handbook of Labor Statistics, 1950," *Bulletin 1016*, p. 178; *Monthly Labor Review*, LXXXIII, No. 4 (April, 1960), 391; LXXXVIII, No. 4 (April, 1965), 419.

But these injuries do not occur evenly throughout all types of work. Table 9.2 indicates on an absolute basis which industries account for the greatest number of disabilities and includes some rather surprising figures.

TABLE 9.2

Estimated Number of Disabling Work Injuries by Industry, 1963–64

Industry	All Disabling Injuries		Deaths	
	1963	1964	1963	1964
All industries	2,202,000	2,050,000	14,200	14,200
Agriculture *	277,000	270,000	3,300	3,200
Mining	44,000	45,000	700	700
Contract construction	214,000	219,000	2,500	2,600
Manufacturing	405,000	429,000	1,800	1,700
Transportation and public utilities	190,000	196,000	1,700	1,800
Trade	372,000	373,000	1,200	1,200
Finance, service, government, and miscellaneous	518,000	518,000	3,000	3,000

* The total number of work injuries in agriculture is based on cross-section surveys by the U. S. Department of Agriculture in 1947 and 1948, with adjustments for changes in employment. These are considered to be minimum figures. Injuries experienced in performing chores are excluded, and there are some indications of under-reporting.

Source: *Monthly Labor Review*, LXXXVIII, No. 4 (April, 1965), 419.

According to these data, more deaths occur in agricultural employments than in manufacturing, a fact reflecting the improved accident prevention programs of manufacturing industries and the effect of mechanization of farms. Work in finance, service, and government is responsible for more injuries than any other single industrial classification. Before judgments can be made about the magnitude of the occupational disability problem in any given employment, however, these aggregate data, of course, must be standardized. This is done by calculating accident "frequency" and "severity" rates.

The Accident Frequency Rate. The accident frequency rate is calculated to show the number of accidents that are occurring and is stated in number of man-hours of exposure to make it comparable from time to time and place to place within and between industries. It is defined as the number of disabling accidents per one million man-hours worked.[3]

While the frequency rate indicates the trend of accidents and enables comparisons between industries, plants, and even between departments within a firm, it does not distinguish serious accidents from less serious ones. All disabling work injuries, regardless of severity, enter the numerator of the frequency rate calculation. Hence, accident data include a second calculation—the severity rate—which states on a standard basis the relative seriousness of occupational injuries.

The Accident Severity Rate. The accident severity rate is an average-time-lost-per-accident measure. It is defined as the average days lost per one million man-hours worked.[4]

For injuries resulting in only temporary disability, the "days lost" figure is the actual number of days the injured worker is forced to be away from his job. Permanent disability and death cases require that days lost be stated in terms of standard time charges varying with the degree of disability. Actual days lost could not otherwise be calculated meaningfully in these two categories. A standard table of time charges is prepared for this purpose by the American Standards Association[5] and is used in severity rate calculations.

---

[3] Frequency rate $= \dfrac{\text{Number of disabling injuries} \times 1,000,000}{\text{Employee-hours of exposure}}$. Thus, if a small manufacturing firm that employed, say, 250 workers for a regular work year of 2,000 hours each, had six disabling accidents, its accident frequency rate would be $\dfrac{6 \times 1,000,000}{500,000}$ or 12, which would place the firm close to its industry's average.

[4] Severity rate $= \dfrac{\text{Total days lost (charged)} \times 1,000,000}{\text{Employee-hours of exposure}}$. (For years before 1955, the severity rate was defined as the average number of days lost for each 1,000 employee hours worked.)

[5] See "American Standard Method of Recording and Measuring Work Injury Experience, 1954."

Frequency and severity rates for selected industries (and industry groups) are presented in Table 9.3. These data show that there are vast differences in frequency and severity rates from industry to industry.

TABLE 9.3

Injury Rates for Selected Industries, 1963

Industry or Group	Injury Rates		Severity	Average Days Lost or Charged Per Case				Per Cent of Disabling Injuries Causing		
	Frequency			All Cases	Permanent Partial Disability	Temporary Total Disability	Death	Permanent Impairment	Temporary Total Disability	
	1963	1962								
All manufacturing	11.9	11.9	689	55	381	18	0.3	5.0	94.7	
Lumber and wood products	36.7	36.0	2,943	75	532	19	0.5	4.6	94.9	
Electrical machinery	5.3	5.3	222	39	276	17	0.1	7.0	92.9	
Ordnance and accessories	2.4	2.8	146	34	252	19	0.1	4.5	95.4	
Contract construction	28.6	29.5	2,219	78	607	18	0.7	2.7	96.6	
Trucking and warehousing	31.3	30.2	1,998	64	447	17	0.6	1.8	97.6	
Wholesale and retail trade	12.2	11.6	515	42	608	14	0.3	2.0	97.7	
Hotels	13.5	12.5	427	32	657	17	0.1	1.5	98.4	
Laundries and dry cleaning	9.0	8.7	505	56	626	19	0.4	2.6	97.0	
Local transit systems	16.9	16.1	1,337	79	722	22	0.8	1.6	97.6	
Elementary and secondary schools	9.1	8.4	242	27	674	13	0.1	1.6	98.3	

Source: *Injury Rates by Industry, 1963,* Bureau of Labor Statistics Report No. 295 (July, 1965).

They suggest, too, a fact borne out by fuller study of a larger sampling of rates, that there is no close correlation between accident frequency and severity rates for all employments.[6] Although manufacturing, for example, always shows a fairly high frequency rate, it tends to have a low severity rate. Construction, on the other hand, always shows both high frequency rates and high severity rates. Average frequency and severity rates change considerably from year to year, however, and rarely show any clearly established patterns.

When these rates for 1962 and 1963 are compared with earlier rates, for example, some are substantially higher, some are substantially lower,

[6] Industrial injury data are available from several sources. Nationally, the U. S. Bureau of Labor Statistics, through the *Monthly Labor Review,* is the most important single source. Data covering specific areas are also compiled by the National Safety Council and various federal agencies, such as the Department of Agriculture and the Bureau of Mines. State agencies, typically Industrial Accident Boards and Commissions, are usually responsible for publication of these data on the state level. For detailed bibliographic notes on sources of accident data, see Herman M. Somers and Anne R. Somers, *Workmen's Compensation* (New York: John Wiley and Sons, Inc., 1954), p. 328.

and others are about the same. The average manufacturing rate of 11.9 disabling injuries per million employee-hours worked includes a very great range, varying, as shown, from ordnance to lumber products.

Analysis of the circumstances surrounding accidents can provide some insight into this picture. Accident frequency—that is, the number of accidents—is subject to control by safety and prevention measures. Accident severity, however, tends to be primarily a matter of chance. Thus, although a downward trend in accident frequency can be credited to improved safety performance, it does not follow that these safety activities will have the same effect on severity rates. Other factors enter in too. For instance, the poor accident records of the World War II period are not generally ascribed to poor safety and prevention measures but rather to the influx of many new and inexperienced workers into the labor force.

Nature and Cost

Disability is the most costly and tends to be the most severe of all non-economic barriers to employment. In addition to the opportunity and maintenance cost of unemployed workers and their families, disability brings about considerable costs of its own—both of a monetary and of a personal nature.

Compare disability, for example, with the non-economic employment barrier of advanced age. Loss of work for either of these reasons will shut off wage earnings. However, age barriers to employment are more or less fixed institutionally over fairly long periods of time. To the worker this means that possible economic insecurity because of old age is a cost that must be met at a future date, and within ranges, it is capable of prediction. Furthermore, it will be incurred at a time when family obligations of the wage-earner tend to be smallest. His children will no longer be financially dependent upon him; he will have paid for his housing, furnishings, and insurance; his fixed financial commitments, if any, will be at their lowest level. So that while workers may or may not be able to prepare for this cost successfully, its incidence can be estimated safely.

Occupational disability, on the other hand, can never be predicted for an individual worker. It seems to occur most frequently among younger workers whose financial and family obligations are greater and among the lowest paid workers who are least able to meet these financial obligations.[7] Over and above the cost of a shut-off income supply (which for the severely disabled may be permanent) are medical and hospital costs as well as inestimable personal costs that in cases of severe disability arise from family sacrifices. The pain and suffering of the injured worker are, of course, incalculable.

[7] Somers and Somers, *ibid.,* p. 10.

As a hazard to individual income security, therefore, disability must be viewed more as a risk than a cost the incidence of which can be predicted. This is not to say that direct and hidden dollar costs of industrial disability are not gigantic. Estimates of the total of income losses, medical expenses, workmen's compensation payments, damage awards, damaged property, and production losses have ranged from 1 up to 10 per cent of national income.[8] While this ratio will change from time to time, the latter estimate is undoubtedly too high. These estimates do not include the great amounts of money spent in avoiding occupational disability through safety programs and health measures. For example, non-traumatic loss of hearing due to industrial noise held compensable in a few states not long ago, has been under strong attack by safety- and cost-minded employers. It was estimated that in 1955 employers spent about $100 million in efforts to reduce this disability hazard alone.[9]

The impact of the dollar costs on individual workers is best illustrated in the light of their financial circumstances. Before workmen's compensation, when damage awards were few, charity was the primary alternate source of income to seriously disabled workers. Workmen's compensation has done much to relieve this situation, but serious gaps remain. For example, a study published in 1961 estimated the loss suffered by permanently and totally disabled workers and found that twenty-four states replaced less than 20 per cent of the loss while only seven states replaced over 40 per cent.[10]

To the worker whose arm is amputated in a revolving cutter, the costs, the pain and suffering, and the problems of physical and occupational rehabilitation are no different from those of another worker suffering loss of a leg as a result of a fall in a friend's home. Both encounter the same problems: obtaining and paying for medical and hospital care, continuing to meet non-deferrable expenses of a family, and, finally, returning to productive employment after healing.

For a long time, American public policy made no basic distinction between these two kinds of injuries. In order to recover money damages for his injury, either worker had recourse only in the common law of liability. If he could prove his injury stemmed directly from the negligence or fault of the factory or home owner, he could recover money damages. With the greater risks of occupational disability that accompanied the industrial development of the late nineteenth century, however, and in response to this growing hazard to the economic security of

---

[8] Domenico Gagliardo, *American Social Insurance* (New York: Harper & Row, 1949), pp. 448–52; Somers and Somers, *op. cit.*, pp. 9–15.

[9] *Wall Street Journal,* November 16, 1955, p. 1.

[10] *Injury and Recovery in the Course of Employment* (New York: John Wiley & Sons, Inc., 1961), pp. 172–73.

the nation's workers, social policy began to distinguish between accidents and sickness caused by the work environment and those that were not. This recognition took three forms: (1) employer-initiated safety programs, which, though unimportant at first, have today become significant factors in holding down the toll of industrial injuries; [11] (2) the industrial hygiene movement aimed at industrial sickness, and (3) workmen's compensation legislation (which seeks through insurance to redistribute part of the costs of occupational disability) in which fault or negligence is not an issue.

EMERGENCE OF THE PROBLEM OF OCCUPATIONAL DISABILITY

American history from the Civil War through the close of the nineteenth century is a story of rapidly expanding industrial capitalism. In a single generation the United States changed from an agrarian country which had to import most of its manufactures from abroad into an industrialized nation exporting products all over the world.

Rail transport expanded rapidly; coal, iron, and petroleum resources were exploited vigorously, and the manufacture of cotton, iron, steel, and other products increased phenomenally. In 1890, for the first time in this country's history, the wealth created by manufacturing surpassed that created by farming. By external measures, too, industrial growth was phenomenal. In 1860, America ranked fourth among nations in the volume and value of factory goods; in 1894, it ranked first, with factory production worth more than that of Germany and Great Britain combined.[12]

To operate the factories turning out this record production, employers recruited to the cities more and more workers—many of them women and children—from farms and from abroad. And with the growth of industrial cities came new problems in the mode and character of American life, particularly in the economic and social life of the worker. During the first fifteen years of the twentieth century, much of the country's energies, particularly at local levels, were directed toward adjusting public policy to the needs of the new economic environment. A concentrated attack was launched on the political, social, and economic problems created by an industrial society—child labor, slums, growing health and accident hazards, to name a few—and with remarkable results. More so-

[11] Today, in addition to safety programs aimed at existing employment hazards, new safety regulations are adopted as work processes and materials change. The increased industrial use of atomic energy, for example, has required new regulations to protect against the hazards of radiation. See, for example, Joint Committee on Atomic Energy, Hearings before the Subcommittee on Research and Development, 86th Congress, *Employee Radiation Hazards and Workmen's Compensation*, pp. 172–76.

[12] For a statistical summary of this economic revolution, see Arthur M. Schlesinger, *Political and Social Growth of the American People, 1865–1940* (New York: The Macmillan Co., 1941), p. 43.

cial legislation (including workmen's compensation) was enacted during this period than during any previous time in American history.

Professional concern for occupational health and safety can be traced back to 1837, when the first United States report on occupational health was issued, long before the movement for legislative reform got under way. Between that time and 1900, over fifty discussions and state reports on occupational health and accident hazards appeared, and by 1910 the industrial health movement had gained support from magazines, state agencies, and professional associations.[13]

In 1867, Massachusetts enacted legislation providing factory inspection services; two years later the first Bureau of Labor Statistics was created in that state to study the accident problem; and in 1877 the Massachusetts legislature acted to insure that employers safeguard hazardous machinery. In 1892 a safety department was established in the Joliet Works of the Illinois Steel Company where the American industrial accident prevention movement subsequently was born.[14]

The exact magnitude of the occupational health and accident hazards of the period cannot be determined accurately. The few data available are not comprehensive and are largely estimates. Farm work was by no means "safe." Hours were long, and the work was strenuous and subject to natural physical hazards. Yet its hazards were relatively few compared with those introduced by mechanized work (including mechanized work on farms). Power-driven machines, and machine tools in particular, created new and serious accident hazards. But it would be inaccurate to attribute the rising accident rate to mechanization alone. Each industry, because of its environment or operations, had its own peculiar hazards—cave-ins and explosions in the coal mines, moving locomotives, lead poisons, overhead cranes, and the pace of the new industrial tempo all contributed to the employment hazards. So, too, did the interdependence of employees in the factory system.[15] In addition, there were the problems of the fatigue of long hours, child labor, the use of "cheap" immigrant labor, and the failure of the large factories, which today produce the most enviable safety records, to assume much responsibility for the injured.[16]

[13] John R. Commons and associates, *History of Labor in the United States, 1896–1932* (New York: The Macmillan Co., 1935), III, 359–70.

[14] Ronald P. Blake (ed.), *Industrial Safety* (Englewood Cliffs, N. J.: Prentice-Hall, Inc., 1943), pp. 12–22.

[15] See Crystal Eastman, *Work Accidents and the Law* (Russell Sage Foundation, 1916 ed.; reprinted in Paul H. Douglas, Curtice N. Hitchcock, and Willard E. Atkins (eds.), *The Worker in Modern Economic Society* (Chicago: University of Chicago Press, 1923, pp. 401–12).

[16] Arthur H. Reede, *Adequacy of Workmen's Compensation* (Cambridge: Harvard University Press, 1947), p. 345.

Somers estimates that the "peak in industrial accident rates was reached during the first decade of the century, probably about 1907–1908. In the year ending June 30, 1907, 4,534 workers were killed in railroading alone; 1907 was also the blackest year in mining: 2,534 men were killed in bituminous mines alone."[17] Frederick L. Hoffman of Prudential Life Insurance Company, whose estimates for early accident experience are as good as any available, guessed the total occupational 1908 death toll at between 30,000 and 35,000.[18] A more conservative estimate by Dr. E. H. Downey,[19] put occupationally caused deaths at 25,000, permanent disabilities at 25,000, and temporary disabilities lasting over three days at 2,000,000. Frederick Lewis Allen writes [20] that ". . . in the single year 1901, one out of every 399 railroad employees was killed; and one out of every 26 was injured. Among engineers, conductors, brakemen, trainmen, etc., the figures were even worse than this: in that single year, one out of every 137 was killed."

The Common Law of Industrial Accidents

With the sharp rise in the number of occupational injuries, the costs of disability became an acute problem. The physical losses, of course, were borne by the injured worker in all cases. But what of the financial burden of job-connected disability? Was this also to be the private responsibility of the worker?

Before 1841, there were no rules of law or court decisions to answer this question, although recourse to the law was available to the occupationally injured and the non-occupationally injured alike. As job injuries became increasingly frequent and severe, the courts were called upon to decide how the financial burden of this disability should be distributed. In these decisions the courts developed the nation's first public policy toward occupational disability as a source of economic insecurity.

In retrospect the body of common law of employers' liability that emerged from these cases seems unduly harsh, for the small-scale industrial organization, frictionless labor market, and close employment relationship between master and servant—on which it was based—were all casualties of the economic revolution.

[17] Reprinted by permission from Somers and Somers, op. cit., p. 9.
[18] Frederick L. Hoffman, "Industrial Accidents," Bulletin of the Bureau of Labor Statistics (Washington, D. C.: September, 1908), p. 418. Quoted in Philip Taft, Economics and Problems of Labor (3d ed.; Harrisburg: The Stackpole Co., 1955), p. 123.
[19] Taft, ibid.
[20] Reprinted with permission from Frederick Lewis Allen, The Big Change (New York: Harper & Row, 1952), p. 56.

At common law, an employee injured in an accident in the course of his work could recover damages only through a personal injury suit against his employer. The success of such a suit depended upon showing that the job-connected injury arose from the employer's negligence. Although a master owed his servants due care (the violation of which was negligence), formidable difficulties faced an employee seeking to discharge his burden of proof against his employer. He frequently encountered reluctance on the part of his fellow employees to testify, probable loss of employment, and a serious (often insurmountable) financial burden.

Second, and even more onerous, was the array of common-law rules of master and servant that blocked easy recovery for industrial injuries. The oldest of these was the defense of contributory negligence which was always available in suits based upon a claim of negligence. This tenet had been introduced into the common law of England in 1809.[21] In operation it defeated an employee's claim to damages if he had in any way contributed to the negligence of his employer.

Two further defenses grew out of later cases. In 1842, the leading American case involving master–servant relations was decided. In *Farwell v. Boston and Worcester R.R. Co.*, a Massachusetts court denied an engineer's claim for damages based upon the negligence of a switchman and established "fellow-servant" and "assumption of risk" defenses in America. The court held that "since the engineer was not in the relation of a stranger to the railroad, the employer's liability, if any, was governed by the implied contract of employment entered into with the engineer at the time of hiring and that such a contract does not extend to indemnify the servant against the negligence of anyone but the master himself."

Two important concepts were implied in this holding. First, servants were now denied recovery for injuries arising from a fellow-servant's negligence. This was an exception to the well-established tort doctrine of *respondeat superior* which held a master responsible to third persons for injuries inflicted by his agents. The second principle—the "assumption of risk" doctrine—made the hazards of an occupation non-compensable. For many years hence, cases consistently holding to the "assumption of risk" defense partially justified this position on the theory that the wage rate of an occupation reflected its hazards. This quite painful application of Adam Smith's principle of equal net advantages [22] together with the con-

[21] In the case of *Butterfield v. Forrester*, 11 East. 60 (K.B. 1809) cited in Walter F. Dodd, *Administration of Workmen's Compensation* (New York: The Commonwealth Fund, 1936), chaps. i and ii.

[22] Smith observed that where there was liberty, wages would make the advantages and disadvantages of occupations equal. See Adam Smith, *The Wealth of Nations* (Modern Library ed.; New York: Random House, Inc., 1937), p. 99: "The whole of

tributory negligence and fellow-servant defenses were the cornerstones on which was built the laissez-faire approach of the common law to occupational disability.

Dissatisfaction with the Common Law and the Enactment of Employers' Liability Laws

With occupational injury and death rates reaching alarming proportions, the continued application of these common-law rules was producing tragic results. The vast majority of the occupationally injured or their survivors realized either inadequate damage awards or, all too frequently, no awards at all. In the face of the wastes, uncertainties, delays, and high costs of lawsuits, widespread dissatisfaction arose with this approach to industrial disability. In the late part of the nineteenth century, many legislative attempts were made to find a new remedy. These took the form of employers' liability legislation which was patterned, in part, after earlier attempts made in England to mitigate the effects of common-law defenses to injury claims. Between 1885 and 1910 most of the states enacted such employer liability legislation.

The first of the three common-law defenses to come under legislative attack was the fellow-servant rule. Next, by stating that an employee's knowledge of safety violations is no bar to a suit for recovery, the assumption-of-risk doctrine was weakened. The defense of contributory-negligence, however, yielded most reluctantly under the more liberal legislative (and judicial) attitudes.

In addition to modifying the three common-law defenses, employers' liability laws sought to bring relief to injured workers in two ways.[23] The first of these was a legal denial of the right to "contract out" of liability. No longer would contracts be binding in which workers agreed not to hold their employers liable for injuries sustained at work. And, secondly, the right to suit was extended to death cases.

Employers' liability laws, following one or more of these three forms, were enacted in almost all the states by the time that accident tolls were reaching their peak (1907–08). But they did not provide an adequate solution to the problem of occupational disability.

---

the advantages and disadvantages of different employment of labour and stock must, in the same neighborhood, be either perfectly equal, or continually tending to equality. If in the same neighborhood there was any employment evidently either more or less advantageous than the rest, so many people would crowd into it in the one case, and so many would desert it in the other, that its advantages would soon return to the level of other employments."

[23] Commons, op. cit., p. 567.

Rise of Workmen's Compensation Legislation

While America was experimenting with legislation designed to modify the results of the common-law rules of employers' liability, a far-reaching experiment was taking place in some European countries. Germany took the lead in the early 1880's, and by 1910 virtually all the countries of Europe had adopted some system of workmen's compensation.

These events did not go unnoticed in the United States. The United States Department of Labor took official notice in its 1893 publication of a report on compulsory insurance in Germany. Shortly thereafter, bills following the European models were introduced in several states (but failed to gain passage). It became apparent through the unsuccessful attempts of several states to enact workmen's compensation legislation that a thorough study was necessary to determine the needs of compensation systems, their requirements, how they might relate to our legal system and, important to employers, what their costs might be. Intensive commission investigation of the problem of occupational disability was the next step.

Some thirty-one investigatory commissions were established between 1909 and 1913. Nine others were in operation in the next six years. These investigating bodies, through joint conferences, hearings, and intense study, recommended unanimously that employers' liability be abolished. From these investigating committees emerged: (1) a severe indictment of the record of employers' liability legislation, and (2) the foundation for recommendations that later evolved into workmen's compensation laws. Their recommendations were supported by the American Association for Labor Legislation, the National Civic Federation, the American Bar Association, the American Federation of Labor, and by a poll of the National Association of Manufacturers.

Failure of the Employers' Liability Statutes

Committee data documenting the failure of the employers' liability systems aroused considerable public concern. They showed that: (1) contrary to their purpose, employers' liability laws were not enabling workers to recover damages for injuries. Damage awards were sparse and uncertain, and where they were granted, they came long after the disability, were usually inadequate, and bore no rational relation to the injury. (2) Since employers' liability was still a system based on lawsuits, it was costly and produced ill will between employers and employees, thus failing to produce any stimulus to safety programs. The emphasis still tended to be to conceal accidents rather than to study them frankly and attempt to reduce them. In short, it was little better than the inadequate, uncertain, and costly remedy at common law. A new approach was needed to the problem of occupational injury and disease. It was found in workmen's compensation.

Workmen's compensation laws were enacted in four states in 1911, eleven states in 1912 and 1913. After 1920, only six states (each of which later enacted systems) did not have workmen's compensation legislation; today such laws are in effect in all states and federal jurisdictions. Much credit for this reform must go to the investigatory commissions.

WORKMEN'S COMPENSATION LAWS

Liability Without Fault

New York was one of the first states to take the lead in the movement toward workmen's compensation. In 1910 it enacted a compulsory law covering twelve specified occupations wherein employers were made liable for specified compensation payments to their injured workers, whether or not the injury stemmed from employer fault. The extent of this departure from the traditional common law of employers' liability is nowhere better dramatized than in the language of the New York Court of Appeals [24] which declared the law unconstitutional the following year. Said the New York court in this case:

. . . This is a liability unknown to the common law and we think it plainly constitutes a deprivation of liberty and property under the Federal and State Constitutions . . . if the legislature can say to an employer, "You must compensate your employee for an injury not caused by you or by your fault," why can it not go further and say to the man of wealth, "You have more property than you need and your neighbor is so poor that he can barely subsist; in the interest of natural justice you must divide with your neighbor so that he and his dependents shall not become a charge upon the state"?

A popular referendum and, later, state and United States Supreme Court decisions and legislative devices [25] overcame constitutional objections, however, and today all states have workmen's compensation laws based upon the principle of "liability without fault." Yet, while the constitutional barrier in the Ives case did not deter the movement toward

---

[24] *Ives v. South Buffalo Railway Co.*, 201 N.Y. 271 (1911). Quoted and discussed in Harry A. Millis and Royal E. Montgomery, *Labor's Risks and Social Insurance* (New York: McGraw-Hill Book Co., 1938), pp. 194–96.

[25] Stefan A. Riesenfeld and Richard C. Maxwell, *Modern Social Legislation* (Brooklyn: The Foundation Press, 1950), pp. 153–62.

workmen's compensation, it indirectly weakened the laws of a majority of jurisdictions. Over two-thirds of the states gave employers an "election" of being covered by the Act or remaining exempt—but without full protection of common-law defenses. Today the laws of nearly one-half the states have some form of elective provision. The extent to which they operate to restrict effective coverage of workmen's compensation acts cannot be estimated.

The principle of liability without fault is quite simple. The employer is assessed the compensable costs of job-connected injuries to his employees not because he is responsible for them, not because he caused them, not because he was negligent, but simply because of social policy. The premise has been discarded that behind every disability there is a negligent party. Under modern industrial conditions the employment relationship itself is reason enough for assessing the employer to compensate his injured employees. Since the employment of labor involves the risk of disability, by social policy the employer must defray its costs.

But while the interpretation of liability without fault is clear enough, its theoretical justification has raised some questions. For one thing, if considered apart from its consequences, the common-law principle that an employer should be responsible only for accidents stemming from his fault has an appeal of justice and fair play. Some early acts applied only to hazardous occupations, holding the employer responsible for operating a hazardous business. But as workmen's compensation laws were extended to most kinds of work, liability without fault could be justified only by reference to broader norms.

Many norms have been formulated.[26] An important early theory was that of the "trade risk." This theory held that the employer must bear the costs of the risks of his trade and, implicitly, that these costs would be shifted forward in the product price. (A slogan attributed to Lloyd George proclaimed that "the cost of the product should bear the blood of the workingman.") The implications of this justification (among them that workers are relieved of all accident costs) have been sharply criticized, and a more thorough formulation has been that of the "least social costs" principle, contending that economic losses were reduced to a minimum by workmen's compensation legislation.[27] These theories, and particularly some of the legal justifications, were important to the acceptance and subsequent broadening of workmen's compensation laws.

[26] Discussions of these can be found in E. H. Downey, *Workmen's Compensation* (New York: The Macmillan Co., 1924), pp. 19–20; and in Clarence W. Hobbs, *Workmen's Compensation Insurance* (New York: McGraw-Hill Book Co., 1939), pp. 61–62. See also Riesenfeld and Maxwell, *op. cit.,* pp. 138–40.

[27] Edwin E. Witte, "The Theory of Workmen's Compensation," *American Labor Legislation Review,* XX, No. 4 (December, 1930), 411–18.

The policy of protecting the economic security of the worker by making employers liable for job-connected disability is not a radical policy from the viewpoint of the economics of the labor market. In fact, it can be interpreted simply as a more efficient result economically than would be the case in a perfectly competitive labor market. Let us examine this point.

The Compensation Principle

If all that is implied in the principle of equal net advantages were empirically descriptive of labor supply and demand conditions, employers' common-law defense of assumption of risk would be economically persuasive. For under this condition, wage rates for individual occupations would reflect fully their relative advantages and disadvantages, including the risk of disability. It would follow that, other things being equal, employments where accident rates are relatively high (say agriculture, where the death rate is three times that of manufacturing) would pay correspondingly higher wage rates than less hazardous jobs requiring similar skill and training. Large numbers of workers would be attracted to the better jobs (tending to keep the wage rate down) and employers would have to bid up wages to attract workers to the less attractive (and more hazardous) jobs.

But do wage rates in fact reflect differences in job hazards? To some extent, yes. Structural steel workers, for example, may be paid a higher wage when working on high construction where the danger from falls is great; test pilots receive a high wage reflecting their hazardous work; seamen receive additional pay for duty in war zones. In fact, in any business organization, wage structures based upon standard methods of job evaluation will, in some measure, be influenced by the relative hazard factor of working conditions.

But wage differentials generally bear very little relation to the relative attractiveness of work. The worker in actual labor markets is not informed completely about attractive alternative job opportunities nor would he always be willing or able to accept them if he did know about them.[28] And no one today would contend seriously that wage rates do include a "risk" portion reflecting the value of an occupation's injury risk. "Assumption of risk" at common law denied damages for injured employees because it was assumed that they had knowledge of the risks of their employment, and hence were left to their own resources if they took the work.

[28] Gordon F. Bloom and Herbert R. Northrup, *Economics of Labor Relations* (4th ed.; Homewood, Ill.: Richard D. Irwin, Inc., 1961), pp. 310–18.

But even the most stringent application of this principle assumed only in part that the wage rate had an adequate risk portion. In a famous and frequently cited case in New York in 1924 [29] a girl who had contracted tuberculosis while working in a candy factory was denied recovery. The court concluded it was from the plaintiff's own testimony that:

> . . . We learn that the walls of the cellar were wet to the touch; that a cesspool backed up liquids which wet the floor; that the cellar was devoid of windows to light or air it; that dead rats were left about; that the odors were vile; that no fires were kept in the upstairs room; that the plaintiff worked in a drafty place; that the upstairs was damp. It is common knowledge that such conditions are deleterious to health. The plaintiff was chargeable with such knowledge. We think that the plaintiff, as a matter of law, assumed the risk attendant upon her remaining in the employment. . . .

What if the many conditions needed to make the labor market perfectly competitive were realized? Then to attract labor, employers would have to pay a "risk" premium in the wage rates for hazardous occupations. It would follow therefore that, other things being equal, the average wage rate would be higher under these competitive conditions than in their absence.

But in the actual labor market, employers have an incentive not to pay the full risk rate because (1) their competitors cannot be expected to follow suit, and (2) the incentive to spend money on safety measures is reduced, since the greater portion of the cost of disability is borne by the disabled worker. The employer's private cost of the full "risk" wage exceeds the benefits he would receive from paying this wage.

Under these circumstances, if injuries are to be compensated, it is necessary for government action to assess a social cost that will pay for the full needed social benefits. This could take two forms. Wage rates could be adjusted by legislation in hazardous occupations, or employers could be made liable for the cost of injuries to employees. Of these two approaches, the latter (workmen's compensation) can be shown to be economically more efficient in principle.

Forcing employers by legislation to pay a risk wage rate for hazardous jobs would result in a small increment in the wage rate. But this would provide less protection for the worker in the event of disability than does an insurance-like payment, withheld and paid at the time of the injury. For in accordance with the principle of diminishing marginal utility,[30] the disutility of one great loss would more than offset the added utility of

---

[29] *Wager v. White Star Candy Co.*, 217 N.Y. Supp. 173.

[30] A good brief discussion of the law of diminishing marginal utility applied to insurance is presented by Paul A. Samuelson in *Economics* (6th ed.; New York: McGraw-Hill Book Co., 1964), pp. 421–22.

small increments of income spread over time. Or, conversely, the utility of payment at the time of disability is greater than that of the increments in the wage rate. Hence, liability without fault is not an expensive social reform, but rather a more efficient method, in principle, of achieving what the labor market would achieve if it were perfectly competitive.

Common Law and Employers' Liability Statutes Are Still Important

The emergence of the workmen's compensation principle, however, has not eliminated case law from the field of industrial disability. Wholly aside from the vast numbers of cases interpreting the compensation laws, there are wide areas where liability is determined through litigation.[31] These include employees who are not covered by the compensation acts, either because they are not working in a covered employment or because they are exempt or excluded by law. Elective laws, discussed earlier, remove considerable numbers of workers from coverage, as do some cases of third-party (non-employer) liability and the area covered by employers' liability laws.

Workmen's compensation laws were not enacted in a vacuum. They grew in response to the pressing needs of the occupationally disabled—needs that were not being met by existing institutions. Let us turn now to see how the compensation principle was used to answer these needs.

OBJECTIVE OF WORKMEN'S COMPENSATION

In comparison with the complex workmen's compensation laws of today, the original acts of the states were very simple. They were all based upon the liability-without-fault principle, and each was enacted to provide prompt and adequate relief to victims of industrial accidents and to improve accident prevention. Most state laws were in large measure based upon the experience of Germany and England in workmen's compensation and upon some of the findings of the American legislative commissions.

But despite their original simplicity and the common origins and problems which led to their enactment, workmen's compensation laws have never been nor are they today uniform from state to state. Local problems and constitutional, statutory, and political barriers account for this diversity. Early legislatures were forced to enact provisions which would circumvent some of these problems and make concessions to others. And over the years the modifying forces of local considerations and political opposition have continued to grow rather than to diminish.

31 Railroad employment is the most important example. See Chapter 13 for a discussion of the Federal Employers' Liability Act.

TABLE 9.4

Comparison of Coverage, Insurance, and Exemption Provisions of Workmen's Compensation Acts of All American Jurisdictions

(September, 1964)

Jurisdiction	Coverage [a] (percentage of workers covered)	State Fund	Private Carriers	Self- Insurance	Employers Exempted If Fewer Employees Than
			Insured Through		
Alabama	Less than 65	—	x	x	8
Alaska	75–85	—	x	x	No exemptions
Arizona	65–75	Compet.	x	x	3
Arkansas	Less than 65	—	x	x	5 [b]
California	85 or more	Compet.	x	x	No exemptions
Colorado	75–85	Compet.	x	x	4
Connecticut	75–85	—	x	x	2
Delaware	75–85	—	x	x	3
D. C.	75–85	—	x	x	No exemptions
Florida	65–75	—	x	x	3
Georgia	Less than 65	—	x	x	10
Hawaii	85 or more	—	x	x	No exemptions
Idaho	75–85	Compet.	x	x	No exemptions
Illinois	85 or more	—	x	x	No exemptions
Indiana	65–75	—	x	x	No exemptions
Iowa	65–75	—	x	x	No exemptions
Kansas	Less than 65	—	x	x	5 [b]
Kentucky	65–75	—	x	x	3
Louisiana	Less than 65	—	x	x	No exemptions
Maine	65–75	—	x	x	4
Maryland	65–75	Compet.	x	x	No exemptions
Massachusetts	75–85	—	x	x	4 [d]
Michigan	75–85	Compet.	x	x	No exemptions
Minnesota	85 or more	—	x	x	No exemptions
Mississippi	Less than 65	—	x	x	8
Missouri	65–75	—	x	x	11 [d]
Montana	75–85	Compet.	x	x	No exemptions
Nebraska	65–75	—	x	x	No exemptions
Nevada	75–85	Exclusive	—	—	2
New Hampshire	65–75	—	x	x	2
New Jersey	75–85	—	x	x	No exemptions
New Mexico	Less than 65	—	x	x	4 [b]
New York	85 or more	Compet.	x	x	No exemptions
North Carolina	65–75	—	x	x	5 [b]
North Dakota	65–75	Exclusive	—	—	No exemptions
Ohio	85 or more	Exclusive	—	x	3
Oklahoma	Less than 65	Compet.	x	x	2
Oregon	Less than 65	Compet.	x	x	No exemptions
Pennsylvania	85 or more	Compet.	x	x	No exemptions
Puerto Rico [c]		Exclusive	—	—	No exemptions
Rhode Island	75–85	—	x	x	4

[a] 1960 figures based on 1960 census.
[b] Does not apply to specified employments.
[c] Not available.
[d] Applies only to non-hazardous employments.

TABLE 9.4 (Continued)

Jurisdiction	Coverage [a] (percentage of workers covered)	Insured Through State Fund	Private Carriers	Self-Insurance	Employers Exempted If Fewer Employees Than
South Carolina	Less than 65	—	x	x	15
South Dakota	Less than 65	—	x	x	No exemptions
Tennessee	Less than 65	—	x	x	5
Texas	Less than 65	—	x	—	3
Utah	85 or more	Compet.	x	x	No exemptions
Vermont	65–75	—	x	x	6
Virginia	75–85	—	x	x	7
Washington	65–75	Exclusive	—	—	No exemptions
West Virginia	85 or more	Exclusive	—	x	No exemptions
Wisconsin	85 or more	—	x	x	3
Wyoming	65–75	Exclusive	—	—	No exemptions
Federal Employees	85 or more	Congressional appropriation	—	—	No exemptions
U. S. Long-shoremen	75–85	—	x	x	No exemptions

Sources: "State Workmen's Compensation Laws," U. S. Department of Labor, Bureau of Labor Standards, *Bulletin 161*, revised September, 1964. *Social Security Bulletin*, XXV, No. 6 (June, 1962), 6.

Table 9.4 illustrates the lack of uniformity of the workmen's compensation laws of the fifty-four state, federal, and territorial jurisdictions for three important aspects of the laws: (1) extent of coverage; (2) permitted manner of insuring liability; and (3) exemptions to coverage for small employers. Other important aspects of the laws, such as medical and indemnity benefits, also vary from state to state.[32]

Students of workmen's compensation, dismayed at the diversity of standards, see little likelihood that this situation will soon be remedied,[33] either by state action alone or by federally enacted standards. In the

[32] State industrial accident boards and commissions will furnish interested students with copies of the workmen's compensation laws they administer. Also available is a pamphlet published by the U. S. Department of Labor, Bureau of Labor Standards, "State Workmen's Compensation Laws, A Comparison of Major Provisions with Recommended Standards," *Bulletin 212*, 1964. The student will find it valuable to obtain his state's law and study its provisions in the context of Chapters 9 and 10, and to use the Bureau's pamphlet as a guide in its evaluation.

[33] In 1955 the U. S. Department of Labor, through its Bureau of Labor Standards, published a tentative copy of a "model workmen's compensation bill" which, it hoped, would be followed by the states in the continual process of revising their compensation laws. But the venture provoked such an adverse reaction in Congress and received so little support that it was soon abandoned. The Council of State Governments more recently produced a comprehensive draft act but it has not triggered substantial reforms to date. For an interesting "inside" view, see Arthur Larson's chapter in Earl F. Cheit and Margaret S. Gordon (eds.), *Occupational Disability and Public Policy* (New York: John Wiley and Sons, Inc., 1962), pp. 11–47.

next chapter we will consider the question of how effective and adequate the workmen's compensation remedy can be, both in specific jurisdictions and in general, in the light of differences in standards and administrative practice.

SUMMARY

Unemployment caused by occupational disability is a less serious aggregate problem in economic security than is unemployment due to labor-market causes. But work-connected injuries and sickness are costly non-economic barriers to employment and tend to present a serious threat to individual economic security. Disability shuts off earnings (sometimes permanently) and brings with it extensive hospital, medical, and maintenance costs.

Although work has always produced disabling injuries and sickness, the rate of these disabilities began to rise in this country as it began to be industrialized in the late nineteenth century. Early interest in combating the problem resulted in scattered safety legislation, a few individual employer safety programs, and eventually an industrial hygiene movement aimed at preventing industrial illness. But during the period of the peak rates of occupational disability, injured workers had as their chief recourse a lawsuit at common law in which recovery required demonstrating employers' negligence as a cause of disability.

This system, which permitted employers to defend on the grounds of contributory negligence, the negligence of fellow employees, or the assumption of the risks of employment by the claimant, produced serious hardships. Lawsuits were costly, time-consuming, produced serious antagonisms, and only infrequently resulted in adequate recoveries. Dissatisfaction with this approach to the problem led to the widespread enactment of employers' liability laws which weakened employers' common-law defenses. But, since lawsuits were still required for recovery, they were little improvement over the common law. Against this background, American legislatures turned with interest to a German legislative experiment: workmen's compensation laws, which provided benefits to injured workers on an insurance basis without the need of a lawsuit or proof of fault. The liability without fault principle of workmen's compensation was first enacted early in the twentieth century, and today all states have these laws, though they differ widely in their coverage, benefits, and effectiveness.

SUGGESTIONS FOR ADDITIONAL READING

BOWERS, EDISON L. *Is It Safe to Work?* Boston: Houghton Mifflin Co., 1930.
The impact of industrial accidents and the failures of workmen's compensation and rehabilitation to deal adequately with them are the central themes of this very readable essay.

CHEIT, EARL F. *Injury and Recovery in the Course of Employment.* New York: John Wiley and Sons, Inc., 1961. Chapter 1.
A summary of the basic remedies available to the occupationally disabled.

CHEIT, EARL F. and MARGARET S. GORDON (eds.). *Occupational Disability and Public Policy.* New York: John Wiley and Sons, Inc., 1962.
A critical symposium on American and European approaches to occupational disability.

DOWNEY, E. H. *Workmen's Compensation.* New York: The Macmillan Co., 1924.
Long considered a classic, this volume is a basic work in the field of early workmen's compensation philosophy and development.

REEDE, ARTHUR H. *Adequacy of Workmen's Compensation.* Cambridge: Harvard University Press, 1947.
A detailed examination of the development of the coverage and benefit provisions in workmen's compensation.

WEISS, HARRY. "Development of Workmen's Compensation in the United States." Unpublished Ph.D. dissertation, University of Wisconsin, 1933.
A comprehensive study of the forces which led to the enactment of workmen's compensation laws by the states.

10

Workmen's Compensation

INTRODUCTION

Today in each of the fifty states, the District of Columbia, and Puerto Rico, workmen's compensation is the major economic security program for occupational disability. The laws of all the states are based upon the principle of liability without fault, but because they are individual state laws, their benefit and coverage provisions vary widely from jurisdiction to jurisdiction. Before discussing the provisions of workmen's compensation laws and their effectiveness, it may be useful to state briefly how they operate.

Workmen's compensation laws usually begin by stating which employments they cover—most public and private employments with stated exclusions and exemptions (see Table 9.4, pages 318–19). The laws entitle covered employees who are disabled as a result of injury or disease causally related to their employment to indemnity, medical and hospital benefits. The employee normally files a notice of injury with his state industrial accident board to receive these benefits. When the injury or disease results in death, stated indemnity benefits are paid to survivors.

The benefits paid under workmen's compensation laws are, by law, secured through insurance.[1] As Table 9.4 indicates, in most jurisdictions this insurance is available only from private carriers. Six states sell insurance to the exclusion of all private carriers, and twelve states offer insurance in competition with private carriers. How much employers pay for this compulsory workmen's compensation insurance coverage varies with the type of work in which their employees are engaged. Premiums

[1] Or, as indicated earlier, employers who demonstrate their financial ability are permitted to self-insure in some jurisdictions (see Table 9.4).

are stated per $100 of covered payroll. For clerical employees whose work is relatively safe, the insurance premiums may be as little as 16 cents for $100 of payroll. For hazardous work, such as construction or mining, the rate may be as high as $20 or more per $100 of payroll.[2]

Let us now examine the benefit and coverage provisions of the laws in greater detail.

QUALIFICATION FOR BENEFITS

Although the benefits that an occupationally disabled worker receives under workmen's compensation vary widely from state to state, the right of a worker to these benefits is determined in all jurisdictions by three basic elements.[3]

First, a worker must be an "employee" working in a "covered employment"—as these terms are defined by the state law. The question of who is an "employee" has raised a considerable volume of litigation, particularly in the case of casual employees and those working for independent contractors, but this element of coverage is fairly well established by now. Table 9.4 indicates that in some jurisdictions, employees working for firms with less than a given number of persons on the payroll—usually between three and five, although ranging as high as fifteen in South Carolina—will not be covered. The table also indicates that about one-half the jurisdictions make no such eligibility requirement. The interpretation of the term "covered employment" is more varied from state to state. Typically, covered employments would include most public employments and all private employments except domestic servants, farm laborers, merchant seamen, railroad employees, and the so-called casual employees whose work is not in the usual course of the trade of the employer. The table also shows that some states exclude "non-hazardous" employments, as well as a few specified employments such as professional athletics. In about one-half the states—those with elective laws—the employer may accept or reject the act, but if he rejects it, he loses the three common-law defenses. These clauses were originally inserted to protect the constitutionality of the early laws; in actual practice the vast majority of employers elect to comply with the workmen's compensation provisions.

Second, "employees" working in "covered employments" can receive benefits only for disabling injuries and sickness the nature and origin of which are compensable by statute. In adopting from English law the

---

[2] Possible economic effects of these costs, and their differences, are discussed later in this chapter in the section entitled "Does Workmen's Compensation Produce Undesirable Economic Effects?"

[3] Stefan A. Riesenfeld and Richard C. Maxwell, *Modern Social Legislation* (Brooklyn: The Foundation Press, 1950), pp. 162–291.

phrase "personal injury by accident," a majority of American jurisdictions embraced the concept of injury as associated with a traumatic occurrence. The rigor of this definition became troublesome, however, in cases where disabilities emerged from gradual deterioration of a bodily member due to work causes or from repeated accidents. American courts have developed a liberal definition of the concept of an "accident" so as to compensate cases such as these. In revising the laws, legislatures are increasingly discarding the word "accident." The battle over compensability has largely shifted to the third requirement (discussed below), that the injury is traceable to the employment.

Legislative coverage of occupational diseases developed much more slowly than did other injury coverage. Massachusetts pioneered in this area when in 1910 it followed the Federal Employees' Compensation Act and provided "blanket" coverage for all occupational diseases. Other states developed the "schedule" system, providing coverage only for diseases specified by law. Today blanket or full coverage is provided by thirty-four jurisdictions; schedule coverage is provided by nineteen. Wyoming is the only jurisdiction that provides no coverage of occupational diseases.

Third, the covered employee's disability (caused by either injury or disease), to be compensable, must have resulted from the employment—again as specified by statute. The requirement that there be a proper relationship between the employment and the disability has become a thorny legal question and policy issue. Almost every American law, again borrowing from England, extended coverage to accidents "arising out of and in the course of employment." This phrasing was intended to reduce to a minimum questions about the origin of the injury, but litigation concerning the interpretation of these words is almost endless.

Two types of issues arise. First, should an admittedly compensable disability be compensated when it occurs under "unusual" circumstances? Typically, should workers be covered while traveling for their employer? After or before working hours? Off duty, going to and from work? Or, at work when a worker takes a devious route? And so on. For the most part, court interpretations of these issues have tended to take a liberal view of what is "in the course of employment." [4]

Second, and perhaps more important as far as policy is concerned, are those disabilities where the causal link with the employment is not clear. That is, did the injury "arise out of" the employment? Disabilities such

[4] For conflicting views on effects of the trend toward liberal interpretation of the phrase, "arising out of and in the course of employment," see Samuel B. Horovitz, "The Litigious Phrase: 'Arising Out of' Employment," *NACCA Law Journal*, III and IV (May and November, 1949), 15–67 and 19–90; and Bruce S. Black, "The Anomalies of Workmen's Compensation," *Industrial and Labor Relations Review*, VII, No. 1 (October, 1953), 43–50.

as non-traumatic loss of hearing, coronary and pulmonary afflictions, and radiation diseases may be caused by employment, but, of course, they are also associated with non-work hazards of life. Allocating liability for these types of disability presents serious policy issues,[5] perhaps the major ones facing workmen's compensation today. Let us now turn to the question of what benefits are paid to an eligible disabled employee.

TYPES AND AMOUNTS OF BENEFITS

Two basic types of benefits are provided by workmen's compensation laws: (1) cash or indemnity payments and (2) payments for medical services. Although rehabilitation services, which are an important recent development, consist partly of medical services, ideally they should extend well beyond them. Hence, they are considered separately here.

Cash or Indemnity Payments

Cash benefits are payable to disabled workers in all American jurisdictions only after a "waiting period" which ranges typically from three to seven days after the injury and is designed to reduce compensation costs and to discourage possible malingering. Although the overwhelming majority of job-caused disabilities are of very short duration and hence do not involve benefit payments (because of the waiting periods), they do account for substantial aggregate medical benefits.

Disability extending beyond the waiting period is classified for benefit purposes into "temporary" and "permanent." Temporary total disability payments are made to a worker when he cannot work at his usual occupation during the period when he is recovering from his injury. Cash benefits for temporary total disability are usually weekly payments calculated as two-thirds of the average weekly wage at the time of the injury, subject to weekly maximums and limits on duration of payments and total amount.[6] Table 10.1 shows these limits and indicates the benefits

[5] Studies by the American Heart Association have led one of its members, Dr. Richard J. Clark, to the conclusion that ideal criteria for compensability of these injuries are virtually impossible, and, therefore, that ". . . all heart and degenerative diseases, barring those cases clearly and specifically caused by well defined accidents on the job, should be excluded from Industrial Accident provisions and should be covered by a Sickness Insurance System. . . ." "The Challenge of Occupational Disability," *Proceedings* of the Committee on Workmen's Compensation, Council on Industrial Health, American Medical Association, January 25–26, 1955, p. 34. A lively argument on how best to handle causation problems in radiation disease can be found in *Studies in Workmen's Compensation and Radiation Injury*, Vol. I (Washington, D. C.: U. S. Government Printing Office, 1965), esp. pp. 12–48.

[6] The operation of benefit formulas and the effect of statutory benefit limits are best understood in the context of specific examples. Students will find it helpful, using the laws of their home states, to compute benefits that are payable to injured workers with different incomes and suffering different degrees of disability.

payable in all American jurisdictions at the time of this writing. At the time recovery ceases, the temporary disability ends. Most occupational injuries result in only temporary disability.

Permanent disabilities resulting from more serious injuries are classified by the severity of the disabling condition into minor permanent partial, major permanent partial, and permanent total disability. Permanent total disability, for example, involves injuries such as loss of sight, both arms, or legs, which, except for cases of successful rehabilitation, make further employment impossible. Permanent total disability benefits are also shown in Table 10.1.

Since it is extremely difficult to determine the exact degree of permanent partial disability, most acts set forth "schedule disabilities" that list the maximum amount and duration of compensation payments for specific injuries. The weekly benefits are calculated by the same formula used in cases of permanent total disability.

Thus, *in addition to* the portion of wages made up during the period of disability, a permanent partial disability payment "schedule" might provide the following payments (using but two examples, ranging from one extreme to the other): (1) for the loss of a little finger, 66⅔ per cent of the daily wage at the time of injury for 15 weeks; (2) for the loss of one arm and one leg, 66⅔ per cent of the daily wage at the time of injury for 400 weeks.

Death benefit payments to survivors are also an important benefit provision, and, like indemnity payments, they vary greatly from jurisdiction to jurisdiction. In all but thirteen jurisdictions (which offer annuity-like payments to widows until their death or remarriage), these payments to dependents are limited both in time and amount. Limits often vary depending on whether there are minor children; they may range from a high of $32,000 (Michigan) to a low of $10,000 (South Carolina). A majority of the jurisdictions pay less than $17,000 in cases of death.

In summary, cash or indemnity payments serve two purposes: first, they make up a portion of the wage loss suffered by disabled workers and by dependents of fatal cases; and, second, in the case of permanent partial disabilities, these benefits additionally seek to make up a portion of anticipated future reductions in earnings that the disability is presumed to bring about. Of necessity, the second of these indemnities must be subject to loose estimation; it is not possible to calculate with any degree of precision what reductions in earning power, if any, such disabilities will cause. Hence, the figures arrived at are compromises of various types. There is great debate on how to measure and how to compensate for permanent disability, and the laws differ greatly from state to state.[7]

[7] For a discussion of the varying concepts, see Report of the Workmen's Compensation Study Commission, State of California, 1965, pp. 124–27.

TABLE 10.1

Comparison of Cash and Medical Benefit Provisions for All American Jurisdictions, January, 1966

| | Cash Benefits | | | | | | Medical Benefits (for accidental injury) | |
| | Permanent Total Disability | | | Temporary Total Disability | | | | |
Jurisdiction	Weekly Max.	Maximum Period	Stated Max.	Weekly Max.	Maximum Period	Total Stated Max.	Full Benefits	Dollar Limits*
Alabama	$ 38.00	550 wks a	$15,200	$ 38.00	300 wks			$ 2,400
Alaska	52.65 a	p.d.		100.00	p.d.		x	
Arizona	150.00 a	life		150.00 up b	433 wks		x	
Arkansas	38.50 a	450 wks	14,500 a	38.50	450 wks	$12,500	x c	
California	52.50	400 wks d		70.00	240 wks		x	
Colorado	49.00 e	life	15,288 e	49.00	p.d.	15,288 e		3,500
Connecticut	61.00 f	p.d.		61.00 f	p.d.		x	
Delaware	50.00	p.d.		50.00	p.d.		x	
Dist. of Columbia	70.00 a	p.d.		70.00 a	p.d.		x c	
Florida	42.00 a	p.d.		42.00	350 wks	24,000	x c	
Georgia	37.00	400 wks	12,500	37.00	400 wks	12,500	x	2,500
Hawaii	112.50 a	p.d.	25,000 g	112.50	p.d.	25,000	x	
Idaho	32.00–52.00 b	400 wks b, d		32.00–52.00 b	400 wks b, d		x	
Illinois	58.00–68.00 b	life	15,000–21,000 b, d	62.00–76.00 b, h	8 yrs		x	
Indiana	42.00	500 wks j	20,000	45.00	500 wks	20,000	x c	
Iowa	37.00	500 wks	23,750	40.00–56.00 b	300 wks		x	
Kansas	42.00	416 wks	17,472	42.00	415 wks	17,430		6,000
Kentucky	44.00 k	425 wks		44.00 k	425 wks		x	
Louisiana	35.00	400 wks		35.00	300 wks			2,500
Maine	57.78 m			57.78 m	300 wks		x c	

TABLE 10.1 (Continued)

Jurisdiction	Cash Benefits						Medical Benefits (for accidental injury)	
	Permanent Total Disability			Temporary Total Disability				
	Weekly Max.	Maximum Period	Stated Max.	Weekly Max.	Maximum Period	Total Stated Max.	Full Benefits	Dollar Limits*
Maryland	48.00	p.d.	30,000	55.00	208 wks		x	
Massachusetts	58.00 up b	p.d.		58.00 up b	p.d.	16,000 up b	x	
Michigan	58.00–91.00 b, n	p.d.		58.00–91.00 b, n	p.d.		x c	
Minnesota	45.00 a	p.d.	(g)	45.00 a	350 wks		x	
Mississippi	35.00 a	450 wks	14,500	35.00	450 wks	14,500	x	
Missouri	47.50	300 wks d		52.00	400 wks		x c	
Montana	35.00–56.00 b	500 wks		35.00–56.00 b	300 wks			2,500
Nebraska	42.00	300 wks d		42.00	300 wks d		x	
Nevada	37.50–56.00 a, b	life		48.75–67.50 b	433 wks		x c	
New Hampshire	50.00	312 wks e		50.00	312 wks e		x c	
New Jersey	45.00	450 wks d		45.00	300 wks		x	
New Mexico	40.00	500 wks	20,000	40.00	500 wks	20,000		25,000
New York	60.00 a	p.d.		60.00	p.d.	6,500	x c	
North Carolina	37.50	400 wks a	12,000	37.50	400 wks	12,000	x c	
North Dakota	50.00–65.00 a, b	life		50.00–65.00 b	p.d.		x	
Ohio	49.00 a	life		49.00 o	p.d.	10,750	x c	
Oklahoma	40.00	500 wks		40.00	300 wks	12,000	x c	
Oregon	35.75–70.38 a, b	p.d.		39.23–73.85 b	p.d.		x c	
Pennsylvania	52.50	p.d.		52.50	p.d.		x c	
Puerto Rico	20.76	p.d.		35.00	312 wks		x	

State	Max. weekly	Period	Total $	Max. weekly	Period	Total $		x
Rhode Island	45.00 a	p.d.		45.00–57.00	p.d.			x c
South Carolina	35.00	500 wks	10,000	35.00	500 wks	10,000		x c
South Dakota	38.00	300 wks d	13,500	38.00	312 wks	14,000	20,000	x
Tennessee	38.00	550 wks	14,000	38.00			2,500	
Texas	35.00 a	401 wks		35.00	401 wks			x
Utah	42.00–60.00 a, b	260 wks d		42.00–60.00 b	312 wks			x c
Vermont	41.00 up b	330 wks	12,870	41.00 up b	330 wks	15,600		x
Virginia	39.00	500 wks	15,600	39.00	500 wks		27 months	x
Washington	42.69– 81.23 a, b	p.d.		42.69– 81.23 b	p.d.			
West Virginia	42.00 a	life		42.00	208 wks			x c
Wisconsin	68.00 a	life		68.00	p.d.			x
Wyoming	26.85– 34.62 b		12,000–19,000 b	40.38– 60.00 b	p.d.	12,000		x c
Federal Employees	121.15 a, b	life		121.15 a	p.d.			x
U. S. Longshoremen	70.00 a	p.d.		70.00 a	p.d.	24,000		x

p.d. = period of disability.

* Six of the ten limited benefit jurisdictions provide both dollar and period limits; three provide dollar limits only; one, duration limit only. Dollar limits only are shown in the table, except in the one latter case.

a Added benefits for specific cases, such as for vocational rehabilitation or for those requiring constant attendance or those involving loss of mental faculties.   b Varies with number of dependents.

c Benefits limited by law but may be extended without limit by administrative agency.

d Added benefit payments at reduced rates (under certain conditions).

e If employee is receiving social security disability benefits, compensation may be reduced by 50 per cent of such payments.

f 60 per cent of the state's average production wage, with added benefits in specific cases. Determined annually. Figure shown set August 1, 1965.

g After $18,000 paid, OASDI benefits credited against workmen's compensation benefits.

h For the first 64 weeks. Thereafter reduced to $56.68.

j After $16,500 and 500 weeks, further payments of compensation may be made for an indefinite period from a special fund.

k 55 of 85 per cent of the state's average weekly wage.   m Two-thirds of the state's average weekly wage.

n Maximum will increase to $61.00–$92.00 on September 1, 1966, and $64.00–$93.00 on September 1, 1967.

o During first 12 weeks, $56.00, then $49.00.

Sources: "State Workmen's Compensation Laws," U. S. Department of Labor, Bureau of Labor Standards, *Bulletin 161*, revised September, 1964; *Monthly Labor Review*, LXXXVIII (November, 1965), 1322–24; Analysis of Workmen's Compensation Laws, U. S. Chamber of Commerce, 1966.

Payments for Medical Services

During the early development of workmen's compensation laws, little or no provision was made for medical benefits. Today, however, as Table 10.1 indicates, some forty-four jurisdictions put no limit on medical benefits provided to those disabled by accidental injury. The benefits are provided as they are indicated medically. They include physician and hospital service, surgical and medical care. Workers suffering from occupational diseases, however, are not so well protected. Almost half the states limit medical benefits in these cases.

This liberalization in medical benefits has been characterized as the greatest single improvement or development in workmen's compensation legislation, but ten jurisdictions still have limits of time or amount. Referring again to Table 10.1, time and dollar limits on medical benefits go as low as $2,400 in Alabama and $2,500 in four other states.

Medical benefits account for about one-third of total benefit payments under workmen's compensation, and it is estimated that over seven million disabilities a year are treated under workmen's compensation medical care programs.

Rehabilitation Services

Most promising of the recent benefit developments is the growth of provisions for physical and vocational rehabilitation.[8] Under early workmen's compensation laws, after the limited medical care called for by law had been provided, the disability was "fixed" as it stood. And when treatment ran out or no further benefit from it was apparent, permanent total disability was often presumed. With the advances in the field of physical medicine, of paramedical services, and facilities of vocational training, the area of permanent total disability has been reduced and can no longer be presumed.

But far too few injured workers receive the medical or vocational rehabilitation needed to reduce their disabilities to a minimum and restore them to full economic usefulness. Provisions for making effective rehabilitation services available have been slow in developing in workmen's compensation laws.

This subject is closely related to developing more effective administration of workmen's compensation and provides a logical point at which to begin an evaluation of workmen's compensation.

---

[8] For further information on rehabilitation, see "Workmen's Compensation and the Physically Handicapped Worker," *Bulletin 234*, 1961, and "Medical Care Under Workmen's Compensation," *Bulletin 244*, 1962, both issued by the Bureau of Labor Standards, U. S. Department of Labor.

Today five jurisdictions operate rehabilitation facilities directly under the workmen's compensation program. About twenty more make some provision relating to rehabilitation, usually offering added indemnity or maintenance allowances during retraining. Federal, state, or private facilities are usually utilized for rehabilitation services.

APPRAISING WORKMEN'S COMPENSATION

Protection against the hazards of occupational disability through workmen's compensation was the objective of the first social insurance programs both here and abroad. Its rapid development, due to both the need for such protection and the soundness of the liability without fault principle, ended abruptly within a decade of its introduction in the United States. Today, more than a half-century after the first American law, critical concern with the role and success of this pioneering social insurance is greater than it ever has been. The remainder of this chapter, therefore, will be devoted to a discussion of the problems which have caused this concern.

As we have already seen, the provisions of state workmen's compensation laws are not uniform. However, all jurisdictions initially sought the same objective—economic rehabilitation of the occupationally injured. The objectives outlined by Marshall Dawson, an eminent workmen's compensation scholar, over twenty-five years ago are still quite valid: [9] (1) to pay certain, prompt, and reasonable compensation to victims of work accidents; (2) to eliminate delays, costs, and wastes of personal injury litigation; (3) to study and attempt to reduce the number of accident cases rather than to conceal them. As a result of long years of compensation experience, (4) prompt and adequate medical treatment and (5) rehabilitation for workers unable to return to their former jobs have become added objectives.

But how fully have these objectives been realized? This question cannot be answered without making value judgments about which there may be some legitimate disagreement. Nor can it be answered completely, for unlike all other forms of social insurance, basic data are not collected in one place, nor are they available from jurisdiction to jurisdiction in complete or comparable form. Thus, some of the most elementary questions about the performance of the laws or the fate of injured workers cannot be answered in some jurisdictions. For example, only a few states know how promptly benefit payments are made to injured workers and whether the full payment required by law has indeed been made

[9] Marshall Dawson, "Problems of Workmen's Compensation Administration in the United States and Canada," *Bulletin 672* (Washington, D. C.: U. S. Department of Labor, Bureau of Labor Statistics, 1940), pp. 5–6.

because the states do not actually administer the laws—the individual carriers in effect administer them. Most of the available data show little more than the number of injured workers and the total compensation paid. This paucity of information has been deplored many times at the annual meetings [10] of the administrators of the state laws. Yet most jurisdictions have failed to follow the lead of states like Wisconsin, whose excellent statistical reports draw wide praise.

Does Workmen's Compensation Pay Certain, Prompt, and Adequate Compensation to Victims of Work Accidents?

Few jurisdictions gather and report data on promptness of payment, and for those who do, comparisons are not easy to make because of varying provisions in the systems: different waiting periods, different methods of computing time of accidents, and different methods of administering or non-administering the law. A 1965 Study Commission on Workmen's Compensation in California found that despite a statute requiring payments to be made on the eighth day after onset of disability, only 50 per cent of all claims had been paid by the 27th day after the injury. Wisconsin, on the other hand, in 1961 showed that 87.5 per cent of all cases received first payment within 15 days following disability (compared to 34 per cent in California). The Commission concluded that prompt payment required administrative supervision, and that successful "self-administration" was a "vain hope." [11] The continued use of the "agreement" method of claims administration (discussed below) also leaves open the possibility of defeating intended statutory benefit amounts. These factors make it difficult to judge whether or not benefits are paid promptly and with certainty, and they indicate that there is much room for improvement on this performance standard.

Cash benefits are frequently referred to as the "heart" of a workmen's compensation system, and with good reason, for they provide income which enables a worker and his family to live during the period of disability. Yet, despite its importance to the compensation principle, in most jurisdictions this part of the compensation law has not accomplished its purpose.

Most of the early workmen's compensation laws stated that weekly cash benefits should be one-half to two-thirds of the worker's weekly

[10] Proceedings of the annual meetings of the International Association of Industrial Accident Boards and Commissions (IAIABC) are an important source of data and evaluations of current workmen's compensation experience. They are published by the U. S. Department of Labor as bulletins of the Bureau of Labor Standards under the title "Workmen's Compensation Problems."

[11] State of California, Report of the Workmen's Compensation Study Commission, 1965, pp. 170–89.

wages at the time of his injury. Minnesota, for example, provided in its April 25, 1913, enactment that the weekly maximum benefit be 50 per cent of wages with a maximum payment of $10, not to fall below a weekly minimum of $6. This maximum weekly figure was in fact close to the average weekly wage prevailing at that time, and, with very limited exception, injured workers received the full 50 per cent of their average weekly wage provided by the law.

However, in the years since the widespread enactment of workmen's compensation laws, both the average weekly wage (real and money terms) and the weekly benefits of compensation have increased. Unfortunately, the former have tended to outstrip the latter. Thus, although today most jurisdictions seek to restore about 60 per cent to two-thirds of the average weekly wage and post higher dollar and duration limits than did their earlier laws, benefits have not kept pace with rising wages. As a result, the maximum dollar limits provided by most laws become in effect upper limits on benefits. As Table 10.1 shows, about one-fourth of the states set maximum weekly benefits at $40 or less. Thus, very few injured workers actually receive benefits amounting to from 60 per cent to two-thirds of their lost weekly earnings. It is clear that, in general, injured workers today are heavier coinsurers than they were under the original workmen's compensation laws.

Since the benefits in some jurisdictions fall below what many consider to be a minimum budget, or even an adequate one by relief standards, it is obvious that over-all benefit performance cannot be judged adequate by any standard.

What is an adequate benefit? How high should cash benefits be? The standard-setting organization of compensation administrators, the IAIABC, proposes that the maximum be set, without weekly dollar limits, at two-thirds of the average gross weekly wages of all covered employees in the state.[12]

Practical considerations guided benefit decisions in the earliest compensation laws. Benefits could not be so high as to be too costly to employers or to give workers an incentive to feign injury or to malinger. On the other hand, they could not be so low as to be inadequate for the support of the injured worker and his family. Admittedly, these outside limits cannot be translated readily into dollars-and-cents statements.[13]

---

[12] The *IAIABC Handbook*, p. 39. The IAIABC also recommends full coverage of all industries and all employees, including agricultural; full rather than scheduled coverage of occupational diseases; unlimited medical benefits, with employee choice of physician and agency supervision of medical care and rehabilitation; additional maintenance benefits during rehabilitation; broadened subsequent injury funds; permanent total disability benefits for life; death benefits until widow's death or remarriage; waiting periods of only three days; penalty for illegal employment of minors.

[13] For a discussion of this issue, see Earl F. Cheit, "Adequacy of Workmen's Compensation," *Insurance Law Journal*, No. 387 (April, 1955), 247.

Yet it seems clear that today's benefit levels are in the aggregate closer to the lower limits than they are to the upper limits. Of course, both sides of the benefit issue must always be considered in shaping policy, but today's benefit levels focus primary attention on the dangers to the living standards of injured workers rather than on the possibility of malingering or of excessive costs.

A discussion of the "reasonableness" or adequacy of indemnity benefits should take into account three additional factors, the first of which has already been mentioned briefly.

There Are Wide Variations Between States. As we have emphasized several times earlier, differences are considerable from jurisdiction to jurisdiction. Thus, workers injured in Wisconsin or Arizona and those covered by the Federal Employees' Compensation Act will receive benefits which restore a considerably greater portion of their wage loss than workers suffering identical injuries in most other states.

There Are Differences Within Jurisdictions Depending on Extent of Disability. Even within a given jurisdiction, the percentage of the wage loss restored differs greatly among degrees of disability. Studies have demonstrated repeatedly that benefits restore a larger portion of lost wages to workers suffering temporary disability than they do in many cases involving death, permanent total, or severe permanent partial disability.

The most recent study, based on actual field interviews with disabled workers,[14] showed that a surprisingly large number of workers with permanent disability ratings suffered no permanent wage losses: 80 per cent of the minor partial disability cases, 57 per cent of the major partial disability cases, and even 18 per cent of the permanent total disability cases. But if the number of cases who sustained permanent wage losses seems relatively small, the estimated losses themselves do not. In dollars, the median losses (for those who suffered losses) for the three groups ranged from $27,500 to $46,562. Measured as a percentage of the total earnings the injured workers might have expected if their injuries had not occurred, the losses totaled 25 per cent for the minor permanently disabled, 49 per cent for the major permanently disabled, and 93 per cent for the permanent totally disabled.

How much of this loss was offset by workmen's compensation payments? For the first group, benefits replaced a median of 7 per cent of the wage losses; for the second, 10 per cent; and for the most seriously

---

[14] Earl F. Cheit, *Injury and Recovery in the Course of Employment* (New York: John Wiley and Sons, Inc., 1961), chap. 6.

disabled, 36 per cent. This compares with a loss replacement of over 40 per cent for the temporarily disabled group mentioned earlier.

The System Cannot Be Judged by Indemnity Benefits Alone. No attempt should be made to conceal the inadequacy of workmen's compensation indemnity benefits, but because the whole performance of workmen's compensation is so frequently judged by reference to this criterion alone, it is important to recognize that the systems have tended to become more liberal in other respects. Broader coverage, more lifetime benefits for permanent total cases, improved benefit duration and rehabilitation progress—these improvements should also be considered in judging the adequacy of the system. Yet in these areas, too, there are serious inadequacies.

If we accept E. H. Downey's premise that the "compensation system should comprise all industries, all persons employed therein and all personal injuries which arise in the course of industrial pursuits," [15] then all state systems must be judged deficient in compensation coverage of work accident victims. For, as we have noted before, exclusions, exemptions, and other eligibility requirements restrict the scope of workmen's compensation. Actually, the scope of compensation protection has been widened considerably over the years; all jurisdictions today have laws; their numerical exemptions have been reduced and in some cases eliminated; the hazardous employment requirement has been dropped from some laws. Nevertheless, substantial numbers of employees remain outside the protection of workmen's compensation.

Six requirements limit workmen's compensation coverage. Benefits can be paid only to (1) "employees" (2) working in covered employments (3) who suffer injuries covered by statute (4) and are incapacitated for a period longer than the waiting period (5) by an injury caused by and sustained in the course of the employment, and (6) who elect or whose employers elect coverage in jurisdictions offering the option. How many victims of work accidents are denied benefits by the combination of these limiting factors is not known accurately, since adequate data are not available.

The most recent estimate [16] reveals that, exclusive of the unemployed, unpaid family workers, the self-employed, and other groups for whom coverage is not normally contemplated by state workmen's compensation jurisdictions (such as railroad workers and federal employees), almost 80 per cent of the remaining "eligible" employees were covered in 1965.

---

[15] E. H. Downey, *Workmen's Compensation* (New York: The Macmillan Co., 1924), p. 21.

[16] Cheit, *op. cit.,* chap. 1.

This figure shows little improvement over estimates made twenty years earlier.

There are wide differences, however, within these broad national estimates. Urban areas and industrial states, for example, have much higher coverage than the rural and non-industrial states (see Table 9.4).

Furthermore, covered workers receive compensation only for injuries specified by statute. This further reduces coverage in some states, especially in the case of occupational diseases. Also, the link between injury and employment must be established legally, and the waiting period requirement must be fulfilled.[17] This latter provision alone takes perhaps two-fifths of all temporary injuries out of coverage. In some states, poor enforcement, as well as elective provisions, tends to reduce coverage.

In sum, remarkable strides have been made in providing compensation to victims of industrial accidents. All state and territorial jurisdictions and the federal government provide coverage against the hazard of occupational disability. Some early restrictions, such as those applying to "non-hazardous" occupations, have been legislated away; other restricting forces such as a rigorous definition of accident have been liberalized by court and legislative action. Yet coverage is still denied to many victims of work accidents. It may be that Downey's criterion is too inclusive. Short waiting periods, though costly to individual workers, do permit allocation of benefit resources to the more seriously disabled. But there are no compelling reasons to exclude employers on the basis of numbers employed or, for that matter, to exempt agricultural, casual, or domestic employees, if these groups are carefully defined. Therefore, although we seem to be moving slowly in the direction of improved coverage, much work remains.

Has Workmen's Compensation Eliminated Delays, Costs, and Waste?

By introducing the concept of liability without fault, workmen's compensation laws eliminated many of the delays and costs made necessary by the common law. In fact, the administrative approaches of workmen's compensation are sometimes suggested as possible solutions to the many automobile accident claims which today cause court delays, costs, and wastes not unlike those associated with occupational injuries at common law. Despite the transfer from court to commission determination of injury claims, however, prompt and efficient benefit payment is not yet

17 Many laws provide that if the disability continues for a certain period the payment of benefits is retroactive to the date of injury. The period ranges from five days to six weeks or more. In California, if the worker is hospitalized, payments are retroactive to the first day the employee leaves work.

ideal because of problems in administration and because of legal contests, which play an ever increasing role in the administration of workmen's compensation. These problems are discussed later in this chapter together with the administration of workmen's compensation laws.

Has Workmen's Compensation Helped to Reduce Accidents?

Accident Facts, published annually by the National Safety Council, indicates that since shortly after the widespread enactment of workmen's compensation in America, the long-run general trend in accident frequency and severity rates has been downward. There is some disagreement, however, about whether or not workmen's compensation laws have contributed substantially to this trend.[18] There are several reasons why we might assume that they have.

First, it is obviously to an employer's self-interest to install safety measures for prevention of accidents when he is liable for the payment of compensation benefits. His insurance premiums, if he is not a small employer, will be "merit rated"—that is, if he produces a good accident record, he will be rewarded with lower insurance costs.

Secondly, it is to the self-interest of the insurance carrier to prevent accidents, and compensation carriers allocate a portion of their premium collections to safety services for their assureds. Some states have sought to stimulate preventive measures by enacting provisions which assess penalties against employers for accidents stemming from safety code violations.

Finally, workmen's compensation systems in themselves make accident control more possible, since the assembling of accident data is a part of their operation.

At the same time, however, it must be noted that the employer's self-interest in reducing accidents is strong whether or not he is covered by workmen's compensation. Benefit costs are but a fraction of total accident costs to employers; furthermore, smaller employers are not eligible for merit rating, and many of those who are can, on small premiums, realize only small incentive savings from a good safety record. The value of penalty provisions is not clear, and the poor reporting of accident data in many states leaves this promising avenue of control unexploited in

---

[18] W. F. Dodd says: "It is perhaps safe to say that workman's compensation has had little effect" [on the industrial accident rate]. See W. F. Dodd, *Administration of Workmen's Compensation* (New York: The Commonwealth Fund, 1936), p. 698. The Director of the Bureau of Labor Standards, however, writes that "the greatest contribution which workmen's compensation has made to the economic and physical well-being of workers is the stimulus it has given to accident prevention efforts." See "Workmen's Compensation in the United States," *Bulletin 1140* (Washington, D. C.: Department of Labor, Bureau of Labor Statistics, 1954), p. 29.

many areas. Even the self-interest of insurance carriers has been known to give way when it becomes a matter of rejecting possible assureds because of questionable safety records.

On balance, therefore, we can do little more than hazard some guesses about the effects of workmen's compensation on accident prevention. First, whether or not they provided great incentives, workmen's compensation laws did, in fact, stimulate initial employer interest in accident prevention. And, to a lesser degree, the workmen's compensation movement has provided a measure of continued drive and direction to the safety movement, now supplemented by the work of many other safety agencies, voluntary and governmental.

Second, it seems safe to assume that compensation incentives, with all their weaknesses, have provided some impetus to prevention. An excellent illustration is the estimated $100 million per year employers have spent to reduce the noise associated with various jobs—partly as a result of the decision holding that non-traumatic occupational "loss-of-hearing" is compensable.

However, there is still elective coverage in many jurisdictions; there are exemptions; and small employers have little, if any, insurance incentives. Some industries, like manufacturing, have produced good over-all results. Others, like coal mining, still tend to be very hazardous. Moreover, the largest companies are producing excellent safety records, but the smaller firms are producing poorer ones. While workmen's compensation may have contributed to accident prevention, accident rates offer little grounds for complacency.

Does Workmen's Compensation Provide Prompt and Adequate Medical Treatment?

We have already seen in Table 10.1 that, either by law or in practical operation, forty-three American jurisdictions provide full medical treatment—that is, the degree of care medically indicated, without legal limitation to a specified time or amount.[19] Even in those jurisdictions where limitations apply, employers and insurance carriers frequently report that they provide unlimited medical treatment to seriously injured workers.

When one considers that the original workmen's compensation acts provided little or no medical benefits, the progress that has been made in this area is probably the greatest single achievement of workmen's compensation since its inception in this country. Furthermore, since

---

[19] Detailed examination of the statutes indicates, however, that medical benefits may be more restricted than is always apparent. See Bureau of Labor Standards, *Bulletin 244, Medical Care under Workmen's Compensation*, for a full study, not only of limitations on care but problems of administration of medical treatment.

there is now a well-established trend toward acceptance of medically indicated medical treatment as the only "adequate" treatment, it appears
that all jurisdictions will move toward employing this benefit policy in
the future.

This optimism is based not on humanitarian considerations, but rather
on the principle of the economy of full medical treatment. It has often
been demonstrated that the maximum medical treatment is also the optimal one; that prompt adequate medical care reduces compensation costs
in at least three ways. First, it reduces the number of cases of "avoidable
disability"—cases of a minor nature which might otherwise become more
serious. Secondly, it reduces the degree of disability. And, finally, it
reduces the period of care, thereby avoiding prolonged indemnity and
other costs.

The most significant problems of medical care in workmen's compensation are problems of quality and administration. For example, fee schedules of charges permitted by some states may be too low to attract the
best medical practitioners to compensation cases. The quality of medical
care may be poor because of the injured worker's ignorance in his choice
of a physician in jurisdictions where such free choice is permitted or because of the pressure of an insurance carrier on a physician where it is
not. Particularly there are too many cases of workers who could have
been rehabilitated if more competent initial treatment had been provided.
All these problems require more statutory supervision over medical care.

In many states, there is an increasing tendency for injured workers to
bargain away their right to unlimited medical care in a compromise settlement which is final and ends the carrier's liability for any future medical aid that may be required. Many state commissions are authorized to
disapprove these compromises if they are against the worker's best interests, but they usually face no real scrutiny.

In addition, partisan medical testimony may have the effect of defeating the ends of efficient claims administration.[20] Yet, on balance, this
phase of workmen's compensation, more than any other, must again be
cited as having most nearly achieved its purposes.

Does Workmen's Compensation Provide Rehabilitation Services for Workers Unable to Return to Their Former Jobs?

Probably in no phase of workmen's compensation does the performance fall so short of the promise than in the area of rehabilitation. A
relatively early concept in the history of workmen's compensation, the
idea of rehabilitation as its major goal, is now widely endorsed, yet at the

[20] *Medical Relations Under Workmen's Compensation in Illinois* (Chicago: American Medical Association, 1953).

same time one-third of the laws make no provision of any kind for re-habilitation, and most of the others are not directed at the central problem.

Most of the present laws [21] merely direct the agency to refer cases to the federal–state vocational rehabilitation program and set up a fund to pay maintenance allowances for a limited period during retraining. In almost no cases does the workmen's compensation agency follow up its referrals, and the vocational rehabilitation agencies, overburdened with non-occupational disability caseloads (80 per cent of their referrals), a shortage of funds, and a mounting backlog, have no mandate to accept them.[22]

Rehabilitation needs to be viewed first and foremost as a *preventive* approach to extended disability—one of the most difficult problems in workmen's compensation. Definitive medical treatment alone, no matter how good its quality, when it provides the disabled worker no guidance or attack on the disuse of his affected parts, or on his fear and discourage-ment, may not be adequate to restore his maximum function. A con-certed effort by the physical therapist, the social caseworker, the brace-maker, and the psychologist, centered in a rehabilitation facility, can often produce what would once have been considered miracles in the total restoration of disabled workers. These often make *vocational* re-habilitation unnecessary. Many insurance carriers (and physicians) have realized these possibilities and discovered their long-run economic advantages,[23] but many more have not. Only strong administrative lead-ership from the workmen's compensation agencies can make this the nor-mal, usual, and expected approach rather than the too rare exception.[24]

In very serious cases of disability, where compensation is extremely costly, the necessary expenditures for maximum restoration of the indi-vidual are clearly worthwhile to insurance carriers. The Liberty Mutual Insurance Company, for example, reports that by putting thirty-five para-plegics back to work through rehabilitation, it saved over 1.5 million dollars in compensation costs. But in many other cases, including minor disabilities, where rehabilitation expenditures might not so clearly be of economic advantage to the carrier, they are still of great value to the in-dividual, as well as clearly worthwhile social investments. If employers and carriers cannot be expected to cover such costs, workmen's compen-

[21] See State Workmen's Compensation Laws, *Bulletin 161, op. cit.,* pp. 59–73.
[22] See Jerome Pollack, "Medical Care and Rehabilitation Under Workmen's Com-pensation," *American Journal of Public Health,* XLV, No. 5 (May, 1955), 648–50.
[23] Willis C. Gorthy, "Rehabilitation: Its Effects in Reducing Compensation Costs," in "Workmen's Compensation Problems," *Bulletin 180* (Washington, D. C.: U. S. Department of Labor, Bureau of Labor Standards, 1953), pp. 35–43.
[24] *Medical Care Under Workmen's Compensation, op. cit.,* chap. 3 and refer-ences cited there.

sation must find other ways to assure this objective of maximum restoration of all injured workers.

Where workers are unable to return to their former jobs, vocational rehabilitation becomes necessary. Here, too, administrative attention is required to assure its success. The federal Vocational Rehabilitation Service has expanded its grants to training centers, established traineeships for training in workshops, and supported many rehabilitation groups. Private centers, too, have made great contributions toward rehabilitating the disabled, and five jurisdictions have set up their own facilities. But not only are the resources and personnel woefully inadequate to their task, but referrals without follow-up and encouragement have proved ineffective.

Further, there are some disincentives to rehabilitation in the laws themselves,[25] to which we now turn.

IS THE SYSTEM STRUCTURED RATIONALLY?

Since workmen's compensation laws do not operate independently of the industrial disability problem which they seek to alleviate, it follows that if the system is structured rationally it should exert a positive influence on industrial injury experience. The merit rating and penalty provisions discussed earlier were adopted with this goal in mind. Although the effects of these provisions are in dispute, other provisions have achieved their purpose—for example, the "nurse credit" in insurance rates to companies which make nursing service available to their employees. To this extent the system is rationally structured.

Under some compensation laws, instances arise of resisting claims through litigation, of paying lump-sum benefits in place of regular payments, of shoddy medical practices and benefit abuse; but, for the most part, these are due to inadequate supervision and administration, rather than to structural failures of the laws. They are more faults of omission than commission.

One serious structural shortcoming of workmen's compensation laws is that they may unwittingly offer disincentives to speedy rehabilitation of injured workers. Two situations arise.

First, *workmen's compensation laws may tend to deter seriously injured workers from seeking rehabilitation aid,* and second, *workmen's compensation laws have tended to deter employers from hiring handicapped workers.* Under present laws, which base permanent disability ratings on a prediction of the worker's future reduction in earning capac-

[25] See Cheit, *op. cit.,* chap. 10.

ity, injured workers often see in rehabilitation the possible forfeiture of their maximum cash benefit claims. Since these cases are costly to insurers, many of them result in litigation where the degree of disability as evidenced by earnings loss is the issue in dispute. When an injured worker is disputing an insurance carrier's contention that he is not as disabled as he claims, he will not readily seek rehabilitation services or do anything else to show that he may not be disabled.[26]

In order to be resolved, this apparent conflict between maximum cash benefits and rehabilitation will require not only more enlightened claims administration, but possibly a major overhaul of present methods of compensating permanent disability. Since it has not proved possible to predict reliably the effect of a given injury on a worker's future earning power, it has been proposed that permanent disability ratings be based solely on the degree of physical impairment; and further, that a new benefit be offered the injured worker, an assurance of reemployment with his former employer.[27]

Employers have avoided hiring handicapped workers for many reasons, one being their fear that further injury could result in a total disability claim. In a well-known case in Oklahoma in 1925,[28] it was held that an employee who had previously lost sight in one eye could bring a claim against his employer for permanent total compensation for loss of the other eye in the course of his employment. It is reported that "Seven thousand one-eyed, one-armed and one-legged workmen were fired over night in that state. Oklahoma employers were unwilling to take on handicapped workers for fear that additional injury would cost them permanent total disability awards." [29]

Second-injury funds have been adopted to meet this situation in all but four states. Money for these funds is collected by a moderate assessment on employers (in most states for death cases where there are no dependents eligible for benefits; in a few states, in each case of serious disability). The second-injury fund operates to protect employers from

[26] Rehabilitation authority Dr. Howard A. Rusk reports that he succeeded in rehabilitating only 3 per cent of 300 back cases in litigation, whereas his usual success with rehabilitation cases is 90 per cent. *Medical Aspects of Compensation* (New York: Commerce and Industry Association of New York, 1953), pp. 68–69. See also Morton Lane, *The Effect of the New York Workmen's Compensation Law Upon the Employment of the Handicapped*, Rehabilitation Monograph XI (New York: The Institute of Physical Medicine and Rehabilitation, New York University Bellevue Medical Center, 1956), pp. 5–16.

[27] Cheit, *op. cit.*, pp. 344–53.

[28] *Nease v. Hughes Stone Co.*, 244 Pac. 778.

[29] Address of Under Secretary of Labor Arthur Larson, "Highlights of the Proposed Model Workmen's Compensation Law," November 17, 1955 (U. S. Department of Labor Press Release No. 1360).

total disability claims in cases involving second injuries. Employers are made liable only for the disability of the second injury and the fund pays the rest of the benefits for total disability.

This remarkable device, if broad enough in its coverage, provides an important incentive to employment of handicapped workers. Moreover, it has proved to be relatively inexpensive, since experience shows that not a great many charges are made against the second-injury funds.

However, the effectiveness of this program has fallen far short of its potential. According to a survey conducted by the Bureau of Labor Standards, "Many employers, especially in small firms, mistakenly thought that hiring handicapped workers would increase their workmen's compensation premiums." [30] At the same time, various restrictions and limitations imposed on these funds in most states have served to limit sharply their application. It is clear that until these statutes are broadened and their application more clearly understood, unnecessary barriers to meaningful employment will continue to confront the handicapped worker.

IS THE SYSTEM ADMINISTERED SOUNDLY?

Sound administration is as important to an adequate workmen's compensation program as are substantive provisions of the law. Adequate benefits lose their value if they are not promptly paid or are not paid in full.

Fewer evaluative data are available to review this aspect of workmen's compensation than any other. We do know that some jurisdictions, most notably Wisconsin, win repeated acclaim as models of good administration. We know, too, that studies of administration do not present a very satisfactory over-all picture. The problems that arise are summarized below.

First, in five jurisdictions the legislation has never been given over to administrative determination. And where workmen's compensation laws are court-administered, the results have not been good. They have provided poor and inadequate records, and, except in contested cases, they have provided no administration at all. The administrative machinery is lacking for the detailed work required of an injury compensation program.

Second, administrative procedures in the remaining jurisdictions follow three basic approaches. Claims are paid by direct settlement; by agreement; or, after a hearing. The direct-settlement method enables cheap and speedy claims payments since claims in non-contested cases are paid

[30] Lloyd W. Larson, "Workmen's Compensation Laws and the Employment of the Handicapped," *Monthly Labor Review,* LXXXV, No. 2 (February, 1962), 145–48.

directly upon notice of disability. But quick and economical claims administration alone does not insure that claims are paid justly. The "hearing" system, used only in New York, seeks to insure just payment by providing a hearing for almost every claim. The "agreement" method, most widely used of the claims techniques today, seeks to gain equity on the assumption that workers can agree with a settlement proposed by employers or carriers and assume essentially that the system will administer itself. Serious problems of cost and waste arise under the hearings approach, and the greatest weakness of the agreement system is its possibilities for abuse. Students of administration seem agreed that a closely supervised direct-settlement method is probably the best approach. But this raises the next problem.

Third, workmen's compensation administrative offices in a majority of jurisdictions are frequently without adequate personnel and budgets, nor do they enjoy the status and tenure protection needed for completely independent judgment. As one of them reported recently, "the toll of top state administrators through political euthanasia is horrendous." [31] It is impossible to operate a closely supervised direct-settlement system under these circumstances.

Fourth, partly because of the lack of professional administrative direction and partly because of the incentives to do so, far too many compensation claims (about 10 per cent) are contested and result in the kind of lengthy and costly litigation which the system was designed to circumvent in the first place. In California, recently, an effort was made to restructure the state's system, with the aim of reducing litigation. The previous self-administration of the law by carriers and self-insurers was rejected; an administrative director was appointed with the new duties of monitoring benefit payments, establishing an advisory service for claimants with a mediating function as well, and supervising a voluntary rehabilitation program and a new medical advisory committee. The elements in the system other than self-administration which produce litigation were not affected by the new legislation and opinions are divided as to its probable effects,[32] since many of the administrative problems and litigiousness grow out of more basic conceptual difficulties of workmen's compensation. These pose some theoretical issues of great importance, such as the proper standards for determining the measure of benefits and disability rating.[33]

[31] *ABC Newsletter, the Journal of Workmen's Compensation Administrators,* II (Winter, 1965), 2.

[32] *Ibid.,* pp. 9–11. The new administrative director comments on the California law.

[33] Stefan A. Riesenfeld, "Basic Problems in the Administration of Workmen's Compensation," *Minnesota Law Review,* XXXVI, No. 2 (January, 1952), 119–42. See also Somers, *op. cit.* and Cheit, *op. cit.,* chaps. 6 and 11.

DOES WORKMEN'S COMPENSATION PRODUCE
UNDESIRABLE ECONOMIC EFFECTS?

According to Social Security Administration estimates, the cost to employers of workmen's compensation insurance (and self-insurance) is about 2.7 billion dollars a year, or about 1 per cent of their total payrolls. Since insurance can be provided more efficiently to larger companies, and since it will reflect safety records, premiums may vary widely among individual employers. Moreover, in any given state, insurance costs will differ from employer to employer depending upon the degree of work hazards. In California, for example, employers presently pay insurance premiums of 16 cents per $100 of payroll to insure clerical workers. They pay $19.52 per $100 of payroll to insure building, wrecking, and demolition crews. Insurance costs vary from state to state, too, depending upon the benefit provisions of the law and the distribution of employments in a given area.

At the time workmen's compensation laws were first being enacted, a major opposing argument was that they would put home industry at a competitive disadvantage, deter location of industry within the state, and possibly even drive business firms away. Although all states have workmen's compensation laws today, the argument is still an important one in legislative debate over liberalization of the laws.

Do interstate cost differentials in fact produce such undesirable economic effects? It seems fairly well agreed that workmen's compensation costs at an average of 1 per cent of payrolls (in contrast, for example, to the estimated more than 25 per cent spent for all fringe benefits) are not sufficiently significant to play an important role in location decisions or in competitive advantage—in the short run. Long-run effects, too, are probably exaggerated. Yet it must be recognized that along with other factors such as taxes, power resources, and labor, employers take workmen's compensation costs into account when deciding where to locate their firms.

A more serious economic effect on individual firms or industries as well as on their insurance carriers arises when workmen's compensation coverage is extended to heretofore non-compensable injuries. It is possible that the full cost impact of new claims would be assessed against the firms or industry in which the majority of claims arise. This possibility has been averted by rating procedures which spread these new costs in part throughout all employers in the state.

Another phase of workmen's compensation insurance costs—one which is not so wholly related to the benefit level and the distribution of industry—has raised questions about economic impact. That is, these costs seem to move counter-cyclically. With rising employment and prosperity, costs tend to go down; with declining levels of employment, they tend to rise. This movement is sometimes attributed to abuse of the system. It is argued that workers have an incentive to malinger when benefits may restore much of their lost earnings and when re-employment opportunities are few; and they may be helped in this process by dishonest physicians, who, during periods of economic decline, are willing to prolong treatment of compensation cases where payment is assured by the compensation system. Also, workers who are laid off may seek to gain compensation for injuries (real or feigned) incurred while they were employed.

There is some evidence that the system is sometimes abused. But there are no data to show that this problem is a serious cost burden or that it is outside of administrative control.

Insurance costs are sometimes criticized as being excessive for the amount of benefits paid by workmen's compensation. The exact proportion of insurance premiums that reaches disabled workers is the subject of some disagreement. How much of every net premium dollar collected is paid out to workers in the form of indemnity and medical benefits? Insurance sources estimate 62.5 cents; labor sources contend 47 cents.

More important than the fact of this difference, which is in part due to definition of losses and premium income, are the questions that it raises: Is workmen's compensation liability being insured efficiently? Or, more directly, do the acquisition and administrative costs of workmen's compensation put an unreasonable cost burden on this social insurance program? The choice of a stock or a mutual carrier may make some cost differences, but insurance authorities are inclined to minimize "legal-organizational structure" per se and to put more emphasis on an individual company's performance for such factors as service, financial strength, and record of cost allocation.[34]

The issue is made far more complex when the alternatives are private carriers on the one hand and state insurance on the other. For in addition to the difficulties of measuring the many variables involved (such as service to policyholders and claimants, safety engineering, and other components of insurance costs), ideological preferences tend to make the issue more a political one than an economic one. Private insurance, as we have seen earlier, is the dominant method by which workmen's compensation liabilities are insured today, although twelve jurisdictions offer the state fund alternative, and seven have state insurance exclusively.

Two recent legislative skirmishes have renewed interest in the question: Should social insurance benefits be privately insured? In Oregon,

[34] C. A. Kulp, *Casualty Insurance* (3d ed.; New York: The Ronald Press Co., 1956), chap. 15.

critics of the exclusive state fund succeeded in passing legislation to permit private insurance; in Alaska advocates of an exclusive state fund sought unsuccessfully to establish one.

The arguments were essentially the long-standing ones: on the one hand, a state fund has smaller administrative and supervisory expenses, and, on the other, private insurance is more efficient.[35]

If insurance premiums one day become a more significant percentage of payrolls, the issue will probably assume more significance, although it seems unlikely that it will ever be resolved with certainty on economic grounds alone.

SUMMARY

The principle of liability without fault has more than proved its *utility* in the field of occupational disability. But problems have arisen out of the *application* of this principle. In no jurisdictions are the benefits and administration of workmen's compensation laws wholly adequate to the needs of an occupational disability program. Not surprisingly, workers have turned to attorneys to protect their interests.[36] As a result, there are many workers today who would prefer to have their injury claims processed through the courts—who are convinced that the tort remedy available in the railroad field is superior to workmen's compensation. Compensation claimants' attorneys oppose extension of the compensation principle into the railroad, tort, or admiralty fields; indeed, despite all its drawbacks, court administration in some states is defended by trade union groups because of the higher awards being gained.

Lagging workmen's compensation benefits have made court awards in damage suits very attractive. Therefore, if all the objectives sought in workmen's compensation are to be gained more fully, widespread reform in the laws is indicated. Although trade unions have succeeded in negotiating supplemental benefits [37] (discussed in Chapter 12), the tort alternative to providing adequate compensation to the occupationally disabled will remain attractive [38] until widespread reform is accomplished. Such

[35] For a more extensive discussion of these arguments, see J. G. Turnbull and C. A. Williams, Jr. (eds.), *Report of the Governor's Advisory Committee on Workmen's Compensation Costs and Benefits,* State of Minnesota, December, 1960.

[36] To see the sort of administration early workmen's compensation scholars and practitioners envisaged, administration which could have prevented litigiousness, it is most refreshing to read E. H. Downey's pioneering work written in 1924. Downey, *op. cit.*

[37] See Harland Fox, "Company Supplements to Workmen's Compensation," in *Occupational Disability and Public Policy* (New York: John Wiley and Sons, Inc., 1962).

[38] See Arthur J. Altmeyer, "The Future of Social Security in America," *Social Service Review,* XXVII, No. 3 (September, 1953), 251–68. Altmeyer makes the argu-

reform has been slow in coming. It remains to be seen whether or not it will succeed in bringing those jurisdictions which have neglected their workmen's compensation programs up to "model" standards.

SUGGESTIONS FOR ADDITIONAL READING

BERKOWITZ, MONROE. *Workmen's Compensation: The New Jersey Experience.* New Brunswick, N. J.: Rutgers University Press, 1960.
The most thorough of the individual state studies of compensation.
CHEIT, EARL F. *Injury and Recovery in the Course of Employment.* New York: John Wiley and Sons, Inc., 1961.
The most recent evaluative study of the performance of workmen's compensation, especially its effectiveness in restoring economic losses of disabled workers. Includes a comparative study of employers' liability systems, together with policy proposals for the future of workmen's compensation.
CHEIT, EARL F., and MARGARET S. GORDON (eds.). *Occupational Disability and Public Policy.* New York: John Wiley and Sons, Inc., 1962.
A symposium of many leading scholars and practitioners in this field expressing their diverse views. Includes a discussion of foreign experience.
DODD, WALTER F. *Administration of Workmen's Compensation.* New York: The Commonwealth Fund, 1936.
Many of the generalizations and insights of this valuable book are important today to an understanding of workmen's compensation administration.
KULP, C. A. *Casualty Insurance,* 3d ed. New York: The Ronald Press Co., 1956. Chapters 5, 6, 7, 17, 18.
Chapter 6 is a good, brief discussion of workmen's compensation. The other chapters present the various aspects of workmen's compensation insurance and rate-making.
New York University Workmen's Compensation Study. New York: New York University Center for Rehabilitation Services, 1960.
A valuable study of medical care and rehabilitation problems with proposals for improving medical administration in New York.
RIESENFELD, STEFAN A., and RICHARD C. MAXWELL. *Modern Social Legislation.* Brooklyn: The Foundation Press, 1950. Pp. 162–440.
A legal presentation of problems in benefits, coverage, and administration, including case materials.
SOMERS, HERMAN M., and ANNE RAMSAY SOMERS. *Workmen's Compensation.* New York: John Wiley and Sons, Inc., 1954. Chapters 3–8.
Comprehensive analysis of workmen's compensation. Excellent treatment of benefit adequacy, insurance, and rehabilitation.

---

ment that a partial re-introduction of the tort remedy is necessary to overcome inadequacies in benefits. See also Benjamin Marcus, "Advocating the Rights of the Injured," in *Occupational Disability and Public Policy* (New York: John Wiley & Sons, Inc., 1962). But see Jerome Pollack, "A Policy Decision for Workmen's Compensation," *Industrial and Labor Relations Review,* VII, No. 1 (October, 1953), 61. Pollack argues that "proposals favoring the availability of both remedies would perpetuate the evils under both systems."

11

Non-occupational Illness Problems

INTRODUCTION

The nature and importance of occupational injuries and disease and the legal responsibility of employers for these illnesses were discussed in the last two chapters. This chapter deals primarily with the economic problems created by non-occupational illness and public approaches to their solution. Most of the public programs to be discussed will also pay benefits for job-connected illness, but these benefits will commonly be offset by any workmen's compensation payments received.

We shall treat first the types of losses caused by non-occupational accidental injuries and sickness, their frequency and severity as revealed by some recent surveys, and the total costs of non-occupational illness.

A general discussion of the various private and public methods of attacking the economic problems created by non-occupational illness will be followed by a more detailed discussion of public alleviative programs. The programs to be considered include the special or categorical state public assistance plans, special hospitals, the total and permanent disability provisions under OASDI, and temporary disability insurance legislation.

The chapter will conclude with a description of the historical background and the major provisions of the two public medical expense insurance programs for the aged established under the Social Security Amendments of 1965. The implications of these programs for the future will also be explored.

LOSSES CAUSED BY NON-OCCUPATIONAL ACCIDENTAL INJURY AND SICKNESS

Nature and Importance

As in the case of occupational illness discussed in Chapter 9, an accidental injury or sickness may cause a financial loss through loss of income and through medical expenses. The potential loss of income may be estimated in the manner outlined in Chapter 2 for computing the income loss caused by death, but the cost of maintenance should not be subtracted and the income loss may be partial or temporary. The income loss caused by total and permanent disability will exceed the income loss caused by death because the maintenance cost continues.

Medical expenses themselves take the form of hospital bills, physicians' and surgeons' charges, nurses' fees, medicines, and appliances. The loss potential is great.

Probability of Accidental Injury or Sickness

The probability of an accidental injury or sickness loss is much more difficult to state than the probability of death for at least three reasons.

First, it is relatively easy to tell whether a person has suffered an accidental injury, but it is almost impossible to determine whether certain individuals are sick. Some persons will claim for various reasons that they are sick while apparently they are not. Others are sick, but they will not admit it.

Even if this problem did not exist, what is illness? Is a slight cold a sickness? Is a minor cut on a finger an accidental injury? Someone has stated that we are all ill; it is just a matter of degree. For statistical purposes it is necessary to draw a definitional line somewhere but unfortunately the available data are not all based upon the same definition. Often this definitional problem is resolved by not recognizing the illness unless it prevents the insured from performing his regular duties for at least one day but, because of differences in character or occupation, we must recognize that the same illness may disable one person but not another.

Second, a person may be ill more than once during a year, and each illness may last for a different period. The probability structure would be a complex one to describe even if the exact probabilities were known. Furthermore, the economic loss depends not only upon the frequency and duration of the illness, but also upon its seriousness in terms of income loss and medical expenses.

Third, births, deaths, and certain illnesses are reported on a regular basis to public authorities, but most illnesses are not so reported. Until recently, the only information on the health status of our population came from several local studies and two extensive, but dated, sample surveys —the 1928–31 investigation by the Committee on the Costs of Medical Care and the National Health Survey of 1935–36.[1]

Since that time at least three comprehensive studies have been published which add greatly to our knowledge of the probabilities of disability income losses and medical expenses.[2]

The first study is the population sample survey of 1949–50 which provided estimates of the prevalence of disabling illness in the United States in February, 1949, and in September, 1950. This survey was conducted by the Public Health Service, the Social Security Administration, and the Office of Vocational Rehabilitation.[3] The second study, which compares the results of three separate surveys by the Health Information Foundation in 1953, 1958, and 1963, was concerned with nationwide charges for personal health services, the distribution of these charges among families and individuals, and the utilization of hospital care and other medical service.[4] These surveys also studied various relationships between vol-

[1] For the results of these two surveys, see (1) I. S. Falk, M. C. Klem, and N. Sinai, *The Incidence of Illness and the Receipts and Costs of Medical Care Among Representative Family Groups* (Chicago: University of Chicago Press, 1933) and (2) U. S. Public Health Service, *Illness and Medical Care Among 2,500,000 Persons in 83 Cities, with Special Reference to Socio-Economic Factors* (Washington, D. C.: U. S. Government Printing Office, 1945).

For a summary of some important results of these surveys, see J. G. Turnbull, C. A. Williams, Jr., and E. F. Cheit, *Economic and Social Security* (first ed.; New York: The Ronald Press Co., 1957), pp. 293–97.

[2] Strictly speaking, the studies do not usually tell us the probability of incurring these losses. For example, the studies often tell us the proportion of persons who were disabled or incurred medical expenses on a certain date or over a specified time, i.e., the prevalence of illness. This is not the same as the probability of loss during a stated period because not everyone who will suffer such losses during that period (say, a year) has to endure them within a selected part of the period (say, a month). Moreover, persons who are disabled or are incurring medical expenses now may be the victims of a long-term illness which started several periods ago.

Another type of information presented in the studies is the average number of workdays or medical expense dollars that were lost per person during a given period. In addition to being subject to the observations presented in the preceding paragraph, these figures reflect directly the severity of the losses as well as their frequency.

[3] Theodore D. Woolsey, "Estimates of Disabling Illness Prevalence in the United States," *Public Health Monograph 4*, U. S. Public Health Service Publication 181 (Washington, D. C.: U. S. Government Printing Office, August, 1952).

[4] Odin W. Anderson with Jacob J. Feldman, *Family Medical Costs and Voluntary Health Insurance: A Nationwide Survey* (New York: McGraw-Hill Book Co., 1956).

Odin W. Anderson, Patricia Collette, and Jacob J. Feldman, "Family Expenditure Patterns for Personal Health Services, 1953 and 1958: Nationwide Surveys," Research Series 14 (New York: Health Information Foundation, 1960).

Preliminary information on the 1963 survey was presented in "Trends in Personal Health Services," *Progress in Health Services*, XIV, No. 5 (November–December, 1965), pp. 1–6.

untary health insurance and medical expenses but this phase of the study is not relevant to the present discussion. The third survey, which is the most recent, is also the most comprehensive. In 1956 Congress authorized a *continuing* National Health Survey by the Public Health Service. This survey has already resulted in the publication of numerous valuable reports on disability income and medical expense losses based on information collected in a continuing nationwide sample of households in the civilian non-institutional population. For example, the sample for the twelve-month period ending in June, 1965, included about 134,000 persons from 42,000 households. For the most part, these three studies will be used to indicate the frequency patterns for disability income and medical expense losses.[5]

Recent Data on the Prevalence of Illness

According to the 1949–50 population survey, 4.19 per cent of the civilian non-institutional population, aged fourteen to sixty-four, were disabled; 4.72 per cent in the February survey and 3.67 per cent in the September survey. A person was assumed to be disabled if he was prevented from doing his regular work or performing other duties on the day of the interview or if he had been able to work only occasionally.

In the February survey, among the disabled,

25 per cent were disabled for one week or less,
24 per cent were disabled for over one week but not over three months,
14 per cent were disabled for over three months but not over one year, and
37 per cent were disabled for over one year.

The corresponding figures in the September survey were 18 per cent, 21 per cent, 15 per cent, and 46 per cent.

In a report[6] based largely upon this population survey, the Social Security Administration estimated that on an average day in 1954 approximately 2.9 million persons, aged fourteen to sixty-four, had been disabled for six months or more. Including children under fourteen and

[5] Unless otherwise noted, the sources for the data cited in this text are the following: U. S. Department of Health, Education, and Welfare, Public Health Service, *Current Estimates From the Health Interview Survey, United States—July, 1964–June, 1965,* Public Health Service Publication No. 1000—Series 10—No. 25 (Washington, D. C.: U. S. Government Printing Office, 1965), Health Insurance Institute, *Source Book of Health Insurance Data* (annual), and U. S. Department of Health, Education, and Welfare, *Health, Education, and Welfare Trends* (Washington, D. C.: U. S. Government Printing Office, annual).

[6] "Estimated Prevalence of Long-Term Disability, 1954," *Social Security Bulletin,* XVIII, No. 6 (June, 1955), 20–21.

persons aged sixty-five and over increased the estimate to 5.3 million or about 3.3 per cent of the total civilian population in the United States. About 1.2 million of these disabled persons were in institutions.

The National Health Survey provides data on the number of days per year the average person in the civilian non-institutionalized population was disabled. During 1964–65, a fairly typical survey year, the average person was forced to restrict his activity on about 16.4 days and had to remain in bed most of the day on about 6.2 days. The average worker lost about 5.7 complete workdays and the average person, aged six to sixteen, about 5.2 school days. Chronic conditions (conditions that had lasted three months or more prior to the interview or which were included in a list of specified conditions expected to last that long) were reported by 46.3 per cent of the population but fortunately only about 10 per cent had their activity limited in any degree by a chronic condition.[7]

Data on the distribution of medical expenses provided by the Health Insurance Foundation surveys are summarized in Table 11.1. Although part of the upward shift in the levels of expenditure from 1953 to 1963 can be explained by the 38 per cent increase in the cost of medical care included in the Consumers' Price Index, the resulting increase in average family expenditures from $207 in 1953 to $370 in 1963 is still impressive. The uneven distribution of these expenses is also noteworthy; the 8 per cent of the families with expenditures of $1,000 or more in 1963 accounted for 36 per cent of the total expended by all families.

Special attention has been devoted in recent years to the medical expenses of the aged. According to the 1963 Survey of the Aged by the Social Security Administration, which provided most of the information concerning the aged presented in Chapter 2, aged couples spent on the average $442 for medical care. About 27 per cent had costs under $100, 32 per cent spent between $100 and $299, 30 per cent between $300 and

---

[7] None of these data indicate the *probability* that a person will become disabled. See footnote 2. The Committee on the Costs of Medical Care found that 53 per cent of the population would be ill during the year and among those who became ill, 52 per cent would be disabled. Among those disabled, 3 per cent would be disabled for more than seventy-five days.

Insurance data (based on insured lives only) indicate that the chance of a person suffering a disability lasting three months or longer is .0033 at age thirty, .0054 at age forty, .012 at age fifty, and .027 at age fifty-nine. These probabilities are almost three times the chance of death at the younger ages and about one and one-half times as great at age fifty-nine. The chance that a person aged thirty-five will suffer a three-month disability prior to age sixty-five is about one-third. Estimate by Ben J. Helphand as quoted by Robert A. Brown, Jr. in Davis W. Gregg (Ed.), *Life and Health Insurance Handbook* (Homewood, Ill.: Richard D. Irwin, Inc., 1959), p. 638.

According to the 1964 Commissioners Disability Table prepared by the National Association of Insurance Commissioners, among insured employees who had been disabled for eight days, 8 per cent remained disabled for at least three months and 2 per cent for at least six months.

$999, and 11 per cent $1,000 or more. These costs would have been higher except for the fact that some doctors or hospitals adjusted their charges downward for the aged and many received "free" services from public or private agencies.[8]

TABLE 11.1

Per Cent of All Families With Various Levels of Expenditures,
1953, 1958, and 1963

Level of Family Expenditures	1953	1958	1963
Under $100	46%	34%	30%
$100–299	32	34	32
$300–999	20	27	30
$1,000 and over	2	5	8

Source: "Trends in Public Health Services," XIV, No. 5 (November–December, 1965), pp. 1–6.

From 1954 to 1964 annual admissions to non-federal short-term general and other special hospitals, which account for over 95 per cent of total admissions have risen steadily from about 116 per 1,000 persons in the civilian population to 137 per 1,000 persons. The average length of stay in a hospital declined over the same period from about ten days to nine days. From July, 1963–June, 1964 the average person made about 4.5 visits to the doctor and 1.6 visits to a dentist. Persons over seventy-five years of age made 7.3 visits to the doctor and only 0.6 visits to a dentist.

Factors Causing Variation in the Prevalence of Illness

The prevalence of illness depends upon age, sex, race, income, employment status, residence, marital status, and the season of the year. The sample surveys are not always in agreement on the effects of these factors but the more common findings are summarized below.

1. The very young and the aged are ill more often than the average person, but age is a relatively unimportant factor for persons aged twenty to forty-five or fifty. The probability of a *long-term* illness, however, increases markedly as a person ages, the illnesses of the aged being of much longer duration than the average illness.
2. Females are more likely to be ill than males, but they are less likely to be disabled for long periods of time.

[8] Elizabeth A. Langford, "Medical Care Costs for the Aged: First Findings of the 1963 Survey of the Aged," *Social Security Bulletin*, XXVII, No. 7 (July, 1964), 4.

3. Disabling illnesses of all durations are more common among non-whites than whites.
4. Low-income groups suffer more frequent and more serious illnesses than the middle- and upper-income groups, but otherwise income does not appear to be an important factor.
5. Employed persons are, on the average, a much healthier group than the unemployed. Certain occupations are more hazardous than others, while some are associated with undesirable moral and economic characteristics.
6. The effect of a rural or urban residence upon the probability of illness is not clear, but the urban group appears to be more healthy.
7. Unmarried persons are more likely to be ill than married persons, especially at the older ages.
8. Illness is much more common in the winter than in the summer, primarily on account of the numerous short-term illnesses in the winter caused by mild respiratory diseases.

Causes of Illness [9]

According to National Health Survey interviews during 1964–65, acute conditions were responsible for about 8.3 days of restricted activity per person, about half of the average number of restricted-activity days reported. Data are not available on the contribution of the various chronic conditions to restricted-activity days but the number of days of restricted activity associated with the five major classes of acute conditions were as follows:

Respiratory conditions	3.6
Injuries	1.7
Infective and parasitic conditions	1.2
Digestive system conditions	.4
All other acute conditions	1.4

Among chronic conditions, it is known that the following cause the most important limitations of activity:

Heart disease
Arthritis and rheumatism
Impairment of vision.

Note that injuries account for only a small fraction of the restricted-activity days. Another fact which emphasizes the much more important role of sickness is that, of the 2.1 acute conditions affecting the average person, only about 0.3 were injuries. Less than one-fifth of the injuries

[9] For a more detailed analysis of the causes of illness than is possible here, see O. D. Dickerson, *Health Insurance* (Homewood, Ill.: Richard D. Irwin, Inc., 1959), pp. 30–38. rev. ed., 1963), pp. 43–58.

were work injuries. Clearly non-occupational illness is a much more important problem than occupational illness.[10]

TOTAL COSTS OF NON-OCCUPATIONAL ILLNESS

The Social Security Administration makes periodic estimates of (1) the aggregate loss of earning power due to temporary non-occupational disability and (2) private expenditures for medical care, except in workmen's compensation cases.[11]

Temporary non-occupational disability includes all disabilities lasting six months or less and the initial six months of disabilities which last longer. It is estimated that this form of disability causes the average wage and salary worker in private employment to lose about seven working days a year. Federal civilian employees lose about eight days, state and local government employees about 7.5 days, and self-employed persons about seven days. On this basis, the estimated income loss due to non-occupational short-term illness in 1964 was $10.2 billion. Ten years earlier the estimated loss was $6.1 billion.

It has also been estimated that temporary non-occupational disability is responsible for about one-fifth of the non-occupational disability income losses, partial disability accounting for about one-half and long-term total disability losses for the remainder.[12] If this estimate is cor-

[10] The 1935–36 National Health Survey also shed some light on the causes of illness. According to this survey, the six leading causes of illnesses disabling a person for a week or more and the per cent of disabling illness caused by them were as follows:

Respiratory diseases	30 per cent
Communicable diseases	17 per cent
Accidental injuries	9 per cent
Confinements	9 per cent
Degenerative diseases	9 per cent
Digestive diseases	8 per cent

Fortunately the causes of long-term disability were among the less frequent causes of disability. The following were associated with the longest average periods of disability:

Orthopedic impairments	344 days
Tuberculosis	246 days
Nervous and mental diseases	189 days
Cardiovascular-renal diseases	122 days
Rheumatism and allied diseases	120 days
Cancer and other tumors	100 days

[11] For the latest estimates, see the January issues of the *Social Security Bulletin*.

[12] Commission on Health Needs of the Nation, *Building America's Health*, IV (Washington, D. C.: U. S. Government Printing Office, 1952), 303. The complete report of five volumes summarizes the statistical findings of many studies.

Professor Dickerson has suggested that in 1961 temporary non-occupational disability accounted for almost 39 per cent of the total non-occupational disability, long-term total disability losses almost 40 per cent, and partial disability the remainder. See Dickerson, *op. cit.*, pp. 16–17.

rect, the total non-occupational disability income loss in 1964 was about $51 billion.

Private consumer expenditures for medical care in 1964 totaled almost $25 billion, or 5.7 per cent of disposable personal income.[13] Ten years earlier the estimated loss was about $12 billion or 4.5 per cent of disposable personal income. Of the $25 billion spent in 1964, about 30 per cent was incurred for hospital services, 27 per cent for physicians' services, 9 per cent for dentists' services, 3 per cent for other professional services, 18 per cent for drugs and drug sundries, 4 per cent for eyeglasses and appliances, 3 per cent for nursing home care, and 5 per cent for "net cost of insurance" (insurance premiums or charges less claim or benefit expenditures).[14] Hospital services and nursing home care have accounted for an increasing proportion of the expenditures during the past decade while the other components have decreased in relative importance.

Thus the total private cost of non-occupational illnesses in 1964 can be estimated at about $76 billion, or over $400 for each person in the civilian population. The aggregate loss to the economy is much greater because of many indirect effects, such as decreased efficiency, expenditures not included in the above totals (vendor payments by philanthropic organizations, industrial in-plant health services, and funds for construction of medical facilities), and about $9 billion in public expenditures for health service and supplies and for medical research and medical facilities construction.

METHODS OF ATTACKING THE PROBLEMS OF ILLNESS

The methods used to attack the problems created by non-occupational accidental injuries and sicknesses are preventive and alleviative, both private and public.

Preventive Efforts

The methods used to prevent premature death also help to reduce the number and duration of accidental injuries and sicknesses. Since these methods were discussed in Chapter 2, they need not be reconsidered here.[15] One preventive method that was not discussed in Chapter 2,

---

[13] For a discussion of the limitations of this estimate, see Oscar N. Serbein, *Paying for Medical Care in the United States* (New York: Columbia University Press, 1953), pp. 47–52.

[14] Whether part or all of this net cost of insurance is properly a cost of medical care is debatable. For example, part of this cost is incurred in order to make advance preparation for future medical expenses. See Dickerson, *op. cit.*, p. 23.

[15] Medical expense programs are considered to be alleviative programs in this discussion but they clearly have preventive aspects as well.

but which reduces the wage loss due to permanent disability, is vocational rehabilitation. Individuals, private non-profit agencies, insurers, employers, unions, and government have all been active in this area, as has been indicated in Chapter 10. Further expansion of these activities is needed and can be expected.

Alleviative Methods

The increasing industrialization of our society and the loosening of family ties have had an even greater effect upon the role of the sick and injured than they have had upon the dependents of deceased persons and the aged. The sick and injured can seldom be absorbed easily into some relative's household. They must either assume the loss themselves, collect insurance payments, or accept aid from outside sources.

Self-assumption is the most economical and most satisfactory way to meet losses that are small relative to the person's income, but insurance or outside aid is essential when the economic impact of the illness is serious. Thus, for the lower income groups, such aid is generally needed.

Voluntary private insurance is, by far, the most important private method of alleviating the financial burden of non-occupational illness. This method and the degree to which it provides protection against income losses and medical bills will be considered in detail in the next chapter. It will be sufficient here to note that although private protection has been expanded to cover many more persons in the past two decades and the quality of this protection has improved greatly, there is still a clear need for some form of public protection.

Public alleviative methods have been limited until recently to public assistance programs based upon need, the provision of medical facilities to deal with certain illnesses such as tuberculosis and mental disease, and programs benefiting special groups such as the armed services, veterans, Indians, and prison inmates. Until the 1954 authorization of the OASDI disability "freeze" and the 1956 addition of limited OASDI disability income benefits, which were liberalized in 1960 and 1965, the only social health insurance program covering the general public was that established by temporary disability insurance legislation in four states. The 1965 amendments to the Social Security Act also established two public medical expense insurance programs for the aged—Hospital Insurance and Supplementary Medical Insurance.

The United States has been slow to adopt public medical expense insurance programs and even today has a more limited program than many other nations for a number of reasons. Chief among these reasons are the potentially high costs involved, the greater subjectivity involved in administering a public health insurance plan than one covering death and old age, the rapid improvement in private protection, and the fear of many that freedom of choice of doctors would be restricted and the quality of medical care lowered. Nevertheless since 1954 the proponents of public health insurance have scored some important victories.

CURRENT PUBLIC ALLEVIATIVE APPROACHES

The most important public alleviative programs include (1) the public assistance plans providing medical care for the aged, income and medical care for families with dependent children, income and medical care for the blind, and income and medical care for the totally and permanently disabled; (2) medical facilities, principally hospitals, for the treatment of special diseases such as mental illness; (3) the disability freeze and disability income protection under OASDI; (4) temporary disability insurance legislation in four states; (5) Hospital Insurance; and (6) Supplementary Medical Insurance.

Public Assistance Programs

All levels of government participate in public assistance programs for needy persons in poor health. One major source of assistance has been the general assistance programs to be described in Chapter 13 and special medical funds, both of which are financed and administered at the state and local government level. Many states, cities, and counties operate general hospitals to help the needy.[16]

The public assistance program providing aid to families with dependent children that was described in Chapter 3 also provides some protection against loss of income caused by accidental injury or sickness because physical or mental incapacity of the parent may be the reason for the dependency. In addition medical care allowances may be included in the cash payments or there may be direct payments to vendors of medical services such as doctors and nursing homes. Protection against these losses, however, is only part of this program, less than one-fifth of the cases being attributable to physical or mental incapacity of the parent and only about 7 per cent of the total payments under the state plans being vendor payments for medical care. Attention here will be concentrated upon those categorical public assistance plans in which poor health plays a very prominent part. These plans include (1) *separate* programs providing (a) medical care for the aged, (b) aid to the blind, and (c) aid to the totally and permanently disabled and (2) more recently in-

---

[16] The federal government also provides some medical services for the needy but on a more limited scale; e.g., there are special programs for needy Indians and Eskimos.

troduced *combination* programs providing under one plan (a) aid for the aged, the blind, and the disabled or such aid and medical assistance for the aged, or (b) medical assistance for all four categories covered under the federal–state categorical public assistance plans. By 1970, all vendor payments for medical care are to be provided under this last combination medical assistance plan, which can be extended to cover children of *any* poor family.

Plans Providing Medical Care for the Aged. The first of these plans provides medical care for the aged. Like the aid-to-families-with-dependent-children program, the old-age assistance program described in Chapter 3 permits the inclusion of medical care allowances in the cash payments or direct payments to vendors of medical services. In 1960 Congress provided substantially liberalized federal grants to the states to enable them (1) to improve or establish medical care benefits under their old-age assistance plans and (2) to establish medical assistance plans for aged persons with limited resources who are not old-age assistance recipients. The grants have since been further increased.

Under the *program for those receiving old-age assistance,* if the states' average old-age assistance payment, including medical care benefits, exceeds the $75 maximum under the grant formula described in Chapter 3, the federal government pays 50–80 per cent (depending upon the state per capita income [17]) of (1) the average *vendor* payments for medical care up to $15 a month or (2) the amount by which the total average assistance benefit (cash maintenance and medical care benefits plus vendor medical payments) exceeds $75, *whichever is less.* For example, if a state has a total average assistance benefit of $100 including a $15 average vendor payment, the federal government will pay 50–80 per cent of $15. If the total average benefit were $80 instead of $100, the appropriate percentage would be applied to $5. If the state's total average payment is $75 or less, the federal government contributes an additional 15 per cent to the average vendor payments up to $15 a month.[18] This 15 per cent is in addition to the federal percentage of 50–65 per cent which, as described in Chapter 3, is applicable to that portion of the total average payment in excess of $37. The formula, therefore, favors vendor payments over cash payments for medical care.

---

[17] $1.00 - .50 \left[\dfrac{\text{State per capita income}}{\text{National per capita income}} \right]^2$ but not less than 50 per cent or more than 80 per cent.

[18] This approach is also available for states with average total monthly payments in excess of $75 if it would improve their position. To illustrate, a state with a high per capita income paying a total average benefit of $80, $15 of which consisted of vendor medical payments, would be better off under the 15 per cent approach. Such cases are unusual.

Participation in the program on the part of the states is optional. Subject to the basic minimum requirements established for federal approval in connection with old-age assistance, each participating state determines the nature and scope of the benefits as well as "reasonable" standards for determining eligibility for assistance and the extent of that assistance.

Under the *program for those not receiving old-age assistance* (called medical assistance for the aged), the federal government pays, in addition to half the administration costs, 50–80 per cent of the cost of the benefits, the exact percentage being computed under a formula based primarily on state per capita income.

Participation in this program is also optional. The basic minimum requirements for federal approval include those applicable to old-age assistance except that the state plan cannot exclude any current resident and, although the program is designed for medically indigent persons, there is no specific requirement that the state must consider an applicant's other income and resources, including aid from relatives, in determining his need for assistance. It is required in addition that the state (1) impose no enrollment fee or charge as a condition of eligibility, (2) furnish assistance to residents absent from the state under regulations prescribed by the Secretary of Health, Education, and Welfare, (3) establish "reasonable" standards consistent with the objectives of the program for determining eligibility for assistance and the extent of that assistance, and (4) impose no liens while the recipient lives nor make any recoveries from his estate until after the death of any surviving spouse.

Unlike the program for those receiving old-age assistance, the sections of the law establishing this separate program (1) specify a broad scope of medical services among which a state may choose and (2) require that the state plan include both institutional and non-institutional care. The medical services which may be provided are the following: in-patient hospital services; skilled nursing-home services; physicians' services; out-patient hospital or clinic services; home health-care services; private-duty nursing services; physical therapy and related services; dental services; laboratory and X-ray services; prescribed drugs, eyeglasses, dentures, and prosthetic devices; diagnostic screening, and preventive services; and any other medical care or remedial care recognized under state law.[19] It is clear that the restrictions imposed by this list are slight.

Under either of these two programs providing medical assistance for the aged or, in fact, under any of the public assistance vendor payment plans, the benefits may be payments for services rendered or for protection under some insurance or prepayment service plan. Other possible

---

[19] As under old-age assistance, however, the federal government does not participate under either medical assistance program in the cost of medical services furnished an inmate in a non-medical public institution.

arrangements include pooled funds administered by the state agency and prepayment agreements with state health departments. Combinations of these methods may also be used.

The law establishing the two programs also directs the Secretary of Health, Education, and Welfare to develop and maintain recommended standards concerning the level, content, and quality of medical services which the states may use in evaluating and improving their own programs. The Secretary is also to report on the scope and content of the state programs.

By April, 1964, all jurisdictions (the fifty states plus the District of Columbia, Guam, Puerto Rico, and the Virgin Islands), encouraged by the promise of additional federal financial participation under OAA, were making the necessary payments to suppliers of medical goods and services to OAA recipients. Fifteen of these jurisdictions (fourteen states plus Puerto Rico) had chosen one of the combination programs to be discussed below. Summarization of the remaining plans is difficult because of their diversity, but some comments can be made concerning the services provided and the methods of making the vendor payments.

The major types of services provided were in-patient hospital services, nursing home care, services by medical practitioners, dental care, and pharmaceutical services.[20] All but a few jurisdictions provided in-patient hospital services and nursing home care. Each of the other types of services was provided in at least forty jurisdictions.

The most common method of paying the suppliers of medical goods and services was to make direct payments to these suppliers for services rendered. About ten jurisdictions maintained a pooled fund into which deposits are made in behalf of all recipients and out of which bills are paid. A few states have made group prepayment arrangements with insurance companies or organizations of suppliers.

By August, 1965, all but eight jurisdictions had in operation medical-assistance-for-the-aged programs. Of the thirty-seven plans on which information was available in April, 1964, all provided hospital services. Each of the other types of benefits was provided in at least twenty-two jurisdictions, with services by medical practitioners being the second most common type of benefit. For example, the Minnesota program provided that an otherwise qualified applicant who had spent $200 for health care within the twelve months before the date of his application was entitled to hospital care, nursing home care, physicians' services, out-pa-

[20] For detailed information, see U. S. Department of Health, Education, and Welfare, Welfare Administration, Bureau of Family Services, *Characteristics of State Public Assistance Plans Under the Social Security Act, Provisions for Medical and Remedial Care*, Public Assistance Report No. 49 (Washington, D. C.: U. S. Government Printing Office, 1964).

tient and clinic care, home-health care, private-duty nursing service, physical therapy, dental care, laboratory and X-ray services, drugs, eyeglasses, dentures and prosthetic devices, and diagnostic servicing and preventive devices. The $200 deductible was waived if the applicant and his spouse could not reasonably pay this amount. Gross annual income had to be less than $1,800 for a single applicant and $2,400 for a couple; real property holdings had to be under $15,000, liquid assets under $1,000. Not included in these limitations were household goods, furniture, wearing apparel, burial lots, and some life insurance cash values ($1,000, if single; $1,000 for each of two married persons).

As in the case of OAA, vendor payments were usually made directly to suppliers, but a few jurisdictions used pooled funds or group prepayment arrangements.

Both of these programs have been greatly affected by Hospital Insurance and Supplementary Medical Insurance for the aged. Since the middle of 1966, when the insurance programs started paying benefits, these public assistance programs have been concerned primarily with filling the gaps in the insurance protection and in paying the $3 monthly premium for SMI. By 1970 these programs must be replaced by the combination medical assistance plan described below.

Plans Providing Aid to the Blind. All states (plus the District of Columbia, Guam, Puerto Rico, and the Virgin Islands) have plans providing aid to the blind that have been approved under the Social Security Act. The requirements for federal approval are essentially the same as those established for old-age assistance plans. One unique requirement is that the state agency *must* disregard the first $85 per month of earned income plus one half of the excess. Under OAA the state *may* disregard a much smaller amount of earned income; it was not permitted to disregard any of such income until the 1962 amendments to the Social Security Act.

Over three-fifths of the plans have no age requirement, the usual minimum ages under the other plans being sixteen or eighteen. Almost nine-tenths of the plans have no citizenship requirement. About one-third of the plans use the residence requirement established by the federal government for approval, but almost one-half simply require that the person be a resident of the state for one year preceding his application for benefits. A few states have no residence requirement; some waive their residence requirement if the recipient lost his sight while a resident of the state. Almost all plans limit the property which a recipient may possess, the limits varying greatly with respect to the type and amount of property. A need for assistance is generally presumed to exist if the income or other resources are insufficient to provide a reasonable subsistence compatible with decency and health. About one-fourth of the plans have legal maximum benefits, but almost half have no maximum benefits. Commonly there is no provision for recovery of the amounts paid, but under many plans the state has a claim against the estate.

The federal government computes its share of the expenditures under the aid-to-the-blind programs in the same way that it determines the amount that it will contribute to approved state old-age assistance programs. This formula was discussed on pages 88–89.

Like the old-age programs, the aid-to-the-blind plans have been liberalized from time to time. It is easier to qualify for a benefit now than it was in the thirties, and the benefits are more adequate.

Plans Providing Aid to the Permanently and Totally Disabled. All jurisdictions except Nevada have federally approved plans providing aid to the permanently and totally disabled. In order to be approved, these programs must satisfy essentially the same requirements as the aid-to-the-blind programs. The disability assistance programs are of special interest because they were not authorized until 1950.

All plans have a minimum age requirement of eighteen years; almost half also have a maximum age requirement of sixty-five. A person under eighteen is assumed not to have suffered an income loss, while a person over sixty-five may be eligible for old-age assistance. Almost nine-tenths of the plans have no citizenship requirement. Almost six-tenths of the plans have a durational residence requirement of one year preceding the date of application. About one-fifth require in addition that the person be a resident in five of the last nine years, but the remaining one-fifth have no residence requirement. All plans take income and property into account in determining the need for assistance, with almost all plans having specific property limitations. Legal maximum benefits are found in about one-fourth of the plans but almost half have no maximum. Over half of the plans do not provide for recovery of the amounts paid but more often than under aid-to-the-blind programs, the total assistance constitutes a claim against the estate of the recipient.

The federal government's contribution to these programs is computed in the same way as under the aid-to-the-blind programs.

The federal grants have been increased and the disability programs considerably liberalized in the short time the plans have been in existence.

Combination Plans Providing Aid to the Aged, Blind, and Disabled. As noted on page 91, the 1962 amendments to the Social Security Act provided for the combination of OAA, AB, and APTD or these three programs and medical assistance for the aged into one program. The requirements for federal approval of these combination plans are the same as the requirements for the separate plans except for the additional requirements that there be a common standard of assistance for OAA, AB, and APTD recipients under the single category. However, the program can recognize the special needs identified with blindness or disability.

The two incentives for adopting a combination plan are that (1) the *average* benefit under all three basic maintenance programs combined is used to determine the amount of federal financial participation and (2) the extra federal contribution under OAA toward the cost of vendor payments for medical care is extended to AB and APTD.

By August, 1965, fifteen jurisdictions had adopted such combination plans.

Combination Plans Providing Medical Assistance for the Aged, Blind, and Disabled and for Dependent Children. The 1965 amendments to the Social Security Act established a new program of medical assistance, which is designed to replace (1) medical assistance for the aged and (2) the vendor payments for medical care under OAA, AFDC, AB, and APTD, and under the combination program for the aged, the blind, and the disabled. Participation in this program is optional, but by 1970 states must have a program of this sort if they wish federal financial participation in payments to suppliers of medical care.

Persons eligible for basic maintenance under the four categorical assistance programs must be made eligible for benefits under this combination program. Persons who are only medically needy *may* be included, but if they are to be eligible, comparable requirements should apply to all four categories of persons under this program. Through a provision that *other* medically needy children can also be included, the program can be extended to cover a new category of recipients. No age requirement is permitted that would exclude any person over age sixty-five or under age twenty-one. The program cannot contain a rigid income test that would deny assistance to persons with large medical bills. No income can be imputed to any individual unless it is actually available. Finally, relatives' responsibility may be considered only if the applicant is the relative's spouse or his child under age twenty-one.

Services that must be provided under this program,[21] if it is to receive federal approval, include in-patient hospital services, out-patient hospital services, other laboratory and X-ray services, skilled nursing home services (for recipients aged twenty-one or over), and physicians' services at home, in the doctor's office, or at a hospital or a skilled nursing home. No deductible or other cost-sharing charge may be imposed for the hospitalization services; such charges are permitted on the other services, but they must bear a reasonable relationship to the recipient's income or resources. In keeping with this principle, elderly recipients

[21] MAA is the only other program with minimum benefit requirements for federal approval.

eligible for the Hospital Insurance benefits described on pages 400–02 must receive assistance in meeting the deductibles and other cost-sharing charges under that program.

The formula for determining the amount of federal participation resembles the MAA formula. There is no maximum on the amount of expenditures in which the federal government will participate. States will be reimbursed for 50–83 per cent of their payments to recipients, depending upon their per capita income, which is more liberal for most states than the 50–80 per cent payable under MAA since a state with per capita income equal to the U. S. average gets 55 per cent instead of 50 per cent, and all states with lower-than-average per capita income also get more than under MAA, as do some higher-than-average states.[22] The states will also be reimbursed for 75 per cent of the cost of compensating and training professional medical personnel and for 50 per cent of other administrative costs. The purpose of the additional federal funds is to improve benefits to recipients, not to reduce state dollar costs. Consequently, the law provides that only those states that maintain their own expenditures at their present level will receive the additional federal funds provided under the new formula. The law also states in Title XIX, Section 1903 (e) that federal funds are not to be paid unless "the State makes a satisfactory showing that it is making efforts in the direction of broadening the scope of the coverage and services made available under the plan and in the direction of liberalizing the eligibility requirements for medical assistance with a view toward furnishing by July 1, 1975, comprehensive care and services to substantially all individuals who meet the plan's eligibility standards with respect to income and resources, including services to enable such individuals to attain or retain independence or self-care." This passage has been interpreted to mean that by 1975 this program will provide medical assistance for substantially all medically needy persons.

By 1966 several states had already adopted a combined program of this sort and some were providing medical assistance for children who would not qualify under AFDC. The New York program, which has the most liberal eligibility requirements established at this writing, provides that generally a family of four with one wage earner can receive benefits if its annual income less income taxes and health insurance premiums is $6,000 or less. Savings up to $3,000 and life insurance with a face value of $1,000 for each member of the family need not be used by the family. About one-third of the state's residents may qualify under these condi-

---

[22] The proportion, which is bounded by 50 per cent and 83 per cent, is determined as follows:

$$\text{Proportion} = 1.00 - .45 \left[\frac{\text{State per capita income}}{\text{National per capita income}} \right]^2$$

tions. The benefits include hospital, doctors', dental, nursing, and other health services as well as drugs and appliances.

Operations. The operations of MAA, AB, and APTD as separate programs or as parts of a combined program are summarized in Table 11.2. Because medical assistance for the aged was not established until 1960, only limited data are available on this program but its rapid growth is striking. Until 1958, when the trend was reversed, the number of recipients of aid to the blind increased slowly but steadily, except during World War II when blind persons re-entered active employment in large numbers. Recipients of aid to the permanently and totally disabled have increased more than eightfold in the sixteen years that such aid has been available. The average monthly benefits under both AB and APTD have increased as the cost of living rose and the plans became more liberal.

TABLE 11.2

Assistance Programs Providing Medical Assistance for the Aged,
Aid to the Blind, and Aid to the Permanently and Totally Disabled:
Recipients, Total Payments, and Average Monthly Payments, by Program,
1936–65

(INCLUDES PAYMENTS FOR MEDICAL CARE)

Year	Recipients * (in thousands)			Total Payments (in millions)			Average Monthly Payment *		
	Medical Assistance For The Aged	Aid to the Blind	Aid to the Permanently and Totally Disabled	Medical Assistance For The Aged	Aid to the Blind	Aid to the Permanently and Totally Disabled	Medical Assistance For The Aged	Aid to the Blind	Aid to the Permanently and Totally Disabled
1936	—	45	—	—	$12.8	—	—	$26.11	—
1938	—	67	—	—	19.0	—	—	25.22	—
1940	—	73	—	—	21.8	—	—	25.38	—
1942	—	79	—	—	24.7	—	—	26.54	—
1944	—	72	—	—	25.3	—	—	29.31	—
1946	—	77	—	—	30.7	—	—	36.67	—
1948	—	86	—	—	41.4	—	—	43.54	—
1950	—	98	69	—	52.9	$ 8.1	—	46.56	$45.41
1952	—	99	164	—	61.3	90.9	—	54.91	53.50
1954	—	102	224	—	67.8	137.1	—	56.37	54.93
1956	—	107	269	—	77.0	176.7	—	63.15	58.82
1958	—	110	328	—	87.4	228.2	—	68.29	62.59
1960	15	108	374	$ 5.4	94.2	288.2	$195.84	73.17	67.64
1962	110	100	437	245.9	93.9	360.9	205.18	80.16	73.51
1964	225	96	527	447.6	98.1	474.8	196.87	85.77	80.60
1965	279	95	575	588.8	97.8	561.2	189.73	92.00	87.27

° December of each year.

Sources: *Social Security Bulletin, Annual Statistical Supplement*, 1963, pp. 114–15, and *Social Security Bulletins*.

In 1965 about one-eighth of the total payments under the aid-to-the-blind plans were vendor payments for medical care, while about one-quarter of the total payments under the plans providing aid to the permanently and totally disabled were used for this purpose. Payments to suppliers of medical care accounted for about one-fifth of the OAA payments.

The number of recipients and the total payments under these programs should increase less rapidly in the future and may eventually decrease because (1) disability benefits under OASDI were liberalized in 1965, (2) a Hospital Insurance system and a Supplementary Medical Insurance system were established to provide medical care for the aged, and (3) part of the past increase in the number of APTD and MAA recipients has been caused by the adoption of new state programs and a backlog of eligible cases.

The number of recipients of aid to the permanently and totally disabled is about 0.5 per cent of the population aged eighteen to sixty-four. Variations among the states are great, however. The same is true of average monthly payments and the federal share of the costs of the programs.[23] The average share of the federal government is about 57 per cent. MAA recipients constitute about 1½ per cent of the aged population but this proportion is as high as 5 per cent in some states. Nationwide the federal share of expenditures under this program is about 51 per cent.

Evaluation. The public assistance programs providing aid to the aged (other than medical assistance for the aged) and dependent children were evaluated in Chapter 3, which should be reread because the remarks apply to all public assistance programs. Three additional observations apply to the programs discussed in this chapter.

First, the blind have been singled out for separate and more liberal treatment than totally and permanently disabled persons who are not blind. In part this is due to the more objective tests that are possible; in part it is due to the prevailing attitude in our country toward the blind. In fairness to the other groups, some observers suggest that we explore the possibility of absorbing the aid-to-the-blind programs into those for the totally and permanently disabled.

Second, the combination programs, which are gradually replacing the separate programs, should result in more economical, efficient, and equi-

[23] For detailed information, see *Social Security Bulletins*, the *Annual Statistical Supplement* and U. S. Department of Health, Education, and Welfare, Welfare Department, Bureau of Family Services, Division of Program Statistics and Analyses release dated June 17, 1965, *Source of Funds Expected for Public Assistance Payments, Calendar Year Ended December 31, 1964.*

table operations. By 1970 all vendor payments for medical care must be provided under one consolidated program in each state. This combination may also cause indirectly a more careful consideration of the relative adequacy of the basic maintenance provided under separate programs.

Third, many needy persons who suffer an income loss due to disability, medical expenses, or both, are not eligible for benefits under the federally supported special programs. Consequently, it has been suggested that (1) eligibility requirements under the special public assistance programs be extended to include more bona fide cases of disability and that (2) medical expense benefits be provided for all indigent and medically indigent. The Title XIX combination medical assistance program may provide such protection by 1975. However, this extended program will have to be strictly administered, so as to prevent abuses and accomplish its purpose. Many persons who support such an extended program believe that the eligibility requirements under the New York program are too liberal. As these programs increase in scope, it is possible that more use will be made of group prepayment arrangements.

Special Hospitals

Most of the hospitals dealing specifically with nervous and mental diseases, tuberculosis, and other special diseases are operated by the government, state hospitals being particularly important in this area. The services in these hospitals are either provided free on a non-needs basis or there is a relatively small charge for persons who can afford to pay. Because of this hybrid feature, these hospitals are listed between the public assistance programs discussed previously and the social insurance and related programs which are described next. One reason for the more liberal public attitude toward persons with these illnesses is the belief that the public benefits directly from the treatment of these conditions. One indication of the importance of these hospitals is that about two-thirds of the 1.7 million hospital beds in the United States are governmental and more than half of the governmentally owned beds are in mental, tuberculosis, and veterans' hospitals.

OASDI Disability Benefits

Disability benefits were included under OASDI for the first time in 1954 and extended in 1956, 1958, 1960, and 1965, although many persons had advocated their inclusion as early as the thirties. The disability benefits are the disability freeze, disability income payments, and income payments for disabled children.

Disability Freeze. In order to qualify for the disability freeze benefit, a person must (1) be fully insured and (2) have at least twenty quarters of coverage out of the last forty quarters, including the quarter in which he becomes disabled. These requirements make it more difficult to qualify for disability benefits than for survivorship benefits and thus reduce the cost of the program. In addition to meeting these requirements, (1) the person must have been unable to engage in *any* substantially gainful activity because of a physical or mental impairment for at least six consecutive months and (2) this impairment must be expected to result in death or continue for at least twelve calendar months.

Blindness is assumed to cause this degree of disability even if the person is able to work. Special insured status requirements also apply to the blind. Persons who are disabled by blindness before they reach age thirty-one are considered insured if half the quarters elapsing after the quarter in which they attain age twenty-one and before the quarter in which they are disabled are quarters of coverage. In order to maintain a minimum requirement of six quarters, persons becoming disabled before age twenty-four must have quarters of coverage in half the twelve quarters preceding the quarter of disability.

The disability freeze benefit protects a fully or currently insured worker against losing this status or having his benefit reduced as a result of a period of total and permanent disability. In determining whether a person is fully or currently insured, any calendar quarter, part of which falls in a period of disability, may be excluded. In determining the average monthly earnings, any calendar year, any part of which was included in a period of disability, may be excluded. However, in both determinations the exclusions are made only if this will benefit the applicant.

To illustrate the application of these requirements and rules, consider the following example. Assume that a person reaches age sixty-five in February, 1972. In order to be fully insured on that date he must have twenty-one quarters of coverage (i.e., quarters of coverage equal to the number of years elapsing between December 31, 1950, and January 1, 1972). If this person had worked in covered employment since January, 1963, and had earned four quarters of coverage each year, but became totally disabled on January 1, 1968, he would have earned only twenty quarters of coverage. If it were not for the disability freeze, he would not be entitled to any retirement benefits in 1972. However, he does qualify for the freeze because at the time of his disability he was fully insured and had at least twenty quarters out of the last forty quarters. Because of the freeze, he is entitled to retirement benefits, since the quarters between December 31, 1967, and January 1, 1972, do not count as elapsed time. He has twenty quarters of coverage but only seventeen years have elapsed. Moreover, because of the freeze, the average monthly wage will be computed on the basis of the earnings and the number of months between December 31, 1950, and January 1, 1968, less the five calendar years of lowest earnings.

Disability Income Payments. In order to qualify for disability income payments commencing six months after the disability begins, the person must satisfy the eligibility requirements for the disability freeze. Unlike the situation with respect to the disability freeze, blindness is not *assumed* to cause total disability. However, a blind person between the ages of fifty-five and sixty-five is considered disabled so long as he is unable, because of blindness, to engage in substantially gainful activity requiring skills or abilities comparable to those required in his former occupations. Although the courts have favored a more liberal interpretation, the law states that other disabled persons must be unable to engage in *any* substantially gainful activity.

The monthly payments are equal to the primary insurance amount to which the person would be entitled if he were sixty-five years of age. The payments stop at age sixty-five when the person qualifies for retirement benefits or, if earlier, two months after the end of the month in which the disability ceases. Dependents' benefits are paid under essentially the same conditions and in the same amounts as the benefits paid to the dependents of retired workers.

Several provisions are aimed at removing deterrents to the rehabilitation of disabled beneficiaries. First, all applicants are to be promptly referred to their state vocational rehabilitation agency and benefits are withheld if an applicant refuses without good cause to accept services offered by that agency. Second, persons who return to work under any kind of rehabilitation plan or are rehabilitating themselves are paid benefits during a nine-month trial period as long as they do not recover medically from their disability. If, after the close of the trial period, the worker demonstrates an ability to engage in substantially gainful activity, his benefits terminate three months later. Third, the six-month waiting period requirement does not apply to persons who again become disabled within five years after the termination of disability insurance benefits or an earlier period of disability. Finally, state vocational rehabilitation agencies have since 1965 received payments from the disability insurance trust fund for the cost of rehabilitation services furnished by them to selected disability income recipients.

If a disabled worker is also entitled to workmen's compensation benefits because of an occupational injury or disease, his OASDI benefit is reduced in those months in which the total combined OASDI and workmen's compensation benefits otherwise payable to him and his dependents would exceed 80 per cent of his earnings prior to his disability, subject to an adjustment for changes in national earnings levels. If these combined benefits would exceed this percentage, the OASDI benefits will be reduced by the excess. For this purpose, the worker's average monthly earnings are defined as his average monthly earnings in covered employment during his five consecutive years of highest earnings after 1950 unless the average monthly earnings used to compute his disability benefits are higher, in which case they are used.

Income Payments to Disabled Children. If a child has been totally disabled since before he reached eighteen, is unmarried, and either (1) is dependent upon a parent, step-parent, or adopting parent who is entitled to OASDI retirement benefits or (2) was dependent upon a parent and was entitled to OASDI survivorship benefits, he may receive the appropriate OASDI child's insurance benefit even though he may be now eighteen years of age or more.

For example, a fully insured worker, aged thirty-two, has a son, aged six, who is totally disabled. If the worker should die during the next year, the mother and son would receive survivorship benefits until the son reached eighteen. Because of the disability provisions, the son's benefit would then be continued for life and the mother's benefit would be continued as long as he remained in her care. On the other hand, if the father should live to age sixty-five, the son would receive a child's benefit at that time, although he would then be thirty-nine years of age. There would also be a mother's benefit if the child was in her care.

Financing. The OASDI payroll tax covers the costs of these disability benefits. To meet the costs of the *income* benefits for disabled workers, their wives, and their children, the OASDI contribution rates applied to the first $6,600 of earnings include a 0.35 per cent tax on employees and on employers and a 0.525 per cent tax on self-employed persons. Unlike the remainder of the OASDI contributions, which, in addition to supporting the old-age and survivorship benefits, finance the disability benefits other than the disability income payments, the 0.35 per cent and the 0.525 per cent rates are not scheduled to increase.

The additional taxes collected for this purpose are appropriated to the Disability Insurance Trust Fund, which operates in essentially the same fashion as the OASI Trust Fund discussed in Chapter 4. The progress of this trust fund is discussed below.

Administration. The most important problem in the administration of the disability benefits is determining whether the applicant is totally disabled and whether this disability is likely to last at least twelve months. Almost all disability determinations are made by state agencies (where possible, state vocational rehabilitation agencies) under agreements between the states and the Secretary of Health, Education, and Welfare. The Bureau of Disability Insurance makes determinations only for persons living outside the United States and a few other cases specifically excluded from state jurisdiction. State agencies are used most often because it is assumed that these agencies have had more experience in this area than the federal agency and to facilitate rehabilitation contacts with the disabled persons.

In order to promote uniformity among the states, the Bureau of Disability Insurance sets standards to guide the state agencies. The Bureau also reviews the state determinations for consistency and for conformity with the national standards and checks on such matters as age, insured status, and dependency status. The Bureau cannot as part of this review process reverse a state finding that no disability exists; it *can* find that *no* disability exists. However, if the applicant appeals a state determination of no disability, the state determination may be reversed by the hearing examiner or the Bureau of Hearings and Appeals of the Social Security Administration. Decisions at this level may in turn be appealed to the federal courts.[24]

Trends. When disability benefits were first added to OASDI in 1954, they were limited to the disability freeze. Furthermore, only disabilities that were expected to result in death or continue for a long indefinite period qualified a person for this benefit. The disability income payments and the income payments to disabled children were added in 1956, but no disability income payments were made until the worker was at least fifty years of age. Workmen's compensation benefits, if any, were deducted from the OASDI payments. Dependents of disabled workers first became eligible for benefits under the 1958 amendments and at the same time the deduction for workmen's compensation benefits was eliminated. The requirement that the disabled worker be at least age fifty before he started to receive benefits was dropped in 1960. The 1965 amendments liberalized the definition of disability to the present requirement and introduced the current treatment of workmen's compensation benefits.

Operations. Because of the rapid introduction of new or more liberal benefits described above, the increases in the number and the amount of benefits since 1960 have been substantial. Table 11.3 presents information for 1957–1965 on the rapid growth in the number of persons receiving OASDI disability income benefits (at the end of each year) classified by type of recipient, the total monthly payments to each class of

[24] For more details on the administration of these benefits, see Arthur E. Hess, "Five Years of Disability Insurance Benefits: A Progress Report," *Social Security Bulletin*, XXV, No. 7 (July, 1962), 3–14.

recipient, and the average monthly benefits in current benefit status. The average monthly benefits have remained fairly stable because there was no change in the formula used to determine the primary insurance amount from 1958 to 1964. The average benefit increased because of the 1965 amendments.

TABLE 11.3

Old-Age, Survivors, and Disability Insurance:
Number of Disability Income Beneficiaries at End of Year,
Monthly Benefits Received, and Average Benefit Received,
by Type of Recipient, 1957–65

(Numbers in Thousands; Amounts in Millions)

Year	Disabled Workers			Dependent Spouses			Dependent Children		
	Number	Amount	Average Benefit	Number	Amount	Average Benefit	Number	Amount	Average Benefit
1957	150	$10.9	$72.76	—	—	—	—	—	—
1958	238	19.5	82.10	12	$0.4	$33.95	18	$ 0.5	$27.28
1959	334	29.8	89.00	48	1.7	36.05	78	2.4	30.95
1960	455	40.7	89.31	77	2.6	34.41	155	4.7	30.21
1961	618	55.4	89.59	118	3.9	33.09	291	8.5	29.13
1962	741	66.7	89.99	147	4.8	32.41	387	11.1	28.56
1963	827	74.9	90.59	168	5.4	32.23	457	13.0	28.39
1964	894	81.5	91.12	179	5.8	32.23	490	14.0	28.48
1965	968	96.6	97.76	193	6.8	34.96	558	17.6	31.61

Source: *Social Security Bulletins.*

Because of the reduction in the number of quarters required for fully insured status, the disability freeze is much less important in preserving this status for disabled workers than it was in 1954. On the other hand, the freeze continues to increase old-age and survivorship benefits for disabled persons by freezing their earnings records. At the close of 1955 almost 29,000 persons were receiving higher benefits because of the disability freeze; by the close of 1963 this number had increased to over 419,000 persons.[25]

During the period 1955–1963 disability allowances were granted to about 1.7 million workers but denied to about 1.3 million others. The proportion of denials to allowances has tended to decrease over time, the allowances in 1963 being 224,229 persons and the denials 146,325. The leading causes of disability among those granted benefits in 1963 were diseases of the circulatory system (29.6 per cent), diseases of the nervous system and sense organs (14.6 per cent), neoplasms (11.2 per cent), mental, psychoneurotic, and personality disorders (10.9 per cent), diseases of the bones and organs of movement (9.7 per cent), and diseases of the

[25] *Social Security Bulletin, Annual Statistical Supplement,* 1963, p. 87.

respiratory system (8.5 per cent).[26] Among the 146,325 denials, about 78 per cent failed to meet the medical standards for disability.[27] About 12 per cent were not disabled at the latest time they satisfied the quarters of coverage requirement. About 4 per cent failed to furnish sufficient evidence and another 4 per cent met the medical standards but were able to engage in substantially gainful activity. The remaining 2 per cent were denied benefits for still other reasons.

TABLE 11.4

Receipts, Expenditures, and Assets of DI Trust Fund,
1957–65

(IN MILLIONS)

	Receipts		Expenditures		
Year	Net Tax Contributions *	Interest	Benefit Payments †	Administrative Expenses	Total Assets
1957	$ 702	$ 7	$ 57	$ 3	$ 649
1958	966	25	249	12	1,379
1959	913	40	457	50	1,825
1960	1,015	53	568	36	2,289
1961	1,038	66	892	64	2,437
1962	1,046	68	1,116	66	2,368
1963	1,099	66	1,230	67	2,235
1964	1,154	64	1,328	79	2,047
1965	1,188	59	1,597	90	1,606

* Includes transfers from the railroad retirement account to the disability insurance trust fund in 1959 ($22 million) and 1960 ($5 million).

† Includes transfers from the disability insurance trust fund to the railroad retirement account from 1961 to 1965. The transfer in 1961 was $5 million and in 1965 $24 million.

Sources: *Social Security Bulletin, Annual Statistical Supplement,* 1963, p. 30. *Social Security Bulletin,* XXIX, No. 4 (April, 1966), p. 51.

The progress of the Disability Insurance Trust Fund since its formation is shown in Table 11.4. The decline in the trust fund assets, which started in 1962, has been explained by the fact that benefits have not been terminated by death or recovery as rapidly as had been originally assumed.[28] Consequently the Board of Trustees recommended that the contributions allocated to this trust fund be increased. Accordingly the

[26] *Ibid.*, p. 99.
[27] *Ibid.*, p. 105.
[28] Robert J. Myers and Francisco Bayo, "Hospital Insurance, Supplementary Medical Insurance, and Old-Age, Survivors, and Disability Insurance: Financing Basis Under the 1965 Amendments," *Social Security Bulletin,* XXVIII, No. 10 (October, 1965), 19.

original .25 per cent tax imposed on employers and on employees and the .375 tax on self-employed persons were raised to the present levels by the 1965 amendments. Some of the increase, of course, was also necessitated by the liberalizations in the disability provisions as a result of those same amendments.

The estimated progress of the Disability Insurance Trust Fund under the 1965 benefit and contribution levels is presented in Table 11.5. Except for the fact that assumptions concerning disability rates play a more prominent role in the results, the assumptions and the methodology are the same as those discussed earlier in conjunction with Table 4.6. Note that according to the intermediate-cost assumptions the decline in the trust fund would be reversed in 1966.

Under the low-cost estimate, the benefits were expected to increase to .65 per cent of taxable payroll by 2040. The equivalent high-cost and intermediate-cost estimates were .86 per cent and .73 per cent respectively. The level-contribution rate (see pp. 146–47) required to keep the system self-supporting to at least 2040 was .60 per cent under the low-cost assumptions, .78 per cent under the high-cost estimates, and .67 per cent under the intermediate-cost assumptions. Because the level-equivalent of the present contribution schedule is .70 per cent, there is an estimated favorable actuarial balance of .03 per cent according to the intermediate-cost estimate. As noted on p. 147, the actuarial balance for the total OASDI system is $-.07$ per cent, the actuarial balance for OASI being $-.10$ per cent. This $-.07$ per cent is less than the $-.10$ per cent within which the system is considered to be substantially in actuarial balance.

Evaluation. Few persons object to the inclusion of the disability freeze benefits under OASDI, but some persons were and are still strongly opposed to the addition of any disability income payments. Others are not opposed to some limited disability income payments, but they believe that the benefits have been liberalized too rapidly. They are particularly concerned about the 1965 change in the definition of disability. Many private insurers are in this category. They argue that what was formerly a limited total and permanent disability insurance program has been replaced by liberal "temporary" disability benefits. Consequently the market for private disability insurance, particularly long-term disability income insurance, has been considerably reduced. Situations have also been created in which the OASDI benefit plus outstanding private insurance benefits, which cannot be reduced because they have been guaranteed under a contract, will approach or exceed the income lost.

At the other extreme are those who would favor reducing still further the twelve-month requirement to, say, three or six months and changing

TABLE 11.5

Estimated Progress of DI Trust Fund Under 1965 Act,
Low-Cost, High-Cost, and Intermediate-Cost Estimates

(IN MILLIONS)

Calendar Year	Receipts		Expenditures		Assets at End of Year
	Net Tax Contributions *	Interest †	Benefit Payments ‡	Administrative Expenses	
		Low-Cost Estimate			
1975	$2,300	$ 201	$1,886	$ 94	$ 5,911
1980	2,516	311	2,050	95	8,986
1990	2,978	655	2,283	94	18,647
2000	3,547	1,252	2,723	103	35,267
		High-Cost Estimate			
1975	$2,200	$ 55	$2,157	$112	$ 1,824
1980	2,257	36	2,372	117	1,217
1990	2,600	**	2,661	120	**
2000	2,919	**	3,091	137	**
		Intermediate-Cost Estimate			
1965	$1,187	$ 51	$1,624	$ 85	$ 1,576
1966	1,821	49	1,759	102	1,585
1967	2,048	52	1,856	108	1,721
1968	2,132	58	1,919	112	1,880
1969	2,207	64	1,984	115	2,052
1970	2,282	70	2,039	119	2,246
1971	2,356	78	2,094	122	2,464
1972	2,433	87	2,145	125	2,714
1975	2,250	121	2,022	103	3,834
1980	2,436	166	2,211	106	5,177
1990	2,789	291	2,472	107	8,965
2000	3,233	509	2,907	120	15,443
2025	4,009	1,113	3,970	156	33,236

* Includes payments to the trust fund from the Railroad Retirement account. Under all three estimates, some small payments are expected from about 1975 on.

† On rates of 3.75 per cent under the low-cost estimate, 3.25 per cent under the high-cost estimate, and 3.50 per cent under the intermediate-cost estimate.

‡ Includes payments up to about 1975 from the trust fund to the Railroad Retirement account.

** Fund exhausted in 1986.

Source: Robert J. Myers and Francisco Bayo, "Hospital Insurance, Supplementary Medical Insurance, and Old-Age, Survivors, and Disability Insurance: Financing Basis Under the 1965 Amendments," *Social Security Bulletin*, XXVIII, No. 10 (October, 1965), 23–24.

the "any substantially gainful activity" requirement to a more liberal standard.

A more moderate position accepts the 1965 liberalization as a way of including more bona fide cases of serious disability. Those who hold this view foresee further liberalizations later, but they believe that only serious disability income losses should be covered under the system and that further significant liberalizations should come only after the impacts of the 1965 changes have been carefully analyzed. The variables in the costing process are too subject to error to permit rash experimentation. Many moderates, however, would support a liberalization in the eligibility requirements for young disabled workers. The special treatment of young blind workers provides a precedent for such a change. Other extensions that are receiving serious consideration would provide benefits for a dependent child who becomes disabled after he reaches age eighteen, for dependent parents of disabled workers, and for a widow who is disabled at the time of her husband's death, before her youngest child reaches eighteen, or within a limited period after either of these events.

One of the reasons that some of the early opposition to disability income payments has disappeared is that, unlike the expectations of many opponents and proponents, the system has been tightly administered.

The emphasis on rehabilitation in the system is highly commendable but a much smaller proportion of disabled persons actually receives rehabilitation services than expected. A large proportion claim that they are not aware of the existence of such services.[29]

The removal of the deduction for workmen's compensation benefits in 1958 generated a storm of protest from many quarters. The major reason for the elimination of this deduction apparently was the belief that the worker should not lose the benefits to which he had contributed and that in most states the combined benefit would still be considerably less than the income loss. However, as a result of the removal of this deduction, it became possible in some states for a seriously injured worker to receive combined benefits that would exceed his wages prior to his disability. With the liberalized definition of disability now in effect, this problem could have become more significant in the years ahead. Some observers also feared that by overlapping workmen's compensation benefits, the federal OASDI system was encroaching upon state workmen's compen-

---

[29] In a 1960 survey, only 7 per cent of the disability income beneficiaries and 28 per cent of the workers with a disability freeze had received such services. Eighty-seven per cent of the disability income beneficiaries and 73 per cent of the workers with a disability freeze did not know about these services. On the other hand, young men tend to seek these services more often than older persons, and since 1960 the young have become a larger proportion of the disabled. Donald S. Frank, "Disabled Workers and Rehabilitation Services," *Social Security Bulletin*, XXVI, No. 6 (June, 1963), 3–6.

sation legislation and might eventually supplant the state programs. If this were to happen, according to these observers, the role of the states and of private insurers would be reduced, workers would have to contribute to the cost of industrial accidents, the incentive provided by experience rating for loss prevention would disappear, and the employers' liability approach might be reintroduced to provide additional benefits. The reinstatement of this deduction in 1965, whenever the combined OASDI and workmen's compensation benefits exceed 80 per cent of the worker's average monthly earnings prior to his disability, represents a compromise approach to this problem. When the disabled person's savings in taxes and work expenses are considered, the maximum possible benefit might still be attractive relative to wages, but the seriously disabled person may incur many extra expenses and relatively few will obtain this maximum benefit. The problem is much less acute than it was formerly. One strong supporter of workmen's compensation has argued that through this provision Congress "reversed the course upon which it embarked in 1958. . . . Congress has said that it does not want to take over the state system by legislative fiat. But, it also has said that it wants disabled workers to be compensated adequately, and it has provided a built-in mechanism for the Social Security system to pick up the slack if the states default on their responsibilities." [30]

Temporary Disability Insurance Legislation

Historical Development. Only four states—Rhode Island, California, New Jersey, and New York—have laws providing cash payments for employees who are *temporarily* disabled because of an accidental injury or sickness.[31] This legislation is aimed *primarily* at the economic problems associated with *non-occupational* illnesses; but three of the laws pay benefits in certain cases *when the illness is job-connected;* here the subject matter might have been discussed in the last two chapters were it not for complexities of presentation.

The basic emphasis is different, however, from both unemployment and workmen's compensation. The latter is an economic security program providing protection against *job-connected* illness. The former, through its "able to work" and "available for work" requirements provides indemnification for the *healthy* person who is unemployed.

Rhode Island adopted the first law of this type in 1942. California passed its act in 1946, New Jersey in 1948, and New York in 1949. In-

---

[30] Address by Paul S. Wise before the American Association of State Compensation Insurance Funds, *The Mutual Memorandum,* XLVIII, No. 8 (August 31, 1965), pp. 1–2.

[31] The federal law covering railroad workers is discussed in Chapter 13.

terest in this type of legislation dates back, however, to the 1915–20 era when workmen's compensation was being introduced.[32] Bills advocating the passage of temporary disability income legislation were debated in many states, but none passed. During the twenties, interest in the subject waned.

The depression years saw a renewal of interest in this type of coverage, and many persons felt that temporary disability insurance should be provided under the Social Security Act. The problems of unemployment and old age seemed much more important at the time, however, and the opposition to the inclusion of any form of health insurance was strong. As a result, the Act as passed contained no reference to disability insurance.

However, the Committee on Economic Security in its deliberations considered the matter of health insurance and suggested further study of this problem. It pointed out that it might be desirable to coordinate unemployment insurance and temporary disability insurance. A similar recommendation was made in 1939 by the President's Interdepartmental Committee to Coordinate Health and Welfare Activities.

In 1939 the late Senator Robert Wagner introduced a bill that provided, among other things, for federal grants-in-aid to states having approved temporary disability insurance legislation. The bill was not reported out of the Senate Committee on Education and Labor, but it received much publicity, and many states began to study the problem seriously.

Most of those who favored the passage of temporary disability insurance legislation felt that this insurance should be combined with unemployment insurance for several reasons. First, unemployment insurance provides protection against loss of income due to lack of work but not due to disability. Therefore, temporary disability insurance is a natural extension of unemployment insurance. Furthermore, the two systems should be related because it is logical to continue the checks of an unemployed person on the same basis if he becomes disabled after the date of unemployment. Second, some states had required employees to contribute to the cost of unemployment insurance and had discovered that these taxes were not necessary. In these states the cost of temporary disability income insurance could be met through the diversion of part or all of an existing tax instead of through the imposition of a new tax. And third, administrative expenses would be reduced if the two programs were integrated.

[32] Alfred M. Skolnik, "Temporary Disability Insurance Laws in the United States," *Social Security Bulletin*, XV, No. 10 (October, 1952), 11–24. Much of the material which follows is based upon this article and a more recent comprehensive analysis by Grant M. Osborn, *Compulsory Temporary Disability Insurance in the United States* (Homewood, Ill.: Richard D. Irwin, Inc., 1958).

For these reasons, Rhode Island, California, and New Jersey patterned their temporary disability insurance plans along the lines of their unemployment insurance plans. Six other states—Idaho, Maryland, Montana, Nevada, Tennessee, and Vermont—did not pass temporary disability income legislation, but amended their unemployment insurance laws as a partial solution to the problem. The amended laws provided that unemployment insurance benefits would not be terminated simply because an unemployed worker was disabled after he had filed his claim and registered for work.

Washington passed a temporary disability insurance law in 1949, which was similar to those in New Jersey and California, but it was defeated in a public referendum in 1950.

New York, on the other hand, passed a law patterned after its workmen's compensation act. Those who favored this approach argued that temporary disability is more closely related to occupational disability than to unemployment. Furthermore, since New York employees did not contribute to the cost of unemployment insurance, a new tax would be required in any event. Finally, unemployment insurance is strictly a government operation, while workmen's compensation insurance may be underwritten by commercial insurers and the New York legislators preferred to have these insurers participate.

The opposition to temporary disability insurance legislation maintains that such legislation reduces the responsibility and freedom of choice of the individual; creates additional tax needs through extra administrative expenses; and is unnecessary because of the important advances in private insurance protection.

Since 1939, over half the state legislatures have debated the merits of temporary disability insurance legislation, but only four states have laws. No state has passed an act of this type since 1949, but each year temporary disability insurance is introduced in several state legislatures.

The space devoted to this subject in this text is not justified by the number of persons directly affected by this legislation nor by the likelihood that this number will increase. The programs, however, represent interesting and diverse attempts to deal with an important problem and the lessons to be learned from an analysis of these programs may point the way to better solutions.[33]

Coverage. The employment covered under the Rhode Island, California, and New Jersey acts are the same or almost the same as those

[33] Many of the important detailed provisions of these laws have been omitted for the sake of brevity and clarity of exposition. For a detailed summary of the laws, the student is referred to the latest edition of the U. S. Department of Labor, Bureau of Employment Security, *Comparison of Temporary Disability Insurance Laws.* This section is based upon material supplied in early 1966 by each of the four states with plans.

covered under their unemployment insurance acts except that individual workers can elect not to be covered on religious grounds. The employments covered under the New York act differ in several respects from those covered under either the New York Unemployment Insurance Act or the Workmen's Compensation Act.

The types of employees excluded under all four laws are interstate railroad workers, government employees, and some employees of some non-profit institutions. Domestic employees are excluded under all acts other than that of New York. Employers, self-employed persons (even if they have no employees) and agricultural workers are covered only in California and only as a result of recent legislation.

The New Jersey law also excludes service for persons who do not employ four or more workers in each of twenty weeks in a calendar year. The California law excludes service for persons whose quarterly payroll is less than $100.

Qualifications for Benefits. In addition to working in covered employment, a person must satisfy the following types of requirements:

1. *Qualifying wages.* In Rhode Island a worker must have earned either $1,200 or at least $20 for twenty weeks in the base period, which is the fifty-two calendar weeks ending with the second week immediately preceding his application for disability benefits.

A California worker must earn $300 during the base period, which is approximately the first four of the last five calendar quarters preceding his application for unemployment or disability benefits.

A New Jersey worker must have earned $15 or more from one employer in each of seventeen weeks during, roughly, the fifty-two-week period preceding his application for either disability or unemployment benefits.

A New York worker must have completed four or more consecutive weeks of employment prior to the commencement of disability. If he terminates his employment, in most cases he will retain his eligibility for twenty-six weeks.

2. *Labor force status.* The purpose of the temporary disability insurance legislation is to make income payments to those persons who cannot work or cannot seek work because of disability. The wage qualification does not always accomplish this objective because a person may qualify on the basis of a past employment record. Therefore, all states other than Rhode Island require that claimants who have been unemployed for more than a few weeks prove their continued attachment to the labor force.

3. *Definition of disability.* In general, a person is assumed to be disabled if he is unable to perform his regular or customary work because

of a mental or physical condition. New Jersey requires that *unemployed* workers be unable to perform the duties of *any* occupation. Unemployed workers in New York must be unable to perform in any employment for which they are reasonably qualified.

New York is the only state that specifically limits the coverage to non-occupational illnesses, but workmen's compensation benefits usually reduce the disability benefits in the other states. New Jersey and Rhode Island cover routine pregnancies, but California and New York pay benefits only for certain disabilities following the termination of normal pregnancy.

4. *Disqualifying income.* The purpose of temporary disability insurance legislation is to replace income that has been lost. The worker should not be placed in a position where he is almost as well off disabled as not, for this leads to false claims and malingering. For this reason the states may disqualify a claimant with other sources of income.

Until 1946, workmen's compensation benefits were ignored in Rhode Island, but at present the workmen's compensation benefit plus the disability benefit is not permitted to exceed 85 per cent of the worker's average wage or $62 (exclusive of dependents' benefits), whichever is less. In California only the difference between the disability benefits and a temporary workmen's compensation benefit is paid but full disability benefits are paid even if the worker is receiving workmen's compensation cash payments for permanent disability. No disability benefits are payable in New York or New Jersey if the claimant is receiving workmen's compensation benefits other than permanent partial benefits for a prior disability.

In California and New Jersey, wages which are continued plus the disability benefit may not exceed the worker's wage prior to the disability. In New Jersey benefits are also reduced by any other benefits to which the most recent employer contributed. In New York, no benefit is payable if the worker is *entitled* to receive from his employer (or from a fund to which the employer has contributed) an amount equal to or greater than the disability benefit. Voluntary aid from the employer does not affect benefits.

5. *Other disqualifications.* All states disqualify a person who is receiving unemployment insurance benefits.

Except in Rhode Island, if a person is ineligible for unemployment compensation for such reasons as involvement in a labor dispute or discharge for misconduct, he is usually ineligible for disability benefits.

Benefits. The benefits are determined by three factors: the benefit amount, the duration of the benefits, and the waiting period.

1. *Benefit amount.* In California the weekly benefit is a function of the total earnings during the base-period quarter of highest earnings. The minimum weekly benefit is $25, the maximum $80. The California act also provides hospital benefits of $12 a day.

Weekly benefits in Rhode Island are 55 per cent of average weekly wages [34] during the base period, plus $3 for each dependent child under eighteen or disabled, the maximum dependents' allowance being $12. The minimum weekly benefit, exclusive of dependents' allowances, is $12; the maximum benefit is 50 per cent of the average weekly wage in covered employment during the preceding calendar year.

In New Jersey the disability benefit for employed workers is a function of the average weekly wage during the eight weeks preceding the disability. Weeks in which the employee earned less than $15 from one employer are excluded. For unemployed workers, the same formula, but a longer and more distant base period, is used. Under this formula the weekly benefit ranges from $10 for an average weekly wage of $18 or less to $50 for an average weekly wage of more than $98.

The New York benefit is one-half the average weekly wage during the last eight weeks in covered employment. The minimum benefit is $20 or the average weekly wage if less. The maximum benefit is $55.

2. *Duration of benefits.* In Rhode Island and New Jersey, benefits can be paid for up to twenty-six weeks in a twelve-month period but the benefit duration cannot exceed a specified fraction of the weeks of employment during the base period. Pregnancy benefits, however, are limited to fourteen weeks in Rhode Island and to eight weeks in New Jersey.

In California the benefits are payable for twenty-six weeks for any one period of disability or until the claimant has received one-half his base period wages if this is a shorter period. Hospital benefits are limited to twenty days for any continuous period of unemployment. In New York the uniform limit is twenty-six weeks in any fifty-two-week period.

3. *Waiting period.* A waiting period reduces the cost of the program by eliminating the frequent small losses which add up to a large total. Claims adjustment expense and the temptation to feign claims are also reduced.

Rhode Island has established a waiting period of seven consecutive days in each benefit year, which is the fifty-two-week period starting with the filing of a valid claim. California, New Jersey, and New York require a waiting period of seven consecutive days at the beginning of each uninterrupted period of disability. California, however, requires no waiting period for hospitalized patients.

[34] The average weekly earnings equal the total earnings divided by the number of weeks in which the worker earned $20 or more.

Type of Insurer. Three different methods have been used to insure these benefits. All eligible employers in Rhode Island are insured under a monopolistic state fund. In California and New Jersey all eligible employers are insured under a competitive state fund *until* the appropriate agency approves a self-insured plan or a privately insured plan. New York requires that the employer actively purchase approved benefits from a competitive state fund or a private insurer unless he can satisfy the appropriate agency that he can safely self-insure this obligation. Disability benefits for unemployed workers formerly covered under a private plan and for persons working for an employer who failed to purchase the required insurance are paid by a special state fund in New York and by the state disability fund in California and New Jersey.

California will not approve a private plan unless it is more liberal than the state plan in at least one respect and at least equal in all other respects. Furthermore, a majority of the employees must consent to the private plan. Even if the plan is approved, those employees who prefer to retain their membership in the state plan may do so. A regulation effective in 1963 (reinstating a provision in effect from 1947 through 1954) prevents private insurers from selecting only employee groups whose sex, age, and wage level composition would leave the state fund with only the less desirable groups. Self-insured plans are not subject to this regulation, which is designed to prevent adverse selection against the state fund.

New Jersey requires that approved private plans be as liberal as the state plan in all respects. A majority of the employees must agree to the plan if the plan is contributory. If the majority agree, all employees are automatically covered.

New York approves a private plan if it provides benefits which are at least as favorable from an over-all point of view as the state plan. The temporary disability income benefits must be at least 60 per cent of the statutory benefits. If these benefits are less than 100 per cent of the statutory benefits, there must be other benefits such as medical expense benefits to make up the difference. Private plans existing on the date the disability benefit was enacted were permitted to continue throughout the term of the contract and could be extended by collective bargaining agreements even if they did not provide the equivalent of the statutory benefits. As a result of these two requirements, the plans in New York are more heterogeneous than those in the other states.

The New York employer decides how he will insure his obligation. No majority vote of employees is necessary. Workers who terminate their employment are insured under the private plan for four weeks after they leave covered employment.

Financing. Rhode Island requires that employees pay a tax of 1 per cent on the first $4,800 of wages to finance the disability benefits. Employers pay nothing. Prior to the enactment of temporary disability income legislation, Rhode Island had required its employees to contribute to the cost of unemployment insurance. The disability tax was at first a diversion of part of this unemployment tax. At the present time, there is no unemployment tax on employees.

In 1946 the federal Unemployment Tax Act was amended to permit states which had required employee contributions for unemployment insurance to recover these contributions for the purpose of financing disability income plans. Rhode Island, California, and New Jersey benefited from this amendment.

California levies a 1 per cent tax on the first $7,400 of earnings of employees covered under the state plan. Employers pay nothing.

A California worker insured under a private plan is not permitted to contribute more toward the cost of this plan than the rate for coverage under the state plan. Most employees pay this 1 per cent tax, but sometimes employers pay part or all of the cost under the private plans. The total cost may be more or less than 1 per cent because private insurers, unlike the state insurer, take into account the underwriting characteristics and loss experience of the group in determining the premium. Also, the benefits under the private plan must be more liberal and this affects the total cost.

The state fund pays all the benefits to qualified workers who have been out of covered employment for more than fourteen days. These benefits are financed out of a portion of the statutory tax rate and a quarterly assessment on private plans. Private plans are also assessed for the cost of the added administrative work caused by their existence.

The New Jersey plan is financed in essentially the same way as the California plan except for the following important differences. (1) An employee covered under the state plan pays a tax of ½ per cent on the first $3,000 of wages, while his employer pays a tax of ¼ per cent. (2) The employer's contribution to the state plan is subject to modification through a form of experience rating.

In New York, employees may not pay more than ½ per cent on the first $60 of weekly earnings toward the cost of the plan, unless there is a special agreement to the contrary approved by the state in recognition of superior benefits. The employer pays the additional cost, if any. Both the state fund and the private insurers use premiums which reflect in approximately the same way the underwriting characteristics and loss experience of each insured group. Consequently, adverse selection against the state fund is much less likely.

Benefits for unemployed workers are financed by assessments on the New York state fund, self-insurers, and private insurers.

Administration. In Rhode Island, California, and New Jersey, the unemployment insurance agency administers the law, while in New York the Workmen's Compensation Board is the administrator. In all four states, under both private and public plans, provision is made for appeal to several administrative boards and eventually to the courts if a claimant is dissatisfied with the award he receives.

The state funds are operated essentially on a pay-as-you-go basis. However, some monies have been accumulated because the employee contributions, interest earnings, and recoveries from the Federal Unemployment Trust Fund have exceeded the benefits and administrative expenses. These amounts are invested in interest-bearing government securities, and the interest and principal can be used to reduce the current tax, improve the benefits, or serve as a contingency fund.

Operations.[35] About twelve million workers or more than one-fourth of the workers covered under unemployment insurance in the United States are covered under these state laws. The New York law covers almost half this number.

In California less than 8 per cent of the covered employees are insured under private plans, most of which are self-insured. The regulation against adverse selection, coupled with the requirement that the private plan be superior to the state plan, which itself has been experiencing some financial difficulties, have been cited as the reasons for the drastic decrease in the proportion of employees covered under private plans from over 30 per cent in 1960. In New Jersey the proportion covered under private plans is 50 per cent, which is also less than the 60 per cent reported in 1960. The requirement that the private plan be at least as good in all respects and the experience rating approach used by the state plan may explain the increasingly important role of the state plan. In New York, on the other hand, over 90 per cent of the covered employees are insured under private plans. In both New Jersey and New York, all but a relatively few private plans are insured plans.

Including payments under the Railroad Unemployment Insurance Act, to be described in Chapter 13, cash benefits under temporary disability insurance laws have increased from $66 million in 1948 to almost $460 million in 1964.[36]

[35] For more details, see the *Annual Statistical Supplement* to the *Social Security Bulletin.*

[36] Since 1962 the amount provided by private insured plans has decreased from $144 million to $124 million.

Private plans are more liberal than public plans in terms of the average weekly benefit. This result is not unexpected because of the criteria established for the approval of private plans.

In recent years disbursements have exceeded receipts for the state funds in California, New Jersey, and Rhode Island, but except in California the balances in the trust funds still exceed several years' disbursements. The California fund at the close of 1964 had a $13.4 million balance, the cash disbursements in that year being almost $218 million ($179 million for disability income, $30 million for hospital benefits, and $9 million for administration). Measures adopted to counter this trend include the adverse selection regulation noted earlier, raising the taxable wage ceiling, repealing a provision that related the maximum weekly benefit to wage levels, and limiting the duration of benefits to one-half the total base period wages if this duration is less than twenty-six weeks. According to the plan's consulting actuaries, these measures should halt the fund's decline but further consideration must be given to strengthening the fund.[37]

Evaluation. Temporary disability insurance legislation was designed to provide a minimum income during periods of temporary disability (primarily non-occupational) to persons who were attached to the labor force: that is, employed or temporarily unemployed at the time they were disabled. The general objective of this legislation has been achieved without any apparent serious adverse economic effects. The original Rhode Island legislation had many obvious defects, but all these have been corrected, at least in part.

Numerous issues[38] have arisen in connection with temporary disability insurance legislation, only a few of which can be discussed here. The basic issue, of course, is whether the coverage is necessary at all. The arguments here usually center on the adequacy of private insurance. In this connection it is interesting to observe that the passage of the legislation in these four states contributed to the growth of private insurance elsewhere because interstate employers often extended the same protection to all their employees, labor unions often pressed for such uniform coverage, and insurers learned how to deal with small groups. The interest of labor unions in this legislation has been somewhat reduced by the success that they have experienced in private negotiations with em-

[37] *Report of the Actuaries for Calendar Year 1964, California Unemployment Compensation Disability Fund* (Los Angeles: Woodward and Fondiller, Inc., 1965).

[38] For a more complete discussion of the issues, see the following:

Osborn, *op. cit.*

"Issues in Temporary Disability Insurance," *Social Security Bulletin*, XII, No. 6 (June, 1949), 3–8, 14.

Monroe Newman, "Issues in Temporary Disability Insurance," *The Journal of Insurance*, XXIV, No. 1 (September, 1957), 61–72.

ployers on similar protection. Private arrangements, they have discovered, are more flexible. Furthermore, the role of the union in improving the protection is more direct and obvious to the union's membership.

Eligibility requirements and benefit formulae have been subject to the type of criticism noted with respect to unemployment insurance. Lack of coordination with unemployment insurance and workmen's compensation has led to some adverse selection against the program with the most liberal benefit schedule. Like the maximum benefits under these two older programs, the temporary disability insurance maximums have also tended to lag behind increases in statewide average wages.

Mention was made earlier of the arguments favoring the attachment of a temporary disability income program to unemployment insurance or workmen's compensation. Some persons favoring the unemployment insurance approach and the adoption of temporary disability insurance legislation in all states would levy a federal tax against which the employer would be permitted to offset his contribution to a state program. Others would make temporary disability insurance a part of OASDI.

One of the most debated issues is the role of private and public insurers. Many of the arguments are similar to those presented with respect to workmen's compensation. Private insurers, it is argued, incur more administrative expenses and the state incurs extra supervisory costs. On the other hand, private insurers claim greater efficiency and argue that decreased benefit costs will offset increased administrative costs. However, because of the unique nature of the temporary disability insurance programs, a few additional arguments are presented on both sides.

In favor of a state fund of *some* type it is argued that there must be some way to handle payments to persons who become disabled while temporarily unemployed. Those favoring a *compulsory* fund support their position by observing that employees contribute to the cost; the plan under this system would be easier to explain to employees; and it would be possible to charge all groups a uniform rate, which they consider to be socially desirable. A competitive state fund cannot successfully charge a uniform rate because of the adverse selection problem encountered in California, which has been only partially solved through the special regulation noted earlier and which *in itself* introduces administrative complications. Opponents of *any* state fund reply that payments to unemployed persons should be handled directly by the unemployment insurance systems. They do not agree that there should be a compulsory state fund because the employees contribute and they do not consider state plans to be more easily understood. Uniform pricing, they believe, is unfair and provides no stimulus for loss prevention and reduction. Finally, they argue, with a private insurer the temporary disability insurance benefits can be made a part of a "package" plan providing death, medical expense, and disability benefits which cuts costs and improves consumer satisfaction. They also fear that a compulsory state fund in this area interferes with the development of all forms of private health insurance.

In states where temporary disability legislation seems advisable, the New York plan offers a compromise between varying objectives. Eligibility requirements and benefit levels are a compromise between equity and administrative ease. Joint financing recognizes that the employer and the employee both benefit from the program. Private insurers are given the maximum opportunity to develop their own coverages, but the state plan is an ever present fair yardstick. Costs are distributed partly on the basis of pooling and partly on the basis of the experience of the individual group. The case for experience rating under this program is stronger than under unemployment compensation but weaker than under workmen's compensation.

The current financial difficulties experienced by the California fund are caused primarily by a benefit structure that is not supported by the contribution schedule. This gap is also partly responsible for the exodus of private insurers from California. Contribution increases or, less likely, benefit decreases are almost certain in all states because of the failure in recent years of receipts to keep pace with disbursements.

One basic question is whether temporary disability insurance legislation of the current type, although extremely important, makes the best use of our limited resources. Many would argue that relatively more attention should be directed, on the private and public levels, toward more adequate long-term disability insurance. Recent changes in OASDI and private insurance are encouraging steps in this direction.

SOCIAL MEDICAL EXPENSE INSURANCE

Historical Trends

Until Hospital Insurance and Supplementary Medical Insurance for the aged were established by the 1965 amendments to the Social Security Act, no general social insurance scheme in the United States included non-occupational *medical expense* insurance except the plans established under the California temporary disability insurance legislation and some of the plans established under the New York law. The other general social insurance programs, other than workmen's compensation, froze the eligibility status of the insured for death and retirement benefits or paid a disability *income*. They did not pay medical expenses or provide medical services.

Opposition to social medical expense insurance has been much stronger than opposition to disability income insurance, because more segments of the population, especially the medical profession, believe that they may be adversely affected. However, there has always been intense interest in the subject during this century, particularly in the thirties and forties.

It has already been stated that interest in non-occupational temporary disability insurance legislation dates back to the introduction of workmen's compensation in the United States. Compulsory medical expense insurance also first attracted widespread public attention in 1912 following the enactment in a few states of the first workmen's compensation legislation. Several state legislatures considered bills that would have required most employers to provide medical expense insurance for their employees, but none passed. The issue continued to attract some attention until the twenties when it was almost dropped.

In 1929 the Committee on the Costs of Medical Care was formed in response to increasing dissatisfaction with medical costs and medical resources. This committee, which was privately financed, included a distinguished group of leaders in the fields of medical practice, public health, and the social sciences. The committee report emphasized the uneven incidence of medical expense, but the majority of the committee felt that, although compulsory medical expense insurance "may ultimately be necessary and desirable in some states, . . . for most states and probably for almost all of them at the present time, it is much more desirable . . . to develop voluntary insurance for medical care." [39] The committee approved the group-practice principle and suggested grants-in-aid to increase the medical resources in certain areas.

The Depression intensified public interest in the problem because the average family was hard-pressed if there were *any* medical expenses. In 1935 President Roosevelt's Committee on Economic Security concluded that health insurance, including medical expense insurance, should be included as part of a federal social insurance system, but the committee made no specific proposals and the Social Security Act itself contained no reference to health insurance.

The year 1935 marked the beginning of the National Health Survey and the appointment by the President of an Interdepartmental Committee to Coordinate Health and Welfare. The National Health Survey produced some extensive information on the frequency and severity of illness. The Interdepartmental Committee submitted a report that was largely responsible for the 1939 Wagner bill already referred to in connection with temporary disability insurance.

[39] Committee on the Costs of Medical Care, *Medical Care for the American People* (Chicago: University of Chicago Press, 1932), p. 130.

The Wagner bill provided for federal grants-in-aid to states having approved temporary disability insurance programs and medical expense plans.[40] The bill emphasized the provision of medical care for the needy, but it also provided that temporary disability insurance plans would not be approved unless all those covered under temporary disability insurance were also covered under an approved compulsory medical expense insurance plan. Although the bill died in committee, it was widely discussed.

The appearance of the Beveridge Report in England in 1942 was the next stimulus, and in 1943 Senators Robert Wagner and James Murray introduced a bill that would have created a "unified" national social insurance program. The same bill was introduced in the House. A second Wagner-Murray-Dingell bill was introduced in 1945. Both bills called for a federal system of medical expense benefits and compensation for temporary disability. President Truman recommended the passage of a National Health Act in November, 1945, and the third Wagner-Murray-Dingell Act was introduced to carry out his recommendations. This third bill was the high spot in the movement for compulsory medical expense insurance for citizens of all ages.

Although this Wagner-Murray-Dingell bill did not pass, its major provisions are of interest because they influenced later proposals including the two programs for the aged enacted in 1965. Under this bill, persons who satisfied requirements similar to those for OASDI currently insured status or who were OASI beneficiaries would have been eligible for hospital services; care by physicians, including surgeons and specialists, in the patient's home, the doctor's office, or a hospital; care by a dentist; nurses' services; laboratory and related services; eye examinations; and appliances, including eye glasses. Hospital benefits were to be limited to a stated amount per day for no more than sixty days, but it was hoped that this limit could be increased later to 120 days. Other benefits were to be limited only if this appeared necessary to prevent abuses, to limit the use of scarce resources such as dental and home nursing services, or to reduce the cost of the program.

All legally qualified hospitals, physicians, dentists, and nurses were eligible to participate, but they did not have to serve under the plan. Except for a limitation on the number of patients that each participating hospital, doctor, dentist, or nurse could serve, patients would have been able to select their own hospital, doctor, dentist, or nurse from among those who chose to participate in the plan. Participants were to be reimbursed on a fee-for-service, per-capita, or salary basis depending upon the preference of each class of participants in a local area. Patients preferring non-participation would receive no benefits under the program.

[40] The Wagner bill and others are discussed in detail in Domenico Gagliardo, *American Social Insurance*, rev. ed. (New York: Harper & Row, 1955), chap. 18.

It was estimated that the benefits could be provided for insureds and their dependents if covered employees and their employers each paid a tax of 1.75 per cent on the first $3,600 of the employee's earnings.

Senators Taft, Ball, Donnell, and Smith were opposed to the Wagner-Murray-Dingell bill, but they felt that some action was necessary. They sponsored proposals that, in effect, would have provided federal grants-in-aid to the states with approved plans providing medical care for the indigent and the medically indigent. These bills and the successors to the Wagner-Murray-Dingell bill all failed.

During most of the fifties, interest in social medical expense insurance was considerably diminished, but starting in 1952, bills were introduced in every Congress that would have added medical expense benefits to OASDI. These bills attracted only scattered support. In 1954 the Eisenhower Administration introduced a bill that would have created a federal reinsurance pool, the purpose of which was to encourage the extension of private insurance plans, particularly with respect to aged persons, substandard lives, and catastrophe losses. This bill and amended versions in 1955 and 1956 were either defeated or died in committee as a result of the combined efforts of those who were disturbed by the vagueness of the proposals, those who believed that the bill was a weak solution to the problem, and those who felt that it provided an opening wedge for "socialized medicine." Private insurers feared the federal controls that they thought would accompany any subsidy under the plan.

In 1958 at public hearings before the House Ways and Means Committee on some proposed amendments to the Social Security Act, new interest was generated in social medical expense insurance when Representative Forand proposed an extension of the OASDI program to include hospitalization, nursing-home, and surgical service benefits for aged and survivor beneficiaries only.[41] As a result of the hearings, the Committee asked the Secretary of Health, Education, and Welfare to prepare a report on hospitalization and nursing care insurance for OASI beneficiaries.

In 1959 the Ways and Means Committee considered this report and held hearings on a new, but almost identical, bill proposed by Representative Forand. The bill would have provided up to 60 days of hospital care; up to 120 days, less the number of days in the hospital, of care in a skilled nursing home; and necessary surgical services. Any hospital or nursing home qualified by the state could enter into an agreement to provide the services and would receive the reasonable cost of providing full-service benefits. The patient was to have freedom of choice in selecting among participating hospitals, nursing homes, and surgeons. In the

[41] This section on the developments in 1958, 1959, and 1960 reviews the comprehensive discussion in William L. Mitchell, "Social Security Legislation in the Eighty-Sixth Congress," Social Security Bulletin, XXIII, No. 11 (November, 1960), 5–18.

administration of the program, the Secretary could utilize non-profit organizations representing providers of these services or operating prepayment plans. The benefits were to be financed by an increase of .25 per
cent in the OASDI tax on employers and employees (.375 per cent for
self-employed persons). Representative Forand later amended the combined employer-employee rate from .50 to .75 per cent when the Social
Security Administration estimated that this increase would be necessary
to make the system self-supporting into the indefinite future.

The two Forand proposals marked the beginning of a strong push for
some medical expense insurance program for the aged. In favor of such
programs, it was argued that (1) the aged had high medical expenses
and low incomes, (2) requiring the demonstration of individual need
under public assistance programs made that approach unattractive except as a supplement to a social insurance system, (3) state public assistance programs varied greatly in the adequacy of the protection they
afforded, (4) although private medical expense insurance for the aged
had made great strides, a sizable proportion of the aged would never
have adequate private insurance coverage, (5) a social medical expense
program for the aged would enable private insurers to provide better
protection for other groups thus making an extension of the social insurance program to cover these people unnecessary, (6) freedom of
choice among hospitals and doctors would be preserved with government
controls being held to a minimum, (7) the costs would be reasonable
considering the improvement in the health of the aged and the reduction
in public assistance and private insurance costs, and (8) although young
persons would have to pay more because of the immediate benefits to the
aged who have contributed nothing to these benefits, many would gain
immediate financial advantages through assistance in meeting the medical
costs of their aged parents.

Against such programs it was argued that (1) the financial position
of the aged was better than claimed by the program's supporters, and
even if their claims were true, increasing OASDI cash benefits could
provide the aged with resources to buy private insurance or pay their
own medical expenses, (2) some of the aged who would become eligible
for insurance benefits were in a better financial position than some of the
workers who would have to contribute to the program, (3) it would be
better to provide comprehensive care on an assistance basis to those who
need it than to provide limited care on an insurance basis to all, (4)
private medical expense insurance would soon cover most of the aged and
the remainder could be cared for under public assistance programs, (5)
although the program was limited at present to the aged, it would soon
be extended to include other groups in the population, (6) government
controls, which would cause widespread dissatisfaction among doctors

and hospitals, were an inevitable feature of any program involving government payments for medical services, (7) the estimated costs were high and the true costs would be even higher, and (8) granting benefits to aged persons who had made no contributions toward these benefits would represent a radical departure from social insurance philosophy and was unfair to the younger generation.

In 1960, a presidential election year, this issue was one of the most important considered by Congress. In addition to the Forand bill, several other proposals were considered by the House of Representatives, of which only a few can be described here. In April, Senator Javits introduced a bill that would have provided federal matching grants to states to help subsidize the cost of *private* health insurance for aged persons. The amount of the premium charges to be paid by the aged person was to increase to $13 a month as his annual income increased up to $3,600. In May, the Eisenhower Administration proposed a bill under which federal matching grants would be made to states with programs which, in return for a $24 fee, would pay 80 per cent of the medical expenses of *low-income* aged persons in excess of $250 in a year ($400 for a couple). The bill placed no maximum on the dollar benefits available, but it did limit annual hospital care to 180 days, X-ray charges to $200, and prescribed medicine costs to $350. Participants could choose instead to be reimbursed for up to 50 per cent of the premium they paid for private major medical expense insurance policies, but this reimbursement was not to exceed $60. Special provisions were made for covering Old Age Assistance recipients without a fee or the cost-sharing provision. Major arguments in favor of these proposals were their voluntary nature and their use of general revenues. Major objections related to the reluctance of states to act, the financial burden placed upon the states, and the inequities resulting from the income tests. The Administration plan was both supported and attacked because of its emphasis on catastrophic illnesses.

After concentrating mainly on the Forand bill and the Administration's proposal and specifically rejecting the Forand approach, the House Committee in June reported out a bill sponsored by Representative Mills, chairman of the Committee, which, instead of establishing a social medical expense insurance system, liberalized the medical expense provisions under Old Age Assistance, and established Medical Assistance for the Aged. The House passed the bill under a closed rule.

The Senate Finance Committee then held public hearings on this legislation and alternative proposals.[42] In August it reported out the House

---

[42] One proposal by Senator McNamara would have included the aged who were not OASDI beneficiaries with the cost for this group being paid out of general revenues.

bill with a number of changes adopted under the leadership of Senator Kerr. On the floor of the Senate two major amendments were proposed. Senator Javits proposed an amendment which combined his original proposal and the Administration proposal. For example, each participant was to be given a choice among a diagnostic and short-term illness plan, a long-term illness plan, and an optional private insurance benefit plan. The income-limit principle of the Administration plan was retained but the limit was raised.

After defeating this proposal, the Senate turned to the Anderson-Kennedy amendment, which attracted considerable attention because Senator Kennedy had just become his party's nominee for President. This amendment resembled the Forand proposal except that the benefits were available only for beneficiaries aged sixty-eight or over, surgical benefits were omitted, home health services by a non-profit or public agency were included, and the limits on hospital and nursing care were changed. For example, hospital services were to be covered for 120 days in a year after the individual paid the first $75. This amendment was defeated by a vote of 51 to 44. A few weeks later the amendments to the Social Security Act establishing the Kerr-Mills program were adopted and signed by the President.

During the 1960 presidential campaign, medical care for the aged was a key issue, with the nominees divided along the lines of the two Senate proposals. Following his inauguration in 1961 the late President Kennedy pressed strongly for a program based upon the same principles as the Anderson-Kennedy proposal. Consequently, several bills were introduced which would extend the OASDI system to provide medical care for the aged. A bill sponsored by Representative King and Senator Anderson resembled the earlier Anderson-Kennedy proposal and received Administration support. This bill would have made the following payments to OASDI and Railroad Retirement System beneficiaries who were sixty-five or over:

1. In-patient hospital services for up to ninety days. Beneficiaries, however, would have to pay the first $10 per day of hospital costs for the first nine days, with a minimum deductible of $20.
2. Skilled post-hospital nursing home services for up to 180 days.
3. Out-patient hospital diagnostic service, subject to a $20 deductible.
4. Home health services (intermittent nursing care, therapy, and part-time homemaker services) for up to 240 visits during a calendar year.

The hospital and nursing home services would have been subject to a maximum of 150 "units of service," a unit of service being equivalent to one day of hospital service or two days of nursing service. The benefit costs would have been met by increasing the OASDI payroll taxes, effective in 1963, by ¼ per cent for employees and for employers, and by ⅜ per cent for the self-employed. In addition, the earnings subject to tax would have been increased in 1962 from $4,800 to $5,000.

The House Ways and Means Committee conducted extended hearings on the King-Anderson proposal but the first session of the Eighty-Seventh Congress ended with the bill still in committee. The pressure of other legislation, intense opposition from some quarters, including Chairman Mills of the House Ways and Means Committee, and the Berlin crisis have been cited as reasons why the bill failed to reach the floor of either house of Congress.

In 1962 Senator Anderson, acting for himself, twenty other Democratic senators, and five Republican senators, including Senator Javits, tried to have a modified version of his original proposal adopted by the Senate as an amendment to a public welfare bill. This bill, which made extensive changes in the federal–state public assistance programs, later became law as the Public Welfare Amendments Act of 1962, but the Anderson-Javits Amendment, as it became known, was tabled by a narrow vote. The four major modifications from Senator Anderson's earlier proposal would have (1) made all aged persons eligible for benefits with general revenues being used to meet the cost of those who were not OASDI or railroad retirement beneficiaries, (2) permitted groups of "providers" to designate a private organization of their own choice to receive and pay provider bills for services (the object of this provision was to take advantage of the experience of such organizations as Blue Cross and commercial insurers in administering health insurance programs and to reduce some of the anxiety about government intervention), (3) permitted individuals who had an "approved" private health insurance policy in effect before reaching age 65 to elect to keep that policy and have the government reimburse the insurer for the cost of the statutory benefits used, and (4) created a separate health insurance trust fund. The private insurance option did not win much support from the private insurance business because the requirements for approving individual contracts would have excluded many such contracts and private insurers would have become reimbursement agents for the government benefits and insurers for only the excess.[43]

Other defeated amendments would have (1) provided federal assistance in meeting the cost of approved state group insurance programs for the aged underwritten by private insurers with contributions by the aged themselves varying inversely with their income, (2) paralleled the

[43] For a more complete discussion of the private insurer position, see O. D. Dickerson, *Health Insurance*, rev. ed. (Homewood, Ill.: Richard D. Irwin, Inc., 1963), p. 265.

1961 Javits proposal, or (3) simply reimbursed OASDI beneficiaries for premiums paid for guaranteed renewable health insurance up to $9 a month.

In 1963, Representative King and Senator Anderson introduced a hospital insurance bill which resembled the Anderson-Javits proposal but did not permit beneficiaries to elect to keep their private insurance policies. This new King-Anderson proposal also presented two new options concerning hospital benefits—(1) 45 days with no deductible or (2) 180 days with a flat deductible equal to 2½ times the average daily hospital cost under the program. Public hearings were held but no bill was reported out of committee.

In 1964, the House Ways and Means Committee did send to the floor of the House a bill that would have liberalized many features of OASDI but did not establish a hospital insurance system. The measure was passed overwhelmingly by the House. The Senate Finance Committee made some changes in the House bill but, although it devoted much time to hearings on a hospital insurance system, it did not change the House bill in this respect. On the floor of the Senate, however, an amendment was made and adopted by a close vote that established a hospital insurance system for the aged. The amendment was basically the King-Anderson proposal, but it included a provision suggested by Senator Ribicoff that would have caused the beneficiaries to pay part of their hospital costs after 1968 if average daily hospital costs increased faster than the earnings base. The Senate bill also included a suggestion by Senator Javits that would have made it possible to establish a national association of private insurers under federal supervision to provide supplementary medical insurance for the aged. There was serious discussion of proposals that would have required OASDI beneficiaries to waive some of their cash benefits if they elected hospital benefits, but his idea was not adopted. This amendment by the Senate proved to be a stumbling block for the Conference Committee and the entire bill died in that committee despite the fact that the other provisions in the bill were apparently generally acceptable to both legislative bodies.

Early in 1965, Representative King and Senator Anderson again introduced companion bills (H.R. 1 and S. 1) that, in addition to liberalizing the OASDI and medical assistance programs, would have established a hospital insurance system providing hospital care for sixty days in a benefit period less a deductible equal to the national average cost of one day of such care.[44] The system would also have provided post-hospital extended care, home health services, and out-patient hospital diagnostic services. Provision was made for the non-profit association of private

---

[44] This discussion of developments during 1965 is based largely on Wilbur J. Cohen and Robert M. Ball, "Social Security Amendments of 1965: Summary and Legislative History," *Social Security Bulletin*, XXVIII, No. 9 (September, 1965), 5–9.

insurers proposed in 1964 by Senator Javits. The prospects for passage of this legislation were now considered to be much improved because the 1964 presidential election results favored candidates pledged to support a hospital insurance bill, the composition of the House Ways and Means Committee had changed, and Chairman Mills had adopted a more favorable attitude to the new proposals.

Three proposals commanded most of the attention of the Ways and Means Committee during early 1965: (1) the King-Anderson bill, (2) an Eldercare bill introduced by Representatives Herlong and Curtis and supported by the American Medical Association, and (3) a proposal by Representative Byrnes, which was supported by five of the eight Republican Committee members.

The Eldercare proposal would have amended the Kerr-Mills bill to provide additional federal support to states providing medical assistance for the aged, the blind, and the disabled in the form of private health insurance. In support of this proposal, it was argued that limiting the program to those who need assistance would cut the cost sharply and that for this more limited group, the benefits would be more adequate because they would not be limited to hospital services.

The Byrnes proposal would have established a voluntary federal health insurance program covering all types of medical expenses. Participants would pay a premium that varied directly with their OASDI benefits, but Congress would also have to appropriate some funds from general revenues. This insurance program would involve private insurers as servicing agents.

In March the Committee introduced its own bill which embodied some of the characteristics of all three proposals. First, it proposed hospital insurance benefits similar to those supported by Representative King and Senator Anderson, but unlike their proposal, the Committee established a separate program supported by a separate tax. This position was consistent with Chairman Mills' desire that the hospital insurance benefits not threaten in any way the established OASDI system. Second, in order to plug the gaps in the benefits provided by this system, it established a voluntary insurance program supported by participants' premiums and government general revenues. Third, the Committee also approved liberalization in the OASDI and medical assistance programs. Although the Committee's total proposal was much more far-reaching than even the supporters of the King-Anderson proposal had reason to expect one year earlier, on April 8 the House passed this bill without amendment by a vote of 313 to 115.

Public hearings were then held by the Senate Finance Committee, which reported out a modified version of the bill on June 30. With some amendments, this bill was passed by the Senate on July 9 by a vote of 68 to 21.

Later in July, a conference committee of the House and the Senate met to resolve their differences. Because these differences did not involve the fundamental features of the proposal, they were resolved in less than two weeks. The committee recommendation was adopted by the House on July 27 by a vote of 307 to 116 and by the Senate on July 29 by a vote of 70 to 24. On July 30, President Johnson signed the bill making it Public Law 89–97.

Hospital Insurance

The major features of Hospital Insurance (HI) will be summarized according to whether they affect (1) coverage, (2) benefits, (3) financing, or (4) administration of the system.

Coverage. Covered employment under this program includes all employments covered under OASDI plus railroad employment.

Benefits. HI benefits are payable to persons aged sixty-five or over who are eligible for any type of OASDI or Railroad Retirement System monthly benefit. For example, the person may be eligible as a retired worker, a dependent wife, or a surviving widow. Also eligible are those persons who would qualify for OASDI benefits except for the fact that their annual earnings cause them to lose all of their monthly benefits under the earnings test. Finally, because there are at present a considerable portion of the aged (about 10 per cent) who are not covered under OASDI and because it was deemed desirable to include these persons under this program, all other individuals aged sixty-five or over before 1968 are eligible for HI benefits if they are (1) citizens or (2) aliens lawfully admitted for permanent residence who have resided in the United States for at least five consecutive years and if they are not (1) subversives or (2) retired federal employees or their dependents who are covered or could have been covered under the Federal Employees Health Benefits Act of 1959.[45]

This provision of benefits for persons who have not made any contributions toward the program constitutes a distinct departure from the social insurance philosophy that had prevailed in the United States up to this time. The departure, however, is not as great as it might at first appear. Only those persons reaching age sixty-five before 1968 receive "free" benefits. Those persons reaching age sixty-five after 1967 must have contributed to the OASDI or Railroad Retirement systems to be eligible for benefits. To qualify, these people must have three quarters of cover-

[45] Under this Act, the federal government contributes toward the cost of medical expense benefits for its employees and their dependents.

age for each year after 1965 and before age sixty-five. To illustrate, a person reaching age sixty-five in 1970 will have to have at least twelve quarters of coverage. After 1973 (1971 for women) this special provision will no longer apply because by that time it will be easier for the person to qualify by becoming fully insured under the OASDI system.

The types of benefits to be provided include (1) hospital benefits, (2) extended care facility benefits, (3) home health services benefits, and (4) out-patient hospital diagnostic services benefits. All benefits began on July 1, 1966, except the extended care facility benefits which started on January 1, 1967.

The system covers the cost of almost all types of hospital services normally furnished to in-patients including such items as room and board, operating room, laboratory tests and X-rays, drugs, dressings, general nursing services, and the services of interns and residents in training. Not covered are the services of private-duty nurses or hospital-employed radiologists, anesthesiologists, pathologists or physiatrists. Only the cost of semi-private accommodations is covered unless a private room is medically necessary. Other limitations on the benefits provided include (1) a duration limit—up to ninety days in a single "spell of illness," which is defined as the period beginning with the first day of hospitalization and ending after the person has not been an in-patient in a hospital or an extended care facility for sixty consecutive days and (2) deductible and cost-sharing provisions (called "coinsurance" provisions in the law). Under the deductible provision, the patient must bear the first $40 of the cost plus the charges, if any are incurred, for the first three pints of blood. Under the cost-sharing provision, the patient must bear, in addition, a cost of $10 per day for all days after the first sixty days in a spell of illness. The purpose of these provisions is to reduce the cost of the system and to encourage the patient who does not need the services to deny them. An interesting feature of these deductible and cost-sharing provisions is that the $40 deductible and the $10 cost-sharing amounts are to be adjusted to reflect changes in hospitalization costs after 1966, but no change is to be made before 1969. This automatic adjustment feature is especially important because there is no dollar maximum on the benefits payable. In-patient psychiatric hospital care is covered under the system but there is a *lifetime* limitation of 190 days of service.

After a patient has been hospitalized for at least three days, he becomes eligible for services in an extended care facility such as a skilled nursing home or the convalescent wing of a hospital for post-hospital care of the condition for which he was hospitalized. The service must be of a type that would be covered if it were furnished to a patient in a hospital. These benefits are limited to 100 days in each single spell of illness. There is no deductible provision, but the patient must bear a cost of

$5 per day for all days after the first twenty days in a spell of illness. This $5 amount is also subject to adjustment to reflect changes in hospital costs.

A patient who has been hospitalized for at least three days also becomes eligible for certain home health services. To receive these benefits, the person must be under the care of a physician; a plan calling for these services must be established within fourteen days after the patient is discharged from a hospital or an extended care facility; the services must be provided by a qualified home health agency; and the services must be such that they would be covered if provided to a patient in a hospital. Intermittent visiting nursing care and physical therapy are examples of the services covered. Although these benefits are designed for homebound persons, they may include services furnished at a hospital, extended care facility, or rehabilitation center when the services require equipment that is not ordinarily taken to patients' homes. The duration limit on these services is 100 visits in the next 365 days after the patient is discharged from the hospital or extended care facility or, if earlier, the beginning of the next spell of illness.

The final benefit covers out-patient hospital diagnostic services. There is no maximum limitation on the amount of these services, but with respect to the diagnostic services provided by a particular hospital during a 20-day period, the patient must pay the first $20 plus 20 per cent of the costs incurred in excess of this $20. The $20 deductible and the 20 per cent cost-sharing provision will be changed over time to reflect changes in hospital costs.

Excluded under all four types of benefits are services obtained outside the United States (except for emergency services required in connection with an illness occurring in the United States), the extra cost of "luxury" services such as a private room or television, custodial care, hospitalization for services such as elective cosmetic surgery not required for the treatment of an illness, services performed in a federal institution such as a Veterans Administration hospital, and workmen's compensation cases.

Financing. The HI benefits are to be financed primarily through contributions by employers, employees, and self-employed persons computed on the same maximum taxable earnings base as OASDI, that is, $6,600. Unlike OASDI, however, the HI system imposes the same rate on self-employed persons as on employees and on employers. In 1966, the rate for all three was .35 per cent. The scheduled contribution rates for 1967 and later years are as follows:

1967–72	.50 per cent
1973–75	.55 per cent
1976–79	.60 per cent
1980–86	.70 per cent
1987 and after	.80 per cent

This schedule of rates appears in a different subsection of the Internal Revenue Code than the OASDI rates.

According to Social Security Administration actuaries, contributions developed using these rates will be sufficient for the HI program to be self-supporting over the twenty-five-year period beginning in 1966. According to their intermediate cost estimates, the level premiums required are 1.23 per cent of taxable payroll, which is the level-premium equivalent of the proposed contribution schedule.[46] The relative importance of the hospital and extended care facility benefits is illustrated by the fact that the level-cost of these benefits alone is 1.19 per cent. Unlike the OASDI cost estimates, HI cost estimates have been prepared on the assumption that earning levels and hospitalization costs will both rise in the future and by making estimates for a twenty-five-year period instead of a seventy-five-year period. The shorter period was selected because it is difficult to make reasonable assumptions concerning trends in medical care costs and practices for a longer period. Under the intermediate-cost estimate, it was assumed that hospitalization costs would rise more rapidly than wages by 2.7 percentage points per year from 1966–70, after which the differential will, over a five-year period, be reduced to and remain at zero. In other words, hospitalization costs and wage increases are assumed after ten years to grow at the same rate. Although some experts believe that the Social Security Administration estimates understate hospital utilization and per diem rates.[47] Administration actuaries believe that their cost estimates are conservative because (1) although they have assumed that earnings will rise at a rate of 3 per cent annually during the next twenty-five years, the $6,600 earnings base has been assumed to remain constant, and (2) increasing productivity of hospital personnel, greater emphasis upon preventive measures, shorter hospitalization periods, and the improving economic status of hospital employees (which will relieve pressures to "catch up" with other employees) may cause hospital costs to rise much less rapidly than assumed. Because of the possible wide margin of error in the actuarial estimates, the experience of a small continuing sample of perhaps 0.1 per cent of all eligible individuals will be studied closely to reveal as quickly as possible any significant departures from the underlying assumptions.

The HI contributions are to be placed in a separate Hospital Insurance Trust Fund with its own Board of Trustees, but the Board has the same

[46] Myers and Bayo, op. cit., pp. 24–27. Although alternative sets of assumptions were considered, there are no formal low-cost and high-cost estimates.

[47] See, for example, Barkev S. Sanders, "What Would 'Medicare' Cost?," Journal of Risk and Insurance, XXXII, No. 4 (December, 1965), 579–94. Dr. Sanders predicts that the hospital utilization rate and the per diem cost for hospitals have been greatly underestimated. He believes that unless the present tax schedule is revised, there will be a substantial deficit from 1967 on.

membership as the OASDI and DI trust funds and follows the same investment procedures.

In 1966, the contributions under an intermediate-cost estimate were expected to total about $1,637 million, out of which $987 million would be paid in benefits and $50 million in administrative expenses. Because interest on the fund was expected to be $18 million, the fund at the end of the first year of operation was expected to be $618 million. By 1990, the contributions are expected to reach $9,015 million, the benefit payments $8,797 million, the administrative expenses $264 million, and the fund $10,426 million, which is expected to be 1.2 times the expected disbursements at that time.

As stated earlier, during a transitional period, benefits will be paid to certain aged persons who have not contributed to the system. Benefits for these persons will be supported from general revenues with the monies passing through the HI Trust Fund as needed. The cost of these benefits in 1966 has been estimated at $140 million. After reaching a peak of $278 million in 1967, they are expected to decline gradually.

Administration. The Department of Health, Education and Welfare administers this system through the Bureau of Health Insurance of the Social Security Administration, which bureau also operates the Supplementary Medical Insurance system. Payments for services rendered can be made directly to providers of these services on a "reasonable cost" basis [48] but each provider can and usually does elect to receive its payments through a fiscal intermediary nominated by the provider and approved by the government instead of dealing directly with the government. This fiscal intermediary may be a state agency, Blue Cross, or some other health insurer. Use of these intermediaries is encouraged because their experience in adjusting health insurance claims should help to prevent over-utilization of the services and provide a check on the reasonableness of the charges made for these services. Most, but not all, hospitals have nominated Blue Cross associations. Several commercial insurers have

---

[48] A controversial accounting system known as RCC (ratio of charges to costs) has been developed to determine the plan payments. Under this system the hospitals must determine the ratio of the charges for aged persons to the charges for total patients, preferably for each type of service. The government payment is equal to this ratio times the costs of these services plus an extra 2 per cent of allowable costs for hospital "growth and development." The government believes that because of longer stays in the hospital, the daily hospital costs for the aged are less than the daily costs for other patients and that this system will produce a lower cost for the program. The American Hospital Association favored the Blue Cross approach described in Chapter 12 because it was simpler, would not upset traditional practices, and would in their opinion produce about the same results. Hospitals have been granted a grace period up to eighteen months to adopt this system. The charges for patients other than the aged will probably also be affected by this system.

been selected. These fiscal intermediaries are reimbursed for the reasonable costs of their services.

Providers of services may elect not to participate under the program. Those who wish to participate must meet certain standards. Because one of the major concerns associated with this insurance is over-utilization of the services, utilization review committees must be established for hospital and extended care facilities. Extended care facilities must develop transfer agreements with hospitals.

Supplementary Medical Insurance

The second medical expense insurance program established under the 1965 Amendments is Supplementary Medical Insurance (SMI), which differs in many ways from the other insurance programs under the Social Security Act. The major features of this system will be discussed under the same general headings as HI.

Coverage. A major difference between this program and the others is that participation is voluntary. Subject to a few exceptions, all aged persons can participate, but in order to avoid adverse selection against the system, persons wishing to participate must so indicate during specified enrollment periods. Otherwise individuals in good health might delay their enrollment until they had reason to suspect that their health was deteriorating. Persons in this group who are eligible to enroll include all persons eligible for HI benefits and any other persons who, unless they are subversives, are (1) citizens or (2) aliens lawfully admitted for permanent residence who have resided in the United States for at least five consecutive years. Retired federal employees covered under the Federal Employee Health Benefits Act of 1959 are thus eligible for SMI but not HI. A person who attained age sixty-five prior to 1966 had to elect coverage before March 31, 1966, unless he could show good cause for his failure to enroll, in which case the deadline was extended to October, 1966. Coverage started July 1, 1966, if he enrolled before March 31, 1966; otherwise it became effective six months after he enrolled. An amendment enacted in April, 1966, extended the March 31 deadline to May 31.

A person who reached age sixty-five in 1966 or will reach that age in later years must elect coverage in the seven-month period starting three months before the month [49] in which he attains age sixty-five and meets the other requirements and ending three months after that month. If he elects coverage during the first three months, coverage is effective for the

[49] If he has not satisfied the eligibility requirements by that month, the period centers around the first subsequent month when he does become eligible for benefits.

month in which he attains age sixty-five. If he elects coverage during the month of his birth, coverage is effective the following month. Election during the fifth month will delay coverage to the seventh month and election during the sixth and seventh months will defer coverage to nine and ten months after the start of the period. If a person in this group fails to enroll in this seven-month period, he has one more chance to enroll during the next "general enrollment period," which is scheduled for October through December of each odd-numbered year. Coverage elected in this way is effective the following July 1.

Once a person has elected coverage he can terminate his participation if he is not an OASDI or RR beneficiary by failing to pay his premiums when due. Otherwise, he must specifically elect during a general enrollment period not to participate in the future. A person who terminates his coverage has one opportunity to re-enroll, but he can do so only in a general enrollment period and must act within three years.

These enrollment procedures are similar to those used by private insurers in connection with voluntary group insurance.

Benefits. The far-reaching benefits under this program supplement those under HI. They include the services of physicians and surgeons in a hospital, a clinic, the doctor's office, the patient's home, or elsewhere; home health services of the type covered under HI but there is no requirement that the patient be previously hospitalized; diagnostic X-ray and laboratory tests, and other diagnostic tests; X-ray, radium, and radioactive isotope therapy; ambulance services; surgical dressings and splints, casts, and other devices for reduction of fractures and dislocations; rental of durable medical equipment used at the patient's home, such as iron lungs, oxygen tents, hospital beds, and wheelchairs; prosthetic devices (other than dental) that replace all or part of an internal body organ; and braces and artificial legs, arms, eyes, etc. Not covered are drugs, private duty nursing, dental services, skilled nursing home and custodial care, routine physical and eye examinations, elective cosmetic surgery, services performed by a relative or household member or by a governmental agency, eyeglasses and hearing aids, and workmen's compensation cases.

Home health services are limited to 100 visits in a calendar year. Payments for outside-the-hospital treatment of mental, psychoneurotic, and personality disorders is limited during any calendar year to $250 or, if smaller, 50 per cent of the expenses. Otherwise, there is no maximum limitation on the benefits, but the patient must bear the first $50 of expenses incurred in a calendar year plus 20 per cent of the excess.

Financing. Aged persons electing to participate in the SMI program pay monthly premiums of $3. The government provides a matching payment from general revenues. If a person fails to enroll during his initial enrollment period, his premium, and the matching government contribution, is increased by 10 per cent for each year that has elapsed since his initial enrollment period.

Premiums are automatically deducted from OASDI, RR, or Civil Service Retirement monthly benefit checks if the aged person is currently receiving such benefits. Other persons pay their premiums directly, subject to a grace period to be determined by the Secretary of HEW but not to exceed ninety days.

The $3 premium rate is intended to keep the system self-supporting during 1966 and 1967 and to provide some margin for contingencies. The $3 premium rate and the matching government contribution are subject to change if the costs of the program increase, but these changes cannot be made more than once every two years. The "actuarial soundness" of this system is judged on a "current cost" basis instead of a long-range basis because the system provides immediate benefits for all premium payers and the annual premiums are subject to change depending upon short-run indications. The initial $3 premium was based on data gathered under the Federal Employees Health Benefits Act of 1959, the Connecticut 65 program (a private group insurance program underwritten by an association of insurers operating in that state), and the National Health Survey. Cost estimates have been prepared on the basis of both "high" and "low" per capita costs and on the basis of an 80 per cent participation rate and a 95 per cent participation rate. Almost all state public assistance agencies were assumed to enroll their old-age assistance recipients. Although the possibility of some adverse selection under the 80 per cent participation rate was recognized by the actuaries, they argue that many of the non-participants would be uninformed rather than in poor health. They have also observed that a 75 per cent participation rate is considered adequate protection against adverse selection in private insurance. The present $3 premium with a matching government contribution is based on the high cost estimates. As in the case of HI, a sample of insureds will be carefully studied on a continuous basis in order to detect as soon as possible any significant cost trends.

These premiums and contributions are placed in a separate Supplementary Medical Insurance Trust Fund, out of which all benefits and administrative expenses are paid. This Fund, like the HI Trust Fund, has its own Board of Trustees, but this Board has the same membership as the OASI and DI Trust Funds and follows the same investment procedures. Because it was desirable to have an operating fund and a contingency reserve as soon as the program became effective, authorization was provided for the government to make available until December 31, 1967, a non-interest-bearing loan equal to six months' government contributions ($18) for all those estimated to be eligible on the effective date of the plan (about 19 million persons).

If 80 per cent of those eligible participated, contributions by participants were expected to be $275 million in 1966 and $560 million in 1967. By the end of 1967, the trust fund assets were expected to be $435 million under the low-cost estimate and $90 million under the high-cost estimate. If 95 per cent participated, contributions were estimated at $325 million in 1966 and $665 million in 1967. By the end of 1967, the trust fund assets under the low-cost and high-cost estimates would be $510 million and $110 million respectively. The actual proportion enrolled when the program went into effect was about 90 per cent.

Administration. This program, like HI, is administered by the Bureau of Health Insurance of the Social Security Administration. Providers of covered medical services can be paid directly by "administrative intermediaries" or by the patient who then seeks reimbursement from the government or its intermediaries. The intermediaries are insurers such as Blue Shield plans or commercial insurers who have been selected by the Bureau of Health Insurance from among those insurers expressing a desire to participate in this fashion. Because of their experience with private insurance, these intermediaries are in a favorable position to determine whether (1) the charges by individual suppliers of services and supplies and the costs of institutional services and supplies and (2) the utilization of the benefits by the participants are "reasonable." For their services, these intermediaries will be paid their reasonable costs of administration. Physicians and other providers of services may elect not to participate under the program, but the opportunity to bill the patient directly and have the patient apply for the plan benefits has eliminated one of the major obstacles to complete participation. Despite its earlier opposition, the American Medical Association gave advice and counsel to the Secretary of Health, Education, and Welfare concerning administrative procedures.

Evaluation. Because no benefits were provided under these two medical expense programs until the middle of 1966, an evaluation of their operations at this time would be premature. The arguments presented for and against these programs before their adoption will not be reviewed in this section because these arguments are now historical and have been presented in summary pages 394–95. On the other hand, it is important to note that the private insurance business and the American Medical Association, both of whom strongly opposed the bills establishing these programs, have indicated their willingness to cooperate in their administration. Such cooperation is essential if the programs are to be given a fair test. Of particular interest in evaluating these programs at a later date will be their impacts on the health status of the aged, the quality of medical care, and their costs.

Pressures to expand the programs have already appeared. Some persons favor an extension of the types of benefits covered [50] and minor changes in the benefits are probably to be expected. Other proposals would increase the number of persons covered under the program. Relatively few persons favor a program that would include the entire population, but apparently a substantial number of persons favor extending the program to include some other OASDI beneficiaries such as disabled persons and their dependents, young widows, and surviving children. The reader may recall that the 1958 and 1959 Forand proposals were not limited to aged beneficiaries. In support of these extensions it may be argued with considerable force that the average economic status of these groups is so low that many of their members cannot afford adequate medical care. Many disabled beneficiaries may, in addition, be ineligible for any private health insurance even if they could afford it. On the other hand, it can be argued that the private insurance protection available to these groups, other than to some disabled persons, is more adequate and less expensive than that available to the aged. Consequently, the case for extending HI and SMI to include these persons is not as persuasive as the case for medical care for the aged. Disabled beneficiaries who are not eligible for private insurance are admittedly a special problem but even these persons should be encouraged to seek such protection before they become disabled. This argument assumes the purchase of the non-cancellable or guaranteed renewable insurance described in Chapter 12. Finally, even if it is desirable to extend the program eventually, it may be wiser first to gain administrative experience and to determine the cost implications under the present more limited approach, with the expanded medical assistance programs being used to handle needy families in these other groups.

In the past it has been customary to believe that social insurance and closely related programs favor the lower-income groups. Despite its regressive payroll tax, for example, OASDI is generally considered to favor workers with low average monthly earnings and many dependents. In practice, HI and SMI *may* work in the opposite direction. As Professor Richard Titmuss has observed recently concerning the British National Health Service, "The higher income groups know how to make better use of the Service; they tend to receive more specialist attention; occupy more of the beds in better equipped and staffed hospitals; receive more elective surgery; have better maternity care; and are more likely to get psy-

---

[50] For example, by eliminating the deductible and cost-sharing provisions, by increasing the time limits on hospital and nursing home stays, by including the cost of psychiatric care, and by adding payments for drugs and appliances.

chiatric help and psychotherapy than low-income groups—particularly the unskilled." [51]   Although Professor Titmuss' observation does not apply with equal force to HI and SMI, it does provide some food for thought.

The impact of these two programs upon private insurance programs will be explored in more detail in Chapter 12 but a few remarks are relevant here. Many special private insurance programs for the aged have been supplanted or reduced by the government programs, but private insurers have developed new coverages designed to supplement the public protection. Private insurers have expressed concern over the duplication of benefits under the government programs with those under some private policies issued prior to 1965 which cannot be cancelled because of contract provisions stating that they can be renewed at the insured's option up to and during old age. These duplicate benefits could affect adversely both the public and the private programs. Some observers predict beneficial results on the whole for the private insurance business because of the insurance consciousness that is being created by these programs, because of the contacts and good will that private insurers will acquire in their role as intermediaries, because private insurers can now concentrate their attention on improving coverage for groups they are better able to handle, and because there is still room to supplement the government protection for the aged. Many others, however, regret the loss of a substantial market, believe that supplementing the government protection for the aged poses some difficult underwriting and marketing problems, and fear that the public program will eventually be expanded in such a way as to reduce significantly the opportunities for private insurance. They observe that in 1966 a worker earning at least $6,600 a year already contributed $377.20 to OASDI and HI, which amount is matched by his employer, and that this contribution will rise even if the benefit structure remains unchanged.

Employee benefit plans have had to be changed because of the two new medical expense insurance programs. Many employee benefit plans provided medical expense benefits for the aged, which would have duplicated the HI and SMI benefits to a large extent. Some plans have terminated these benefits; others have reduced them. As a result, employer contributions to these plans were reduced. In part these contributions have been offset by increased OASDI and HI contributions, but many of the affected employers have either unilaterally or under pressure from labor unions used the "savings" plus additional funds to provide such benefits as the payment of the $3 a month SMI premiums for retired

---

[51] Richard M. Titmuss, "The Role of Redistribution in Social Policy," *Social Security Bulletin*, XXVIII, No. 6 (June, 1965), 19. Professor Titmuss also believes that the private pensions of the rich are more heavily subsidized than the pensions of the poor for a variety of reasons.

workers, to introduce new coverages designed to supplement the private protection, or to improve plans for active workers, many of whom at present have benefits inferior to those provided under HI and SMI. Employers who did not previously provide benefits for retired persons have been similarly affected.

One final observation on the many ramifications of these programs is concerned with the nature of medical care. Some observers believe that the provision of hospital insurance on a compulsory basis will accelerate the trend away from the present system of medical care, which is doctor-oriented, toward one which centers around a hospital or institutional complex. Nursing homes and home nursing programs will probably increase in importance as long hospital stays become less common.

A NOTE ON TERMINOLOGY

Hospital Insurance and Supplementary Medical Insurance pose some interesting questions for persons concerned with social insurance terminology. The Committee on Social Insurance Terminology of the American Risk and Insurance Association is currently considering these questions. For a temporary period many persons will receive Hospital Insurance benefits who did not contribute to HI although some of these persons did contribute to OASDI. Some regard this absence of contributions to be sufficient to suggest that HI is not social insurance or that the proposed definition of social insurance itself (see pages 24–25) should be revised. Similar statements can be made about OASDI since the 1966 amendment that made some persons, aged seventy-two or over, eligible for special benefits even if they never worked in covered employment. Others believe that this transitional characteristic of the system should not obscure its fundamental character and that indeed the program can be divided conceptually into two parts—a permanent program based on contributions and a temporary program supported by general revenues. SMI, on the other hand, is clearly not social insurance according to the proposed definition because, among other things, it is a voluntary program. These observations illustrate why any definition must be regarded as somewhat arbitrary, but attempting to pose a definition clarifies the nature of the concept and the programs.

SUMMARY

Non-occupational accidental injuries and sicknesses are much more important than job-connected injuries and disease as a cause of income losses and medical expenses. In 1964 the average private cost of non-occupational illness was over $400 per person in the civilian population and this cost was distributed unevenly among American families.

Preventive and alleviative methods, both private and public, have been used to attack the financial problems caused by non-occupational illnesses. This chapter is primarily concerned with public alleviative approaches.

The important public programs are the general assistance programs, the special federally supported state public assistance programs which provide medical assistance for the indigent and medically indigent aged, medical assistance for needy families with dependent children, aid for the blind, and aid for the permanently and totally disabled; hospitals for special diseases; the disability freeze and disability income programs under OASDI; temporary disability insurance legislation in four states; and two new medical expense insurance programs for the aged under the Social Security Act.

The OASDI disability freeze enables a person who is expected to be totally disabled for at least twelve months to retain the insurance status and average monthly wage he had earned at the date of disability. OASDI disability income benefits enable such a disabled person and his dependents to receive a monthly income. Children who are disabled prior to age eighteen also receive a monthly income under certain conditions after they reach age eighteen.

Temporary disability insurance legislation in four states protects workers against short-term disability income losses. Three of the states coordinate temporary disability insurance with unemployment insurance; the fourth regards it as a supplement to workmen's compensation. One state requires insurance in a monopolistic state fund; the other three states permit commercial insurers to compete with a state fund. Two states tax the employee only, while the other two tax both the employer and the employee. No two plans have the same eligibility requirements or benefit formulas.

Hospital Insurance provides hospital benefits, extended care facility benefits, home health service benefits, and out-patient hospital diagnostic service benefits for the aged. Supplementary Medical Insurance, a voluntary program for the aged subsidized by the government from general revenues, provides primarily physicians' care.

SUGGESTIONS FOR ADDITIONAL READING

BURNS, EVELINE M. *Social Security and Public Policy.* New York: McGraw-Hill Book Co., 1956. Chapter 8.
An excellent discussion of the National Health Service and other social insurance approaches to the problem of medical care.

DICKERSON, O. D. *Health Insurance.* Homewood, Ill.: Richard D. Irwin, Inc., 1963.

Chapters 1 through 3 contain an extensive analysis of the costs of poor health. Chapter 14 and pp. 85–93 review and evaluate public assistance and social insurance programs dealing with poor health.

GAGLIARDO, DOMENICO. *American Social Insurance,* rev. ed. New York: Harper & Row, 1955. Chapter 19.

An extensive discussion of the arguments for and against social medical expense insurance and the legislation that was introduced during the thirties and forties.

HABER, WILLIAM, and WILBUR J. COHEN (eds.). *Social Security: Programs, Problems, and Policies.* Homewood, Ill.: Richard D. Irwin, Inc., 1960.

This book of selected readings contains several excellent articles dealing with the topics covered in this chapter.

MYERS, ROBERT J. *Social Insurance and Allied Government Programs.* Homewood, Ill.: Richard D. Irwin, Inc., 1965.

Of particular interest in this recent text by the Chief Actuary for the Social Security Administration are Chapter 2 on public assistance programs and Chapter 7 on health benefits proposals.

OSBORN, GRANT M. *Compulsory Temporary Disability Insurance in the United States.* Homewood, Ill.: Richard D. Irwin, Inc., 1958.

A comprehensive discussion of the problems arising in connection with the temporary disability insurance programs in four states and the federal program for railroad workers.

SPIEGELMAN, MORTIMER. *Ensuring Medical Care for the Aged.* Homewood, Ill.: Richard D. Irwin, Inc., 1960.

A complete and careful analysis of the economic and health status of the aged and the various public and private approaches to their medical care problems.

TASK FORCE ON ECONOMIC GROWTH AND OPPORTUNITY. *Poverty: The Sick, Disabled and Aged.* Washington, D. C.: Chamber of Commerce of the United States, 1965.

A recent report by a Chamber of Commerce task force which contains interesting background material and recommendations for keeping down the cost of medical care, fostering health and rehabilitation, and achieving economic security for the sick and disabled.

U. S. DEPARTMENT OF HEALTH, EDUCATION, AND WELFARE. *Annual Report.* Washington, D. C.: U. S. Government Printing Office, latest edition.

The annual reports of the Department comment on the current operations of the federal public assistance and social insurance programs.

U. S. HOUSE OF REPRESENTATIVES, Executive Hearings Before the Committee on Ways and Means, 89th Congress, 1st Session. *H.R. 1 and Other Proposals for Medical Care for the Aged.* Washington, D. C.: U. S. Government Printing Office, 1965.

U. S. SENATE, Hearings Before the Committee on Finance, 89th Congress, 1st Session. *Social Security.* Washington, D. C.: U. S. Government Printing Office, 1965.

Hearings on the latest amendments to the Social Security Act. Earlier hearings before these two committees on the Social Security Act are also valuable references.

12

Private Approaches: Accidental Injury and Sickness

INTRODUCTION

Social insurance and related programs providing benefits for accidental injury or sickness have been discussed in Chapters 9, 10, and 11. These programs include workmen's compensation laws, which provide disability income and medical expense benefits for job-connected injury and disease; OASDI, which freezes the eligibility status of totally and permanently disabled persons and provides them with a monthly income; HI and SMI, which provide medical expense protection for the aged; and, in four states, temporary disability insurance legislation, dealing essentially with non-job-connected accidents and sickness.

Important gaps in this social insurance protection against accidental injury and sickness remain. For example, OASDI disability income benefits are payable only under certain special conditions, and only one state program requires medical expense benefits for non-occupational illness for the general population. Voluntary private health insurance, therefore, is extremely important in covering non-job-connected illnesses and, in many cases, job-connected illnesses.

In this chapter we shall consider the voluntary protection provided by private insurers. We shall classify private health insurance plans according to the type of insurer, for each type of insurer has a different underwriting philosophy and we are interested in the important characteristics of each approach.

The three major types of insurers are commercial insurers,[1] Blue Cross and Blue Shield associations, and independent insurers. The last class includes all types of insurers not included under the first two classes.

Under each category we shall discuss the benefits currently available, their role in the economic security system, and important trends in their development.

COMMERCIAL INSURANCE CONTRACTS

The commercial insurer is the most important type of insurer in the private health insurance field. Commercial insurers underwrite almost all the protection against loss of income caused by disability and they share with Blue Cross and Blue Shield associations the leadership in underwriting medical expense coverages.

Commercial insurers write both individual and group coverages. The major characteristics of each of these major classifications of coverages are discussed below.

Individual Insurance

Individual insurance contracts may be divided into three classes: income contracts that protect insureds against loss of income only, income-medical expense contracts that protect insureds against both loss of income and medical expenses, and medical expense contracts that protect insureds against medical expenses only. Included in the first two groups are commercial,[2] guaranteed renewable, non-cancellable, industrial, and limited policies. Included in the third group are basic medical expense, major medical expense, and comprehensive medical expense policies, which, as will be observed later, can also be subclassified according to the nature of their cancellation provisions. We shall discuss the major provisions of the most typical contracts under each classification, but the reader should remember that there are a very large number of different forms available. Our discussion is primarily intended to indicate the major types of protection available.

[1] The term "commercial insurers" is not a satisfactory way to distinguish stock and mutual insurers from the other two types. If "commercial" implies a profit-making concern, mutual insurers are not profit-oriented, but some independent plans are organized for this purpose. However, this terminology is in common use and no better term has been suggested. One alternative approach is to use a three-fold classification of insurance companies, Blue Cross and Blue Shield associations, and independent plans. See O. D. Dickerson, *Health Insurance*, rev. ed. (Homewood, Ill.: Richard D. Irwin, Inc., 1963), p. 310.

[2] These policies are called commercial policies because of the market they were intended to serve, not because they are issued by "commercial" insurers. They are to be distinguished from industrial policies, which are designed for a different market.

Individual Income and Income-Medical Expense Contracts. *Commercial policies* are the most frequently sold income and income-medical expense contracts. They are issued primarily to persons engaged in the less hazardous occupations. The policy may protect the insured against losses due to accidental injury and sickness or the coverage may be restricted to accidental injuries.

In the past, accidental injury benefits were usually payable only if the insured suffered a bodily injury effected solely through accidental means. The cause had to be accidental. Today, however, most leading insurers simply require that the claimant have suffered an accidental bodily injury. The distinction is clearly important if the insured does not also have a sickness policy; it is also important if the insured has a sickness policy because the accidental injury benefits are much more liberal, as indicated in the following paragraphs.

The most important accidental injury benefits include disability income benefits, benefits for dismemberment and loss of sight, and medical expense benefits. Usually the insured selects from a schedule which of these benefits he would like to purchase but sometimes the contract is sold only as a package or provides only one benefit.

There are two types of disability income benefits—total disability benefits and partial disability benefits. A person who is totally and continuously disabled within a specified period, such as ninety days, following the date of an accident will receive a specified weekly indemnity. He is considered to be totally disabled if he is completely unable to engage in his regular occupation. The test is not whether his income stops. The requirement that the disability commence within a stated period after the accident is included because, as the interval between the accident and the date of disability increases, it becomes more difficult to determine whether the disability was caused by the accident. Payments are usually continued for some stated period such as 104 weeks or until recovery, if earlier. Payments will be continued for life if the insured is unable to engage in *any* occupation for which he is reasonably fitted by education, training, or experience.

A person who is partially and continuously disabled within some period, such as ninety days, following an accident or immediately following a period of total disability will receive a specified weekly indemnity which is commonly half of the total disability weekly indemnity. Partial disability is defined as one which renders the insured able to perform one or more but not all of the duties of his occupation. The payments are generally continued up to twenty-six or fifty-two weeks, never for life.

Insureds who lose one or more members or the sight of one or both eyes within a certain period following the accident may commonly elect to receive a lump-sum payment equal to the weekly indemnity for a number of weeks; for example, one hundred weeks for the loss of a hand or foot. The payments may be in addition to the disability income payments or establish the minimum amount to be paid under the disability income provisions. In less liberal contracts, these payments replace the total disability income payments and may affect adversely a seriously injured person.

Medical expense benefits, which are often not included, may be written on a blanket or on a specified basis. Under the blanket coverage there is one aggregate limit for all types of expenses covered. For example, one policy pays hospital bills, nurses' fees, and charges for treatment by a physician or surgeon incurred within twenty-six weeks following the accident up to the limit specified in the policy. Under the specific coverages, there are separate limits for each type of expense covered. For example, under one policy the insureds may purchase one or more of the following specific benefits: (1) actual hospital room and board charges up to $15 per day for not more than one hundred days plus miscellaneous hospital expenses up to $200; (2) surgical fees according to a schedule of allowances; (3) nurses' fees up to $6 per day for not more than one hundred days; and (4) charges for a physician's care in the hospital up to $5 per day for not more than one hundred days. Blanket coverage is more liberal than the specific coverages because the types of covered medical expenses included in the insured's claim do not affect his recovery from the insurer.

Accidental injuries caused directly or indirectly by suicide or war are excluded. Moreover, no benefits are paid for injuries sustained while the insured is in the armed services in time of war or while the insured is riding in an airplane other than as a fare-paying passenger on a scheduled airline. There are usually other minor exclusions.

Sickness benefits, which are almost always written only in conjunction with accidental injury benefits, include only a total disability income benefit and medical expense benefits. Sickness losses are much more difficult to underwrite than accidental injury losses because of the possibility of feigning sickness. Therefore, insurers are more cautious when they underwrite this type of insurance.

A person who is totally and continuously disabled by sickness will generally receive a specified weekly indemnity for some specified period such as 104 weeks beginning with the eighth or later day of total disability. Longer durations can be purchased, but lifetime benefits are rare. An increasingly popular contract continues the benefits to age sixty-five. The seven-day waiting period (or some other waiting period) reduces the cost of the insurance considerably because it eliminates the frequent short-term illnesses. Total disability is defined in the same manner as under the accidental injury benefit. A recurrent disability from the same or related causes is considered a new disability if the insured performed all the duties of a gainful occupation for some specified period such as six months following the final disability.

Partial disability benefits are seldom included, but some contracts distinguish between total confining disability and total non-confining disability benefits. A disability is confining if the insured must stay indoors. These contracts are usually less liberal than the more common contract because the total confining disability benefit is the same as the usual total disability benefit, while the total non-confining disability benefit is less liberal in duration and sometimes in amount. Some contracts will continue the payments for life if the insured is house-confined.

The medical expenses in the sickness policy are almost always written on the less liberal specific basis.

No sickness benefits are usually payable during the first two or three years the contract is in force if the sickness was contracted prior to the fifteenth day of the policy period. Moreover, no benefits are payable if the insured is not under the care of a physician or if the loss is incurred while the insured is a member of the armed services. Sometimes the latter exclusion applies only in time of war.

Commercial accidental injury and sickness contracts are issued on a yearly basis and are renewable at the option of the insurer. Sometimes the contract is conditionally renewable; for example, the insurer may agree that it must state certain reasons other than the deterioration of the insured's health for the refusal to renew. On the other hand, under many contracts the insurer not only has the right not to renew the policy but it also reserves the right to cancel the contract during the policy period. This cancellation right in itself is undesirable from the insured's point of view, but it enables the insurer to offer more liberal benefits than would otherwise be possible or to offer the same protection at lower cash. Several states prohibit by law cancellation during the policy period. North Carolina requires insurers to give prior written notice of their intention not to renew thirty days to two years in advance of this action depending upon how long the policy has been in effect.

Premiums for the accidental injury benefits are dependent primarily upon occupation and sex. Age is not important. Premiums for sickness insurance depend primarily upon sex. There may also be broad age groupings such as eighteen to forty-nine and fifty to fifty-four. The premiums are quoted on an annual basis, but they may be paid semi-annually, quarterly, or monthly.

Each applicant must pass the underwriting standards established by the insurer. Factors considered by the underwriter are the applicant's age, his physical condition, his occupation, and his moral and financial reputation.

Non-cancellable contracts and *guaranteed renewable contracts* are extremely important. The insurer may not cancel the contract within the policy period, and in addition the insurer must renew the contract at the insured's request up to some advanced age specified in the contract. This right to renew adds greatly to the economic security of the individual. Guaranteed renewable contracts differ from non-cancellable contracts in that under non-cancellable contracts the premium on outstanding contracts cannot be changed. Under guaranteed renewable contracts the insurer does have the right to change the premium rates on outstanding policies, but the change must affect broad classes of insureds—not only a single insured. The rate increase might be sufficient to cause the insured to discontinue his protection but it is the intention of most insurers issuing these contracts to exercise this right only in unusual situations.

Non-cancellable contracts and guaranteed renewable contracts provide a specified weekly indemnity if the insured is totally and continuously disabled by disease or by an accidental injury within some specified period, such as ninety days, following the accident. The sickness benefits are not payable until after a waiting or "elimination" period, and the average waiting period exceeds the average commercial sickness contract waiting period.

If an accidental injury makes it impossible for an insured to perform the duties of his usual occupation, benefits are payable for some maximum period such as twelve months or sixty months. If the insured cannot perform the duties of *any* gainful occupation for which he is reasonably fitted, the benefits may be continued for life.

If sickness caused the disability, the benefit duration depends upon the type of contract written. Short-term contracts provide benefits for three years or less; intermediate-term contracts for about five years; long-term contracts for about ten years; and extra-long-term contracts for fifteen years or, most commonly, to age sixty-five. Lifetime benefits are extremely rare.

Almost all these contracts provide for the waiver of future premiums in case of total and permanent disability. Most contracts provide short-term benefits in case of partial disability caused by an accidental injury, but long-term contracts restrict the payments to periods of partial disability following a period of total disability. Medical expense benefits are uncommon.

Many of these contracts, particularly the long-term and extra-long-term contracts, contain provisions for reducing the benefit if the total disability income insurance available to the insured exceeds a specified percentage of his earnings at the time he was disabled. Without this clause a moral hazard might be created if the insured's earnings dropped.

The exclusions in non-cancellable contracts and guaranteed renewable contracts are approximately the same as those found in commercial contracts.

The premiums for these contracts are level premiums similar to those paid for life insurance contracts. Sex and occupation are important rating factors, but the most important factor is age, because of the level premium and long term. Underwriting practices are strict, and a physical examination by a doctor is required of about half the applicants.

Industrial contracts are designed primarily for low-income groups. Premiums are payable weekly or monthly and are usually collected at the home of the insured. The benefits are essentially the same as those provided under the commercial contracts, but they are much lower in amount and somewhat more restricted.

Limited policies are policies which protect the insured for a very short period of time or against special types of illnesses. Examples are the railway travel policy and dread disease insurance contracts.

Commercial policies, non-cancellable policies, and guaranteed renewable policies play major roles in the search for economic security because they provide valuable protection for many persons against both loss of income and incurred medical expenses. Industrial policies provide less protection, but this protection is important to the low-income groups. The limited policies play a relatively minor role in our economic security system, but they may be helpful in individual cases.

Individual Medical Expense Contracts. *Basic medical expense insurance contracts* are the most frequently sold individual health insurance contracts. They may protect an individual or a family. The probability of incurring medical expenses looms greater than the probability of a loss of income, and the average person insures against unexpected medical expenses first. His principal concern is hospital expenses.

A typical hospital expense policy pays daily hospital room and board charges up to a specified amount, such as $10 or $15, for a specified period, such as thirty or 100 days. Hospital expenses other than room and board charges incurred during the same specified period are covered up to a specified dollar amount or some multiple, such as ten or fifteen, of the daily room and board allowance. Maternity benefits are limited to some multiple, such as ten, of the daily room and board allowance.

Typical exclusions are treatments for mental disorders, injuries covered under a workmen's compensation law, injuries or sickness for which care is provided by or in a federal government hospital, and injuries caused by war or attempted suicide. Mental disorders, however, are increasingly covered for any treatment received in a general hospital. No benefits are payable for injuries sustained while the insured is engaged in air travel other than as a fare-paying passenger on a scheduled airline. Maternity confinements are not covered unless the policy has been in force nine or ten months, and sometimes treatments for appendicitis, tonsillitis, and similar illnesses are also excluded during the first few months. On the other hand, the maternity coverage continues for nine or ten months following the expiration of the contract.

The contract may be written on a family basis. Dependent children are usually covered from age two weeks to eighteen or twenty-one years.

An addition to the hospital policy or, infrequently, a separate policy may provide surgical benefits, physicians' care benefits, or both. The surgical benefit is a schedule of allowances toward the actual cost of several specified surgical operations. An in-hospital physicians' care benefit provides $4 to $6 per visit beginning with the first or fourth visit for a specified number of days, such as 100 days, or until a maximum amount, such as $250, has been paid. Sometimes benefits are payable on essentially the same basis even if the physician treats the patient in his office or at the patient's home. The exclusions under all of these coverages are about the same as those under the hospital expense coverages.

Basic medical expense coverages are usually renewable only with the consent of the insurer. Some medical expense contracts, like disability insurance contracts, are conditionally renewable by the insurer but others may be cancelled with proper notice at any time. Hence, under most contracts, the insured faces the possibility of losing the coverage if his health deteriorates. Cancellation, however, does not affect the benefits payable on account of illness commencing while the policy is in force. The state laws limiting cancellation of commercial disability income contracts also apply to medical expenses. New York, in fact, imposes an additional requirement with respect to medical expense contracts in that it requires insurers to state an approved reason for cancellation. Deterioration of the insured's health is not an acceptable reason. Fortunately, noncancellable contracts and especially guaranteed renewable contracts have become much more readily available on a voluntary basis in recent years.

Basic medical expense rates vary primarily according to the sex of the insured, especially when maternity and obstetrical benefits are included. Age becomes important only at advanced ages.

Basic medical expense insurance enables the insured to budget systematically the medical expenses associated with less costly illnesses. It provides valuable protection if the insured becomes ill shortly after the policy is issued. Like the medical expense coverages in the income-medical expense contracts, it has a limitation in filling the economic security gap in that it provides little protection against the sizable medical expenses associated with long-term serious illnesses unless the insured is willing to pay the premiums necessary to purchase extremely high limits.

If he has that much money to spend, it would probably be more economical for him to self-insure the less costly, more frequent illnesses himself because these losses are relatively expensive for an insurer to adjust.

Major medical expense insurance contracts are designed for the person who wants to insure against sizable medical expenses at a reasonable cost. Individual and family contracts are issued. The main features of this important form of protection may be summarized as follows: (1) Almost every type of medical expense such as hospital bills, nurses' fees, medicine costs, surgical fees, and physicians' charges is covered. There are few, if any, limits on specific types of medical expenses. (2) The insurer agrees to contribute to the medical expenses only when they exceed a specified amount called the "deductible." The insured may select the deductible in accordance with his financial resources and desires. The deductible may apply to each illness or to the total expenses during some period. (3) Usually the insurer promises to pay only part, commonly 75 or 80 per cent, of the excess expenses in order to give the insured some incentive to keep the costs down. (4) The maximum contribution of the insurer is limited to some stated amount, such as $5,000, $10,000, or $20,000. These maximums may apply to each illness or to total expenses during a lifetime. In the latter case, it is usually possible to restore the maximum amount if the insured person incurs no expenses over a specified period.[3]

Treatments for mental or nervous disorders, except when treated in a general hospital, and for injuries covered by workmen's compensation are generally excluded. Other exclusions tend to be of minor importance.

Most major medical expense policies are cancellable or conditionally renewable, but guaranteed renewable contracts have increased considerably in importance in recent years.

Age is the most important factor affecting premiums even if the contract is cancellable. Other factors include income, sex, and occupation.

Comprehensive medical expense insurance contracts fall into two groups. The first is a major medical expense contract with a low deductible. The second commonly provides first basic hospitalization and surgical expense protection up to some specified amount such as $500. The other medical expenses are subject to a deductible and the insurer pays, say, 75 per cent of the expenses in excess of the basic coverage and the deductible amount. Comprehensive insurance has proved highly marketable and is considered to be major medical expense insurance even though it departs from the basic principle underlying that type of insurance—the assumption of all small losses by the insured.

[3] For a current comprehensive survey of major medical expense insurance, see Harry M. Johnson, "Major Medical Expense Insurance," *Journal of Risk and Insurance*, XXXII, No. 2 (June, 1965), 211–36.

The establishment of HI and SMI has led to the development of new individual coverages designed to supplement this government protection for the aged. These *coverages supplementing HI and SMI* usually take one of three forms: (1) They pay part or all of the cost of certain items not covered under HI or SMI such as prescription drugs, private duty nursing service, and hospital service beyond the HI limit plus some or all of the cost of the HI or SMI benefits that would otherwise be borne by the insured because of the deductible and coinsurance provisions. (2) They include most types of medical expense, including those covered under HI and SMI, but HI and SMI benefits are deducted under any amounts paid under these policies. (3) They pay a stated dollar benefit per day while the insured is in a hospital or a nursing home or is receiving some other specified type of medical care.

Medical expense policies cover only one of the two types of losses caused by accidental injury and sickness, but this type of loss has been a matter of great concern to the American public. Major medical expense insurance and comprehensive medical expense insurance are relatively recent innovations, but they have already established themselves as important parts of our economic security system.

Disability Provisions in Individual Life Insurance Contracts. Individual life insurance contracts also provide some disability benefits. Most life insurance contracts provide in the policy itself or through a rider for the waiver of future premiums if the insured is totally and permanently disabled prior to age fifty-five or sixty. About half of the largest one-hundred life insurers will also promise to pay $5 or $10 per month per $1,000 of insurance usually beginning with the sixth or seventh month of disability either for life or until some advanced age at which time the life insurance contract is converted into a matured endowment contract. This coverage is always provided through a rider attached to the life insurance policy and an additional premium is charged. The benefit is attractive because it is non-cancellable, relatively low in cost, and available for persons disabled by either an accidental injury or sickness. The major disadvantages are that this benefit is usually written only in conjunction with non-term insurance and that in order to obtain adequate disability income insurance, a person may have to purchase more non-term insurance than he desires or can afford.

Group Insurance

The advantages, nature, and history of group insurance have already been discussed in Chapter 5. Several additional factors are peculiar to group health insurance. First, the fact that an individual's protection cannot be cancelled unless the group contract is cancelled is especially valuable in health insurance. Second, because age is a much less important factor in health insurance than in life insurance, group health insurance is written on groups that would not be eligible for group life insurance. Third, group health insurance grew less rapidly than group life and pension plans until the forties. Now it is the most rapidly growing field of group insurance because of an increasing awareness by the public of the need for this form of protection, the more frequent inclusion of this protection in collective bargaining agreements, and the increased interest of private insurers.

Group health insurance includes temporary disability income insurance (often called group accident and health insurance), long-term disability income insurance, dismemberment insurance, and medical expense insurance: basic, major, and comprehensive. Usually the plans cover only non-occupational illnesses, but occupational illnesses are sometimes included. The only exclusion may be self-inflicted injuries.

Unlike group life contracts, most group health contracts do not permit a terminating group member to convert his group coverage to an individual contract. However, the medical expense benefits are usually continued for a three-month period if the insured terminates his membership because of total disability and remains totally disabled for that period. Furthermore, most insurers will today upon request include conversion rights in their group contracts. New York requires the inclusion of such conversion rights in group hospital and surgical expense contracts.

Premiums depend upon the percentage of females in the group and, in the case of the disability income and dismemberment coverages, upon the industry. The age and income composition of the group are important in group major medical expense insurance. Premiums are adjusted partly according to the experience of the particular group and partly according to the total group experience of the insurer. In addition to the rate for employees, there may be one rate for dependents, one for one dependent and another for two or more dependents, or one rate for a spouse only, another for children only, and a third for spouse and children.

Group Temporary Disability Income Insurance Contracts. These contracts provide an income for the person who is temporarily disabled. The insurer promises to pay a specified weekly income for a maximum period of thirteen or twenty-six weeks, or sometimes fifty-two or 104 weeks. Payments usually begin with the first day of disability due to an accidental injury and with the fourth or eighth day of disability due to sickness. The weekly income is usually two-thirds of the employee's wage, but typically does not exceed $60. If the plan covers occupational illnesses, workmen's compensation payments are deducted from the group insurance benefits. Maternity benefits, if included, are usually limited to six weeks.

According to a survey by the Health Insurance Institute of new group protection issued in 1964, 62 per cent of the employees covered by short-term plans were insured under thirteen-week contracts and 36 per cent under twenty-six-week contracts. Four out of five employees would receive benefits beginning with the first day of disability caused by an accident and the eighth day of disability caused by sickness. The maximum weekly benefit was $35 or more in about three-quarters of the plans.[4]

Group Long-Term Disability Income Insurance Contracts. This relatively new kind of protection pays totally and permanently disabled employees an income to some advanced age, such as sixty-five, after the completion of a lengthy waiting period. This insurance usually supplements paid sick leave and group temporary disability income plans and is usually restricted to the firm's higher-paid employees. This insurance is expected to grow rapidly in the years ahead but its progress, at least among the lower-paid workers, has probably been slowed by the 1965 liberalizations in the disability provisions of OASDI. Proper coordination of long-term disability benefits with other disability income payments such as OASDI benefits is an important feature of this insurance.[5]

Group Accidental Death and Dismemberment Contracts. These contracts provide for the payment of a lump sum if there is a loss of life, limb, or sight through solely external, violent, and accidental means within ninety days after an accident.

Group Basic Medical Expense Contracts. Included here are group hospitalization contracts, group surgical contracts, different forms of group physicians' care contracts, and minor coverages.

Typical group hospitalization insurance contracts promise to pay daily room and board charges up to $10–$20 for a period of hospital confinement up to 31–70 days. Sometimes the daily benefit is paid even if the actual charge is less. Reimbursement for other hospital expenses incurred within the covered period is limited to ten to thirty times the daily room and board allowance. A few plans place no dollar amounts on these expenses. There is a trend toward sharing with the insured the loss above twenty times the daily allowance. Maternity benefits are usually included, but the benefit is limited. For example, the maximum covered

[4] *Source Book of Health Insurance Data, 1965* (New York: Health Insurance Institute, 1965), pp. 29–30.

[5] For a comprehensive discussion of recent long-term disability insurance plans, including the methods used to coordinate these benefits with OASDI benefits, see J. Philip Starr, "Plan Design in Group Long Term and Disability Insurance," *Journal of Risk and Insurance,* XXXII, No. 4 (December, 1965), 509–23.

confinement is commonly fourteen days or ten to fifteen times the daily room benefit.

According to the 1964 survey of new group cases by the Health Insurance Institute, 40 per cent of the employees were entitled to daily room and board allowances of less than $16, 22 per cent to $16–$19.99, and the remainder to $20 or more. Eight per cent were covered for the full cost of semi-private or ward accommodations. About 36 per cent were entitled to maximum durations of thirty-one or thirty-five days, another 36 per cent for seventy days, 19 per cent for 100, 120, or 150 days, and 3 per cent for 180 days or more. Five per cent were in other categories.[6]

Group surgical insurance contracts promise to pay the cost of surgical operations up to the limit specified in a schedule. The maximum allowance is usually $200 or $300. In a few states, participating doctors have agreed to charge low-income groups a scheduled fee established by a local medical society, and the group surgical contract may provide these scheduled amounts. New group policies issued in 1964 had an average maximum benefit of $330.[7]

There are three group insurance plans covering the charges for a physician's care. The group in-hospital plan pays $4–$6 per day of confinement to cover the costs of physicians' visits (non-surgical) in the hospital. The group total disability insurance plan may pay $3 for an office call and $4 for a home call if the insured is totally disabled. Charges for hospital calls may be reimbursed up to $4 per call or $4 per day of confinement. The group comprehensive insurance contracts pay essentially the same benefits as the group total disability contracts, but total disability is not required and periodic health examinations and immunizations may be included in the protection. Under all three plans, the maximum payment is usually 50 to 100 times the maximum daily benefit rate provided.

Dependents, including a wife or husband and children from fourteen days to nineteen or twenty-two years of age, may be insured for the same or slightly less liberal benefits under each of the medical expense plans except the total disability plan because it would be difficult to tell if a dependent were totally disabled.

Group Major Medical Expense Insurance (*including group comprehensive insurance*). This is the most rapidly growing form of group medical expense insurance because of the important need it fills and because of its recent introduction. Its principal characteristics have already been noted in connection with individual contracts. It is sufficient to note here two

[6] *Source Book of Health Insurance Data, op. cit.,* p. 29.
[7] *Ibid.*

additional facts: First, group major medical expense and comprehensive contracts are more liberal than the individual equivalents. For example, most individual major medical contracts limit the period within which the expenses associated with an illness must be incurred to a stated period such as two or three years; there are usually no time limits in the group contracts. Second, the deductible in a major medical plan superimposed over a basic plan commonly assumes one of two forms. Under a *corridor* deductible, the deductible is the basic plan benefits plus a specified amount. Under an *integrated* deductible, the deductible is the basic plan benefits or the specified amount, whichever is greater.

Group Insurance Supplementing Hospital Insurance and Supplemental Medical Insurance. Group insurance contracts have been developed to supplement the medical expense insurance protection for the aged under HI and SMI. This insurance takes the three forms described earlier in connection with individual supplementary insurance policies.

Group Life Insurance Contracts. These contracts commonly provide that life insurance will be continued in force without charge for twelve months if a person under age sixty-five terminates his membership because of total disability and remains totally disabled. Most new contracts, however, provide for the waiver of premiums for life in case of total and permanent disability. A few provide for the payment of the face amount in case of death or total and permanent disability.

Group Pension Plans. Such plans may provide some assistance for a disabled person through their early retirement provisions. Under some plans, only totally disabled persons can retire early. Under others the amount of the early retirement pension is greater for a totally disabled person. Some plans include total and permanent disability income insurance as a separate feature. Usually they provide a specified income beginning within a few months after the occurrence of the disability and continuing to the date of normal retirement. A relatively few plans also waive future premium payments in case of total and permanent disability. Some of these waiver-of-premium benefits enable the insured to retire at the normal retirement age with the same income that he would have received had he continued to participate in the plan at the same salary up to that time.

In summary, the most frequently issued forms of group health insurance are temporary disability income insurance, the medical expense coverages, and dismemberment insurance. The last form is too limited to be considered a vital part of the economic security system. Long-term disability income losses are covered under relatively few group insurance plans.

Trends in Commercial Insurance Contracts

The first commercial health insurance contracts were issued about the middle of the nineteenth century, but it was not until the latter part of that century that the coverages were broadened and the industry became established. About the same time, life insurers introduced waiver-of-premium riders in their contracts.

The next important development was the writing of the first non-cancellable policy in 1915 in response to criticisms of the cancellation provisions in commercial contracts. In 1917, some life insurers added total and permanent disability income riders to their contracts. As competition became intense in the twenties, the contracts were further liberalized and lifetime income payments for total and permanent disability became common.

Group disability income insurance was first written in 1912 as a result of the Montgomery Ward group life insurance negotiations discussed in Chapter 5, but this form of insurance did not make much progress until the late twenties because both insurers and employers were directing most of their efforts toward the problems caused by premature death and old age. Meanwhile some group life and group pension plans included total and permanent disability income protection.

The thirties witnessed disastrous experience with lifetime indemnity coverages because of a combination of inadequate premiums, inadequate reserves, inadequate underwriting, and many improper claims. Almost all insurers withdrew from that field or seriously restricted their coverages. On the other hand, medical expense insurance began to grow because the Depression emphasized the need for this form of protection and a new competitor—the Blue Cross movement [8]—was born. Group hospitalization policies were issued for the first time in 1934; group surgical policies, in 1938.

As economic conditions improved during the forties, commercial life insurers cautiously re-entered the lifetime indemnity field, and health insurers began to liberalize their coverages. These liberalizations were made on a much sounder basis than they had been made in the twenties. The interest in medical expense coverages continued to grow rapidly, and group policies covering charges for physicians' care appeared in 1943. The most significant development was the first writing of a major medical expense policy in 1948. This policy was written on a group basis at the request of a society of employees of the General Electric Company, which was seeking this form of protection for its members.

[8] See pp. 433–34 for the history of the Blue Cross movement.

During the fifties and early sixties, further improvements occurred, reflecting increased competition, experience, and consumer interest. Policies are becoming more standardized and easier to read; more guaranteed renewable and non-cancellable policies are being issued; policy provisions are being liberalized with respect to definitions of disability, duration of benefits, and exclusions; more substandard lives are being insured; major medical expense and comprehensive insurance is being improved; and small deductibles are being included in basic medical expense coverages. This is an important period of experimentation, and many new approaches will be tried in the quest for economic security.

BLUE CROSS AND BLUE SHIELD PLANS

The most important competitors of the commercial insurers are the Blue Cross associations and the Blue Shield associations.[9] Their underwriting philosophy and their contracts differ significantly from those of commercial insurers. We shall now consider the contributions of these associations to our economic security system.

Blue Cross Plans

Blue Cross associations and commercial insurers are about equally important in the field of hospitalization insurance. A Blue Cross association is a voluntary non-profit hospital expense prepayment plan that has applied for and received the approval of the American Hospital Association and the Blue Cross association.[10] There are nearly eighty locally autonomous Blue Cross associations in the United States. Almost all the associations cover a state or part of a state, and, except in North Carolina, the plans are not competing. The promoters of most associations are hospitals in the plan area. Member hospitals usually elect the board of directors whose members represent the hospitals, the medical profession, and the public. Generally the member hospitals guarantee the plan benefits.

9 For an excellent discussion of the advantages which Blue Cross and Blue Shield enjoyed in their competition with commercial insurers and how they are losing those advantages, see C. A. Kulp, *Casualty Insurance* (3rd ed.; New York: The Ronald Press Co., 1956), pp. 359–60.

For a discussion of some recent problems, see Donald L. MacDonald, "Blue Cross Troubles: a Price of Delusion," *The Weekly Underwriter*, CLXXV, No. 20 (November 17, 1956), 1134–37, and Robert D. Eilers, *Regulation of Blue Cross and Blue Shield Plans* (Homewood, Ill.: Richard D. Irwin, Inc., 1963).

10 This non-profit corporation provides many services for the member plans and coordinates certain of their activities. It is responsible, for example, for administration of the Inter-Plan Service Benefit Bank Agreement and the Inter-Plan Transfer Agreement. It is also the national spokesman for the plans.

Initially, Blue Cross contracts were sold only to members of eligible groups. Most subscribers are still covered on that basis but increasing emphasis is being placed upon non-group enrollment. At the end of 1954, about three-fourths of the persons covered under Blue Cross contracts were enrolled through employee groups and another 15 per cent were former members of employee groups.[11] Each association has its own standards, but groups as small as two persons have been covered. The percentage of the group which is required to participate decreases as the size of the group increases.

Each association makes contracts with its subscribers and its member hospitals. All associations do not use the same contracts, and most of them offer more than one form of contract to their subscribers.

Subscriber Contracts. A "typical" Blue Cross contract with a subscriber promises to provide certain hospital *services* in a member hospital for a stated period of time, regardless of the cost of the services. This is one of the major differences between Blue Cross contracts and those issued by commercial insurers. If a subscriber wants better accommodations than those provided under the plan, he receives a limited cash allowance to help cover his expenses. In either case the subscriber receives no cash directly; his hospital bill is reduced.

For example, the contract may provide subscribers with room and board, general nursing service, use of the operating room, and a broad list of other hospital services in ward or semi-private accommodations of member hospitals for some specified number of days, such as 70 or 180, in each period of separate and unrelated disability in each membership year. Thus if the subscriber is hospitalized for the specified number of days or less, he may have no hospital bill to pay except for those services not listed among the covered hospital extras. Occasionally Blue Cross's practice of listing these extras results in lower benefits than the blanket approach of commercial insurers. At the close of 1962, 7 per cent of the Blue Cross subscribers were entitled under these "basic" certificates to 365 or more days of "full" service benefits.[12]

Partial benefits such as a 50 per cent allowance on all specified benefits are sometimes provided for an additional specified period, such as ninety days. Maternity benefits are usually limited in time or amount. If the subscriber wants private accommodations, some specified amount, such as the hospital's usual charge for semi-private accommodations, is

[11] Sol Levine, Odin Anderson, and Gerald Gordon, *Non-Group Enrollment for Health Insurance* (Cambridge: Harvard University Press, 1957).

[12] For a detailed summary of all the contracts issued by Blue Cross associations, see the latest issue of *Blue Cross Guide* published by the Blue Cross Association.

Blue Cross Association, *Special Blue Cross Enrollment Report,* March 5, 1964 (Statistical Bulletin No. 2B), Table 1.

allowed on the charges for room and general nursing services. All other benefits are generally provided on a full-service basis.[13]

The most common variation of the typical contract provides essentially the same benefits, but there is a dollar limitation, say $10 or $15 per day, on the charge for room and board and general nursing service. Other variations have dollar limitations on some or all of the hospital extras or small deductibles, such as $10 and $25, applicable to these charges. Under these contract variations, the subscriber is much more likely to have some hospital bill to pay.

Special benefits are provided for Blue Cross subscribers who may be hospitalized in a non-member hospital or in an institution which belongs to a different Blue Cross plan. Not many Blue Cross subscribers are hospitalized in non-member hospitals, because less than 10 per cent of the hospital beds fall in that category. Benefits in these non-member hospitals are limited to some specified amount, and the money is often paid to the insured after he has paid the hospital bill.

Because of the local autonomy of Blue Cross associations and territorial variations in hospital costs, a subscriber hospitalized in a member institution in a different area used to receive the same benefits that he would have received in any non-member hospital. Today an Inter-Plan Service Benefit Bank plan makes it possible for a participating plan to provide the service benefits of the plan in the area in which the subscriber may be hospitalized for the number of days to which he is entitled under his own plan. When a person moves from one area to another, an Inter-Plan Transfer Agreement enables him to maintain continuous coverage.

A Local Benefit Agreement for National Accounts provides a uniform basis for enrolling and administering national accounts which want local plan benefits in each area. Firms which wish to provide uniform coverage for employees in two or more plan areas can purchase a contract from a stock insurer, Health Service, Incorporated, which is owned by the member plans through their Blue Cross Association. In most cases, Health Service passes on to the individual plans the entire coverage underwritten. Health Service itself writes only that portion of the coverage which a local plan is unable or unwilling to provide.

Most contracts exclude workmen's compensation cases, cases where hospitalization is obtainable without cost from any governmental agency, hospitalization primarily for diagnostic studies, and rest cures. Other common exclusions or limitations apply to care for tuberculosis, nervous and mental diseases, venereal disease, alcoholism, and drug addiction. Pre-existing conditions may be excluded entirely or for the first six to twelve months. A waiting period may also apply to treatment for ton-

---

[13] Coverage for X-ray services is usually limited to a specified dollar amount

sillitis or adenoiditis, or, less often, appendicitis. Group contracts contain fewer limitations and exclusions than individual contracts.

Dependents may be insured for the same or slightly less liberal benefits. Dependents include the husband or wife and children, usually from birth to age nineteen or twenty-two.

Although Blue Cross contracts do not guarantee subscribers leaving an employee group the right to convert their group coverage, they have usually permitted these persons to secure an individual contract providing the same protection without proving insurability. This ease of continuing this protection may explain why maternity coverage terminates when the Blue Cross protection ends instead of being continued for, say, nine more months.

The premium structure is usually very simple. In addition to rates for the employee, there may be a rate for dependents or there may be two rates for dependents—one for a spouse only and a second for a spouse and children. Philosophically, the Blue Cross associations would prefer to add nothing more to this pricing structure than a distinction between group and individual insurance. This preference for "community rating" is based on the belief that in order for the benefits of private medical expense insurance to cover all or most of the population, some members of the population will have to subsidize other members of the population. This could be termed a quasi-social-insurance philosophy. Competitive pressures from private insurers, however, particularly with respect to groups among whom actual experience may vary widely, have forced most plans to experience rate groups with more than a specified number of members.[14]

Since the advent of major medical expense insurance, Blue Cross plans have become increasingly interested in providing protection against the more serious illnesses. "Extended benefit" contracts may simply provide additional hospital coverage for days beyond the basic contract, or they may cover 80 per cent of the hospital charges and physicians' fees incurred after the exhaustion of the benefits provided under basic contracts and the satisfaction of some "corridor" deductible. If physicians' services are covered, the contract is usually written in conjunction with a Blue Shield plan. Other expenses often included are drugs, appliances, nursing services, and out-patient diagnostic X-ray and laboratory service. These extended benefits can be purchased only in conjunction with a basic program.

[14] For an analysis of the relative merits of community rating and experience rating, see Duncan M. MacIntyre, *Voluntary Health Insurance and Ratemaking* (Ithaca, N. Y.: Cornell University Press, 1962).

Recent activities of Blue Cross associations with respect to experience rating are described in Robert D. Eilers, *Regulation of Blue Cross and Blue Shield Plans, op. cit.*

Blue Cross plans also underwrite contracts providing medical expense protection for the aged to supplement HI and SMI benefits.

Contracts with Member Hospitals. The contracts with the member hospitals prescribe the schedule of payments that these hospitals will receive for the services rendered Blue Cross subscribers. In some areas the plan pays all or part of the billed charges but the most common procedure is to base payments upon service cost statements provided by the hospitals, but to limit these payments to the charges to non-members. Costs are interpreted liberally to include depreciation and obsolescence, interest, and an increase in the contingency fund. Some plans have used average cost statements instead of individual cost statements in order to provide an incentive for more efficient hospital administration. The fact that Blue Cross may and often does pay less than the charges to the public has been justified partly by the fact that the hospital's cost of billing Blue Cross is low and there is no collection problem. The "community responsibilities" assumed by Blue Cross, however, are considered an even more important justification. Blue Cross, it is claimed, performs functions which would otherwise have to be performed by the hospitals and community agencies (1) when it provides payment for *all* care under a high-level service-type contract and (2) when it continues coverage throughout the lifetime of the subscriber because otherwise many of the current services rendered by hospitals would not be insured and the persons receiving the services would be unable to meet the charges out of their own funds.[15] This latter argument lost some of its force with the passage of Hospital Insurance and Supplementary Medical Insurance.

Trends in Blue Cross Contracts

Hospital expense prepayment plans have been traced back to 1880 in Minnesota and Oregon, but the modern movement is considered to have started with the Baylor University Hospital Plan in 1929. A group of teachers in the Dallas city schools who were impressed by the need for protection against hospital expenses approached the hospital administrators with the original idea. As a result of their talks, all Dallas teachers who belonged to a Sick Benefit Fund were promised twenty-one days of hospitalization in a semi-private room for a premium of 50 cents a month. Other groups joined the plan as its popularity grew.

Hospital administrators throughout the country studied the plan and many of them adapted the underlying principles to their own situation. They discovered that through such plans they could provide a valuable

[15] Basil C. Maclean, "Blue Cross Payments to Hospitals," Speech at the Eighth New York Institute for Hospital Administrators, Columbia-Presbyterian Medical Center, New York, N. Y., June 24, 1958.

form of protection and cut down the amount of free service that they were providing. The Depression and increasing hospital services had intensified their financial problems.

The fear of excessive competition among two or more plans in a given area and the disadvantages of limiting coverage to one hospital suggested the joint participation of several hospitals in a single plan. The first joint plan was established in 1932 in Sacramento, California, and was followed in 1933 by plans in six other cities.

In 1933 the American Hospital Association approved the principle of prepaid hospital expense and appointed a special committee to study the growing movement. The committee reported a few months later on the essentials of an acceptable plan. In 1936 the AHA established a Commission on Hospital Service as a clearing house and center for information and advice. In 1937 the Commission, which is now the Blue Cross Association, began to approve plans meeting their standards and Blue Cross was born.

Contracts have been improved from time to time. As in the case of the commercial insurers, increased competition, experience, and consumer interest are responsible for these improvements. The number of days of coverage has been increased to as many as 365 days or more, the list of hospital extras has been lengthened, and out-patient diagnostic service has become more common. Many plans have ventured into the comprehensive version of major medical expense insurance. The independent plans are learning to work together, and today the Blue Cross subscriber can receive service benefits in a different plan area. The community-rating concept has been replaced to some extent by experience rating. Individual contracts are becoming more common.

Blue Shield Plans

Blue Shield associations are voluntary non-profit prepayment plans covering surgical fees and charges for physicians' care which have applied and qualified for membership in the National Association of Blue Shield Plans.[16] This association is governed by eleven directors, three of whom are appointed by the American Medical Association. There are about seventy-five locally autonomous plans, most of them organized on a statewide basis. A local medical society usually initiates and controls the plan, the daily operation of the plan generally being handled by the staff of the local Blue Cross plan. Most of the plans are underwritten by the participating physicians.

[16] A few Blue Cross plans include surgical and physicians' care benefits in their hospital contracts, while several Blue Shield plans include hospital benefits in their contracts. In a few areas Blue Cross and Blue Shield plans compete.

Most Blue Shield contracts are sold to members of eligible groups, but individual contracts are receiving increasing attention. Conversion rights are granted under the group contracts.

Subscriber Contracts. The variations among the subscriber contracts offered by a given plan are minor, but there are significant variations among the different plans. All plans cover charges for surgical services and for non-surgical physicians' care in the hospital. About two-thirds cover X-ray examinations and therapy for in-patients or out-patients. Sometimes these latter services are covered instead under the Blue Cross plan; in other cases both the Blue Cross and Blue Shield plans provide this benefit on a cooperative basis. Over one-fourth of the plans will cover charges for physicians' care at the doctor's office or at the patient's home. The benefits are approximately the same as those provided under commercial group contracts, but there are usually more exclusions and no coverage during a specified period for pre-existing illnesses, tonsillitis, and adenoiditis. Dependents are eligible for the same or slightly less liberal benefits and children are usually considered dependents from birth to age nineteen or twenty-two.

Most contracts are partial service contracts. The patient is responsible for the difference between the benefit and the doctor's regular charge, but if the subscriber's family income from all sources is less than a specified amount, say, $4,000 for single subscribers and $6,000 for family subscribers, participating physicians agree to accept the benefit as full payment. Almost half of the plans now permit persons in an intermediate income group—higher than the income level eligible for service benefits in the basic plan but lower than some specified amount, say, $6,000 for single subscribers and $8,000 for famliy subscribers—to receive service benefits if they are willing to pay an additional premium.

In 1965 thirteen plans were written on a cash indemnity basis; six plans provided full-service benefits.[17]

About 90 per cent of the physicians in the United States are participating physicians, but in certain plan areas the percentage is much less than the average. About five-sixths of the plans promise to pay 50 or 75 per cent of the cash indemnity if the subscriber is treated by a non-participating physician. Most of the other plans pay the same cash indemnity to participating and non-participating physicians, but a few pay no benefits to non-participating doctors.

[17] The National Association of Blue Shield plans would like to have the plans provide full-service benefits for at least 75 per cent of the subscribers.

Several plans have recently developed a procedure under which a doctor files his regular fee schedule. If his charges are within the ninth decile of the charges of all physicians in the area, the plan will pay him his regular charges if he agrees to accept this amount as full payment for *all* patients.

If a subscriber covered under a full service or partial service plan is treated by a participating physician in another plan area, there is no guarantee that the physician will accept the benefit as full payment, but in practice this is what usually happens.

A stock insurer, Medical Indemnity of America, Incorporated, corresponds to Health Service, Incorporated, the Blue Cross insurer providing nationwide coverage.

The premium structure for Blue Shield contracts resembles that used by the Blue Cross associations.

Blue Shield plans have issued "extended benefit" contracts similar to or in conjunction with Blue Cross plans. They have also issued policies extending the protection afforded by HI and SMI.

Trends in Blue Shield Contracts

Medical society sponsored prepayment plans covering surgical fees and charges for physicians' care date back to 1929 in Washington and Oregon. They were an outgrowth of earlier prepayment plans controlled by lay persons which started in the 1880's when employers entered into contracts for the provision of service to workers injured on the job. Because the physicians found that the lay associations were forcing the doctors to compete for their subscribers on a price basis, county medical societies organized their own medical service bureaus.

The movement did not grow rapidly until 1939 when the California Physicians Service was established on a statewide basis by the California Medical Association. The governor of California had proposed a social medical expense insurance bill and the doctors resolved to prove that a voluntary plan would work. Soon plans were being formed in other areas.

Blue Cross plans encouraged the movement, for their subscribers were requesting coverage against doctors' bills, and commercial insurers were providing this protection. In 1942 the American Medical Association approved the principle of prepayment plans sponsored by medical societies. During the next three years the Council on Medical Service and Public Relations coordinated the existing plans and gave guidance to local medical societies which were interested in establishing new plans. Some plans began to display the Blue Shield symbol. In 1946 a definite set of standards was made public and the formal approval program, which is now controlled by the National Association of Blue Shield Plans, was started.

The coverages are gradually being liberalized. Physicians' care in the hospital, in the doctor's office, or at home is being provided in more contracts; benefit amounts are being increased; exclusions and waiting periods are becoming less numerous; and service benefits are becoming more common. Many Blue Shield plans now issue comprehensive medical expense insurance contracts similar to those being sold by commercial insurers.

INDEPENDENT PLANS

The independent plans include all accidental injury and sickness plans other than those underwritten by commercial insurers and Blue Cross and Blue Shield associations. The plans may be divided into three major categories: (1) paid sick leave plans, (2) supplementary workmen's compensation benefit plans, and (3) medical expense plans.

Paid Sick Leave Plans

Paid sick leave plans are the only important non-occupational disability income plans in addition to those underwritten by commercial insurers. These sick leave plans may be formal or informal: the benefits may be paid according to a predetermined formula or they may be awarded on some discretionary basis at the time of need. The plans are self-insured by the employer.

The plans usually continue the employee's salary in full, beginning with the first day of absence from work. There is usually a maximum number of days of sick leave per year and this maximum may be a function of the length of service. More than half the firms with paid sick leave plans also have an insured temporary disability insurance plan.

Supplementary Workmen's Compensation Benefit Plans

Plans under which a firm seeks to supplement workmen's compensation payments have become more common in recent years because workmen's compensation benefits have lagged behind temporary disability insurance payments. A variety of practices are used in these supplementary payment plans.[18] The most common single practice is to pay the employee his full compensation, from which workmen's compensation is deducted.[19] Most companies also tend to maintain a distinct, separate, self-insured program for such supplemental payments. Sometimes a paid sick leave plan or group temporary disability income insurance is used.

[18] Harland Fox, "Company Supplements to Workmen's Compensation," *Occupational Disability and Public Policy* (New York: John Wiley and Sons, Inc., 1962).

[19] Interestingly enough, this type of supplement does not appear to have given rise to any of the legal, ethical, and economic issues that have arisen in conjunction with unemployment supplements. Nor, so far as we know, has anyone studied the effects on incentives of the 100 per cent benefit, which was the most common practice, as noted in the paragraph above. These plans merit further investigation.

Medical Expense Plans

In 1962 there were about 800 independent medical expense plans in the United States.[20] About half of these plans had enrollments of less than 5,000. Because the plans are a very heterogeneous group, their operations and benefits will be discussed only in general terms.

Two-thirds of the independent plans are industrial plans whose membership is restricted to the employees of a single establishment or union and to their dependents. Independent industrial plans differ from other industrial plans in that they have elected to self-insure their benefits instead of purchasing coverage from some health insurer. Most of these plans are controlled and operated directly by a union or group of unions, the funds usually being provided at least in part by employers. The second most common group is jointly financed and controlled by the employer and the employee or union. Employee-sponsored plans are the third most common, and employer-sponsored the least common.

An example of a liberal industrial plan is the medical program of the United Mine Workers of America Welfare and Retirement Fund. This program provides medical care and rehabilitation services for miners and their dependents and survivors of deceased miners. Services provided by approved physicians and hospitals (located primarily in coal mining areas) are covered almost completely. The welfare and pension programs of the fund are financed by employer payments equal to a specified royalty rate per ton of coal mined.

The non-industrial plans include plans sponsored by a community or some consumer organization, a medical society, a dental society, or a private group clinic. Community plans are sponsored by the public and are open to groups or to individuals in the community. Consumer plans resemble community plans, but each member must belong to the consumer organization operating the plan. Medical society plans resemble the Blue Shield plans, but their sponsors either have not applied for or have not gained Blue Shield approval. Dental society plans are prepayment dental care plans sponsored by dental societies. Private group clinic plans are prepayment plans operated under the direction, control, and ownership of a group of doctors or dentists.

An example of a liberal non-industrial community plan is the Health Insurance Plan of Greater New York, a non-profit corporation that contracts with various medical groups owned and controlled by their mem-

[20] Louis S. Reed, *The Extent of Health Insurance Coverage in the United States*, Research Report No. 10, Social Security Administration, U. S. Department of Health, Education, and Welfare (Washington, D. C.: U. S. Government Printing Office, 1965), p. 39. Data on a 1965 survey are expected to become available soon.

ber doctors to provide the service. The plan provides medical care by a doctor and home nursing service. Service provided within one of the plan group practice areas by approved physicians is covered in full (except that a small charge may be made for night calls by a doctor) with limited cash payments being made if for any reason the subscriber cannot be served by his medical group. Each subscriber is entitled to one physical examination per year. Subscribers are required to purchase hospital insurance from a Blue Cross association or some other health insurer.

Group Health Insurance of New York City, another well-known independent plan, uses a different approach. Subscribers may choose between two contracts—one covering only surgery, in-hospital medical care, and X-ray and laboratory services and the other comprehensive medical care. Any physician is eligible to participate if he agrees to accept the plan benefits as full payment for his services. Hospital insurance must be purchased from some other health insurer.

Four Kaiser Health Plans in the western part of the United States provide hospital care through their own hospitals. Members can choose to receive comprehensive service benefits from a closed panel of physicians and surgeons or to retain complete free choice of doctors and receive reimbursement benefits. Originally designed as industrial plans, these four plans now serve the communities in which they are located.

Other large non-industrial plans include the Group Health Association of Puget Sound, the Group Health Association of Washington, D. C., and the Ross-Loos Medical Group of Los Angeles.

Dental society plans are limited to dental services. Although these plans presently account for a small proportion of the total enrollment under independent plans, they are the fastest growing component.

About two-fifths of the enrollees in the independent plans receive at least one type of benefit on a service basis through a group practice arrangement.[21] The prepayment plan may provide the service itself or it may have a contractual arrangement with a community hospital or a group practice clinic owned or operated by private physicians.

Group practice arrangements are much more popular among industrial plans than non-industrial plans. Dental and diagnostic benefits are the types of benefits most likely to be provided through a group practice arrangement; hospitalization is the benefit which is least likely to be provided in this fashion.

About three-fifths of the enrollees in non-industrial plans are dependents of subscribers while less than one-half of the industrial plan enrollees

[21] Medical society plans which may provide service benefits to low-income subscribers do not provide their benefits through group practice arrangements and are not included in this fraction.

are dependents. Most of the railway hospital plans and many of the union plans do not provide benefits for dependents.

Most of the persons covered under the independent plans will be able to supplement their protection under Hospital Insurance and Supplementary Medical Insurance with benefits provided by the independent plans.

Premiums do not generally vary among subscribers, but an additional premium is charged for each dependent, up to three or four dependents.

Trends in Independent Plans

Four significant trends have been noted since 1950. First, enrollment in independent plans has changed only slightly in recent years but benefits have increased substantially, especially for physicians' services. Second, union-sponsored plans, private group clinics, and community plans have experienced the greatest expansion. Medical society plans have become a relatively unimportant component, but dental society plans are becoming more significant. Third, more plans are providing benefits through their own group practice clinics and hospitals. Finally, most plans supplement public medical expense insurance benefits for retired workers.

The independent plans include many novel approaches to the medical expense problem, and the more popular plans will continue to adopt some of their ideas. However, in some states, legislative barriers have been erected which hinder this type of useful experimentation.

OPERATIONS OF PRIVATE HEALTH INSURERS

The recent past has witnessed a remarkably rapid increase in voluntary private health insurance. As evidence of this progress two types of data will be presented—the number of persons insured and the percentage of illness losses covered by private health insurance benefits.

The Health Insurance Council, an organization of various commercial insurance trade associations, reports annually on the number of persons covered under private insurance contracts. Although reported by the Council, the estimates are made by the largest of its member trade associations, the Health Insurance Association of America. The figures do not include persons covered under workmen's compensation insurance, total and permanent disability riders on life insurance contracts, or commercial contracts covering accidental injuries only. The figures do include workers covered under private plans in the four states with temporary disability insurance legislation.

The first annual report indicated the number covered as of December 31, 1947, while the latest report available as of this writing depicted the situation as of December 31, 1964. Table 12.1 presents and compares data on the number covered at the close of 1950 and 1964.

Data are not available on the number of persons protected against major medical expenses but there are data on the number of persons with commercial insurance protection against these expenses. At the close of 1951 only 108 thousand persons were so insured, about 89 per cent under group policies. By the end of 1964, 47,001 thousand had this coverage, about 91 per cent under group policies.

The data indicate (1) a tremendous growth in all forms of coverage, especially the physicians' care and major medical expense coverages; (2) the greater popularity and more rapid growth of medical expense coverages as compared with loss of income coverages; (3) the dominant role of commercial insurers and the Blue Cross-Blue Shield movements; and (4) the large and increasing importance of group insurance.

Information concerning the number of persons protected under private health insurance has also been gathered by six national household interview surveys during the past twelve years. Some of these surveys were conducted by private groups; the others by public agencies. In a recent Social Security Administration research report comparing the data in Table 12.1 with the results of the household interview surveys, the analyst concluded that "the HIAA findings run consistently higher by 3 to 7 percentage points—or 6 to 10 per cent. While both sets of data are approximations, the available evidence would seem to indicate that (a) the true extent of health insurance coverage may be closer to the findings of the household surveys than to the HIAA estimates and (b) any overstatement in the HIAA figures results from overstatement by insurance companies of the number of gross enrollments, probably largely under individual policies and/or insufficient allowance for duplicate insurance company coverage." [22]

In a report on private health insurance in the *Social Security Bulletin,* the Social Security Administration presented its own estimates on the number of persons enrolled for the different types of benefits with the various types of insurance. These estimates are based on enrollment data, not household surveys. The Social Security Administration accepted the HIAA report for commercial insurance but developed its own enrollment figures for Blue Cross and Blue Shield and revised the earlier estimates for independent plans. The major difference between the two tabulations is that under the government report the number enrolled

[22] Louis S. Reed, *The Extent of Health Insurance Coverage in the United States, op. cit.,* p. 32.

TABLE 12.1

Number of People Protected Under Private Health Insurance, End of 1950 and End of 1964

(In Thousands)

Plan	End of 1950	End of 1964	Per Cent Increase
Loss of income:			
Commercial insurance			
Group insurance	15,104	24,434	61.8%
Individual insurance	13,067	15,443	18.2
Total	28,171	39,877	41.6
Paid sick leave *			
Private industry	4,500	3,700	-17.8
Civilian government service	3,900	1,200	84.6
Total	8,400	10,900	29.8
Union administered plans *	1,500	550	-63.3
Employee mutual benefit associations *	1,400	550	-60.7
Grand Total	39,471	51,877	31.4
Deduct for duplication	2,178	3,706	
Net Total	37,293	48,171	29.2
Per cent of civilian population	25%	27%	

	Hospital Expense	Surgical Expense	Physicians' Care Expense	Hospital Expense	Surgical Expense	Physicians' Care Expense	Hospital Expense	Surgical Expense	Physicians' Care Expense
Medical expense:									
Commercial insurance									
Group insurance	22,305	21,219	5,587	64,506	64,939	47,446	189.2%	260.0%	749.2%
Individual insurance	17,296	13,718	2,714	39,724	34,775	12,318	129.7	153.5	353.9
Blue Cross plans and plans sponsored by medical societies	38,822	19,690	11,428	62,922	54,028	50,746	62.1	174.4	344.0
Independent plans:									
Industrial	2,392	2,073	2,121	4,800	4,800	4,400	100.7	131.6	107.4
Community–consumer	801	396	302	2,090	3,400	3,300	160.9	758.6	992.7
Private group clinics	326	350	350	60	250	250	−81.4	−28.6	−28.0
University health plans	100	100	100	400	300	900	300.0	200.0	800.0
Grand Total	82,042	57,546	22,602	174,502	162,492	119,360	112.7	182.4	428.1
Deduct for duplication †	5,403	3,390	1,013	23,379	21,825	10,643			
Net Total	76,639	54,156	21,589	151,123	140,667	108,717	97.2	159.8	403.6
Per cent of civilian population	51%	36%	14%	79%	74%	57%			

* Net figures after adjustment for duplication of other coverage.

† Duplication among persons with more than one commercial insurance policy accounts for about one-half of these totals. For example, in 1964 the net total of those persons with each of the three types of coverage was 93,209, 89,558, and 55,174.

Sources: The Health Insurance Council, *A Survey of Accident and Health Coverage in the United States* (New York: 1951), and *The Extent of Voluntary Health Insurance Coverage* (New York: 1965). The data also appear in the Health Insurance Institute, *Source Book of Health Insurance Data, 1965* (New York: 1965). The 1950 data used in the table are the latest revised estimates.

TABLE 12.2

Private Insurance Benefits in Relation to Disability Income Losses and Private Consumer Expenditures for Medical Care, 1950 and 1964

(In Millions)

Type of Loss	1950			1964		
	Loss	Insurance Benefits	Per Cent of Loss Covered by Insurance	Loss	Insurance Benefits	Per Cent of Loss Covered by Insurance
Income loss: *						
Disability income loss	$4,795	$940	19.6	$10,216	$3,068	30.0
Net cost of disability income insurance †	307	—	—	640	—	—
Total	$5,102	$940	18.4	$10,856	$3,068	28.3
Medical expenses:						
Hospital services	$1,965	$680	34.6	$ 7,552	$5,205	68.9
Physicians' services	2,597	312	12.0	6,775	2,602	38.4
Dentists' services	961	—	—	2,341	—	—
Other professional services	370	—	—	850	—	—
Drugs and drug sundries	1,716	—	—	4,341	—	—
Eyeglasses and appliances	482	—	—	1,043	—	—
Nursing home care	110	—	—	789	—	—
Total	$8,201	$992	12.1	$23,691	$7,808	33.0
Net cost of medical expense insurance †	300	—	—	1,151	—	—
Total	$8,501	$992	11.7	$24,842	$7,808	31.4

*Short-term non-work-connected disability (lasting not more than six months) and the first six months of long-term disability.
† Premiums earned less benefits incurred.

Sources: Louis S. Reed and Ruth S. Hanft, "National Health Expenditures, 1950-65," *Social Security Bulletin*, XXIX, No. 1 (January, 1966), 14–15; and Saul Waldman, "Income-Loss Protection Against Short-Term Sickness, 1948–64," *Social Security Bulletin*, XXIX, No. 1 (January, 1966), 26.

under independent plans in 1950, particularly community-consumer plans, was greater than under the HIAA report, thus reducing the rates of growth for these plans. For example, omitting university health plans, which are not considered in the government report, hospital insurance enrollment under independent plans increased from 3,945 thousand in 1950 to 6,950 thousand in 1964, an increase of 76 per cent. HIAA data showed an increase of 97 per cent from 3,519 thousand to 6,950 thousand.[23] Notice that both enrollment estimates for 1964 are the same.

Data from the National Health Survey indicate that medical insurance coverage is closely related to family income. Only 34 per cent of the families with less than $2,000 annual income had hospital or surgical insurance in 1962–63. The educational level of the family head, which is highly correlated with the family income, is also an important factor, especially in the lower income groups. Other influencing factors include age, occupation, and race.[24]

The Social Security Administration also uses a different yardstick to determine the growth of private health insurance. It reports annually the total non-occupational short-term disability income losses and medical expenses and the percentage of the losses covered by private insurance benefits. Table 12.2 summarizes the record of private insurance according to this measure in 1950 and 1964. The data are presented in such a way that it is possible to compare the benefits with the losses including or excluding the expenses, contingency reserves, and profits of insurers.

The growth of all forms of private health insurance is impressive.[25] The percentage of medical expenses covered in 1950 was considerably less than the percentage of disability income losses covered, but medical expenses are now more fully covered than disability losses. Hospital bills are the most nearly completely covered type of expense, but the most rapidly growing type of insurance covers doctors' charges.

[23] Louis S. Reed, "Private Health Insurance in the United States: An Overview," *Social Security Bulletin*, XXVIII, No. 12 (December, 1965), 15.

[24] U. S. Department of Health, Education, and Welfare, Public Health Service, *Medical Care, Health Status, and Family Income*, Vital and Health Statistics, National Center for Health Statistics, Series 10, No. 9 (Washington, D. C.: U. S. Government Printing Office, 1964), 5–10.

[25] The disability income insurance benefits include benefits under state temporary disability insurance legislation and the Railroad Unemployment Insurance Act. In 1964 group insured plans paid $124 million in benefits under these laws, self-insurers paid $71 million, and publicly operated funds $264 million. The insurance protection against medical expenses includes the insurance benefits provided by private insurers under the New York and California temporary disability insurance legislation. The data, therefore, overstate the role of voluntary private insurance. On the other hand, to omit these benefits would understate this role because many of the persons covered under this legislation would be covered by private plans even if these acts did not exist. Many were already insured under private plans when the legislation was passed.

Of the insurance benefits covering income losses, 52 per cent were paid by sick leave plans, 39 per cent by commercial insurers and self-insurers, and 9 per cent by publicly operated cash sickness funds. These data emphasize the liberal individual payments under the sick leave plans because relatively few people are covered under these plans. Of the medical expense benefits, about 46 per cent were paid by Blue Cross-Blue Shield associations, 48 per cent by commercial insurers, and 6 per cent by the independent insurers.

In interpreting these data it should be remembered that complete coverage is impossible for underwriting reasons. In fact if the expenses of the insurer are included in the losses, the per cent would be less than unity even if all losses were paid. Furthermore, complete coverage may not be desirable if it is more economical to retain some of the losses as operating expenses. Finally, one very able exponent of the private insurance viewpoint has observed that many people do not feel any need for health insurance because (1) they do not have to pay for the care they receive (servicemen, for example), (2) their religious views make them opposed to insurance, or (3) their income is so high that they prefer to meet their expenses out of current income or savings.[26]

The Social Security Administration recognizes that complete coverage may not be a fair benchmark. Consequently, with respect to disability income losses, they also compute insurance benefits as a percentage of the income loss that may be considered insurable or compensable under prevailing insurance practices. First they recognize that insurance plans are not designed to cover the first few days or the first week of disability. Eliminating the first three days cuts the income loss 30 per cent; eliminating the first week reduces the loss 45 per cent. They also exclude the income losses of those workers who are covered exclusively under paid sick-leave programs, which on the average cover 74 per cent of the income losses of those workers. In 1950 insurance benefits met 15.4 per cent of the income loss excluding the first three days and 19.5 per cent of the income loss excluding the first seven days. In 1964, the percentages were 25.0 and 31.8 respectively. In 1959, the peak year, these two percentages were 25.4 and 32.4. The Social Security Administration further recognizes that insurers prefer to compensate the disabled person for less than his total insurable loss in recognition of the fact that a disabled person's non-medical expenses including taxes are reduced and that there must be some incentive to return to work. The Social Security Administration assumes that two-thirds of the wage loss is a reasonable standard. On this basis, the percentage of the income loss covered by insurance benefits in 1950 was 23.0 excluding the first three days and 29.3 excluding the

[26] J. F. Follman, Jr., "Some Medico-Economic Trends," *The Journal of Insurance*, XXVII, No. 2 (June, 1960), 49.

first week. In 1964 the respective percentages were 37.5 and 47.7. No reliable data are available on private protection against long-term disability income losses but it is small.

With respect to medical expenses, the Social Security Administration formerly computed the percentage of "currently insurable" expenditures and of "potentially insurable" expenditures met by insurance. Currently insurable expenditures omitted the costs of nursing homes, nursing care, and care from other non-physicians plus nine-tenths of the expenditures for drugs and appliances. These expenses are not included under most health insurance contracts. In 1949 insurance benefits were only about 14.9 per cent of these expenditures but by 1959 this proportion had increased to 36.0 per cent. Potentially insurable expenditures include the types of benefits included under the newer, broader forms which comprise about 80 per cent of the total medical expenses. On this basis, the proportion of the expenses covered by insurance was 13.4 per cent in 1949 and 32.4 per cent in 1959. In its 1961 report on 1960 expenses, the Social Security Administration stopped providing this measure "because of recent developments in medical care insurance," which have covered losses formerly considered not insurable.

Unfortunately, these data do not tell us to what extent some families benefited more than others from private insurance benefits. The benefits may be widespread in their impact or a small percentage of the families may have a large percentage of their losses covered. Furthermore, there is no information on the types of benefits paid. It makes a difference both to the family and to society whether the benefits were used to pay for a few serious losses or for many non-serious losses.

The Health Information Foundation study, noted in the preceding chapter, does provide some information on this score with respect to medical expenses. Among the insured families incurring total expenses in 1963 in excess of $500,

64 per cent had 20 per cent or more of their charges met by insurance,
34 per cent had 50 per cent or more of their charges covered, and
12 per cent had 80 per cent or more of their charges covered.

The three percentages were, respectively, 56, 24, and 4 in 1958, and 49, 19, and 2 in 1953.[27]

[27] "Trends in Voluntary Health Insurance," *Progress in Health Services*, XV, No. 1 (January–February, 1966), 5.

Odin W. Anderson with Jacob J. Feldman, *Family Medical Costs and Voluntary Health Insurance: A Nationwide Survey* (New York: McGraw-Hill Book Co., 1956), pp. 49–50.

Odin W. Anderson, Patricia Collette, and Jacob J. Feldman, "Health Insurance Benefits for Personal Health Services, 1953 and 1958: Nationwide Surveys," Research Series 15 (New York: Health Information Foundation, 1960), pp. 7–8.

Data from the continuing National Health Survey present a more favorable picture with respect to hospital expenses. Among insured families with hospital expenses in 1958–60, 7.9 per cent reported less than half of these expenses met by insurance, 16.6 per cent had one-half to three-quarters of their expenses covered, and 75.4 per cent three-quarters or more. Higher income groups had a greater proportion of their expenses covered than lower income groups.[28]

EVALUATION [29]

Private health insurance has expanded significantly but few people would claim that there are no important unsolved problems. In this section we shall consider separately the protection afforded, underwriting practices, the problems of overutilization and overinsurance, premium structures, and the type of control.

Protection Afforded

Private insurance contracts are available that protect insureds against long-term disability income losses, short-term disability income losses, and medical expenses.

Under most individual disability income policies, the insurer will pay lifetime benefits for a total disability caused by accidental injury. If the disability is caused by sickness, however, most policies limit the benefit duration to a few years although benefits to age sixty-five are becoming more common. Partial permanent disability payments are always limited to a relatively short period. Disability income riders on life insurance policies protect the insured against long-term total disability income losses, regardless of the cause, but it is necessary to purchase a sizable amount of life insurance before the disability income amount is reasonably adequate. Group plans seldom provide any long-term disability income protection but this type of protection is becoming more common.

At present long-term disability is the weakest area in private health insurance, but commercial insurers appear to be gradually solving some

---

28 *Medical Care, Health Status, and Family Income, op. cit.,* p. 21.

29 For an extensive objective critique of commercial health insurance, see Kulp, *op. cit.,* pp. 391–98 and Dickerson, *op. cit.,* pp. 218–301, 328–33, 365–67, and 407–10.

For an often-quoted comprehensive analysis of all forms of private health insurance, see Herman M. Somers and Anne R. Somers, "Private Health Insurance, Part I: Changing Patterns of Medical Care Demand and Supply in Relation to Health Insurance," and "Part II: Problems, Pressures, and Prospects," *California Law Review,* XLVI, Nos. 3 and 4 (August and October, 1958), 376–410 and 508–57. Also see Herman M. Somers and Anne R. Somers, *Doctors, Patients and Health Insurance* (Washington, D. C.: The Brookings Institution, 1961).

of their important underwriting problems and long-term disability income protection should be continually improved. The 1965 liberalization in OASDI eligibility requirements and benefit amounts has caused some insurers to look less favorably upon this field, particularly with respect to low-income workers. Others believe that the government program will increase the demand for their product and that possible overinsurance problems can be solved through suitable offset provisions. Further extensions of the government program may depend to a large extent upon private insurance progress.

Temporary disability income benefits are readily available from commercial insurers on an individual or group basis and under paid sick leave plans. The cause of the disability may be an accidental injury or sickness. Waiver of premium benefits is also readily available in individual life insurance and guaranteed renewable contracts.

Under almost all disability income contracts, disability is not defined in terms of a loss of income. Administrative reasons have been cited to justify the definitions used, but, in the opinion of the authors, a more logical definition based upon the loss of income is needed. The need for a change in the present definitions is being discussed more frequently both within and outside the insurance industry.

Individual sickness contracts almost always require that the sickness commence during the policy period. Therefore, a claim may be denied on the grounds that the illness was pre-existing even though the insured was unaware of its existence at the time he purchased the contract. However, most states do not permit commercial insurers to deny claims on this basis after the policy has been in effect for two or three years. Many insurers follow this practice voluntarily in the other states. The other exclusions under most disability income contracts are not too important for the average person.

Many types of medical expense coverages are available. The prospective insured may choose among commercial individual and group insurance contracts, Blue Cross and Blue Shield plans, and independent plans.

Some medical expense plans usually provide complete protection for non-serious illnesses, but most contracts always require the insured to pay part of the bill himself. When the medical facilities are costless, the insured is more likely to seek early treatment, which should reduce the severity of the illness. On the other hand, complete protection may encourage overutilization of the medical resources.

Many plans provide full or partial service benefits. The loss of freedom of choice of medical facilities is slight under most of these contracts, but some are very restrictive in this respect. In fact, some plans require treatment in one hospital by a limited group of doctors. To some persons, however, even this restriction is not important.

Until recently, medical expense insurance was primarily a device for budgeting the cost of non-serious illnesses over a number of years. Protection against financial catastrophes at a reasonable cost is a recent innovation, but it is growing rapidly.

Insurance against the costs of non-surgical care by a physician, nursing-home care, various forms of home care, dental services, and the like needs to be more fully developed and marketed. There is reason to believe and some evidence to indicate that hospital utilization is reduced when non-hospitalized illness is covered under the same plan.[30] In addition, as Somers and Somers have pointed out, in our country chronic and mental illnesses are becoming increasingly important for a variety of reasons, including the growing proportion of the aged in our population. This trend has increased the demand for more comprehensive benefits.[31] Private insurers already are active in some of these fields and experimenting in others.[32] Independent plans have often pioneered in these and other areas and their activities, including the use of group practice arrangements, should not be hindered by artificial barriers.

Benefits covering diagnostic and preventive services and vision care are more debatable. At present most plans do not provide these benefits but some diagnostic services such as those provided in the out-patient department of a hospital are already common. In most cases it may be cheaper for an insured to pay for such services as periodic health examinations and immunizations at the time he incurs the expense because the expense is certain and the insured saves the expense loading of the insurer. On the other hand, (1) insureds are more likely to take advantage of these preventive services when they have paid for them, thus reducing the other services which are necessary, and (2) the cost per examination is reduced by distributing the overhead expense among more persons.

The exclusions under medical expense contracts are more numerous and more important than those under disability income contracts, but they are being reduced. Group insurance contracts tend to be more liberal than individual contracts. Treatment for mental and nervous disease is limited or excluded under most contracts.

Age limitations are common in both disability income and medical expense contracts, especially those of commercial insurers. These limitations are not too important in the case of disability income insurance because the insured's earning power would normally stop at some advanced

---

[30] According to Somers and Somers, "Private Health Insurance . . . ," *ibid.*, p. 392, the hospital utilization rate for members of some comprehensive independent plans was about 60–80 per cent of that for members of the "Blues."

[31] *Ibid.*, p. 554.

[32] For example, see Dickerson, *op. cit.*, pp. 287–301.

age, but the need for medical expense insurance increases at advanced ages. Until the establishment of Hospital Insurance and Supplementary Medical Expense Insurance, insurers were devoting much study to this problem and age limits were increased under many contracts. Some contracts were guaranteed renewable for life. Now that these two government programs are in operation, insurers have turned their attention to providing protection that will supplement the government protection.

Opinions as to the adequacy of the present plans vary, depending upon the standard desired. Those who believe that the plans should provide complete protection against all types of medical expenses would consider the present plans inadequate. Ideally private health insurance should be available that would pay all the losses that the insured family cannot, without more than temporary inconvenience, handle out of its current income and small savings accounts. On this score, private insurance rates fairly high and its record is improving, but there are still some important gaps and weaknesses to be overcome.

Underwriting

A larger percentage of applicants is ineligible for private health insurance than for private life insurance. Advanced age and poor health are the principal reasons for the rejections. Moreover, individual contracts can usually be cancelled or not renewed if the insurer finds it necessary to take this step.

Much more attention is now being paid to substandard lives and the rural population. Although the aged are now eligible for extensive medical expense benefits under HI and SMI, private insurers sell contracts supplementing this government protection. Most leading insurers also sell disability income and medical expense insurance on a guaranteed renewable or a non-cancellable basis under which they relinquish their right to cancel or to refuse to renew the contract to some advanced age.

Group insurance is another solution to the problem of individual uninsurability because all members of an eligible group are insurable. Although group protection cannot, for underwriting reasons, be extended to cover all persons in the population, insurers have broadened their concept of eligible groups to include smaller groups and new types of groups such as trade associations, professional associations, employer associations, and unions. One version of group insurance is the "mass enrollment" technique offered by several insurers under which aged persons in an area are invited to enroll during a specified period for protection supplementing Hospital Insurance and Supplementary Medical Insurance. Eligibility for individual medical expense insurance is also increased through group insurance because under most non-commercial plans and an increasing number of commercial insurance plans, terminating members are permitted to purchase individual insurance contracts without proving insurability.

There will always be some persons who will be ineligible for private insurance. Others will not choose or be able to afford the protection, and the protection purchased will probably always be incomplete for many others. Most persons agree that, for these reasons, there will be a continuing need for public assistance programs covering the expenses of medical care for all age groups. Some believe that these gaps will result in an extension of existing public disability income and medical expense insurance programs.

Overutilization and Overinsurance

The twin problems of overutilization and overinsurance have received considerable attention in recent years. Overutilization of medical services consists of a more frequent use of these services than necessary, the use of more expensive or extended services than required, and unreasonable charges by suppliers. Various studies have indicated that insured persons are more likely to overutilize health services than are non-insureds.[33] Hospitals, physicians, insurers, and patients have all contributed to this overutilization, but all four groups would gain from some improved controls. Only insurer approaches will be considered here.

Insurers can exercise some control through investigation of applicants' moral qualities but the right of individual selection is relinquished under group insurance and moral qualities are difficult to evaluate. Insurers may also attempt to control overutilization through policy provisions that force the insured to share part of the loss. For example, certain types of expenses may not be covered, internal limits may be placed on specified expenses such as hospital room and board, or the policy may contain a deductible or a percentage participation provision. These provisions, however, should not exclude or limit coverage of expenses against which it is reasonable to insure. They should also not discourage insureds from seeking early treatment or from obtaining adequate treatment for extended illnesses.

A special problem that affects both disability income and medical expense insurance is overinsurance resulting from duplicate insurance protection. In the past it has been customary to assume that the possibility of overinsurance had been considered prior to the issuance of the policy and that the insured was entitled to collect from all insurers with whom he had policies. However, overinsurance may result from

---

[33] See the discussion of overutilization by Dickerson, *op. cit.*, pp. 270–87.

narrow coverages that apply only in certain instances (such as automobile medical payments insurance), from later enrollment under a new group plan, or from later liberalizations in an existing group plan. Moreover, as benefits have been improved, it has become more likely that a person with two or more contracts is overinsured. Consequently, more insurers are inserting provisions in their policies providing for some sharing of the losses with duplicating insurance. Non-cancellable and guaranteed renewable disability income insurers are for similar reasons making more frequent use of a provision that limits total recoveries from all insurers to a specified per cent of the insured's average earnings.[34]

Some authorities have questioned whether private insurers might not be encouraging overutilization of health services by the aged by offering private protection against the HI deductibles. Others argue that the aged need assistance in meeting these charges and that the aged will still share some of the expenses of more serious illnesses in the form of uncovered types of expenses.

Premium Structures

As stated in Chapter 5, private insurance premiums should not, on the average, be excessive and they should distribute the cost equitably. One indication as to whether the premiums are excessive, on the average, is the benefit ratio or ratio of benefits incurred to earned income. Other things being equal, a high ratio is favorable, for it indicates that most of the premiums are being returned to policyholders in the form of benefits.

Table 12.3 lists the 1964 benefit ratios of each type of insurer. Paid sick leave plans are not included. The ratio exceeds 79 per cent in each case except commercial individual insurance where the insured receives more individual attention and, consequently, the cost of selling and servicing the protection is greater.[35] Since these ratios vary from year to year, slight differences among the ratios should be ignored. On the whole, the picture is favorable to private insurance, but it can be improved.

There are two schools of thought concerning the equitable distribution of insurance costs. The arguments of both schools have some merit.

[34] For a comprehensive discussion of the most recent versions of these provisions dealing with duplicate insurance, see William H. Wandel, "Overinsurance in Health Insurance," *Journal of Risk and Insurance*, XXXII, No. 3 (September, 1965), 427–34.

[35] Kulp points out that the quality of the agent and the service he provides must be considered in deciding whether acquisition costs are too high. See Kulp, *op. cit.*, p. 396. Unfortunately many health insurers do not train their agents adequately, and some individual agents are much more interested in commissions than in service to policyholders.

Taxes, primarily 2 per cent state premium taxes, constitute a larger per cent of the premiums of commercial insurers than of the other types of insurers.

TABLE 12.3

Expenditures for Income and Medical Expense Benefits as a Per Cent
of Earned Income, by Type of Insurer, 1964

Benefit and Type of Insurer	Benefits as Per Cent of Income
Loss of income:	
Commercial insurers	
Group insurance *	80.5
Individual insurance	51.7
Others †	79.6
Medical expenses:	
Commercial insurers	
Group insurance	91.7
Individual insurance	54.5
Blue Cross associations	96.1
Blue Shield associations	90.3
Independent plans:	
Employer–employee–union	89.9
Community–consumer	90.5
Medical society	85.7
Private group clinics	84.3

* Includes private insurance written in connection with temporary disability insurance legislation.

† Excludes self-insured unfunded employer-administered plans in states without temporary disability insurance legislation.

Source: *Social Security Bulletin,* December, 1965, p. 18, and January, 1966, p. 23.

One school maintains that it is socially and economically desirable to use an average premium for all insureds, regardless of their age, sex, and group experience. The objective of this community-rating school is the widest possible pooling of risks and extension of coverage. The other school argues that a uniform distribution of the costs is not a fair distribution according to private insurance standards. The members of this school also believe that a uniform premium will work only if the insurer has a monopoly or if all insurers charge the same uniform premium, because otherwise the insureds will seek out the insurer charging the lowest premium. Even if the premium were uniform, it might be higher than some of the healthier insureds would be willing to pay. Hence compulsion might be necessary if these people are to be insured.[36]

[36] John H. Miller, "Rates and Reserves—Personal Commercial and Non-cancellable Contracts," *Accident and Sickness Insurance* (Philadelphia: University of Pennsylvania Press, 1954), pp. 190–91.

For a more recent statement on the social utility and limitations of both pricing systems, with special emphasis on medical expense insurance for the aged, see Duncan M. MacIntyre, "Rate Philosophy and Health Insurance Competition," *Journal of Risk and Insurance,* XXXII, No. 4 (December, 1965), 525–37.

Type of Control

The insured usually has little or no direct control over the types of contracts offered. Stockholders, the present management, physicians, and hospitals control most of the plans. However, this lack of control by the insureds is not too important as long as the plans continue to experiment and to liberalize their coverages. Competition has forced the plans to listen to the demands of insureds.

However, as noted in Chapter 5, in the late fifties, several significant abuses were discovered in connection with some employee welfare plans that resulted in some federal and state legislation requiring the filing of disclosure information and the bonding of administrators. Most of the abuses arose out of the health insurance features of the plans. It has also been claimed with some justification that some doctors and hospitals have abused health insurance. On the whole, however, the administration of private health insurance appears to be honest.

Service benefit plans are generally considered to have greater opportunities to control the cost and quality of the services rendered because of the close relationship between the insurers and the purveyors of the services. In many cases they are the same people. On the other hand, supporters of indemnity plans argue that in practice doctor- and hospital-controlled plans do not police their colleagues adequately. Small independent plans can rely to some extent upon group pressures.

A CONCLUDING NOTE

The most obvious characteristic of private health insurance is at the same time a strong point and a weakness. The multitude of contracts available with their heterogeneous benefits and costs gives the insured considerable freedom of choice. Moreover, the competition among insurers has produced many important improvements. On the other hand, the field is so complicated that relatively few insureds understand it well enough to make intelligent choices.

SUMMARY

Private health insurance is underwritten by three major classes of insurers: (1) commercial insurers, (2) Blue Cross associations and Blue Shield associations, and (3) independent insurers.

Commercial insurers underwrite both disability income and medical expense benefits. The three most important forms of individual insurance providing both types of benefits are commercial insurance, which is cancellable by the insurer, non-cancellable insurance, and guaranteed renewable insurance. The income benefits vary depending upon whether the disability is partial or total and whether the disability is caused by an accidental injury or sickness. The medical expense benefits may be written on a general or on a specific basis and are often not included in the contract.

Most individual medical expense insurance contracts issued by commercial insurers are basic medical expense insurance contracts. These contracts protect the insured against small and moderate medical expenses, usually on a specific basis. An important relatively recent development is major medical expense insurance which usually pays, on a blanket basis, all or most of the medical expenses in excess of a specified deductible up to some specified maximum amount. Comprehensive insurance, which was introduced in the late fifties, is a hybrid of basic and major medical expense insurance. Insurance for the aged supplementing HI and SMI is also available.

Group insurance underwritten by commercial insurers protects more persons than individual insurance. The most common benefits protect the insured against a temporary disability income loss, specific types of basic medical expenses, such as hospital expenses, and major medical expenses. Group protection against long-term disability income losses is growing rapidly. Medical expense insurance for the aged supplementing HI and SMI is also available.

Blue Cross associations and Blue Shield associations are the most important competitors of the commercial insurers. A Blue Cross association is a non-profit hospital expense prepayment plan approved by the Blue Cross Association. There are many types of Blue Cross contracts, but the typical contract provides a specified number of days of service in ward or semi-private accommodations of member hospitals. The subscriber receives dollar benefits if he wants better accommodations or if he is hospitalized in a non-member hospital.

A Blue Shield association is a non-profit prepayment plan covering surgical fees and charges for physicians' care that has been approved by the National Association of Blue Shield Plans. There are many Blue Shield contracts, but the typical contract provides specified dollar amounts for surgical operations. Participating physicians agree to accept the benefit as full payment if the subscriber's income is below a certain amount.

Independent insurers underwrite medical expense plans primarily, but paid sick leave plans self-insured by employers are important disability income plans. The independent insurers include the non-industrial insurers—community–consumer plans, medical society plans not associated with Blue Shield, private group clinics, and dental society plans—and the industrial insurers—unions, employers, and groups of employees. Most of these plans provide some service benefits, and in some plans the protection is very comprehensive.

SUGGESTIONS FOR ADDITIONAL READING

ANDERSON, ODIN W., PATRICIA COLLETTE, and JACOB J. FELDMAN. *Health Insurance Benefits for Personal Health Services, 1953 and 1958: Nationwide Surveys.* Research Series 15. New York: Health Information Foundation, 1960.
A detailed analysis and comparison of the role of private health insurance in meeting the costs of medical care during two different twelve-month periods.

DICKERSON, O. D. *Health Insurance,* rev. ed. Homewood, Ill.: Richard D. Irwin, Inc., 1963.
A recent comprehensive text on health insurance.

EILERS, ROBERT D. *Regulation of Blue Cross and Blue Shield Plans.* Homewood, Ill.: Richard D. Irwin, Inc., 1963.
An interesting analysis of Blue Cross and Blue Shield plans, as well as their regulation.

EILERS, ROBERT D., and ROBERT M. CROWE (eds.). *Group Insurance Handbook.* Homewood, Ill.: Richard D. Irwin, Inc., 1965.
A handbook covering the principles and practices of group life and health insurance.

FAULKNER, EDWIN J. *Health Insurance.* New York: McGraw-Hill Book Co., 1960.
Another recent comprehensive text on health insurance.

FOLLMANN, J. F., JR. *Medical Care and Health Insurance.* Homewood, Ill.: Richard D. Irwin, Inc., 1963.
An authoritative account of the role and development of group health insurance.

GREGG, DAVIS W. (ed.). *Life and Health Insurance Handbook,* 2nd ed. Homewood, Ill.: Richard D. Irwin, Inc., 1964.
A handbook of current practices and procedures in the life and health insurance fields.

HABER, WILLIAM, and WILBUR J. COHEN (eds.). *Social Security: Programs, Problems, and Policies.* Homewood, Ill.: Richard D. Irwin, Inc., 1960.
Selections 36, 37, 38, and 39 of this useful book of readings deal with private health insurance.

HERRICK, KENNETH. *Total Disability Provisions in Life Insurance Contracts.* Homewood, Ill.: Richard D. Irwin, Inc., 1956.
This book traces the history of total disability provisions in life insurance contracts and discusses the present status of this coverage.

ILSE, LOUISE WOLTERS. *Group Insurance and Employee Retirement Plans.* Englewood Cliffs, N. J.: Prentice-Hall, Inc., 1953. Chapters 1, 2, and 7 through 10.
This text describes group health protection underwritten by commercial insurers and Blue Cross–Blue Shield associations.

KULP, C. A. *Casualty Insurance,* 3d ed. New York: The Ronald Press Co., 1956. Chapter 14.
An objective description, analysis, and evaluation of private health insurance.

MACINTYRE, DUNCAN M. *Voluntary Health Insurance and Rate Making.* Ithaca, N. Y.: Cornell University Press, 1962.

A detailed analysis of the methodology, relative merits, and effects of experience rating and community rating.

PICKRELL, JESSE F. *Group Disability Insurance,* rev. ed. Homewood, Ill.: Richard D. Irwin, Inc., 1961.

A study in depth of commercial group health insurance.

Problems and Solutions of Health and Welfare Programs, Study No. 1, Parts A, B, C, and D. New York: Foundation on Employee Health, Medical Care and Welfare, Inc., 1957 and 1961.

A clear exposition of the differences among commercial insurers, Blue Cross and Blue Shield associations, and independent plans. Part D considers the pros and cons of insurance and self-insurance.

REED, LOUIS S. "Private Health Insurance in the United States: An Overview," *Social Security Bulletin,* XXVIII, No. 12 (December, 1965), 3–23, 48.

A comprehensive summary of all forms of private health insurance, which includes a new series on enrollment data.

SERBEIN, OSCAR N., JR. *Paying for Medical Care in the United States.* New York: Columbia University Press, 1953.

This authoritative volume analyzes in detail all types of medical expense insurance.

SKOLNIK, ALFRED M. "Ten Years of Employee-Benefit Plans," *Social Security Bulletin,* XXIX, No. 4 (April, 1966), 3–19.

The latest in a series of reports by the Social Security Administration on the growth, scope, and adequacy of private employee-benefit plans.

SOMERS, HERMAN M., and ANNE R. SOMERS. *Doctors, Patients and Health Insurance.* Washington, D. C.: The Brookings Institution, 1961.

A penetrating analysis and evaluation of the organization and financing of medical care.

SPIEGELMAN, MORTIMER. *Ensuring Medical Care for the Aged.* Homewood, Ill.: Richard D. Irwin, Inc., 1960.

A comprehensive discussion of a major problem; includes an extensive discussion of the private and public mechanisms for financing medical care for the aged.

13

Economic Security
Programs for
Special Groups

INTRODUCTION

In addition to the programs created under the Social Security Act and the related economic security measures discussed in earlier chapters, five other major systems, underwritten by governmental units, deal with the old-age, illness, and unemployment risks to economic security. These are special programs for veterans, railroad workers, federal civil servants, state and local government employees, and individuals receiving aid under the general assistance programs.

These programs differ in two respects from those considered earlier. First, their coverage is limited to these specific groups of workers; and, second, the objective of the benefits paid under these programs is in some cases somewhat different from that of the Social Security Act. We have omitted from this discussion still other special programs, such as the Merchant Marine Act, which extends to seamen the same rights railroad workers enjoy under their Federal Employers' Liability Act, and the Longshoremen's and Harbor Workers' Act, which provides workmen's compensation benefits similar to those of the Federal Employees' Compensation Act. Each of these, and others, while they are important to their industries, were omitted to enable more adequate discussion of the programs which, by the standard of numbers of workers protected, are the most important ones applying to special groups.

TABLE 13.1

Persons Receiving Payments and Amount of Such Payments Under Social Insurance and Related Programs, 1963

	Average Monthly Number of Persons Receiving Payment (in thousands)	Annual Amount of Payments (in millions)
Old-age benefits		
Old-Age, Survivors, and Disability Insurance	13,038	$10,795
Railroad Retirement	489	654
Federal Civil Service and other federal	618	1,628
State and local government retirement	655	1,145
Veterans' programs	20	27
Old-age assistance	2,194	2,029
Survivorship benefits and aid to dependent persons		
Monthly benefits:		
Old-Age, Survivors, and Disability Insurance	4,227	3,216
Railroad Retirement	275	244
Federal Civil Service and other federal	196	161
State and local government retirement	85	130
Veterans' programs	1,707	105
Workmen's compensation	a	125
Lump-sum survivorship payments:		
Old-Age, Survivors, and Disability Insurance	81	206
Railroad Retirement	2	24
Federal Civil Service and other federal	2	16
State and local government retirement	2	90
Veterans' programs	17	51
Aid to dependent children	3,989	1,477
Disability		
Old-Age, Survivors, and Disability Insurance	1,380	1,210
Workmen's compensation	a	905
Veterans' programs	3,160	2,819
Railroad Retirement	101	159
Federal Civil Service and other federal	231	499
State and local government retirement	67	130
State programs for temporary disability	145	390
Railroad temporary disability insurance	27	49
Aid to the Permanently and Totally Disabled	479	417
Aid to the Blind	98	96
Unemployment		
State unemployment insurance	1,623	2,926
Railroad unemployment insurance	50	99
Area Redevelopment Act and Manpower Development Training Act allowances	27	22
General assistance (cases)	353	280

a Not available.

Sources: *Social Security Bulletin, Annual Statistical Supplement,* 1964, pp. 6, 114; and *Statistical Abstract of the U. S., 1965,* pp. 288, 306.

In Table 13.1 these economic security measures for special groups are compared with the systems we have been discussing in terms of the risks with which they deal and the size of their coverage and benefits.

It is apparent from this table that the programs for special groups are indeed important in relation to our better known economic security measures. This is particularly true of some of the veterans' and the general assistance programs that, in terms of the scope and degree of coverage they provide, are the major programs applying to special groups.

VETERANS' ECONOMIC SECURITY PROGRAMS

A system of veterans' benefits has been maintained by this country since the Revolutionary War. In fact, pension precedents established at that time are still used today in appeals for veterans' pensions. In times of war, veterans' benefit programs have always been re-examined and usually have been extended.

Although the veterans' benefit program includes economic security measures protecting against the hazards of death, old age, dependency, and illness (which are in some respects comparable to our regular social insurance programs covering these hazards), the whole program, both in scope and nature, goes far beyond the system of job-oriented economic security dealt with in this book. It is instructive, however, to enumerate some of the veterans' benefit programs that have been provided by our government over the years: *disability compensation to veterans and dependents; pensions; aids in land acquisition; cash bounties; domiciliary care; Civil Service preference; insurance; medical and hospital care; vocational rehabilitation; guardianship service; retirement of disabled emergency officers; readjustment benefits (G. I. Bill) providing re-employment rights, education benefits, readjustment allowances, unemployment insurance, and loans.*[1] This list does not include veterans' benefits provided under state laws.

Changing Philosophy of Veterans' Benefits

From the period of the American Revolution, the government has always accepted the view that it is responsible in some measure for the economic security of those who served it in time of war. There has never been any question about compensating the survivors of war casualties or veterans who were disabled in the service of their country. But how to discharge this responsibility to other veterans in their best interest has

[1] For a complete study of veterans' benefits programs, see House Committee on Veterans' Affairs, 84th Congress, 2d Session, *A Report on Veterans' Benefits in the United States* (Washington, D. C.: U. S. Government Printing Office, 1956), Committee Prints 243, 244, 246, 247, 259–62, 270, 275.

been debated, not without the influence of strong political and economic pressure groups since the Revolutionary War, and changing concepts of this responsibility have led to a new approach in veterans' benefits.

A long-prevailing philosophy, particularly as evidenced by the various pension acts, was that the government ought to help the veteran because he is a veteran. In part, there has always been the desire to protect veterans from indigency, to pay them a debt of gratitude, or simply to reward them for faithful service. Basically, this philosophy governed veterans' benefits until World War II. The veteran was largely left to make his own economic adjustment on return from duty to civilian life, and if he failed, the government sought to come to his aid. Under this approach, the emphasis was on picking up the pieces of economic wreckage, rather than on avoiding them if possible.

An attempt to replace the automatic pension approach with a better program after World War I failed because of the deeply imbedded concept that something was owed to the veteran. Veterans were a minority group, had no general social security system, and could point to much precedent for pension benefits. But World War II, and the legislative programs for economic security that preceded it, changed this picture. Veterans were no longer a small minority group. In 1955, they represented 13.5 per cent of the total population, or 20.5 per cent of the population eighteen and over. Including wives and children of veterans, nearly 45 per cent of the population is now eligible for veterans' benefits. Furthermore, after World War II, veterans had gained protected status under the Social Security Act.

By this time, it was thus possible successfully to introduce a new approach to veterans' benefits—one which most observers feel has worked well. A program of benefits was designed to launch the veteran in his civilian role and to help him compete on equal terms with non-veterans. Readjustment benefits, including education benefits, unemployment allowances, job counseling and re-employment rights replaced the pension approach as the attempt was made to bring the veteran into the mainstream of competitive economic activity on a forward-looking basis.

Readjustment Benefits

The Servicemen's Readjustment Act of 1944—best known as the G. I. Bill of Rights—was the central piece of legislation in this new philosophy of veterans' benefits programs. As amended and later applied to Korean War veterans, it provided a variety of benefits to aid the veteran in readjusting to civilian life. In 1966, legislation extended eligibility retroactively to all veterans who had served in the armed forces at any time after January 1, 1955.

Education benefits under the first G. I. Bill of Rights expired on July 26, 1956, after providing education opportunities to nearly eight million veterans at a total cost of about $14.5 billion. An estimated two million veterans attended colleges and universities, and some 600,000 disabled veterans became self-supporting through the program. Similarly, eligibility for Korean War veterans expired January 31, 1965. Two million four hundred thousand veterans had entered training and 294,000 exhausted their entitlement.

A major innovation of the 1944 Act was the loan guaranty program which was devised as an alternative to the bonus. It was less expensive for the government and was designed to serve better the ends of the veteran by providing credit to enable him to get started in farming, in a business, or in buying a home. The system also provided an investment outlet for large amounts of savings accumulated at the end of World War II.

Readjustment allowances—payments to unemployed or partially employed veterans—were also provided under the Act with the purpose of providing minimum income during readjustment. Nearly ten million veterans filed claims, and total expenditures of around $4 billion were made.

Service-Connected Disability and Death Compensation

As Table 13.1 indicates, compensation for service-connected disability is one of the most important veterans' programs. This type of payment has existed in some form since before the American Revolution. Today, these benefits, paid without regard to other income or resources, are as follows: total disability, $300 per month, with rates for partial disability ranging down to $20 per month for a 10 per cent disability. Totally disabled veterans who are permanently housebound or hospitalized may receive up to $200 per month additionally. Veterans 50 per cent or more disabled receive additional compensation for dependents. Also, there are statutory awards ranging as high as $500 per month for specific losses of bodily members and for disease. Veterans who become disabled during peacetime service receive compensation at a lower rate—80 per cent of wartime rates.

For service-connected death, the following schedule of monthly benefits is paid to widows: $120 per month plus 12 per cent of basic pay of the rank held by the veteran at the time of his death. Other rates of payment apply to dependent parents and children. There are also educational allowances for children of both of these groups of veterans that pay $130 per month for full-time study, less for part-time, for as long as 36 months.

TABLE 13.2

Beneficiaries and Benefits Under Veterans' Programs, 1940–63

(In Thousands)

| Year | Retirement | | Survivorship | | |
| | Beneficiaries | Benefits | Beneficiaries | Benefits | |
				Monthly	Lump Sum
1940	29.2	$19,770	323.2	$ 105,696	$ 3,960
1941	36.6	24,423	318.5	111,799	4,352
1942	42.0	28,956	315.9	111,193	4,120
1943	46.8	32,632	322.7	116,133	4,350
1944	59.1	49,250	372.7	144,302	4,784
1945	59.1	54,730	542.1	254,238	5,049
1946	62.5	57,370	790.5	333,640	7,491
1947	61.6	54,285	901.5	382,515	13,270
1948	59.8	64,221	950.0	413,912	12,358
1949	57.4	61,731	971.2	477,406	12,427
1950	53.5	57,586	991.7	491,579	12,709
1951	57.3	62,350	1,011.2	519,398	12,885
1952	78.4	87,220	1,044.2	572,983	15,142
1953	71.8	86,284	1,086.0	613,475	16,118
1954	65.7	79,096	1,122.2	628,801	16,193
1955	59.6	75,472	1,152.9	688,426	16,827
1956	55.9	70,850	1,173.9	699,204	17,494
1957	50.2	63,900	1,176.9	748,660	20,218
1958	44.3	56,522	1,190.0	794,253	24,674
1959	38.8	49,690	1,215.4	818,984	37,688
1960	33.2	42,655	1,262.0	864,555	39,515
1961	28.8	37,372	1,492.7	956,476	42,821
1962	24.3	31,727	1,595.5	976,669	44,144
1963	20.5	26,868	1,706.7	1,018,316	50,650

Sources: Federal Security Agency, *Social Security Yearbook,* 1945, p. 18; and 1948, p. 4; *Social Security Bulletin,* Annual Statistical Supplement, 1963, p. 6.

Pensions—Non-Service-Connected

Pensions for non-service-connected disability and death are still being paid by the Veterans' Administration to veterans of wars prior to World War I and to some veterans of that war, and the Veterans Pension Act of 1959 greatly liberalized the availability and size of these pensions for veterans of World Wars I and II and the Korean War and their survivors. All benefits under this act are paid on a sliding scale based on need.[2] As of 1966, for example, single veterans or survivors with annual incomes

[2] The disability pension ranges from $43 per month to $115, varying with amount of income and number of dependents. In 1961 automatic cost of living increases were added, as in civil service annuities.

over $1,800 were ineligible for them; for veterans or widows with one or more dependents, the maximum permissible income was $3,000. However, the pensions payable to veterans of earlier wars and certain veterans of World War I are not related to need.

Table 13.2 lists retirement and survivorship benefits paid under the veterans' program from 1940 through 1963. Retirement benefits and beneficiaries are on the decline, since veterans of the most recent wars are no longer entitled to such benefits.[3] Survivorship benefits and the number of beneficiaries have increased considerably, especially in the post-World War II period. Since benefits are paid from Congressional appropriations, there is no trust fund or actuarial reports.

Insurance

The Veterans' Administration issued United States Government Life Insurance policies to servicemen from World War I until 1940 when National Service Life Insurance policies were introduced. If they wanted the coverage, the servicemen paid for this insurance. The contract was very similar to that issued by commercial insurers, except that there was no exclusion of war deaths. The original policy was a term policy which paid only in case of death, but servicemen had the right to renew the policy at the expiration of the term without proving insurability. They could also convert the term policy to a level-premium contract with a cash value at any time. Both plans provided for participation in dividends resulting from gains and savings derived from favorable mortality experience and excess interest earnings.

Because the expenses of the operation were to be paid by the government out of tax revenues, the initial premiums were low. The actual cost was much less than the initial premium because the actual death claims were far fewer than the estimated death claims. The mortality table used was too conservative, and insurance funds were not used to pay claims if the death occurred in service or was service-connected.[4]

Because it was expensive for the government, because commercial insurers argued that coverage after service was not justifiable, and because of numerous administrative and personnel problems, National Service Life Insurance was replaced by the Servicemen's Indemnity Act

[3] The sudden increase in 1952 is misleading, since in 1951 the Veterans' Administration began to classify under old-age pensions both disability pensions and old-age pensions awarded to veterans prior to World War I.

[4] For more information on government life insurance, see Dan M. McGill, *An Analysis of Government Life Insurance* (Philadelphia: University of Pennsylvania Press, 1949); Charles K. Reid, *Fundamentals of Government Life Insurance and Related Benefits* (Philadelphia: American College of Life Underwriters, 1958) and *Annual Report,* Administration of Veterans Affairs, 1965, pp. 95–102.

of 1950. This Act provided $10,000 of protection free to every serviceman in a non-participating program. For all but disabled servicemen, the only policy to which they could convert was five-year renewable term. The premiums were lower than those of commercial insurers because there was no loading for expenses, but the insurance funds were used to pay all death claims. As a result of Congressional action in 1956, issuance of all *new* insurance protection by the government ceased. In 1958, provisions were made for those already insured to change to a lower-priced term policy, non-renewable after age 50, and for conversion to permanent plans.

In 1964, new legislation reopened the NSLI program for one year to certain disabled veterans, especially those who would have difficulty obtaining private life insurance, and offering a modified life plan encouraging conversion from term policies.

In 1965, group life policies were again made available to all servicemen on active duty on or after September 29, 1965. At a rate of $2 per month for the maximum of $10,000, premiums were made automatically deductible unless servicemen preferred a $5,000 premium for $1 or rejected the program entirely. The insurance continues 120 days after separation and may be converted to individual policies with commercial life insurers without a medical examination. This current plan, unlike earlier plans, is administered entirely by commercial insurers, but with government reimbursement for added risk of death in combat.

The earlier insurance programs were justified on the social grounds that servicemen had devoted part of their lives to serving their country. However, their bonus feature should be acknowledged and appreciated.

Table 13.3 presents some data on veterans' life insurance. In 1944, the amount of veterans' life insurance in force was almost equal to the total amount of commercial life insurance in force during that year. Apparently, many veterans did not recognize the bonus feature of the insurance, for two years later the amount of insurance in force was only about 30 per cent of the 1944 figure. Veterans of the Korean conflict reacted in the same way, but with a somewhat better reason. The death benefits were sizable; other benefits such as cash values and disability payments were much less important.

The Veterans' Administration establishes a full legal reserve on these contracts similar to those maintained by commercial insurers. Their assets are invested in special 3 per cent government bonds.

The insurance program administered by the Veterans' Administration, though gradually declining since 1957, is still the fourth largest insurance operation in the United States, based on total amount of insurance in force. During fiscal year 1965, living policyholders received $223 million in dividend payments, $36 million in disability benefits, $31 in surrender value, and $14 in matured endowments. A total of about $354 million was paid to beneficiaries of deceased policyholders. From the inception of the program through 1965, payments have totaled about $19.4 billion, about half paid to living policyholders and half paid to beneficiaries.

TABLE 13.3

Veterans' Life Insurance in Force

(IN THOUSANDS)

Year	Number of Policies	Amount
1940	609	$ 2,565,000
1945	16,512	126,034,000
1950	6,113	37,973,000
1955	6,449	42,623,000
1960	6,320	42,382,000
1961	6,215	41,659,000
1962	5,999	40,057,000
1963	5,936	39,665,000
1964	5,886	39,470,000
1965	5,824	39,103,000

Source: U. S. Veterans' Administration, *Annual Report, 1965*, p. 302.

Armed Services Program

Members of the armed forces are covered by OASDHI but, in addition, the armed services provide a liberal non-contributory retirement plan for their career members. Not all branches have exactly the same plan, but, in general, a serviceman who has completed twenty years of service may retire (with the consent of his branch) on a monthly income for life equal to 2½ per cent of his highest base pay, plus the allowance for length of service times the number of years of service. The maximum annuity is 75 per cent of his present pay.

The annuity continues during the lifetime of the annuitant but not after his death. If the serviceman dies while on active duty, his family is entitled to a lump sum equal to six months' pay and the burial benefits and service-connected death compensation available to the families of veterans. If the serviceman dies after he has left the service, his status is that of a veteran.

All these benefits are provided without cost to the members of the armed services. They are paid out of annual Congressional appropriations.

A Concluding Comment

Although veterans' benefit programs have been reshaped to follow a more forward-looking approach to the problems of economic security, they are still beset by many difficulties. Attempts to revise and modernize measures such as disability compensation and medical benefits still meet with strong (and often successful) resistance. Thus, while an improved system of veterans' benefit programs has slowly evolved over the years, it remains a program shaped as much by power and politics as by sound economic and public policy.

ECONOMIC SECURITY PROGRAMS FOR RAILROAD EMPLOYEES

Old Age, Death, and Permanent Disability

In 1875 the American Railway Express Company established the first formal private pension plan for railroad workers; by 1934, almost ninety such plans had been instituted, and the railroad industry was considered a leader in the private pension field. These plans typically provided a pension of 1 per cent of the worker's average salary over the ten-year period preceding his retirement for each year of service. Most of these plans were self-insured, and few, if any, were fully funded. Consequently, they encountered financial difficulties during the Depression. In 1934, because the orderly operation of these pension plans was essential at a time when employment opportunities for younger men were scarce, Congress enacted legislation which created a liberal compulsory retirement system underwritten by the federal government and financed by taxes levied on the railroads and their employees.

In enacting this law, the Congress argued that the safety of passengers and freight was endangered by the continued employment of older workers. But the United States Supreme Court declared the law unconstitutional on the grounds that certain provisions took property without due process of law, and the power to regulate interstate commerce did not include the power to establish a compulsory retirement system for workers in interstate commerce. A 1935 Act creating essentially the same system was declared unconstitutional by the Supreme Court of the District of Columbia, but the decision was ambiguous and the system actually started to operate in a small way in 1936. Operations under this system and litigations concerning its operations ceased in December, 1936, following a joint conference of railroads and railroad unions. At this conference the details of a mutually satisfactory compulsory retirement system were worked out, and in 1937 Congress enacted these details into law. The

1937 Act has since been amended nine times; the discussion herein is based on the 1965 law.[5]

Benefits

The railroad retirement system provides four basic types of benefits: retirement annuities; death and survivorship annuities; annuities for total disability; and medicare. There is a close relationship and financial interchange between the system and the OASDHI program, and all railroad workers with less than ten years of railroad service have their earnings treated as covered wages under OASDHI for benefit purposes. Also, the railroad retirement system has a "Social Security Minimum" applicable to all benefits so that benefits payable under this system will always be in effect at least 10 per cent more than the OASDHI benefits that would have been payable if the railroad wages had been covered by OASDHI. Most railroad survivors' benefits are payable under this "Social Security Minimum," but at present only about 10 per cent of the annuities come under the guarantee.

Retirement Annuity. To be eligible at age sixty-five for a retirement annuity, a railroad worker must have had at least ten years of creditable service in covered railroad and related work. At age sixty he is eligible with thirty years of service (but, for men, at a reduced rate). Credit is provided for military service. The program includes benefits for wives of retired workers, which were liberalized in the 1965 amendments.

The retirement annuity for a worker retiring at age sixty-five is determined by applying the following formula to his average monthly compensation: 3.35 per cent of the first $50 of average monthly compensation, plus 2.51 per cent of the next $100, plus 1.67 per cent of the next $400, the sum to be multiplied by the years of service.

In addition to the "Social Security Minimum," there is another minimum benefit provision which may provide more liberal benefits. Under this provision, the minimum annuity is the smallest of the following amounts: $83.50, $5 times years of service, or 110 per cent of the average monthly compensation.

In 1964, the average annuity paid to employees was $136.90, and to wives, $55.60.

Survivorship Benefits. Under a survivors' benefit program, payments are made to specified survivors of workers who were "completely" or "partially" insured. At least ten years of service with the industry and

---

[5] See *Social Security Bulletin*, XXIX, No. 2 (February, 1966) for details of the 1965 Amendments to the Railroad Retirement Act and a full statement of the provisions of the Act, as well as the relationship of the program to the OASDHI.

current connection with the industry for a stated number of work quarters are required. A formula is prescribed for the computation of a "basic amount" and the benefits are percentages of this amount.

Disability Benefits. Disability annuities are payable to workers who are permanently disabled for any regular gainful employment if the disabled worker has had ten years of covered railroad service. Workers who are permanently disabled for their regular occupations (but not necessarily for other work) are eligible for a disability annuity at age sixty, if they are currently connected with the industry at the time of disability and have had ten years of service, or under age sixty with twenty years of service covered by law.

Disability annuities are computed in the same way as retirement annuities.

Health Benefits. When hospital insurance was added to the social security system in 1965, railroad annuitants, pensioners, and employees over 65 were all covered. The protection provided was identical for all (see Chapter 11 for details). The voluntary supplementary medical insurance program also extends to railroad groups, and the monthly premium, initially $3, will be deducted from OASDHI or Railroad Retirement cash benefits where possible. The Railroad Retirement Board determines eligibility of railroad annuitants and employees for hospital benefits, and the Social Security Administration pays for the services. In addition, the Railroad Retirement Board arranges for reimbursement for hospital expenses incurred in Canada to the extent that they are not covered by Provincial insurance programs.

Unemployment and Temporary Disability

As early as January, 1933, the Railway Labor Executives' Association proposed a federal law designed to stabilize employment and pay unemployment compensation through payroll reserves. Their desire for a national law was based on the whole historical pattern of railroad labor relations. Wages, hours, and conditions of work in the railroads were not governed by state boundaries, but were set for the whole industry. Experience under the state unemployment compensation acts convinced the Association that a federal approach was needed, and the efforts of this Association (and others) were rewarded when, in June, 1938, the Railroad Unemployment Insurance Act was put into effect. The law has been amended several times since. Its most important amendment (in 1946) extended the system to provide cash sickness benefits, similar to those paid for unemployment, for workers temporarily unable to work because of sickness (which included maternity sickness) or injury.

Benefits paid under the Act are designed to protect workers against income losses from unemployment caused by labor market fluctuations or temporary disability—occupational or non-occupational. Benefits are administered much like the unemployment benefit programs of the states. The system provides for disqualifications for several causes (such as failure to apply for work, leaving suitable work without cause, fraud, or participation in a strike) and stipulates a seven-day waiting period for disability benefits. Benefits are payable after the fourth day of unemployment. Special maternity benefits may be paid for 57 days before confinement and for a maximum of 116 days. These are in addition to general disability benefits.

Eligibility and Benefit Level

To qualify for benefits, a covered worker (note that coverage is the same as under the Railroad Retirement Act) must, under more stringent rules adopted in 1963, have received at least $750 in pay from an employer covered by the Act in the calendar year preceding his benefit year. New entrants to railroad employment must have seven months of service in the base year. The benefit rate is not less than 60 per cent of the employee's daily rate of pay for his last railroad employment in the base year, subject to a maximum of $10.20. Thus, at the maximum rate, weekly unemployment and sickness benefits now amount to $51, and the average payment is $39 for normal unemployment, $44 for extended unemployment, and $45.50 for sickness. Extended unemployment benefits are provided for beneficiaries with ten or more years of railroad service who exhaust rights to normal benefits.

Coverage and Operations of the Railroad Retirement System and Unemployment Insurance Act

Although the Railroad Retirement and Unemployment systems do not affect nearly as many workers as the Social Security Act, they do cover all employees in an important industry. Both programs are administered through the Railroad Retirement Board, membership to which is gained by Presidential appointment with Senate confirmation. The retirement system is financed by joint contributions of employers and employees at a rate which is gradually rising. From 1966 to 1987, the combined rate will rise from 15.9 per cent to 20.3 per cent of the employees' compensation, up to $550 a month (thus coordinating the earnings base with that of the Social Security Act). Taxes collected from workers and employers are placed in a special account in the treasury's general fund, and that part of the account which is not needed to pay current benefits and administrative expenses is invested in interest-bearing United States government obligations. At least once every three years the Railroad Retirement Board is required to make an actuarial report and to estimate the tax rate required to make the system self-supporting. The contribution rates set in the 1965 amendments have been estimated to be insufficient by about .62 per cent of payroll.

The unemployment and temporary disability programs are financed wholly by a payroll tax on employers. The rate of contribution varies from .5 per cent to 4 per cent depending upon the size of the balance in the Railroad Unemployment Insurance account.

In 1963, an average of 790,000 workers per month worked in employments covered by the Railroad Retirement and Unemployment Insurance Acts. A total of 1,003,000 employees worked in covered employment. Coverage figures for the Act for the past decade are presented in Table 13.4.

TABLE 13.4

Employees Covered by Railroad Retirement and
Railroad Unemployment Insurance Acts

(IN THOUSANDS)

	Number of Employees	
Year	Average [a]	Total
1949	1,403	2,112
1950	1,421	2,073
1951	1,476	2,103
1952	1,429	2,045
1953	1,405	1,982
1954	1,250	1,690
1955	1,239	1,694
1956	1,220	1,647
1957	1,150	1,510
1958	984	1,321
1959	949	1,242
1960	909	1,177
1961	836	1,082
1962	815	1,037
1963	790	1,003

[a] Average of twelve mid-monthly employment figures.

Source: Railroad Retirement Board, *Annual Report* (Washington, D. C.: U. S. Government Printing Office, 1964), p. 179.

The table reveals that the average monthly coverage of the Act is dropping steadily. Although these figures indicate the secular decline in employment in the railroad industry, the system is nevertheless important in terms of its coverage.

Occupational Disability

As indicated in Chapter 9, work on the railroads has always been among the most hazardous occupations and once had the worst accident record. Hence, it is not surprising that accident compensation should long have been a concern among railway workers. They were active in the fight for compensation legislation, and in 1908 won enactment of the Federal Employers' Liability Act which, although it has been amended many times, is the basis for occupational injury compensation on the railroads today.

It is important at the outset to stress that the Federal Employers' Liability Act is not a workmen's compensation law. It does not include the principle of liability without fault. Compensation for occupational injury on the railroads must still go through the regular court channels, and the injured employee (with some exceptions) has the burden of proof of negligence. But that burden has been considerably lightened because the common-law defenses of assumption of risk and fellow servant have been denied the employer by law. Furthermore, even contributory negligence will not wholly deny a claim, but will merely reduce it.

Injured railway workers take their claims to the courts, and usually depend upon jury awards for their compensation. This situation is condemned as archaic, in view of the compensation principle; yet the failure of compensation laws to keep pace with rapid changes in wages and other costs, together with the liberal jury awards of recent years, have caused the railway worker to defend the system of employers' liability. If it were to be changed to a compensation system, it would be over the strenuous objection of railway unions and compensation claimants' attorneys who are convinced that workmen's compensation is not sufficiently liberal to compete with the success of jury awards.[6]

It should be noted that the occupationally injured have two other sources of income: (1) the temporary disability benefits under the Railroad Unemployment Insurance Act, and (2) the disability benefits under the Railroad Retirement Act. Should an injured worker win a damage settlement for work injury, however, he must repay any benefits received from these programs.

ECONOMIC SECURITY PROGRAMS FOR FEDERAL EMPLOYEES

The federal government, in its role of employer, has done much to insure the economic security of its many thousands of civilian employees.

[6] For a comparison of the two systems, see Earl F. Cheit, *Injury and Recovery in the Course of Employment* (New York: John Wiley and Sons, Inc., 1961), chap. vii.

Programs protecting against the risks of death, old age, and occupational illness have long been part of the terms of federal employment, and in 1955, for the first time, unemployment compensation was made available to federal employees.

Occupational Illness

The oldest of the federal programs is the Federal Employees' Compensation Act—the workmen's compensation system for federal government workers. In fact, it is the oldest of the American workmen's compensation systems, dating back to 1908 in its original form. Since the law covers employees of all branches of the federal government, its total coverage is in excess of 2.5 million workers.

Like the state workmen's compensation systems considered earlier, the federal system provides indemnity and medical benefits for disability that is causally linked to employment—due either to disease or accidental injury. The federal system differs from the state laws in several respects, particularly in benefit administration, but its most significant difference is that the federal system is generally more liberal. Its full medical benefits and liberal death and indemnity allowances (with no limit on total disability length or amounts) are considered by many to be a "model" of achievement in the workmen's compensation field.

The Act is financed by Congressional appropriations and administered by the Bureau of Employees' Compensation in the Department of Labor. All administrative functions of claims adjustment and administrative supervision are conducted by the Bureau. Administrative costs of the federal Act are often discussed, for, while they are not comparable to private insurance expense ratios, they are nevertheless sufficiently lower (running about 4 per cent of total benefits) that they are sometimes cited as evidence of the advantage of a state-financed program.

Unemployment

Until 1955, federal employees were not eligible for unemployment compensation benefits under the state unemployment compensation laws. As of January 1, 1955, however, they gained coverage under the state laws and are eligible for benefits with the same status—for purposes of the system—as employees of private industry.

Old Age, Death, and Disability

Actually, there are several different retirement plans covering civilian employees of the federal government and quasi-governmental agencies. Special plans cover groups such as foreign service officers. The most important of these plans is the Civil Service Retirement System which was established in 1920. This system covers 2.3 million, over 90 per cent of all federal employees, including all non-elective officers and employees in the three branches of the federal government except those excluded by an executive order (part-time workers, dollar-a-year men, temporary employees) and those included under some other retirement plan. Special eligibility requirements and benefits apply to Congressmen and persons dealing with criminals. There is a tendency to bring these special groups under OASDHI coverage.

Retirement Annuities. Retirement is compulsory at age seventy, but annuities are payable to persons fifty-five or sixty years of age with thirty years of service or sixty-two years of age with five or more years of service. Individuals involuntarily separated without cause on their part may retire at fifty years of age with twenty years of service. All annuities paid to those under sixty are reduced. Optional retirements now constitute about four-fifths of all retirements under the plan. The annuity is calculated at 1½ per cent of the average annual pay during the highest five consecutive years for the first five years of service (or, alternatively, 1 per cent of such average pay plus $25 for each year of such service), plus 1¾ per cent of such pay for the next five years of service (or, alternatively, 1 per cent of such pay plus $25 for each year of such service), plus 2 per cent of such pay times the remaining years of service (or, alternatively, 1 per cent of such pay plus $25 multiplied by such years of service). In all cases the maximum annuity is 80 per cent of the highest five-year average salary. In 1963, a cost-of-living adjustment in annuities for already retired persons was added to the plan, providing that each 3 per cent rise in the Consumer Price Index automatically triggers a corresponding increase in the annuity. An increase was paid in 1963 and 1965. In addition, in 1965, all retirement annuities were increased by 6.1 per cent or 11.1 per cent, depending on commencing date.

Disability Annuities. Disability annuities are payable to workers with over five years of service who are disabled (and unable to follow their usual occupations). The annuity is calculated in the same way as the retirement annuity, with a minimum benefit of 40 per cent of the highest five years' average annual pay or, if less, the annuity that would arise if the individual continued in service until age sixty with his same "final salary."

Survivorship Benefits. The most important survivorship benefits were made available in 1948, and have since been extended in some cases to widows of employees and retired employees who died before 1948. These are payable if an employee has completed five years of service and is either an active employee or an annuitant, but only if the annuitant so elects and takes a reduced annuity. Benefits were increased 10 per cent in 1963.

Health Benefits for Retired Workers. Beginning in 1961, health benefits were made available on an elective basis to retired workers with 12 years of federal service or disability annuitants with five years of service. The government contributes $3 monthly for a single retiree and twice this amount for a family; and the annuitant contributes a like amount. The annuitant may elect coverage under a government-wide health program or some private health plan. Workers retiring after the program went into effect in 1961 can continue their preretirement health plan with more generous benefit protection, though at a greater employee cost.

Financing the Civil Service Retirement System

The Federal Civil Service Retirement System is jointly financed. Employees today contribute 6½ per cent of their regular compensation.[7] A matching contribution is made by governmental departments, and, when necessary, Congress appropriates additional funds. The amounts of the Congressional appropriations are not fixed by law.

The system is administered by the United States Civil Service Commission through a retirement division. It is the largest single-employer retirement system in the United States. When it began in 1920, it had a membership of approximately 330,000 with an annual covered payroll of about $400 million, and only employees in classified Civil Service and certain special groups were eligible for membership. With more liberal eligibility provisions, the system today covers more than 2.3 million civilian employees.

As is the case with the OASDHI and Railroad Retirement funds, the annual receipts to the Civil Service Retirement and Disability Fund exceed the annual expenditures. Each year the Board of Actuaries makes its estimates of the annual appropriation necessary to make the system self-supporting, but the Congressional appropriation is often less than the recommended amount or non-existent.

The 1964 report of the Civil Service Commission indicates that, despite a sizable fund ($14,374,417,526), the deficiency under the fund is increasing. In fact, in 1963 the report estimated that "practically all the funds now held" at the end of that fiscal year would be needed merely to pay benefits to persons already on the benefit rolls if the system were to be

---

[7] This rate of contribution has risen over the years as follows: 2.5 per cent in 1920; 3.5 per cent in 1926; 5 per cent in 1942; 6 per cent in 1948; 6½ per cent in 1956. Workers who have left their jobs after five years of government service, but with less than twenty years, may request a refund of their contributions, plus interest. Or they may be eligible for benefits at age sixty-two. The refund option is not available to workers after twenty years of service.

terminated at that time and "urgently" recommended a graduated scale of increasing employment agency contributions, calling an improvement of the funding provisions of the system "increasingly imperative." [8] Earlier, the system's Board of Actuaries had recommended that the fund be placed on a full reserve basis: Not only should the deficiency be prevented from increasing, but it should eventually be liquidated. It was feared that the present system makes younger employees too dependent upon future Congressional appropriations; that benefits might be reduced when the true costs of the program were realized; and that if the system were not fully funded, the benefits for present beneficiaries might be unjustifiably increased, thus increasing the cost even further. The following observation of the Board of Actuaries should be of interest to students because of its importance to this program and also because it is partially applicable to the Railroad Retirement Act as well:

The argument has been made that reserves should not be built up to meet the Government's obligations, that since any moneys set aside are to be invested in the Government's own securities, the Government is in effect borrowing from itself and in the end the outlay will be the same whether the Government set aside a lesser amount now and paid its interest or appropriated a great amount later. In support of this argument the hypothetical case of a government without a debt was cited and it was stated that in order to have a reserve fund such a government would need to go into debt in order to issue the bonds in which to invest. This argument is novel and it would seem to mean one of two things.

It might mean that a government, without a debt, would have the privilege of incurring any deferred pension liabilities for the public to meet that it wishes to incur, because if it does not take such deferred liabilities into account in its bookkeeping, it is in a good financial position.

We would assume that in such case any system would have to be non-contributory because there would be no way of investing reserves from employees' contributions. This theory has operated to the disadvantage of taxpayers in many cases where it has been used, and to a loss to employees in others. The other alternative would seem to be that such a government should set aside funds to meet its obligations, when it incurs them, but not invest them but hold them in case.

Perhaps there is a third possibility, namely, that if no provision to meet pension costs is made as the costs accrue, future benefits may be cut if future costs are too high. This argument may be sound in a system like the Social Security System, where almost the entire public is involved, but it hardly applies to a staff pension system where employees are rendering definite service to the employer in return for a definite promise of a stated pension. In the latter case, the pension is not like social insurance, but it is in the nature of deferred compensation.[9]

[8] Board of Actuaries of the Civil Service Retirement System, *Forty-third Annual Report* (Washington, D. C.: U. S. Government Printing Office, 1965), p. 13.

[9] Board of Actuaries of the Civil Service Retirement and Disability Fund, *Thirty-Second Annual Report* (Washington, D. C.: U. S. Government Printing Office, 1952), p. 31.

While these views are perhaps not generally accepted, they merit attention and thought. Many would probably argue that it is sufficient to prevent the deficiency from increasing, since the system will almost certainly operate indefinitely.

ECONOMIC SECURITY PROGRAMS OF STATE AND LOCAL GOVERNMENTS

State and local government employees are protected by widespread economic security programs today. It is estimated that over 87 per cent of the 6.4 million persons employed by these governments are currently insured under one of several retirement programs. These employees are covered by their respective state workmen's compensation laws, and although many such governmental units elect to act as self-insurers of their workmen's compensation liabilities, their employees receive the same protection as they would in private covered employment.

State and Local Government Retirement Systems

Although state and local government retirement systems vary widely from one locality to another, a few generalizations can be made about their coverage, benefits, and operations. Most of the governmental units establish three types of retirement plans—in the order of liberality of their benefits. These plans cover policemen and firemen, teachers, and all other employees. In general, all three of these plans are contributory, but they differ in type and amount of benefits. Typically, only the plans applying to policemen and firemen provide survivors' benefits. Eligibility requirements tend to be high for all the plans, and the benefits are less liberal than those received by federal civil servants. Finally, although eligibility requirements are high, most of the plans offer both disability and old-age annuities.

Operation of State and Local Retirement Systems

The estimated 4.4 million workers covered by these programs are more than the number covered under the Railroad Retirement and Civil Service Retirement plans combined. Table 13.5 indicates the number of beneficiaries and the amount of benefits paid under state and local retirement systems in selected years from 1940 through 1963. Both number of beneficiaries and benefits paid have mounted steadily.

These steady increases over time reflect graded increases in the number of plans, the number of employees, their salary and benefit levels, and the maturing of existing plans. Total lump-sum benefits have increased substantially. Average retirement and survivorship benefits have increased as well, but only generally and less markedly than in the case of other plans.

Because these plans are operated at the state and local levels, national figures would not indicate any sudden over-all changes in coverage or benefit levels. No national figures are available on the actuarial status of these plans, but it is generally agreed that many of them are being operated essentially on a pay-as-you-go basis, while others are fully funded.

TABLE 13.5

Beneficiaries and Benefits Under State and Local Retirement Systems

Fiscal Year Ending June 30	Retirement		Survivorship		
	Beneficiaries	Benefits	Family Beneficiaries	Monthly	Lump Sum
1940	113.0	$ 103,000	25.0	$ 16,000	$12,500
1945	155.0	143,000	32.0	20,000	15,500
1950	222.0	250,000	40.0	26,000	20,000
1955	335.0	460,000	50.0	40,000	40,000
1960	535.0	850,000	62.0	70,000	63,000
1961	575.0	950,000	66.0	80,000	70,000
1962	665.0	1,140,000	81.0	105,000	75,000
1963	655.0	1,145,000	85.0	105,000	90,000

Sources: *Social Security Bulletin, Annual Statistical Supplement,* 1959, p. 6; Federal Security Agency, *Social Security Yearbook,* 1945, p. 18; and 1948, p. 4; *Social Security Bulletin, Annual Statistical Supplement,* 1963, p. 6.

Today the Social Security Act permits states to enter voluntary agreements with the federal government to accept federal OASDHI coverage for employees of the state or of its political subdivisions. As of January, 1961, about 3.8 million, or 60 per cent of the persons employed by state and local governments, were covered by such agreements. Somewhat over 2.5 million of these were also members of state and local retirement systems. Thus, protection is being extended beyond the scope of the state and local systems.[10]

GENERAL ASSISTANCE

Under the provisions of the Social Security Act discussed in Chapters 3 and 11, five special public assistance programs provide aid to four speci-

[10] "State and Local Government Employees Covered by OASDHI and Staff Retirement Systems," *Social Security Bulletin,* XXV, No. 3 (March, 1962), 17–20.

fied groups: the aged, dependent children, the blind, and the permanently and totally disabled. Many persons who lack money to meet their basic needs, however, are not eligible for assistance under these provisions because of their inability to meet age, disability, residence, or other requirements. For these persons, the state and local aid program—commonly referred to as general assistance—is the only source of aid. All states but three (Idaho, Indiana, and Nebraska) provide a general assistance program.

Although the general public assistance program is the most basic and the oldest of assistance programs in this country, today it is essentially a "residual" program. That is, it comes to the aid of those persons who are not included in federally aided programs or who are not getting sufficient aid from these programs to meet their needs. For this reason, the types of persons on general assistance rolls tend to change with the times and with the adequacy and scope of coverage of other programs.

For example, during periods of depression, one can expect to find on these rolls persons who are able-bodied and fully capable of full-time gainful employment, but who are unable to find work due to labor market conditions. During periods of economic prosperity, the persons on general assistance rolls tend more to be those who are disabled or sick or who are survivors or dependents of such persons. Federal programs, such as the Social Security Act amendments providing aid to the permanently and totally disabled and their dependents, aided in lightening the load, as did unemployment compensation and the other programs of the Social Security Act before it. Nevertheless, while these programs have tended to take the major burden from the general assistance program and have made it essentially a residual one, experience reveals that there will still be many persons who will be unable to meet the criteria of these other programs and must rely for their basic needs on general assistance. The means test that must be met to qualify, however, is often so severe that one must be virtually destitute to receive help.

Table 13.6 indicates the number of general assistance cases and amount of benefits paid them for the years 1936 through 1964.

Just as special assistance programs should become less important as the OASDHI first line of economic security defense becomes more extensive in its coverage and more liberal in its provisions, so, too, should general assistance programs carry a smaller and smaller load of the burden as all these programs expand. Table 13.6 indicates that this has tended to be the case. It must be remembered that only three decades ago, general assistance was, in fact, the *major* economic security program. The gradual reduction in case loads from 1936 through the present period is due to the fact that other programs have taken over the burden. The most recent illustrations are the extension of the aid to dependent children programs to include certain unemployed and some of the specific programs of the antipoverty war. (The system still increases and decreases its load with changing economic circumstances.)

TABLE 13.6

General Assistance Cases and Benefit Payments, 1936–64

Year	General Assistance Cases (in thousands)	Average Monthly Pay, Per Case	Total Payments (in millions)
1936	1,510	$24.13	$439.0
1937	1,626	25.36	406.9
1938	1,631	25.06	476.2
1939	1,558	24.89	482.7
1940	1,239	24.28	405.0
1941	798	24.40	272.6
1942	460	25.23	180.6
1943	292	27.76	111.0
1944	258	28.77	88.8
1945	257	32.72	87.0
1946	315	39.47	120.9
1947	356	42.79	164.8
1948	398	47.39	198.8
1949	562	50.47	282.3
1950	413	46.65	295.4
1951	323	47.09	195.3
1952	280	49.82	171.8
1953	270	50.53	151.4
1954	351	57.27	198.1
1955	314	55.04	214.3
1956	305	56.14	197.7
1957	345	59.74	213.4
1958	434	68.88	307.2
1959	399	69.44	344.5
1960	431	71.62	322.5
1961	411	67.95	356.0
1962	354	66.80	292.7
1963	352	67.95	279.6
1964	346	68.60	272.7

Sources: *Social Security Bulletin, Annual Statistical Supplement,* 1963, pp. 114, 115; *Welfare in Review, Statistical Supplement,* 1965, p. 3.

Administration of General Assistance

General assistance programs are truly local in nature. They receive no federal aid, and their cost is distributed between the states and localities, with the localities bearing slightly under one-half of it. Since administration is wholly local, the system is administered in many thousands of localities—counties, town, and villages.

General assistance evolved from the local poor relief systems that existed in the colonial period, and has not completely shaken some of its features of those days. One of these is the principle of local responsibility based on the doctrine that towns and settlements would be responsible for their own paupers, but not for those of other communities. Some states maintain residence requirements today which have the effect of denying payments to new residents.

Another feature of the early relief systems—the imposition of primary responsibility on the family—is today an important part of general assistance in many states, with the right of suit for enforcement available in some of them. Finally, the fear that welfare recipients would not seek employment has kept payments minimal.

Adequacy of General Assistance Payments

General assistance payments are made on the basis of needs and are intended to fill the gap between the recipient's resources and his needs. But the limited funds of the local agencies often put a lower limit on benefit levels than this theoretical level. Table 13.6 indicates that the long-term tendency for average monthly payments per case is upward and has almost tripled (in money terms) from 1936 through 1963. (The average monthly payment per recipient is much lower; in 1963, it was about $28.) In general, however, payments under this program tend both to be smaller than comparable special assistance programs and to show greater diversity from state to state, as is shown in Table 13.7.

TABLE 13.7

Range of Average Benefit Payments Under Unemployment Insurance, Special Assistance and General Assistance, December, 1964

	Average Payment	
Program	Highest State	Lowest State [a]
Unemployment Insurance (weekly)	$ 43.68 (Calif.)	$23.15 (N. C.)
Old-Age Assistance (monthly)	110.67 (Wis.)	39.14 (Miss.)
Aid to the Blind (monthly)	136.44 (Mass.)	44.79 (Miss.)
Aid to Permanently and Totally Disabled (monthly)	159.83 (Mass.)	43.41 (Miss.)
Medical Assistance for the Aged (monthly)	382.57 (Ill.)	25.08 (Ky.)
General Assistance (per case) (monthly)	122.79 (N. J.)	12.00 (Okla.)

[a] Omitting territories outside continental United States.

Source: *Statistical Abstract of the U. S., 1965*, pp. 302, 309.

Suggested Reforms in General Assistance

Plagued by ancient traditions, a wide diversity of administrative regulations and standards, and inadequate funds, the general assistance program operates under a heavy handicap in its important role as our residual economic security program. As noted above, the program has improved its benefit levels and has been relieved of some of its obligations by the Social Security Act. Also, there is a distinct trend among states to reduce residence requirements. Aside from the benefit levels, there is still need for vast improvement, especially in its administration, which is often humiliating and punitive to the recipient.

The American Public Welfare Association has gone on record in favor of several specific reforms. These include: (1) further reduction in the residence requirements; (2) establishment of reciprocity between the states; (3) the inclusion of all needy persons under the program, regardless of the cause of their need; and (4) a unified public assistance program. The idea of several categorical relief programs sponsored or aided by the federal government, and a general relief program without that aid has been under critical attack for some time. The American Public Welfare Association has recommended that a single federal general assistance program be adopted to replace all categorical programs. The Advisory Council on Public Assistance established under 1958 amendments to the Social Security Act has recommended that federal aid be extended to include general assistance and that the states be permitted to administer public assistance as a single program.[11]

A Concluding Comment. In some respects, the general assistance program raises the basic issue in economic security: To what extent does an individual who lacks basic resources have an enforceable right to receive from society a minimum standard of living?[12] Historically, no such common-law right existed. And although, after 1900, states began to single out certain categories of needy individuals and to give them assurances of basic income, the assistance program has always maintained its relief aspects. It has been indigency relief rather than enforcement of rights. Perhaps it is inevitable that the residual program should maintain this character, but it is not necessary that it remain so wholly inadequate. It could be modernized and made to reflect an ". . . affirmation of worth, not a testimony of inadequacy."[13]

[11] "Public Assistance: Report of the Advisory Council," *Social Security Bulletin,* XXIII, No. 2 (February, 1960), 11.

[12] See A. Delafield Smith, "Public Assistance as a Social Obligation," *Harvard Law Review,* LXIII, No. 2 (December, 1949), 266–88. See also Ellen J. Perkins, "Unmet Needs in Public Assistance," *Social Security Bulletin,* XXIII, No. 4 (April, 1960), 3–11.

[13] Smith, *ibid.*

SUMMARY

Despite many differences among the economic security programs for special groups, all of them (with the exception of the veterans' and general assistance programs) have one striking similarity. Each originally sought to provide essentially the protection that most workers engaged in private industry would have received from a combination of the Old-Age, Survivors, and Disability Insurance program and group insurance and pension plans. Inevitably, this raised the question of whether it might not have been more logical for purposes of equitable treatment and cost of administration to have included the special groups under the OASDI programs and use the special programs for providing the additional coverage deemed desirable.

As we have seen, the railroad system has worked out its special form of accommodation with the OASDHI, and the state and local systems are increasingly coordinating their programs. The civilian employees of the federal government remain the last major group that does not have OASDHI coverage, and several studies and recommendations have been made of possible ways to provide them social security protection.[14] In all likelihood, we may expect some legislative action in this direction.

Clearly, of the special groups, the veterans' programs are the most liberal. In view of the combined roles that their benefits seek to play, however, they cannot be compared to the programs of the social insurance type, although the programs of the Veterans' Administration and the armed forces resemble the social assistance programs in some respects.

For all the special programs, both those of the assistance and of the social insurance nature, the economic effects seem clearly desirable and comparable to those of the general social insurance and assistance programs.

SUGGESTIONS FOR ADDITIONAL READING

CHEIT, EARL F. *Injury and Recovery in the Course of Employment.* New York: John Wiley and Sons, Inc., 1961.
See Chapter 1 for description of Federal Employees' Compensation Act, Chapter 7 for Federal Employers' Liability Act.

GRIGSBY, MARJORIE W. "Workmen's Compensation Under the Federal Laws," *Archives of Industrial Hygiene and Occupational Medicine,* American Medical Association, IX (June, 1954), 451–75.

[14] An excellent examination of the problems involved in coordinating OASDHI with the Civil Service Retirement Act can be found in *Social Security and Federal Employment,* A report requested by the Committee on Ways and Means, U. S. House of Representatives (Washington, D. C.: U. S. Government Printing Office, 1965).

A careful analysis of the operation of the Federal Employees' Compensation Act.

HOGAN, JOHN D., and FRANCIS A. J. IANNI. *American Social Legislation.* New York: Harper & Row, 1956.
Chapter 5 on social assistance is useful.

RIESENFELD, STEFAN A., and RICHARD C. MAXWELL. *Modern Social Legislation.* Brooklyn, N. Y.: The Foundation Press, 1950. Pp. 685–747.
Legal background and foundations for the present-day public assistance programs are presented here. Also case materials on legal issues in administration of the program.

U. S. HOUSE OF REPRESENTATIVES, COMMITTEE ON VETERANS' AFFAIRS, 84th Congress, 2d Session. *A Report on Veterans' Benefits in the United States.* Washington, D. C.: U. S. Government Printing Office, 1956. Committee Prints 243, 244, 246, 247, 259–62, 270, 275.
Detailed report on the operation and historical background of present-day veterans' benefit programs.

Note: Operating statistics for the Railroad Retirement and Unemployment programs can be found in the *Annual Reports* of the Railroad Retirement Board; those for the Civil Service program in the *Annual Report* of the Civil Service Retirement Board; and those for the veterans' programs in the *Annual Reports* of the Veterans' Administration. The *Social Security Bulletin* and *Welfare in Review,* especially the statistical supplements for each year, contain operating data on all programs and detailed statistics on public and general assistance.

14

Economics of Security Programs

INTRODUCTION

In previous chapters we have discussed the problems of economic insecurity arising out of old age, death, unemployment, and accidental injury and sickness. And we have likewise looked at the ways in which society has adjusted itself to these problems through both public and private economic security programs. This process of social adjustment includes various administrative, economic, legal, political, and other issues. In this chapter we shall focus upon basic economic issues and analyze them in greater detail.[1]

In analyzing the economic implications, separate treatment must be accorded preventive as against alleviative programming. This is true for two reasons: (1) the programs tend to be markedly dissimilar in nature, (2) their impacts and consequences are likewise varied.

PREVENTIVE PROGRAMS

Preventive programs, as noted earlier, are found in both public and private sectors. In the public sector they tend to be of two types, the general and the specific. Monetary and fiscal policies designed to generate high levels of economic activity exemplify the first type; manpower training and development the second. Private approaches tend essentially to be of the specific variant: plant safety programs afford a good illustration.

[1] The student specializing in law, political sciences, sociology, or social work may wish to append materials from his own discipline to this analysis.

Public policies such as those aimed at fostering high levels of employment tend to be both general in nature and indirect in impact. They *are* economic security programs in the broadest sense of the word. But they frequently are multi-purposed, designed to achieve goals broader than, say, a reduction in the level of unemployment. For example, policies designed to increase the rate of economic growth may be desirable from the standpoint of improving the international position of the United States and of increasing the possibility of assistance to other economies, as well as reducing the level of unemployment at home.

The detailed analysis of the nature of such economic policies and of their impacts is outside the scope of this volume, but several points may be noted.

1. Unemployment is not the only problem an economy faces. Inflation, international competition, and balance of payments are but a few of the others that are relevant. Frequently it appears to be the case that policies designed to get at one problem may produce side effects that increase another. For example, massive doses of deficit financing would no doubt go a long way toward bringing down the level of unemployment. But what of the impact upon prices and upon the balance-of-payments situation? There is little doubt they would be adversely affected. Hence, the life of a policy maker is most difficult; he must reconcile different goals and must consider "trade-offs": how much in the way of possible price increases is one willing to accept for, say, a given reduction in unemployment? The economic world is complex and it is nowhere better illustrated than in this case.

2. An illustration of general public policy and of side effects is to be found in the income-tax reduction of 1964. Such fiscal policy has come to be regarded as a primary weapon in the attack upon unemployment. What *were* the economic impacts of this tax cut? [2] One estimate is that a "total" gain of $36.2 billion in gross national product will have accrued from the cut. Federal tax revenues will total nearly $10 billion over and above what they would have been in the absence of the reduction; state and local taxes, $2.2 billion. Unemployment at the end of 1965 was close to the 4 per cent level—the intermediate "full-employment" goal. [3] But such gains were not without their problems: specific price conflicts in aluminum, copper, and steel, and an ever increasing concern about the imminence of inflationary pressures (though it need be noted that the international situation was also an important contributing factor).

[2] The analysis herein is based upon Arthur M. Okun (Member, Council of Economic Advisers), "Measuring the Impact of the 1964 Tax Reduction," a talk given before the American Statistical Association, September, 1965.

[3] The rate was well below this (as low as 2 per cent) for some age groups and certain geographic areas.

"Specific" economic security public policies and programs are increasingly to be found. These include such variants as area redevelopment, manpower training and retraining, economic opportunity, civil rights. In some cases (area redevelopment and economic opportunity), the approach borders upon the more general policies—such as fiscal methods—discussed above, and can be treated in somewhat similar fashion.[4] The tentative conclusion one might reach at this point is that while such programs are beset by political and other pressures, they are instruments of economic policy which, on balance, yield positive results.[5] One would be venturesome indeed, though, to try to quantify the extent of the results.

Programs—both public and private—that relate to such issues as manpower training and development are increasingly being subjected to "cost-benefit" analysis. What were the costs of the programs? The benefits? [6] The returns are not yet in—by any means—but they suggest that on-the-job training yields a rate of return not markedly different from that on the total costs of college education. The evidence on "retraining" and "manpower development" is much less complete, but here also the evidence appears positive in its nature.

In general, then, one might conclude that:

1. "General" public economic policy is capable of producing desired results (as in reducing the level of unemployment) but it may produce other consequences (such as rising prices). Hence delicacy is required in its application. This problem was nowhere better illustrated than in the state of the economy in mid-1966.

2. "Specific" public and private programs such as manpower training do yield positive rates of return, though the evaluation of such techniques is still at a relatively primitive state.

ALLEVIATIVE PROGRAMS: THE BASIC QUESTIONS

Alleviative programs—in effect, income maintenance programs—require a different analytical approach. This is true for a number of reasons. First, such programs tend to be pinpointed toward a specific peril; thus workmen's compensation and occupational illness. Second, these

---

[4] For an example of such evaluation see Sar A. Levitan, *Federal Aid to Depressed Areas: An Evaluation of the Area Redevelopment Administration* (Baltimore: Johns Hopkins Press, 1964).

[5] For an example of political pressures see William F. Haddad, "Mr. Shriver and the Savage Politics of Poverty," *Harper's,* CCXXXI, No. 1387 (December, 1965), 43–50.

[6] For an example of such analysis, see Jacob Mincer, "On-the-Job Training: Costs, Returns, and Some Implications," *The Journal of Political Economy,* LXX, No. 5 (October, 1962), 50–73. The entire issue (Part 2) deals with the topic of investment in human beings.

programs involve "ear-marked" contributions and benefits; hence there is a collection-distribution problem.

The initial questions to be asked with respect to these income-maintenance programs are: What are their economic impacts, if any? What "differences" do they make?

"Operationally" it is easy to see the differences made by such programs. The economically insecure are cared for in a different manner: instead of relatives, friends, or charities providing assistance as a matter of need, formalized and impersonal income or service programs extend it as a matter of right.

"Economically" does this mean there is also a difference? Are these programs economically neutral? If they are, there is, of course, nothing further to be said and no need for any analysis. But we contend they are not neutral; we hold that they are large-scale resource allocation and income distribution programs and hence that in two ways they alter the pattern of economic activity. First, on the benefit side they distribute income with varying accompanying impacts. Second, such benefits must be "collected," and here patterns of consumption, saving, and investment activity are affected. In essence, these programs are major collection and distribution activities.

Fundamentally, how do the programs operate? On the preventive side, as noted earlier, they change government and business practices: a company introduces a safety program, a political unit subsidizes medical research, and expenditure patterns are thus altered. On the alleviative side the programs can be regarded as large-scale "savings"-"transfer" processes. In private programs the transfers and savings may be "voluntary" for individual cases, or "compulsory" in group systems. Public programs are primarily "compulsory" in nature. Both approaches—the preventive and alleviative—fundamentally involve resource reallocation.

Prior to examining these issues in greater detail let us raise a question or two about how much "economic security" our society can afford. In seeking to provide an answer, we shall introduce a series of ideas which will be helpful to us as we analyze further in this chapter the twin problems of benefits and costs in economic security programs.

HOW MUCH ECONOMIC SECURITY CAN OUR SOCIETY AFFORD?

The word "afford," used in the heading above, can be defined in at least two ways. First, it should be reiterated that the economically insecure are an "overhead cost" to society. The employer can reduce his work force in a depression; labor is a variable cost to him. But, society cannot do this; we have no magic way of making the unemployed, the aged, the destitute "disappear." Hence one interpretation is budgetary: How much of an individual's (and of the nation's) income can be "devoted" to economic security? That is, at what level is it possible to "maintain" the economically insecure? Second, "afford" can be viewed as psychological-operational: How much economic security can society "tolerate" before adverse effects upon incentives appear?

For the second of these problems we can offer only conjectures. As was noted in Chapter 1, there is a dearth of evidence—theoretical or empirical—as to the impact of security upon incentive and hence upon the motivating forces of a dynamic economy. In that chapter several conclusions were suggested. First, as indicated in Chapter 1, economic security programs apparently have not had any demonstrably detrimental aggregative effects upon incentive, though, certainly, individual examples of abuse can be found. (But conversely, neither can it be shown that such programs have had any markedly beneficial effects upon incentives.[7]) Second, merely because such economic security programs have been "neutral" up to now in their incentive effects, it should not be taken to imply that they will continue to be neutral regardless of the scope or form of the program. For example, economic security program benefits that restore all or nearly all of wage losses would have potentially dangerous (and detrimental) effects upon incentive.[8]

But what of the first problem, the budgetary aspects of economic security? How much economic security can society afford? The answer is twofold: (1) as much as its resources will allow, and (2) given this limiting factor, beyond that as much as it is willing to spend. Both monetary and physical-productivity factors are involved.

Any economic security program presupposes a given "standard" or "level" of protection or care for those persons covered. And the height of the standard that can be adopted is restricted, in the limiting case, to the productive capabilities of the society. For example, it is difficult to visualize the aged being provided for in the backwoods-frontier regions of the early United States under the equivalent of our present-day Old-Age, Survivors, and Disability Insurance system (even if the frontier philosophy had been willing to accept such an approach). The aged were taken care of, but "retirement at sixty-five" could not be tolerated, and when a person finally had to stop work, he was cared for in the same cabin as was occupied by the rest of the family. Productive capacity simply was not such as to permit separate facilities to be built or for the

---

[7] But see Arthur Larson, *Know Your Social Security* (New York: Harper & Row, 1955), p. 23, where he argues that while it cannot be proved statistically, it is generally agreed that the "secure worker is the better worker."

[8] Much interesting work is being done in an allied area, that of taxation and the incentive to work. Higher taxes may cause people to work harder: the income effect is more powerful than the substitution.

retired person to "live in style," supported by the family.[9] In a real sense we could not have had an OASDHI program of today's dimensions one hundred years ago; the productive capacity of the country could not have supported it. To be sure, the aged had to be taken care of (they *were* an overhead cost to society); but instead of "retiring in their own homes," as is increasingly true today, they were frequently provided for by more intensively utilizing the capacity of the family homestead.[10] Or, if provided for in public institutions, the care was minimal in most cases.

Given the fact that the productive capacity of the economy ultimately limits the level at which economic security can be provided, it is nevertheless true that society has considerable choice within this limit as to the level or standard it wishes to select.[11] Thus, another answer to the question of how much it can afford is how much it is willing to pay, and this is a cultural as much as an economic answer. "Willingness to pay" additionally involves two specific questions.

The first of these questions is: How much present income (in the real sense) is the *individual* willing to forego for protection in the future against the risks of economic insecurity?[12] What level of security is he willing to provide? In the individual case this becomes a matter of individual determination, and one finds a range of such choices from persons with no protection to those who are "insurance poor." In the case where the economic security program is of a negotiated type, as in an employer-union relationship, the individual may have a choice (or vote) in the initial deliberations on whether or not to attempt to negotiate such a program. Once the program has been accepted, the individual is restricted in the freedom he has in choosing present as against future goods. The same restraints apply in the case of any compulsory program.

The second specific question relates to the level of security *society* is willing to provide (and is economically capable of providing). Private and public retirement programs give an individual the right to claim

[9] Just as fiction is frequently more revealing than fact in many instances, it is also the case here. For an account, less rigorous than the backwoods illustration given above, of the way a somewhat later generation cared for the aged, see Mildred Walker, *The Southwest Corner* (New York: Harcourt, Brace & World, Inc., 1951). (Thus, succinctly, on page 11, Miss Walker notes: "The southwest corner was the way New England handled social security in the very early days.") For a still later account, see the short story by Edna Ferber, "Old Man Minnick," in *Your Town* (World Reprint ed.; Cleveland: World Publishing Co., 1948).

[10] For a humorous and nostalgic account of this, see James Thurber's tales of his grandfather's life in the family homestead in *My Life and Hard Times* (New York: Harper & Row, 1933). For a different but also pleasantly humorous tale see Samuel Hopkins Adams, *Grandfather Stories* (New York: Random House, Inc., 1960).

[11] See the discussion in Gerhard Colm, "The Economic Base and the Limits of Social Welfare," *Monthly Labor Review*, LXXXVIII, No. 6 (June, 1963), 695–700.

[12] See the interesting discussion in John J. Corson and John W. McConnell, *Economic Needs of Older People* (New York: The Twentieth Century Fund, 1956), chap. xiii.

goods and services at a later date in exchange for goods and services fore-gone now. (Thus, under OASDI an individual gives up—pays—so many dollars a year in exchange for the right to collect benefits at a later age.) The individual, therefore, has a "legal" claim which he has the right to exercise in the future. But, in the future, those in society who have not retired are the people who will have to produce the goods and services which the retired person can claim. And, for a variety of reasons the non-retired group may not be able to do this. The problem is not one of money but of real resources. One could visualize, for example, a so-ciety in which the majority of persons were in the older age group. In such a case the productive segment of the population, even if provided with considerable capital equipment, may not be able to produce the needed goods. A more realistic case of the same nature arises out of a state of war and a war economy. Here it may not be possible to permit the aged to exercise their claims; the productive segment of the economy simply may not be able to turn out military and civilian goods in sufficient quantity. Hence we come around the full circle again to the earlier noted idea that the productive capacity of a society looms importantly in the question of how much economic security can be afforded. And while one notes an increasing amount of our economy's resources formally being devoted to economic security, the process is not unidirectional. It could well be that the pressure of future events might require a reversal of the trend.

ISSUES IN ECONOMIC SECURITY PROGRAM BENEFITS

We noted previously that economic security programs "redistribute" income. Such redistribution may occur in a number of ways: (1) among individuals at any given time or (2) over time, as when income is "stored up" for a given period and then released. In the second example an in-dividual may merely distribute his own income over time, or in addition to the time dimension there may also be distribution among individuals.

If economic security programs increase the total output of the econ-omy, a larger "pie" is available for redistribution. Such an increase could come about, for example, when "surpluses" arising out of the program (the excess of "receipts" over "benefits" at any period) are invested and yield a larger future return than would otherwise be the case. If output does not increase, income is redistributed simply from those who work to those who do not (or from those who do not experience the insecurity to those who do).

"True" actuarial benefits pose few problems either at a given time or over time. To be sure, redistribution exists: monies are paid to "he who has the accident" and "taken from" those in the system who do not experience the undesired event. But such redistribution is a matter of impersonal statistical probabilities. (We leave to the reader the oft-raised issue as to whether the only way one can "gain" in this redistribution is to have the accident.)

Social insurance benefits do, however, raise additional questions. Such benefits are frequently based upon factors other than actuarial relationships. In particular, these benefit structures tend to be weighted in favor of the lower income groups. Thus, under OASDI the maximum primary benefit, compared to the average monthly wage upon which it is based, is a smaller percentage than the minimum benefit similarly compared. Or, in Minnesota for many years the unemployment insurance benefit structure averaged out to $8 plus 1 per cent of one's base period earnings, up to a stipulated maximum. The flat $8 weights the benefit structure toward its lower end.

Why should such social insurance systems redistribute income in this manner? The essential reason is that there is a budgetary minimum necessary to keep body and soul together. It is this minimum which tends to be "built into" the benefit structure. There exists other than an "actuarial" return: people with low incomes get relatively more for what they (or their employers) pay into the system than do those with higher incomes. Ethical and moral considerations are intertwined with the economic.

What are the economic impacts of such economic security program redistribution? For "actuarial" redistribution, once a program gets under way, it is relatively simple: you and I forego a definite "loss" (the premium) in exchange for protection against a bigger loss. Assuming the event, say an accident, would happen and assuming we would wish to "remedy the damages," the insurance system simply provides a specific way of doing it. For social insurance the case may vary. Here there tends to be a redistribution in favor of lower income groups. In such cases, the net effect is probably to increase consumption and reduce saving: the lower income groups who receive benefits are likely to spend them; the higher income groups might have saved some of the monies collected from them by the economic security program. In cases where "reserve funds" are built up, such as under OASDI, the rate of collections may be such that the "forced savings" accumulation outweighs, at the first stage, whatever consumption impact might arise out of the transfers themselves.

One study, made in 1958, suggests the quantitative impact of income redistribution.[13] This study indicates a net transfer of $4.5 billion from

[13] See J. J. Carroll, *Alternative Methods of Financing Old-Age, Survivors, and Disability Insurance* (Ann Arbor: University of Michigan, Institute of Public Administration, 1960).

those with incomes above $3,000 to those below. About $2.5 billion accrued to those in the $1,000–$1,999 income class. On balance a net amount of $2.5 billion was transferred from "middle income" ($3,000 to $7,500) to "low-income" (below $3,000) groups. One increasingly hears that "the poor are supporting the aged." While the above does not quite bear this out, it does suggest that the regressive nature of OASDI contributions lends some credence to the allegation.

Social insurance redistribution may create some incentive problems though they are likely to be the deterrents of poverty rather than affluence. Thus, again using Minnesota as an example, as late as 1966, a person with base-period earnings of $520 could be imagined as having worked at $10 a week for fifty-two weeks. If unemployed and eligible for benefits, he could receive $12 a week for eighteen weeks. Here is a case where weekly benefits are higher than wages: where benefit restoration is *over* 100 per cent (granted benefits last only eighteen weeks and not fifty-two). One might ask himself, however, how real such problems are in these times.

But, as noted earlier, economic security programs also redistribute income through time. In one case—such as old age—the purchase of a deferred annuity provides an example of this distribution. We deliberately use it as an example since it typifies a class of distributive cases which are independent of the level of economic activity. In a second case such redistribution *is* linked to the level of economic activity, as in unemployment compensation. Let us examine both of these types, concentrating upon the second and asking the question: How much of a counter-balancing force do such economic security programs exert in "evening out" purchasing power through time—in skimming it off in periods of prosperity and feeding it back during recessions?

Compensatory Influences of Economic Security Programs

First, in the case of accidents, sickness, death, and old age, it is difficult to speak of the "compensatory" or "counter-balancing" influences of economic security programs. This is true because, unlike unemployment, it is not customary to view accidental injury, sickness, death, or old age as accompanying (or causing or resulting from) changes in the level of economic activity. Hence, it is likewise not customary to view such economic security program benefits as compensatory influences in the way that unemployment insurance payments are.

But, the injured, the dependent, and the aged are an overhead cost to society. And payments made under private and public economic security programs for accidents, death, and old age are one means through which these overhead costs can be met. Hence, while such payments may not be necessarily compensatory in, say, a counter-cyclical manner, they do provide an income flow which permits a more socially desirable way of caring for those dependent, and which in turn helps maintain the level of economic activity.

There is evidence, however, that certain of these programs may have cyclically compensatory impacts, relatively minor though they may be. Thus, during an upswing, OASDI contributions tend to rise, while benefits, though they may not fall, will rise relatively less insofar as beneficiaries (actual or potential) may be able to take advantage of more favorable employment opportunities. The reverse tends to operate in a recession.[14] Thus far, however, it is probably the case that programmatic changes have washed out any counter-cyclical possibilities.

Table 14.1 summarizes social welfare expenditures for three selected years: 1935, 1950, and 1963. The data indicate the trends in economic security payments, not only in absolute dollar amounts, but on a per-capita basis, and as compared to various indexes such as gross national product. The magnitude of such payments is apparent. As a percentage of personal income, social insurance and related payments have also increased, running currently at over the 7 per cent level, as compared with less than half that a quarter-century ago.

Second, unemployment insurance is, however, more relevantly viewed against the backdrop of changing levels of economic activity. What is the economic significance of unemployment compensation? The most thorough investigation of this subject has been made by Richard A. Lester, whose study is summarized here.[15]

Among others, Lester asks the following two questions for the period 1949–59:

1. What percentage of the wage loss, resulting from unemployment, was restored by unemployment compensation?
2. How much of the earnings loss caused by recessions was met by the additional benefit payments resulting from recession unemployment?

These two questions can be combined and restated: For the period 1949–59, unemployment compensation restored what portion of wage loss

---

[14] For a detailed analysis see Ida C. Merriam, "Social Security Programs and Economic Stability" in *Policies to Combat Depression: A Report of the National Bureau of Economic Research* (Princeton: Princeton University Press, 1956); M. O. Clement, "The Quantitative Impact of Automatic Stabilizers," *Review of Economics and Statistics*, XLII, No. 1 (1960), 56–61.

[15] See Richard A. Lester, "The Economic Significance of Unemployment Compensation, 1948–1959," *The Review of Economics and Statistics*, XLII, No. 4 (November, 1960), pp. 349–72. See also the other studies cited by Lester in his article.

TABLE 14.1

Trends in Social Welfare Expenditures Under Public Programs,
Fiscal Years 1935, 1950, and 1963

Item	Fiscal Year			Per Cent Increase		
	1935	1950	1963 [a]	1935–50	1950–63	1935–63
Total social welfare expenditures (in millions):						
Current prices	$ 6,503	$23,189	$65,904	257	184	913
1963 [b] prices	$15,265	$29,353	$65,904	92	125	332
Per capita social welfare expenditures:						
Current prices	$ 50.33	$150.89	$345.67	200	129	587
1963 [b] prices	$118.15	$191.00	$345.67	62	81	193
Ratio of:						
All welfare expenditures to:						
Gross national product	9.5	8.8	11.6	—	—	—
Total government expenditures	49.4	36.7	38.7	—	—	—
Federal welfare expenditures to all federal expenditures	47.8	24.3	28.4	—	—	—
Federal welfare expenditures from general revenues to all federal expenditures from general revenues	47.6	21.3	13.7	—	—	—
State and local welfare expenditures to all state and local expenditures	50.8	61.7	59.8	—	—	—

[a] Preliminary estimates.
[b] Fiscal year.

Source: Ida C. Merriam, "Social Expenditures and Worker Welfare," *Monthly Labor Review*, LXXXVI, No. 2 (June, 1963), 688.

(1) for the over-all period and (2) for that caused specifically by the recessions of 1949–50, 1954–55, and 1957–58?

Lester's answers to these questions run as follows:

1. Benefits under regular state and railroad programs of unemployment compensation appear to have restored no more than 20 per cent of the wage loss from total unemployment. If the wage loss from partial unemployment is included, the compensation rate, including partial benefits, averages about 15 per cent. (Interestingly, the rate of compensation appears to have followed a horizontal trend during the period in question.)
2. Unemployment compensation during the first three post-war recessions appears to have provided no higher a rate of restoration for the recession-caused wage loss than did such compensation for the period as a whole. Such compensation for recession-caused unemployment would, however, be additive to the compensation provided for "basic" unemployment existing at the time. Hence, if one takes all public unemployment insurance programs and looks at their compensating effects, the restoration runs between 25 and 30 per cent during recession peaks (closer to 25 in the earlier recessions and 30, because of temporary unemployment compensation, in the 1957–58 recession).

We may raise here one additional question as to the counter-cyclical nature of unemployment compensation. How successful have economic security programs been in skimming off purchasing power in prosperity and feeding it back in recessions? The Lester data just presented indicate that there is benefit "feedback" in recessions. But, for unemployment insurance, may it not be that the sums paid out as benefits are collected in the same period in which they are distributed, rather than in an earlier time? Hence, may it not be the case that there are compensatory benefits, but not counter-balancing financial impacts?

We believe the answer to these last two questions may well be "yes." Because of the influence of experience rating (discussed below in this chapter) unemployment insurance collections exhibit little counter-cyclical influence. Wisconsin has a financing system by means of which tax rates are lowered as payrolls decrease, and a few other states have exhibited counter-cyclical patterns. But most states operate in the opposite direction: if the reserve funds decrease (indicating high out-payments), the tax rates increase. This is just the opposite of what is desirable.

Two further comments might be made. First, because of processing problems, it takes time to introduce changes in state unemployment insurance tax structures. Given the relative shortness of the post-war recession cycles, "accidental" counter-cyclical influences have been exerted. These have resulted since the change to a higher tax structure cannot be made administratively instantaneous; and by the time it is introduced, the recession may be over.

Second, in the post-war period, counter-cyclical influences have been minimized by the drawing down of state unemployment insurance trust funds. In 1950 they stood at 7 billions; in 1955 at 8.3 billions; in 1960 at 6.6 billions; and in 1965, 7.8 billions. Hence, compensation payments have been financed in part in the last decade by using a previously accumulated savings fund. And, this savings fund has been drawn on in good times as well as poor.[16]

Four conclusions appear from the investigations of Lester and others. The first is that in the relatively mild post-war recessions, payments to the unemployed were important in maintaining purchasing power. Second, if wages and salaries become more resistant to downturns in a recession, it becomes more important to calculate compensatory influences in terms of what growth rates such wages and salaries would have exhibited in the absence of a recession. (This is the method Lester uses in his analysis.) Third, in more severe business recessions, compensating payments may be less effective than they were in 1948–49, 1953–54, and 1957–58 (and 1960–61). Fourth, economic security programs of all types are "built-in stabilizers." They may not work as effectively as we had hoped from a counter-cyclical point of view. But they provide a steady stream of income payments to various classes of recipients. This stability factor has a usefulness all its own.

ISSUES IN ECONOMIC SECURITY PROGRAM FINANCING

What of the other side of the coin: the cost or financing side of economic security programs? Benefits do not fall, like manna, from heaven. They must be "paid for." Who *does* pay for them? What are the economic consequences of various methods of financing? Let us now consider the collection rather than the distribution phases of the problem.

Costs and Burdens in Economic Security Programs

Financing economic security programs involves a number of problems, some of which are related to the individual, others to the economy. We shall analyze briefly a number of these problems.

[16] See the paper by George E. Rejda, "Unemployment Insurance As An Automatic Stabilizer," given before the American Risk and Insurance Association, September, 1965. Rejda concludes that during three of the four postwar downswings unemployment insurance offset 24 to 28 per cent of the decline in national income. He also notes that unemployment taxes are not automatic *destabilizers* as is commonly believed.

Who Bears the Costs of Economic Security Programs? "Bear" is defined here in terms of the individual or group upon whom the burden ultimately falls; we are not concerned with the legal or financial mechanics of who initially pays or how the payment is made. Three different situations may be recognized.

First, as noted earlier, economic security programs like the Employment Act of 1946 are financed out of general revenues, and hence the burden is diffused through the economy, dependent upon the ways in which revenues are produced. The same or parallel analyses can be used with respect to public works programs, to the costs of administering governmental intervention in substandard conditions, and to other cases where there is no direct relation of payments to benefits or where there are no compulsory, earmarked taxes involved.

Second, where the individual provides for his own economic security, such as through the purchase of accident and sickness insurance or of a retirement annuity, he in turn bears the cost. This is done by the individual's giving up present goods and services (or reducing savings) in exchange for "future protection."

Third, there are cases where the program is compulsory and where the employee and/or employer pays a premium or a tax. This is the incidence problem. In the case of private programs—health, welfare, pension—the employer may initially pay the entire "premium" or only some part of it. Does this imply that he likewise bears the burden? The answer to this question depends upon whether one believes that the employees would have received the equivalent of the premium or tax in higher wages had there been no economic security program. It may be conjectured that the employees would have received, via wage increases, some portion—perhaps a major portion, though not necessarily all—of the premium or tax.[17] Hence a portion—and perhaps a major one—of the costs of employer-employee security programs is borne by the employees themselves.[18] In the case of public programs, the analysis appears to

[17] This would perhaps vary from time to time. Thus, in a period when a direct wage increase would not or could not have been forthcoming, "fringes," as in an economic security program, might have been. Hence in some cases (wage stabilization periods or "depressed" periods such as 1960–61) the burden is not shifted (at least not immediately) to employees. In such cases the employees have the choice of accepting the economic security program or "nothing," since a direct wage increase would be unlikely. *But,* economic security programs may be a method through which some gains can be negotiated by labor organizations. Hence there is the problem not only of cost but also of ingenuity in presenting and securing demands.

[18] Since the employer pays an income tax on income *after* his security program tax (or premium) has been deducted (as a "wage cost") while the employee pays an income tax on an amount *including* his security program contribution, there is a certain logic in the belief that the employer contributions are deferred pay, and hence paid for by employees.

indicate that the burden is more fully diffused, with some belief that employees again bear the major share of the burden.[19]

Is the Financing of Economic Security Programs Deflationary? Inflationary? In the case of compulsory public programs, any in-payment made to the government is a tax, and as such its collection is deflationary.[20] If the tax receipts were in some way sterilized, or were a substitute for monies that would be raised through credit expansion, the net result would also be deflationary. But the collected tax is not sterilized; it passes into the flow of economic activity. If the tax is used to effect a transfer payment (that is, if it is paid out to a recipient of an economic security program) then the situation that develops is equivalent to that which existed prior to the collection of the tax, providing the propensities to consume and save are equal for taxpayer and recipient. There is a lag problem involved inasmuch as collection and distribution are not coincidental in time. Since public economic security program taxes are collected regularly through the year, this lag is likely to be regularized and minimized. If the collected tax is paid out to government employees, there results a production of goods and services, and under specified conditions there may actually be an expansion of production.[21] Thus the net impact of the collection of economic security program premiums or taxes need not be deflationary.

In the case of private programs where the premium payment is compulsory and where the service received is not necessarily or continuously equal to the in-payment, the type of analysis used above can be applied.

---

[19] This is the conclusion of a study by R. A. Musgrave, J. J. Carroll, L. D. Cook, and L. Frane, "Distribution of Tax Payments by Income Groups: A Case Study for 1948," *National Tax Journal*, IV, No. 1 (March, 1951), 1–53. See particularly pp. 23–25, where the authors present their summaries. Musgrave and his associates conclude that in a competitive system, the entire burden is borne by wage earners, but that in the realistic case complete backward shifting is unlikely for various reasons, among them being the fact that unions may cite the intent of the law and restrain employers from such shifting. For analysis, as well as a useful summary of the literature, see S. E. Harris, *Economics of Social Security* (New York: McGraw-Hill Book Co., 1941), Part III, particularly chap. xiii. Harris concludes (pp. 440–41) that a substantial part of the burden falls elsewhere than on the wage earner. For a more recent summary see Richard A. Lester, "Financing of Unemployment Compensation," *Industrial and Labor Relations Review*, XIV, No. 1 (October, 1960), 52–82. Older analyses tended to emphasize more fully the fact that the employee bore the full burden; the modern tendency is less so.

[20] For an extended discussion of this question, see Harris, *ibid.*, Part I. Some authorities hold that the recession of 1937–38 was caused in part by the imposition of Social Security taxes. See Kenneth D. Roose, *The Economics of Recession and Revival* (New Haven: Yale University Press, 1954), pp. 210–12.

[21] For a useful discussion, see T. Haavelmo, "Multiplier Effects of a Balanced Budget," *Econometrica*, XIII, No. 4 (October, 1945), 311–18; and the further discussion by G. Haberler, R. M. Goodwin, E. E. Hagen, and T. Haavelmo in *Econometrica*, XIV, No. 1 (January, 1946), 148–58.

If the program is voluntary and/or if there is a close correspondence of benefit and payment, a different approach must be used. In this case the analytical treatment is the same as is used for any personal expenditure on consumer goods.

What Are the Implications of Alternative Methods of Financing Economic Security Programs? Certain types of economic security programs inherently call for financing on a pay-as-you-go basis. Thus, except for accumulating contingency reserves, this would be true (with minor exceptions) of insurance programs such as accidental injury and sickness, and workmen's compensation, whether private or public. Conversely, the very nature of private pension programs calls for the accumulation of reserves (although in some cases in the past, companies operated on an out-of-pocket basis). In the case of public old-age and unemployment programs, either approach could be used.[22]

The choice made on these latter two programs has been dictated in part by other than economic considerations and is moreover in part a result of the sheer accidents of historical development. If unemployment insurance is to be financed from sources other than general revenues, then it is logical to build up reserves in years of great plenty to carry over in years of famine.[23] But partly because employment experience since 1940 has been much different than was anticipated and partly because of various pressures upon state legislatures, the size of the reserve, its growth to 1950–51 and subsequent decline, bear little relation to any particular set of logical economic criteria.[24]

In the case of the old-age program, there have been various shifts between pay-as-you-go and full-reserve approaches, and the present system stands somewhere between either extreme, probably closer to the former.[25] Proponents of pay-as-you-go have taken their positions either out of a belief in the economy of such an approach (or related approaches) or out of a conviction that the states rather than the federal government should administer such a program.[26]

[22] Students interested in the public finance aspects of economic security programs should consult the *National Tax Journal* which publishes relevant items.

[23] *Genesis,* 41: 25–36.

[24] Various states have, however, undertaken detailed studies in an attempt to bring some actuarial rationality into cost calculations. See the references in Chapter 7.

[25] This does not mean that the Social Security Administration has been capricious in its approach to the problems involved. Far from it! Under the direction of Chief Actuary Robert J. Myers and others, numerous actuarial studies have been undertaken for a series of differing situations. See Chapter 5 of this text for additional discussion.

[26] The student should check such sources as L. Meriam, K. T. Schlotterbeck, and M. Maroney, *The Cost and Financing of Social Security* (Washington, D. C.: The Brookings Institution, 1950); Chamber of Commerce of the United States, *Improving Social Security* (Washington, D. C.: 1953); and the papers presented in the sym-

If it is the factual case that both public old-age and unemployment programs have resulted in the accumulation of combined reserves at the end of 1965 of over $29 billion, what are the economic implications of such accumulations? What of the private pension counterparts? We shall not consider here such issues as investment outlets, effects on the interest rate, liquidation problems, and the like.[27] We are rather concerned with the general economic implications of fund accumulation and reduction.

If public program receipts exceed benefit payments, the excesses are required under law to be invested in United States obligations. Given this fact, a number of possible alternatives can be discerned. If the funds now provided the government via economic security program in-payments were raised alternatively by other types of personal taxes, the net impact on the level of economic activity would be likely the same, lags excepted, if propensities to consume and save of the two taxable groups were similar. If the funds were raised by government borrowing, then the results would depend upon the source from which the loans were obtained. If the banking system were the source, then the results would be inflationary; hence, in this case, an economic security program would contribute to stability. If the public were the source, then the results would depend upon the propensities to save and consume, and any of a number of alternatives would be possible.[28] Conversely, if the fund were reduced (if out-payments exceed in-payments) the above analysis would be applicable, except that results in the opposite direction might be expected in given cases. Thus, fund reduction (and hence debt repayment) may be deflationary in the same sense as is general public debt reduction.

In the case of private economic security programs where funds are accumulated, a major determinant is the savings-investment relation. In-payments to such a program arbitrarily increase the level of savings. Investment (in the real sense, not merely in the purchase of securities) is, however, likely to be undertaken by other groups in the economy. And, unless these groups are willing to make use of the larger accumulation of savings, the impact of fund increases is deflationary. Thus, such economic security programs can be a valuable source of savings for the in-

---

posium on "Social Security—A New Look" in *Proceedings* of the Sixth Annual Meeting, Industrial Relations Research Association, 1953, pp. 163–99, for illuminating discussion on these issues. See also the October, 1960 issue of the *Industrial and Labor Relations Review*.

[27] See for example, Paul P. Harbrecht, S. J., *Pension Funds and Economic Power* (New York: The Twentieth Century Fund, 1959).

[28] The student should construct cases where borrowing from the public is inflationary in the above case and where it is not. Hint: Vary the propensities to save and consume of the different groups in question, and assume in one case that the savings are automatically invested; in the other, that they are not.

vestment required by economic progress; on the other hand, in the early thirties, they would have added fuel to the deflationary spiral.

One final comment: Pay-as-you-go programs are less subject to the vicissitudes of economic change than are funded programs. While pay-as-you-go may be impractical (or impossible) in some types of private programs, the alternative is always available for public programs. And even if hyper-inflation should wipe out the assets of private program funds, public programs would be unaffected and could continue operating (or start operating again). This factor is not necessarily decisive in choosing the program type (there are advantages to funded systems, in leveling out the premium or in providing for contingencies), but it is worth calling attention to in light of economic activity and price level movements over the last generation.

Economic Security Trust Funds and the Taxation Question

An additional problem, relating to financing methods, has appeared over the years. This involves the attack on (and defense of) economic security trust funds.

The trust fund "fraud" thesis is usually spelled out in the following steps. (We will use the OASDI fund as the example.)

1. The government taxes employers and employees covered under the OASDI program. But it taxes (at present, at least) more than is needed to meet current out-payments. Therefore a reserve (a trust fund) is built up and by law is invested in United States government securities. This is the first taxation stage—single taxation.

2. The securities held in the reserve (trust fund) are interest-bearing. In order to pay the interest on these obligations, the government taxes the general public. This is the second taxation stage—"double" taxation, and the stage which is viewed as "fraudulent" by certain critics.

A variety of minor rebuttals have been made to this argument: that if the excess of taxes over out-payments were invested in private rather than in government securities we would have government ownership of private industry (and hence "socialism"); or that the contention might have some merit only if the excess receipts caused the government to spend more than it otherwise would have.

But these rebuttals do not get at the core of the false reasoning involved in this type of argumentation. That there are two stages of taxation is obviously the case. But this is not double taxation. Nor is it fraudulent. Assume that present taxes were lower—that they were just sufficient to meet present benefit requirements, and hence that no trust fund could be built up. Assume that the system remains on such an annual "pay-as-you-go" basis. Now "pay-as-you-go" has a particular connotation here. What it means is that each year those who are actively covered under the system pay the benefits of those who have become eligible to retire. As the percentage of the retired aged increases (which is the developing case in this country) those actively covered under the system will have to pay increased taxes to meet the obligations imposed by the given benefits structure. Disregarding discount complexities, one can show that the interest paid on the trust fund and raised by taxation is equal to the increase in taxes that would be required to meet obligations in the absence of such a fund. Thus there is no "double taxation." There might be some legitimacy to the criticism that the taxes are paid by different groups; that in the case of a trust fund, the "general public" helps support the OASDI beneficiary, whereas on a pay-as-you-go approach the OASDI group finances itself. But this is not the same as double taxation or fraud.

A simple arithmetic example will bring out the above. Assume $1,000,000 is needed this year to pay benefits, and $1,002,000 next year. Using the trust fund approach, $1,100,000 is raised via OASDI taxes this year, and the excess $100,000 invested in United States securities at 2 per cent. Next year $1,000,000 will be raised from OASDI coverage and $2,000 via general taxation as interest on trust fund securities. Thus, $2,000 comes from general taxation. In the absence of this fund, the $2,000 would have to be raised via OASDI taxes. Hence $2,000 = $2,000 and there is no double taxation. It may be argued that an extra $100,000 was levied in the first year to build up the trust fund. But, ultimately if the trust fund is reduced to zero, the process of its reduction means that additional funds will be available, thus permitting taxes to be reduced in that year. Hence, again the two alternative systems balance each other out.

The Social Security Advisory Council's rebuttal to the "double taxation" thesis was a "half-taxation" argument, which while interesting also is not wholly valid. This rebuttal ran as follows:

Assume that in a future year, OASDI benefit payments exceeded taxes collected by $2,000. If there were a $100,000 trust fund invested in 2 per cent United States securities, $2,000 would be earned, and total receipts from taxation and interest would equal benefit payments. But assume there was no reserve fund. Then it would be necessary to raise the $2,000 via, say, additional OASDI taxes. *And* (and this is the core of the argument) another $2,000 would have to be raised to pay interest on $100,000 of public debt that would now be held by someone other than the OASDI trust fund. Therefore, the trust fund results in half, rather than double taxation.

One does not, however, get something for nothing in this case; if one did it would be profitable to pursue this policy and thus achieve one-fourth, one-eighth, and subsequent geometric reductions in the tax load. Counter-balancing factors negate this "something for nothing" possibility. If no reserve had been created, the excess taxes (or tax base) that would have been used in building it up could have been used for other purposes. Hence there would have been no need to have public debt in the hands of others (there would have been no public debt) and in turn no need to levy taxes to make interest payments. But assume that a public debt did exist and it was in the hands of others. If this were the case, then taxes would have been less in an earlier period (or periods) since public borrowing was used instead. Thus the additional tax burden now (to meet public debt interest payments) would have been balanced by the lower earlier tax load. There is, of course, a difference in who pays the taxes. But this is not a "half-taxation" argument. Again arithmetic examples could be used to illustrate the problems involved.[29]

Whether a trust-fund approach should or should not be used for the various social insurances has been endlessly debated.[30] There are valid arguments for and against such an approach. But we are not convinced that the double-taxation (or half-taxation) argument is one of them.

Let us now turn to a final problem in the area of financing, that of experience rating in unemployment compensation.

Experience or Merit Rating in Unemployment Compensation

"The primary and announced purpose of experience rating . . . is to provide a financial incentive, in the form of a reduced contribution rate, for the individual employer to make a real effort to stabilize his employment."[31] While Great Britain experimented with this approach prior to 1920 and then abandoned it, the "merit rating" idea was incorporated into the Wisconsin Act in 1932. Today all state laws make provision for some

[29] As an exercise the student might wish to work out several such examples.

[30] See Harris, *op. cit.*, chap. ix, and "Financing Old-Age and Survivor's Insurance," Report on Issues in Social Security to the Committee on Ways and Means of the House of Representatives, 79th Congress, 1st Session (Washington, D. C.: U. S. Government Printing Office, 1946), particularly pp. 103 ff. See also Chapter 4, this text.

[31] Charles A. Myers, "Experience Rating in Unemployment Compensation," *American Economic Review*, XXXV, No. 3 (June, 1945), 339. This article, along with the following by Professor Myers, provides an excellent analysis of the subject: *Employment Stabilization and the Wisconsin Act* (Washington, D. C.: Social Security Board, September, 1940).

form of merit or experience rating. (While the two terms are technically interchangeable, the latter has become the more customary.) The necessity for such adoption was discussed in Chapter 7, along with experience rating formulae and the employer contribution rate changes resulting from the utilization of this system.

But, the mere fact that all states have experience rating plans does not mean that the approach is economically logical (though this had led to the oft-repeated statement that "experience rating is indefensible in theory but thoroughly acceptable in practice"). What are the presumed advantages of experience rating? The disadvantages? The following discussion seeks to get at the more relevant issues.[32]

The major contentions for experience rating are two in number, as follows:

1. On an economy-wide level, such a system is viewed as a way of allocating or distributing the social costs of unemployment among industries in the order in which they are "responsible" for unemployment. This is held to be analogous to the way in which, for example, the costs of industrial accidents are distributed among companies in order of their safety "experience."

2. On the individual-enterprise level, the purpose of experience rating is, as was noted in the opening paragraph of this section, to stabilize employment in the individual firm by providing a monetary incentive in the form of a reduced contribution rate. (If employment stabilization were a cost-free process, one would presume that the entrepreneur would carry it to the point where his unemployment compensation tax was minimized. If it were not cost-free, then economic logic would dictate that it be carried to the point where its marginal costs would not be greater than the marginal tax savings.)

The arguments arrayed against experience rating are more numerous. Whether they are also more persuasive is a matter we shall analyze further.

1. It is held to be economically and ethically undesirable, as well as operationally impossible, to allocate the social costs of unemployment via experience rating. Assume a highly unstable industry, and assume that the employer is thus able to do little in the way of stabilizing his employment. Further assume his contribution rate is therefore high. If the em-

---

[32] Perhaps still the two best sources in this topic are Herman Feldman and Donald M. Smith, *The Case For Experience Rating in Unemployment Compensation and a Proposed Method;* and Richard A. Lester and Charles V. Kidd, *The Case against Experience Rating in Unemployment Compensation,* both published by Industrial Relations Counselors, New York, 1939. The analysis herein leans heavily upon these studies. For a more recent study see Clinton Spivey, *Experience Rating in Unemployment Compensation, Bulletin 84* (Urbana: Bureau of Economic and Business Research, University of Illinois, 1958).

ployee bears the burden of the high rate he is really paying the cost of unemployment inherent in his own job. If the tax is shifted to consumers and the employer bears none of the burden, there is no incentive for him even to attempt to stabilize. If the employer bears the burden, he is a victim of economic happenstance. And even if the burden is shared, there is little justice; it merely means that three parties carry the yoke, and injustice is compounded. Moreover, say the critics, the analogy with workmen's compensation is not valid, since unemployment is largely a *market* phenomenon, unlike industrial accidents which occur because of conditions within the plant.

2. Rather than being counter-cyclical in nature (and hence acting as a stabilizing force), experience rating "adds fuel to the flames." In boom periods, when employment is high (for reasons inherent in the functioning of the economic system), tax rates are low (when they should be high). Conversely, in depressed periods, the contribution rate is high (when it should be low). Thus the entire system operates out of phase.

On the individual firm level the principal counter-arguments are three in number.

1. The major criticism rests upon the contention that the employment experience of a business is largely beyond its control; that market forces and not employer activities are the critical causal factors. Hence, experience rating is a misdirected form of social policy, since it rewards one employer for a record not of his doing and penalizes another on the same basis.

2. Experience rating may in part tend to be self-defeating. Employers, in attempting to secure more favorable tax rates, are likely to engage in a variety of practices (some ethically defensible, others not so) that *may* increase employment stability for a small core of employees, but which *will* greatly increase instability for another group. For example, an employer can increase his use of part-time employees, can discharge individuals before they become eligible for unemployment insurance, or can utilize other practices that at one and the same time decreased employment stability for given employees and yet that do not in any way officially blemish the employer's records. Hence it is held that experience rating may actually increase unemployment for that marginal group of employees who can stand it least.

3. Finally it is contended that such a system will prove administratively cumbersome if not unworkable. Experience rating implies the keeping of detailed and perhaps voluminous reports on each employer's accessions and separations. Moreover, it is now to the economic interest of an employer to challenge unemployment insurance payments to individuals in specified cases; a successful challenge means a better employment record and hence a lower contribution rate. Therefore, unemployment insurance may become a legalistic battleground, defeating in part its operation. This legalism may, additionally, be carried over into struggles to prevent benefits from rising so as to keep the contribution rate low.

Let us take a more critical look at various of these contentions, recognizing that we do not have a clean slate upon which we can trace an ideal system, but rather that the system of experience rating is a reality in all states.

Can an employer stabilize his employment? What degree of control does he have? What forces, operating through the market, are beyond his ability to regulate? This is perhaps the most important of all the questions involved, since answers to the others depend in no small measure upon the answers to it.

The customary answer is that the employer has little control over his total employment experience, particularly that arising from cyclical and secular causes where market forces are the more crucial, although he does have more control over other unemployment types. While there has been little recent empirical research in this field, earlier studies tend to support this position. Thus Charles A. Myers concludes by noting that employers can do something in the way of ironing out day-to-day or intermittent irregularities in employment or reducing seasonal unemployment. And Myers also indicates that a reduced contribution rate is a tangible financial incentive *initially,* though he wonders if it need be continued once a firm has seen the inherent desirability of stabilized operations.[33]

Thus, the general conclusions to which one comes are as follows: First, the stabilization of employment is a multi-layered matter. Second, over the basic and quantitatively more important employment layer (secular, cyclical) the employer has relatively little control. Third, over the layer of daily and seasonally changing levels of employment, he has a higher degree of control. Fourth, a financial incentive may help to reduce unemployment of the latter type, though there is some doubt as to whether a continuing incentive is necessary.

If these arguments have merit, then one can in turn reach certain conclusions on experience rating as a social policy. Such a system should not be used to allocate the social costs of that unemployment included in the basic layer, since such unemployment is largely outside the employer's control. But, such a system might well be used in conjunction with the secondary layer of unemployment. The relationship of this approach to commercial insurance premium structures is readily apparent. Given this approach, there would be a minimum rate *all* employers would pay. Above that, reductions of a supplementary rate would be possible, contingent upon the employer's experience.

The organizational and administrative difficulties of such a system should not be minimized, however. Critical decisions would have to be

---

[33] See the previously cited works by C. A. Myers, particularly "Experience Rating in Unemployment Compensation," p. 347.

made on the choice of the basic rate and the supplementary rate, and this would involve a variety of inter-industry and inter-firm comparisons. Day-by-day administration of such a system would be far from routine. Moreover, such an approach would not of itself equalize the burden among the various states, and federal minimum-maximum specifications would be desirable. Whether such a system would be self-defeating (a criticism noted above) is difficult to answer without experience as a guide; one may conjecture that it would not. Nor would such an approach have the desirable counter-cyclical characteristics; to achieve this would involve, at the very least, a complicated lag-formula system.

But, if the present system does not operate as envisaged above, and if, in fact, we have a miscellany of experience rating plans, what practical suggestions can be given? One would be that the federal government enact a set of minimum standards for experience rating. Such standards would require uniformity among the states and would meet in part the multi-layered nature of the unemployment problem.[34]

SOME GENERAL IMPACTS OF ECONOMIC SECURITY PROGRAMS

In addition to the benefit and cost implications of economic security programs, other influences—upon business enterprise and its location, upon pricing, upon general economic activity—may be found. Let us look at several of these problems.

Impacts upon Business Enterprise

Do economic security programs of the formalized type, whether public or private, discourage entrepreneurship? Formal economic analysis of a firm would indicate that the costs of such a program would change the position of the cost curve of that firm. But, while formal analysis is capable of indicating the consequences of the change in the cost curve, it does not itself tell us about the effect upon entrepreneurial activity, partly because this is a problem of a different order.

Several different impacts on entrepreneurial activity may be found. First, in the short run, there may be a sort of negative "shock" impact arising out of the instituting of an economic security program. And this may have "slightly" unfavorable consequences for the entrepreneur, a "discouraging" influence on his "outlook." Observations would lead one

[34] See Feldman and Smith, *op. cit.*, p. 59. See also *Unemployment Insurance,* Senate Document No. 206, 80th Congress, 2d Session (Washington, D. C.: U. S. Government Printing Office, 1948), pp. 30–42. One improvement was made in federal specifications as of January 1, 1955, in that an employer could qualify for reduced benefits with only one rather than three years' experience. Hence the "new" firm is not discriminated against.

to believe, however, that these "unfavorable" or "discouraging" consequences are not necessarily translated into specific business activity.
There are no recorded instances in which a businessman deliberately
closed his doors or another decided not to enter business because of the
introduction of, say, the Old-Age, Survivors, and Disability Insurance program. Nor would such programs appear markedly to influence the fields
of economic activity which an entrepreneur chooses to enter; we would
not feel that the absence of an unemployment insurance tax would be
critical in influencing an entrepreneurial decision to enter the field of
agriculture, for example. All this should not be taken to imply that the
government can act with impunity; there may be levels at which the
programs might be self-defeating. And "differentiated" programs, discussed below, may have important impacts.

Second, in the long run, it is probable that the influence is even minimized as far as the psychological aspects are concerned. Thus, economic
security programs become an ingrained part of the environment within
which business is done; and they are accepted as an integral element of
the business framework. This should not be taken to imply that entrepreneurs are thereby oblivious to the costs involved or to *changes* in these
costs. Far from it; all the proof one needs can be obtained from business
responses in hearings on proposed changes in workmen's compensation
rates, for example. But the fundamental program tends to grow into the
framework within which economic activity takes place, and it becomes
a customary factor in doing business.

Third, "differential" economic security programs do, however, have
an influence upon entrepreneurial decision-making and hence upon the
location of industry and pricing. These programs are only one of many
factors considered, for example, in plant location. But, as one factor, they
do contribute to decisions made with respect to location and pricing, and
in some cases they may be the critical factor. And while, as noted above,
such programs may not have a marked influence upon fields of economic
endeavor entered or not entered, they do influence the choice of geographic area in which to locate. "Differential" programs are "differentiated" essentially on a state-by-state basis. This is one reason why
we find states generally unwilling to be very far in the forefront in economic security programs, for these programs customarily involve a premium or a tax of some type, and a state is usually not desirous of increasing these costs for fear of driving out established businesses or failing to
attract new businesses.[35]

[35] See various issues of the magazine *Industrial Location* for a discussion of concrete location factors. For a regional analysis of the problem see The Commonwealth
of Massachusetts, *Report* of the Special Commission Relative to the Textile Industry
. . . Boston: May 12, 1950), pp. 43–49, 51; and *Report* on the New England Textile

Indirect Economic Security Program Impacts

The structure, content, and the administrative operation of a security program may have an important effect upon economic activity. A given program, even if it is designed wholly and only as a security measure, may have discernible economic impacts of various types. Moreover, some programs have had incorporated into them, deliberately or otherwise, features designed to accomplish other purposes than economic security itself. Here the impact may be even more pronounced.

Several examples may be cited to illustrate these possibilities. Take private pension programs, for example. Such programs generally have not incorporated vesting rights for the employee. That is, the employer's contribution generally has not belonged to the employee; the latter could not take the contribution with him when he left the employ of a given employer.[36] Hence, non-vested pension programs probably have the effect of restricting labor mobility, or conversely, of tying the employee to the employer. As was noted in Chapter 8, employment guarantees as well as pension plans may restrict mobility. While we need to know more about "desirable" *versus* "undesirable" levels of labor mobility, and while it is one of the industrial relations functions of management to reduce labor turnover, it is nevertheless true that the artificial erection of walls retarding the free flow of economic activity is undesirable.[37] This holds true not only for labor mobility, but for resource allocation, pricing, distribution, and for all the other phases of economic activity. Good cases can be made for regulating certain types of economic activity,

---

Industry by the Committee Appointed by the Conference of New England Governors (Cambridge: 1953), pp. 245–55. One of the authors has sat as a member of a state unemployment insurance advisory council, and an argument frequently heard during council meetings was that relating to social insurance costs and plant location.

[36] This would appear to be a denial of the belief that it is the employee who bears an important share of the burden of economic security programs. In the non-vesting case, the employer retains his (the employer's) contribution; if the payment were merely a foregone wage increase, one would assume it belonged to the employee and he should be able to take it with him. The fact that vested rights are slowly but surely on the increase makes it appear, however, that there is some logic to the assertion that certainly a part of the burden of economic security programs rests upon the employee.

[37] Professor George P. Shultz has pertinently noted to us that, while employee services are generally available on a "here and now basis" to all employees, this is not true of certain classes of financial services. In the latter case, there is a "time-lock" wherein the employee must remain with the company to benefit from the service. In the extreme case (a non-vested pension) he "loses all" if he leaves the company. There are modified "time-locks" in many employee services: vacations graduated on the basis of length of service, or employee discounts similarly graduated. But here the employee does not lose all if he leaves the company, since he has "collected" in the interim.

but an economic security program hardly seems the appropriate vehicle for such control.

A second example is found in the Old-Age, Survivors, and Disability Insurance program provision which limits benefits if earnings by a retired person exceed a given amount. At present, the law provides that between the ages of sixty-five and seventy-two a benefit recipient can earn up to $1,500 a year without loss of benefits. After $1,500 has been earned, benefits are withheld contingent upon earnings above that figure and the months in which earned. Such "retirement earnings" have been liberalized greatly through the years, and the age limit has come down from seventy-five to seventy-two.

The original purpose of this provision is not difficult to discern, resting upon the "lump of labor" theory. This theory, in one version, assumes that there is only so much work available, and hence only so many employees needed. One way, therefore, in which new entrants into the labor force can get jobs is through the relinquishing of jobs by the retirement of older workers. But, at present, the view appears to be that earnings below $1,500 annually are not sufficient to pose a threat to the younger worker; that is, it is only after $1,500 that the potential displacement threat becomes actual. Likewise, after age seventy-two, an individual apparently is not presumed to threaten the jobs of others.[38]

One may ask the question, however, whether an economic security program should have as an integral purpose the regulation of the supply of labor. J. Douglas Brown contends that it should not, noting that "the essential purpose of social insurance is to afford security and not to regulate the supply of labor."[39] Dean Brown notes, however, that the contingency of dependency is likely to be reduced by earnings, and hence that the amount of benefit above a modest sum should be reduced by an amount equivalent to the earnings received. Thus the result tends to be a compromise, with present trends indicating a liberalization of earnings and a lowering of the age. Both these factors in turn tend to lessen the influence of an economic security program in regulating the supply of labor. These are moves in the right direction. An economic security program need not necessarily be economically neutral (nor is it possible for it to be "neutral" in many situations). But a program is perhaps most rationally structured when it does not implicitly or explicitly seek to accomplish, or in fact does not accomplish, the regulation of other phases of economic activity.

[38] Arthur Larson holds that cost is an important factor in these provisions, and that if benefits were payable to people if they continued to work, the cost would skyrocket, increasing an estimated two billion dollars a year. Larson, *op. cit.*, p. 31.

[39] J. Douglas Brown, "Concepts in Old-Age and Survivors' Insurance," *Proceedings* of the First Annual Meeting, Industrial Relations Research Association, 1948, p. 102.

A Final Comment on Alternative Economic Security Approaches

The previous discussion has centered upon problems related primarily to the *present* United States economic security system and to alternative ways of structuring security programs within that system. In closing this section it may be well to comment briefly upon more basic alternatives–those of differing systems.

One basic question is whether economic security should be a matter of complete private action and initiative or should involve the government. But, government *is* an active participant in present programs and during our lifetime is not likely to remove itself. Moreover, it has been clearly demonstrated that there is a useful role to be played by the government in providing the *basic* layer of protection against economic insecurities.

If it be assumed that the government, broadly defined, has a legitimate place in formal economic security programs, a second question is whether the federal government, state governments, or some combination should exercise jurisdiction. Here one can also take a somewhat deterministic view, but there is perhaps more freedom of choice. What criteria would one apply in making such a decision? On the one hand would be the yardsticks of economy and uniformity; here an all-federal program would probably best fit the specifications. On the other hand, if one applies the criterion of states' rights, then a combined program fits better. Which of these criteria one does apply is a matter for one's own value judgments. Our own preference would be for a combined program, even if it sacrificed some economy and uniformity. But this does not mean that lack of economy and uniformity should be at a premium. Far from it. We have commented at various places in this text on ways of undertaking voluntary action toward efficiency and standardization.

If federal and state governments undertake programs of economic security, what form should such programs take? The range of possibilities is great, from a Townsend Plan at one extreme through a rigid insurance program to the setting of individual wage rates at levels which compensate for the risks of economic insecurity involved. For reasons developed in Chapters 7 and 9, a "tax" system is preferable economically to a wage adjustment program. Administratively, the tax system is much to be preferred; the difficulties in wage adjustment appear incredibly difficult, in addition to which there are the ethical problems inherent in this type of control.

If a tax system is preferable, should it be the type which uses general revenues, the type which applies special taxes such as transaction taxes, or the type in which all groups are blanketed on some sort of complete pay-as-you-go basis? Or should it be of some "social insurance form," such as we now have? Considering costs only, good cases can be made for the first three types, although there are some hidden dangers. But the latter approach, utilizing the social insurance basis, appears more compatible with our cultural mores, and hence is much more acceptable to the populace at large. For the present at least, tempering economics with social reality, the existing system is the most operable.[40]

SUMMARY

In this chapter we have presented a number of the more important and interesting economic issues involved in programs of economic security. It is difficult to treat these issues within a formal analytical framework, such as might be done when examining, say, business price policy in light of the theory of the firm. A welfare economics approach might be used, but this requires a degree of sophistication in presentation and utilization that is hard to achieve. Yet the relative absence of a formal framework does not mean that an economic approach cannot be used. Far from it; we have tried in the above to indicate ways in which such an approach can be employed.

Thus, in trying to answer the question of how much security a society can afford, we noted that this involves first the question of the productive capacity of that society, and given more than minimal capacity, it involves secondly a choice by society as to what proportion of its resources it wishes to devote to economic security programs. The choice might well vary under different conditions; thus in a war economy, economic security programs might have to be restricted.

A variety of financial problems are created through the operation of economic security programs. Who pays the costs of such programs? There is some reason to believe that employees finance their own security in large measure although not completely. The specific method of financing such programs creates its own problems, particularly where reserves are utilized, and deflationary or inflationary pressures may be built up depending upon the method chosen.

Economic security programs may have impacts other than those of a financial nature as noted above. What of the impact upon entrepreneurship? It is our feeling that "differentiated" programs may have marked consequences (or at least may be a factor of importance) upon businessmen's behavior, but that programs comprehensive in nature tend to

[40] See J. Douglas Brown, "The American Philosophy of Social Insurance," *The Social Service Review*, XXX, No. 1 (March, 1956), 3–8.

become part of the setting within which economic activity takes place and hence their effect is minimized. Similarly, such programs may have various "side effects" as, for example, in influencing labor supply. We would feel that such side effects should be minimized, and if it is desirable to control these other economic activities it should be done by direct means rather than through an economic security program.

Economic security programs are important built-in stabilizers in the economy; the benefit payment record under unemployment compensation illustrates this. Yet, some programs work contrary to economic balance, as in the case of the tax structure under experience rating. Conversely, it is not valid to conclude that the accumulation of trust funds under various security programs has the contrary result of "double taxation."

But, in all these matters, the economist's verdict is not final. It should be taken into account, but only along with relevant legal, political, psychological, and social considerations.

SUGGESTIONS FOR ADDITIONAL READING

ALLEN, DONNA. *Fringe Benefits: Wages or Social Obligation?* Ithaca: Cornell University Press, 1964.
This volume provides an analysis of fringe benefits, with an historical focus upon the paid vacation. The discussion is useful on the question of the incidence of payments for fringes. The book also can be read profitably in conjunction with Chapter 8 of this volume.

BURNS, EVELINE M. *Social Security and Public Policy.* New York: McGraw-Hill Book Co., 1956.
A social, political, economic, and operational analysis of many of the facets of economic security. Very useful as a constant reference when studying the American economic security system.

GORDON, MARGARET S. *The Economics of Welfare Policies.* New York: Columbia University Press, 1963.
An analysis of the nature of economic security programs and their impacts. The volume includes an extensive reference list. If one peruses this work and the references cited, he will have covered all that is currently available on this most important topic.

HARRIS, SEYMOUR E. *Economics of Social Security.* New York: McGraw-Hill Book Co., 1941.
While this book is factually dated, it provides one of the most comprehensive treatments existent on the economic phases of security problems.

LESTER, RICHARD A. *The Economics of Unemployment Compensation.* Princeton University, Industrial Relations Section, 1962.
An analysis of the economic impacts of this important economic security program. The treatment is particularly useful in the area of benefits and income maintenance, although financing issues are also discussed.

RICHARDSON, J. H. *Economic and Financial Aspects of Social Security.* London: Allen and Unwin, 1960.

TITMUSS, RICHARD. *Essays on the Welfare State.* New Haven: Yale University Press, 1959.

Both of these volumes are useful in their analyses of the macroeconomic aspects of economic security policies and programs.

U. S. DEPARTMENT OF LABOR. *Selected Bibliography on Manpower and Employment.* U. S. Department of Labor, Manpower Administration, Bureau of Employment Security, United States Employment Service, October 4, 1965. (Mimeographed.)

This is a bibliography, not a "reading" in itself. It contains over 250 entries, which provide references useful in connection with the topics in this chapter and in Chapters 6, 7, and 8 of this volume.

15

Problems of Substandard Conditions

INTRODUCTION

The working and living conditions of American workers became a matter of widespread concern for the first time around the turn of the twentieth century. There were being generated employment and living conditions which a changing public opinion would not long tolerate. We discussed earlier the deplorable accident record of this period. Conditions of work were equally poor (although not all of them were as harsh as in the case of the candy girl whose fate was described in Chapter 9). Frederick Lewis Allen writes of this period that to read "reports of qualified observers of poverty at its worst in the big city slums and grim industrial towns at the beginning of the century is to hear variation after variation upon the theme of human misery, in which the same words occur monotonously again and again: wretchedness, overcrowding, filth, hunger, malnutrition, insecurity, want." [1]

What were employment conditions at the time? First, there was widespread employment of children which increased steadily until 1910. Census records reveal that 16 per cent of all children ten to fifteen years old were gainfully employed in 1880, and 18.4 per cent in 1910. These estimates are probably conservative, since child labor in home work and street trades could not easily be recorded. Much of this child labor was most heavily concentrated in agriculture and manufacturing, where accident rates among children were high. The average earnings of em-

[1] Reprinted with permission from Frederick Lewis Allen, *The Big Change* (New York: Harper & Row, 1952), p. 57.

ployed children, except for the war years, was reported at from three to five dollars a week.[2]

Second, adult American workers of the period labored under similarly adverse conditions. Allen writes[3] that the average annual wage of the period for American workers was between $400 and $500, with unskilled workers averaging under $460 in the North and $300 in the South. A report[4] of male earnings in the "principal trades and industries" for the decade preceding World War I reveals that one-fourth of the heads of families earned less than $400 a year; and one-half of them earned less than $600. One-fourth of regularly employed women in the "principal manufacturing industries" earned less than $200 a year and two-thirds earned less than $400. Women and children were employed in greatest proportions in the low-paid industries, such as textiles and glass. For women, a work week in excess of fifty-five to sixty hours was not uncommon.

NATURE OF THE PROBLEM

Oppressive working conditions, such as those briefly sketched above, pose a problem in economic security which cannot be resolved by approaches such as the social assistance and insurance measures considered in earlier chapters. Rather, they must be dealt with through direct control and intervention. This is true because the problem is associated with employment rather than with unemployment.

In the preceding chapters, the problems in economic security which were discussed were problems of unemployment. That they should be of great importance is not surprising, for in an industrial society the only means by which a worker can earn a livelihood is through the sale of his personal services in a free labor market. Whether unemployment arises directly out of labor market operation or is caused indirectly by other factors such as accidents, illness, or old age, social insurance measures seek primarily to alleviate its undesirable consequences. Protection against substandard working conditions cannot be provided by these methods, however, for it is not the inability of workers to get a wage contract that is at issue here, but rather their inability to get a wage contract that meets the minimum standards under which a society will per-

[2] S. Howard Patterson, *Social Aspects of Industry* (New York: McGraw-Hill Book Co., 1929), p. 200.

[3] Allen, *op. cit.*, p. 55.

[4] These data are taken from an interesting compilation of studies on working conditions for the period from 1900 to World War I by W. Jett Lauck and Edgar Sydenstricker, *Conditions of Labor in American Industries* (New York: Funk and Wagnalls, 1917), chap. 2.

mit its members to be employed. Hence a different type of labor market functioning is involved.

This distinction has significance beyond its use as a definition. For unlike unemployment-caused insecurity, control of substandard conditions requires, and has indeed involved, intervention into the wage contract and intervention directly into the labor market. And so, two questions arise: Should the government intervene in the freedom of individuals to enter contracts for employment? Can it intervene? The courts permitted qualifications of this freedom in the name of economic security only after extended resistance.

Changing Attitudes Toward Substandard Conditions

Because of the vast improvement in the conditions of work over the past one hundred years, most working conditions during this period would probably be termed "substandard" by today's standards. The terms of employment which free societies accept as reasonable have changed enormously over the years, as have educational, health, and living standards —and they are continuing to do so.

The changing attitudes toward child labor are illustrative. Of eighteenth-century England, Professor Herbert Heaton writes that ". . . a child of four or five years could, if well brought up, 'earn its own bread.' In the straw-plaiting regions they began work at four years, and by their sixth birthday were (in 1801) earning 2/- to 3/- a week, climbing to a wage of 10/- to 12/- by the time they were eight or nine." [5]

In the American colonies, one of the chief benefits derived from manufactures was considered to be the job opportunities created for children. As recently as 1910, it was estimated that about one-fifth of all boys between ten and fifteen years of age were employed. Today the Fair Labor Standards Act prohibits the employment in interstate commerce of children under sixteen in all employments and under eighteen in hazardous work.

Similarly, the acceptable minimum standards for working conditions, working hours, and pay have changed with a changing social and economic environment. These changes have been achieved through legislation, the efforts of trade unions, the actions of employers and, in the case of improved hours and wages, were made possible by advances in productivity. Today, our increased concern about poverty has come about not because there is anything strikingly new about the problems of the poor but because we have become more sensitive to the painful contrast

[5] Reprinted with permission from Herbert Heaton, *Economic History of Europe* (New York: Harper & Row, 1936), p. 350.

of poverty in the midst of affluence. As one writer pointed out, "in a time when the boon of prosperity is more general, the taste of poverty is more bitter." [6]

DEVELOPMENT OF PROTECTIVE LEGISLATION

Before considering the provisions of the protective labor laws which are in effect in all American jurisdictions today, it is useful to note several generalizations about their development.

Historically, movements for improving working standards have been directed more at a specific situation which had aroused public interest than at goals based on abstract principles. Definitions of minimum acceptable working conditions have been determined by contemporary economic, social, and political circumstances. Clyde Dankert notes that arguments for reduced hours at any particular time ". . . usually bear a close relationship to the objective conditions prevailing at that time." [7] The appearance early in the twentieth century of a child labor movement in the South, for instance, was due less to a belief that children should be educated as well as protected from working conditions interfering with their adult development, than it was to the realization of the inhumane effects of the widespread employment of children by the new southern mills.

For these reasons, arguments in support of government intervention into substandard conditions have changed with the times and the conditions. Thus we may note that shorter hours were first advocated as necessary for leisure and for better citizenship. But later, with the coming of the factory system, this approach was abandoned for the argument that shorter hours were necessary to protect the worker's health. In the 1960's adoption of a shorter workweek is being urged as a means of reducing unemployment and cushioning the effects of advancing technology.

Experience under the Fair Labor Standards Act has been similar. Both the original 1938 Act and its subsequent amendments were justified by arguments which are traditionally offered in support of minimum wage legislation—the need to provide minimum living standards, to reduce poverty, to increase purchasing power, and to lessen employer exploitation of the worker. Important to the 1938 law, however, was the argument that the overtime penalty provisions would aid in spreading employ-

---

[6] Mollie Orshansky, "Counting the Poor: Another Look at the Poverty Profile," *Social Security Bulletin*, XXVIII (January, 1965), 3.

[7] Clyde E. Dankert, *An Introduction to Labor* (Englewood Cliffs, N. J.: Prentice-Hall, Inc., 1954), pp. 519–20.

ment in that immediate post-depression period. The 1955 amendment, which increased minimum wages during a period of high, full employment, found important justification in the arguments that since the low wages paid in southern states were acting as an inducement to northern industry to migrate south, they were an unfair competitive advantage against northern employers and a threat to trade union wage standards.

In short, demands that certain working conditions be declared substandard have varied at different times and have been based on many grounds, including those of civic improvement, safety, health, morals, and more recently, economic effects.[8] Although these demands at all times had the specific objective of improving the conditions of work, they did not necessarily focus on an abstract goal or on a single set of principles.

Behind this condition of objective and value judgment criteria for improved working conditions, there occasionally lurked the selfish motive of setting job standards for women which would reduce their competitive threat to men.

Support for protection has come from many and varying sources. Sometimes an aroused public opinion was the initiating factor, as in the case of the child labor movement in the South. Trade union support, which today is frequently at the head of campaigns to improve legislative standards, dates back to the interest of the Knights of Labor in child labor legislation and the eight-hour day, which this union gained for its members for a short time. Yet trade union support has by no means been uniform. In fact, trade unions never gave much support to men's hours movements, and for a time actively opposed the enactment of minimum wage legislation, for fear minimum wages would become "maximum" wages and because they feared the government's entry into the wage-fixing arena.

Employers have improved working conditions on their own initiative, partially in response to the pressures of trade unions and of competition, and in part when the economies of such action were apparent. Finally, reform movements frequently had as their nucleus of support organizations like the Consumers' League and Women's Trade Union League (in the case of women's hours) and various public-spirited middle-class individuals and groups who carried the brunt of the fight for minimum wage legislation.

Cultural, economic, and social philosophy, in the broad sense, appear to have played a more minor role in the movements for legislative pro-

[8] H. A. Millis and R. E. Montgomery, *Labor's Risks and Social Insurance* (New York: McGraw-Hill Book Co., 1938), p. 249; Frank T. de Vyver, "Regulation of Wages and Hours Prior to 1938," *Law and Contemporary Problems*, VI, No. 3 (1939), 323–24.

tection. Humanitarian considerations, it is true, were responsible for the recognition that, particularly with respect to children and women, conditions of work were cruel and inhuman by virtually any standard. From these premises came the regulation of child labor. Other arguments came to be more significant, and the movement eventually extended to hours regulation for women and men, and finally to wage regulation.

ORIGINS OF THE PROBLEM OF SUBSTANDARD CONDITIONS

Also, prior to analyzing the standards set by protective labor laws, several questions should be asked. Why do working conditions fall to "low" levels? Who or what is responsible? The answers to these questions have, of course, changed from the time of the master-slave relationship to the present-day wage system.[9] Since slaves were owned by a master who could buy and sell them, they were wholly at their master's disposal. The status of the serf in the period of feudalism was only slightly better. While a lord did not own his serfs, their freedom was narrowly limited by their legal obligations in a lord's service, and government action was used to insure that economic force did not give the serf power to change these conditions.[10]

None of these legal ties bind today's workers, since the essence of the contemporary wage system is the workers' freedom of choice. Workers are legally free to choose their occupations and to change them; to accept or reject working conditions that please or fail to please them; to change employers, to work in any part of the country that they choose, or indeed, to refuse to work altogether.

Given these legal labor market freedoms and concomitantly those of the employer to hire and fire, it should follow that under competitive labor market conditions employers would be the custodians or administrators of working conditions determined by the basic market forces of competition. It was one of Adam Smith's premises in his theory of equalizing differences (referred to in Chapter 9) that under a free wage system, competing bids for labor would regulate working conditions effectively in different occupations. The regulating force of competition lies in the threat to an employer posed by his employees' alternative opportunities.[11]

---

[9] Discussed by Maurice Dobb, *Wages* (London: Pitman Publishing Co., 1948), pp. 1–17.

[10] Thus the first real government regulation of working conditions was the oppressive fourteenth-century Statutes of Laborers which set maximum wages—a policy followed in the later Elizabethan Statutes of Apprentices.

[11] The effect of competition on restricting the scope of bargained terms is presented concisely by Tibor Scitovsky in *Welfare and Competition* (Homewood, Ill.: Richard D. Irwin, Inc., 1951), chap. 2.

Employees who are informed of job alternatives and who are willing and able to accept them, will force employers to offer wage contracts at least equal to these alternatives.

If it is assumed that labor market competition will regulate working conditions in a free economy, and the government intervenes in a free labor market to prohibit certain pay or employment practices that would prevail in the absence of such intervention, one is saying in effect that competition as a regulating force of working conditions has failed. Yet, this statement seems to conflict with common sense.

Competition appears to play a paradoxical role in its effects on working conditions. On the one hand, our competitive system leads all nations of the world in its ability to amass capital and to become increasingly productive. Furthermore, the gigantic increases in real national income due primarily to productiveness have, over the years, been distributed generously to American workers in the form of reduced hours of work and higher (real) wages. Working hours during the past century have been shortened from an approximate sixty-nine-hour week to the present forty-hour week with lower hours in an increasing number of occupations. Average non-agricultural wages have increased from about 9 to 10 cents an hour to current levels of about $2.60. Our competitive economy has produced a situation which led the manager of Buick Division of General Motors to comment that "the man on the assembly line can buy what he makes." [12]

On the other hand, various social, political, and economic criteria have been used over the years to demonstrate that an unregulated wage system produces substandard conditions, and that at the beginning of the twentieth century, deplorable working conditions existed in this country.

These two apparently contradictory situations can be reconciled, however, when the distinction is made between labor market competition on the one hand and product market competition on the other. In part, the reasons that labor market competition does not always bring about acceptable working conditions [13] are similar to the reasons that it fails to bring about wage rates that fully reflect the accident hazard of occupations. The reasons are not wholly the same, however, and since they involve the effects of the product market, let us examine them more fully. There are three general reasons why competition may not adequately regulate working conditions, to which a fourth may be added. These are as follows.

[12] First National City Bank *Monthly Letter,* March, 1956, p. 35.

[13] For a discussion of labor market competition as a regulator of working conditions, see Francis M. Boddy (ed.), *Applied Economic Analysis* (New York: Pitman Publishing Co., 1948), chap. 5.

Barriers to Labor Market Competition

Although workers enjoy full legal rights to choose among labor market alternatives, they are not always willing or able to exercise these rights fully. Hence, the competitive regulating force of working conditions is seriously weakened by the labor market imperfections referred to earlier: poor knowledge of alternatives, institutional (non-economic) barriers to accepting alternatives, economic barriers to geographic mobility, and economic and social barriers to upward occupational mobility. To expect of free *legal* labor market choice the full exercise of *economic* labor market choice which will fully regulate working conditions is, in Dobb's words, to depend upon so "one-sided a picture as to contrast in some respects grotesquely with reality." [14]

Superior Bargaining Power of Employers

Partly because of these barriers to labor market competition and partly because of the very nature of the employment relationship, employers enjoy bargaining advantages over their employees in setting conditions of work.[15] In the absence of trade unions, competition among workers for jobs tends to be greater than competition among employers for workers. Employers have better information about alternatives; moreover, they control revenues and payments.

Labor is much more difficult to move than is capital, and it is much more perishable. Since most workers with little savings cannot store their services, they have poor waiting power. These and other reasons explain in large part why our present-day public policy toward collective bargaining encourages the development of trade unions as a means of gaining equality in bargaining power between employer and employee.

It must be stressed in considering the above two points that they are by no means applicable without exception. For instance, the employment of women was once opposed as a social evil on the grounds that women were being underpaid and exploited. Yet today women represent about one-third of the labor force. And in the secretarial and other office jobs in which demands for their skills are highest, women's working conditions

---

[14] Dobb, *op. cit.*, p. 6; for an interesting picture of the relation of the worker to his labor market in 1923, see Paul H. Douglas, Curtice N. Hitchcock, and Willard E. Atkins (eds.), *The Worker in Modern Economic Society* (Chicago: University of Chicago Press, 1923), pp. 226–28. For a more recent analysis see Herbert S. Parnes, "Research on Labor Mobility," *Bulletin 65* (New York: Social Science Research Council, 1954).

[15] Discussed by K. W. Rothschild, *The Theory of Wages* (New York: The Macmillan Co., 1954), chap. 9.

tend to be excellent by almost any standard. Another illustration is that, despite possible labor market imperfections, the current keen competition for the services of engineers has forced employers to bid up their working conditions. This happens wherever demands for labor are strong. During periods of rising prosperity, the overwhelming majority of workers enjoy working conditions far better than the statutory minimums. Yet, even in these times there are many who do not.

While our competitive system has produced the highest standard of living in the world, certain aspects of the system, in the absence of regulation, do produce substandard working conditions. Using $3,000 per family as the poverty standard, the Council of Economic Advisers found 33.4 million Americans living in substandard conditions in 1963. The Department of Health, Education, and Welfare, using a more flexible standard designed to take into account individual differences in need, came up with an estimate of 34.6 million needy persons in 1963.[16]

Keen Product Market Competition [17]

Despite the obvious virtues of competition among sellers of goods and services, it is historically true that where such competition is keen and is combined with the labor market imperfections referred to above, substandard conditions of employment tend to result. Employers have a strong incentive to maximize their employees' output during the immediate period of their employment. The Webbs observed that, as a result of the introduction of the factory system, "competition is always forcing him [the employer] to cut down the cost of production to the lowest point. Under this pressure, other considerations disappear in the passion to obtain the greatest possible 'output per machine.'" [18]

The desire to increase productivity and reduce costs by greater employment of the fixed costs of the factory led to long hours of work and to the employment of children. Children were worked without consideration for the subsequent effects on their adult health or lack of education; adults were worked long hours and under serious hazards, with low pay. Over a period of years, workers became less productive and had to be replaced. The result was not only inhumane; it was socially inefficient.

Although maximum short-run productivity may not produce maximum long-run productivity, price competition can force employers to maximize short-run output. And as long as there is an adequate labor supply, em-

[16] Margaret S. Gordon (ed.), *Poverty in America* (San Francisco: Chandler Publishing Co., 1965), pp. 5–6.

[17] Rothschild, *op. cit.*, pp. 51–52.

[18] Sidney and Beatrice Webb, *Industrial Democracy* (London: Longmans, Roberts and Green, 1897), p. 327.

ployers have incentives to follow this policy. The private cost to an employer of doing so is less than the full social cost of depreciating workers. Where labor market competition cannot be counted upon to remedy this situation, government intervention is necessary. By intervening here to achieve improved working conditions, the government performs one of its most important economic functions,[19] and as a result everyone benefits —employers gain greater long-run productivity, and workers enjoy better health and living standards.

Labor Is a Human Commodity

Unequal bargaining power and the lack of competitive regulation, despite their effects on the terms of sale, might be tolerable except for one additional factor—the commodity involved is an unusual one. Like most other commodities in the economy, labor has a price and is bought and sold in a marketing process. But unlike any other commodity, labor is distinctive in that the service can never be isolated from the person who performs the service. In short, it is a human commodity. The attention currently commanded by the "human relations" aspects of employment is ample evidence of how widely this fact is appreciated today. The terms of the sale of labor involve human conditions which are not a part of any other market considerations.

The problem of substandard conditions will be illuminated if we look more closely at one special group, the hired farm laborers.

THE SPECIAL PROBLEM OF FARM LABOR

In 1939, as the greatest depression the American economy has ever experienced was drawing to an end, John Steinbeck's *Grapes of Wrath* was published, depicting the plight of the migrant farm laborer. A quarter of a century later the condition of the domestic farm laborer still requires special attention in a book on economic security. Though some progress has been made, especially in the past five years, the hired farm worker, and the migrant in particular, remains the most economically deprived occupational group in our society. In the recent words of a U. S. Senate Subcommittee, "The migratory worker lives and works in conditions that must be recognized for what they are—a national disgrace." [20]

[19] An excellent discussion of this function, an issue basic to much of the material in this book, appears in William J. Baumol and Lester V. Chandler, *Economic Processes and Policies* (New York: Harper & Row, 1954), pp. 119–34.

[20] "The Migratory Farm Labor Problem in the United States," 1965 *Report* of the Committee on Labor and Public Welfare, Subcommittee on Migrant Labor, 89th Cong., 1st Sess., p. vii.

TABLE 15.1
Selected Characteristics of Farm Workers, 1964

Selected Characteristics	Farm Wage Workers		Workers Who Did Farm Wage Work Only		
	Total (in thousands)	Percentage Who Also Did Some Non-Farm Wage Work	Total (in thousands)	No. Days Worked	Wages Earned per Year
All workers, 1964	3,370	38	2,094	100	$ 698
Color and sex					
White	2,322	40	1,385	102	812
Non-white	1,048	32	709	95	475
Male	2,398	40	1,439	123	898
White	1,796	43	1,026	125	1,003
Non-white	603	32	413	118	638
Female	972	33	655	49	257
White	527	32	359	38	267
Non-white	445	33	296	63	246
Chief activity					
Farm work	1,036	24	791	198	1,499
Farm wage work	818	23	629	238	1,818
Without non-farm work	629	—	629	238	1,818
With non-farm work	190	100	—	—	—
Other farm work [1]	218	26	162	44	267
Non-farm work [2]	412	98	11	—	—
Unemployed [2]	96	66	33	—	—
Not in labor force	1,826	31	1,259	40	205
Keeping house	548	26	404	42	211
Attending school	1,122	33	756	39	195
Other	155	36	100	38	256
Duration of farm wage work					
Less than 25 days	1,369	47	723	10	58
25 days and over	2,001	31	1,371	147	1,035
Residence					
Farm	1,130	23	869	116	682
Non-farm	2,240	45	1,224	88	709
Migratory status					
Migratory	386	44	218	109	935
Non-migratory	2,984	37	1,876	99	670
Region					
Northeast	292	50	145	140	1,007
North Central	632	44	353	93	651
South	1,797	32	1,225	95	529
West	649	43	370	106	1,183

[1] Includes operating a farm and unpaid family labor.
[2] Averages not shown where base is less than 50,000 persons.

Source: "The Hired Farm Working Force of 1964," U. S. Department of Agriculture, Economic Research Service, *Agricultural Economic Report No. 82*, August, 1965, p. 21.

The labor market conditions which underlie many of the problems of the agricultural work force will be discussed in Chapter 16 when the Fair Labor Standards Act and the extension of its minimum wage provisions to agriculture will be analyzed. In this section we will examine the composition of the domestic farm labor force, its economic position, and its protection or non-protection under the relevant state and federal laws.

Profile of the Farm Labor Force

In 1964 about 3.4 million persons did some work on farms for which they received cash payment. Only about 25 per cent of these were chiefly engaged in farm work, however. The migrant labor force numbered approximately 386,000 and about 600,000 persons lived in households headed by migratory-workers.[21] Table 15.1 provides a breakdown of the farm labor force by selected characteristics.

In 1964 the average hired farm laborer earned only 91 cents per hour (see Table 15.2), and those whose chief activity was farm work averaged only $1,523 per year. The comparable figure for migratory workers was even lower—$1,240.[22]

TABLE 15.2

Average Hourly Earnings in Agriculture
and Other Selected Industries, 1964

All manufacturing	$2.53
Lumber and wood products	2.14
Canning and preserving	2.03
Apparel and related products	1.79
Laundries	1.44
Agriculture:	
Composite rate per hour	.904
Rate per hour without board or room	1.08

Source: "The Migratory Farm Labor Problem in the United States," 1965 Report of the Committee on Labor and Public Welfare, Subcommittee on Migrant Labor, 89th Cong., 1st Sess., p. 25.

Further, the farm laborer is excluded from the protection of much of the economic and social legislation which plays such an important role in the lives of workers in other sectors of the economy. It is to this legislation which we shall now turn.

[21] "Characteristics of the Population of Hired Farmworker Households," U. S. Department of Agriculture, Economic Research Service, *Agricultural Economic Report No. 84*, August, 1965, p. 5.
[22] "The Hired Farm Working Force of 1964," p. 15.

Status of Agricultural Workers
Under Selected State and Federal Laws [23]

Workmen's Compensation. As we have seen, the first type of social insurance to be enacted in America was workmen's compensation.[24] Yet, agricultural workers are fully covered in only five states; the statutes of many states either deny coverage to agricultural employees, or have extremely restrictive statutes, as Table 15.3 indicates. The seriousness of these omissions can best be appreciated if one looks back at the figures presented in Table 9.2 which show for 1963 *minimal* estimates of disabling injuries and deaths in agricultural employment for one year only of 2,020,000 and 14,200, respectively, the highest of any occupational grouping. A recent study shows California farm workers have the highest rate of occupational disease in the state, more than double the rate of the construction industry and nearly three times that of manufacturing.

Unemployment Insurance. Only two jurisdictions, Hawaii and Puerto Rico, have any provisions specifically covering agricultural employees. All other laws with the exception of those of Alabama, Massachusetts, and New York permit voluntary coverage. Only in North Dakota, however, has voluntary coverage been very significant.

Temporary Disability Insurance. Of the four jurisdictions which provide temporary disability insurance coverage (New York, New Jersey, Rhode Island, and California), only California's includes farm laborers.

Minimum Wages. The federal Fair Labor Standards Act specifically exempts agricultural workers from its minimum wage provisions (see Chapter 16). Of 32 jurisdictions with state minimum wage laws, only Hawaii and Puerto Rico provide statutory protection for both men and women farm workers. A recently enacted Michigan statute will cover a small number of that state's agricultural work force. While eight other laws permit coverage for agriculture by administrative action, only Wisconsin and California have done so. In Wisconsin there is a minimum of $1.00 an hour for employment of women and minors 16 years of age and over, and a minimum of 75 cents for minors under 16. Two wage orders in effect in California provide a minimum of $1.30 an hour for

[23] Except where otherwise indicated, all data in this section are taken from "Status of Agricultural Workers Under State and Federal Labor Laws," U. S. Department of Labor, Bureau of Labor Standards, *Fact Sheet No. 2,* December, 1964.

[24] For further details, see "Agricultural Workers and Workmen's Compensation," *Bulletin 206* (Washington, D. C.: U. S. Department of Labor, Bureau of Labor Standards, 1964).

TABLE 15.3

Agricultural Coverage Under State Workmen's Compensation Acts

All Farm Employment	All Farm Employment Except Employers With Less Than Number of Employees Indicated		Voluntary Coverage	No Coverage	Workers Engaged in Certain Machine Operation Only, Except for Employers With Less Than Number of Employees Indicated	
Alabama [a]	Connecticut	2	Alaska	Oklahoma	Arizona	3
California	Florida	4	Arkansas	Tennessee	Kentucky	3
Hawaii	Ohio	3	Colorado	Texas	Louisiana [c]	
Massachusetts	Vermont	6	Delaware		Minnesota	
New Jersey	Wisconsin [b]	6	Georgia		New York	
Puerto Rico			Idaho		South Dakota	
			Illinois		Wyoming	
			Indiana			
			Iowa			
			Kansas			
			Maine			
			Maryland			
			Michigan			
			Mississippi			
			Missouri			
			Montana			
			Nebraska			
			Nevada			
			New Hampshire			
			New Mexico			
			North Carolina			
			North Dakota			
			Oregon			
			Pennsylvania			
			Rhode Island			
			South Carolina			
			Utah			
			Virginia			
			Washington			
			West Virginia			

[a] Except part-time workers.
[b] And who work less than 20 days during a calendar year.
[c] Except while being transported to or from such work.

Source: U. S. Department of Labor, Bureau of Labor Standards, "Status of Agricultural Workers Under State and Federal Labor Laws," December, 1964, *Fact Sheet No. 2*, pp. 5–7.

women and minors employed in packing sheds on farms, and $1.30 an hour for women and $1.10 for minors employed in other agricultural occupations.[25]

Labor Relations Acts. The federal Labor–Management Relations Act specifically excludes agricultural workers from its provisions. Of the fourteen jurisdictions with labor relations acts, ten specifically exclude agricultural workers. Those of Kansas, Puerto Rico, and Wisconsin would appear to include them. Hawaii's statute covers all workers with the exception of those employed in feeding and milking cows.

OASDI. Under the original provisions of the Social Security Act, most farm workers were excluded. As a result of several amendments to the Act during the 1950's, farm workers are presently covered, "if the worker receives cash wages amounting to at least $150 from one employer during the year, or if the worker works for one employer on 20 days or more during the year for cash renumeration computed on a time basis."[26] However, since a great number of migratory workers are paid on a piece-rate basis this latter provision has had limited practical effect, and the $150 cash minimum is most often controlling.[27]

Special Programs for Farm Workers

As the above section indicates, farm workers simply do not enjoy the statutory protection to which most American workers have become accustomed. However, their vulnerability to economic misfortune has been somewhat alleviated by a series of federal, state, and community programs developed specifically for them. The major federal programs are described below.

Migrant Health Act. The Act authorizes the Public Health Service to make grants to public and other non-profit agencies to pay part of the cost of establishing and operating family health-service clinics, and other special projects to improve health services and conditions of domestic agricultural migratory workers and their families, and generally to encourage and cooperate in programs for the purpose of improving migrant health services and conditions. Currently, health projects are in operation under this program in twenty-nine states and Puerto Rico.

[25] State of California, Department of Industrial Relations, Division of Industrial Welfare, Wage Order 14–65, issued June 24, 1965.

[26] For a detailed statistical report on social security coverage of farm workers, see "Social Security Farm Statistics, 1955–61," U. S. Department of Health, Education, and Welfare, September, 1964.

[27] "The Migratory Farm Labor Problem in the United States," p. 37.

Housing Act. Under this federal program, grants have been given to "states or political subdivisions, or public or private non-profit organizations, to assist in providing housing and related facilities for domestic farm labor." Applicants must agree not to charge rentals exceeding amounts approved by the Secretary of Labor; to maintain the housing in a safe and sanitary condition; and to give domestic farm labor absolute priority for occupancy.

Economic Opportunity Act. One provision in the 1964 Act authorizes assistance to states and subdivisions and public and non-profit agencies by direct loans to establish programs of housing, sanitation, education, and day care of children for the benefit of migrant and other seasonally employed agricultural workers and their families. The Act also authorizes funds for the states to develop programs concerned with employment, job training, counseling, health, vocational rehabilitation, housing, home management, welfare and special remedial education to meet the needs of low-income rural families. An unlikely proposal which has been suggested by anti-poverty officials in New York is "to take migrant laborers off local farms and put them aboard salt water trawlers as commercial fishermen." [28]

Federal Farm Labor Contract Registration Act. This Act was designed "to prevent the exploitation of migrant agricultural workers by farm labor contractors." Farm labor contractors are required to obtain a certificate of registration from the U. S. Secretary of Labor, if the crew includes ten or more migrant workers who will be used in interstate agricultural employment. The Act prescribes certain duties for the contractor, lists certain undesirable practices which are prohibited, and provides machinery for refusing or revoking a certificate of registration.

In addition to the above legislation, there has been federal and state action in the areas of transportation of farm workers and regulation of farm labor camps.

As necessary as this special legislation is, however, it represents merely a peripheral approach to the economic insecurity of the farm worker. A necessary, though clearly not sufficient, condition for ending the poverty of the farm laborer, and the second-class citizenship which is a by-product of this poverty, is the inclusion of the farm worker in the economic and social security programs which are now enjoyed by almost all other wage-earning groups in our society.

Ultimately, more far-reaching solutions to the peculiar problems posed by the agricultural labor market (to be discussed in Chapter 16) will have to be found. Meanwhile, these "forgotten people" continue to be, in the Senate's words, "a national disgrace."

[28] *New York Times*, February 14, 1966, p. 21.

APPROACHES TO THE PROBLEM OF SUBSTANDARD CONDITIONS

Recognition of the need for regulating working conditions developed along similar lines in America and in England, although at different times. In both countries the government intervened to protect those least able to protect themselves—those whose lack of bargaining strength prevented them from a full exercise of their legal labor market freedoms.

Dissatisfaction with substandard working conditions in England came in the late eighteenth century shortly after formalized adoption of laissez-faire policies and was soon followed by legislative efforts to correct them. The first such enactment was the (1802) Factory Act designed to protect pauper children who had been made apprentices. Only a few such laws were enacted for some time, but after 1850 the area of regulative control expanded, until by World War I all the leading industrial countries of Europe exercised extensive controls over working conditions, hours, and wages.

WORKING CONDITIONS

Almost all states, and many municipalities and other jurisdictions, have sought to regulate conditions of work to insure certain minimum standards—particularly in the case of working women and children. Since there is very little uniformity in this type of legislation, it is difficult to estimate the degree or quality of protection that it affords,[29] but certain generalizations about the laws can be made.

Most of the laws apply primarily to women and children. For these two groups, most states prohibit work in specified industries or occupations—those declared hazardous or a health menace; and require that seating, rest, and toilet facilities be available. Some jurisdictions require lunchroom facilities, stated meal periods, and that sanitary drinking water be provided by the employer. Twenty-seven states have enacted "equal pay" legislation seeking to attain for women the pay status of men.

Some of this legislation reflects the needs of particular geographic areas. Alaska's law, for instance, requires that employers provide physical examinations for all employees recruited outside of Alaska and return transportation for those rejected on physical grounds. Mining states—Arizona, for example—prohibit payment of wages in scrip and forced purchases at the "company store."

Where this protective legislation has been extended to include men, it sometimes requires "safe employment devices and safeguards" and, in

---

[29] A state-by-state summary of legislation affecting working conditions appears in *Labor Policy and Practice Manual,* III (Washington, D. C.: Bureau of National Affairs, Inc., 1961).

a few states, provides for minimum pay for call-ins and split-shift work. Other regulations require approved ventilation standards (particularly in laundries), payment of wages at least twice monthly, time off for voting, and adequate lighting.

Because of enlightened personnel administration, trade union pressures, and the cost savings to an employer of a satisfied working force, many of the standards of these laws are not as high as the "going practice." Yet, for some employees, particularly those in unorganized areas, these laws can be a genuine source of protection, when adequately enforced.

Child Labor [30]

In America the first protective measures—also child labor laws—were enacted during the nineteenth century. Although a few states adopted such laws during this period, major protective labor legislation in America did not appear until after 1900.

Of all labor legislation, the need for laws regulating the employment of children was most generally accepted and received the most early widespread support. Nevertheless, the development of child labor legislation was piecemeal and slow. It was hampered by problems of law and enforcement as well as by powerful, though limited, opposition. In addition, the problem of child labor was extremely complex. Elizabeth Sands Johnson writes that from the time of the earliest nineteenth-century laws, it became apparent that adequate protection of children required: "(1) a minimum age below which they should not be allowed to work; (2) a minimum of education which they should acquire before entering employment; (3) a maximum number of hours for their employment; and (4) some rules to protect them against especially hazardous or unhealthful occupations." [31]

Let us examine state and federal legislative efforts to achieve protection for children in these areas.

Action by the States Before 1900. During the nineteenth century there was some support for the protection of children (some of which came from the Knights of Labor) and, in fact, a substantial number of laws were enacted. Following the early leads of the New England states, most notably Massachusetts and Connecticut, other states also adopted child

[30] For an excellent review of child labor legislation from its beginnings through the middle 1930's, see John R. Commons, *History of Labor in the United States* (New York: The Macmillan Co., 1935), III, 403–56. A more recent treatment of the legal problems of regulating child labor may be found in Glenn W. Miller, *American Labor and the Government* (Englewood Cliffs, N. J.: Prentice-Hall, Inc., 1949), pp. 146–48 and 245–65. Both sources were drawn upon in preparing this section.

[31] Reprinted by permission of The Macmillan Co. from John R. Commons, *op. cit.*, pp. 403–04.

labor measures, and by the turn of the century, twenty-eight state laws had been enacted. These early laws were recognized as a justifiable exercise of a state's police power, since the welfare of children (minors) as wards of the state was bound up with the welfare of the state.

Early child labor laws embodied a variety of standards, but were, for the most part, limited to work in manufacturing. They set the minimum age limit at twelve years and the workday at ten hours. Only a few of the laws made some provisions for required education.

Despite this apparent progress in regulating the employment of children, census data for the period indicated that the percentage of employed children ten to fifteen years old was increasing. This was partly due to poor enforcement and limited coverage of the laws and, in part, to the new industrial expansion of the South, an area in which labor laws were yet to be enacted (and in which they were to encounter their stiffest opposition).

Action by the States After 1900. A great deal of state child labor legislation was enacted after the turn of the century and until the period of the first federal action in 1916. A Child Labor Committee was formed in the South in reaction to the widespread employment of children in that area. Later another committee was formed in New York, and eventually a national group began operation. By 1909, all but six states had minimum age requirements for factories. And during the period of greatest growth of labor and protective legislation (from 1911 to 1913), thirty-one states took action to improve child labor legislation.

These laws sought to: (1) create administrative devices which would enable conclusive evidence of age that could not be circumvented by parents; (2) set up hours provisions that bore a rational relation to the amount of work that a child could (reasonably) do; and (3) make some educational provisions.

All states now have child labor laws. Like workmen's compensation laws, they are constantly being revised, and (again, like workmen's compensation) certain elements are common to all of them, although their standards differ considerably.[32] State child labor laws seek to:

1. Set a minimum age at which a child may legally accept work, qualified occasionally by school hours requirements
2. Limit the maximum hours per day that a youth may be employed
3. Limit employment during night hours
4. Set age limits on certain dangerous occupations
5. Require employment certificates
6. Require school attendance

[32] Summaries of state child labor laws are published from time to time by the U. S. Department of Labor, Bureau of Labor Standards. The most recent is "State Child-Labor Standards," *Bulletin 158*, revised 1960.

TABLE 15.4

Major Standards Recommended by the International Association of Governmental Labor Officials for State Child Labor Legislation and the Extent to Which Existing State Child Labor Laws Meet These Standards

	Recommended Standards	Extent to Which State Child Labor Laws Meet Recommended Standards
Minimum age	*16 years*, in any employment in a factory; 16 in any employment during school hours; 14 in non-factory employment outside school hours.	23 states and Puerto Rico approximate this standard in whole or in part (Ala., Alaska, Conn., Fla., Ga., Ill., Ky., La., Maine, Md., Mass., Mont., N. J., N. Y., N. C., Ohio, Pa., R. I., S. C., Tenn., Va., W. Va., Wis.)
Hazardous occupations	*Minimum age 18* for employment in a considerable number of hazardous occupations.	Few, if any, states extend full protection in this respect to minors up to 18 years of age, though many state laws prohibit employment under 18 in a varying number of specified hazardous occupations.
	State administrative agency authorized to determine occupations hazardous for minors *under 18.*	23 states, D. C., and Puerto Rico have a state administrative agency with such authority (Alaska, Ariz., Colo., Conn., Fla., Hawaii, Kans., La., Maine, Md., Mass., Mich., N. J., N. Y., N. C., N. Dak., Ohio, Ore., Pa., Utah, Wash., W. Va., Wis.)
Maximum daily hours	8-hour day for minors *under 18* in any gainful occupation.	16 states, D. C., and Puerto Rico have an 8-hour day for minors of *both sexes* under 18 in most occupations (Alaska, Calif., Ky., La., Mont., N. J., N. Y., N. Dak., Ohio, Ore., Pa., Tenn., Utah, Va., Wash., Wis.)
		7 other states have this standard *for girls* up to 18 (Ariz., Colo., Ill., Ind., Nev., N. Mex., Wyo.)
Maximum weekly hours	40-hour week for minors *under 18* in any gainful occupation.	6 states (Alaska, Ky., N. J., Tenn., Va., Wis.) and Puerto Rico have a 40-hour week for minors *under 18* in most occupations; 4 states (La., Ore., Pa., Utah) a 44-hour week for such minors.
		10 other states (Ala., Fla., Ga., Hawaii, Md., Mo., N. Y., N. C., R. I., W. Va.) have a 40-hour week for minors *under 16* in most occupations, and 2 states (Miss., N. Mex.) a 44-hour week for such minors.
		Washington has a 40-hour week for minors under 16 when school is not in session.

TABLE 15.4 *(Continued)*

Recommended Standards	Extent to Which State Child Labor Laws Meet Recommended Standards
Work during specified night hours prohibited — 13 hours of nightwork prohibited for minors of both sexes *under 16* in any gainful occupation.	11 states and Puerto Rico meet or exceed this standard, at least for most occupations (Hawaii, Iowa, Kans., N. J., N. Y., N. C., Ohio, Okla., Ore., Utah, Va.). The Virginia law prohibits 13 hours of nightwork on nights preceding schooldays. (Kentucky prohibits 13 hours of nightwork for minors under 15.)
	13 states and D. C. prohibit 12 or 12½ hours of nightwork for minors *under 16* (Ala., Ariz., Ill., Md., Mass. (12½ hours), Minn., Mo., N. Mex., N. Dak., Pa., R. I., Tenn., Wyo.). The Alabama law prohibits such work for 12 night hours during the regular school term, and "after 7 P.M." at other times. The Missouri law prohibits 12 hours of nightwork on nights preceding schooldays.
8 hours of nightwork prohibited for minors of both sexes *between 16* and *18* in any gainful occupation.	10 states, D. C., and Puerto Rico meet or exceed this standard, at least for most occupations (Ark., Conn., Kans., Ky., La., Mass., Mich., N. J., Ohio, Tenn.).
Employment certificates — Required for minors *under 18* in any gainful occupation.	23 states, D. C., and Puerto Rico require employment or age certificates for minors *under 18* in most occupations (Calif., Conn., Del., Fla., Ga., Hawaii, Ind., Ky., La., Md., Mass., Mich., Mont., N. J., N. Y., N. C., Ohio, Ore., Pa., Utah, Va., Wash., Wis.). Two other states (Ala. and Nev.) require such certificates for minors *under 17*.

Source: U. S. Department of Labor, Bureau of Labor Standards (Washington, D. C.: August, 1960).

The International Association of Governmental Labor Officials (IAGLO), an organization of the state administrators of laws relating to labor, has prepared standards which it considers to be minimum required regulations, and from time to time the Bureau of Labor Standards issues a tabulation indicating the number of jurisdictions which meet these minimum standards. The latest comparison for state child-labor laws (August, 1960), is reprinted in Table 15.4.

This table reveals both the gains that have been made in the regulation of child labor and the gaps that remain. Factory employment, which was the focal point of the initial drives against the evils of child labor, is now regulated approximately up to recommended minimum age standards in twenty-four jurisdictions. But hazardous occupations, including agriculture where child labor violations are most frequent and accident rates highest, are not at all well regulated.

The table indicates further that less than one-third of the states meet IAGLO recommended standards for maximum weekly hours (a forty-hour week for minors under eighteen in any gainful occupation), and for the prohibition of work during specified night hours. Ironically, the best regulation (in twenty-three states, D. C., and Puerto Rico) is achieved in connection with required employment certificates.

Federal Approaches to Regulation of Child Labor. Because of the diversity in state child labor standards and the failure of some states to enforce their laws adequately, it became apparent that genuinely effective control could be achieved only by federal legislation. Even before 1900 pressure was building, and despite the fact that the states had enacted considerable legislation, by 1914 demands for federal action could no longer be ignored.

By 1916, support was so widespread that Congress, by a great majority, enacted the first federal child labor law. It was the first in a series of federal attempts at regulation. Of these, the first four failed to survive legal hurdles, and the fifth provided little protection.

The first federal attempt to regulate child labor was based upon the constitutional power of the Congress to regulate interstate commerce. It declared unlawful and punishable by fine and/or imprisonment the interstate shipment of mined products on which children under sixteen had been employed and cannery or manufactured products on which children under fourteen had been employed. It also prohibited a workday longer than eight hours, a workweek longer than forty hours, and night work.

To base this federal regulation on the commerce clause of the Constitution was a rather novel use of this power, but it was not an unreasonable approach, since there was convincing precedent that federal regulation of this type could meet court approval. Earlier laws had successfully regulated the shipment of lottery tickets and the transportation of women across state lines for purposes of prostitution.

Since major opposition to the passage of the law came from the South, it was no surprise that the new law received its first test in North Carolina. In 1918 the United States Supreme Court held [33] the law unconstitutional on the grounds that Congress had exceeded its authority under

[33] *Hammer v. Dagenhart*, 247 U. S. 251 (1918).

the commerce clause; that however desirable the purpose of the law and undesirable the situation it was meant to correct, this was a matter for the local police power of the states.

Congress responded promptly to the challenge of this decision by enacting a new child labor law in the same year. Its standards were the same as the first law, as were the arguments raised for and against it. But its enforcement provisions were quite different. The new law was based on another (and the only other regulative) constitutional authority of the Congress to regulate labor—the power to tax. Its connection with the child labor problem was even less direct, but there was a somewhat analogous precedent for control based on this power. It had been used to prohibit the manufacture of white phosphorous matches. The new law provided a penalty of a 10 per cent tax on the net profits of violators.

The bill was passed as an amendment to a revenue act, and became a law in 1919. It was challenged immediately and successfully—again in North Carolina. Upon appeal, the United States Supreme Court ruled [34] the child labor law unconstitutional on the grounds that it was not a tax that imposed incidental restraints, but that it was in fact a regulation using the power to tax as a penalty. The court concluded that its provisions went far beyond the taxing authority in supervising a course of conduct in business.

The poor standards of state child labor legislation in the year of the *Bailey* case (1922) impelled supporters of federal regulation to seek a new approach. In only thirteen states were child labor standards comparable to those of the unsuccessful federal laws, and the employment of children was still widespread. Since the only two apparent avenues of congressional authority had been blocked by the Supreme Court's interpretation of the Constitution, the only possibility that remained was to change the Constitution specifically to authorize federal child labor regulation. A child labor amendment giving Congress "power to limit, regulate and prohibit the labor of persons under 18 years of age" was presented to the states for ratification in 1924.

Despite its apparent strong support, it failed because of local opposition based on the fear that it would give Congress too much authority. Only twenty-one of the required thirty-six states ratified it by 1933, and only six more had done so by 1939 when the issue arose whether or not its long delay still left it open to further ratifications. Although the Supreme Court ruled favorably, it was of no importance, since the federal control of child labor had finally been achieved by that time with the passage of the Fair Labor Standards Act in 1938.

[34] *Bailey v. Drexel Furniture Co.*, 259 U. S. 20 (1922).

An early federal control which did succeed, although briefly, set minimum age standards for the employment of children in the Codes of Fair Competition of the National Industrial Recovery Act. The standards of the Codes varied, but typically they provided for a minimum age of sixteen, although some went as low as fourteen. Eighteen was set as the minimum age in hazardous employment. The Codes succeeded in curtailing the employment of children,[35] but the regulations fell in 1935 along with the rest of the NIRA when the United States Supreme Court held [36] that in enacting the Codes, the Congress had exceeded its powers to regulate interstate commerce.

Following the *Schechter* decision, Congress acted to control child labor in an area which seemed safely within its powers, namely, contractors supplying the federal government. In 1936 the Walsh-Healey Public Contracts Act was passed prohibiting contractors who supply the federal government (with manufactures or products or finished materials) in values over $10,000 from employing children under sixteen and women under eighteen. It does not apply to agriculture, retail trade, or the service occupations. This was the only successful enactment of federal child labor regulation before the passage of the Fair Labor Standards Act, which marked the end of a twenty-two-year period of unsuccessful federal action in this field.

HOURS

Attempts to regulate working hours of adults, particularly women's hours, were in many cases linked to the child labor regulations discussed above. In fact, in some states the same law controls working hours of both women and children, and in a few states, general laws cover all workers.

Although movements to control working hours for women and men are related both in time and in motivating forces, because of some differences in timing, theory, scope and coverage, hours regulation for these two groups will be discussed separately here. Although hours regulation prior to the Fair Labor Standards Act was primarily a matter of state legislation, the federal government in its role as employer was actually the first to limit hours and undoubtedly influenced the actions of some employers and legislative groups. But federal regulation comparable to that of child labor has never been attempted in this field. The discussion below, therefore, concerns state regulations, with a brief added comment on federal action.

[35] Miller, *op. cit.*, p. 255.
[36] *Schechter Poultry Corp. v. U. S.*, 295 U. S. 495 (1935).

Women's Hours

Successful regulation of women's working hours dates back almost as far as the first child labor laws. New Hampshire enacted a ten-hour law in 1847, and a few other New England states followed. By 1896, thirteen such regulatory laws had been passed. These laws were, for the most part, limited to manufacturing, and by and large were not very effective, either because they were unenforceable or because they lacked realistic hours limits. Moreover, a court decision in 1895 declared an Illinois eight-hour law for women unconstitutional.[37] The court ruled that such laws interfered with the right of freedom of contract and liberty and that there was not present the necessary protection to health, safety, or morals which might make such interference justifiable.

In the view of this Illinois court, at least, the theory that hours protection should be extended to children by the state as their guardian did not apply to women. The court did not agree that special protection for women was needed on the grounds that women were unable fully to gain their rights in the labor market. But it was the recognition of these differences in women's bargaining ability that played a prominent part in the thinking of the United States Supreme Court when, in 1908, the first women's hour law reached the court.[38] In declaring an Oregon ten-hour law for women constitutional, the court brushed aside the arguments of the Ritchie case (as did an Illinois court in a later decision) and upheld the law which applied to mechanical establishments, factories, or laundries.

As a result, there was from 1909 to 1917 a great flood of state legislative activity in this field. The principle had been firmly established, had won legal acceptance, and most states enacted women's hours laws. After World War I, however, the movement never regained its pre-war momentum, and the legislative revisions were limited to newer rules such as prohibitions against night work and required rest periods.

The current status of hours regulation is summarized from time to time by the United States Department of Labor publications. The most recent summary [39] indicates that, while almost every jurisdiction has in some way regulated the hours of women, the extent and quality of coverage (as in the case of working conditions legislation) tends to vary

---

[37] *Ritchie v. People,* 155 Ill. 98 (1895).

[38] *Muller v. Oregon,* 208 U. S. 412 (1908).

[39] "State and Federal Hours Limitations," *Bulletin 116* (Washington, D. C.: U. S. Department of Labor, Bureau of Labor Standards, 1950). (This bulletin includes all hours regulations.)

widely among jurisdictions. However, the following generalizations about them appear to be warranted: (1) for reasons of health and safety, most women's hours laws limit work in specified industries or occupations; (2) almost all the women's hours laws provide for maximum hours—only a few do not. Frequently there is a stated maximum of an eight-hour day and a forty-eight-hour week, but there are many exceptions, particularly in the South; (3) the effect of the maximum hours requirement is considerably weakened by the exemptions (most frequently domestics, agricultural workers, and waitresses) which appear in virtually all the laws. Coverage in some of the laws is limited to certain industries or establishments.

Men's Hours

Regulation has never been as comprehensive in its scope or coverage of men's working hours as it has of the hours of women and children. Until fairly recently, laws were enacted almost exclusively in those employments where protection was very badly needed because of hazardous conditions or where they were fairly easy to enact because of advantageous political or administrative situations.

In 1840 a presidential order stipulated a ten-hour maximum workday in government Navy yards.[40] As early as 1868, Congress, with some success, limited the workday on contracts for government buildings and roads to ten hours. An early case [41] upheld state and municipal employees' hours laws and those covering state workers under contract.

Regulation of hours in hazardous work was first approved by the Supreme Court in 1898,[42] when the court upheld a Utah law which regulated the hours of men working in mines. Later cases upheld the right to regulate hours of special groups such as railroad employees, mining workers, bus drivers, and others on the grounds of safety.

In *Holden v. Hardy*, the court stated that ". . . the fact that both parties are of full age and competent to contract does not necessarily deprive the State of power to interfere where the parties do not stand upon an equality or where public health demands that one party to a contract shall be protected against himself." [43] This doctrine, as we have seen, found general application in the case of women's hours laws. Men's hours laws, however, except for those applying to state and federal government employees, tended to remain limited to those situations in which the addi-

[40] Discussed by Matthew A. Kelly, "Early Federal Regulation of Hours of Labor in the United States," *Industrial and Labor Relations Review*, III, No. 3 (April, 1950), 362–74.

[41] *Atkin v. Kansas*, 191 U. S. 207 (1903).

[42] *Holden v. Hardy*, 169 U. S. 366.

[43] *Ibid.*, p. 397.

tional grounds of health or safety were present. And with but one important exception,[44] courts recognized these bases as proper for the regulation of men's working hours.

Although men's hours laws gained recognition and approval between 1911 and World War I, they did not play a part in that period of vigorous legislative activity. Public interest in men's hours laws was never great, and no particular movement to enact this legislation ever developed.

Attempts to achieve shorter hours have been an important part of trade union programs since the 1890's. Since unions have been successful in gaining this objective and because of the general feeling that men are better able than women to protect themselves in the labor market, this area of regulation has not been one of major legislative or public interest in the over-all movement to improve substandard conditions. Little has been done by the states since the passage of the Fair Labor Standards Act. Only a few states today have general maximum hours laws for men.

Federal Regulation of Women's and Men's Hours

With the exception of work on railroads, Congress has never sought to enact legislation which would state maximum hours of work for men or for women. Its approach in the few areas in which it has attempted regulation has always been not to prohibit excessive hours of work, but rather to make excessive hours expensive through penalty "overtime" payments. The Codes of Fair Competition of the National Industrial Recovery Act provided for overtime payments, as did the 1916 Adamson Act and the Walsh-Healey Act. Each of these set the workday and provided for overtime payments. Apart from the instances in which the federal government was acting as employer, these were the only federal regulations in this field prior to the Fair Labor Standards Act.

WAGES

Wages were the last of the conditions of employment to be regulated by government intervention. In working to the wage core of the employment relationship, state governments had regulated the length of the workday, its conditions, and the time and method of wage payments. Child-labor and hours movements were well under way by the time Massachusetts enacted the pioneer minimum wage law in this country in 1912 —one which set nonmandatory minimum wages for women and children. In many respects the minimum wage laws were to be an extension of these movements. With but limited exception, they applied exclusively

[44] *Lochner v. New York*, 198 U. S. 45 (1905). The Supreme Court refused to uphold a New York ten-hour law applying to bakery workers.

to women and children and were justified as protecting these two groups from low wages resulting from competitive labor market conditions.

State Attempts at Regulation

Although eight states quickly followed the lead of Massachusetts in enacting minimum wage laws (most of which called for enforcement), and despite apparent Supreme Court approval,[45] the movement never gathered much momentum. Only fifteen states had enacted such laws when the movement encountered a serious legal setback. In 1923, the minimum wage law of Washington, D. C. was held [46] unconstitutional as an interference with the freedom of contract.

The effect of this decision was nearly ruinous. Laws in six other jurisdictions were declared unconstitutional; other states avoided court tests at the cost of full compliance; and by 1933, wage laws existed in only nine jurisdictions, and some of these were not in effective operation.

Most early minimum wage laws were based upon a concept of the minimum wage needed for living. In the Adkins case the court implied that a criterion more directly related to the value of the services performed by the employee might be a more appropriate basis for such legislation. Laws which embodied this concept and set minimum wages for "reasonable value of services" were enacted in some states. The New York law, however, was challenged and held [47] unconstitutional despite its new basis. It was not until 1937 that the United States Supreme Court gave full approval to state minimum wage laws by holding [48] the Washington law a valid exercise of state police power.

Some favorable legislative response followed this decision, and state legislatures enacted laws or broadened existing ones, in some cases even extending coverage to men. Yet for a number of years there was little legislative action on this front. Then with the poverty program providing the incentive, there was a flurry of activity beginning in 1964, when Michigan enacted a minimum wage law, the first state to do so for five years. In 1965, three states (Delaware, Indiana, Maryland) passed laws for the first time, two states amended their laws to bring men under coverage, and many states increased their statutory rates.[49]

---

[45] In *Stettler v. O'Hara*, 243 U. S. 629 (1917), the U. S. Supreme Court split evenly, J. Brandeis abstaining, on the constitutionality of Oregon's minimum wage law, leaving intact its approval by the lower court.

[46] *Adkins v. Children's Hospital*, 261 U. S. 525 (1923).

[47] On the grounds of a violation of the due process clause of the Fourteenth Amendment. *Morehead v. New York ex rel. Tipaldo*, 298 U. S. 587 (1936).

[48] *West Coast Hotel Co. v. Parrish*, 300 U. S. 379 (1937).

[49] *State Minimum Wage Legislation, A Major Weapon in the War on Poverty* (Washington, D. C.: U. S. Department of Labor, Women's Bureau, 1965).

Current Status of State Minimum Wage Regulation [50]

Minimum wage laws exist today in thirty-nine jurisdictions, as Table 15.5 shows. Twenty-three statutes apply to both men and women. The thirteen states that do not have minimum wage laws are, by and large, southern and border states.[51] Standards required by these state minimum wage laws vary greatly. They range from $.16 an hour in Arkansas, to $1.75 an hour in Alaska. These standards are somewhat deceiving, however, since some of the laws restrict coverage to certain industries, and in three states (Kansas, Illinois, and Louisiana), although there is a minimum wage law, no wage orders are currently in effect.

Situations such as these have focused attention on a problem of long standing—namely, how shall state minimum wages be set? There are three alternative methods, all of which are in use today. Minimum wages may: (1) be set by the legislature which, as a matter of law, declares the minimum figure—Alaska follows this procedure; (2) be fixed or revised by the agency responsible for administration of the law—this practice is followed in Arkansas; or (3) be set by a wage board which hears recommendations of an appointed tripartite commission, and then sets the minimum—Minnesota now employs this method.

Although it is sometimes argued that the use of legislative procedures results in a less flexible and somewhat more haphazardly set minimum, which agency sets the wage is less important than how a criterion of wage adequacy can be translated into dollars and cents. All the standards to which agencies refer (such as the "necessary cost of living") produce results about which there may be legitimate value judgment differences when they are converted to an actual wage.

For an estimated 10 million workers who are outside the coverage of federal minimum wage regulation, therefore, state laws offer a wide variety of standards—in some cases better protection than under the federal law, and in others no protection at all. For the most part, however, state minimum wage protection falls far below federal standards.

[50] For the current status of state minimum wage laws and other provisions affecting working conditions, see "Analysis of Coverage and Wage Rates of State Minimum-Wage Laws and Orders," *Bulletin 291* (Washington, D. C.: U. S. Department of Labor, Women's Bureau, 1965). This bulletin presents the detailed laws, titles of orders, dates, occupation or industry covered, class of employees covered, minimum wage rates for each, and hours of work. A companion study shows the history of State minimum wage legislation and an analysis of the basic provisions of minimum wage statutes—e.g., authority of minimum wage administrator, appointment of wage boards, promulgation of wage orders and related provisions. See "State Minimum-Wage Law and Orders," *Bulletin 267, Part I* (Washington, D. C.: U. S. Department of Labor, Women's Bureau, 1963).

[51] Alabama, Florida, Georgia, Iowa, Mississippi, Missouri, Montana, Nebraska, South Carolina, Tennessee, Texas, Virginia, and West Virginia.

TABLE 15.5

Summary of State Minimum Wage Law Provisions, August 1, 1965

State	Law Covers		Type of Law			Rates in Effect for		Law With Numerical Exemptions	Statutory Overtime After 40 Hours a Week
			Statutory						
	Men and Women	Women and/or Minors	Rate of $1.25 or More	Rate Less Than $1.25	Wage Board	Most Industries	Few Industries		
Alaska	X		X			X			X
Ariz.		X			X		X		
Ark.		X		X		X			
Calif.		X			X	X			
Colo.		X			X		X		
Conn.	X		X			X	X		
Del.	X			X		X	X		
D. C.		X			X	X			
Hawaii	X		X			X			X
Idaho	X			X		X			
Ill.*		X			X				
Ind.	X			X	X	X		X	
Kans.*		X			X				
Ky.		X			X	X			
La.*		X			X				
Maine	X			X		X		X	
Md.	X			X			X	X	
Mass.	X		X			X			X
Mich.	X			X	X	X		X	
Minn.		X			X	X			
Nev.	X		X			X			
N. H.	X		X			X	X		
N. J.		X			X		X		
N. Mex.	X			X		X		X	
N. Y.	X		X			X			
N. C.	X			X		X		X	
N. Dak.	X				X		X		
Ohio		X			X		X		
Okla.	X			X			X		
Oreg.		X			X	X			
Pa.	X			X		X	X		
P. R.	X			X		X	X		
R. I.	X		X			X	X		
S. Dak.		X		X		X			
Utah		X			X		X		
Vt.	X		X *			X	X		X
Wash.	X		X			X	X		
Wis.		X			X	X			
Wyo.	X			X		X			

* Law inoperative.

Source: Women's Bureau, U. S. Department of Labor.

Federal Approaches

Prior to the enactment of the Fair Labor Standards Act, attempts to intervene in the wage area were made almost wholly by the states, although from time to time there had been pressure for federal action— some as early as World War I.

Proponents of federal wage regulation argue that a uniform standard overcomes interstate cost differentials which are always cited in opposition to increasing a state minimum wage level. A novel state approach to this problem [52] was initiated in 1931 by Franklin D. Roosevelt. As Governor of New York, he succeeded in persuading seven states (Connecticut, Maine, Massachusetts, New Hampshire, New York, Pennsylvania, and Rhode Island) to sign an interstate wage compact. It provided for uniform wages and hours and was ratified by three of the states when passage of the Fair Labor Standards Act made its operation seem unnecessary. It later became ineffective.

Federal minimum wage action prior to 1938 was limited to the Davis-Bacon Act (1931), which provided for the payment of prevailing wages on federal construction contracts over $2,000; to the Walsh-Healey Act (1936), which required overtime and "prevailing wage" payments for industries holding government contracts in excess of $10,000; and to the NIRA Codes.

SUMMARY

Government intervention into conditions of employment began as a movement to protect women and children. Although some state protective legislation applies to men today, the state laws, generally speaking, have neither gone far beyond this scope, nor have they fully achieved the original objective. Wage and hour laws are still the continuing business of state legislatures, but interest in them has subsided substantially since the enactment of the Fair Labor Standards Act. In the past twenty-five years, rising levels of income and a public policy favorable to collective bargaining have brought working conditions for many workers in intrastate commerce well above the minimum levels which existing state regulation could properly achieve. But for significant numbers of workers, particularly in some areas of the South, and especially among agricultural workers, improved legislative standards could achieve better conditions of work. Let us next consider the development of present-day federal standards in the Fair Labor Standards Act.

[52] de Vyver, op. cit., p. 330.

SUGGESTIONS FOR ADDITIONAL READING

BUREAU OF NATIONAL AFFAIRS, INC. "Wages and Hours," *Labor Relations Reporter*. Washington, D. C.
  Presents a summary of legislation, regulations, and court decisions, both state and federal, covering working conditions, wages and hours. Current service.
COMMONS, JOHN R. *History of Labor in the United States,* Volume III. New York: The Macmillan Co., 1935.
  The entire third volume of this classic series is devoted to working conditions. It presents a detailed and comprehensive analysis of the development of legislation in this field.
——— and JOHN B. ANDREWS. *Principles of Labor Legislation,* 4th ed. New York: Harper & Row, 1936. Chapters 2, 3, 4, and 6.
  This book is still valuable for its expert insights into principles and administrative problems of labor legislation.
CULLEN, DONALD E. *Minimum Wage Laws.* Bulletin 43 of the New York State School of Industrial and Labor Relations, Cornell University, 1961.

[Current literature in substandard conditions is much less common today than it was, say, fifty years ago. The interested student would be advised to look at various economic histories and to dip into the labor novel of a half-century ago.]

16
Fair Labor Standards Act

INTRODUCTION

In 1938 government regulation of child labor, working hours, and wages was brought together under the Fair Labor Standards Act.[1] The inclusive provisions of the Act were unique in comparison with the scope and operation of the state protective labor laws which preceded it.[2] It is true that as early as 1913 in a few states (Oregon, California, and Washington) minimum wage laws for minors and women provided wide administrative discretion in establishing "'standard conditions of labor' demanded by their well being." [3] None of these laws, however, prohibited child labor or established a fixed minimum wage applicable to women and men alike.

Not only was the Fair Labor Standards Act comprehensive, but each of its several standards tended to be more rigorous and more inclusive than previous state protective labor legislation. Its child labor requirements were higher than those of the provisions of many of the 1938 state laws; it fixed an absolute wage minimum, departing from the administrative arrangement of flexible minimum wage-setting to which all state minimum wage laws had adhered; and while its hours provisions did not set absolute maximums, it was the opinion of students at the time that the law would probably give more impetus to a movement toward a shorter workweek than had been generated by the state hours laws. Fur-

[1] 52 Stat. 1060 (1938). The law is most widely referred to as the "Wage and Hour Law."

[2] Strictly speaking, this cannot be said when comparing the Act with earlier federal laws, since "... The Fair Labor Standards Act is a reenactment of subsection (3) of Section 7(a) of Title I of the National Industrial Recovery Act." Orme W. Phelps, *The Legislative Background of the Fair Labor Standards Act* (Chicago: University of Chicago Press, 1939), p. 5.

[3] Louise Stitt, "State Fair Labor Standards Legislation," *Law and Contemporary Problems*, VI, No. 3 (Summer, 1939), 454. Copyright 1939 by Duke University.

thermore, the new law extended wage and hour protection to men, discarding the widely held theory that, except for special cases where health or safety were involved, only women and children required government protection against the economic pressures of the labor market.

Finally, it extended regulation of working conditions far beyond the narrow limits of earlier federal control which, it will be recalled, was limited to situations in which the government was the employer, or was being furnished goods by contractors, or was interested in safety. Based on the constitutional authority of Congress to regulate interstate commerce, the Fair Labor Standards Act covered employees who were engaged in (1) "commerce," and (2) "the production of goods for commerce." In short, it covered all employees in interstate commerce activities except those who were specifically exempted.

Despite its comprehensive and far-reaching provisions and its new extension of federal authority into working conditions, however, the Fair Labor Standards Act was but an extension of a movement for improved labor standards legislation which, as noted in the last chapter, had begun over 100 years earlier in this country and over one and one-half centuries earlier in England. Federal intervention, though narrowly circumscribed, originated in the ten-hour order of President Van Buren in 1840 and encompassed a long history of federal attempts at control of child labor as well as the action of governmental agencies in helping the states obtain sound and workable protective labor legislation.[4] Of these influencing forces, the primary antecedents of the Fair Labor Standards Act were the National Industrial Recovery Act, the President's Re-Employment Agreement and the Codes of Fair Competition.[5]

THE FAIR LABOR STANDARDS ACT

Legislative History [6]

The National Industrial Recovery Act was held [7] unconstitutional in 1935, and in the following year the United States Supreme Court refused

[4] See, for example, "Criteria for Minimum-Wage Determination," *Monthly Labor Review*, XLVI, No. 1 (January, 1938), 201–04. This is the report of a study designed to aid state agencies in formulating criteria that go into the cost-of-living bases for many state minimum wage laws.

[5] A comparison of the provisions of the NIRA, the Agreement, and the Codes with the Fair Labor Standards Act reveals how closely they correspond. See Phelps, *op. cit.*, pp. 5–8.

[6] For a detailed and thorough presentation of the general legislative history of the Act and an analysis of the legislative fate of the many proposals that were considered before its final passage, see John S. Forsythe, "Legislative History of the Fair Labor Standards Act," *Law and Contemporary Problems, op. cit.*, pp. 464–90. This material was drawn upon in the preparation of this section.

[7] *Schechter Poultry Corp. v. U. S.*, 295 U. S. 495 (1935).

to uphold New York State's minimum wage law.[8] As a result, an important plank in the platform of the Democratic party in the 1936 presidential election was the enactment of federal wage and hour controls, by constitutional amendment if necessary. The party's victory brought immediate attention to the question of how this pledge would be fulfilled.

Eighteen months elapsed between the time the seventy-fifth Congress convened and June 25, 1938, when President Roosevelt signed the Fair Labor Standards Act. The first six months of this period were marked by intensive administrative maneuvering and momentous decision-making for each of the branches of government. The Administration and the Congress were faced with the problem of fulfilling the campaign pledge for federal wage and hour standards. President Roosevelt, deeply concerned about possible opposition from the judiciary and the probable refusal by the Court to uphold a federal protective labor law, sought to obtain enactment from the Congress of his Court reorganization measure as well as the labor standards legislation. Forsythe observes that the President considered the wage and hour bill to be "one of his strongest weapons available to force passage of the Court bill. For this reason it was indicated that the legislation would not be submitted until after there had been action on the Court plan." [9]

Meanwhile, the United States Supreme Court upheld the constitutionality of the Railway Labor Act of 1926 as revised in 1934, the newly enacted National Labor Relations Act, and a minimum wage law of the state of Washington.[10] Since these decisions reduced much of the pressure for the Court reorganization bill, the Administration decided to introduce a wage and hour bill. Some thirteen months later the President signed a bill which had been buffeted through three sessions of Congress and had "undergone amendment after amendment until practically the only point in common with the original bill was the legislative number." [11] The Fair Labor Standards Act became law on June 25, 1938, and began effective operation on October 24th of that year.

Basic Provisions

In its statement of findings and policy, Congress declared that it was the purpose of the Fair Labor Standards Act:

. . . to correct and as rapidly as practicable to eliminate . . . labor conditions detrimental to the maintenance of the minimum standard of living necessary

[8] *Morehead v. New York ex rel. Tipaldo,* 298 U. S. 587 (1936).

[9] Forsythe, *op. cit.,* p. 465.

[10] *Virginia Railway Co. v. System Federation #40,* 300 U. S. 515 (1937); *National Labor Relations Board v. Jones and Laughlin Steel Co.,* 301 U. S. 1 (1937); *West Coast Hotel Co. v. Parrish,* 300 U. S. 379 (1937).

[11] Forsythe, *op. cit.,* p. 466.

for health, efficiency, and general well being of workers . . . without substantially curtailing employment or earning power.

To achieve this purpose, the law established labor standards for (1) minimum wages, (2) maximum hours, and (3) control of child labor. The original provisions have been amended several times—a major revision was effected in 1949, a more limited one in 1955. In 1961, the law's coverage was generally extended for the first time since its adoption; in 1963, a new labor standard was added, equal pay for equal work for women; in 1966, coverage was greatly broadened and the minimum wage raised.

General Coverage. The original law extended protection to "employees" who were "engaged in commerce" or in the "production of goods for commerce" and who were not specifically exempted from coverage. A multitude of legal issues and uncertainties are involved in these standards.[12] In 1939, reflecting early uncertainties with the law, a lawyer wrote with respect to coverage that at least one question ". . . can be answered with certainty. When an employer inquires whether the wage and hour requirements of the law apply to his business, an attorney can with comparative safety always answer in the negative." [13]

Despite legal vagaries, however, some elements of the test of coverage became well-established. Until the 1961 amendments, coverage was made to depend upon the activities of the individual employee—not upon his employer's over-all business, nor on the work of fellow employees, nor on the industry involved. Thus, one of two employees working side by side might be engaged in commerce while the other might not. The definition of "employee" was broadly interpreted, so that the designation of a worker as an "independent contractor," for example, would not deny him protection of the Act if he worked in the usual employer–employee relationship. Although there evolved no definitive tests of what is commerce, employees have been held covered even when they have worked only part-time on work going into interstate commerce for an employer whose interstate commerce activities constitute less than 1 per cent of his total business. In 1961, the employee test was changed by statute to an employer test—extending protection to all employees of any employer who met the coverage criteria.

Specific groups of employees, however, are exempted, and these exemptions have always been more important numerically than the fringe cases of coverage and will be considered in detail later in this chapter.

---

[12] For an analysis of the legal problems involved in coverage, see Stefan A. Riesenfeld and Richard C. Maxwell, *Modern Social Legislation* (Brooklyn: The Foundation Press, 1950), pp. 606–37.

[13] Frank E. Cooper, "The Coverage of the Fair Labor Standards Act and Other Problems in Its Interpretation," in *Law and Contemporary Problems, op. cit.,* p. 333.

Minimum Wages. Section 6 (a) of the Fair Labor Standards Act provided that:

Every employer shall pay to each of his employees who is engaged in commerce or in the production of goods for commerce wages at the following rates—(1) during the first year from the effective date of this section, not less than 25 cents an hour, (2) during the next six years from such date, not less than 30 cents an hour, (3) after the expiration of seven years from such date, not less than 40 cents an hour, or the rate (not less than 30 cents an hour) prescribed in the applicable order of the Administrator . . . whichever is lower, and (4) at any time after the effective date of this section, not less than the rate (not in excess of 40 cents an hour) prescribed in the applicable order of the Administrator . . .

The Fair Labor Standards Act set a goal of a 40-cent-an-hour minimum wage rate, to be attained over a seven-year period in order to reduce any possible adverse employment effects of the legislated minimum wage. It should be recalled that in 1938, 10,390,000 workers—19 per cent of the civilian labor force of 54,610,000—were unemployed.[14]

Not all, nor even a major portion of the 1938 wage rates were subject to immediate revision as a result of the new minimum. In manufacturing, for example, average gross hourly earnings were 63 cents; in bituminous coal mining, 88 cents; and in wholesale trade, 70 cents.[15] Yet, for the estimated eleven million workers covered by the Act in September, 1938, at least 300,000 were earning less than 25 cents an hour; 550,000 were earning below 30 cents an hour; and 1,418,000 below 40 cents.[16]

In order to attain the minimum wage rate for each covered industry as rapidly as possible, at the same time retaining flexibility through the period of transition, the Act instructed the Administrator to appoint a committee for each industry. These committees were to investigate and recommend to the Administrator the highest wage that the industry could afford to pay without curtailing employment. Industry committees began to function shortly after the Act was passed.[17] Their valuable work was abetted by World War II's effects on wages and prices, and the committees reached the 40-cent objective before the October, 1945 deadline.

Maximum Hours. Section 7 (a) provided that:

No employer shall, except as otherwise provided in this section, employ any of his employees who is engaged in commerce or in the production of goods for commerce—

[14] *Economic Report of the President* (Washington, D. C.: U. S. Government Printing Office, January, 1955), p. 153.

[15] *Ibid.*, p. 162.

[16] *Monthly Labor Review*, XLIX, No. 6 (December, 1939), 1439–46.

[17] Z. Clark Dickinson, "The Organization and Functioning of Industry Committees Under the Fair Labor Standards Act," *Law and Contemporary Problems, op. cit.*, pp. 353–67.

(1) for a workweek longer than forty-four hours during the first year from the effective date of this section,

(2) for a workweek longer than forty-two hours during the second year from such date, or

(3) for a workweek longer than forty hours after the expiration of the second year from such date

unless such employee receives compensation for his employment in excess of the hours above specified at a rate not less than one and one-half times the regular rate at which he is employed.

This section of the Act followed the same gradual approach as the wages section, although the goal was to be attained in this case the second year after the Act went into effect. It is estimated that of the eleven million workers covered by the Act as of September, 1938, 1,384,000 were working more than forty-four hours per week; 1,751,000 were working more than forty-two hours per week; and 2,184,000 were working more than forty hours per week.[18]

This provision (with one exception discussed below) sets no maximum daily or weekly hours beyond which work is prohibited. Rather, it assesses an overtime penalty on long working hours. Also, it is noteworthy that the overtime penalty of one and one-half times is based upon the regular rate of pay, and not upon the statutory minimum rate.

The United States Supreme Court has emphasized several times that the hours section of the Fair Labor Standards Act has a dual purpose.[19] On the one hand, it is designed to compensate workers for the duress of long hours worked in excess of the statutory minimum; and on the other, it is designed to spread employment through its overtime penalties.

Control of Child Labor. Section 12 (a) provided that:

. . . no producer, manufacturer or dealer shall ship or deliver for shipment in commerce any goods produced in an establishment situated in the United States in or about which within thirty days prior to the removal of such goods therefrom any oppressive child labor has been employed.

"Oppressive child labor" is defined by Section 3 (1) as the employment of children under sixteen, unless employed by parent or guardian. Employment in mining and manufacturing is prohibited in all cases for employees under sixteen. For children fourteen to sixteen, employment is not oppressive if it does not interfere with schooling, health, and well-being—as determined by the Chief of the Children's Bureau. Work in occupations designated as "hazardous" by the Children's Bureau is oppressive for children below eighteen. Appropriate agencies in the states issue certificates of age for children seeking employment.

[18] *Monthly Labor Review*, XLIX, No. 6 (December, 1939), 1439–46.
[19] See Riesenfeld and Maxwell, *op. cit.*, pp. 604–05.

Exemptions from Coverage. A series of four specific provisions exempted otherwise covered employees from each of the three basic labor standards insured by the Act.

1. *Exemptions from minimum wage requirements.* To avoid curtailing employment for groups whose positions might be placed in jeopardy by too high a minimum wage, the Act authorized the Administrator to issue special certificates to handicapped workers, messengers, apprentices, and learners. Certified workers in these groups may be employed at a rate below the statutory minimum. Since this exemption is intended only to avoid possible restriction in employment opportunities, it does not extend to the hours (or overtime) provision of the law. Thus messengers, learners, apprentices, and handicapped workers must be paid one and one-half times their regular rate of pay for hours in excess of those specified by statute—after 1940, forty hours per week.

2. *Exemptions from hours (overtime) requirements.* Three exemptions were provided. First, industries found by the Administrator to be "seasonal" were given an exemption for fourteen weeks in any calendar year. Employees in these industries could work up to twelve hours a day, fifty-six hours a week, without overtime payment. Beyond these limits, overtime applied. Second, a fourteen-weeks exemption per calendar year was provided employees working in "agricultural processing—such as processing milk, processing cream into dairy products, ginning and compressing cotton." Third, employees who come under the Interstate Commerce Commission's jurisdiction with respect to hours (such as motor carriers) were exempt from overtime provisions.

The final hours exemption related to collective agreements. In order to encourage regular employment, exemption from overtime penalties was provided if an employer and a certified union entered into a collective agreement which provided either a maximum of fifty-two weeks of employment for 2,000 hours (changed to 2,080 hours in 1941); or twenty-six weeks of work for 1,000 hours. Where such contracts were bargained, employers were permitted to average out overtime, and to work employees up to twelve hours a day, or fifty-six hours a week without incurring the overtime penalty. If the 2,080 or 1,040 hour maximums were exceeded, the overtime exemption was lost.

3. *Exemptions from child labor provisions.* We have already noted that children working for a parent or guardian were exempt in part. Children working in agriculture, while not legally required to attend school, and children employed as actors in motion pictures or theatrical productions were also exempt.

4. *Exemption for wage and hour provisions.* Complete exemption from the coverage of the Fair Labor Standards Act was provided for some dozen groups of employees. Most important of these are the several classes which fall into the agricultural and white-collar group.

First, employees classified as executive, administrative, professional, outside salesmen, or working in local retailing or retailing primarily intrastate commerce in nature, were exempt. By law the Administrator is empowered to set up regulations which define the scope of these exemptions.

Second, seamen, fishermen (including canning), workers employed in agriculture, and those working in agriculture or horticulture in the "area of production" were exempt.

Finally, employees such as air carriers, switchboard operators, and employees of small local newspapers were given exemptions.

Enforcement Provisions. Three means of enforcement were established. First, willful violation of the Act could be punishable criminally by fine and imprisonment. Second, the right of civil suit was given employees whose employers violated wage and hour provisions. Suits for unpaid amounts as well as for damages, fees, and costs were authorized. Finally, violations of the Act could be restrained by injunctions.

Constitutionality [20]

The first challenge of the Fair Labor Standards Act reached the Supreme Court in 1940, and in 1941, the Court reversed a lower District Court decision and held [21] the new Act constitutional. Darby Lumber, which had been charged with a violation of the wage and hour provisions, claimed that the Fair Labor Standards Act, in violation of the rule in *Hammer v. Dagenhart*, used the power to regulate commerce to regulate essential interstate business. The Court repudiated this narrow view of what was a permissible regulation of commerce and overruled *Hammer v. Dagenhart*. The Court's earlier decision in *West Coast Hotel v. Parrish* had already determined that wage regulation did not violate the Fourteenth Amendment. In the *Darby* case the Court held that the Act did not violate the due process clause of the Fifth Amendment. Another decision [22] upheld the operation of the industry committees as a permissible delegation of powers, and they operated until they completed their work in 1944.

Revisions of the Act

Five important amendments have been made to the original Fair Labor Standards Act. Before turning to the details of the coverage and

[20] In view of past decisions of the U. S. Supreme Court on state laws regulating conditions of work, there was a great deal of speculation about whether or not the Court would uphold the Fair Labor Standards Act. Two opinions, one holding the new Act constitutional, the other holding it unconstitutional, were prepared in 1939 by legal scholars as suggestive of what the Court might do. See Robert L. Stern and R. S. Smethurst, "How the Supreme Court May View the Fair Labor Standards Act," *Law and Contemporary Problems, op. cit.*, pp. 431–53.

[21] *United States v. F. W. Darby Lumber Co.*, 312 U. S. 100 (1941).

[22] *Opp Cotton Mills v. Administrator*, 312 U. S. 126 (1941).

administration of the Act, its rationale, and an appraisal, let us discuss these amendments.

1949 Revisions. In 1944, when the last industry committee had reached the minimum wage goal set forth in the Fair Labor Standards Act, that wage level (40 cents an hour) was already considered by many persons to be obsolete. The inflationary pressures of World War II had pushed gross hourly earnings in manufacturing from a 1938 level of 63 cents to $1.02—some 61 per cent; in construction, hourly earnings had risen from 91 cents to $1.32; in wholesale trade from 70 cents to 99 cents; and in laundries, from 42 cents to 61 cents. During this same period, prices, as measured by the Consumers' Price Index, rose from a 1938 index level of 60.3 to 75.2.[23]

It was with these facts in mind that President Truman in his "State of the Union Message" on January 5, 1949, stated that the minimum wage should be fixed at 75 cents an hour. This major aim was more fully spelled out by William R. McComb, Wage and Hour Administrator, in his testimony in the hearings on proposed legislation. Said Mr. McComb:

> The most vitally required change in the Fair Labor Standards Act is to increase the minimum wage. This proposal should no longer be in the realm of controversy. The 40-cent minimum wage has shrunk to 23 cents in 1938 dollars. It is a modest proposal . . . Most industries could afford to pay a minimum wage well above 75 cents . . . While I estimate that only 7 per cent of the 22,600,000 workers covered by the minimum wage provisions of the Act are earning less than 75 cents an hour, this 7 per cent represents 1½ million human beings. These 1½ million workers desperately need the benefits of a modest 75-cent minimum wage.[24]

In the nine months which elapsed between the time the Administration bill was introduced and the time the measure reached the President's desk, the proposed amendments went through many changes. The President received his recommended 75-cent minimum, but he also received amendments he had not sought.

The 1949 amendments may be summarized as follows:

1. *Wage and hour provisions.* (a) The minimum wage was increased from 40 to 75 cents an hour. (b) Rules governing overtime exemptions for annual wage plans were made more flexible. The maximum of 2,080 hours for fifty-two-week plans was raised to 2,240 hours. Overtime rates are required over the lower figure, but exemption is not lost unless the upper figure is exceeded. Similarly, the ceiling of 1,000 hours on twenty-six-week plans was raised to 1,040 hours. (c) Contracts permitting fixed

---

[23] Wage and price data from the *Economic Report of the President,* January, 1955, *op. cit.,* pp. 162–76.

[24] Hearings Before the House Committee on Education and Labor, 81st Congress, 1st Session, *Amendments to the Fair Labor Standards Act of 1938,* I (Washington, D. C.: U. S. Government Printing Office, 1949), 51–52.

weekly wages for employees with irregular hours were authorized if they were limited to sixty hours a week, guaranteed the minimum statutory rate, and provided overtime for more than forty hours. (d) The concept "hours worked" was defined to exclude wash-up time and clothes-hanging time unless these are covered by contract or custom. (e) "Regular rate of pay" was defined to exclude certain gratuities. The effects of these latter changes are discussed later in this chapter.

2. *Child labor provisions.* (a) Whereas the earlier law simply prohibited shipment of goods on which oppressive child labor had been employed, the new law *specifically prohibited the employment of child labor.* (b) It set the minimum age for hazardous work at eighteen and eliminated the exemption for children working for parents. (c) It added exemptions for minors in radio and television, but limited the agriculture exemption to hours outside required school hours for the district where the child or parents reside.

3. *Coverage.* The 1938 law covered employees engaged in commerce, or in the production of goods for commerce or in any occupation necessary to such production. The amendments reduced coverage to apply to employees engaged in commerce or in the production of goods for commerce or in any *closely related* process or occupation *directly essential* to such production.

4. *Exemptions.* Only two of the original exemptions—fishing and air carriers—were somewhat curtailed. Exemptions to agricultural processing, local newspapers, and telephone exchanges were enlarged, and new exemptions—for agricultural irrigation, taxicab operators, forestry and lumbering, and telegraphic agencies—were added.

5. *Enforcement.* The new law gave the Administrator the authority to sue for an employee's back wages with the consent of the employee. Such suits had not previously been authorized.

1955 Revisions. In his *Economic Report* to the Congress in January, 1955, President Eisenhower proposed that the minimum wage be increased to 90 cents an hour and that ". . . both Congress and the States . . . consider the question of bringing substantial numbers of workers, now excluded from the protection of a minimum wage, under its coverage." [25]

After lengthy hearings, Congress rejected the Administration bill and approved one which increased the minimum wage to $1 an hour, but did not extend coverage of the Act.[26]

[25] *Economic Report of the President,* January, 1955, *op. cit.,* pp. 58–59.
[26] Other 1955 amendments provided that the Wage and Hour Administrator's annual report must make an evaluation and appraisal of the minimum wage set by the Act; that it must also make recommendations for future revisions of the law; and that the reports of industry committees for minimum wages in Puerto Rico and the Virgin Islands must be published in the Federal Register to take effect fifteen days after such publication. Changes became effective March 1, 1956.

An important issue in the hearings on the 1955 amendments was whether or not workers in the retailing industries should be brought under the Act. Although they were not included in the bill, the United States Department of Labor announced plans for an extensive fifteen-month study to determine the feasibility of such coverage for the national retail industry.

1961 Revisions. During the six years following the 1955 amendments, as the cost of living, the average hourly earnings of workers, and national productivity continued to rise,[27] labor pressed for raising the minimum wage to $1.25 and for extending the coverage of the Act to new employees. Extensive hearings on such amendments were held by House and Senate committees in 1957, 1959, and 1960. In the latter year, each house of Congress passed its own version of a bill, the far more generous Senate measure sponsored by the then-Senator Kennedy, but the conferees were unable to resolve the substantial differences in the two bills, and no final measure was enacted. In 1961, the new Kennedy Administration gave early priority to the issue, pushing it with added urgency as an anti-recession weapon.

Again both House and Senate hearings were held on an Administration compromise measure which extended coverage to 4.3 million workers and raised the minimum wage in gradual steps to $1.25. Once more, two greatly differing versions resulted. The Senate measure closely followed the Administration proposal; the House defeated the Administration bill by one vote, however, and went on to pass a very limited bill, raising the minimum wage to $1.15 and extending no overtime standard and only the then-existing $1 minimum to 1.4 million new employees. This time, the conference committee, with an Administration majority, worked out a successful compromise, making two major concessions to the House: the period for bringing newly covered employees up to a $1.25 minimum wage and down to a 40-hour straight-time workweek was lengthened from three to four years, and the coverage extensions were cut down to bring only 3.6 million new workers under protection. Strong White

[27] "Between March 1956 and December 1960, average hourly earnings in manufacturing rose by 19 per cent, to $2.32 an hour. In three of the manufacturing industry groups, ... earnings increased by about 25 per cent. In some nonmanufacturing industries average earnings increased by even larger amounts. Telephone workers received increases averaging 26 per cent; telegraph workers, 29 per cent; and employees of gas and electric utilities, 27 per cent. . . . During the same period, the Consumer Price Index increased by 11 per cent. During the 5 years, 1956 through 1960, real output per man-hour in the private sector of the economy increased by about 13 per cent." From the testimony of Secretary of Labor Arthur Goldberg, Hearings Before the House Committee on Education and Labor, Special Subcommittee on Labor, 87th Congress, 1st Session, *To Amend the Fair Labor Standards Act* (Washington, D. C.: U. S. Government Printing Office, 1961), p. 26.

House efforts propelled the new bill through the House, this time with a comfortable majority. Thus for the first time since the original bill's passage in 1938, substantial new groups of employees finally gained the benefits of minimum wages, hours, and child labor protection.

The 1961 amendments may be summarized as follows:

1. *Wage and hour provisions.* (a) For presently covered employees, the minimum wage was increased to $1.15 (effective September 3, 1961, or four months after signature of Act) and two years later, again increased to $1.25. (b) For newly covered employees, a minimum wage of $1.00 an hour was established for the first three years following the effective date of the Act; the fourth year, the minimum became $1.15; and the fifth year (beginning September 3, 1965), the minimum reached $1.25. (c) For newly covered employees, there was no limitation set on overtime during the first two years; in the third year, overtime was payable after 44 hours; in the fourth year, the ceiling went to 42 hours and after the fourth year, to 40 hours. (However, 312,000 of the employees newly covered as to minimum wages did not receive overtime coverage.) (d) In Puerto Rico and the Virgin Islands, present rates of covered employees were increased by 15 per cent, and two years later, further increased by 10 per cent, unless appealed. Machinery was established for committees to review such appeals and for committees to set rates for newly covered employees.

2. *Coverage.* (a) Retail and service establishments: minimum wage and overtime protection was extended to an estimated 2.1 million employees of retail and service establishments which meet certain tests. First, they must have employees engaged in commerce or in the production of goods for commerce, including handling, selling, or otherwise working on goods that have been moved in or produced for commerce. (This requirement also applies to the enterprises covered by the other categories mentioned later.) Second, they must have an annual gross volume of sales of $1 million or more. Third, they must purchase or receive goods for resale that move or have moved across state lines (not in deliveries from the reselling establishment) which amount in total annual volume to $250,000 or more. Fourth, in chain operations that meet these tests, each individual store to be covered must have annual gross sales of $250,000 or more. This general extension of coverage to retail and service establishments is qualified by certain specific exemptions discussed below. (b) Minimum wage and overtime protection was extended to an estimated 1 million employees of construction enterprises with an annual gross volume of $350,000 or over; and to an estimated 30,000 switchboard operators in public telephone exchanges (unless employed by an independently owned telephone company that has no more than 750 stations). (c) Minimum wage and overtime protection was extended to any establishment that has two or more employees engaged in commerce or in the production of goods for commerce if it

is part of an enterprise which is not specifically exempt and has an annual gross volume of sales of not less than $1 million. This affects an estimated 100,000 workers in previously covered establishments, most of them wholesale firms, who had been unprotected because coverage had previously applied only to workers specifically handling goods in interstate commerce. (d) Minimum wage protection, but not overtime coverage was extended to the following: an estimated 86,000 employees of gasoline service establishments having an annual gross volume of sales of $250,000 or more; an estimated 93,000 employees of local transit companies having an annual gross volume of sales of $1 million or more; an estimated 100,000 seamen on American vessels; and an estimated 33,000 seafood processing workers.

3. *Exemptions.* (a) The coverage of retail and service establishments specifically exempted employees of hotels, motels, restaurants, laundries, auto and farm implement dealers, motion picture theaters, recreational establishments operating on a seasonal basis, hospitals, institutions primarily engaged in the care of the sick, the aged, or the mentally ill or defective, residing on the premises of such institutions, and schools for physically or mentally handicapped or gifted children. Also exempt were all employees of retail or service establishments employed primarily in connection with preparation or offering of food or beverages. (b) In addition, the Act exempted 15,000 cotton ginning employees who had previously been covered, as well as certain employees in tobacco processing, fruit and vegetable transportation, livestock auctions, country elevators, and evergreen wreath-making. Also added were exemptions for overtime only for certain radio and television station employees in smaller cities and certain drivers, drivers' helpers, loaders, and mechanics.

4. *Enforcement.* The Federal District courts were authorized, in injunction actions brought by the Secretary of Labor, to issue court orders requiring employers to cease unlawful withholding of minimum wages and overtime compensation found by the court to be due to employees under the Act. Awards would be limited to wages and overtime dues. In these actions, the Secretary of Labor does not need employee consent, which had previously been required.

5. *Foreign competition.* The new law required the Secretary of Labor to investigate and report to the President and to Congress whenever he has reason to believe that in an industry under the Act, the competition of foreign producers in the United States market or in markets abroad has in fact resulted or is in fact likely to result in increased unemployment in the United States.

6. *Study.* The Act required the Secretary of Labor to study the complicated system of exemptions on handling and processing of agricultural products and also rates of pay of employees in hotels, motels, restaurants, and other food service enterprises, and to make recommendations for legislation designed to simplify and remove inequities in the application of such exemptions.

1963 Revision. In 1963, for the first time since its enactment, a new basic labor standard was added to the Fair Labor Standards Act, guaranteeing equal pay for equal work regardless of sex. The legislation, intended primarily to protect women from discriminatory pay practices, requires employers engaged in interstate commerce to provide equal pay for "equal work on jobs the performance of which requires equal skill, effort and responsibility and which are performed under similar working conditions." Exceptions are provided where differentials are based upon a seniority or merit system or where earnings vary with quality and quantity of production. However, employers must apply any such system equally to men and women. Employers are prohibited from equalizing pay by reducing men's pay. The Equal Pay Act applies to every employer having employees who are subject to a minimum wage under Section 6 of the FLSA. Covered were some 7.5 million women employed by 1.1 million firms engaged in interstate commerce, but since the Act went into effect in mid-1964 no reliable estimates have been made of the number actually receiving wage increases as a result of the pay amendment.

1966 Revisions. As indicated in recent editions of the *Economic Report of the President,* the Administration of Lyndon B. Johnson has expressed the desirability of expanding coverage and raising wage minimums under the FLSA. Labor has been pushing vigorously for a $2 minimum wage and greatly expanded coverage. After extended hearings and legislative debate, and after failure to win Congressional approval on a measure in 1965, House and Senate bills differing in effective dates and coverage provisions were passed in 1966. The conference committee report included the more liberal elements in both bills and a final measure was enacted in the fall of 1966. The major features of the revisions were these:

1. *Wage and Hour Provisions.* (a) For presently covered employees, the minimum wage was increased from $1.25 to $1.40 on February 1, 1967, and from $1.40 to $1.60 on February 1, 1968. (b) For newly covered farm employees, a minimum wage of $1 an hour was set, effective February 1, 1967, rising to $1.15 one year later, and to $1.30 the following year. (c) For other newly covered employees, the same provisions apply to farm workers, except that the $.15 per hour annual increment continues for two more years, bringing these workers to the $1.60 minimum by February 1, 1971. (d) For newly covered workers other than farm workers, overtime payment is required after 44 hours during the first effective year of the Act; after 42 hours during the second year, and after 40 hours beginning February 1, 1968. The overtime provisions do not apply to farm workers.

2. *Coverage.* An estimated 8 million new workers will be brought under the FLSA by the 1966 amendments. (a) A beginning was made

in coverage of agricultural labor. Approximately 500,000 farm workers will be covered for the first time. The Act applies to farms employing 500 man-days of labor in a 3-month period, which generally works out to cover those farms employing seven or more workers. (b) Over 7 million non-farm employees, many in retail and service occupations, will eventually be covered, as the various stages of the Act go into effect. These include a block of elementary and secondary school employees numbering approximately 900,000, and federal employees in the Canal Zone and trust territories. (c) Many of the retail and service establishment employees now receive protection for the first time because the dollar-volume test for covered enterprise (mentioned earlier in the description of the 1961 revisions) was reduced from $1 million to $500,000 in 1967 and $250,000 in 1969.

3. *Age Discrimination.* An effort was made in Congress to include a provision prohibiting discrimination because of age. Although this amendment was not passed, the Act does direct the Secretary of Labor to submit specific legislative proposals on the matter of age discrimination when Congress convenes in 1967.

Coverage of the Act *

According to the most recent United States Department of Labor estimates (January, 1966) the Fair Labor Standards Act sets minimum standards for about 29½ million, or 62.6 per cent of the 47 million [28] American wage and salary workers for whom this protection might be contemplated. Table 16.1 indicates the degrees to which coverage extends to employees of major industry categories, the number covered by state laws only, and the number covered by neither.

Table 16.1 reveals at its extremes that almost all workers in mining, manufacturing, transportation, communication, and utilities are covered by the Fair Labor Standards Act, whereas in agriculture, forestry, fisheries, and domestic service coverage is virtually non-existent. The other groups range from 20 to 80 per cent coverage of their employees. Two factors deny Fair Labor Standards Act protection to these groups: (1) the requirement that coverage extend only to enterprises "engaged in commerce or in the production of goods for commerce," which (a) have an annual gross volume of sales of at least one million dollars; and which, in the case of retail or service establishments, also (b) purchase or receive goods for resale that move or have moved across state lines amounting to more than $250,000 annually; and the further requirement that individual units of chain operations must show sales of $250,000 to be

---

* Before 1966 amendments.

[28] Excludes executive, administrative, professional, government, and self-employed persons as well as armed forces personnel.

TABLE 16.1

Coverage of Non-supervisory Employees Under the Fair Labor Standards Act, 1964

	Per Cent of Non-supervisory Employees Protected by FLSA	Number of Workers Not Covered (in thousands)	Number Covered by State Laws Only (in thousands)	Number Covered by Neither (in thousands)
Mining	99.1	5	1	4
Manufacturing	95.9	644	111	533
Transportation, communications, and utilities	94.8	190	39	151
Contract construction	79.7	616	193	423
Wholesale trade	69.4	923	112	811
Finance, insurance, real estate	74.3	646	96	550
Retail trade	32.5	5,395	2,437	2,958
Services and related industries	22.2	4,862	2,267	2,595
Agriculture, forestry, and fisheries	.0	1,882	56	1,826
Domestic service	.0	2,504	—	2,504
Total, all industries	62.6	17,667	5,312	12,355

Source: U. S. Department of Labor, Wage, Hour, and Public Contract Division, *Minimum Wage and Maximum Hours Standards under the Fair Labor Standards Act, 1966.*

covered, and (2) specific exemptions which exclude many workers who meet coverage requirements.

The effects of these two limitations on Fair Labor Standards Act protection are demonstrated in the second column of Table 16.1, which reveals that over 17½ million workers are not protected by the Act: Approximately two-thirds of them do not meet (interstate) coverage requirements; and about one-third who do meet these requirements are specially exempt by one or more provisions. A detailed breakdown of the exempt workers is presented in Table 16.2. A large percentage of these specifically exempt groups are also excluded by the coverage requirements of the Act.

The full effect of this spotty coverage cannot easily be gauged. Undoubtedly some of the workers who fall outside the protection of the Act are not in need of it. This would apply to employments in which trade union wage and hour standards are in effect. Most organized workers enjoy working standards well above the minimum requirements of the Act. But the exempted groups include some of the nation's lowest paid employees, e.g., farm workers, hotel, restaurant, and laundry workers. In 1966 about 7½ million workers were employed at hourly rates of less than $1.25. This is more than 15 per cent of the non-supervisory work

TABLE 16.2

Exemptions Under the Fair Labor Standards Act Before 1966 Revisions

Exemptions	Number Exempt
Employed by exempt retail trade establishments	3,567,000
Farm workers	1,895,000
Outside salesmen	1,757,000
Employed by restaurants	1,753,000
Employed by miscellaneous services	1,528,000
Domestics	2,504,000
Employed by hotels	549,000
Employed in laundries or cleaning and dyeing plants	505,000
Engaged in handling or processing agricultural commodities in the area of production	90,000
Employed by motion picture theaters	114,000
Taxicab operators	122,000
Employed in small logging operations having 12 or fewer logging employees	87,000
Engaged in fishing	20,000
Employed by local transit companies	15,000
Employed by small newspaper concerns	16,000
Employed by cotton gins	34,000
Switchboard operators of small telephone exchanges	3,000
Total	14,559,000

Source: Hearings Before the Committee on Education and Labor, House of Representatives, General Subcommittee on Labor, 89th Cong., 1st Sess., *Minimum Wage-Hour Amendments, 1965* (Washington, D. C.: U. S. Government Printing Office, 1965), Part I, p. 449.

force. About three-fifths of these workers earned less than $1.00 per hour and more than one-fourth of them earned less than 75 cents. Those whose wages fall under the minimum and who cannot look forward to favorable market forces must depend upon state minimum wage laws. As we have already seen in Chapter 15, thirteen states have no minimum wage protection whatever. Statutes that do exist often apply only to women, and their standards, by and large, are low. As Table 16.1 shows, over 12 million workers are covered by neither federal nor state protection.[29]

[29] Comments William L. Batt, Jr., Secretary of Labor and Industry, Commonwealth of Pennsylvania at the 1961 Hearings: "State action is too slow. At the rate of progress since the first State minimum wage was enacted 50 years ago, it is going to take close to another 50 years to get minimum wages for storeworkers in all the States, if you depend on the States to do the job. . . . It is quite clear that minimum wages by State action can never be sufficiently high and comprehensive to eliminate unfair competition from cheap labor in the United States in our lifetime." *To Amend the Fair Labor Standards Act, op. cit.,* p. 354.

Let us now turn to the qualitative issues in coverage to determine the rationale behind the exemption and limiting provisions.

Rationale of Coverage and Exemptions

At the present time the employed civilian labor force is comprised of about 72 million persons. Of these, 25 million work in occupations for which Fair Labor Standards Act coverage was not intended.[30] For the 47 million who remain, however, we have seen that, even after the 1966 amendments, protection is not available to almost 10 million workers who are either not covered or are exempt. What are the reasons offered for these limits on coverage and exemptions? It may be instructive to look at this matter in some detail so as to get a flavor of political processes.

Limitations on Coverage. Congress cannot legislate beyond its constitutional authority which, in the case of the commerce clause, is "to regulate commerce . . . among the several States. . . ." The Fair Labor Standards Act is limited in application to employers "engaged in commerce or in the production of goods for commerce." Court interpretation has given broad scope to the coverage phrases of the Act to "extend it far beyond interstate commerce . . . to a whole complex of activities which precede commerce, broadly defined as production for commerce." Yet coverage of the Act is restricted by the fact that "It does not . . . extend at all beyond commerce to the other complex of activities which follow commerce. . . . The effect on commerce of labor conditions in production of the article which subsequently moves, is recognized, though the effect on the same commerce of labor conditions in the distribution of the article which has moved, is not." [31]

Exemptions. Fair Labor Standards Act protection is neither intended nor appropriate for workers who are professionals or for those who are identified with management (executives, administrators, and white-collar workers). But why does the law fail to protect the non-managerial groups? [32]

Part of the answer can be found in the legislative history of the Act. Each volume of congressional hearings on this legislation is replete with pleas from trade associations and employer groups predicting financial

---

[30] Proprietors, self-employed, and unpaid family workers; government employees; executive, administrative, and professional employees.

[31] Hearings Before the Senate Committee on Labor and Public Welfare, Subcommittee on Labor, 84th Congress, 1st Session, *Amending the Fair Labor Standards Act of 1938* (Washington, D. C.: U. S. Government Printing Office, 1955), p. 1779.

[32] Listed in Table 16.2.

ruin if their particular group of employees is covered.[33] Frequently these requests for exemptions are transmitted by Congressmen.

Illustrative of the arguments advanced for specific exemptions are these: farm workers and fishery employees—too hard to regulate hours and wages in an industry that is subject to natural and seasonal forces; handlers and processors of agricultural commodities—the costs of processing cannot be passed on to the consumers but must be borne by the farmers and, furthermore, these employees do not work under industrial conditions; small logging operations—need exemption to compete with large operators and also too difficult to enforce.

The unsuccessful Kennedy-Morse-Roosevelt Bill in 1960 originally proposed extension of coverage to 8 million additional employees,[34] over half of them in the retail trade. The coverage criterion was $500,000 in annual sales. The bill included employees of hotels, laundries, and other services, as well as logging, taxicabs, and other presently exempted employees. The Kennedy Administration, in preparing its 1961 bill, trimmed its proposals (despite strong labor protests) frankly in the interests of framing a measure that could be passed. New coverage was cut to 4.3 million new employees. After the one-vote defeat in the House, exemptions eliminating over 700,000 more from coverage were added (primarily laundries and auto dealers). This kind of legislative history, then, helps to explain why the many gaps in coverage seem to fall into no rational pattern.

[33] A random sampling from the 1961 hearings: American Retail Federation; California Laundry and Linen Supply Assn.; National Assn. of Amusement Parks, Pools and Beaches; American Merchant Marine Institute; Transportation Association of America; Florida & Georgia Cigar Leaf Tobacco Assn.; National Association of Motor Bus Owners; National Automobile Dealers Assn.; Liquefied Petroleum Gas Assn.; Council of Motion Picture Organizations; Slack Cooperage Industry; National Retail Furniture Assn.; Association of Retail Grocers; National Retail Hardware Assn.; National Lumber Manufacturers Assn.; United Fresh Fruit & Vegetable Assn.; National Retail Lumber Dealers Assn.; Associated Retail Bakers of America; National Retail Farm Equipment Assn.; Pennsylvania Retailers' Assn.; Conference of American Small Business Organizations; National Retail Merchants Assn.; National Fisheries Institute; National Oil Jobbers Council; National Association of Broadcasters; etc.

On the other hand, there is an occasional discordant note in the chorus. For example, James F. Haley, spokesman for Cluett-Peabody, the nation's largest men's clothing manufacturer, declared: "As long as the legal minimum remains at the low figure of $1 an hour, it will continue to be possible for substandard manufacturers to provide the worst kind of unfair competition to the legitimate and efficiently operated units of the industry." And Lansing P. Shields of the Grand Union Company, one of the largest retail chains, pointed out that retailers "all buy now at about the same price, and competition makes us sell at approximately the same level . . . retailing can no longer afford to be considered to be a second class industry, or be satisfied with attracting second-class help . . . the move to include retailing is welcomed as necessary to the retail industry's growth and development."

[34] Over 3 million of whom received less than $1.25 an hour.

In 1965, the Johnson Administration recommended extending coverage to about 4.6 million additional workers; the House Labor Committee in 1965 approved a bill extending coverage to about 7.9 million additional workers. These two proposals involved:

	Administration Proposal	House Committee Proposal
Retail trade	1,500,000	2,010,000
Hotels	275,000	275,000
Restaurants	425,000	525,000
Laundries	175,000	505,000
Hospitals and nursing homes	890,000	1,353,000
Agriculture	—	1,300,000
All other industries	1,296,000	1,961,000

But these measures failed to win congressional support in 1965, as House Labor Committee efforts also failed in 1964.

A Comment. If an important aim of the Fair Labor Standards Act is to protect workers because they are unorganized and/or in employments in which working conditions are substandard, then the interests of these workers must be brought before the Congress. No one spoke authoritatively for expanded coverage in 1949 when revisions of the minimum wage involved changes which curtailed coverage of the law. Today, however, trade unions strongly back extensions of the Act.[35] It seems likely that the first hesitant steps toward fuller coverage taken in 1961 will continue until the law more nearly fulfills its original policy declaration: "to correct and as rapidly as practicable to eliminate . . . labor conditions detrimental to the maintenance of the minimum standard of living necessary for health, efficiency and general well-being of workers."

To gain further insight into the problem of extending minimum wage coverage, let us look in detail at one of the major groups of workers totally excluded until 1966—those in agriculture.

FLSA AND FARM LABOR

President Franklin D. Roosevelt, in his message to Congress in 1937 first proposing the establishment of a minimum wage, stated, "Legislation can, I hope, be passed at this session of the Congress further to help those who toil in factory and on farm." [36] The passage of the FLSA in the following year placed a floor on wages for millions of Americans, but

[35] See AFL-CIO testimony in 1960 and subsequent hearings.

[36] As quoted in "Data pertinent to determining the scope and level of a minimum wage for hired farm workers," U. S. Department of Labor, Wage and Hour and Public Contracts Division, January, 1964, p. 1.

did little to improve the lot of those who labored on America's farms. Though the Act has been amended and broadened on several occasions, thirty years later most hired farm laborers still do not enjoy the protection of a minimum wage. This absence of a wage floor is a significant factor in explaining both the low level of agricultural wages, as well as the increasing gap between agricultural wages and wages in other sectors of the economy.

The absence of legislation in this area should not be taken either as an indication that a problem did not exist, or that its existence has been ignored. Over the years a number of amendments to the FLSA have been proposed, and in 1962 the President's Committee on Migratory Labor, headed by the Secretary of Labor, voted "support, in principle, for the extension of appropriate minimum wage legislation . . . to agriculture." [37] Though certain adverse economic and social effects of the establishment of a minimum wage are not to be overlooked, the chief reason President Roosevelt's proposal has lain fallow for thirty years appears to be a political one—the disproportionate influence exerted by employers of farm labor in Congress.

An over-all view of farm poverty has been sketched in Chapter 15. Its paramount causes are the seasonal nature of the farm work and the low level of agricultural wages. Even if farm workers were granted the statutory protection which most other workers enjoy, their lot would scarcely improve unless their average hourly wages increased significantly. Extension of the federal minimum wage to agriculture seems clearly indicated as the only feasible method for accomplishing this end, as we shall see below. The 1966 revisions of the Act, which place half a million farm workers under the FLSA, are a first step in this direction.

Factors Influencing Farm Wages

Low wages in agriculture are due primarily to the existence of an excess supply of available farm labor. From 1952 until 1965 the importation of thousands of foreign nationals under Public Law 78 added to this depressing factor on the level of farm wages.

The origins of this labor market imbalance can be traced to supply-and-demand factors in both the farm and non-farm economy. From 1910 to 1963, total farm employment dropped approximately 52 per cent. During the same period, the estimated number of man-hours worked in farming declined by about 61 per cent.[38] Though these figures reflect a

[37] Letter to the President of the United States from Arthur J. Goldberg, Secretary of Labor, Chairman, President's Committee on Migratory Labor, January 17, 1962.
[38] W. Keith Bryant, "Demand and Supply of Agricultural Labor in a Period of Social Change," *Journal of Farm Economics*, XLVI, No. 5 (December, 1964), 1246.

significant decline in the farm labor force, it has not been rapid enough to offset the decrease in demand for hired farm labor. This decline in demand stems from the extraordinarily large productivity increases in agriculture. From 1940 to 1962, output per man-hour in agriculture increased 253 per cent [39]—gains which have only partially been offset by increasing demand for agricultural products.

Most recent studies indicate that the rate of out-migration from the agricultural sector is dependent primarily upon available work in the non-farm sector.[40] Unless there is a sharp increase in the demand for the services of unskilled labor by the non-farm sector, there is little reason to expect the rate of out-migration from agriculture to increase sufficiently to affect the agricultural labor market surplus. A further depressing factor on the supply side is the continued high birth rate in rural areas. Finally, the relatively unskilled nature of most farm work allows large numbers of additional workers to enter the farm labor market during seasonal peaks.

On the demand side, continuing farm mechanization will further decrease the quantity of farm labor required. At the same time, as unskilled labor becomes relatively less important in the non-farm sector, farmers will become more insulated from competition with non-farm employers for the services of the unskilled.

There is little likelihood, therefore, that the natural operation of the labor market will function so as to bring farm wages more in line with wages in the rest of the economy. The disproportionate extent to which agricultural wages have fallen behind those of other industry groupings is shown in Table 16.3.

TABLE 16.3

Increase in Hourly Wages of Major Industry Groupings,
U. S., 1947–62

	Per Cent
Agriculture	56
Mining	84
Retail trade	93
Wholesale trade	94
Manufacturing	96
Contract construction	115

Source: Agriculture—U. S. Department of Agriculture; others—U. S. Bureau of Labor Statistics.

[39] "Data pertinent to determining the scope and level of a minimum wage for hired farm workers," p. 20.
[40] See studies cited by Bryant, *op. cit.*, pp. 1248–49.

State minimum wage laws applicable to agriculture are almost non-existent, as shown in Chapter 15. We would expect this, as the highly competitive nature of the agricultural product market is a strong deterrent to individual state action. Thus, legislative intervention through the extension of the FLSA represents the most realistic hope of hired farm workers to begin their escape from poverty.

Probable Consequences of Farm Coverage

A study made by the U. S. Department of Labor predicting the effects of a minimum wage in agriculture concluded:

> By making farm labor more expensive, a minimum wage would encourage more efficient utilization of manpower and would thus result in some reduction in the demand for hired labor. In addition, increasing mechanization would probably be accompanied by acceleration in the current trend toward increased consolidation of agricultural operations, and would thereby tend to reduce the number of farm operators.
>
> The number of persons in the labor force now working in agriculture who must seek work in other industries would tend to increase as a result of the minimum wage. The problem is to avoid setting the initial rate so high—or advancing it so rapidly—that it could not be achieved "without substantially curtailing employment or earning power." [41]

It is difficult to predict the number of jobs that may be lost or the number of farms that will no longer be profitable, given a minimum wage in agriculture. The effect on the latter will probably be small, however, since most of the bills before Congress exempt smaller farmers—those who use less than a specified number of man-hours during a specific time period. For example, it has been estimated that a bill introduced in Congress in 1965, which would exempt those farmers who used less than 560 man-days during a given quarter, would apply to only 50,000 of the nations 3.2 million farms.[42] Even if the cut-off point were reduced to 300 man-days, only 2 per cent of the nation's farms would be covered, though this criterion would include 42 per cent of the nation's hired farm workers. As we have seen, the 500 man-days test in the 1966 bill is estimated to affect 500,000 farm workers.

No matter what cut-off point is used, there will be a number of farm operators who will no longer find it profitable to continue farming. The social cost to them, their families, and society is not easily ignored. Yet the displacement of the marginal farmer is a phenomenon which has

[41] "Data pertinent to determining the scope and level of a minimum wage for hired farm workers," p. 26.

[42] "The Migratory Farm Labor Problem in the United States," Fourth Report of the Committee on Labor and Public Welfare, U. S. Senate, Subcommittee on Migratory Labor, 88th Congress, 2nd Session, p. 44.

been occurring for many years. In the last 25 years, 2.5 million farm families have left the land, and according to one estimate, "By 1980, the typical family farm that is paying its way will have a total capital requirement ranging from $100,000 to $250,000." [43] Thus the minimum wage would only accelerate slightly a long-established trend resulting from the technological revolution which has swept through American agriculture in the twentieth century, a small price compared to the human cost now exacted from the poverty-stricken farm worker.

In the last analysis, of course, the problems of those who are displaced from the soil, both farm worker and farmer, can be met only by a rapidly growing economy which can provide gainful employment at reasonable wages for all those who seek it.

It is not only difficult to estimate accurately the economic effects of proposed legislation, it is also difficult to determine with any exactitude the effects of minimum wage legislation already enacted, as we shall see in the next section.

Economic Effects of the Act

Earliest United States Department of Labor estimates (referred to earlier in this chapter) of the wage and hour status of workers covered by the 1938 Act revealed that 300,000 covered workers were earning less than 25 cents an hour; 550,000, less than 30 cents an hour; and 1,418,000, less than 40 cents an hour. It was estimated that 1,384,000 workers were working in excess of forty-four hours a week; 1,751,000, more than forty-two hours a week; and 2,184,000, over forty hours a week. A later study [44] concluded that on October 24, 1938, the date the Act became effective, 650,000 workers in manufacturing, wholesale trade, and motor carriers— some 5½ per cent of all covered employees—would be subject to wage increases to 30 cents an hour; that the wage increases would average 1.9 per cent in all manufacturing, 13.5 per cent for cottonseed oil, 8.2 per cent in saw mills, and 4.9 per cent in the canning industry; and that only 30 per cent of some 2,400,000 workers then working more than forty-two hours a week were receiving overtime.

What effects would the required adjustments have on wages, employment opportunities, prices, and profits? These questions were of great concern to the Congress which, it will be recalled, prefaced the new law with the policy statement that it was the purpose of the law to eliminate substandard conditions ". . . without substantially curtailing employment or earning power." As Chapter 17 will indicate, economists have long been concerned about these issues of public policy, but have never been

[43] *New York Times*, February 14, 1966, p. 21.
[44] *Monthly Labor Review*, L, No. 3 (March, 1940), 546.

in agreement as to the probable effects of minimum wage laws. Their differences of opinion are apparently due partly to different points of view regarding the desirability of minimum wage legislation and partly to the notable lack of empirical information on these questions.

The new law raised wage rates and reduced hours (or penalized overtime)—this is agreed. But did it have other (possibly undesirable) economic consequences? Since reliable and comprehensive data are not available, there has been little more than speculation about this question. Nowhere is the lack of empirical information about the effects of the Fair Labor Standards Act more clearly indicated than in the congressional hearings on the 1949 revision.[45]

When the law was amended in 1949 with the 75-cent minimum to become effective January 25, 1950, the Department of Labor undertook a major study [46] to determine its effects. Three avenues of inquiry were followed.

First, field surveys were made in five low-wage manufacturing industries (southern sawmilling, fertilizer, men's dress shirts and nightwear, women's seamless hosiery, and wood furniture except upholstered) to determine the impact of the new law on wage structures.

Second, every complaint of a plant slowdown, shutdown, or job curtailment due to the law was investigated thoroughly. A wide range of firms and industries was covered.

Third, a comparison was made of wage movements for seventeen industries, some high-wage, others low-wage, for several periods to determine the effects of the law.

Results of this study, briefly summarized below, were perhaps partly influenced by the fact that the period after 1950, because of the Korean War, was one of rising prices and employment. The data reveal that, except for the payment of the required increase, the over-all effects of the new minimum were minor for the firms studied.

Wage Changes. Upward wage adjustments in the five low-wage inindustries were extensive. In southern sawmilling, for example, the direct wage bill rose by 14 per cent. With but few exceptions, the increases in the wage bill were greater than any effected by the industry committee under the original Act. As might have been predicted, percentage wage differentials were reduced, both between high- and low-wage industries

---

[45] *Amendments to the Fair Labor Standards Act of 1938, op. cit.*

[46] See Chapter 17, this text, for further discussion of this study. After the 1955 amendments, the Department conducted another study along somewhat similar lines. For a summary of the data on employment effects plus critical comments of the AFL-CIO on the study, see Hearings Before the Senate Committee on Labor and Public Welfare, Subcommittee on Labor, 87th Congress, 1st Session, *Amendments to the Fair Labor Standards Act* (Washington, D. C.: U. S. Government Printing Office, 1961) Appendix B, p. 695.

and regions. Wage rates of employees working at or above the new 75-cent minimum wage were not significantly affected. For employees outside of coverage, wage rates that were below the new minimum increased—in some cases as much as those of covered employees. The study of wage movements in the seventeen industries indicated that low wages increased more in covered industries than in non-covered industries.

Non-Wage Effects. Despite the fact that the new higher minimum required significant wage increases, its effect on employment, plant shutdowns, hiring policies, technological change, and overtime work was minor. In the relatively few instances where minor employment declines did occur, the decisions to reduce employment were influenced by other factors as well as the minimum wage. No plant closings were attributed by their managers solely to the 75-cent minimum wage requirement.

Some firms indicated that the new minimum had the effect on their hiring policies of placing more emphasis on younger, more experienced workers. Although a few cases of curtailed overtime were reported, over-all effects on prices and overtime work were similarly small and insignificant. Finally, no direct evidence could be found that the new minimum accelerated the rate of technological change.

Effects in Firms Reporting Adjustment Problems. These firms, it will be recalled, were those which reported difficulties in adjusting to the new minimum wage. Not only were they untypical of all firms, but were, in fact, those least able to meet the wage and hour requirements of the new law. Even in these firms, however, the new minimum wage law did not have any serious over-all effects.

The hand cigar and oyster canning industries were especially hard hit. Together with a few other industries, they experienced unemployment and even a few closings, although most of the unemployment resulted from job elimination or elimination of slower workers. Even in these extreme cases, however, the causal picture was not clear, since other unfavorable market forces were influential in the employment decisions.

It will be useful for the student to consider the meaning of these findings in the context of the next chapter. Do they indicate, for example, that the new higher minimum wage was returning to workers more than the value of their marginal product? The studies produced by the Department of Labor do not confirm this.

The Secretary of Labor is required to make annual reports to Congress on the administration of the Fair Labor Standards Act with recommendations for its improvement. The Department of Labor, in this connection, carries on continuous economic studies on the results of earlier amendments to amass further evidence on the relationship of minimum wages to employment, prices, and profits. In his 1966 summary of the studies,

Secretary W. Willard Wirtz reported that despite the substantial impact of the 1961 amendments—which raised earnings of between 3½ and 4 million workers by an annual total of approximately $1.2 billion—there is no evidence that these statutory changes have retarded economic expansion, adversely affected employment, reduced profits, or contributed to inflation. This echoes the report of an earlier Senate Subcommittee on Labor that pointed out in 1961,[47] the "transition to the $1 minimum seems to have taken place with no, or only very limited, adverse effects on the employment totals reflected in the Bureau [of Labor Statistics] surveys. This is particularly significant in view of the fact that the industries surveyed were selected because the $1 minimum had its greatest impact on them." [48]

The most effective allegation made against an increase in the minimum wage rate is that it increases unemployment. Study after study attempting to prove or disprove this charge faces the difficulty that in any given situation there are always forces at work which affect employment rates more significantly than the change in the minimum wage law.

For example, the most significant change in the 1961 amendments was its expanded coverage of retail trade. A comparison of retail trade employment in June, 1965, with what it had been in June, 1961, shows an increase of 300,000 (from 2.4 million to 2.7 million); an increase in employment in each of the four broad regions in the country, ranging from 8 per cent in the South to 31 per cent in the West; and reveals further that many retail trade employers put the $1.25 rate and the 40-hour overtime rule into effect prior to the time they were required to do so by the statute. However, during this same period a number of major steps were also taken in the general economy to promote higher private investment (for example, the 7 per cent investment-credit, relaxed depreciation requirements, and a cut in the corporate profits tax) and the economy was beginning the longest period of continuous expansion in its history.

Thus the employment effects of higher minimum wages are extremely difficult to estimate. Although some studies [49] allege that they can be identified, it is a highly problematic venture at best.

[47] *Amendments to the Fair Labor Standards Act, op. cit.,* p. 702.

[48] See also a study by Dr. Paul Brinker, Chairman of the Department of Economics, University of Oklahoma, on the impact of the $1 minimum in 15 Oklahoma industries, which found that "The firms paying below $1 an hour [ended up with] a better record of employment than the firms already paying all employees over $1." Paul A. Brinker, "The $1 Minimum Wage Impact on 15 Oklahoma Industries," *Monthly Labor Review,* LXXX (September, 1957), pp. 1092–95.

[49] See, for example, John M. Peterson, "Employment Effects of Minimum Wages, 1938–50," *Journal of Political Economy* (October, 1957); N. Arnold Tolles, "The Purposes and Results of U. S. Minimum Wage Laws," *Monthly Labor Review* (March, 1960); and David E. Kaun, "Minimum Wages, Factor Substitution and the Marginal Producer," *Quarterly Journal of Economics* (August, 1965).

Administration of the Act

The myriad problems that arise in the administration of the Fair Labor Standards Act can be grouped into problems of how to fix standards and how to enforce them.

Fixing Standards. Although the Fair Labor Standards Act defines basic wage and hour standards, it leaves to the Administrator considerable areas of discretion in defining and delimiting the law's applicability. The Administrator is also called upon to interpret the law for employees who are uncertain of their status. A great many questions must be decided. Who is an executive, an administrator, or an outside salesman within the meaning of the Act? What employments are "closely related" or "directly essential" to the production of goods for commerce? For that matter, who are "employees"? How is overtime to be computed? Who qualifies for the various exemptions? For seasonal industry exemption? What is the "Area of Production"?

The Act gives the Administrator power to issue binding and authoritative regulations in connection with specific provisions of the Act. It also makes provision for employers or others affected by these regulations to appeal to the Administrator for their revision. These important regulations cover the many phases of the law which the Administrator must supervise.[50]

The Administrator must set standards for employment of learners and must revise these standards in the light of current economic conditions. He must issue certificates for the employment of apprentices, messengers, and handicapped workers. In addition, he must maintain wage standards in Puerto Rico and the Virgin Islands, where they are still determined by industry committees.

Shortly after passage of the Act in 1938, the Administrator was besieged by employers and unions seeking authoritative rulings as to the applicability of the Act in specific situations. In lieu of such rule-making power (which was not given to the Administrator in the Act) the Wage and Hour Division began, in November, 1938, to issue interpretative bulletins—a practice which it has followed ever since.

---

[50] A list of the current regulations provides some indication of the scope of this area of administration. They cover: certificates of age, employment of minors, child labor, utilization of state agencies for investigation and inspections, record keeping, vocational training, apprentices, learners, messengers, handicapped workers, sheltered workshops, seasonal industries, student workers, cost of facilities, area of production, white-collar workers, thrift and savings plans, profit-sharing plan or trust, agreed basic rates on overtime, and "talent" fees. For the complete text of these regulations and the interpretative bulletins, see Bureau of National Affairs, Inc., *Labor Relations Reporter,* Wage and Hour Manual, Binder 6 (Washington, D. C.: 1961).

The first interpretative bulletin (October 12, 1938) made clear its non-official status by noting:

. . . interpretations announced by the Administrator, except in certain specific instances where the statute directs the Administrator to make various regulations and definitions, serve only to indicate the construction of the law which will guide the Administrator in the performance of his administrative duties, unless he is directed otherwise by the authoritative rulings of the courts, or unless he shall subsequently decide that a prior interpretation is incorrect.

Today, interpretative bulletins cover such areas as general enforcement policy, coverage, methods of wage payment, overtime compensation, retail and service trades, and agricultural processing. While these bulletins do not have the status of substantive regulations, they do carry weight with the courts, which are faced with the question of interpreting the Fair Labor Standards Act.

Enforcing Standards. Despite the many problems involved in fixing standards, the most difficult task of the Administrator is to enforce them. Although the law has always made private suits for back pay available to workers, experience indicates that enforcement cannot be left to the worker's own initiative. Rather, business establishments are inspected to insure compliance with required standards—through lawsuit if necessary. Enforcement is an especially vexing problem since the number of inspections is relatively small because of limited personnel, and the percentage of violations, although many are good-faith errors, is very large.

Inspections. In the first annual report of the Wage and Hour Division (1939), Administrator Harold J. Jacobs stated:

The Administrator has proceeded on the assumption that the Division should work toward a sustained program of inspecting on a systematic basis the establishments of all employers subject to the provisions of the act. Experience in the enforcement of other labor laws has demonstrated the necessity for such procedure. The goal of the Division is to make annual routine inspection of each covered employer. This goal probably will not be achieved for several years, but it is one which, in fairness to both employers and employees, should not be put in the too distant future.

In 1946, Wage and Hour Administrator L. Metcalfe Walling reported:

It has been conservatively estimated that there are currently about 550,000 establishments with employees subject to the Fair Labor Standards Act, with a total of nearly 20,000,000 covered employees . . . most of the establishments which are inspected are found to be in violation of the major provisions of the Fair Labor Standards Act and Public Contracts Act. Nevertheless, because of budgetary limitations, the Divisions must attempt to obtain compliance in all of these 550,000 covered establishments through inspections of only 45,000, or 8 per cent, of them each year.[51]

[51] U. S. Department of Labor, Wage and Hour and Public Contracts Division, *Annual Report* (Washington, D. C.: U. S. Government Printing Office, 1946), p. 24.

TABLE 16.4

Investigations Under Fair Labor Standards Act and Public Contracts Act (Non-agricultural Establishments)

Fiscal Year	Total Establishments Investigated	Number of Employees Subject to Acts	Percentage Employees Underpaid	Total Amount Underpaid (min. wage & overtime)	Average Amount Under-payment per Employee	Restitution Agreed to or Ordered		
						Percentage of Underpaid Employees	Average Amount per Employee	Percentage of Under-payments Restored
1951	31,899	1,569,866	8.9	$11,202,561	80.57	68.8	69.74	59.5
1952	39,109	2,125,103	9.8	15,663,912	75.27	69.6	58.48	54.0
1953	38,649	2,092,933	9.2	16,652,697	86.23	59.4	72.16	49.7
1954	39,430	2,019,649	7.0	13,744,248	97.44	60.2	76.26	47.1
1955	39,330	1,962,278	6.6	12,151,077	94.37	63.2	75.80	50.7
1956	33,148	1,581,641	7.1	11,085,952	98.36	66.3	80.95	54.6
1957	48,482	2,296,913	7.9	18,834,134	103.54	60.7	83.45	48.9
1958	53,796	1,910,127	8.7	19,655,299	118.05	70.1	93.79	55.7
1959	54,916	1,630,261	10.9	22,403,116	125.93	69.7	103.88	57.5
1960	45,729	1,441,679	13.0	28,033,314	149.91	63.8	116.40	49.6
1961	44,268	1,362,145	14.8	30,942,531	153.33	60.4	118.74	46.8
1962	44,115	1,469,025	14.5	34,004,338	159.94	64.2	118.45	47.8
1963	54,331	1,889,570	16.5	49,110,626	157.19	56.4	114.43	41.1
1964	56,370	1,710,850	21.3	59,709,484	163.95	51.9	120.25	38.1

Source: U. S. Department of Labor, *Annual Report, 1964* (Washington, D. C.: U. S. Government Printing Office, 1964), p. 193, and earlier reports.

In 1955, when an estimated 800,000 establishments were covered by the law, Administrator Newell Brown disclosed that inspections reached 39,300 establishments, or just under 5 per cent of those covered. In 1960, the Department was still able to investigate less than 5 per cent of the firms subject to the Act, a total estimated at 1 million (before passage of the 1961 coverage extensions).

In 1963, the investigation program was expanded somewhat in an attempt to insure more effective enforcement of the enlarged coverage of the Act and, though the number of investigations rose from 44,000 to 54,000, the percentage of firms investigated was still very low.[52]

Violations. A great many firms which are covered by the Fair Labor Standards Act operate in violation of its provisions. Table 16.4 (which presents data for the Fair Labor Standards Act and the Public Contracts Act) indicates just how extensive this problem is. The proportion of investigated establishments found to be in violation of the minimum wage and overtime provisions is about the same today as it was in 1939—an astonishing figure of 50 per cent. Child labor violations, which are not reported in the table, are increasing. In 1964, disclosures of illegal employment of minors in industry and agriculture were the highest in the 25-year history of the Act—more than 13,000 minors in industry and 8,000 on farms during school hours were found employed in violation of the Act.

Wage and Hour officials have always stressed the fact that a large majority of these violations are not intentional. Whether or not they are intentional, however, violations of the standards of the Act deny full protection of the law to employees and indicate how strongly additional inspection and enforcement are needed to bring working standards up to the requirements of the law.

Furthermore, whether the violations are intentional or not, much of the unpaid wage bill remains unpaid as Table 16.4 points out. In the last calendar year reported, for example, violations were found to the extent of $59.7 million unpaid wages and overtime compensation for 364,200 employees. At the end of the year, $27 million of the $59.7 million due had not been repaid.[53] Moreover, as the table indicates, the violations are increasing from year to year in number of employees affected and amount underpaid, and the percentage restored is dropping steadily.

Officials, prior to the 1961 amendments, had been hampered in their efforts to enforce restitution by the requirement that the employee authorize a court proceeding. The Department had found them very reluc-

[52] U. S. Department of Labor, *52nd Annual Report, 1964* (Washington, D. C.: U. S. Government Printing Office, 1966), pp. 175–92.

[53] *Ibid.*, p. 193.

tant to do so, especially in periods of recession. Therefore in 1961, the Department requested and received statutory authority to bring proceedings for restitution of unpaid wages without an employee complaint.

Some Special Problems

Experience under the Act reveals that some of its standards, though clear in definition, present important policy problems when interpreted in specific situations. For example, the requirement that employees covered by the law must be paid overtime pay for all hours worked in excess of forty, at the rate of one and one-half times their regular rate of pay, has produced a series of complicated issues which revolve about the questions: What are "hours worked," and what is "the regular rate of pay"?

Hours Worked. According to the Act, to "employ" means, in part, "to suffer or permit to work." Thus, "hours worked" include not only time an employee is *required* to be on duty, but also time he is *permitted* to be on duty, whether required or not. Two types of questions have arisen: Should "hours worked" include (1) idle time when, say, men are awaiting orders, and (2) time spent by employees getting ready for work, such as underground miners walking between the portals of the mine and the working face at the beginning and the end of each day? The United States Supreme Court held [54] that "hours worked" should include both these instances, and the latter decision gave rise to the important "portal-to-portal" pay problem.

It appears that portal-to-portal pay began during the period of wage stabilization as a "fringe" item won by the United Mine Workers. It was soon adopted in slaughterhouses, bakeries, and powder plants, and employees were being paid for time spent changing uniforms, obtaining tools and materials and traveling to work areas, in addition to regular working time. When the United States Supreme Court held [55] in 1946 that such activities were "hours worked" and refused later to rehear the case, the legal basis for portal-to-portal pay could no longer be questioned.

Employee lawsuits for back pay at overtime rates were instituted against employers in several areas, and management became genuinely alarmed when the United Automobile Workers (CIO) talked of suits against all automobile companies. The United Steel Workers also threatened suit for several hundred million dollars against steel companies.[56]

[54] *Skidmore v. Swift and Co.*, 323 U. S. 134 (1944); and *Tennessee Coal, Iron and R.R. Co. v. Muscoda Local*, 321 U. S. 590 (1944).
[55] *Anderson v. Mt. Clemens Pottery Co.*, 328 U. S. 680 (1946).
[56] *Business Week*, November 23, 1946, pp. 102–06.

In 1947, Congress enacted the Portal-to-Portal Act designed to curtail the basis for portal-to-portal pay claims. The law, which was amended slightly in the 1949 Fair Labor Standards Act changes, was passed on the grounds that the Court holdings in this issue went beyond the intentions of the Act. The Portal-to-Portal Act stated that time spent in preliminary or postliminary activities or in travel to the work site cannot be considered as "hours worked" unless payment for these activities is the custom of the industry or is expressly agreed to in a collective agreement.

Regular Rate of Pay. If a covered employee regularly works a forty-hour week at a wage rate of $2 an hour, and one week works, say, five additional hours on Saturday, his weekly pay is easily established at $95.[57] Suppose, however, that a worker is employed under a union agreement that specifies that work from 8:00 A.M. to 5:00 P.M. Monday through Friday and from 8:00 A.M. to noon on Saturday is to be paid at the "regular rate" of $2 an hour, but that work outside of these hours shall be paid at the "overtime" rate of one and one-half times the "regular rate," and he works thirty hours at the "regular rate," and fifteen hours at the "overtime rate." Should his weekly pay be $105 or $110.70? [58]

Overtime on Overtime. This was essentially the issue that arose between New York longshoremen and stevedoring companies, and which culminated in the famous Overtime-on-Overtime case.[59] In 1938 the Wage and Hour Administrator had ruled that premium payments under contracts could be credited toward the overtime required by the Act. But in the *Bay Ridge* case, the United States Supreme Court upset this position, holding that such premium pay for work outside of "regular hours" was not genuine overtime as required by law and, therefore, that such premium rates would have to be included in calculating the "regular rate" on which the overtime was based. It held that in order to compute overtime, the total weekly compensation must be divided by the number of hours worked. Therefore, in the above example the employee was owed $5.70.

Interestingly, the International Longshoremen's Association joined employer and government lawyers to oppose the workers' claims in this case, fearing that the union would lose an advantageous contract clause. And immediately after the decision, a House subcommittee began work on a measure that would exempt employers from its effects. With the backing of employers (who, with good reason, were fearful of an avalanche of suits for back pay), trade unions, and the Wage and Hour Division, Congress enacted on July 20, 1949, the "overtime-on-overtime"

57 [(40 × $2.00) + (5 × $3.00)].
58 [(30 × $2.00) + (15 × $3.00)] or [(40 × $2.33) + (5 × $3.50)].
59 *Bay Ridge Operating Co. v. Aaron,* 334 U. S. 446 (1948).

law which permitted premium pay of 150 per cent to be excluded from the computation of regular rates. The 1949 amendments to the Fair Labor Standards Act expanded the overtime-on-overtime law—actually they repealed it and reenacted it in a broader form. The amendments forbade claims for overtime-on-overtime and permitted employers to include as overtime, premium pay for work outside the regular workday or workweek, if the premium is fixed by employment contract and is 150 per cent of the "regular rate" on other days.

Belo Plans. When the Fair Labor Standards Act was passed in 1938, some employers—particularly those whose employees worked irregular hours—sought to make pay arrangements which would permit them to pay the same weekly wage as before the Act, despite its overtime requirements. The arrangement of the A. H. Belo Corporation, Texas newspaper publishers, for a fixed hourly rate, time and one-half for hours over forty-four, and a weekly guarantee of $40 was challenged by the Wage and Hour Administrator. The Administrator contended that the $40 weekly minimum and the 67 cents an hour in the pay arrangement were inconsistent; that the weekly $40 guarantee was the only real weekly rate and that the "regular rate" of pay should be $40 divided by the number of hours worked each week. The United States Supreme Court disagreed with this interpretation and held [60] that since the plan specified a basic hourly rate and time and one-half for overtime and was mutually satisfactory to the contracting parties, it carried out the intention of Congress. Thus, "Belo plans" gained official status.

While Belo plans were especially attractive to employers whose employees had to work irregular hours, they provided an opportunity for abuse, and the United States Supreme Court struck down several purported Belo-type plans on the grounds that they were defeating the purposes of the Act.[61]

It became uncertain whether or not Belo-type plans were lawful. In the 1949 amendments, Belo plans were specifically authorized, but were limited to prevent possible abuse. Today an employee whose work requires irregular or fluctuating hours may be paid a regular weekly amount. But these contracts for a regular weekly wage must offer: (1) a wage equal to or better than the minimum wage; (2) time and one-half for all hours over forty; and (3) the guarantee must be limited to sixty hours.

Guaranteed Pay Plans. It will be recalled that in the original Act, union-negotiated annual pay plans had to provide an annual guarantee, but not in excess of 2,080 hours of work in fifty-two weeks to gain the overtime exemption. This rigid requirement was relaxed somewhat in the new 1949 law in the hope that it would make such plans more at-

[60] *Walling v. A. H. Belo Corp.,* 316 U. S. 624 (1942).
[61] See Riesenfeld and Maxwell, *op. cit.,* pp. 646–56.

tractive to employers. Under the amended law, employers may now work employees up to an absolute limit of 2,240 hours without losing the exemption. Time worked during the hours of added flexibility (between 2,080 hours and 2,240 hours) simply requires overtime for hours worked beyond 2,080. Similarly, the twenty-six-week guarantee has a more flexible ceiling—1,040 hours rather than 1,000 hours. However, an annual guarantee plan must provide at least 1,840 hours of employment in order to qualify for eligibility; this is the minimum figure allowed.

OTHER FEDERAL STANDARDS LAWS

Two additional federal measures regulate labor standards, and although their coverage is much smaller than that of the Fair Labor Standards Act, they are nonetheless important in their particular fields. The Davis-Bacon Act of 1931 (amended in 1936) and the Walsh-Healey Act of 1936 regulate firms doing business with the government; and both laws provide the means by which the government's purchasing policies can be used as leverage to protect labor standards.

The Davis-Bacon Act

This law applies to federal public works contracts—government construction projects (construction, alteration, and repair) which exceed $2,000. The law declares that it is government policy to pay to "mechanics and laborers employed directly upon the site of the work" the prevailing minimum wage rates for such work. Since construction work is performed at specific sites, the relevant prevailing wage rates are typically those of the local building trades in individual towns, sites, or civil subdivisions that are affected. By setting a wage floor, the law seeks to achieve two purposes: (1) to protect labor standards, and (2) to prevent unfair competition for government business by contractors who obtain such business by paying low wages.

The prevailing wage for a locality is determined by the Secretary of Labor in accordance with procedures outlined in the Act. Interested persons may obtain the prevailing wage rates for given localities at given times from the United States Department of Labor. A prevailing wage determination, however, does not necessarily mean that labor will be available at that rate. Thus in one case [62] when a contractor had to pay above the "prevailing wage" set by the Secretary of Labor, he was not entitled to recover the difference from the government. In 1964, the Act was amended to include prevailing fringe benefits as part of the required "prevailing wage."

[62] See *Monthly Labor Review*, LXXVII, No. 5 (May, 1954), 558–59.

The law is enforceable by termination of contract, by blacklisting the violators from government business, or by withholding amounts due.

The Walsh-Healey Act

Labor standards protection of the Walsh-Healey Act covers employees of firms ("regular dealers" or "manufacturers") supplying the federal government with new or used materials in amounts exceeding $10,000. It applies to manufacturing, assembling, and handling.

Executives, administrators, professional workers, office, custodial, and maintenance workers, as well as agricultural workers and farm producers are exempt from coverage. For covered firms, the law stipulates standards in five areas: it prohibits child labor (males under sixteen and females under eighteen cannot be employed); it prohibits prison labor; it specifies certain safety and health standards; it sets minimum wages as specified by the Secretary of Labor; and it requires overtime at the rate of one and one-half times the basic rate for more than eight hours a day or forty hours per week.

Administration of the law is assigned to the Wage and Hour and Public Contracts Division. Among the tasks of administration are the granting of exemptions, making final decisions on violations, rulings and interpretations, determining questions of who is a "manufacturer" or "regular dealer." The task of determining minimum wages is the most important of the provisions of the law.

The law provides that ". . . all persons . . . will be paid . . . not less than the minimum wages determined by the Secretary of Labor to be the prevailing minimum wages for persons employed in similar work or in the particular or similar industries or groups of industries currently operating in the locality in which the materials are to be manufactured."

These minimum wages are set after investigation of the industry, consultation with industry and labor officials, and public hearings. In many cases such hearings produce substantial agreement and the rate is agreed upon. The minimum wage determinations of the Secretary of Labor are published in the annual reports of the Director of the Wage and Hour and Public Contracts Division. They show the industry covered, the date of the ruling, the rate, and the employees covered.[63]

In setting the minimum wage, the Secretary has taken the position that in industries like cement and steel where long-distance shipment is too expensive, the government may permit different minimum wage rates for different localities without doing damage to one of the major goals

[63] U. S. Department of Labor, Wage and Hour and Public Contracts Division, *Annual Report* (Washington, D. C.: U. S. Government Printing Office, 1953), pp. 66–69.

of the Act—namely, the prevention of unfair competition for government business by business firms who get the contracts because they pay lower wages than do competitors.

In industries where distribution costs are smaller and where slight labor cost differentials may make considerable differences in the ability to win contracts, the Secretary has sought to prevent wage differences between localities. This has meant the protection of unionized and high-wage bidders in some cases. It was impossible to appeal the Secretary's ruling until 1952, when the law was amended to permit such appeals to the Courts. The Walsh-Healey Act promptly received its most important challenge since its enactment on the question of what, precisely, is a "locality."

In 1953, the Secretary of Labor fixed a $1-an-hour minimum wage for the cotton, silk, and synthetic branches of the textile industry for government contract work. Some 158 textile companies in the South and in the New England areas joined in suit, challenging this action on the grounds that the Walsh-Healey Act gave power to fix wages only for a geographic locality, and therefore could not on an industrywide basis.

On December 1, 1955, the U. S. Court of Appeals ruled in *Mitchell v. Covington Mills* [64] that the federal government has the authority to set minimum wages on a nationwide basis in industries working on government contracts. To do otherwise, said the Court, would "freeze the competitive advantage of concerns that operate in low-wage communities and would in effect offer a reward for moving into such communities." [65] On March 26, 1956, the United States Supreme Court refused to review this decision. Today the power of the Secretary of Labor to set industrywide minimum wages is established.[66] The economic problems in such wage determination are discussed in Chapter 17.

The law is enforceable by government suit for violations and by blacklisting.

SUMMARY

At the time the Fair Labor Standards Act was passed, its comprehensive and far-reaching extension of government authority into working conditions was viewed with some apprehension. For although it was an extension of a century-old state movement for improved labor standards legislation, its child labor and wage and hour provisons set standards well above existing state standards. And subsequent amendments have tended to increase this gap.

[64] Discussed in *Monthly Labor Review*, LXXIX, No. 3 (March, 1956), 325.
[65] *New York Times*, December 2, 1955, p. 6.
[66] *Wall Street Journal*, March 27, 1956, p. 3.

Yet all available data seem to indicate that the Fair Labor Standards Act and its companion legislation—the Davis-Bacon and Walsh-Healey Acts—have had but negligible impact on employment, prices, and profits.

Today there is widespread support for extension of the Fair Labor Standards Act's coverage to groups which are still not protected. The extension of coverage to service employees, begun in 1961 and continued in 1966, was particularly timely, as the number of service employees is increasing much more sharply than the number of industrial workers. It has already surpassed manufacturing and the trend will no doubt continue as technology develops.

Further pressure for raising the minimum wage level may also be expected, if inflationary trends continue. Even the $1.60 minimum results in an annual income far less than that estimated by the Bureau of Labor Statistics as necessary for a modest level of living.

SUGGESTIONS FOR ADDITIONAL READING

BUREAU OF NATIONAL AFFAIRS, INC. *The New Wage and Hour Law.* Washington, D. C.: 1961.
A detailed "operating manual" on the Fair Labor Standards Act.
Law and Contemporary Problems, VI, No. 3 (Summer, 1939).
The entire number of this Duke University law publication is devoted to articles interpreting the original Fair Labor Standards Act.
RIESENFELD, STEFAN A., and RICHARD C. MAXWELL. *Modern Social Legislation.* Brooklyn, N. Y.: The Foundation Press, 1950. Pp. 585–655.
A concise discussion of the history of wage and hour regulation, together with a legal presentation of questions of coverage, benefits, and administration of the Fair Labor Standards Act. (Includes 1949 amendments.)
U. S. DEPARTMENT OF LABOR. *Annual Report.* Washington, D. C.: U. S. Government Printing Office, 1965.
The annual reports of the Department include the results of investigation and enforcement of the Fair Labor Standards Act, the Davis-Bacon and Walsh-Healey Acts, as well as regulations and interpretations under these laws.
U. S. DEPARTMENT OF LABOR, WAGE AND HOUR AND PUBLIC CONTRACTS DIVISION. *Results of the Minimum Wage Increase of 1950: Economic Effects in Selected Low-Wage Industries and Establishments.* Washington, D. C.: U. S. Government Printing Office, 1954.
Report of an extensive study of the economic impact of increasing the minimum wage from 40 to 75 cents an hour.
U. S. HOUSE OF REPRESENTATIVES, HEARINGS BEFORE THE COMMITTEE ON EDUCATION AND LABOR, GENERAL SUBCOMMITTEE ON LABOR, 89th Congress, 1st Session. *Minimum Wage-Hour Amendments, 1965.* Washington, D. C.: U. S. Government Printing Office, 1965.
U. S. SENATE, HEARINGS BEFORE THE COMMITTEE ON LABOR AND PUBLIC WELFARE, SUBCOMMITTEE ON LABOR, 87th Congress, 1st Session. *Amendments to the Fair Labor Standards Act.* Washington, D. C.: U. S. Government Printing Office, 1961.

17

Economic Issues in Substandard Conditions

INTRODUCTION

As has been noted in the previous two chapters, the problems of substandard conditions do not exist apart from the day-to-day operations of labor markets. Nor do the remedies, existing or proposed. Rather, problems and remedies are both embedded in a realistic and changing economic and social framework. A summary of the issues involved follows.

First, society expects a certain minimum performance from its economic institutions. Failure to achieve this level of performance may create economic insecurity.

Second, in western capitalistic countries, the marketing mechanism—the labor market—has been the chief economic institution by means of which wages, hours, and working conditions have been "determined."

Third, since at least the early part of the nineteenth century in England, and later in this country, society has felt that the marketing mechanism has malfunctioned in part or at times, and has not always come up to expected levels of performance. In some cases, society also has held that the marketing mechanism was not designed (or expected) to perform in certain ways.

Fourth, two schools of thought exist on the subject of remedies for these problems. The first generally maintains that interferences with the marketing mechanism are undesirable and likely to be self-defeating (that there are, in effect, "economic laws" with which society should not tamper). Those groups opposing minimum wages fall in this category. The second school holds that society can beneficially intervene and can improve substandard conditions, and that such intervention can take the form of various economic security programs.

Fifth, society has (using the United States now as the example) tended to follow the second school of thought, increasingly so in the twentieth century.

And, lastly, our task in this chapter is to look at the way in which society has intervened in substandard conditions and, using the materials developed in the last two chapters, ask the question: What are the economic issues in, and the implications of, intervention as a type of economic security program? We shall analyze three topics, treating them in the following order: working conditions, hours, wages. While common threads run through all three, there are enough differences to warrant separate discussion.

WORKING CONDITIONS: THE SUPPLY OF LABOR, AND THE WORK ENVIRONMENT

Defined rigorously, working conditions involve the work an employee performs and the environment in which it is done. But the term has come to be applied also to *who* may do the work. In turn, government intervention has been of two types. First is the positive regulation of the work environment: requiring that minimal specifications be met. Second is the negative regulation of the work force: deciding what groups will be excluded from labor force participation and under what circumstances.

Regulation of Labor Supply

The latter topic, "regulation of the labor force," is easier to analyze and we will discuss it first. The basis for this type of regulation is more a matter of social welfare than it is of economics. If society concludes that it is to its best interest to prohibit, say, children under twelve from working at all or children under sixteen from working in mines, the grounds for such a conclusion rest upon concern for the mental, moral, and physical well-being of the young; in effect, for their security.

Such regulation, however, is not directly imposed upon one or more of the "resultants" (wages, hours, working conditions) of the operation of the marketing mechanism. Rather, it is imposed upon one of the causal forces involved in producing these resultants, in this case labor supply. It is doubtful that economists, when speaking about the self-adjusting characteristics of marketing mechanisms, specified any minimum qualifications for labor force participation and hence for labor supplies. The market would adjust to whatever supply existed, but the existing supply was looked upon as a cultural-social datum, rather than as an economic factor. If this were the case, then society might be interested, for reasons noted above, in specifying those individuals and groups who might not be part of the labor supply. As society applied such regulation, it invariably involved curtailing the supply: society was more rigorous than was the market.

The economic effect of this type of intervention expresses itself through a reduction of labor supply which therefore shifts the short-run supply curve to the left, and in so doing increases the price of labor. But in a dynamic economy, such government regulation tends to become intertwined with other economic and social changes. Hence it is doubtful if succeeding generations in the economy are aware of what dimensions the supply curve of labor would have had, had the old system persisted and had society not curtailed labor force participation for certain groups.

The long-run economic effects may, however, be quite different. By such intervention with respect to, say, child labor, the future physical condition of the youth of the nation may be improved and hence the future supply curve of labor may be to the right of what it otherwise might have been.

An analogy from athletics may be appropriate to this whole train of discussion. Disregarding obvious differences, both athletic games and economic pursuits are played under a framework of rules. In the interest of the participants in the game (players, schools, clubs) rules may be imposed and may be changed. Moreover, institution of, and changes in, rules may occur in both the areas discussed in the opening paragraph on working condtions. Thus the athletic "labor supply" may be regulated, as in cases where freshmen are prohibited from engaging in varsity competition. Or the "working environment" itself may be subject to rules and rules change. In football, for example, the flying wedge was abolished in the interest of reducing the number of injuries and deaths. So in economic games, the rules may be changed in what society deems is in its best interest.

Interestingly enough, opposition to government intervention of this type has not been entirely a matter of the economics of short-run increases in costs. Legal and social considerations also have been important. Although these latter arguments may have merely masked a real concern over costs, employers and others often have contended strongly that denial of freedom of contract was at the root of their opposition. Likewise there were oft-repeated moralistic beliefs that "idleness breeds mischief" and that to prevent children and women from working was to put them into the hands of the devil.[1]

[1] For an interesting statement, see William G. Long, "Let's Allow Our Teen-Agers to Work," *Reader's Digest*, LXVIII, No. 405 (January, 1956), 71–74.

Regulation of this type represents the earliest governmental intervention in substandard conditions. In the United States it can be traced back to the first half of the nineteenth century. By now it has become an accepted part of government control of economic activity. And, it is difficult to say that such intervention has detrimental long-run economic implications. There is essentially nothing that can be self-defeating in such regulation. Society has, in the larger interest, simply set up a different framework of rules. Moreover, such intervention may actually be beneficial, in that future labor supplies are more productive than they otherwise would have been.

But, as was noted in Chapter 15 in conjunction with the discussion on protective labor legislation for women, one qualification should be made. All protective labor legislation need not necessarily arise for altruistic social reasons: it may also result from the efforts of various pressure groups to restrict labor-supply competition. Here social rules-making becomes entwined with self-interested "monopolistic" practices. The student should be aware of this in his study of such labor regulation.

Regulation of the Working Environment

Government regulation of the work environment imposes minimum requirements upon the employer. Instead of "negative" behavior, of refraining from hiring child labor, he is obligated to "positive" action, that of maintaining his workplace in accordance with legal specifications. The immediate consequences, those of increased costs, may be the same under both types of regulation, but the routes through which they are reached are different.

The basis for government intervention of this type is the same as that involved in regulating labor supply. The psychological and physical well-being of employees requires certain standards of ventilation, lighting, sanitation, and materials-handling. There is no guarantee that the market will provide such standards. Hence government action may be required to provide the necessary security.

There are several important differences, however, between this case and that previously discussed. Thus, while labor supply is a determinant in market action, the work environment is much more a resultant. As was noted in the last section, it is not necessarily a function of the market to regulate participation in the labor force. But, conversely, the market may both compensate for inherent job differences and regulate the work environment. This the market may do in two ways.

First, it may *regulate*, by "forcing" continuous employer readjustments in the working environment so that it becomes equalized among establishments. For example, if the working conditions of Employer A are substantially below a competitor's, he may have difficulty in retaining his present work force or in attracting new employees. This will "force" a change in the resultant, in Employer A's, and hence, the total working environment.

Second, the market may *compensate* for differences in the inherent characteristics of jobs (including a work environment component) by means of wage differences. If the market does not necessarily *regulate* job content, some economists have held that it *reflects* innate differences in the agreeableness of jobs through differences in wages.[2] Thus the marketing mechanism is at least presumed to be "aware" of job differences.

There are, however, two realistic limitations to the above notions of readjustment. First, wage differentials may not, in fact, compensate for the innate differences in jobs. Certainly penalty rates exist for extra-dirty or hazardous tasks. But economists from Senior's day on have stressed that the market does not always evaluate job differences as one might expect it would.[3] We have commented upon this matter in earlier sections of this book. Second, there is no necessary guarantee that "continuous employer working condition readjustments" will be upward (that they will be improvements). Moreover, even if the adjustment is upward, there is no certainty that the final equilibrium will be at a minimally acceptable level, however this be defined by society.

Social attitudes, and hence actions, have been of two types. First, society has not sought to correct the malfunctioning of the market (where it has malfunctioned) by adjusting wage rates and job content. Wage administration of this type involves incredibly difficult ethical, economic, and administrative problems. It is our judgment that this is not a proper function for the state; we feel that the government should not administratively attempt to set wages so as to reflect innate differences in the agreeability or disagreeability of jobs. Our feeling is that market malfunctioning in this respect would be the lesser of two undesirable states of affairs.

But, second and conversely, the government has in many cases specified minimal work conditions: safety, sanitation, space, ventilation, and comfort requirements such as seating arrangements for female employees. The government, in fact, has acted thus, since the market did not guarantee what society felt were minimally acceptable conditions. The preventive rather than the curative route was followed; society did not accept the view that any type of working environment was satisfactory, provided wage rates (whether set by the market or the government) reflected working condition differences.

    [2] See, for example, Nassau William Senior and his discussion of Adam Smith in *An Outline of the Science of Political Economy* (New York: Farrar and Rinehart, 1939), pp. 200–04.
    [3] See, for example, E. H. Phelps Brown's review of "The Social Foundations of Wage Policy" (by Barbara Wooton) in *Economica,* New Series, XXII (November, 1955), 349–54. See also the discussion in Chapters 7 and 9 of this volume.

In requiring that the employer conform to minimum specifications, the government imposes a "continuous" performance requirement upon him. Such performance customarily involves an increase in expenses, which in turn increases the cost of employing labor. (This is why, for example, an employer may be reluctant to hire women, since the overhead cost of providing minimal working conditions for them may be higher than for men.) Depending upon the ease of substituting other factors of production for labor, there may be a short-run reduction in employment. The long-run impact may be the opposite; the increased well-being of the work force may result in increased productivity more than enough to offset the cost increases. There is a limit, however, to this process; for, no matter how greatly working conditions are improved, the employee's output can only approach a physical maximum.

Under certain conditions in the short run, employment would not be reduced even though, for example, a safety law were enacted. Thus, assume a statute required the employer to install guards upon plant machinery. This involves a fixed cost and does not alter the marginal cost curve of the business enterprise. Hence the level of output is unaffected, as is employment—whether of males or females. It is only when the law is differential in scope (as in requiring certain minimal conditions for female employees, but not for males) and where the employer has an "option" that an employment impact may result. Even here the consequences are by no means certain. Thus, an employer with a skilled female work force would not be likely to replace them with males even if a new working condition law were imposed. Assuming a male force could be assembled, the processes of recruiting, selecting, and training employees are not costless. Numerous variations on this analysis can be worked out.

Even if the employer's long-run costs are increased (assuming not all the burden is passed back to the employee or forward to the consumer), a case still can be made for this social approach. Substandard working conditions are likely to have undesirable mental and physical impacts upon groups in the work force. At a later date it may be necessary for the state to care for these groups: they become an overhead cost to society. Hence it may be not only economical but also more socially desirable to use the preventive rather than the curative approach. The analogy with unemployment and workmen's compensation is clear.

In summary, society demands a certain minimal performance from its economic institutions. If the marketing mechanism, as such an institution, does not meet this performance level (or if it was not designed for such a purpose), intervention by the state may be required. It is hard to see how intervention can be self-defeating in the case of working conditions, for in the long run no one is made worse off, while many may be better off. And even if it could be shown in some way that the output of goods and services was reduced by intervention, it would be a healthy rather than an ailing society that would have the opportunity of consuming them.[4]

HOURS OF WORK

Hours of work, like working conditions, are neither necessarily nor uniquely determined by or with a given wage rate.[5] Hours cannot be changed readily by the unilateral action (or individual bargaining) of individual employees demanding certain hours or working conditions with a given wage rate. Rather, changes are likely to occur as a result of collective action at various levels: the firm, the area, the industry, the economy.

Government intervention on hours has been both preventive and punitive. In the first case, certain classes of employees are prevented (through absolute limits) from working over a given number of hours per given time span. In the second case, the employee may work more than the specified maximum, but only if he is paid penalty rates. Here the first case is the easier to analyze, and we shall examine it first.

Preventive Regulation

The case for preventive regulation is based upon two factors that vary in different situations: (1) the well-being of the employee and/or (2) the well-being and safety of the clientele using the services of the employee. The case involving the well-being of the employee himself is analogous to that discussed in the previous section on working conditions, and it need not be reanalyzed here.

The second situation requires, however, a slightly different type of treatment. Here it is the well-being of the consuming public that is the basis for government intervention. In the rendering of certain services, of which public transportation is the best example, the safety (and the life) of the consumer is entrusted to an employee or an employee group. In rendering the service, the employee must maintain a basic performance level so that the customer is not endangered. Such performance entails a minimum physical well-being which, in turn, requires that "proper" rest be obtained. Conversely, such rest is presumed to be obtainable only if the employee does not work more than a given maximum number of hours in one stretch, or if he has "proper" rest pauses.

---

[4] For a brief but interesting account of the rise of such social regulation in England, see A. P. Usher, *An Introduction to the Industrial History of England* (Boston: Houghton Mifflin Co., 1920), particularly chap. 16, "The Protection of Health and Welfare by the State."

[5] K. W. Rothschild, *The Theory of Wages* (New York: The Macmillan Co., 1954), chap. 4.

Under the pressure of product market competition for business, there is no necessary guarantee that the market will limit maximum hours to this "safe" number, as has been noted in Chapter 15. Hence, society has imposed arbitrary hour restrictions for such groups as locomotive engineers, airline pilots, and bus drivers. While these limits are customarily higher than the actual workday, they may become effective in critical cases. Further, while there are obvious individual differences between employees as to their fatigue "thresholds," society has set down blanket restrictions, in the interest of administrative simplicity.

It is difficult to argue against such regulations. One might be disposed to question the specific maximums in a given case, but the over-all rationality of this approach has been proved by time and experience. In one respect there is no economic basis upon which one can argue. One cannot say that such regulations are self-defeating; there is nothing about which to be self-defeating. One can merely note that society has changed certain phases of market operation, in the interest of the health and safety of the consumer.

Punitive Regulation

Punitive pay regulations had their inception in a lump-of-labor-spread-the-work philosophy. If there was only so much work available at a given time, it was viewed as ethically undesirable to permit some employees to get more than their "share" of it. In the past four decades, an "ethical" share has been most commonly viewed as that done in an eight-hour day or a forty-hour week. If more work than this is available, it should be given to those not receiving their share. To put pressure on the employer to ration out available work, various government regulations require that he pay premium rates (as time-and-one-half) for hours worked over the maximum. This, in turn, would presumably lead him to hire additional help at regular rates and thus to increase employment (and reduce unemployment in the case at hand).

An interesting variant of this thesis was found in the *Economic Report of the President,* January, 1964, in which President Lyndon B. Johnson noted that the regular use of heavy overtime might be unreasonably curtailing job opportunities in some industries and that he intended to ask for legislation authorizing higher overtime penalty rates on an industry-by-industry basis where it could be determined that such rates could create more jobs without unduly raising costs.[6]

[6] See the *Economic Report of the President* (Washington, D. C.: U. S. Government Printing Office, 1964), p. 13; and Sar A. Levitan, *Reducing Worktime as a Means to Combat Unemployment* (Kalamazoo, Mich.: W. E. Upjohn Institute for Employment Research, 1964).

A second basis for punitive wages has become increasingly important, primarily in rates negotiated by employers and unions. This is the "normal life" concept. The employee is presumed to wish to lead a life which, in terms of his work schedule, conforms to the general pattern. Hence, if the employer wishes him to work overtime, or more particularly in this case, Saturdays, Sundays, holidays, or odd hours, the employee should receive premium pay.[7] Here, the emphasis is not upon work-sharing; it is rather on requiring the employer to schedule his work in accord with current work-leisure patterns.

It is difficult to find a basis for judging such punitive wage payments as "self-defeating," although operational complications may result. A number of interesting implications are, however, developed.

First, such requirements reduce employer flexibility in work scheduling. If the business enterprise is on "cost-plus" contracts from a government agency, overtime payments may not be significant. But in competitive situations the opposite may be true, although overtime may indicate a "good" state of business and may more than pay for itself. In the competitive case the employer may try to "cut down" on work done rather than provide overtime, let alone hire extra help. Moreover, there are many situations in which it is more logical to pay overtime than to hire extra help. Hiring and separating additional help is not a cost-free process. Therefore, until the employer is convinced that additional business is permanent, it may be preferable to pay overtime. (Two incidental problems are frequently presented to the employer through the use of overtime. Thus, employees working overtime may find their total take-home cut when overtime is curtailed. They may then press for "maintenance of take-home in the face of a reduction in hours." Again, administering overtime in the plant and "distributing it equitably" is frequently a complicated problem for the employer.)

Second, overtime pay presents problems to the economy-at-large. Thus, in times of full employment when additional output is necessary, it may be forthcoming only at a premium. Such a situation adds fuel to the flames of inflation, or at least makes administrative problems in checking inflation much more difficult.

Third, overtime pay provisions pose interesting questions for wage theory. While overtime pay does not necessarily weaken the logic of marginal productivity theory, it makes for difficulties in its application.[8]

[7] Such premiums are becoming increasingly common.

[8] For an analysis see Richard A. Lester, *Economics of Labor* (New York: The Macmillan Co., 1941), pp. 199–202.

A Note on the Shorter Workweek or Workday

What if the statutory punitive maximum workweek were lowered from forty to, say, thirty hours per week? Under employment conditions of the last fifteen years, no strong views have been expressed that it be undertaken for work-sharing purposes (though it is a method through which adjustments have been suggested for the possible impacts of automation). The general belief exists that we should solve unemployment problems by expanding demand, not by forcing the standard workweek down to, say, 35 hours. This would only redistribute work, not expand it.

If such a decision were made, given recent employment experience, it is likely to be a reflection of public sentiment that gains in productivity should, in part, be realized through a reduction in working hours. It is our belief that such a decision is best made by employees themselves (or employers and unions) rather than by state edict. This is true even though the forces of competition may not lead to the reduction of hours in the same way that they do to increases in real wages.[9] This limitation notwithstanding, we would not be disposed to suggest further governmental intervention. The various problems involving the cultural, economic, and social consequences of such a reduction in hours have been analyzed extensively elsewhere and need not be treated here.[10]

WAGES

Government intervention in substandard wages has been more recent and has provoked more controversy than has either regulation of working conditions or hours. In part, businessmen have joined the controversy because wages have a money dimension easily recognizable, because the impacts of an increase in wages are readily perceived in cost terms, and because wage changes have important economic implications. In part, economists have been much more vocal about the wage question because ethically and logically it is more readily grappled with. Labor leaders, politicians, administrators, and others have contributed to the debate.

Economic analysis on minimum wages falls into three categories: first, arguments against wage setting; second, arguments for wage setting; and third, empirical studies of the impacts of minimum wages. After a brief

[9] See the argument in G. F. Bloom and H. R. Northrup, *Economics of Labor Relations* (5th ed.; Homewood, Ill.: Richard D. Irwin, Inc., 1965), chap. 17.

[10] For a general discussion, see Harry A. Millis and Royal E. Montgomery, *Labor's Progress and Some Basic Problems*, volume I of *Economics of Labor* (New York: McGraw-Hill Book Co., 1938), chap. 9. See also the papers by H. Gregg Lewis and Melvin Reder in *Proceedings* of the Ninth Annual Meeting, Industrial Relations Research Association, 1956, pp. 196–229.

introduction we shall examine each of these categories and then conclude with a number of evaluatory comments.

The Basis for Minimum Wage Setting

In the broadest sense, the basis for setting minimum wages rests upon a belief that the marketing mechanism has malfunctioned. Malfunctioning may occur in two ways which may, but need not necessarily, be connected.

First, the market may not operate in such a way as to provide a "living wage" for those who supply labor services. This failure has important economic and ethical implications: economic in that an institution does not perform optimally; ethical in that the wage earner may be forced into degrading situations of various types. The latter argument is found particularly in the case of minimum wages for women. "Elimination of poverty" is the phrase sometimes used in conjunction with this type of wage-raising legislation.

Second, the employer, deliberately or otherwise, may exploit the worker in the sense of paying him less than "his due." Minimum wage regulation may, therefore, be applied to reduce the degree of employer control in the labor market, and hence to reduce exploitation. In summary, poverty and exploitation are the two major themes most commonly encountered in minimum wage arguments.

The Contemporary Case Against Minimum Wage Regulation

While well-developed positions against minimum wages can be found in the writings of such earlier twentieth-century American economists as John Bates Clark and F. W. Taussig, the most general argumentation has been developed by George J. Stigler.[11]

While aggregative effects of minimum wage setting are considered (particularly by Stigler), the general emphasis of this group of economists is upon the economics of the individual firm. Both competitive and non-competitive cases are analyzed. Two basic assumptions, whether explicitly stated or implicitly introduced, are important for the argumentation. The first is that the firm follows marginal principles in its profit maximizing efforts. The second is that restrictions are placed upon discontinuities in both demand and cost functions.[12]

[11] George J. Stigler, "The Economics of Minimum Wage Legislation," *American Economic Review*, XXXVI, No. 3 (June, 1946), 358–65. See also R. G. Hawtrey, *Cross Purposes in Wage Policy* (New York: David McKay and Co., Inc., 1955), pp. 87–88, 91–95, 124–25.

[12] For an excellent analysis of the application of marginalism in discontinuous cases, see R. L. Bishop, "Cost Discontinuities, Declining Costs, and Marginal Analysis," *American Economic Review*, XXXVIII, No. 4 (September, 1948), 607–17.

Given these assumptions, the argument can be presented simply. We shall use a graphic rather than arithmetic method, but the logic is the same in either case.

Let us take the competitive case first.

Using Figure 17.1, assume the employer purchases his labor in a competitive labor market. In such a case the supply of labor to him will be perfectly elastic, and average outlay (AO) and marginal outlay (MO) will be the same. D is the demand curve for labor (value of the marginal product or marginal value product, whichever is lower). In the case at hand, given a wage of W_1, the employer will hire Q_1 units of labor.

Assume now the state sets a minimum wage of W_2. Under such conditions, employment will decrease from Q_1 to Q_2; this consequence is inevitable in the nature of the situation. Who becomes unemployed? Those who are the less efficient, whose services are less than the minimum wage. Hence, unless one does not view a decrease in employment as undesirable, the imposition of a minimum wage is self-defeating.

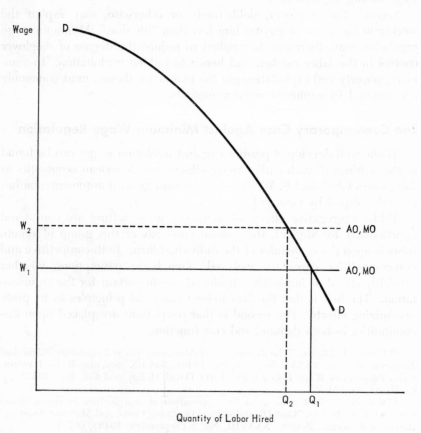

Figure 17.1. Quantity of labor hired in a competitive market.

Is there any way out of this dilemma? A number of alternatives present themselves, all of which are based upon increases in labor productivity to offset the higher wage. First, the workers themselves may become more efficient or work harder. Second, employers may introduce previously unprofitable techniques or they may be "shocked out of lethargy" to become more efficient. (If one assumes a given demand for goods and services, such adjustments may also be self-defeating in that *fewer* workers are needed if they become more efficient.)

It is Stigler's contention, however, that neither of these means is likely to provide much of a counter-force to the unemployment impacts of the minimum wage. He notes in particular that the shock theory seems inapplicable to low-wage-paying industries, where the impact of the regulation is the greatest.

In the case of employer control (monopsony) in the labor market, a skillfully set minimum wage may increase both wages and employment. Figure 17.2 illustrates this.

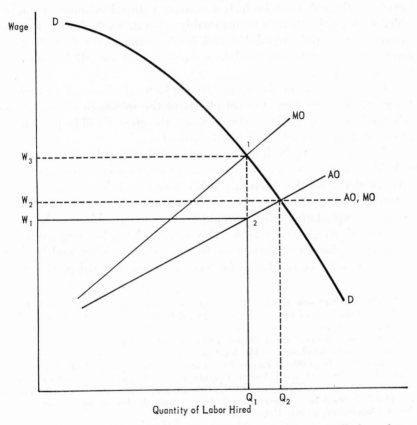

Figure 17.2. Quantity of labor hired in an employer-controlled market.

Under monopsony, the supply curve of labor to the employer is not a horizontal line, but positively sloped. Marginal and average outlays diverge. Using the logic of marginalism, the employer will hire labor to the point where the demand and marginal outlay curves are equated (point one). The wage paid will be W_1 (point two); the employer moves down from the marginal to the average curve.[13]

Assume again that the state sets a minimum wage. The supply curve now becomes a horizontal line for its effective length, and average and marginal outlays again coincide. A minimum, W_2, set just above the going wage would maximize the possible increase in employment. At W_3 the maximum has been reached; up to that point an increase in wages will also result in an increase in employment. At a wage higher than W_3, employment would fall to less than what it was under the non-regulated market.

Stigler is not very optimistic, however, about the possibilities of administratively setting wages so as to achieve the results desired. Because of diversities of conditions among occupations and firms, and because of variations through time, he feels a uniform national minimum is unsuitable. Conversely, there is no reasonably accurate method to derive such demand and supply schedules, and hence administratively setting different rates for different conditions would be an incredibly difficult if not impossible job.[14]

On the question of the aggregate employment effects of a minimum wage, Stigler feels that "the net effects of the minimum wage . . . are adverse." The higher the minimum wage, the greater will be the number of covered workers who will be discharged.

Thus, considering both the economy and the firm, the minimum wage is held to be an undesirable type of state intervention. To reduce poverty, Stigler feels that there are other, more desirable means, such as granting assistance to the poor with regard to their need. To reduce employer exploitation, Stigler would remove the condition of labor immobility which gives rise to it. This can be done, he suggests, by increasing employment information, by vocational training, and by loans to cover moving costs. These, he feels, are more rational procedures to

[13] This involves one species of "exploitation." The student might wish to (1) think about the logic of this variant and (2) ask himself what other types of exploitation might be found.

[14] A "kinky" demand curve creates a discontinuity within which wages may move appreciably with no change in the level of employment. Again, however, there are incredibly difficult problems involved in setting minimum wages in such cases. See Paul M. Sweezy, "Demand Under Conditions of Oligopoly," *Journal of Political Economy*, XLVII, No. 4 (August, 1939), 568–73; and Raymond F. Mikesell, "Oligopoly and the Short-Run Demand for Labor," *Quarterly Journal of Economics*, LV, No. 1 (November, 1940), 166.

achieve the purposes that the minimum wage is not capable of accomplishing.

The Contemporary Case for Minimum Wage Regulation

The leading spokesman against the previously noted position has been Richard A. Lester, whose criticisms have been directed not only against conventional minimum wage doctrines but also against the basic principles of marginalism.[15]

Lester's minimum wage criticisms can be summed up under three major headings: that the economists typified by Stigler have an inadequate understanding of first, labor market operation, including wage determination therein; second, policies and functioning of management in manufacturing concerns; and third, the economic effects of minimum wage fixing as observed in practice.

Labor markets, contends Lester, are not like commodity markets, in large measure because of a complex of job factors, and because psychological, social, and institutional (union) pressures are absent in the latter type of market. Hence, demand, supply, and price considerations are considerably tempered in labor markets. Unlike a reduction in commodity purchases, a reduction in the work force of an employer frequently involves significant costs: separation costs, adverse effects upon morale, transfers, increases in unemployment tax rates. Conversely, a firm may increase its wage level for various non-market reasons. Moreover, in the labor market itself, Lester contends that it is simply not the case that each worker receives the value of his marginal product under competition. Hence, there is frequently a range within which wages can move without any damaging effects. Finally, institutional rules in the labor market (such as seniority) may make it impossible for the employer to separate the least efficient employees if a minimum wage is introduced.

The view on managerial policies and actions is also criticized by Lester. It is his contention that employers do not react to an increase in wages in the way Stigler says they would—namely, through a reduction in labor employed. Lester asks first how a minimum wage is supposed to lead to a curtailed output and the "discharge of a large number of workers." Through increased prices? On the basis of marginalist reasoning, Lester holds this unlikely. Through the substitution of machinery for labor? In the short run there may be fixed coefficients and the possibility of sub-

---

[15] See particularly R. A. Lester, "Shortcomings of Marginal Analysis for Wage-Employment Problems," *American Economic Review,* XXXVI, No. 1 (March, 1946), 63–82; and "Marginalism and Labor Markets" (including rejoinders by Fritz Machlup and G. J. Stigler), *American Economic Review,* XXXVII, No. 1 (March, 1947), 135–57.

stitution is small. Through cutbacks in production? But costs increase in the general case under such conditions, and if a firm is wedded to a given sales volume, this is unlikely. Conversely, Lester holds that "better management" is an adjustment technique that has been widely used to counteract increased wage scales due to unionism or governmental intervention.

Finally, Lester contends that the empirical evidence simply does not substantiate the position of these economists. As we shall discuss this in detail in the next section, it is not necessary to enlarge upon the matter here.

In summary, Lester contends that "marginalism has become suspect" for both pecuniary and non-pecuniary reasons. Therefore, its applicability to minimum wage issues is also suspect, and on this basis Lester contends that it should not be used as a tool to assess the impact of government intervention in substantial wage conditions.

Empirical Studies of the Impacts of Minimum Wages

A number of studies have sought to assess the impacts of minimum wages. These studies fall into three classes relating to (1) state minimums for women for periods as early as 1913–14 in Oregon and as late as 1934–35 in Ohio, which studies have been recently re-examined, and more recent laws such as in New York in 1957; (2) experience under the U. S. law, 1938–50, also since re-examined and (3) experience under the U. S. law, 1950 on, broken into three subperiods, 1950–56, post-1956, and post-1961. Let us look at each of these in turn.

State Laws. The conclusions reached in the various original state studies were that the minimum wages as set had little if any effect on employment of women. Not so, says John M. Peterson who argues that the employment effects were relatively adverse.[16] In so doing Peterson also tilts lances with Lester. Peterson concludes that for Oregon retail stores 1913–14, New York power laundries 1933–35, and Ohio dry-cleaning 1934–35, "the limited empirical evidence . . . is consistent with the orthodox hypothesis that employment is inversely related to the wage level."

Lester challenges this in a communication (replied to by Peterson). Lester argues that (1) in some cases the results (unemployment) were not what Peterson claimed them to be, or, more importantly (2) where unemployment increased, factors other than the minimum wage were

---

[16] The basic article to be consulted is John M. Peterson, "Employment Effects of State Minimum Wages for Women: Three Historical Cases Re-examined," *Industrial and Labor Relations Review*, XII, No. 3 (April, 1959), 406–22. This article not only presents Peterson's argument but cites many of the earlier studies.

responsible. More recent research reported on by N. Arnold Tolles tends to uphold the Lester viewpoint.[17]

A still later study analyzes the impact of the New York State retail trade order of 1957, which established a $1.00 an hour minimum for stores in New York City, Nassau, Suffolk, and Westchester counties, and outstate communities with 10,000 or more inhabitants.[18] The previous minimums had been 75, 70, or 65 cents, depending upon location. Two-step increases to $1.00 were instituted for smaller outstate communities.

Three-quarters of the stores in the state were not affected by the order. Approximately one-quarter of one per cent of all retail jobs were lost, at least temporarily; 951 employees were laid off, and 517 were not replaced when they quit. Stores tended to use a variety of other adjustment techniques of a cost-reducing nature, both of a direct payroll nature, and of indirect services such as abolition of free alterations. Withal, however, the direct employment impact was of a very small order.

After reading and rereading the materials and trying to sift the evidence we would conclude that (1) Lester has weakened the Peterson thesis by pointing up the importance of "other causes" but that (2) the thesis is valid. We would hope, given the development of increasingly powerful statistical techniques, that more rigorous appraisals of this problem can be made in the future.

The FLSA, 1938–50. This is the period in which the 40-cent minimum was reached early and then maintained. Some four principal and initial empirical studies were reported for this period, none dating later than 1941–42. Then in 1957 there appeared an article by John M. Peterson in which, as in the previously noted state laws, he re-examined certain of the 1938–50 data.

Let us look at each of these studies.

Harry M. Douty, reporting on the seamless hosiery industry, notes that the establishment of a wage minimum of 32.5 cents an hour had an appreciable effect upon the industry's wage structure. Almost half the workers in the industry were directly affected by the wage order. Yet, Douty concludes that there is no evidence to show that the minimum wage resulted in the dislocation of employment through plant failures.

[17] See "Communications" by Richard A. Lester and John M. Peterson, *Industrial and Labor Relations Review*, XIII, No. 2 (January, 1960), 254–73; N. Arnold Tolles, "The Purposes and Results of U. S. Minimum Wage Laws," *Monthly Labor Review*, LXXXIII, No. 3 (March, 1960), 238–42; and "American Minimum Wage Laws: Their Purposes and Results," *Proceedings* of the Twelfth Annual Meeting, Industrial Relations Research Association, 1959, pp. 116–33.

[18] See "Effects of Minimum Wage on Employment and Business," *Monthly Labor Review*, LXXXVIII, No. 5 (May, 1965), 541–43.

There was some transfer of employment from low-wage to high-wage firms. But available data do not indicate that the total volume of employment was materially affected. Douty is of the opinion that managerial performance was stimulated and improved.[19]

Robert J. Myers and Odis C. Clark reach somewhat similar conclusions for the cotton garment industry.[20] Few displacements resulted from the introduction of the 30-cent and the 32.5-cent minimum rates in the cotton garment industry in 1939 and 1940, and most of the separated workers experienced little hardship in occupational readjustment. (The Myers-Clark analysis focuses upon workers in those firms existent at both the beginning and terminal dates of the study. Hence, the analysis does not reveal anything about possible unemployment arising from firms which went out of business. But within this limitation the inquiry does not indicate any serious unemployment impacts of the minimum wage.)

John F. Moloney holds that the minimum wage has tended toward some reduction in employment in southern industries, but this has been more than offset by a rising volume of production.[21] Moloney further notes that the Act has encouraged better management practices and the installation of labor-saving equipment. He feels, however, that the full impact of the law will not be realized until the volume of production again declines.

Other commentary runs in the same vein as the above. Herbert R. Northrup, in a useful survey article, summarizes the experiences of a number of industries and concludes that minimum wages did not produce the dire results expected, in no small part because of the impact of other employment-increasing forces.[22] Lloyd Reynolds notes that the only large group of workers displaced were several thousand pecan shellers who had been receiving as little as 8 cents per hour, and who were replaced by machinery.[23]

[19] See Harry M. Douty, "Minimum Wage Regulation in the Seamless Hosiery Industry," *Southern Economic Journal*, VIII, No. 11 (October, 1941), 176–90. See also A. F. Hinrichs, "Effects of the 25-Cent Minimum Wage on Employment in the Seamless Hosiery Industry," *Journal of the American Statistical Association*, XXXV, No. 209, Part 1 (March, 1940).

[20] Robert J. Myers and Odis C. Clark, "Effects of a Minimum Wage in the Cotton Garment Industry, 1939–1941," *Monthly Labor Review*, LIV, No. 2 (February, 1942), 318–37.

[21] John F. Moloney, "Some Effects of the Federal Fair Labor Standards Act upon Southern Industry," *Southern Economic Journal*, IX, No. 1 (July, 1942), 15–23.

[22] See Herbert R. Northrup, "Minimum Wages and Employment," *The Conference Board Business Record*, VII, No. 4 (April, 1950), 141–47. Northrup's article contains a useful theoretical summary also.

[23] Lloyd Reynolds, *Labor Economics and Labor Relations* (2d ed.; Englewood Cliffs, N. J.: Prentice-Hall, Inc., 1954), p. 663. In later editions of his book Reynolds omits this material and deals instead with the results of subsequent amendments.

Peterson has re-examined the data in two of the earlier studies—men's cotton garments, and seamless hosiery—and has introduced a new analysis on southern sawmills.[24] Peterson concludes here that a

. . . re-examination of the FLSA minimum-wage experience during 1938–50 in the Southern sawmill, men's cotton garment, and seamless hosiery industries supports the hypothesis that employment changes will be inversely related to wage increases imposed by a minimum among firms in the same industry making similar products.[25]

The FLSA, 1950–56. With the 40-cent minimum all but meaningless after World War II, pressures arose to have it increased. The change was finally made and became effective January 29, 1950, with the minimum increased to 75 cents an hour. A number of studies have been made for this period; again, however, their usefulness is limited by the course of history after June, 1950, and by subsequent "full-employment" and inflationary movements. The period is a small-scale replica of 1938–50.[26] A Department of Labor study summarizes the impacts of the 75-cent minimum thus:

. . . Though causing significant payroll increases, the 75-cent rate had only very minor determinable effects on employment and other non-wage variables in the five low-wage manufacturing industries surveyed. [These included: southern sawmilling, fertilizer, men's dress shirts and nightwear, men's seamless hosiery, wood furniture.] Even within as selected a group of establishments as those with reported adjustment problems, the non-wage consequences of the 75-cent requirement were on the whole not very substantial. *The Korean development undoubtedly helped the affected firms meet their higher wage bills.*[27] [Italics supplied.]

Again Peterson and Lester differ over the validity of these conclusions, taking the particular points of view we would expect.

The FLSA, Post–1956 Experience. In 1959 the U. S. Department of Labor issued an analysis of experiences under the $1 minimum wage.[28] Twelve industries were surveyed and in all but three the findings were

[24] John M. Peterson, "Employment Effects of Minimum Wages, 1938–50," *Journal of Political Economy*, LXV, No. 5 (October, 1957), 412–30.

[25] *Ibid.*, p. 430.

[26] A useful summary of various Department of Labor Studies is found in U. S. Department of Labor, Wage and Hour and Public Contract Divisions, *Results of the Minimum-Wage Increase of 1950: Economic Effects in Selected Low-Wage Industries and Establishments* (Washington, D. C.: U. S. Government Printing Office, 1954).

[27] *Ibid.*, p. 19.

[28] U. S. Department of Labor, Wage and Hour and Public Contracts Division, *Studies of the Economic Effects of the $1 Minimum Wage* (Washington, D. C.: U. S. Government Printing Office, 1959). For a concise summary see H. M. Douty, "Some Effects of the $1.00 Minimum Wage in the United States," *Economica*, New Series, XXVII, No. 106 (May, 1960), 137–47.

such that the Secretary of Labor reported to Congress that the surveys provided evidence of dis-employment apparently related to the increase in the minimum wage to $1.[29]

In 1961 the Congress amended the law.[30] On May 3, both the Senate and House approved a measure which raised the minimum wage to $1.15 an hour in four months after passage, and to $1.25 two years later. Protection was extended for the first time into the retail and service areas, with 3,600,000 additional workers coming under the Act.[31]

It is interesting to note the philosophy of the Eisenhower Administration on minimum wages:

. . . Minimum wage laws do not deal with fundamental causes of low incomes. Accordingly, this condition can be corrected only to a limited extent by such laws. However, as pointed out in the last *Economic Report,* minimum wage laws can assist the comparatively small number of workers who are at the fringes of competitive labor markets.[32]

The FLSA, Post–1961 Experience. Preliminary studies of the impacts of this increase indicate the following. First, two and one-half million employees received wage increases as a consequence of the amended statute. Second, there were no immediately evident employment effects except in retailing and the sawmill industry, both in the South. In the former case, there was an 11 per cent decline in employment in covered retail stores (in non-metropolitan areas) between June 1961 and June 1962, while employment increased in non-covered retailing in the same area. In sawmilling, employment also declined, but this was merely a continuation of a previous pattern, though perhaps accentuated by higher labor costs resulting from the higher minimum wage. Subsequent analyses suggest that a generally rising wage structure tended to wash out whatever impacts might have resulted.

Proposals were introduced in the Congress in 1965 to further raise the minimum; one figure suggested was $1.75. In the hearings on these proposals, evidence was developed to show the possible adverse em-

[29] See Lester and Peterson, "Communications," *op. cit.,* particularly pp. 260–63 and 269–71 for contrary views on these conclusions. There is little doubt that real conceptual differences exist between these two; unfortunately they seize upon diverse bits of evidence to prove their points. Hence it is not easy to weigh the merits of each position.

[30] See *New York Times,* May 4, 1961, p. 1.

[31] For a fascinating account of the thinking which goes into such legislation see House Committee on Education and Labor, 84th Congress, 1st Session, *Proposed Legislation to Increase the Minimum Wage* (Washington, D. C.: U. S. Government Printing Office, 1955). See also the hearings on the 1961 and 1965 legislation.

[32] *Economic Report of the President,* January, 1956 (Washington, D. C.: U. S. Government Printing Office), p. 67. The same philosophy is expressed in subsequent *Reports.*

ployment effects. Since such evidence involved considerable conjecture, and since the proposals were not enacted into law, the problems remain, at the moment, in the realm of speculation.[33]

What conclusions do these studies yield? That the unemployment impact of a minimum is exaggerated and hence not to be feared? Or conversely, that the impact is such as to make intervention self-defeating? Or, that some unemployment results but not enough to destroy the usefulness of substandard condition controls?

Let us try to summarize our answer under a number of major headings.

1. No "valid" test has ever been made of the impacts of a minimum wage. This is true for three reasons. First, such minimums have been imposed during periods of an upward wage drift which largely cancelled the impact. Second, other forces were at work and no statistical appraisal has been made of their influence. Third, so far as we know there has been no specific research framework set up ahead of time designed to test the impacts.

2. We would conclude that the various studies show that some unemployment was associated with the imposition of the various minimums. Note we do not say here that the unemployment was "caused" by the minimum wage.

3. Peterson would conclude that the resulting unemployment (where found) *was* "caused" by the wage control; Lester, that it was not. Peterson would admit other forces were at work, but after cancelling out their possible influence he would hold that the minimum wage did have an impact. His reasoning rests upon the notion of a downward sloping demand curve for labor. Lester would hold that other forces were responsible for such unemployment as developed. His reasoning rests in part upon a belief that management has ways of adjusting to a wage increase other than cutting employment.[34] A careful reading of Lester indicates that he does not deny the possibility that a minimum wage will have some effect but rather: "My position is that, for a number of reasons, the orthodox model (such as accepted by Peterson) lacks good predictive value with a limited zone or range of wage change."[35] Our personal value judgment based upon sifting the evidence is that unem-

[33] For information see *Hearings Before the General Subcommittee on Labor of the Committee on Education and Labor,* House of Representatives, 89th Cong., 1st Sess., on H.R. 8259 (Washington, D. C.: U. S. Government Printing Office, 1965), Parts 1–4. (Minimum Wage-Hour Amendments, 1965.)

[34] For a fuller exposition of his views see his "Economic Adjustments to Changes in Wage Differentials" in G. W. Taylor and F. C. Pierson (eds.), *New Concepts in Wage Determination* (New York: McGraw-Hill Book Co., 1957). For a recent summary of research tending to uphold the Lester position see the previously cited articles by N. Arnold Tolles.

[35] Lester, "Communications," *op. cit.,* p. 254.

ployment did result *from* the minimum but it was less than economic theory indicated could occur.

4. If we assume some unemployment results from a minimum wage, the critical question that has not been raised—let alone answered—is whether or not on balance the gains outweigh the costs. N. Arnold Tolles suggests they do; the "built-in stabilizer" value of minimum wages is significant.[36]

The Social Minimum Wage

A new "variant" of the minimum wage has been developed by Clarence D. Long.[37] This is the "social minimum wage," a "wage below which custom, employer ethics, or law forbids workers to be employed." Long contends that such a wage causes unwanted workers—those whose productivity lags behind—to be priced out of the market. In contrast to a statutory minimum wage, whose impact is sudden and sharp, the social minimum is less obvious and its effects operative over longer periods of time. Moreover, while it may not necessarily cause job separation, it may "prevent" certain classes of workers from obtaining employment.

The impacts of this kind of minimum (if one accepts its existence) are much more difficult to appraise than the statutory minimum, difficult as that is. One appraisal has, however, been undertaken by Richard C. Wilcock and Walter H. Franke.[38] Their data lead them to conclude that the social minimum wage argument is not tenable unless one assumes that labor demand in recent prosperity periods has been adequate and unemployment entirely frictional. Thus, the argument harks back to the "aggregate demand deficiency" discussed in earlier chapters. If one holds—as a majority of economists do—that such a deficiency was basic to the unemployment levels of the period 1960–65, then the social minimum thesis does not hold up.

Whether empirically supportable or not, the Long hypothesis provides an interesting illustration of (1) the economic impacts of an economic security "policy," policy in this sense arising from custom and ethics as well as law, and (2) the fact that economic security approaches, even if "implicit," are not neutral.

---

[36] Tolles, *op. cit.*, p. 242. For a summary on another economy see Karl O. Mann, "The Fair Labor Standards Act and Economic Security in Puerto Rico," in *Proceedings* of the Tenth Annual Meeting, Industrial Relations Research Association, 1957, pp. 122–28.

[37] See "A Theory of Creeping Unemployment and Labor Force Replacement," a paper delivered before the Catholic Economic Association, St. Louis, Missouri, December 27, 1960.

[38] See "Will Economic Growth Solve the Problem of Long-Term Unemployment?" a paper given before the American Economic Association, December 28, 1961.

An Evaluation

We can pull together the minimum wage discussion with the following comments.

First, wages are a cost of production. Other things being equal, an increase in wages increases production costs. Under static conditions, where competition exists, unemployment will result. In the static-imperfect competition case, a skillfully set minimum wage may increase employment.

Second, minimum wages are imposed in a dynamic rather than in a static economy, and one in which imperfect competition is the rule rather than the exception. Four possibilities follow from such conditions.

1. Unemployment need not result if the entrepreneur increases his selling efforts or in other ways tries to market the same amount of goods at higher prices.
2. Conversely, he may try to become more efficient so as to keep costs the same for a given level of production. How much of this activity is undertaken or can be done is an empirical problem about which we have relatively little information. It is our hunch, however, that the possibilities are greater than sometimes visualized.
3. Management reaction to the minimum may develop along directions other than that of the wage-employment axis.
4. However, the possibility of substituting capital for labor is greater over the long run, and this may be a negative offset to the two positive forces noted above.

Third, if society is willing to accept an alteration in the level of returns to the factors of production, minimum wages need not result in unemployment. Thus, if entrepreneurs will accept a reduced rate of profit, the impact of a minimum wage can be absorbed. Here is a case where realistic pressures shift the forces operating in economic markets. Such alterations, if they do occur, are likely to take place only over a longer period of time.

Fourth, the relatively optimistic statements of the last two paragraphs should not be taken to imply that society can act without restraint in setting wage minimums. Far from it. Any attempt to, say, take the economy's "average" wage and make it the minimum would result in serious economic problems. Structural dislocations of many types and price rises would occur that would cancel much of the wage increase. And such minimum wages tend to increase the unemployables by imposing higher standards of employability. One cannot lift oneself economically by this type of bootstrap; minimum wages are neither a substitute for productivity nor a panacea that will produce a utopian wage structure.[39]

Fifth, if the minimum wage approach appears to be restricted in its usefulness in raising the basic wage, it also appears to us to possess limitations as a technique to prevent exploitation in imperfect labor markets, or to raise wages where discontinuities make a wage-range possible. To be done efficiently and justly, such wage setting requires industry-by-industry and firm-by-firm treatment. We would agree with Stigler that there is no "tolerably accurate method" of deriving the demand and supply schedules necessary to fix such a wage. Moreover, even if there were, we would be concerned about the administrative bureaucracy that might become necessary to implement the program. We would feel that trade unionism is a more suitable institution for correcting such malfunctioning along with mechanisms to increase the degree of competition in labor markets.

Finally, if these minimum wage limitations appear, does the mechanism possess any justification as a device of economic policy? Our answer would be, yes, that minimum wage law can "help tidy up the ragged lower edge of the wage structure."[40] Such a ragged lower fringe may exist in a number of circumstances: sweated industries in general, inefficient marginal firms, and the employment of women. What society in effect does is to set up minimum specifications and then tell employers that they must either meet these or go out of business. Is this inhumane treatment? Possibly no more so than the rigors of normal business competition.

Can a minimum wage law be self-defeating if it merely seeks to regulate wages at the fringes? In practice, regulation has lagged behind general wage movements. This in itself has minimized the impact. Moreover, in the case of national minimums, increased economic activity and rising prices have minimized the effects of the 1938, 1950, 1956, and 1961 wage settings (and, we suspect, will minimize any future increase.) As

[39] Some contemporary economic thinking does focus, however, upon the problems and possibilities of changing *basic* wage structures through minimum wage legislation. Thus R. G. Hawtrey notes that minimum wage legislation of the general type aims not only at "correcting lapses of wages below the basic wage but at maintaining or raising the basic wage itself." If such legislation is to be successful, monetary policy must provide the mechanism through which adjustments are made. For a provocative discussion, see Hawtrey, *op. cit.*, pp. 91–96. We are less optimistic about the desirability and possibility of monetary policy accomplishing the required adjustments. We do not feel, however, that this contradicts our position in Chapter 6 of this text, where we hold that monetary and fiscal policy *can* be used to maintain high levels of employment.

[40] This is the philosophy consistently expressed in the *Economic Reports of the President* in the 1950's. For a more critical view on all this see "The Economics of Minimum Wage Laws," in George Leland Bach, *Economics* (Englewood Cliffs, N. J.: Prentice-Hall, Inc., 1960), pp. 594–95.

long as care is exercised in rate setting (so that structural distortion is minimized) and insofar as high levels of economic activity are maintained (not necessarily with rising prices) we would feel that the self-defeating possibilities can be minimized.

Hence, we would feel that the minimum wage mechanism is a useful tool of social policy. But we would not agree with its most enthusiastic adherents in holding that it is one of the (if not the) means for achieving an ideal basic wage. Nor would we agree with its critics who can see naught but disaster flowing from its application.

MINIMUM LABOR STANDARDS AND COMPETITIVE CONDITIONS

Does government intervention in substandard conditions jeopardize the competitive position of the firms, industries, regions, and countries affected? Or, conversely, has it no effect? Or is the answer, "It depends"? Let us return to this problem, to which passing attention has been given in many of the chapters of this volume.

It is a well-established principle, if not a truism, in economic theory and business practice that labor is a factor of production and that whatever affects the costs of hiring that factor affects the allocation of resources and the pricing of produced goods and services.[41] Certainly, government intervention in substandard conditions is a force affecting the cost of labor; it was noted in Chapter 14 that other economic security programs have a similar impact.

As a specific example, do high wages and optimal working conditions impose a competitive disadvantage upon the firm, industry, region, or country that provides them? The answer is *no*, if (1) all participants compete under the same set of rules, and (2) the high wages and optimum conditions *flow out of* high productivity. Here productivity precedes and permits the improvements. Thus an American business enterprise, with much higher wages and fringes than its foreign counterpart, need have little fear of foreign competition, if it is higher productivity which makes the wages possible and which sustains the American competitive position.[42]

But the answer may be *yes*, if the higher wages and optimal working conditions are imposed by government edict (or by collective bargaining) upon a system that may not necessarily be able to "afford" them and if they are imposed unequally among firms, industries, regions, and

[41] The literature here is voluminous. For a good summary, see Edgar M. Hoover, Jr., *The Location of Economic Activity* (New York: McGraw-Hill Book Co., 1948).
[42] We omit here, and subsequently, all the details involved in similarities and differences between interregional and international trade.

countries. A system may be able to "afford" such intervention by the government if the other factors entering into the cost of production—abundant natural resources, cheap power and fuel, nearness to market, economical transportation, low taxes—are sufficient to counter-balance the degree of intervention. It is further true that, even if the government does intervene with undesirable immediate consequences, there will be a long-run return to "equilibrium." But such a balancing movement takes time, and may involve painful readjustments.[43]

Is government intervention likely to be the critical element, or only one of several, in determining competitive positions and in affecting the allocation of resources and the pricing of goods and services? The answer depends upon both the degree of intervention and the area in which it occurs. As we have emphasized throughout this book, social insurance programs are likely to be but one of many elements involved. Likewise, the regulation of hours and working conditions is but one of many possibilities, though here intervention may have a more critical impact at times.[44] In the case of wages, the impact may be most pronounced of all. It is "differential" intervention, however, which is important. Interestingly enough, differentiation can arise in two opposing ways. Thus, if State A imposes regulations and B does not, such intervention may work to the detriment of the former. But suppose the federal government imposes a uniform minimum national wage. Though it is "uniform," such a wage minimum yet is differentiating in its impacts; it places a heavier burden upon the low-wage areas, such as the South, and removes one element of competitive advantage from such regions.

All this poses a series of interesting questions, particularly as regards wage regulation. Should nationally set minimum wages, as under the Fair Labor Standards Act, be uniform throughout the country? Or should "regional" minimums be imposed, making exceptions for "low" wage areas? Under the Walsh-Healey Act, which specifies prevailing minimum wages for certain classes of government contracts, should "prevailing" be interpreted on an industry or on a regional basis? [45]

The legislative or judicial answers that have been given to the above questions have had as many political overtones as they have had economic

[43] We are less optimistic here than is R. A. Lester. See his *Economics of Labor* (New York: The Macmillan Co., 1947), chap. 19, "The Economics of Labor Standards." See also his *Labor and Industrial Relations* (New York: The Macmillan Co., 1951), Part III.

[44] Thus it was frequently contended that prohibiting women from working on the third shift in textile mills in Massachusetts placed industry in that state at a competitive disadvantage.

[45] For a discussion of the nature and (from one point of view) the impact of the Walsh-Healey Act, see John V. Van Sickle, *The Walsh-Healey Public Contracts Act*, National Economic Problems Series, No. 445 (New York: American Enterprise Association, Inc., 1952).

ones. Yet it is possible to look at the questions from an economic view-point.

The decision one comes to on these questions is conditioned chiefly by which of two basic sets of assumptions one chooses to accept. Regional differentials may arise from differing natural resources, labor supplies, proximity to markets, and other "inherent" characteristics. *But* they may also arise from all kinds of artificially induced means: plant subsidies, tax concessions, restrictive labor legislation, and the undercutting of other labor standards. Here is a case where the participants do not compete under the same set of rules.[46]

If one views differentials as arising essentially from the first set of causes, then regional variations in minimum wages would be logical. If one views them as developing essentially out of the second set of causes, then a national minimum is the more appropriate.[47] Such a national minimum would tend to counter-balance the artificial inducements.[48] Whether it would also over-balance natural regional advantages would depend in large measure upon where the minimum was set.[49]

In the case of the Fair Labor Standards Act, the minimum wage is national in scope. As such, and even though it is a marginal rather than an average minimum, it impinges more heavily upon the lower-wage South than upon the North. This in turn alters the competitive position of the two areas, presumably offering something of a deterrent to industrial growth in the South, and making it less desirable to shift plants from the North. Can such a minimum be justified? We think yes, if for no

[46] In the above discussion we have extensively utilized the following sources: Seymour E. Harris, *New England Textiles and the New England Economy, Report to the Conference of New England Governors* (Cambridge: February, 1956); *Report on the New England Textile Industry by Committee Appointed by the Conference of New England Governors, 1952* (Cambridge: May, 1953); *Subsidized Industrial Migration: the Luring of Plants to New Locations* (Washington, D. C.: American Federation of Labor, 1955); the previous work cited for John V. Van Sickle; and Gerard D. Reilly, Reuben S. Haslam, and Rudolph Modley, "Threat of the Walsh-Healey Act," *Harvard Business Review*, XXIX, No. 1 (January, 1951), 86–98. See also the *Annual Reports* of the Wage and Hour and Public Contracts Divisions, U. S. Department of Labor.

[47] Ideally, the most "logical" method would be to set the minimums on a regional basis just compensating for the artificially induced means. This is a "sophisticated" sort of neutrality equivalent to the political form which would have us arm nations differentially so as to preserve the balance of strength among them. The incredible administrative difficulties in trying to do this in the wage field are apparent. A case might be made, however, for using industry committees such as was done in the early days of the Fair Labor Standards Act.

[48] In fairness it ought to be said that such a minimum may also subsidize a variety of restrictive union practices. There is little doubt that many such practices promote desirable labor standards. But some may be socially or economically undesirable. The case also highlights the problems involved when a union has organized only a part of an industry; this is true of textiles.

[49] For other argumentation see Bloom and Northrup, *op. cit.,* pp. 552–54, 567–69.

other reason than that it eases the transitional problems faced by a regional economy such as New England, which lost 43 per cent of its textile
employment from 1947 to 1955, in part because of artificial inducements
of other areas.

It is true that such a uniform minimum is a type of internal tariff protecting northern industry. On this basis it might be better not to impose
a national minimum, but to let industry migrate and then to assist, say,
New England by means of subsidies and other measures. Administratively, however, a national minimum is probably a more reasonable way
of achieving the desired result. Therefore, we would conclude that a
case can be made for a national minimum.

In the case of the Walsh-Healey Act, should the "prevailing minimum
wage" be set in terms of industries or localities? The trend has been
increasingly to focus upon the industry rather than upon a series of localities. The Fulbright Amendment of 1952, however, granted judicial
review of prevailing minimum wage determinations and other administrative actions. As a result, a number of determinations made upon an
industry basis have been challenged by affected companies and were
litigated, although by denial of review, the Supreme Court in March,
1956, upheld an industry-wide minimum in cotton, silk, and synthetics.[50]

The Walsh-Healey question is less easily answered, irrespective of the
trend. This is true because the impact of an industry determination is
more pronounced than a national minimum; the former reaches more
completely into many localities than does the latter. As such, there is a
greater possibility of local distortions, *if* the affected firms choose to bid
on government contracts. Again, the results are like the national minimum: northern firms may get a share of government business which they
might find it otherwise hard to secure; southern firms may refrain from
contract bidding.

There are many forces making for wage equalization: the redirection
and relocation of economic activity; industry-wide and pattern collective
bargaining; union policies. Should government action hasten the process?
We would be somewhat less insistent upon industry determinations under
the Walsh-Healey Act because of the possibilities of local distortions. Yet
if various regions undercut what are considered desirable (not "excessive") labor standards, such determinations may serve a useful corrective
purpose. Some of the innocent may get burned along with the non-
innocent; this is probably an unavoidable consequence if various artificial
inducements cannot be reached in other ways.

[50] See *Labor Relations Reporter,* XXXVII, 433–34, and earlier issues for information on company challenges of wage setting in cotton, synthetic, and silk textiles and
for court interpretation. The industry-wide minimum approach has been subsequently upheld.

SUMMARY

We may pull together the threads of thought in this chapter with several concluding observations.

First, the market mechanism does not necessarily or always function so as to provide a minimally acceptable set of rules of the game. Therefore, society may deem it desirable to intervene in what it considers substandard conditions, in an effort to eliminate a source of economic insecurity.

Second, such intervention may serve a variety of useful purposes. But it may have certain self-defeating tendencies, and certainly it is not a process by means of which one can artificially raise oneself by the boot-straps. Improvement at the margin and gradualism are two desirable, if obvious, approaches of economic security programs of this type.

Third, intervention, if imposed on a differential basis by varying regions or states, may change the competitive position of the affected areas, since labor conditions are a factor taken into account in plant location and in the pricing of output. Hence, a "liberal" region may find itself in a dilemma: it would like to raise its labor standards, but it is fearful of doing so if its competing neighbor does not. Complete national regulation is politically unfeasible; hence, the various states must of necessity move modestly in attempting improvements. We have records of states that moved too rapidly, with subsequent local economic difficulties. Persistent education and effort can help materially, however, in gradually improving the level of labor standards. The record is clear on this account.

SUGGESTIONS FOR ADDITIONAL READING

BENEWITZ, MAURICE, and R. E. WEINTRAUB. "Employment Effects of a Local Minimum Wage," *Industrial and Labor Relations Review*, XVII, No. 4 (January, 1964), pp. 276–88.
A theoretical analysis of the possible impacts of a New York City minimum wage (which wage was short-lived).

CHAMBER OF COMMERCE OF THE UNITED STATES. *Economics of Minimum Wage Legislation.* Washington, D. C.: 1955.
A presentation of one point of view on the minimum wage question. Includes comments on economic issues, as well as on matters of coverage under minimum wage acts.

HAWTREY, R. G. *Cross Purposes in Wage Policy.* New York: David McKay Co., Inc., 1955. See particularly pp. 91–96.
This volume should be examined not only for its comments on conventional minimum wage setting, but also for its ideas on changing basic wage structures through legislative means.

MACESICH, G., and C. T. STEWART, JR. "Recent Department of Labor Studies of Minimum Wage Effects," *Southern Economic Journal*, XXVI, No. 3 (April, 1960), pp. 281–90.

An analysis of U. S. Department of Labor minimum wage studies. The authors suggest adverse effects were greater than the studies would lead one to conclude.

MANN, KARL O. "The Fair Labor Standards Act and Economic Security in Puerto Rico," *Proceedings* of the Tenth Annual Meeting, Industrial Relations Research Association, 1957.

An empirical study on the effects of minimum wages in a developing economy.

THOMAS, MAURICE WALTON. *The Early Factory Legislation, A Study in Legislation and Administrative Evolution.* Leigh-on-Sea, Essex: The Thames Bank Publishing Co., Ltd., 1948.

An account of the early development of factory legislation in Great Britain. Particularly helpful in showing how ethics, politics, and other pressures combine with, or temper, economic forces in molding social legislation.

U. S. HOUSE OF REPRESENTATIVES, COMMITTEE ON EDUCATION AND LABOR, 84th Congress, 1st Session. *Hearings on Proposed Legislation to Increase the Minimum Wage.* Washington, D. C.: U. S. Government Printing Office, 1955.

A fascinating study of the way in which the legislative process operates. Useful narrative and statistics. Later Hearings should also be consulted.

18

Some Concluding
Observations

"Want is a needless scandal, due to not taking the trouble to prevent it."   —Lord Beveridge.

"Poverty in the midst of plenty is a paradox that must not go unchallenged."   —John F. Kennedy.

"This nation of abundance can surely afford . . . to assure all citizens of decent living standards regardless of economic reverses or the vicissitudes of human life and health."   —Lyndon B. Johnson.

PUBLIC POLICY TOWARD ECONOMIC SECURITY

The introduction to this book promised not only a description but an evaluation of economic security measures: do they accomplish their purposes; are they soundly structured and administered; do they produce undesirable economic consequences? While these questions have been raised earlier about single programs, in this concluding chapter we will depart from a program-by-program analysis, and look at the aged, the disabled, the unemployed, and the low-wage workers to see how they, as groups, are faring. With the elimination of poverty now accepted as a national goal of social policy in the United States, we must also examine those aspects of poverty that seem to have new dimensions today and explore the effects of our past policies on income redistribution and equality.

617

TABLE 18.1

Public Income Maintenance Program Expenditures and Individuals Receiving Payments

Program	Annual (Fiscal Year) Expenditures [a] (in millions)						
	1934–35	1939–40	1944–45	1949–50	1954–55	1959–60	1964–65
Total expenditures	$3,706.7	$5,172.2	$3,027.2	$9,097.5	$14,992.9	$25,814.2	$36,178.3
Social insurance and related programs	709.1	1,574.1	1,997.5	6,660.0	12,265.2	22,265.0	31,665.6
Old-age, survivors, and disability insurance	—	28.1	266.8	784.1	4,436.3	11,032.3	16,997.4
Railroad Retirement	—	115.7	143.7	304.4	575.6	925.4	1,126.6
Public employee retirement	210.0	254.5	382.8	743.4	1,388.5	2,569.9	4,595.0
Unemployment insurance and employment service	—	570.6	216.7	2,311.5	2,239.4	3,044.8	3,042.0
Veterans' pensions and compensation	390.2	447.8	755.9	2,092.8	2,712.5	3,425.7	4,187.8
Workmen's compensation: net of medical	108.9	157.4	277.1	433.2	627.6	890.6	1,215.0
Temporary disability insurance: net of medical [b]	—	—	5.1	101.1	251.7	376.3	501.8
Public aid	2,997.6	3,598.7	1,030.5	2,438.9	2,729.2	3,549.2	4,512.7
Public assistance, categorical and general: net of medical	624.0	1,124.3	1,028.8	2,438.9	2,729.2	3,549.2	4,501.2
Work programs (including FERA, OEO)	2,373.6	2,474.4	1.7	—	—	—	11.5

Program	Individuals Receiving Cash Payments [c], December (in thousands)						
	1934	1939	1944	1949	1954	1959	1964
Social insurance and related programs							
Old-age, survivors, and disability insurance	—	—	955	2,743	6,887	13,704	19,800
Railroad Retirement	—	139	168	370	586	769	886
Public employee retirement	197	269	343	580	899	1,387	2,075
Unemployment insurance and employment service	—	695	94	2,121	1,586	1,714	1,393
Veterans' pensions and compensation	914	925	1,329	3,314	3,759	4,194	5,053
Public aid							
Public assistance, special types	620	2,739	2,774	4,877	5,065	5,807	7,073
General assistance	5,367	4,675	260	1,337	351	399	778
Work programs (including FERA, OEO)	1,122	3,344					51

[a] Payments to individuals and administrative expenditures. Administrative expenditures under state workmen's compensation laws not included for years before 1950.

[b] Programs in Rhode Island, California, New Jersey, and New York, and for railroad workers. Includes payments under private plans written in compliance with state laws.

[c] Data not available on number of beneficiaries under workmen's compensation and temporary disability insurance.

Source: *Social Security Bulletin,* XXVIII, No. 8 (August, 1965), 6, and XXVIII, No. 10 (October, 1965), 4.

When our present social insurance programs were devised, few could have foreseen our present productivity or the affluence of much of our society; nor could the growing multiplicity and complexity of these and related programs have been predicted. These and other pressures for change have produced a number of new and fertile proposals for meeting the problems of economic security which we will also examine in this chapter.

Growth of Economic Security Programs

It is common to think of our public economic security programs primarily as Depression-born measures designed to meet immediate needs of the times, and to think of them only secondarily as designed to insure against the risk of income interruption. Actually, as we know, social welfare measures began in the colonial period, and although they have been undertaken at all levels of government, they were mainly local programs in their earliest forms. State programs became important in the mid-nineteenth century. Although the Depression shifted emphasis and accelerated federal activity in the field of economic security, it was not the causal force behind the rise of public programs. They arose, as we have seen, as an answer to the problems caused by an industrial society in which an increasing number of persons had to depend for a livelihood upon a wage system, with its inherent hazards beyond the worker's control. All industrial societies have been confronted with the need for programs of economic security and labor protection, and it is helpful in gaining perspective on our own programs to compare them with the experience of other nations.

The Over-all Picture. Table 18.1 shows constantly rising U. S. expenditures for public income maintenance program expenditures, and the number of beneficiaries for every program except public works during the last thirty years. In terms of constant 1965 dollars, the 1965 expenditures are three times those of 1950, four times those of 1935.

Growth of OASDI. The most impressive growth has been that of the OASDI program. In 1943, OASDI expenditures first exceeded those for public aid. Now there are two and one-half times as many recipients under the social insurance program while only 15 years earlier the relationship was reversed with twice as many receiving assistance. This relegation of public assistance to a secondary, supplementary role in public income maintenance has been a major feature of American social insurance policy. As Jerome Pollack has pointed out,[1] just as workmen's

---

[1] "Disability Insurance under Social Security," in Earl F. Cheit and Margaret S. Gordon (eds.), *Occupational Disability and Public Policy* (New York: John Wiley and Sons, Inc., 1963), p. 158.

compensation was divested of its demonstration of fault, social insurance abandoned the demonstration of need. It has grown from a system providing old-age annuities for workers in industry and commerce to a system covering almost all Americans who work for pay, and providing family protection against the risk of income loss from death and permanent disability as well as old-age retirement. On its thirtieth anniversary, it added health insurance protection for persons 65 and over.

Federal-State Contributions. Since the 1930's, state participation in social welfare programs has been strengthened by federal programs administered through states and localities. Today about 71 per cent of expenditures under public programs for social insurance, public aid, and other welfare are contributed by the federal government, and less than 30 per cent by the states and localities. Even if education and health expenditures are included, the federal government now contributes the larger amount, reversing a historic balance in the other direction.

Private–Public Expenditures. Also, showing continuing growth during the last fifteen years, the private employee-benefit plans now represent over 15 per cent of the total expenditure for organized income maintenance and welfare service programs (Table 18.2). In 1950 these

TABLE 18.2

Expenditures from Public and Private Funds for Organized
Income-Maintenance and Welfare Service Programs,
Selected Fiscal Years

(AMOUNTS IN MILLIONS)

Source of Funds	1950	1955	1960	1961	1965 *
Total amount (excluding expenditures for health)	$12,169	$18,602	$32,050	$36,272	$46,758
Public expenditures	10,519	15,857	27,417	31,159	39,698
Social insurance	4,678	9,519	18,839	23,662	27,478
Veterans' programs	2,946	2,908	3,744	4,018	4,674
Public aid	2,445	2,791	3,609	3,855	4,884
Other welfare programs	450	638	1,224	1,409	2,663
Private expenditures	1,650	2,745	4,633	5,113	7,060
Employee-benefit plans	965	1,895	3,545	3,950	5,725
Philanthropy	685	850	1,088	1,163	1,335
Per cent of total:					
Public expenditures	86.4	85.2	85.5	85.9	84.9
Private expenditures	13.6	14.8	14.5	14.1	15.1

* Preliminary estimates. These figures differ from those in Table 18.1 because welfare service programs are included. See source for details.

Source: *Social Security Bulletin*, XXVIII, No. 10 (October, 1965), 15.

private plans accounted for less than 14 per cent of the total expenditures. In 1964–65, private plans paid out $2.9 billion for pensions for retired workers; $1.7 billion for group life insurance; $1.1 billion for temporary sickness benefits or paid sick leave; and $100 million for supplementary unemployment benefits. In addition to the amount shown, private expenditures for health insurance costs amounted to $7.2 billion. The figure shown for philanthropy represents primarily services, such as institutional care, counseling, day care, and some emergency relief.

New Programs. New programs of the Economic Opportunity Act of 1964 which have been initiated as part of the "war on poverty" include the work-experience program (expenditures of $11.5 million in 1964–65), which provides work and training for unemployed parents of dependent children and other needy persons, and is similar to the work relief programs of the 1930's (listed under "public aid" in these tables). Other programs, comprising 20 per cent of the "other welfare" category in Table 18.2, include community action programs ($134 million) providing literacy courses, job training, employment counseling, and homemaker and health services; migrant agricultural employees program ($14.9 million) described in Chapter 15; the Job Corps ($179 million), a youth training program in special residential centers; the Neighborhood Youth Corps ($127.4 million) for work-experience opportunities for unemployed youth in community-work training projects; and finally the Volunteers in Service to America (VISTA), a program for training and subsidizing volunteers for service in programs combating poverty ($2.8 million).

Welfare Priority Still Low. The over-all dollar expenditures for public income maintenance programs are very substantial. But when the aggregate amounts are viewed in the perspective of our expanding economy, as a percentage of gross national product (Table 18.3), the growth appears much less dramatic. Expenditures for social insurance, public aid, veterans' programs and other welfare services were 5.8 per cent of GNP in fiscal year 1934–35; 5.3 in 1949–50 and 6.6 in 1964–65. During the last five years, a period of unexcelled growth, the proportion of GNP spent for welfare remained constant. The massive growth of OASDI represents not only liberalization of the program but, to a greater extent, its maturation, as more insureds become eligible for benefits. Thus, despite the growth of OASDI, the number of recipients of public assistance also continues to climb. Compared with the growth of *state* expenditures for social legislation, especially lagging workmen's compensation, the growth of federal social security legislation has been rapid. Compared with the growth of private employee benefit plans, it has been only moderate. Compared with similar expenditures in other

TABLE 18.3

Civilian Public Social Welfare Expenditures in Relation
to Gross National Product

Fiscal Year	Gross National Product (in billions)	Social Welfare Expenditures as a Per Cent of GNP (excluding education and health expenditures)				
		Total	Social Insurance	Public Aid	Other Welfare Services	Veterans' Programs
1934–35	68.7	5.8	.6	4.4	0.1	.7
1939–40	95.1	5.8	1.3	3.8	.1	.6
1944–45	211.1	1.7	.7	.5	.1	.4
1949–50	263.4	5.3	1.8	.9	.2	2.4
1954–55	379.7	4.8	2.6	.8	.2	1.2
1959–60	495.6	6.0	3.9	.8	.3	1.0
1960–61	506.5	6.6	4.4	.9	.3	1.0
1961–62	541.7	6.7	4.5	.9	.3	1.0
1962–63	574.1	6.7	4.5	.9	.3	1.0
1963–64	608.7	6.5	4.4	.9	.3	.9
1964–65	649.6	6.6	4.3	1.0	.4	.9

Source: *Social Security Bulletin,* XXVIII, No. 10 (October, 1965), 7.

industrialized countries, it has been much less impressive. Table 18.4 presents the relation of social security expenditures to gross national product in 45 countries, based on figures compiled by the International Labor Office.[2] Among the reasons for relatively low United States ranking is that we are the only major nation in the world with no national health service or insurance program, and unlike many other countries, we have no family allowance program. If private benefits, where our nation leads, were taken into account, the picture would be improved, though not as much as one might expect. Harold Wilensky argues persuasively[3] that "the United States is more reluctant than any rich demo-

[2] See *Social Security Bulletin,* XXVIII, No. 6 (June, 1965), 28–32, for full explanation of programs that are included, which differ slightly from those used in computing Table 18.3. See also Margaret S. Gordon, *The Economics of Welfare Policies* (New York: Columbia University Press, 1963), chap. 2.

[3] *Industrial Society and Social Welfare* (New York: The Free Press of Glencoe, 1965), xvi–xvii. Wilensky argues that the problem is not merely that we starve our public sector, but the expenditures we emphasize in our public sector: "How much for improving the technology of missiles, how much for improving techniques of community organization and welfare administration? How much for the further training of scientists and engineers, how much for the staffing of mental hospitals? How much for reaching the moon, how much for reaching the unreached poor? In short, the balance between public and private may be less fateful than the balance between public civilian and public military. Despite heroic economy drives in the defense establishment, despite renewed concern with the quality of American domestic life, our defense budget in 1964 remained about 56 per cent of the total federal budget.

TABLE 18.4

Ratio of Social Security Expenditures to Gross National Product in 45 Countries

Country	1960	Country	1960
Germany (Federal Republic)	16.1	United States	6.3
		Panama	6.2
Czechoslovakia	15.3	Portugal	5.5
Belgium	14.2	Japan	5.2
Luxembourg	14.2	Ceylon	4.5
Austria	14.0	Spain	4.2
France	13.9	South Africa	3.8
New Zealand	13.0	Malagasy Republic	—
Italy	12.7	Cyprus	3.3
Sweden	12.4	Malaya	3.1
Denmark	11.1	Congo (Brazzaville)	—
Netherlands	11.0	Guatemala	3.0
United Kingdom	11.0	Venezuela	2.8
Yugoslavia	11.0	El Salvador	2.2
Norway	10.3	Tanganyika	1.9
Finland	9.6	Upper Volta	—
Ireland	9.4	Viet-Nam	—
Poland	9.0	India	1.4
Canada	8.9	Ghana	1.3
Australia	7.9	Turkey	1.3
Switzerland	7.7	China (Taiwan)	1.2
Iceland	7.2	Philippines	1.1
Israel	7.1	United Arab Republic	—

Source: *Social Security Bulletin*, XXVIII, No. 6 (July, 1965), 30. See the article for detailed explanation (ILO figures).

cratic country to make a welfare effort appropriate to its affluence. Our support of national welfare programs is halting; our administration of services for the less privileged is mean. We move toward the welfare state but we do it with ill grace, carping and complaining all the way." As we examine the specific groups for whom the welfare programs are designed, and see how they are faring, we can better evaluate Wilensky's criticisms.

Inadequacies and Gaps in Public Programs

The Aged. For those persons 65 and over who comprise almost 10 per cent of population of the United States, the overriding economic fact is that their incomes are usually inadequate for even a modest level of

---

So long as we pursue our national interests as a world power, so long as we accent military means in that pursuit, we will lag in the most civilizing of our public expenditures" (p. xi).

TABLE 18.5

Average Payments under Old-Age, Survivors, and Disability Insurance, Unemployment Insurance, and Public Assistance, in December of Selected Years, 1940–64

Program	1964 Dollars				
	1940	1950	1955	1960	1964
Old-age, survivors, and disability insurance:					
Average *monthly* benefit in current-payment status:					
Retired worker	$ 50.10	$ 54.80	$ 72.05	$ 77.55	$ 77.57
Aged widow	44.95	45.65	56.65	60.40	67.85
Widowed mother and two children	104.35	117.30	157.55	196.85	193.90
History of *monthly* old-age benefit of worker retiring in 1940	50.10	51.70	60.05	57.60	55.00
Unemployment insurance (state programs):					
Average *weekly* benefit for total unemployment	24.10	25.95	30.40	35.80	36.81
Public assistance:					
Average *monthly* payment per recipient:					
Old-age assistance	44.90	54.90	62.75	71.70	78.90
Medical Assistance for the Aged	—	—	—	205.05	194.69
Aid to Dependent Children	21.85	26.40	28.35	31.50	33.85
Aid to the Blind	56.25	58.15	67.60	76.60	85.80
Aid to the Permanently and Totally Disabled	—	56.70	65.35	70.85	80.61
General assistance (per case)	53.80	58.25	64.05	75.00	68.60

Source: *Statistical Abstract of the U. S., 1965*, p. 289.

living. Census figures for 1960 showed aged persons living alone to have a median yearly income of $1,055; for a two-person family, $2,530. In 1962 it was estimated that two-fifths, or almost 7 million, of the aged were below the poverty line, despite the fact that six out of every seven received payment under one or more public income-maintenance programs.[4]

Table 18.5, showing the average payments in 1964 under OASDI ($77.57) and old-age assistance ($78.90), helps explain this fact. A 1963 Survey of the Aged showed that the OASDI benefit was virtually the sole source of cash income for nearly one-fifth of the beneficiary couples and for more than one-third of the non-married beneficiaries.

[4] "Social Security Protection after Thirty Years," *Social Security Bulletin*, XXVIII, No. 8 (August, 1965), 9–11. Seventy-seven per cent of the men and 72 per cent of the women 65 and over receive OASDI benefits.

Benefits since 1935 have kept pace with rising living costs but not with the rising productivity of the economy and the consequent rising standard of living of the American worker. Over two million of the eighteen million aged have been forced to resort to public assistance payments. Two-fifths of those on Old-Age Assistance are receiving OASDI payments because their incomes are below the standards of need set by their state, and three-fifths of the new applicants for OAA are already receiving OASDI payments. For many of the aged, the problem of low income is persistent, not temporary, and the OASDI and OAA payments keep them at a level which perpetuates their poverty. The addition of medical benefits under social security in 1965 will certainly improve the economic lot of the aged, and a 7 per cent benefit increase in 1965 brought the average payment in December, 1965, to $83.92; but until the minimum benefits of both programs for the aged are sharply increased,[5] old age will continue to mean economic desperation for many of our elderly citizens.

The Unemployed. Only about half of the unemployed are receiving unemployment insurance benefits. About 40 per cent of the labor force (20 per cent of wage and salary workers) is not covered by the federal-state system, and many of those who are covered cannot meet various qualifying requirements. In addition, there are the long-term unemployed who are without coverage. Since 1958, more than one-fourth of the recipients for every year but one exhausted their benefits. Those who overcome these hurdles receive on the average $36.81 per week. The average weekly benefit has not kept pace, declining from 42 per cent of the average wage in 1939 to approximately 35 per cent in recent years.

The victims of these inadequacies in our unemployment insurance system may attempt to turn in desperation to the public assistance program, but they will find little comfort there. In much of the country, relief is either unavailable or available only on the most meager and humiliating terms. In 17 states, needy families with *employable* parents are not eligible for general assistance; in 1961 Congress extended the program of Aid to Dependent Children to cover needy families with employable parents, but as of December, 1964, only 18 states had adopted this provision and only 67,000 of the unemployed were receiving payments under it. Of course, if there are no minor children, the protection is unavailable.

Thus a large number of the unemployed cannot qualify for any type of public income maintenance payment at all, and benefits that are paid offset less than one-fourth the loss of earnings due to unemployment.

[5] See, for example, proposals of Charles I. Schottland in Margaret S. Gordon (ed.), *Poverty in America* (San Francisco: Chandler Publishing Co., 1965), pp. 238–39.

The Disabled. One of the major risks still inadequately covered by our present programs is that of short-term non-occupational disability. Two-fifths of the nation's private wage and salary workers are without public or private protection, either through insurance or formal sick leave arrangements, against this type of earnings loss. In 1964, benefits paid under public and private cash sickness plans (including sick leave) replaced less than a fifth of the loss, leaving the disabled with an income loss of over $8 billion. Since 1949, no new states have joined the four with temporary disability insurance, and since 1957 there has been little change in the ratio of earnings loss replaced.

Of the 3.3 million persons with long-term disabilities, an estimated 43 per cent were receiving no cash benefits or payments from public income maintenance programs in December, 1964, and very few private programs reach this group. Of those not receiving OASDI disability benefits, roughly 40 per cent worked under OASDI covered employment but failed to meet insured status requirements; 20 per cent failed to meet the definition of disability required; 10 per cent were not covered by OASDI but had worked prior to their disablement; and 30 per cent had no gainful work history. The liberalization of the definition of disability in the 1965 amendments was expected to add about 60,000 disabled to the eligibility list. The average OASDI benefit for disabled workers averaged $91 per month at the end of 1964, with additional benefits for dependents.

Public assistance payments to the permanently and totally disabled and to the blind reached over 670,000 persons in 1964, with lower monthly payments. As in other assistance programs, each state determines the minimum amount needed to live in health and decency, but only a quarter of the states make payments high enough to support the minimum standards they themselves have set (in one or more of the federally aided categories). General assistance is even less adequate.

As far as the occupationally disabled are concerned, Chapters 9 and 10 have pointed out a long series of serious inadequacies. Workmen's compensation covers 17 million fewer workers than are covered by OASDI. Because workmen's compensation is a state program with no strong political group to further its cause, it has lagged seriously in most jurisdictions and as its rehabilitation promise has become greater, the gaps in its relative fulfillment have increased. Arthur Larson points to one of our largest cities where half the compensation recipients have been driven to seek public assistance to bring their benefits up to a subsistence level.[6]

[6] See his "Compensation Reform in the United States," in Cheit and Gordon, *op. cit.*, p. 16.

Nor has a rehabilitation program commensurate with the potential really begun to take shape for the non-occupationally disabled. Herman Somers concludes that the disabled are "likely to remain among the most unfortunate disadvantaged in our population" due in part to a "growing indifference as we become accustomed to living in a labor surplus economy."[7]

The Low-Wage Workers. The President's Council of Economic Advisers estimated in 1963 that the heads of 30 per cent of the families living in poverty were employed all year and another 30 per cent were employed part of the year. Many of these low-wage workers are among the 10 million not covered by the minimum wage provisions of the Fair Labor Standards Act, but the minimum wages set in the Act and even the new minimum wage proposed by the President in 1966 will still result in an income below the poverty level. Most of these low-paid employees work, as we have seen, in hotels and motels, restaurants, laundries, hospitals, agriculture, and domestic service. In restaurants, for example, the average hourly earnings were $1.14; in the South, the figure is 80 cents. One-fourth, or 300,000, earn less than 75 cents an hour.[8]

In New York City, it is estimated that the cost of low wages to the public treasury in the form of welfare payments amounts to over $1 million a month or $13 million a year. In 1964 this involved 7,729 welfare cases who received supplemental assistance because their earnings were less than the welfare budget. In Cook County (Chicago), 3,000 such families received supplemental assistance. In most parts of the country, however, public assistance is not available for these families.

The Profile of Poverty

With these figures in mind, the fact that perhaps 35 to 50 million Americans [9] today live under conditions of poverty will come as no surprise. But when Michael Harrington first published *The Other America* [10] in 1963 and referred to the poor as "invisible," they were in fact hidden in ways that were new to American experience. The flight of the middle class to the suburbs had left the poor largely isolated and

[7] "Poverty and the Disabled," in Gordon, *Poverty in America, op. cit.,* pp. 246, 252.

[8] "The Low Paid Worker," in Louis A. Ferman, Joyce L. Kornbluh, and Alan Haber (eds.), *Poverty in America* (Ann Arbor: University of Michigan Press, 1965), p. 125.

[9] Mollie Orshansky, "Counting the Poor: Another Look at the Poverty Profile," *Social Security Bulletin,* XXVIII, No. 1 (January, 1965), 3–29.

[10] Michael Harrington, *The Other America* (New York: The Macmillan Co., 1963).

out of sight in the cities. The first minority poor in history, as J. K. Galbraith points out, they were also politically invisible, easily ignored by politicians as they were not joiners and were largely unorganized. The growing numbers of aged and disabled among them were not easily seen. Nor today does their clothing or appearance set them apart.

Harrington raised some penetrating questions: Why, despite our expanding economy and our large social welfare expenditures, does one-fifth of the nation remain impoverished? Why isn't the welfare state more helpful to the poor? Why is the drift toward equality in income distribution so slow? Finally, exactly who are the poor today?

To answer the last question first, the poor are not always those we might expect. Although families headed by a woman, for example, are especially vulnerable to the risk of poverty, actually about three-quarters of poor families live in a home with a man at its head. Two-thirds of all the children in poor families also live in such homes. We know many of our aged are impoverished, but almost four-fifths of the poor families are headed by someone *under* 65. Non-white families are three times as likely as white families to be under the poverty line, and the average income of non-white families is only 56 per cent of the average income of the white family, but 70 per cent of poor families are white. Though unemployment looms large in the statistics of poverty, the head of more than one-half of all poor families is currently working.[11]

When the majority of the population was poor, not only was there less stigma attached to the condition, but their very numbers made them politically powerful. As technology advanced, the more skilled moved ahead, but there was still plenty of work for the unskilled. General economic progress was the major factor in the gradual conquest of poverty. But Harrington and Galbraith argue this is no longer true. The poor today, says Harrington, "made the mistake of being born to the wrong parents, in the wrong section of the country, in the wrong industry, or in the wrong racial or ethnic group . . . for reasons beyond their control, they cannot help themselves. All the most decisive factors making for opportunity and advance are against them. They are born going downward and most of them stay down."[12] The easy cases have

[11] See Orshansky, *op. cit.*, for a full discussion of the criteria used to determine poverty—a set of variable income standards depending upon size and location of family, averaging $3,130 for a family of four, $1,540 for an unrelated individual. Using these criteria for 1963, a total of 7.2 million families and 5 million individuals "lacked wherewithal to live at anywhere near a tolerable level." Of the 34½ million persons, 15 million were children, 5 million aged.

[12] Harrington, *op. cit.*, pp. 14–15. James Tobin argues that there may be something to this "backwash" thesis as far as whites are concerned but it definitely does not apply to Negroes, whose economic progress is peculiarly sensitive to general economic growth. "On Improving the Economic Status of the Negro," *Daedalus*, XCIV, No. 4 (Fall, 1965), 879.

been eliminated by prosperity, leaving a hard core beyond the reach of national economic trends.

The social legislation of the 1930's, though stimulated by the mass misery of the Depression, ironically contributed to this process by aiding primarily the rising group and aiding least and isolating further the poor. For example, the coverage gaps in unemployment compensation, temporary disability, workmen's compensation, or the Fair Labor Standards Act [13] largely omit from protection those who need it most. OASDI does not now present coverage problems [14] but benefits alone have never been adequate for subsistence and it is the middle third of the population again who can supplement social security with private benefits. The long-term unemployed, as we have seen, have no protection. As Robert Lampman says, "our system of public income maintenance . . . is aimed more at the problem of income insecurity of the middle class and at blocking returns to poverty than in facilitating exits from poverty for those who have never been out of poverty." [15]

It has been argued that the total effect of all welfare programs on redistributing income in the direction of more equality is negligible; [16] that the largest, OASDI, is the most regressive public program while the most egalitarian, public assistance, is the most starved. Private employee benefits, tied to employment, seniority, and occupational achievement, are the most regressive of all, and foster the illusion that stingy public programs are adequate.[17] Further, employers paying generous fringe benefits resist the expansion of public services.

Income Distribution. Whatever the over-all effect of welfare programs, it is true that in spite of the great changes which have occurred in our economic structure and income and wealth levels, there has been a

[13] Secretary of Labor Willard Wirtz, for example, recently wrote that two-thirds of all white workers come within the present minimum wage coverage of the FLSA, but less than half of all non-white workers are covered.

[14] However, in earlier phases of social security there were coverage problems and higher requirements for insured status which disqualified many of the less fortunate aged and disabled from receiving social security benefits.

[15] Ferman, Kornbluh, and Haber, op. cit., p. 417.

[16] Wilensky, op. cit., pp. xiii–xvi (who cites Gordon and Titmuss). See also Roy Lubove, "Social Work and the Life of the Poor," Nation, CCII, No. 21 (May 23, 1966), 609–11, and Richard M. Titmuss, "The Role of Redistribution in Social Policy," Social Security Bulletin, XXVII, No. 6 (June, 1965), 14–21. Titmuss examines British social security policy and concludes with a plea for extending the welfare state to the poor. Myrdal observes, "In almost all respects . . . American economic and social policies show a perverse tendency to favor groups that are above the level of the most need."

[17] Since most are paid for by untaxed or lightly taxed income, their ultimate cost is borne by the government. Titmuss, e.g., has estimated that private tax-exempt pension schemes cost the British government far more in uncollected taxes than the entire exchequer cost of national pensions.

remarkable stability in over-all distribution of wealth and income. Wealth has remained highly concentrated, with the top 10 per cent of families ranked by wealth holding over 50 per cent of the total and the lowest one-third holding only 1 per cent. In the postwar period the top 10 per cent continued to receive 30 per cent of income and the lowest 10 per cent (whose highest income is $2,000) continued to receive 2 per cent.[18]

THE FUTURE OF ECONOMIC SECURITY SYSTEMS:
I. FORCES FOR CHANGE

Equality and income redistribution are just two of a whole array of new issues that the declaration of war on poverty has introduced into the discussion of economic and social security. If the war on poverty is seriously prosecuted, it will inevitably involve such issues. As we try to chart the course ahead, it might be useful to see what we can learn from the lengthier experience of European nations. Gunnar Myrdal in his book, *Beyond the Welfare State*, makes three relevant points: first, that the need for planning a rational program of economic security is forced on modern nations, arising out of earlier governmental intervention; second, that strong political differences on these questions tend to fade in time; and third, that pressures from the less privileged groups in society for equality and more state intervention tend to increase in a democratic society. These generalizations provide a useful framework within which to evaluate the American experience and we will look at each.

Irrationality Forces Planning

Myrdal identifies a historical trend toward planning, which follows, not precedes, state intervention, and which is found necessary to co-ordinate and rationalize measures growing out of bounds in volume and complexity.

Such attempts at coordination were forced upon the state: when it turned out to have been an illusion that the need for a particular intervention was only temporary; when the acts of intervention proved to have disturbing effects, often far outside the field where they were applied, effects which had not been taken

[18] Robert J. Lampman, "Income Distribution of American Labor," in William Haber (ed.), *Labor in a Changing America* (New York: Basic Books, Inc., 1966), pp. 58–68.

into account at the time the measures had been decided upon; when their lack of compatibility with each other and with other aims and policies of the national community stood out as irrational and damaging; and when they created serious administrative difficulties.[19]

The pressure for a more rational system has a familiar ring to American students of social insurance, who have been increasingly concerned with the mounting complexities, unaccountable effects, incompatible policies, and administrative impasses in what has been called our own "non-system." In earlier chapters, we encountered some of these irrationalities. In the next few pages, we will list a series of them, to illustrate and underscore the need for a new look at the over-all design of our present system.

Multiplicity. We observed that at least seven federal and state social insurance or public assistance programs pay benefits for old age; that at least eight provide survivors' benefits for dependent persons; that at least six alleviate the effects of unemployment due to labor market causes; and that at least a dozen systems pay disability benefits. In the latter case, Jerome Pollack's comments are singularly appropriate:

> Disability has been carved categorically into many camps: according to the extent of disability—permanent versus temporary; according to sponsorship—public versus private and state versus federal; according to origin—occupational versus nonoccupational; and according to program elements—income versus rehabilitation versus medical care. These are essentially spheres of influence caused by the pluralistic development of programs and services and solidified in the course of numerous jurisdictional disputes.
>
> The separation of diagnosis, treatment, temporary income restoration, and permanent income maintenance, and of income maintenance from care and rehabilitation; and the division of responsibility for determining disability from that of maintaining the disabled—all militate against the highly coordinated attack that is essential in dealing more effectively with disabilities of utmost severity.[20]

The identical injury to a railroad worker, a merchant seaman, a longshoreman and a government clerk, for example, is compensated under at least four separate legal systems and involves different concepts and legal issues of liability, as well as varying amounts of compensation. A farmhand and a factory worker receiving the same injury would have to turn for protection to two entirely different remedies in most of the states, with striking variations in the laws governing each of them from state to state.

[19] Gunnar Myrdal, *Beyond the Welfare State* (New Haven: Yale University Press, 1960), p. 22.
[20] Cheit and Gordon, *op. cit.*, p. 184.

The existence of these separate systems is being questioned not only because of the administrative complexities they create but also because the distinctions between them often seem to create more problems than they solve. For example, one of the most difficult problems in workmen's compensation is distinguishing between (compensable) occupational and (non-compensable) non-occupational disability. In heart and radiation cases, among others, it is often actually impossible to distinguish, and the attempt has frequently split the medical profession into opposing camps. But as Pollack points out, once society accepts a liability to insure against disability having nothing to do with employment, the question arises whether the distinction between occupational and non-occupational disability should be maintained. He argues that the distinction has always been programmatic, arbitrary, and, as we have said, in numerous instances indeterminate. Although Margaret Gordon argues the case for maintaining the distinction, she also points out that unless workmen's compensation systems are far more effective in rehabilitating injured workers and restoring them to employment, "the case for their survival as separate systems falls apart." [21]

Overlapping. The faults of multiplicity are compounded by the inevitable overlapping benefits which may occur alongside them. For example, it is possible for the widow of a worker killed on the job to have no recourse but common law or, in many states, a very small benefit payment. At the same time in a different jurisdiction or under different dependency circumstances, it is possible for her benefit payments under the OASDI survivors' program and workmen's compensation to exceed her husband's lost earnings. These overlapping benefits often weaken the benefit structure of the laws. The inadequate widows' benefits in all but thirteen workmen's compensation jurisdictions, for example, are undoubtedly influenced by legislative awareness of the overlap possibilities. But this method of avoiding overlap leaves the many widows who may not be covered by OASDI poorly protected indeed. A proposal has been made to offset survivors' payments under workmen's compensation by the amount of OASDI benefits, at the same time raising widows' benefits to an adequate level, for the duration of widowhood, so that those widows not covered by OASDI will not suffer as they do at present,[22] but no state has taken such action to date.

There are many other examples of overlapping, and some of the programs have sought to avoid the inequities that can arise from dual

[21] *Ibid.*, pp. 162, 422.
[22] Earl F. Cheit, *Injury and Recovery in the Course of Employment* (New York: John Wiley and Sons, Inc., 1961), chap. 5.

payments. The unemployment compensation laws of most jurisdictions and the temporary disability laws have "offset" provisions, and the 1965 social security amendments included an offset when total benefits payable to the disabled worker and his dependents under OASDI and workmen's compensation exceed 80 per cent of his average monthly earnings before the onset of disability, but with the reduction periodically adjusted to take account of changes in national average earnings levels. Although this overlap affected only a tiny fraction of workmen's compensation recipients, a fervor out of all proportion to the size of the problem was organized by employer groups and state administrators to pressure Congress, alleging that the survival of workmen's compensation was threatened by the federal program.[23] Similar problems of overlapping have occurred in connection with private health insurance and have been discussed in Chapter 12. Overlapping, however, is not currently a serious over-all problem, but it underscores the need for a more rational relationship among our various economic security programs.

State-by-State Variations. The variations in benefit payments in all the programs administered by the states make little sense by any standards. But the inconsistencies in compensation of permanent disability are perhaps most puzzling of all. As Jerome Pollack points out in an extreme example, maximum workmen's compensation payments for the loss of a thumb in Wisconsin exceed that for an arm at the shoulder in Arizona, Maine, and Wyoming, or the loss of an entire hand in eleven additional states.[24] These wide and difficult-to-rationalize differences exist in all the state programs. Eligibility standards in all programs differ from state to state. Unemployment insurance pays workers with similar employment histories greatly differing benefits, in amount and duration; and in public assistance, the variations are even more glaring, the average benefits in some states being twice that paid in others.

Two-Class System. Many critics have warned of the widening chasm separating the "first class workers," who have every kind of public social insurance plus numerous private supplementations, from "second class workers," who have none of these except basic social security, if that. Arthur Larson draws a graphic picture of this situation:

Picture two industrial establishments side by side in the same city. Suppose that one is a great factory having 2,000 employees, while next to it is a small

[23] See Somers, in Gordon, *Poverty in America, op. cit.,* pp. 250–51; also Earl F. Cheit, "Workmen's Compensation, OASDI: The Overlap Issue," *Industrial Relations,* III, No. 2 (February, 1964), 63–80.

[24] Jerome Pollack, "A Policy Decision for Workmen's Compensation," *Industrial and Labor Relations Review,* VII, No. 1 (October, 1953), 56.

machine shop having two employees. In a typical state, it is quite conceivable that the worker in the larger factory, if disabled, would draw not only workmen's compensation but a private supplementation under the union contract. On top of this he would probably have various hospital and medical benefits in addition to those provided by the compensation act. If he became economically unemployed, he might draw unemployment insurance and quite possibly supplementary unemployment insurance negotiated under contract. But the worker in the small machine shop doing the same kind of work under the same kind of conditions must, when disabled or unemployed, seek public relief or the poorhouse.

This sort of discrimination is intolerable in our free society. There were many disparities between individuals before the era of social insurance; but what makes the present disparity intolerable is that it has been imposed upon our society, not by ruthless "robber barons," but by the beneficient and remedial ministrations of a governmental social insurance system in a democratic state and by the provisions of private employee-benefit plans.[25]

Floor of Protection. Because of the existence of this layer of private benefits, social insurance benefits have theoretically always been intended to provide only a floor of protection on which additional protection can be built, and have not been extended to meet the full need of beneficiaries. But the theory is far from clear, and the practice is, as we have seen, far from equitable, since social security is often the sole source of assured income. Among the aged, for example, nearly half (47.4 per cent) are supported by OASDI benefits with no income from employment, public assistance, or veterans' benefits. At most, onefourth receive private pensions, and they are often meager.

As for the theory, Pollack attacks its vagueness. It has not been "structured to cover identifiable necessities or to meet a specified percentage of total need. It is a legislative fiction. Benefits in fact have been set according to the political realities of the time." [26]

Another difficulty with the floor-of-protection theory is that it also presupposes an adequate subflooring—the public assistance program, prepared to protect those whose needs are not otherwise met. Here, need alone should be the test of eligibility. But public assistance, as we have seen, is the most inadequate program of all. In spite of all these criticisms, the concept still affords a useful basis for distinguishing between public and private responsibility.

Reverse Incentives in Public Assistance. James Tobin has pointed out that the means test forces recipients out of the labor force or gives them the incentive to withdraw, causing needless waste and demoralization, since a person on public assistance cannot add to his family's standard of living by working. "This application of the means test is bad economics

[25] In Cheit and Gordon, *op. cit.,* p. 25.
[26] *Ibid.,* p. 178.

as well as bad sociology. It is almost as if our present programs of public assistance had been consciously contrived to perpetuate the conditions they are supposed to alleviate." Tobin presses his attack further:

Of course, the means test provides a certain incentive to work in order to get off public assistance altogether. But in many cases, especially where there is only one adult to provide for and take care of several children the adult simply does not have enough time and earning opportunities to get by without financial help. He, or more likely she, is essentially forced to be both idle and on a dole. The means test also involves limitations on property holdings which deprive anyone who is or expects to be on public assistance of incentive to save.

In a society which prizes incentives for work and thrift, these are surprising regulations. They deny the country useful productive services, but that economic loss is minor in the present context. They deprive individuals and families both of work experience which could teach them skills, habits, and self-discipline of future value and of the self-respect and satisfaction which comes from improving their own lot by their own efforts.

Public assistance encourages the disintegration of the family, the key to so many of the economic and social problems of the American Negro. The main assistance program, Aid for Dependent Children, is not available if there is an able-bodied employed male in the house. In most states it is not available if there is an able-bodied man in the house, even if he is not working. All too often it is necessary for the father to leave his children so that they can eat. It is bad enough to provide incentives for idleness but even worse to legislate incentives for desertion.[27]

Reverse Incentives in Workmen's Compensation. Maximum rehabilitation of the injured worker and his restoration to employment should obviously be the two primary (and complementary) goals of workmen's compensation. Yet, as the litigious aspects of the system have developed, the handling of permanent disability cases often frustrates these goals, so that the injured worker does not want to be rehabilitated; the insurance carrier does not want to recognize his claim; the employer does not want to retain the injured worker in his employ.[28] The system is also geared to take little or no cognizance of the actual economic effect of the disability on the injured worker. Thus, a California study found that there was no significant difference between workmen's compensation payments to workers with no permanent wage loss and to those with staggering permanent wage losses.[29]

Coordination of the Poverty Program. Hundreds of new coordination problems have emerged with the development of the poverty program. In mid-1965, 150 separate programs were operating under the aegis of the "war on poverty," and by March, 1966, 600 community action agencies

[27] Tobin, op. cit., p. 890.
[28] See Cheit and Gordon, op. cit., pp. 67–68.
[29] Ibid., p. 76.

in that many cities and counties across the country were attempting to coordinate activities of the Office of Education, the Welfare Administration, the Labor Department, the Agriculture Department, and other old-line agencies on a local level—not to mention local governing bodies, school boards, city housing agencies, local voluntary agencies, and so on. While a degree of communication has sometimes been achieved, significant cooperation and coordination often have not.[30]

Conflicting Economic Goals. In the economic security field, our economic goals are often in conflict with each other or with other desirable social goals. An example is minimum wage legislation. Though society may feel that minimum wages are too low, the possibility of increasing unemployment serves as an effective constraint to raising minimum wages to whatever the socially desired level may be.

Again, it is generally agreed that the single most effective action we could take to improve the economic position of the poor, especially the Negroes, would be to operate the economy with a tight labor market. We know well enough how to create a low rate of unemployment. But we have not stimulated the economy sufficiently because of a fear of inflation and because of its adverse effect on the balance-of-payments problem.

This conflict between price stability and aggregate demand policy underlies the concern in recent years over the question of whether the high unemployment rates of the late 1950's and early 1960's were due to inadequate demand or structural changes in the economy. Even if there have been no significant structural changes (the economy did reduce the unemployment rate to 3.7 per cent by 1966 without suffering significant inflation), the fact that we generally define full employment at a 4 per cent level of unemployment is a reflection of a well-founded belief that we could not achieve the low levels of unemployment of many Western European countries without suffering an "unacceptable rate" of inflation. There is dispute, of course, about which social value should take precedence.[31]

One result of this conflict has been the proliferation of programs designed to increase labor mobility and the skill levels of certain groups in the labor force through such programs as the Manpower Development and Training Act and certain sections of the Economic Opportunity Act. If successfully combined with measures to stimulate aggregate demand these programs help decrease unemployment without any concomitant increase in the price level. Yet, these programs as presently

[30] *Wall Street Journal*, March 1, 1966.
[31] See for example, Tobin, *op. cit.*, pp. 878–98 and Hyman Minsky, "The Role of Employment Policy," in Gordon, *Poverty in America, op. cit.*, pp. 175–201.

structured only reinforce the pattern of gap and overlap outlined above. Especially significant in this respect is the *selective ad hoc* nature of these programs. Undoubtedly, many who could profit from them will be denied the opportunity.

Many other irrationalities, conflicting policy goals of public programs, and examples of administrative blindness could be cited; differential treatment in our tax system undermining welfare objectives and the less favorable treatment accorded children in our public aid programs are two which will be mentioned later. But enough has been said to indicate that the present system is more makeshift than tailormade, that though intricate, it is far from comprehensive, and that the need for rationality which Professor Burns began asserting many years ago is driving more and more students to search for simpler approaches. In the need for coordination and planning which Myrdal cites as characteristic of the evolution of the welfare state in modern industrial society, the United States is no exception.

Political Attitudes Toward Economic Security

A second trend cited by Myrdal, also applicable to the American scene, is that political attitudes toward these issues tend to converge and

> . . . that many divisions of opinion, once of burning importance, now tend to fade away, or to change character and thereby to become much less important. . . . Nobody nowadays gets very excited about the issue of whether or not there should be progressive taxation. The disagreement . . . concerns . . . to what extent and by what devices taxation should be used to influence the distribution of wealth and income. Similarly, the discussion about whether there should be a system of social security has ended. The practical problem is now only how much money should be devoted to this purpose, who should pay it, and how it should be used.[32]

In 1936 social security was branded as a "fraud" and "a cruel hoax" by the Republican Presidential candidate; in 1954 it was called the "cornerstone of the government's program to promote the economic security of the individual" by a Republican president.[33]

In 1956, in the debate over addition of disability benefits to social security, experts testified that "the ultimate cost and waste of a disability program . . . would . . . jeopardize the economic, the psychological and the moral stability or our social order . . ." and "the payment of disability benefits for any length of time, even in modest amounts, undermines human personalities, destroys incentive and the will to seek

[32] Myrdal, *op. cit.*, pp. 72–73.
[33] Arthur J. Altmeyer, *The Formative Years of Social Security* (Madison: University of Wisconsin Press, 1966), p. 263.

work fitted to one's capabilities." But the arguments were met by a Southern Democratic senator who argued that "we want to rely on the tried and tested method of contributory social insurance to meet the major economic hazards of our industrial society." [34] Senator Goldwater, when running for President in 1964, retracted his earlier opposition to social security. Thus, this program is almost universally accepted in America today, but it should be noted that one of the major reasons for its ultimate acceptance by business and conservative groups has been the emphasis on the contributory earnings-related features of the system. OASDI can be viewed as a conservative program, providing a small measure of economic security for selected risks, with a minimum of income redistribution. In fact, one of its major architects, Edwin Witte, explained that it was not designed to "modify the distribution of wealth and it does not alter at all the fundamentals of our capitalistic and individualistic economy." [35]

The difficulty is that if the war on poverty is to be pursued in earnest, it will inevitably involve more serious income redistribution, requiring real changes in the institutions and power relationships of American society. It is far from clear that Americans are prepared to move very rapidly in this direction. There are deep roots of resistance to the idea of the Welfare State. The traditional belief in economic individualism, and the virtues of thrift and self-reliance, fears of the effect of "handouts" on weakening the moral fiber of the people, the fear of increasing power of the state with its threat to individual liberty—all are still an important part of the American ideology.[36] (And concerns about the mixed bless-

[34] Quoted by Pollack in Cheit and Gordon, op. cit., p. 167.
[35] Quoted in Lubove, op. cit., p. 611.
[36] It should be remembered, of course, that state intervention in economic affairs goes far beyond measures to protect individual economic security. In an instructive staff report entitled "Subsidy and Subsidylike Programs of the U. S. Government," the Joint Economic Committee of Congress in 1960 sought to determine the scope and amounts of government subsidies. It found that subsidy payments to labor are less than one-fourth those made to business, or to agriculture. (Joint Economic Committee, 86th Congress, 2d Session, "Subsidy and Subsidylike Programs of the U. S. Government," 1960.)

In an earlier survey entitled "The Spreading of State Welfare," Fortune magazine (February, 1952) sought to trace the extent of "government welfare." It reported that "the endlessly staggering fact about the United States government . . . is the number of things it has a policy about. . . ." Admittedly, definitions of welfare or welfare state are in large measure a function of political disposition, but no matter what views one holds, the vast array of state services to business organizations cannot be ignored when questions of state interference in economic affairs are raised. Fortune listed twenty-eight federal departments and agencies which ". . . render services of distinct benefit to business, exclusive of contracts (for example, munitions) or business generated by foreign aid." These services range from ". . . stocking inshore ocean beds with young lobsters . . . [to] . . . furnishing isotopes."

ings of government interference into private lives are not limited to "conservative" circles.) Further, the growing middle class, with its rising living standards, has not evinced great concern for the less successful. On the contrary, they are more concerned with getting ahead themselves [37] and have often been receptive to the cries of "welfare scandals" and "welfare chiseling" that are favorite themes in mass circulation magazines.[38] But, in addition, certain groups obviously have a stake in preventing broader programs which go beyond their political philosophy. Many private insurance carriers, for example, would resist moves to make the government an insurer of risks they now insure. State and local governments would not yield their pivotal positions in administering the present system without a struggle. Many trade unionists would resist a national program of income maintenance because of the threat it would pose to their role in collective bargaining.

Nevertheless, old views are changing. The passage of medical care for the aged signaled also the passing of an historically effective lobby opposing change. Another example is the 1966 Report of the National Commission on Technology, Automation, and Economic Progress, established by the Congress with broad representation from business, labor, and academic life. It unanimously recommended both a basic annual income for every family in the United States (discussed later in this chapter) and that the government become "an employer of last resort" for people who cannot find jobs elsewhere. Rather compelling confirmation of the changing attitudes comes from a *Wall Street Journal* editorial attacking the National Commission's report as "welfarism running rampant" and "neo-feudalism." "Only a few years ago," the editorial complained, "the current welfarist thinking would have been deemed unacceptable by the American people. Today there seems little in the way of an effective counterforce." [39]

[37] Daniel Moynihan has pointed out that in this country we find the idea of a high minimum for all much less attractive than the opportunity of high income for some. Nathan Glazer adds that we do have a lower, or more irregular floor, than Europe but we also have higher plateaus on which very substantial numbers are located. Gordon, *Poverty in America, op. cit.,* p. 16.

[38] A. J. Liebling wrote, "There is no concept more generally cherished by publishers than that of the Undeserving Poor . . . one way to rationalize the inadequacy of public aid is to blackguard the poor by saying that they have concealed assets, or bad character, or both." See, for example, Earl and Anne Selby, "Why the Dole Doesn't Work," *Reader's Digest,* March, 1965, p. 79 or Fletcher Knebel, "Welfare —has it become a scandal?," *Look,* November 7, 1961.

[39] *Wall Street Journal,* February 8, 1966. See also Robert Heilbroner, *The Limits of Capitalism* (New York: Harper and Row, 1966), especially pp. 76–88, for a broader but pertinent view of these questions.

Pressures for Equality

This brings us to the final trend that Myrdal reports, the pressure from the less privileged groups in a democratic society for "ever more state intervention in practically all fields."

The rational basis for this general interest of people in the lower income brackets in intervention is that, when private relations become public relations in the Western countries, now so firmly dedicated to equality, there is a better chance that the poor man's concerns will be looked after.[40]

This pressure is becoming evident in the United States, and will no doubt grow in strength as the results of the Supreme Court's "one man, one vote" reapportionment decision gradually are felt. For, as Glazer has pointed out, "It is the civil rights revolution that makes poverty a great issue in America." [41] As voting rights for Negroes are won, it is likely that the civil rights movement will turn its attention more prominently to economic issues, since, as noted earlier, half of the Negro population is below the poverty line, compared with one in every seven whites.

The poverty program itself is generating new pressures in its community action programs, providing for "maximum feasible participation" of the poor. The success of Saul Alinsky and the Industrial Areas Foundation in organizing poor communities to press their demands with militance is an indication that the often deplored "apathetic" response of the poor is not necessarily a permanent phenomenon.[42] The United Automobile Workers are attempting to organize the poor in community groups and the United Steelworkers are backing efforts to organize migrant workers in Florida. The voice of the farmworker, so long silent, is also beginning to be heard. And the poor have been heard in other ways than political activity and unionization. The riots in Watts in the summer of 1965, in a tragically effective manner, made the "invisible" poor at least briefly visible.

It is possible, of course, that as the lot of the poor improves and they are able to participate in the mainstream of American political life, the political power of those who remain poor will diminish. Also, the efforts of organized spokesmen for the poor to control poverty program

[40] Myrdal, *op. cit.*, p. 38.

[41] Gordon, *Poverty in America, op. cit.*, p. 20.

[42] Perhaps more important, the psychological changes produced by this kind of self-help organization may have more long-run effect in eliminating poverty than any government programs. See, e.g., Glazer, in Gordon, *Poverty in America, op. cit.*, pp. 12–26, especially p. 26. See also *Wall Street Journal*, February 18, 1966.

funds have evoked a counter-attack by established political forces when the poor threatened to upset existing power relationships.

But a shift in the balance of power is underway. There is a new recognition that the whole community bears the costs of poverty and slums, of dependency, crime, delinquency, disease; that the total bill may be higher than the costs of prevention; and that the political explosiveness of the ghetto is not necessarily containable within its borders.

Professor Burns in analyzing the evolution of worldwide welfare programs finds that "The policy issue that seems to be everywhere emerging is not whether all members of a large community, such as a nation, should be assured some roughly uniform minimum real income under circumstances which are not regarded as demeaning, but rather how best to bring this about." [43]

THE FUTURE OF ECONOMIC SECURITY SYSTEMS:
II. PROPOSALS FOR CHANGE

In discussing proposals for "how best to bring this about," a distinction between two primary groups among the poor today should be kept in mind: first, the victims of the natural forces of the labor market; and second, those whose poverty is largely due to the absence of ties with the labor market. The poor with no labor market attachment are, of course, likely to be worse off, since they are cut off not only from wages, but from the whole structure of private security systems. But not everyone, of course, is a potential member of the labor force. The aged, the disabled, and mothers of small children without a breadwinner must seek an improvement in their situations through some kind of income maintenance program.

Among the various alternatives which have been suggested for the future, and which will be considered briefly here are the following: (1) an overhauling and upgrading of our present income maintenance programs, minimum wage programs, etc., with no major structural changes in or integration of our economic and social security programs; (2) a system of family allowances along the lines of those in most other major nations; (3) a minimum income allowance or negative income tax; (4) a massive job creation program, or use of the government as an employer of last resort; and finally, (5) programs which place emphasis on changing the poor, rather than, or in addition to, changing the society, an approach exemplified by most of the present war-on-poverty programs.

[43] Eveline M. Burns, "Welfare Programs in Evolution," *Monthly Labor Review,* CXXXVIII, No. 2 (March, 1965), 294–95.

Upgrading Our Present Programs

Clearly the line of least resistance is to continue our economic and social security programs along the same general lines of development we have been following, filling gaps, meeting inadequacies, strengthening standards, adding new programs to meet specific new needs as they become pressing. Many of the problems outlined in this book, at least with respect to employment-related programs, could be solved by expansion of private and public coverage and benefits (as in the Fair Labor Standards Act, unemployment insurance, and OASDI benefits) and by better coordination where overlapping occurs. Robert M. Ball, Commissioner of Social Security, argues that one-third to one-half of our present poverty—the easier part to cure, he admits—could be prevented by improvement and broader application of the social insurance principle and he outlines the steps he thinks are needed.[44] Any change which sought to remove the contributory feature of the social security system would undoubtedly meet with strong opposition. In defending the present system against change, conservatives will have the benefit of arguing the position espoused for years by liberals—that benefit payments as a matter of right should stem from a contributory source.

Sar Levitan, doubtful that the society will decide in the foreseeable future to allocate the resources needed to win total victory over poverty, partly because of the many pressing and competing goals, proposes a series of short-run priorities within the present framework. He places wide dissemination of birth control information as the first priority; and as the second, a radical overhauling and boosting of benefits of the Aid to Families with Dependent Children, using the Veterans Administration pension system as an administrative model, since its simplified methods avoid harassment and degradation and do not discourage initiative of recipients; he proposes, third, a work relief program with the goal of creating 300,000 jobs; and finally a vigorous program of public subsidized housing.[45]

Eveline Burns points out that extensive social security coverage has led to the discovery of two new risks to income maintenance which need to be met: the risk of family breakup from causes other than death, and the risk of long-term unemployment.[46] She points out that unemployment insurance (with employer financing) is unsuitable as a tech-

---

[44] "Is Poverty Necessary?" *Social Security Bulletin*, XXVIII, No. 8 (August, 1965), 18–24.

[45] *Programs in Aid of the Poor* (Kalamazoo, Mich.: W. E. Upjohn Institute for Employment Research, 1965), 44–59.

[46] Burns, *op. cit.*, p. 295.

nique for handling this risk, and public assistance with its means test is unacceptable. But both of the risks could conceivably be handled without major changes in program structure. The same is true of proposals to extend medical care under social security to those under 65.

A Family Allowance System

With the recent discovery that children form a much larger proportion of those living below the poverty level than had heretofore been thought, there has been wider recognition of the fact that our children are one of our most neglected groups.[47] They receive social security only if their OASDI breadwinners die or are permanently and totally disabled, but not if they desert, separate but do not support the family, or never married in the first place. Then public assistance is the only recourse, and as we have so often seen, the low payments, uncertainties, and means test make this at present an unacceptable alternative. Then there are millions of children living in homes with both parents, often with the father employed, who are still below the poverty line (5.7 million children); often these are families with especially large numbers of children, as there are many more of these, proportionately, in the lowest income groups.[48]

It has been proposed to meet the needs of these children through a family allowance system, which the United States, almost alone among Western nations, lacks. The justifications offered are that the well-being of children should be the concern of society as a whole; and that since the wage system is not adapted to take account of the diverse needs of workers, it alone is an inadequate basis for distribution of income. Expenditures for AFDC account for 0.3 per cent of national income; a number of countries spend ten times this percentage or more for family allowances.[49] In France the allowances are financed by employers and amount to 13.5 per cent of total payrolls; in Canada, they are paid by the government from the general revenue and pay a smaller proportion of family income. Thus far, this plan has received only limited support in this country.

[47] See Eveline Burns, in Haber, *op. cit.*, pp. 279–80, and Levitan, *op. cit.*, p. 2.

[48] One-half of families with six children were in the poverty group; nearly half of the 15 million children of the poor were in families with 5 or more children.

[49] Levitan, *op. cit.*, pp. 44–45. See also Lampman, in Ferman, *et al.*, *op. cit.*, p. 418.

The Guaranteed Minimum Income:
Negative Income Tax

A much more far-reaching suggestion that is receiving a great deal of discussion is that of direct cash subsidies to the poor (guaranteed minimum income) of which the "negative income tax" is one method of implementation. Although there are many variants of this proposal, they all involve the same principle: those whose income falls below a designated level would receive cash payment from the Treasury, just as those whose incomes today are above a given level pay taxes. Thus, a minimum income would be assured to all members of society.

Eveline Burns makes some interesting points in this connection:

. . . now that the coverage of the general tax system is so extensive, it may well be asked whether instead of two income tax collecting systems it might not be preferable to have a single system, especially as the national tax structure is distinctly more progressive than that of the social security system. (It would still be possible, as is done in some countries, to earmark for social security a percentage of the tax payable for each individual.)

The wide population coverage of the income tax return and its use as a means of discrimination between those who do and who do not have to pay taxes inevitably raises also the question whether this same machinery could be used to discriminate between those who should and should not receive income security payments. In other words, cannot the income tax return, as is, or modified, become a substitute for the needs test in its many forms?

Another development which cannot fail to influence thinking about the future nature of our income maintenance system is the increasing use of the tax system as a welfare instrument . . . (with) . . . the special deductions or exemptions which have a welfare objective. Among these are the exemptions for dependents, the double exemption for persons 65 and over, the liberal medical deductions allowed the aged, and the complete exemption from tax liability of social insurance and other forms of socially provided income. . . . As these tax concessions for special groups and needs increase in number, attention is inevitably directed to the pros and cons of substituting a nationally determined single payment for these many and often arbitrary concessions. We may expect this question to be asked with increasing frequency as the current rediscovery of poverty focuses attention on income deficiency (as opposed to income interruption which has been the major concern of public social policy for the last 30 years). For the ironical aspect of the present use of the tax system as a welfare instrument is that the greatest gain is secured by those in the highest tax brackets while those whose incomes are most deficient are often unable to take advantage of all the exemptions and deductions which are legally available.[50]

Robert Theobald points out that at its inception, the income tax exemption was set to exempt from taxes that part of income required for a reasonable standard of living. This policy was set aside during

[50] Burns, op. cit., p. 295.

World War II to increase revenue for the war and has been further reduced since then by the effects of inflation.[51]

Most proposals deal with the question of diminishing work incentives through some sort of schedule which would partially lower payments as additional income was earned, and Tobin suggests that the scale of allowances by family size should contain some disincentive to the creation of large families.[52]

The country's leading conservative academic economist, Milton Friedman, has joined those on the other end of the political spectrum in endorsing one version of this proposal, and as has been mentioned, the National Commission on Technology, Automation, and Economic Progress, which included men from such diverse backgrounds as Walter Reuther and Thomas J. Watson, Jr., endorsed the idea unanimously.

Aside from the opposition to this proposal on policy or ideological grounds, the main problem is cost. The cost estimates vary with the many alternative versions from $2 billion to $23 billion.[53] Of course, there would likely be considerable indirect savings because the dependence on existing security measures such as public assistance would greatly diminish. Even assuming the costs were manageable, it must be recognized that providing the poor with basic income allowances is only one aspect of combating poverty. Also needed are a broad battery of services to the poor to improve their ability to compete for jobs in the labor market.

Margaret Gordon also argues that the negative income tax would be no substitute for a more adequate system of income maintenance for the unemployed or for needed improvements in the social security system generally, although its heavy costs would in all likelihood militate against such improvements. Further, she points out that unemployment insurance benefits, inadequate as they are, have been very effective and prompt in maintaining purchasing power in recessions, a function the negative income tax would perform much less successfully.[54]

Government as Employer of Last Resort

It is generally recognized that the single goal which would produce the most desirable effects in eliminating poverty would be a tight labor

[51] *Free Men and Free Markets* (New York: Clarkson N. Potter, Inc., 1963), pp. 192–93.

[52] See Tobin, *op. cit.*, pp. 891–94; Levitan, *op. cit.*, pp. 46–47; Ferman, *op. cit.*, pp. 418–19, 483–96; and see a symposium on the subject in *Industrial Relations*, VI, No. 2 (February, 1967).

[53] See Robert Lampman, *Approaches to the Reduction of Poverty*, Papers and Proceedings of the Seventy-seventh Annual Meeting of the American Economic Association, May 1965, pp. 521–29; Levitan, *op. cit.*, pp. 46–47.

[54] Gordon, *Poverty in America, op. cit.*, p. 259.

market, in which unemployment would be low and short in duration and job vacancies plentiful; which would mean not just jobs, but better jobs and higher wages. Various proposals have been made for programs of job creation, massive social spending for public works, "hiring the poor to abolish poverty," as Harrington says, inventing new kinds of jobs for the poor, raising performance standards in municipal facilities and services, in medicine, social work, and the war on poverty by hiring and training the poor to function as "subprofessionals." But perhaps the most imaginative suggestion in this area is the "Wage Support Law" of Hyman Minsky, directed specifically at the 60 per cent of the poor who are either employed or, if not employed, are in the labor force.

Work should be made available for all able and willing to work at the national minimum wage. Ideally I would repeal the minimum wage law. In its place I would have a wage support law, analogous to the laws supporting agricultural commodities. With such a law anybody who has an hour of labor to sell, can sell it to the government for $1.25. You don't have to worry about trade union contracts for exempt laundry workers at 70 cents an hour. They can all go to work for the government at $1.25 an hour. Under this law, no one is going to work for 70 cents an hour. The problem of what kind of labor is "covered" and what kind is "uncovered" is eliminated. All workers have jobs available for them at $1.25 an hour.

To qualify for employment at these terms, all that would be required would be to register at the local USES. Part time and seasonal work should be available: this will be a special boon to students, low income farmers, working wives and farm workers. National government agencies, as well as local and state agencies would be eligible to obtain this labor. They would bid for labor by submitting their projects, and local "evaluation" boards would determine priorities among projects.[55]

Several arguments have been made against this type of proposal for creating a tight labor market. It would clearly be inflationary. Anticipating this, Minsky argues as follows, ". . . a wage support law would raise the wages of hospital orderlies and licensed vocational nurses relative to other workers. . . . A rise in their wages would raise hospital costs. But given the social importance we attach to medical care, why should a rise in the wages of hospital employees raise hospital fees? Rather than do this the government could subsidize hospital wages."[56]

Clearly such a wage support law would have numerous side effects and would no doubt involve government intervention, as Minsky shows, in many other areas. Still, such a proposal would virtually eliminate low-wage poverty and will no doubt receive serious study in the future.

[55] Hyman Minsky, *Labor and the War Against Poverty* (Berkeley, Calif.: Institute of Industrial Relations, 1965), pp. 12–13. See also Tobin, *op. cit.*, pp. 878–98.

[56] *Ibid.*, pp. 13–14. For full argument see also Minsky, *The Role of Employment Policy*, in Gordon, *Poverty in America, op. cit.*, pp. 175–200.

Investment in Human Capital

What differentiates the poor, in the view of Oscar Ornati,[57] is the lack of personal assets that produce income. Thus, "in a high income economy such as ours, different rates of investment in human beings determine who in our sociey is or who is not poor. . . . If unplanned inadequate investments in human capital have created much unwanted poverty, deliberate, planned differentiated investment in human beings ought to rectify the situation (provided of course, a continued high rate of economic growth and employment). . . . What is significant about added expenditures on human beings and what is not the case with income guarantees is that they produce future income streams."

This general view underlies many of the present programs of the war on poverty, and its emphasis on preventive expenditures, especially among the young, for education, health, retraining, etc. The basic idea is to enlarge the ports of entry into the market society. Nathan Glazer tries to answer the question of why we see the "poverty problem in this country as demanding much more than tinkering with benefits and eligibilities? Here radicals, liberals, and even some conservatives call for a social and psychological revolution, requiring us to develop a completely different attitude to the casualties of industrial society, an attitude capable of remaking them rather than providing simply better care." [58] Similarly, a psychologist views the problem of poverty as the problem of powerlessness, and suggests that all social arrangements which take responsibility out of the hands of the poor feed this psychology of powerlessness, while the best antidote is social action of the poor themselves in their own interests.[59] Ornati and others argue not for this approach only, but a "judicious mixture of personal and social reconstruction."

CONCLUDING COMMENTS

The war on poverty has been the victim of much criticism, especially that its expenditures to date and its projected budget do not scratch the surface when the magnitude of the problem is considered.[60] But we

[57] "Two Approaches to Welfare," *Monthly Labor Review*, CXXXVIII, No. 3 (March, 1965), 296–97.

[58] In Gordon, *Poverty in America, op. cit.,* pp. 14–15.

[59] Warren C. Haggstrom, *The Power of the Poor*, in Frank Riesman, Jerome Cohen, and Arthur Pearl (eds.), *Mental Health of the Poor* (New York: The Free Press of Glencoe, 1964).

[60] Sargent Shriver estimated total expenditures the first year at 2 billion, the second at 1.5 billion, and the budget request for 1966–67 is 1.75 billion. This is a generous estimate, including programs in all agencies with any relation to the effort, not just OEO.

would argue that the fact of overwhelming importance is that the war has been declared. Do Americans really care? A review of this book makes clear that Americans have made a significant commitment to the solution of problems of economic security, but this chapter also indicates that the work left undone is equally significant. The first annual report of the Social Security Board asserted, "An attempt to find security for a people is among the oldest of political obligations and the greatest task of the state." Unquestionably, we have undertaken that obligation, and if we have not met it to the extent of our economic capacity, we have made giant strides in that direction.

Our progress has been painfully uneven. There have been inspiring jumps forward and discouraging periods when we fall behind. In describing this process, Arthur Larson cites an analogy from Ralph Waldo Emerson: if you take a jar of honey and hold it upside down, three quarters of the contents rush out. But if you were turned into marble and held the inverted jar into eternity, the last one-quarter would never come out. So it is with perfection in all kinds of social insurance, he asserts. "Most . . . reforms are swept in on a wave of white-hot public indignation. A long accumulation of needs and grievances eventually produces powerful pressure groups capable of driving through the greater part of the needed program. But because of the political need for compromise or because of administrative difficulties alleged to exist in the new program, the one-fourth of the problem is left unsolved. Then the pressure eases; the white-hot indignation cools off." [61] And a long, frustrating deterioration often sets in.

But the declaration of war on poverty can mark the beginning of one of the most creative periods in our history. Already the 1965 social security legislation, with the launching of "Medicare," and the initial activities of the Office of Economic Opportunity have broken new ground, and fertile new suggestions are percolating again after a long period of legislative neglect and public disinterest in the field. In the private area, too, new departures may be in the making, with the announcement of the United Automobile Workers that its basic contract demand in 1967 will be to obtain salaried status for hourly workers.

A great many unsolved and difficult questions await us. Clearly, multiple approaches are going to be called for, and one fundamental condition of success will be a healthy and growing economy. What priorities we will assign to the elimination of poverty remain to be seen. What role we assign to private measures, what role we assign to social insurance, how bold we will be in experimenting with new devices, it is too early to tell. But a great debate is beginning, and this is a first necessary step, without which the paradox of poverty in the midst of plenty will never be effectively challenged.

[61] In Cheit and Gordon, *op. cit.*, pp. 11–12.

SUGGESTIONS FOR ADDITIONAL READING

Burns, Eveline M. "Social Security in Evolution: Toward What?" *Social Security Review*, XXXIX (June, 1965), 129–40.
A leading student of social insurance examines its progress to date and the problems it will face in its further evolution.

Ferman, Louis A., Joyce L. Kornbluh, and Alan Haber (eds.). *Poverty in America.* Ann Arbor: University of Michigan Press, 1965.
A comprehensive and diverse anthology, describing and analyzing the multi-faceted problems of poverty.

Gordon, Margaret S. (ed.). *Poverty in America.* San Francisco: Chandler Publishing Co., 1965.
A very useful collection of policy-oriented essays prepared for a conference on poverty held at the University of California, Berkeley.

Haber, William, and Wilbur J. Cohen (eds.). *Social Security: Programs, Problems, and Policies.* Homewood, Ill.: Richard D. Irwin, Inc., 1960.
A valuable compendium of current and historical items, both facts and analysis.

Harrington, Michael. *The Other America: Poverty in the United States.* New York: The Macmillan Co., 1962.
The passionate but fact-filled book that sparked the war on poverty.

Levitan, Sar A. *Programs in Aid of the Poor.* Kalamazoo, Mich.: W. E. Upjohn Institute for Employment Research, 1965.
A description and appraisal of our current welfare system and various anti-poverty proposals.

Myrdal, Gunnar. *Beyond the Welfare State.* New Haven: Yale University Press, 1965.
A view of economic planning and the welfare state from a world perspective.

Office of Economic Opportunity. *A Nation Aroused.* 1st Annual Report. Washington, D. C.: 1965.
A review of war on poverty programs, combining pictures and statistics.

———. *Catalog of Federal Programs for Individual and Community Improvement.* Washington, D. C.: 1965.
A detailed explanation of the nature and purpose of federal anti-poverty programs.

Seligman, Ben B. (ed.). *Poverty as a Public Issue.* New York: The Macmillan Co., 1965.
Another collection of papers presented at a seminar on poverty, this one held by the Institute for Policy Studies, Washington, D. C.

Social Security Bulletin, published monthly by the Social Security Administration, is a useful compendium of current analysis in the social insurance field, with a monthly bibliography and operating statistics. The August, 1965, issue reviews the first thirty years of social security legislation.

Technology and the American Economy. Report of the National Commission on Technology, Automation, and Economic Progress. Vol. I. 1966.
Discusses public and private policies needed for facilitating the nation's adjustment to technological change.

Wilensky, Harold, and Charles N. Lebeaux. *Industrial Society and Social Welfare.* New York: The Free Press of Glencoe, 1965.
The introduction to the 1965 edition is a very interesting sociologist's view of the problems and prospects of the welfare state.

Index of Authors and Sources Cited

(Italicized entries refer to first citation of sources quoted by title only. Annual reports, court cases, hearings, proceedings, and serial items are not included in this listing.)

Index of Subjects

"Able to work," 252
Accidental injury and sickness
  alleviative programs, 31–33
  approaches to, 32–33, 414–58, 357–90
  insurance plans, 414–58
  loss caused by non-occupational, 350–56
  public assistance, 32
Accidents; *see also* Disabilities and injuries; Illness; Insurance
  common law of industrial, 309–11
  frequency rate, 303
  industrial, 15–16
  prevention programs, 303, 308, 337–38
  severity rate, 303–5
  work injuries, 301–2
Adamson Act, 543
Administration of Aging, 69
Aged; *see* Old age; Old-age assistance; Old-Age, Survivors, and Disability Insurance (OASDI)
Aid to Families with Dependent Children, 30, 32, 49, 359, 635, 642
  administration of, 108
  benefits, 95, 101–2, 105, 460
  causes of dependency, 106
  effect of OASDI on, 148–49
  evaluation of, 102–8
  federal grants to states for, 94–97
  inadequacies in, 625
  number of recipients, 100, 149, 460
  operations, 99–102
  requirements for federal approval, 95
  state programs, 97–98, 105
  trends in, 98–99
  unmet needs, 105, 625
Aid to the Blind, 32
  combination plans, 364–65
  federal grants, 91
  operations of, 367–68
  public assistance programs, 363–64
  range of benefit payments, 482
Aid to the Permanently and Totally Disabled, 364
  federal grants, 91

  operations of, 367–68
  range of benefit payments, 482
Alleviative programs, 12–13, 29–39, 48
  accidental injury and sickness, 31–33
  death and old age, 30, 69–71
  economics of, 488–89
  private, 14
  unemployment, 30–31
Anderson-Kennedy amendment, 396
Annuity contracts, 170–72
Area Redevelopment Act (1961), 227
Area redevelopment programs, 43, 227, 460
Armed Services program, 467
"Availability for work," 252–53

"Base period" or "base year," 252, 254
Benefits; *see individual programs*
  public assistance versus social insurance, 19–20
  qualifications for collection of, 37–38
Blind; *see* Aid to the Blind
Blue Cross plans, 32, 404, 428, 429–33, 456
  benefits, 430–31
  contracts with member hospitals, 433
  eligibility requirements, 430
  exclusions and limitations, 431–32
  subscriber contracts, 430–33
Blue Shield plans, 32, 429, 456
  subscriber contracts, 435–36
British National Health Service, 409
Built-in economic security stabilizers, 229–32
  unemployment insurance, 298
Burden of economic security program, 498–501
Bureau of Employment Security, 217, 249
Business enterprise, impact of economic security programs on, 298, 509–10

California, temporary disability insurance legislation, 379–90
Caseworkers, role of, 108

659